Theatre
Brief Version

Also by Robert Cohen

Theatre, Sixth Edition
(0-7674-3006-9)

For the Acting Sequence:

Acting in Shakespeare
(0-87484-951-9)

Acting One, Fourth Edition
(0-7674-1859-X)

Acting Power
(0-87484-408-8)

Acting Professionally: Raw Facts About Careers in Acting, Fifth Edition
(1-55934-941-7)

Advanced Acting: Style, Character, and Performance
(0-7674-2542-1)

Anthologies:

Eight Plays for Theatre
(0-87484-850-4)

Twelve Plays for Theatre
(1-55934-144-0)

Other:

Giraudoux: Three Plays of Destiny

More Power to You

Creative Play Direction (with John Harrop)

Theatre
Brief Version
SIXTH EDITION

ROBERT COHEN

Claire Trevor Professor of Drama
University of California, Irvine

McGraw-Hill

Boston Burr Ridge, IL Dubuque, IA Madison, WI New York
San Francisco St. Louis Bangkok Bogotá Caracas Kuala Lumpur
Lisbon London Madrid Mexico City Milan Montreal New Delhi
Santiago Seoul Singapore Sydney Taipei Toronto

McGraw-Hill Higher Education

A Division of The McGraw-Hill Companies

2 3 4 5 6 7 8 9 0 VNH/VNH 0 9 8 7 6 5 4 3 2

Library of Congress Cataloging-in-Publication Data
Cohen, Robert
    Theatre : brief version / Robert Cohen.—6th ed.
      p. cm.
    Includes bibliographical references and index.
    ISBN 0-7674-3007-7
    1. Theater. I. Title.

PN2101 .C632 2002
792—dc21   2002016543

Sponsoring editor, Allison McNamara; *production editor,* Jennifer Mills; *manuscript editor,* Margaret Moore; *design manager,* Jeanne Schreiber; *cover designer,* Susan Breitbard; *art manager,* Robin Mouat; *photo researcher,* Brian J. Pecko; *manufacturing manager,* Pam Augspurger. This text was set in 9.5/12 Stone Serif Regular by Thompson Type and printed on acid-free, 45# Pub Matte by VonHoffmann Press.

Cover images: Top left, The Lantern Acrobat, courtesy Press Office, Hong Kong Kultural Centre, Serene Lai; *top right, Hamlet,* © Stephanie Berger; *middle left, When We Dead Awaken,* © Richard Feldman; *middle, The Producers,* © Paul Kolnik; *middle right, Amy's View,* © Joan Marcus; *bottom left, The Tempest,* © David Cooper; *bottom right, The Blue Room,* © Robbie Jack/Corbis.

Credits appear on a continuation of the copyright page, pages C-1–C-3.

www.mhhe.com/cohen

To Whitney Cohen

Preface

I am sitting in a darkened theatre correcting the galley sheets for the book you are about to read. A technical rehearsal for a play I am directing is in progress; I am seated at a make-shift desk in the back of the house, my reading illuminated by a tiny covered gooseneck lamp. Onstage stand several actors, silent and motionless, as light plays over their faces and bodies. Above me, unseen and unheard, technicians operate, adjust, and record the settings for another of the play's hundred and fifty light cues. To the outside observer, it is the dullest situation imaginable; nothing observable happens for twenty or thirty minutes at a stretch. A pool of light intensifies and then recedes, muffled conversation crackles over headsets, footsteps clang on steel catwalks lacing the ceiling, and a spotlight is carefully repositioned. This has been going on now since eight in the morning, and it is already past dinnertime.

And yet my eye is continually pulled from these pages to the dance of light upon the stage. The violet and amber hues are rich with color, and the sharp shafts of incandescence dazzle with brilliance. I am fascinated by the patient weariness of the actors, alternately glowing in and then shadowed by the lights, endlessly holding the positions that, in performance, they will occupy for only a few transitory seconds. I gaze with admiration at the followspot operator, his hands gloved, as he handles his instrument with the precision and sensitivity of a surgeon.

The silence, the stasis, is hypnotic. All is quiet but profound with held-back beats, incipient torrents of passion and exhilaration. The potential is riveting—I am alive with excitement—and I look back to these cold galley sheets with alarm.

How can I have thought to express the thrill of the theatre in these pages? How can I have hoped to make recognizable the joy and awe I feel in theatrical involvement?

The theatre is not merely a collection of crafts, a branch of literature, a collaboration of technique, or even an all-encompassing art form. It is a life. It is people. It is people making art out of themselves. Its full reality transcends by light-years anything that could be said or written about it.

What I have tried to do in these pages is not so much to introduce the theatre or to survey it as to *present* the theatre with its liveliness and humanness intact, with its incipient passion and exhilaration always present, with its potential for joy, awe, wisdom, and excitement as clear to the reader as they have been made clear to me.

Features

This is a brief version of a larger book that is published simultaneously. The larger volume includes five chapters on theatrical history that do not appear here and three chapters (instead of two) on the modern theatre. The goal of this brief version is to provide students surveying the theatrical arts and collaborative theatrical crafts—but not dramatic history—with a comprehensive text in the dramatic arts as they exist today.

I have included more than 200 theatre photographs—mostly in color—collected from all five continents. The vast majority of these are of significant recent stage productions from around the world. Other photos illustrate the processes of theatrical creation or the historical and current contexts of theatre presentation. Completing the book's art are a dozen drawings by scholar/architects that illustrate theatres both past and present as accurately as current research and skilled reconstruction can make possible. Extended captions should help readers better appreciate these images of theatre worldwide and make stronger connections to the text examples.

The text offers a number of pedagogical aids. Terms commonly used in theatre and theatre history are defined in the glossary at the back of the book, and further sources of information for the curious can be found in the selected bibliography. To help students enjoy performances, I have included an appendix that offers advice on observing and writing critically about plays.

To help students enhance their playgoing experience further, we have prepared a brief guide—*Enjoy the Play!* Co-authored with Lorna Cohen, the guide includes suggestions as to how and where students may attend live theatre—at low cost—either in their own hometowns or in major theatre centers here and abroad. It also includes pointers on how to write a play report.

To help busy instructors, there is a Test Bank, written by Marilyn Moriarty, which includes 50 multiple-choice questions and several short-answer or essay questions per chapter. A computerized version of the Test Bank is available to qualified adopters.

No study of the theatre can be truly comprehensive without seeing and reading plays. It is my belief that regular playgoing and play reading, supported by the discussions in these pages and in the classroom, will provide a good foundation for the student to develop an in-formed and critical enthusiasm for the art of drama.

What's New?

For this edition, the chapter on "Theatre Today" has, naturally, been completely revised, with new and substantially augmented sections on dance theatre, performance art, and important trends and emerging artists in America and Europe. Chapters on musical theatre and playwriting have also been substantially revised and modestly expanded, and the photo essays on Tony Award-winning scenery and costume designers have now expanded from two to three, with a new one on lighting designer Chris Parry. Readers of the previous edition will also immediately notice more than seventy-five new color photographs of important stage productions, mostly from the current millennium, which have been individually selected from studios of leading theatre photographers in Europe and America. And, naturally, the scholarship and reportage in virtually every chapter in the book has been updated and, where necessary, corrected.

Acknowledgments

In all of these revisions, I have profited from literally hundreds of valuable suggestions from readers and from a dozen reviews solicited by the publisher from around the country. These include: Joe Aldridge, University of Nevada at Las Vegas; Carol Burbank, University of Maryland; George Caldwell, Washington State University; Kurt Daw, Kennesaw State University; Richard Devin, University of Colorado; Cliff Faulkner, University of California at Irvine; Stephen Hancock, University of Memphis; Mark Harvey, University of Minnesota; Richard Isackes, University of Texas at Austin; Robert Gerald Levy, Clarion University of Pennsylvania; Diane McNeil, University of Rhode Island; Dean Mogle, College Conservatory of

Music, University of Cincinnati; Rebecca Morrice, Slippery Rock University; C. Ronald Olauson, Mankato State University; Mikell Pinkney, University of Florida; Rebecca Rumbo, University of Connecticut; Terry Donovan Smith, University of Washington; Jeffrey Stephens, Oklahoma State University; Janet Swenson, Brigham Young University; and Edmond Williams, University of Alabama.

I am also deeply grateful for the counsel of my University of California colleagues Madeline Kozlowski and Cameron Harvey (at Irvine) and John Rouse and Chris Parry (at San Diego), in addition to the collaborative assistance of many people in acquiring the new photographs for this edition, including Laurencine Lot at the Comédie Française in Paris; Jagoda Engelbrecht at the Berlin Theatertreffen 2001; Charlotte Webb at the Performing Arts Library in London; Amy Richards at the Oregon Shakespeare Festival; James Loder at A Conservatory Theatre in Seattle; Julia Oberschneider at the Berliner Ensemble; Ana Sokol at GAle GAtes et al. in New York; Ann B. Goddard at the Utah Shakespearean Theatre; Thomas Aurin in Berlin; Barbara Higgs at the Zurich Schauspielhaus; Carol Rosegg, Joan Marcus, Paul Kolnik, and Stephanie Berger in New York; Gina Lutterman at the Goodman Theatre in Chicago; Barbara Schindler at the Berliner Volksbühne; Cris Gross at South Coast Repertory; and David Lincecum and Shannon Forcier at ETC Products.

Finally, I would like to note that this edition is the first I have conceived and written entirely under the guidance of McGraw-Hill Higher Education, which in 2001 absorbed Mayfield Publishing Company with which I published not only the five previous editions of *Theatre* and *Theatre: Brief Version* but also fourteen editions of seven other books during the past thirty years. One hardly expects such transitions to be seamless, but this one proved to be exactly that, and for that I am profoundly grateful to this edition's astute Sponsoring Editor, Allison McNamara, whose steadfast counsel and encouragement have proved extraordinary, as did that of the entire publishing team, many of whom moved over from Mayfield. This team included the very careful Margaret Moore, whose copyediting saved me (and you) from a great many egregious mistakes; the resourceful Brian Pecko, who sorted out all the photographic permissions from several countries; the artful Robin Mouat who coordinated the art and photo program; and the book's masterful assembler, Production Editor Jen Mills.

Support for Instructors

Please note: The supplements listed here and below in Support for Students *may accompany this text. Please contact your local McGraw-Hill representative for details concerning policies, prices, and availability as some restrictions may apply. If you are not sure who your representative is, you can find him or her by using the Rep Locator at www.mhhe.com.*

INSTRUCTOR'S MANUAL   McGraw-Hill offers an *Instructor's Manual* to all instructors who adopt *Theatre, Brief Version* for their courses. Each chapter of the *Instructor's Manual* includes:

- an overview and outline of the text chapter
- a list of significant names and terms found in the chapter
- questions for student essays or discussions

The last section of the *Instructor's Manual* contains a sample *Test Bank*, organized by chapter, for in-class quizzes and testing.

COMPUTERIZED TEST BANK   The test questions from the *Instructor's Manual* are available on MicroTest, a powerful but easy-to-use test-generating program. MicroTest is available for Windows and Macintosh personal computers. With MicroTest, you can easily view and select the test item file questions, then print a test and answer key. You can customize questions, headings, and instructions, you can add or import questions of your own, and you can print your test in a choice of fonts allowed by your printer.

ONLINE LEARNING CENTER: WWW.MHHE. COM/COHEN   The Online Learning Center is an Internet-based resource for students and faculty alike. The Instructor Resources are password protected and offer the complete text of the *Instructor's Manual* and a link to our customizable database of plays. To receive a password for the site, contact your local sales representative or email us at theatre@mcgraw-hill.com.

Additionally, the Online Learning Center offers chapter-by-chapter quizzes for student testing. These brief quizzes are separate from those offered in the *Instructor's Manual*, generate instant grades, and the results can be emailed directly to the instructor with the click of a button (see Student Resources below). This special quizzing feature is a valuable tool for the instructor who requires a quick way to check reading comprehension and basic understanding without using up valuable class time.

Student Resources

MAKING THE GRADE CD-ROM   This CD-ROM, packaged free with the text, provides students with an excellent resource that offers enrichment, review, and self-testing. The following components are included:

- Internet primer
- Study skills primer
- Guide to electronic research in theatre
- Multiple-choice questions for each chapter—graded automatically
- Learning assessment
- Links to the book's Web site

ENJOY THE PLAY!   This free theatre guide is packaged with every copy of the text. From getting to the theatre to what to write in a theatre report, *Enjoy the Play!* is an excellent introduction to the art of attending a play.

ONLINE LEARNING CENTER: WWW.MHHE. COM/COHEN   McGraw-Hill offers extensive Web resources for students with Internet access. Students will find the Online Learning Center of particular use with the sixth edition of *Theatre Brief Version,* as each chapter is equipped with: glossary terms, chapter objectives, discussion questions, and online testing. In addition, the site hosts links to promote getting involved in theatre and in conducting research on the Web.

THE MCGRAW-HILL GUIDE TO ELECTRONIC RESEARCH IN THEATRE   This brief booklet is designed to assist students in locating theatre sites on the Web, evaluating the onsite information, and provides guidelines for referencing online sources. This supplement can be packaged with the text for free.

I would like to express my appreciation to Doug Cummins of Furman University for his contributions to the *Making the Grade* CD-ROM and the Online Learning Center and Dennis Beck of Bradley University for creating the *Instructor's Manual.*

Contents

Chapter 7 Theatre Traditions: East and West   211

Chapter 8 The Modern Theatre   241

Chapter 11 The Critic   365

Introduction

It is evening in Manhattan. On Broadway and the streets that cross it — from 42nd to 54th — marquees light up, "Performance Tonight" signs materialize in front of double doors, and beneath a few box-office windows placards announce "This Performance Completely Sold Out." At Grand Central and Penn Stations, trains disgorge suburbanites from Greenwich, Larchmont, and Trenton; students from New Haven and Philadelphia; daytrippers from Boston and Washington. Up from the Times Square subways troop denizens of the island city and the neighboring boroughs. At the Duffy Square "TKTS" booth, hundreds line up to buy the discount tickets that go on sale a few hours before curtain time for those shows with seats yet to be filled. Now, converging on these few midtown blocks of America's largest city, come limousines, restaurant buses, private cars, and taxis, whose drivers search for a curbside slot to deposit their riders among the milling throng of pedestrians. Financiers and dowagers, bearded intellectuals, backpack-toting teenagers, sleek executives, hip Harlemites, arm-in-arm widows, out-of-town tourists and conventioneers, between-engagement actors, celebrities, honeymooners, and the precocious young — all commingle in this bizarre aggregation that is the New York Broadway audience. Even during (and perhaps *especially* during) troubled times in this vibrant city, it is as bright, bold, and varied a crowd as is likely to assemble at any single place in America.

It is eight o'clock. In close to forty theatres within two dozen blocks of each other, houselights dim, curtains rise, and spotlights

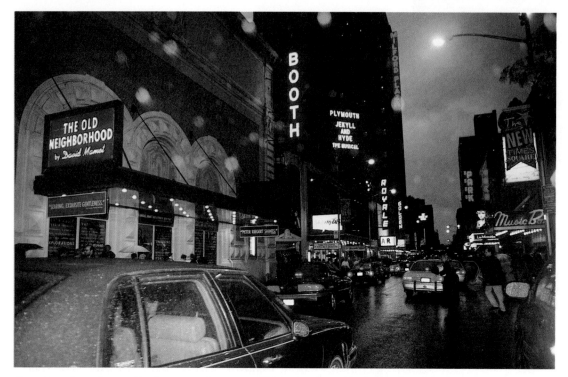

About three dozen theatres line the streets of a mere two blocks in midtown Manhattan; five of them – the Booth, the Plymouth, the Royale, the Music Box, and the Martin Beck – are shown here in a single half block of 45th Street. Most Broadway theatres date from the beginning of the twentieth century, and several are currently being restored. This convergence of playhouses makes Broadway the most concentrated – and consequently the most lively – theatre district in the world.

pick out performers whose lives center on this moment. Here a new musical, here a star-studded revival of an American classic, here a contemporary English comedy from London's West End, here a new play fresh from its electrifying Seattle or Atlanta premiere, here a one-woman show, here an off-Broadway hit moving to larger quarters, here a new avant-garde dance-drama, here a touring production from eastern Europe, and here the new play everyone expects will capture this year's coveted Pulitzer Prize. The hours pass.

Eleven o'clock. Pandemonium. All the double doors open simultaneously, as if on cue, and once again the thousands pour out into the night. At nearby restaurants, waiters stand by to receive the after-theatre onslaught. In Sardi's private upstairs room, an opening-night cast party gets under way; downstairs, the patrons rehash the evening's entertainment and sneak covert glances at the celebrities around them and the actors heading for the upstairs sanctuary: there to await the reviews that will determine whether they will be employed next week or back on the street looking for new jobs.

Now let's turn back the clock. It is dawn in Athens, the thirteenth day of the month of Elaphebolion in the year 458 B.C. From thousands of low mud-bricked homes in the city, from the central agora, from temples and agricultural outposts, streams of Athenians and visitors converge upon the south slope of the Acropolis. Bundled against the morning's dampness, carrying with them breakfast figs and flagons of wine, they pay their tokens at the entrance to the great Theatre of Dionysus and take their places in the seating spaces allotted them. Each tribe occupies a separate area. They have gathered for the Great Dionysian festival, which celebrates the greening of the land, the rebirth of vegetation, and the long sunny days that stretch ahead. It is a time for revelry, for rejoicing at fertility and all its fruits. And it is above all a time for the ultimate form of Dionysian worship: the theatre.

The open stone seats carved into the hillside fill up quickly. The crowd of 17,000 people here today comprises not only the majority of Athenian citizens but thousands of tradesmen, foreign visitors, slaves, and resident aliens as well. Even paupers are in attendance, thanks to the two obols apiece provided by a state fund to buy tickets for the poor; they take their place with the latecomers on the extremities of the *theatron,* as this first of theatres is called. Now, as the eastern sky grows pale, a masked and costumed actor appears atop a squat building set in full view of every spectator. A hush falls over the crowd, and the actor, his voice magnified by the wooden mask he wears, booms out this text:

> I ask the gods some respite from the weariness
> of this watchtime measured by years I lie
> awake . . .

And the entranced crowd settles in, secure in the knowledge that today they are in good hands. Today they will hear and see a new version of a familiar story — the story of Agamemnon's homecoming and his murder, the revenge of that murder by his son Orestes, and the final disposition of justice in the case of Orestes' act — as told in the three tragedies that constitute *The Oresteia.* This magnificent trilogy is by Aeschylus, Athens's leading dramatist for more than forty years. The spectators watch closely, admiring but critical. Tomorrow they or their representatives will decide by vote whether the festival's prize should go to this work, or whether the young Sophocles, whose plays were presented in this space yesterday, had better sensed the true pulse of the

time. Even forty years later, the comic playwright Aristophanes will be arguing the merits and demerits of this day's work.

It is noon in London, and Queen Elizabeth I sits on the throne. Flags fly boldly atop three of the taller buildings in Bankside, across the Thames, announcing performance day at The Globe, The Rose, and The Swan. Boatmen have already begun ferrying theatre-bound Londoners across the river. Meanwhile, north of town, other flocks of Londoners are headed by foot and by carriage up to Finsbury Fields and the theatres of Shoreditch: The Fortune and The Curtain. And though public theatres have been banned within the city for some time now by action of the aldermen, an ensemble of trained schoolboys is rehearsing for a private candlelight performance before the queen in the royal palace.

Now, as the morning sermon concludes at St. Paul's Cathedral, traffic across the river increases. London Bridge fills with pedestrians hurrying to Bankside, where players at The Globe will present a new tragedy by Shakespeare (something called *Hamlet,* supposedly after an old play by Thomas Kyd). And The Rose promises a revival of the late Christopher Marlowe's *Dr. Faustus.* The noisy crowds swarm into the theatres, where the price of admission is a penny; another penny is needed for a pint of beer, and those who wish to go upstairs and take a seat on one of the benches in the gallery — the best place to see the action, both on the stage and off — must plunk down yet more pennies.

At The Globe, 2,000 spectators are on hand for the premiere. A trumpet sounds once, then again, and then builds into a full fanfare. The members of the audience exchange a few last winks with friends old and new — covert invitations to postperformance intimacies of various kinds — then turn their attention to the pillared platform stage. Through a giant door a guard bursts forth, lantern in hand. "Who's there?" he cries. Then through another door a voice responds, "Nay, answer me: stand

and unfold yourself," and another guard enters. In 2,000 imaginations, the bright afternoon has turned to midnight, Bankside has given way to the outskirts of Elsinore. And a shiver from the actors onstage sets up an answering chill among the audience as the second guard proclaims to the first, "'Tis bitter cold, and I am sick at heart." The audience strains forward. The new tragedy has begun.

It is 1629 in Edo (Tokyo), and the Shōgun has called together his advisors to discuss, with the utmost urgency, Japan's wildly popular *kabuki* drama. First performed by women in Kyoto, this explosive music-drama now employs performers of both sexes and has become fabulously licentious: "Men and women sing and dance together! Their lewd voices are clamorous, like the buzzing of flies and the crying of cicadas!" an outraged Confucian has reported. Somberly, the Shōgun delivers his edict: henceforward, kabuki can be performed only by males. Little does the Shōgun realize that his edict will be absolute law at least through to the next millennium.

It is 5 A.M. in Moscow, 1898. At a cafe in the shadow of the Kremlin wall, Konstantin Stanislavsky and Vladimir Nemirovich-Danchenko hotly discuss the wretched state of the current Russian theatre. It is too declamatory, they agree; it is also too insensitive, too shallow, too inartistic. Out of this all-night session the Moscow Art Theatre will be formed, bringing to the last days of czarist society the complex, gently ironic masterpieces of Chekhov and an acting style so natural as to astonish the world.

It is midnight in a basement in the East Village, or a warehouse in Brooklyn, or a campus rehearsal room, or a coffee shop in Pittsburgh, Seattle, Sioux Falls, or Berlin. Across one end of the room, a curtain has been drawn across a pole suspended by wires. It has been a long evening, but one play remains to be

seen. The author is unknown, but rumor has it that this new work is brutal, shocking, poetic, strange. The members of the audience, by turns skeptics and enthusiasts, look for the tenth time at their programs. The lights dim. Performers, backed by crudely painted packing crates, begin to act.

There is a common denominator in all of these scenes: they are all theatre. There is no culture that has not had a theatre in some form, for theatre is the art of people acting out — and giving witness to — their most pressing, most illuminating, and most inspiring concerns. Theatre is at once a showcase and a forum, a medium through which a society displays its ideas, fashions, moralities, and entertainments and debates its conflicts, dilemmas, and struggles. Theatre has provided a stage for political revolution, for social propaganda, for civil debate, for artistic expression, for religious conversion, for mass education, and even for its own self-criticism. It has been a performance ground for witch doctors, priests, intellectuals, poets, painters, technologists, militarists, philosophers, reformers, evangelists, prime ministers, jugglers, peasants, children, and kings. It has taken place in caves, in fields and forests, in circus tents, in inns and in castles, on street corners, and in public buildings grand and squalid all over the world. And it goes on incessantly in the minds of its authors, its actors, its producers, its designers, and its audiences.

For theatre is, above all, a *living* art form — a process, an event that is fluid in time, feeling, and experience. Theatre is not simply a matter of "plays" but also of "playing"; and a play is composed not simply of "acts" but also of "acting." Just as *play* and *act* are both noun and verb, so theatre is both a thing and a happening. It is continually forming, continually present in time. In fact, that very quality of "presentness" (or, in the actor's terminology, "stage presence") defines great theatrical performance.

Unlike the more static arts, theatre presents us with a number of classic paradoxes:

It is spontaneous, yet it is rehearsed.

It is participatory, yet it is presented.

It is real, yet it is simulated.

It is understandable, yet it is obscure.

It is unique to the moment, yet it is repeatable.

The actors are themselves, yet they are characters.

The audience believes, yet it does not believe.

The audience is involved, yet it remains apart.

The theatre's actors, as you will see in later chapters, both "live in the moment" during performance, yet carefully study, plan, and rehearse the details of their roles beforehand. And the audience responds to this performance by rooting for dramatic "characters" to achieve their goals, then applauding the "actors" who play those roles during the curtain call. Yet these paradoxes do not represent a flaw or weakness in the logic of theatrical construction; rather, they show the theatre's essential strength, which lies in its kinship and concern with the ambiguity and irony of human life. For it is *we* — the people of the real world — who are at the same time spontaneous yet premeditating, candid yet contriv-

ing, unique yet self-repeating, comprehensible yet fundamentally unknown and unknowable. The theatre shows us, and *is* us, in all of our living complexity.

Theorists of dramatic literature and of dramatic practice often ignore the theatre's paradoxes in their attempts to "explain" a play or the art of the stage; in this they do a disservice to art as well as to scholarship, for to "explain" the theatre without reference to its ambiguities is to remove its vital dynamic tension — in other words, to kill it. And although much valuable information can certainly be discovered at an autopsy table, it is information pertinent only to the appearance and behavior of a corpse.

In this book we shall not be overly concerned with corpses. Our task will be the harder one — to discover the theatre in being, *alive* and with all its paradoxes and ambiguities intact. From time to time it will be necessary for us to make some separations — between product and process, for example — but we must bear in mind at all times that these separations are conveniences, not representations or fact. In the end we shall be looking at the theatre as part of the human environment and at the ways in which we fit into that environment — as participants and observers, artists and art critics, role models and role players, actors and persons. As such, this book about the theatre is also about ourselves.

1

What Is the Theatre?

W hat is the theatre? The word comes from the Greek *the-atron*, or "seeing place." It is a place where something is seen. And the companion term *drama* comes from the Greek *dran*, "to do." It is something done. An *action*. Theatre: Something is seen, something is done. An action is witnessed.

Today we use the word *theatre* in many ways. We use it often to describe the building where plays are put on: the architecture, the structure, the space for dramatic performance — the place where "something is seen." We also use the term to indicate where films are shown, as in "movie theatre." And we use it metaphorically to refer to a place where wars and surgeries occur: the "theatre of operations" and the "operating theatre."

But that's just the "hardware" definition of *theatre*. The "software" definition — the *activity* involved in theatre — is far more important. For *theatre* also refers to the company of players (and owners, managers, and technicians) who perform in such a space and to the body of plays that such a company produces. This is the "something that is done." When we speak of "the Guthrie Theatre," we are referring not merely to a building in Minneapolis but also to the stage artists and administrators who work in that building and to the body of plays produced there. We are also referring to a body of ideas — a vision — that animates the artists and integrates them with the body of plays. Theatre, in this sense, is a combination of people, ideas, and the works of art that emanate from their collaboration.

7

The Guthrie Theatre in Minneapolis was founded in 1963 by celebrated British director Tyrone Guthrie, who oversaw the architectural design, which – like sixteenth-century Shakespearean playhouses – thrusts the actors in the midst of the audience. Shown here is Chekhov's *The Three Sisters*, directed by Mr. Guthrie and designed by Tanya Moiseiwitsch for the theatre's initial season.

And, finally, we also use the word *theatre* to summon up an *occupation* that is the professional activity — and often the passion — of thousands of men and women all over the world. It is a vocation, and sometimes a lifetime devotion. *A Life in the Theatre* is the title of one theatre artist's autobiography (Tyrone Guthrie, in fact, for whom the Guthrie Theatre is named), as well as the title of a play about actors by modern American dramatist David Mamet. But *A Life in the Theatre* is more universally known as the unwritten title for the unrecorded biographies of all theatre artists who have dedicated their professional lives to perfecting the special arts of acting, direct-ing, designing, managing, and writing for "the theatre" in all the above senses.

Theatre as a building, a company, an occu-pation — let's look at all three of these usages more closely.

The Theatre Building

Sometimes a theatre is not a building at all but merely, in English director Peter Brook's term, an empty space. The most ancient Greek theatron was probably nothing but a flat circle where performers chanted and danced before a hillside of seated spectators. The minimal requirement for a theatre "building" is nothing but a place to act and a place to watch. And when there is a text for the performance, it is a place to hear as well as to watch. Hence the word *audience,* from the Latin *audientia,* "those who hear."

The empty space needs some definition, then. This includes some attention to seating a large number of people so that they can see the performers, hence the hillside presenting a bank of seats, each with a good view. It also includes some attention to *acoustics* (from the Greek *acoustos,* "heard") so that the sound is protected from the wind and directed (or reflected) toward the hearers.

This watercolor depicts the opulent interior of Booth's Theatre in New York at its 1869 opening. This grand "temple of theatre" was built by America's finest actor of the time, Edwin Booth (the brother of Lincoln's assassin). Booth staged and performed in a classical repertory of Shakespearean plays at his theatre for four years. The side boxes, similar to those that still exist in older Broadway theatres today, had poor sight lines: spectators electing to sit there were more interested in being seen than in seeing the play. The luxurious seating in the orchestra made this a particularly comfortable as well as an elegant way to see classic theatre. Charles Witham, Booth's original stage designer, painted this watercolor; part of Witham's scenery (a street scene) is shown onstage.

THEATRE AND DRAMA

The words *theatre* and *drama* are often used interchangeably, yet they can also have distinct meanings. Although both are very general terms, *theatre* often denotes the elements of the whole theatrical production (architecture, scenery, acting), and *drama,* a more limited term, tends to refer mainly to the plays produced in such a "theatrical" environment. To use a modern metaphor, theatre is the "hardware" of play production, and drama is the "software." This reflects on the words' separate etymologies: theatre is that which "is seen," and drama is that which "is done."

Theatre can mean a building; *drama* cannot. *Theatre* is used to include all the theatrical arts — architecture, design, acting, scenery construction, advertising, marketing, and so on — whereas *drama* is often used in a more limited sense to refer to plays and to dramatic texts (or dramatic literature). Therefore, drama-derived terms such as *dramatic* and *dramaturgy* are often used to refer to the verbal aspects of theatre; *theatrical* tends to suggest visual aspects, as well as "effects" that generate audience impact. (Detractors of the theatre sometimes use the word *theatrical* in a pejorative sense, implying gaudiness and sensationalism, as in "mere theatricality.")

In some parts of North America, particularly in Canada, a further distinction is made: *theatre* is used more to denote stage plays (the product), and *drama* refers more to the acting and improvising of situations (the process).

The audience gathers at a matinee performance at the ornate Kabuki-za Theatre in Tokyo, the principal home of Japan's kabuki drama. Matinees begin at eleven o'clock here and last until four o'clock, with the audience enjoying snacks or full meals during the play's several intermissions.

Theatre buildings may also be very elaborate structures. Greek theatres of the fourth century B.C. — the period immediately following the "golden age" of Greek playwrights — were gigantic stone edifices, capable of holding upwards of 17,000 spectators. Magnificent three-story Roman theatres, complete with gilded columns, canvas awnings, and intricate marble carvings, were often erected for dramatic festivals in the time of Nero and Caligula — only to be dismantled when the festivities ended. Grand freestanding Elizabethan theatres dominated the London skyline in the illustrated sixteenth-century pictorial maps of the town. Opulent proscenium theatres were built throughout Europe and in the major cities of the United States in the eighteenth and nineteenth centuries. Many are in full operation today, competing with splendid new stagehouses of every description and serving as the urban focus for metropolitan areas around the world. Theatres (the buildings) are central to modern urban architecture, just as theatre (the art) is central to contemporary life.

The Company, or Troupe, of Players

Theatre is a collaborative art, usually involving dozens, even hundreds, of people for a single performance. Historically, therefore, theatre practitioners have worked together in long-standing companies, or troupes, of such theatre artists. Since the third century B.C., troupes of players (actors, or, more literally, "playmakers") have toured the countrysides and settled in cities to present a repertory (or repertoire) of plays as a means of earning their livelihood. Generally such players have included actor-playwrights and actor-technicians as well so that the company becomes a self-contained production unit, capable of writing, preparing, and presenting whole theatrical works that tend to define the "theatre" named

Often these spaces — for performing and for seeing and hearing — can be casually defined: the audience up there, the actors down there. Occasionally, the spaces are even merged together, with the actors mingling with — and sometimes interacting with — the watchers and listeners. When the practice of selling tickets and paying actors began (more than twenty-five hundred years ago), rigid physical separation of these spaces began to be employed.

after it. Some of these troupes — and the works produced by them — have become legendary: the Lord Chamberlain's Men of London, which counted actor-playwright William Shakespeare as a member, for example, and the Illustrious Theatre of Paris, founded and headed by the great actor-writer Molière. These theatres — these companies of players — have proven more long-lasting than the buildings that in some cases survived them; they represent the genius and creativity of theatre in a way that stone and steel alone cannot.

In a more general sense, we may also use the term *theatre* to indicate a general category of associated dramatic works, such as the American theatre, the Elizabethan theatre, dance-theatre, musical theatre, the theatre of the absurd, the theatre of Neil Simon, and black theatre. Any or all of these terms may serve to represent a specifically defined grouping of plays, players, authors, and buildings that form a broad identity in the minds of theatre students, critics, and enthusiasts.

The Occupation of Theatre

Finally, theatre is a principal occupation of its practitioners. It is a vocation for professionals and an avocation for amateurs, yet in either case, theatre is *work*. Specifically, it is that body of artistic work in which actors impersonate characters in a live performance of a play. Each aspect of theatre as occupation — work, art,

Improvisational theatre is performance without a script. Here, Paul Sills and company present *Story Theatre*, popular children's stories improvised and acted by adult performers at the Mark Taper Forum in Los Angeles.

One of the excitements of theatregoing is seeing plays of the past come vividly to life in our own times. The job of the contemporary theatre artist is to make the genius of the past speak persuasively in the present. In Andrei Serban's radically contemporized production of Shakespeare's *Twelfth Night*, Duke Orsino arrives, with his bodyguards, by helicopter. This 1989 American Repertory Theatre production featured sets by Derek McLane and costumes by Catherine Zuber.

impersonation, and performance — deserves individual attention.

Work

The "work" of the theatre is indeed hard work. Rehearsals alone normally take a minimum of four to six weeks, which are preceded by at least an equal amount of time — and often months or years — of writing, researching, planning, casting, designing, and creating a production ensemble. The labors of theatre artists in the final weeks before an opening are legendary: the ninety-hour workweek becomes commonplace, expenditures of money and spirit are intense, and even the unions relax their regulations to allow for an almost unbridled invasion of the hours the ordinary world spends sleeping, eating, and unwinding. The theatre enterprise may involve hundreds of people in scores of different efforts — many more backstage than onstage — and the mobilization and coordination of these efforts is in itself a giant task. So, when we think of the "work" embodied in the plays of Shakespeare or Neil Simon, for example, we must think of work in the sense of physical toil as well as in the loftier sense of *oeuvre,* by which the French designate the sum of an artist's creative endeavor.

The work of the theatre is generally divisible into a number of crafts:

Producing, which includes securing all necessary personnel, space, and financing; supervising all production and promo-

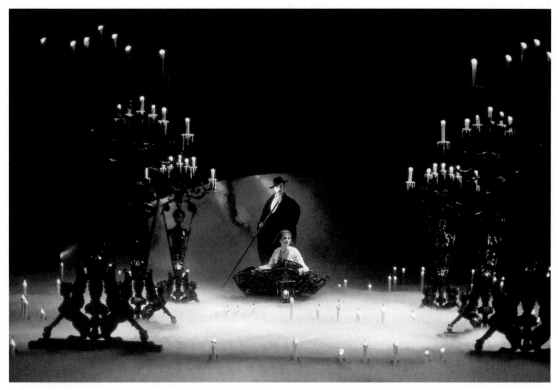

Andrew Lloyd Webber's *Phantom of the Opera* is the most commercially successful theatre production in history, having been seen by more than 63 million people at the time of this writing, and earning, in ticket sales alone, well over three *billion* dollars since its 1986 London opening. Part of the play's success is its spectacular staging, including a famous falling chandelier and a boat ride on a lake existing underneath the Paris Opera house (which actually exists — the remains of an old water system). The celebrated production design (scenery and costumes) is by Maria Björnson, with admirable lighting by Andrew Bridge.

tional efforts; fielding all legal matters; and distributing all proceeds derived from receipts

Directing, which includes controlling and developing the artistic product and providing it with a unified vision, coordinating all its components, and supervising all rehearsals

Acting, in which actors perform the roles of characters in a play

Designing, in which designers map out the visual and audio elements of a production, including the scenery, properties, costumes and wigs, makeup, lighting, sound con-

cepts, programs, advertising, and general ambience of the premises

Building, in which carpenters, costumers, wigmakers, electricians, makeup artists, recording and sound engineers, painters, and a host of other specially designated craftspeople translate the design into reality by constructing and finishing in detail the "hardware" of a show

Crewing, in which technicians execute in proper sequence and with carefully rehearsed timing the light and sound cues and the shifting of scenery, as well as oversee the placement and return of properties and the assignment, laundering, repair, and changes of costumes

Stage managing, which includes the responsibility for "running" a play production in all its complexity in performance after performance

House managing, which includes the responsibility for admitting, seating, and providing for the general comfort of the audience

And above all there is *playwriting,* which is in a class by itself. It is the one craft of the theatre that is usually executed away from the theatre building and its associated shops — indeed, it may take place continents and centuries away from the production it inspires.

Of course, the work of the theatre need not be divided exactly as the preceding list indicates. In any production, some people will perform more than one kind of work; for example, many of the builders will also crew. And it is not uncommon for playwrights to direct what they write, directors to act in their own productions, and designers to build at least some of what they design. There are indeed celebrated occasions where multitalented theatre artists have taken on multiple roles at the same time: Aeschylus, in ancient Greece, and Molière, in seventeenth-century Paris, each wrote, directed, and acted in their own plays, probably designing them as well; William Shakespeare was playwright, actor, and co-owner of the Lord Chamberlain's Men in Elizabethan times; Bertolt Brecht revolutionized both playwriting and acting when writing and directing his plays in Berlin after World War II; and Mel Brooks, in our own times, wrote the text and lyrics, composed the music, and produced his celebrated 2001 Broadway show, *The Producers.*

Theatre is also work in the sense that it is not "play." This is a more subtle distinction than we might at once imagine. First, of course, recall that we ordinarily use the children's word *play* in describing the main product of theatre work: while children "play games," adults may "play roles" or "put on a play." This is not merely a peculiarity of the English language, for we find that the French *jeu,* the German *Spiel,* and the Latin *ludi* all share the double meaning of the English *play,* referring both to children's games and to dramatic plays and playing. This association points to a relationship that is fundamental to the understanding of theatre: theatre *is* a kind of playing, and it is useful for us to see how and why this is so.

Theatre and games have a shared history. Both were developed to a high level of sophistication in Greek festivals: the Dionysian theatre festivals and the Olympian game — or sport — festivals were the two great cultural events of ancient Greece, each embodying the legendary Greek competition for excellence. Centuries later, the Romans merged sports and theatre in public circuses, where the two were performed side by side, often in competition with each other. And more than a millennium later, the Londoners of Shakespeare's time built "playhouses" that could accommodate dramatic productions on one day and bear-baiting spectacles (somewhat akin to more modern bullfights) on the next. The association — and popularity — of dramatic and sports entertainment continues today, where dramatizations (sitcoms like *Friends* and *Frasier,* dramas like *ER* and *Law and Order*) and games (sports contests, quiz shows, "reality" competitions) utterly dominate television fare around the world. Even most television commercials are "minidramas" that, during their fifteen or thirty seconds, manage to introduce characters, plot, and an all-important theme or "message." And professional athletes and stage entertainers are among the foremost (and most highly paid) celebrities of the modern age. Many a retired sports hero has even found a second career in the other type of play: acting.

This link between games and theatre is formed early in life, for "child's play" usually manifests both gamelike and dramalike aspects. Much child's play includes "dressing-

The link between sports and theatre has led to many plays about sports, including *The Great White Hope* about boxing, *That Championship Season* about basketball, *Fences, Cobb,* and *Bleacher Bums* about baseball, *The Beautiful Game* about English football (soccer), and *The Changing Room* about rugby. Here the Utah Shakespearean Festival stages one of the classic American musicals of the 1950s, *Damn Yankees,* in 1999.

up" and "acting-out," where children create improvisations they may call "playing doctor" or "playing cops and robbers." Like drama, this play is also educational, as it helps children prepare for the necessary role-playing of adult life. Structured games are similarly instructional: hide-and-seek, for example, while a playful and engrossing game, is also an opportunity to act-out one of childhood's greatest fears — the terror of separation from the parent, or "separation anxiety," as psychologists term it. Hide-and-seek affords the child a way of dealing with separation anxiety by confronting it "in play" until it loses much of its frightening power. Such "child's play" is often grounded in serious concerns, and through the act of playing the child gradually devel-

ops means of coping with life's challenges and uncertainties. The theatre's plays and playing often serve the same role for adults.

Drama and games are likewise linked in that they are among the very few occupations that also attract large numbers of wholly *amateur* "players," individuals who seek no compensation beyond their sheer personal satisfaction. This is because both drama and games offer wonderful opportunities for intense physical involvement, friendly competition, personal self-expression, and emotional engagement — within limits set by precise and sensible rules. And both sport and drama also generate an audience to their activities, because the energies and passions expressed by each — common enough on children's playgrounds but rarely

> ### NEITHER A BOOK NOR A WORK BUT AN ENERGY
>
> Theatrical representation is finite and leaves behind it, behind its actual presence, no trace, no object to carry off. It is neither a book nor a work, but an energy, and in this sense it is the only art of life.
>
> – Jacques Derrida

seen in daily adult life — can prove immensely engaging to nonparticipating spectators.

But the theatre must finally be distinguished from child's play, and from sports as well, because theatre is by its nature a calculated act from beginning to end. Unlike adult games, which are open-ended, every theatre performance has a preordained conclusion. The Yankees may not win the World Series next year, but Hamlet definitely will die in the fifth act. The work of the theatre, indeed, consists in keeping Hamlet alive up to that point — brilliantly alive — to make of that foreordained end a profoundly moving, ennobling, even surprising climax.

We might say, finally, that *theatre is the art of making play into work* — specifically, into *a work of art*. It is exhilarating work, to be sure, and it usually inspires and invigorates the energies and imaginations of all who participate; it transcends more prosaic forms of labor just as song transcends grunts and groans. But it is work. That is its challenge.

Art

As we have suggested, the work of the theatre goes beyond the mere perfecting of skills, which is, after all, a goal of professionals in every field. The theatre is *artistic* work. The word *art* brings to mind a host of intangibles: creativity, imagination, elegance, power, aesthetic harmony, and fineness of form. Furthermore, we expect a work of art to capture something of the human spirit and to touch upon sensed, but intellectually elusive, meanings in life. Certainly great theatre never fails to bring together many of these intangibles. In great theatre we glimpse not only the physical and emotional exuberance of play but also the deep yearnings that propel humanity's search for purpose, meaning, and the life well lived.

Art, of course, is one of the most supreme pursuits of humanity, integrating, in a unique fashion, our emotions with our intellects and our aesthetics with our revelations. Art is empowering, to both those who make it and those who appreciate it. Art sharpens thought and focuses feeling; it brings reality up against imagination and presses creativity to the ever-expanding limits of human potential. Although life may be fragmented, inconclusive, and frustrating, a beautiful painting, choral hymn, jazz rendition, or dance video can provide us with near-instant integration, synthesis, and satisfaction. One might, of course, find similar values in religion as well, but art is accessible without subscribing to any particular set of beliefs; it is for everyone: an open-ended response to life's unending puzzles. It is surely for this reason that all great religions — Eastern and Western — have employed art and artworks (including dramatic art) in their liturgies and services from the earliest of times.

Impersonation

The theatrical art involves actors impersonating characters. This feature is unique to the theatre and separates it from other art forms such as poetry, painting, sculpture, music, performance art, cabaret acts, and like activities. Further, impersonation is the single most important aspect of the theatre; it is its very foundation.

Try to imagine what extreme conceptual difficulties the ancient creators of the theatre encountered in laying down the ground rules for dramatic impersonation. For how was the audience to distinguish the "real person" from the "character" portrayed — the actor-as-himself from the actor-as-character? And

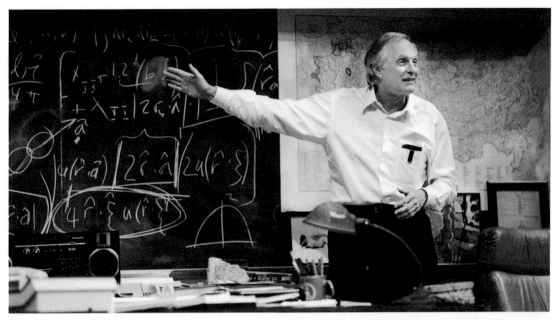

The characters that actors impersonate are often based on real people. In Peter Parnell's *QED*, premiering at the Los Angeles Mark Taper Forum in 2001, distinguished actor Alan Alda plays the late, Nobel Prize–winning physicist Richard Feynman, essentially lecturing the theatre audience – mostly in Feynman's actual words – on physics, politics, relationships, creativity, and the ever-imminence of death. Alda doesn't look like Feynman, but former Feynman associates agree that the actor captures Feynman's mental buoyancy to perfection.

when the playwright was also an actor, how could onlookers distinguish between the thoughts of playwright-as-himself and those of the playwright-as-character? Questions such as these are often asked by children today as they watch a play. Indeed, in face-to-face encounters, soap opera fans will address actors by their character names and ask them questions pertinent only to their stage lives. Given this confusion in what we like to think of as a sophisticated age, it is easy to see why the ancients had to resolve the problem of actor-character separation before the theatre could become a firmly established institution.

The solution the ancient world found was the mask. Western theatre had its true beginning that day in ancient Greece when an actor first stepped out of the chorus, placed an unpainted mask over his face, and thereby signaled that the lines he was about to speak

were "in character." The mask provides both a physical and a symbolic separation between the impersonator (the actor) and the impersonated (the character), thus aiding literal-minded onlookers to temporarily suspend their awareness of the "real" world and to accept in its place the world of the stage. In a play, it must be the *characters* who have apparent life; the actors themselves are expected to disappear into the shadows, along with their personal preoccupations, anxieties, and career ambitions. This convention of the stage gives rise to what Denis Diderot, an eighteenth-century French dramatist (and author of the world's first encyclopedia), called the *paradox of the actor:* when the actor has perfected his or her art, it is the *simulated* character, the mask, which seems to live before our eyes, while the real person has no apparent life at all. The strength of such an illusion still echoes in our

Left: Full-face masks are used for gods and humans alike in Peter Hall's extraordinary Royal Shakespeare Company/Denver Center Theatre 2000 production of John Barton's *Tantalus*, which takes the twenty-first-century audience back to the times of ancient Greece. Scenic and costume design by Dionysis Fotopoulos; lighting design by Sumio Yoshii.

Below: Contemporary avant-garde theatre often uses masks as well, as in this highly experimental version of *1839*, created by the GAle GAtes et al. company (see chapter titled "Theatre Today") in Brooklyn, New York, in 2000.

use of the word *person,* which derives from the Latin word (*persona*) for mask.

But of course we know that the actor does not die behind the mask, and herein lies an even greater paradox: we *believe* in the character, but at the end of the play we *applaud* the actor. Not only that — as we watch good theatre we are always, somewhere in the back of our minds, applauding the actor. Our appreciation of theatre rests largely on our dual awareness of actor and character and on our understanding that they live inside the same skin. Masks are rarely used in modern theatre, but they can be seen, even today, in the *nō* drama in Japan, the masquerade dramas of Nigeria, and many of the other ritual dance-dramas of Africa, Asia, and the Americas. But the mask remains the symbol of impersonation, at once hiding the face of the performer and projecting that of the character, and as such the mask is often seen as the symbol of the theatre — usually in the form of the double masks of comedy and tragedy that adorn many theatres and theatre company letterheads.

Performance

Theatre is performance, but what, exactly, does *performance* mean? Performance is an action or series of actions taken for the ultimate benefit (attention, entertainment, enlightenment, or involvement) of someone else. We call that "someone else" the audience.

A strictly private conversation between two people is simply "communication." If, however, they engage in a conversation to impress or involve a third person who they know is in a position to overhear it, the "communication" becomes a "performance" and the third person becomes its "audience."

Obviously, performance is a part of everyday life; indeed, it has been analyzed as such in a number of psychological and sociological works. When two teenage boys wrestle on the schoolground, they may well be "performing" their physical prowess for the benefit of their

The masked chorus cringes in awe during a 1992 production of Euripedes' *Iphigeneia at Aulis*, directed by the late Garland Wright at the Guthrie Theatre in Minneapolis. The costumes and masks, by Susan Hilferty, echo ancient tragic wear.

peers. The student who asks a question in the lecture hall is frequently "performing" for the other students — and the professor "performs" for the same audience in providing a response. Trial lawyers examining witnesses invariably "perform" — often drawing on a considerable repertoire of grunts, snorts, shrugs, raised eyebrows, and disbelieving sighs — for the benefit of that ultimate courtroom audience, the jury. Politicians kiss babies for the benefit of parents (and others) in search of a kindly candidate. Even stony silence can be a performance — if, for example, it is the treatment a

woman metes out to an offensive admirer. We are all performers, and the theatre only makes an art out of something we all do every day. The theatre reflects our everyday performances and expands those performances into a formal mode of artistic expression.

The theatre makes use of two general modes of performance: presentational (or direct) and representational (or indirect). Presentational performance is the basic stand-up comedy or nightclub mode. Club performers directly and continuously acknowledge the presence of the audience by singing to them, dancing for them, joking with them, and responding overtly to their applause, laughter, requests, and heckling. Dramatic forms of all ages have employed these techniques and a variety of other presentation methods as well, including asides to the audience, soliloquies, direct address, plays-within-plays, and curtain calls.

Representational performance, however, is probably the more fundamental mode of drama. It is certainly the mode that makes drama "dramatic" as opposed to simply "theatrical"; in the representational mode of performance, the audience watches behavior that seems to be staged as if no audience were present at all. As a result, the audience is encouraged to concentrate on the *events* that are being staged, not on the nature of their presentation. In other words, the members of the audience "believe in" the play and allow themselves to forget that the characters are really actors and that the apparently spon-

Star perfomer Bebe Neuwirth exemplifies the very notion of "performance" as she sings, dances, and flirtatiously dazzles the audience in the 1997 Broadway revival of *Chicago*.

Above left: Masks remain a major theatrical device worldwide. *Umabatha,* a Zulu version of Shakespeare's *Macbeth,* created and directed by Welcome Msomi in Johannesburg, South Africa, employs such masks to create a larger-than-life persona for an army-chorus. This photograph is from the 1997 world tour.

Left: Actors don't impersonate just human beings. In the 1998 *Lion King,* masked actors portray elephants, lions, gazelles, and, as shown here, prancing zebras. The masks and costumes (designed by Julie Taymor, who also directed) do not hide the actors' faces entirely but rather show the artists and their art simultaneously.

taneous events are really a series of scripted scenes. This belief — or, to borrow Samuel Taylor Coleridge's famous double negative, this "suspension of disbelief" — attracts audience participation through empathy: our feeling of kinship with certain (or all) of the characters which encourages us to identify with their aspirations, sympathize with their plights, exult in their victories, and care deeply about what happens to them. When empathy is present, the audience experiences what is often called the "magic" of theatre. Well-written and well-staged dramas make people *feel,* not just think; they draw in the spectator's emotions, leaving him or her feeling transported

and even somewhat changed. This is as much magic as the modern world provides anywhere, and its effect is the same all over the world.

Occasionally, presentational and representational styles are taken to extremes. In the late nineteenth century, a radically representational movement known as *naturalism* sought to have actors behave onstage exactly as real people do in life, in settings made as lifelike as possible (on one occasion, a famous New York restaurant was completely disassembled and reconstructed on a stage, complete with its original moldings, wallpaper, furniture, silverware, and linens). At times the representational ideal so dominated in certain theatres that actors spoke with their backs to audiences, directors encouraged lifelike pauses and inaudible mumblings, playwrights transcribed dialogue from fragments of randomly overheard conversations, and house managers timed intermissions to the presumed time elapsing in the play's story.

Top left: In this example of presentational performance, the characters of Robert Schenkkan's Pulitzer Prize-winning play, *The Kentucky Cycle,* share the play's political and social concerns directly with the audience. This 1993 Broadway production was directed by Warner Shook.

Left: Representational performances look like real life. In *Jitney,* one of August Wilson's earliest and most straightforwardly realistic plays, we see a hardworking father who owns a low-cost taxi (jitney) service in Pittsburgh, and his son, an ex-con who returns home for forgiveness — and does not receive it. Immensely powerful performances by Paul Butler as the father (*seated left*) and Carl Lumbly as the son (*standing*) make this 2000 pre–New York production, at the Mark Taper Forum in Los Angeles, a portrayal of real life that is both heartbreaking and eloquent. Costumes by Susan Hilferty.

Above: Bertolt Brecht's work takes a direct approach, often with shocking (and nonrealistic) images, lecture-mode presentations, songs, slide shows, and bold graphics. The nastiness of urbanization is the subject of his 1923 *Jungle of Cities* (set in Chicago), here presented by the American Repertory Theatre in 1998, directed by Robert Woodruff, with scenery by Robert Pyzocha.

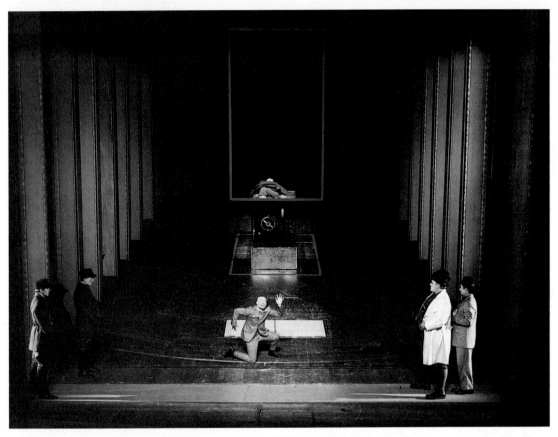

The theatre created by the great German director, theorist, and dramatist Bertolt Brecht is frankly presentational in all respects. His *Resistible Rise of Arturo Ui*, a parable of Hitler's rise to power written in 1941 (although not performed until much later), abstracts, exaggerates, and "distances" the story by setting it among some Chicago gangsters and turning it into a semifarce. Directed by Heiner Müller in 1999 at the Berliner Ensemble, the theatre Brecht founded.

Rebelling against this extreme representationalism, the twentieth-century German playwright-director Bertolt Brecht created its opposite: a presentational style which, seeking to appeal directly to the audience on a variety of social issues, featured lettered signs, songs, slide projections, chalk talks, political arguments directly addressed to the house, and an "alienated" style of acting which was intended to reduce empathy or theatrical "magic." These extremes, however, exist more in theory than in practice. We are always aware, during naturalistic performances, that we are watching actors perform for us, and the plays of Brecht and his followers, despite his theories, generate empathy when well performed; the fact is that theatrical performance is always *both* presentational and representational, though often in different degrees.

Two other aspects of performance distinguish theatre from certain other forms of performance: theatre is *live* performance, and it is in most cases a *scripted* and *rehearsed* event.

LIVE PERFORMANCE   Unlike video and cinema (although sometimes employing elements of both), the theatre is a living, real-time event, with performers and audience mutually interacting, each fully aware of the other's immediate presence. This turns out to be an extremely important distinction. Distinguished film stars, particularly those with theatre backgrounds (as most have), routinely return to the live dramatic stage, despite the substantially greater financial rewards of film work, and invariably prefer stage acting because of the immediate audience response theatre provides, with its corresponding sensations of excitement and "presence." Beyond question, fundamental forces are at work in live theatre.

The first of these forces is the rapport existing between actor and audience. Both are breathing the same air; both are involved, at the same time and in the same space, with the stage life depicted by the play. Sometimes their mutual fascination is almost palpable: every actor's performance is affected by the way the audience yields or withholds its responses — its laughter, sighs, applause, gasps, silences. Live theatrical performance is always — even in naturalistic theatre — a two-way communication between stage and house.

And second, live theatre creates a relationship among the audience members. Having arrived at the theatre as individuals or in groups of two or three, the audience members quickly find themselves fused into a common experience with total strangers: laughing at the same jokes, empathizing with the same characters, experiencing the same revelations. This broad communal response is never developed by television drama, which is played chiefly to solitary or clustered viewers who (because of frequent commercials) are only intermittently engaged, nor is it likely to happen in movie houses, where audience members essentially assume a one-on-one relationship with the screen and rarely (except in private or group-oriented screenings) break out in a powerful collective response, much less applause. By contrast, live theatrical presentations generate audience activity that is broadly social in nature: the crowd arrives at the theatre at about the same time, they mingle and chat during

Nothing is more immediate, in the theatre, than a live animal, who (presumably at least) has virtually no self-consciousness about "acting." One of Shakespeare's classic roles is Launce in *Two Gentlemen of Verona*, who shares stage with his dog, Crab; the actor (Michael Fitzpatrick here) must seem to be as "real" and unaffected as his very real dog. From the 2001 Utah Shakespearean Festival production.

intermissions, and they all depart together, often in spirited conversation about the play. Moreover, they communicate *during* the play: laughter and applause build upon themselves and gain strength from the recognition that others are laughing and applauding. The final ovation — unique to live performance — inevitably involves the audience applauding *itself,* as well as the performers, for understanding

A Script Is Not a Play

A play in a book is only the shadow of a play and not even a clear shadow of it.... The printed script of a play is hardly more than an architect's blueprint of a house not yet built or [a house] built and destroyed. The color, the grace and levitation, the structural pattern in motion, the quick interplay of live beings, suspended like fitful lightning in a cloud, these things are the play, not words on paper nor thoughts and ideas of an author.

— Tennessee Williams

and appreciating the theatrical excellence they have all seen together. And plays with political themes can even generate collective political response. In a celebrated example, the depression-era *Waiting for Lefty* was staged as if the audience were a group of union members; by the play's end the audience was yelling "Strike! Strike!" in response to the play's issues. Obviously, only a live performance could evoke such a response.

Finally, live performance inevitably has the quality of *immediacy*. The action of the play is taking place *right now,* as it is being watched, and anything can happen. Although in most professional productions the changes that occur in performance from one night to another are so subtle that only an expert would notice, the fact is that each night's presentation is unique and everyone present — in the audience, in the cast, and behind the scenes — knows it. This awareness lends an excitement that cannot be achieved by theatrical events that are wholly "in the can." One reason for the excitement, of course, is that in live performance, mistakes can happen; this possibility occasions a certain abiding tension, perhaps even an edge of stage fright, which some people say creates the ultimate thrill of the theatre. But just as disaster can come without warning, so too can splendor. On any given night, each actor is trying to better her or his previous performance, and no one knows when

this collective effort will coalesce into something sublime. The actors' constant striving toward self-transcendence gives the theatre a vitality that is missing from performances fixed unalterably on videotape or celluloid. But perhaps most appropriately, the immediacy of live performance creates a "presentness," or "presence," that embodies the fundamental uncertainty of life itself. One prime function of theatre is to address the uncertainties of human existence, and the very format of live performance presents a moment-to-moment uncertainty right before our eyes. Ultimately, this "immediate theatre" helps us to define the questions and confusions of our lives and lets us grapple, in the present, with their implications.

Scripted and Rehearsed Performance
Theatre performances are largely prepared according to written and well-rehearsed texts, or playscripts. In this way they are often distinguished from several other forms of performance, such as improvisations, performance installations, and certain other performance art projects. Although improvisation and ad-libbing may play a role in the preparation process, and even in certain actual performances, most play productions are based on a script that was established before — and modified during — the play's rehearsal period, and most of the action is permanently set during these rehearsals as well. Mainstream professional play productions, therefore, appear virtually the same night after night: for the most part, the Broadway production of *The Producers* that you see on Thursday will be almost identical to the show your friend saw on Wednesday or your mother saw last fall. And if you were to read the published text, you would see on the page the same words you heard spoken or sung on the stage.

But the text of a play is not, by any means, the play itself. The play fully exists in its performance — its "playing" — only. The script is

THE FUTURE OF THEATRE?

Since the development of motion pictures, about a hundred years ago, it has been occasionally suggested that theatre is in danger of becoming obsolete. This is sheer lunacy. While the cinema's success has obviously been spectacular in the ensuing years, film has only *increased* the worldwide popularity and importance of live theatre. Immediately prior to the terrorist attacks of September 11, 2001, the Broadway theatre had just concluded its most successful season in history, with nearly 12 million persons filling its theatre seats and standing rooms, while U.S. cinema was experiencing its fourth consecutive year of steadily declining attendance. And after the attacks, which closed all New York theatres for two days and caused attendance to dwindle all over town for two or three weeks, business quickly returned to normal and in some cases above normal. Indeed, the New York theatre virtually dwarfs that of previous eras, with over a hundred professional off-Broadway and off-off-Broadway theatres in Manhattan alone, almost none of which existed fifty years ago. And the number of professional American theatres outside of New York City – largely untouched by the national events – has, in the same fifty-year period, skyrocketed from fewer than five companies to well over four *hundred*. Indeed, many of America's regional theatres are now expanding into performance centers with two, three, and even four complete stages.

In fact, theatre flourishes at both the high and low ends of the economic spectrum. At the top, it is gargantuan: while most people know that the 1999 film *Titanic* broke cinematic records to reach $1.6 billion in worldwide ticket sales, the stage musical of *Phantom of the Opera* has earned fully *twice* that sum, having thus far played 96 cities in 18 countries, been seen by 63 million people, and on its way to its fourth billion in ticket receipts. And while Disney's film of *The Lion King* was the sixth largest box-office success in cinema history, earning $770 million worldwide, the same company's live stage version of the same work will have surpassed that figure by the time you read these words. And Mel Brooks' 2001 Broadway stage hit, *The Producers,* has already surpassed the worldwide earnings of his award-winning 1968 film of the same name on the basis of its Manhattan show-

ing alone. There is no question about it: live theatre is, at the top end, an economic powerhouse.

But the theatre's importance does not, of course, derive primarily from its money-making potential; in fact, the opposite is more important. Theatre really flourishes, and will continue to flourish, because even at the low economic end of the scale some of the greatest, most entertaining, most provocative theatre can be created quickly, simply, and cheaply – with neither expensive technology nor multimedia marketing. At bottom, theatre demands nothing more than brilliance, artistry, and hard work. Life-changing stage productions have been mounted with little more than $50 and a borrowed space; high technology, while surely a boon, is never a necessity. For this reason, in addition to the profusion of professional theatres in virtually every state in America, there are ten or twenty times the number of active community and college theatres, high school theatres, camp and club theatres, street theatres, and Shakespeare festivals just about everywhere you can find a park (or, in New York, a parking lot). Audiences everywhere have, and continue to have, a thirst for live performance and live performances. Immediacy, the hallmark of live theatre, has never gone out of style and never will.

Moreover, live plays even in modest theatres have the capacity to change the entire cultural and political climate of their time. It is incontestable that nineteenth-century performances of *Uncle Tom's Cabin*, performed in theatres and meeting halls around the country, played a major role in bringing slavery to an end in America, and it is equally incontestable that staged depictions of homosexuality, homophobia, and America's public AIDS policies, largely in off-Broadway, college, and regional theatres, radically changed American discourse and action on these sensitive and previously invisible subjects during the 1970s, 80s, and 90s. Theatre's demise has been forecast before – first with the advent of film, and then with radio and television – and Broadway has been called a "fabulous invalid" at least since Moss Hart and George S. Kaufman wrote their play of that name in 1938, but it is by now quite obvious that the theatre's universally admired history will be matched, if not exceeded, by its achievements in the future.

merely the record the play leaves behind after the audience has gone home. The script, therefore, is to the play it represents only what a shadowpainting is to the face it silhouettes: it outlines the principal features but conveys only the outer margins of the complexity, the color, the smell, and the spirit of the living person.

And published scripts are an imperfect record at that. Often they carry over material left out of the actual production, or include new material the author thought of after the production was over. The published texts of Shakespeare's plays include differing versions of many of his plays, including two versions of *King Lear* now thought to have been written several years apart. When American dramatist Tennessee Williams published his *Cat on a Hot Tin Roof* after the play's premiere, he included both the third act that he originally wrote and the third act, written at director Elia Kazan's request, that was actually used, and invited his readers to select their preferred version. Moreover, even a fixed script is often as notable for what it lacks as for what it contains. Plays published before the twentieth century rarely have more than rudimentary stage directions, and even now a published play tells us almost nothing about a play's nonverbal components. For how can a printed text capture the bead of sweat that forms on Hamlet's brow as he stabs Polonius, or Romeo's nervous laugh as he tries to part dueling adversaries, or the throbbing anxiety in Beatrice's breast when she first admits to Benedick that she loves him? The published text gives us the printed but not the spoken words: they largely fail us in providing the sounds and inflections of those words, the tones and facial expressions of the actors, the color and sweep of costumes, the play of light and shadow, the movement of forms in space — and the audience response to all this — that come together in a living production.

The chief value of playscripts, then, is that they generate theatrical production and provide an invaluable, albeit imperfect, record of performances past. Two and a half millennia of play productions have left us a repository of thousands upon thousands of scripts, some awful, many ordinary, a few magnificent. This rich store puts us in touch with theatre history in the making and allows us a glimpse back at the nature of the originals in production. It also suggests ways in which the plays of yesterday can serve as blueprints for vital theatre today.

This, then, is the theatre: buildings, companies, and plays; work, art, impersonation, and performance; living performers and written, rehearsed scripts. It is a production, an assemblage of actions, sights, sounds, ideas, feelings, words, light, and, above all, people. It consists of playing and, of course, plays.

But what is a play? That question deserves a separate chapter.

2

What Is a Play?

A play is, essentially, the basic unit of theatre. It is not a thing but an event, taking place in real time and occupying real space. It is a drama — remember its origin from the Greek *dran*, "something done." It is action, not just words in a book.

Action is not merely movement, of course: it is argument, struggle, persuasion, threats, seduction, sound, music, dance, speech, and passion. It comprises all forms of human energy, including language, spatial dynamics, light, color, sonic shocks, aesthetic harmonies, and "remarkable things happening" from moment to moment. It is *live* action, ordinarily unmediated by videotape or cinematic celluloid.

And yet a play does not merely produce (or reproduce) live action; drama frames and focuses that action around a particular conflict, which lends the action meaning and significance. Life may be, as Shakespeare's Macbeth says, "a tale told by an idiot, full of sound and fury, signifying nothing," but drama, which is also full of sound and fury, signifies all sorts of things: if not exactly answers, then at least perspectives, vocabularies, illuminating arguments, and aesthetic illuminations. Conflict — generally between characters but also within them — shapes the action into purposeful, meaningful (and meaning-filled) human struggles, the composite of which become dramatic stories against which we can judge our own struggles. A play presents us with characters that can serve as role models, both positive and negative; it offers us themes, ideas, and revelations that we can accept, scorn, or store for future contemplation. A play is a piece of life — animated, shaped, and framed to become a work of art. It provides a structured synthesis — sometimes a critique and sometimes a celebration — of both life's glories and life's confusions.

Of course, a play is also a piece of literature. There has been a reading audience for plays at least since the time of the ancient Greeks, and play collections — such as Shakespeare's works — have been published since the Renaissance. Today, plays are often printed in literary anthologies, intermixed with poems, short stories, and even novels. But drama should not be thought of as merely a "branch," or "genre," of literature; it is a live performance, some of whose repeatable aspects (chiefly, the words) may be captured in a written and published text.[1]

Finally, a play is "playing," and those who create plays are "players." The theatrical play contains root notions of "child's play" in its acting-out and adventurism, of "dressing-up" in its costumes and props, and of the thrill of sportive competition in its energy and abandon. Like all play, drama is an exhibition, and its players are, in a real sense, willingly exhibitionistic. These are not fundamentally literary characteristics.

Classifying Plays

Plays may be volatile, but they are also contained. They are framed, with a beginning and

---

[1]If the arboreal metaphor is insisted upon, drama would have to be considered the "trunk" of the literary tree, not merely a branch. Certainly no other literary form — the novel, the epic poem, the lyric poem, the short story — has the sustained level of literary excellence over twenty-five centuries as does the written dramatic work of Aeschylus, Sophocles, Euripides, Aristophanes, Marlowe, Shakespeare, Jonson, Chikamatsu, Webster, Racine, Corneille, Lope de Vega, Calderón de la Barca, Molière, Congreve, Dryden, Farquhar, Fielding, Goethe, Schiller, Ibsen, Wilde, Yeats, Chekhov, Shaw, O'Casey, O'Neill, Pirandello, Giraudoux, Sartre, Brecht, Beckett, Williams, Churchill, Wilson, and so on.

an end, and, no matter how original or unique, they can be seen to fall into a variety of classifications. Two of these are *duration* and *genre*. Although these classifications have been emphasized more in the past than they are today, they still play a part in our understanding of drama.

Duration

How long is a play? American playwright Arthur Miller admitted that when he first thought of writing for the theatre, "How long should it be?" was his most pressing question. The answer is far from obvious.

Historically, in Western drama, a "full-length" play has usually lasted somewhere between two and four hours. This is not an entirely arbitrary period of time; it represents roughly the hours between lunch and dinner (for a matinee) or between dinner and bedtime. The Jacobean playwright John Webster wrote that the actor "entertains us in the best leisure of our life, that is between meals, the most unfit time either for study or bodily exercise." Webster was thinking of the afternoon performances in the outdoor theatres of his day (c. 1615). A few years earlier, speaking of candlelit evening performances at court, Shakespeare's Theseus (*A Midsummer Night's Dream*) asks for a play "to wear away this long age of three hours between our after-supper and bed-time."

But plays can also be much shorter or longer. One-act plays of an hour or less, or, increasingly today, "ten-minute plays," are often combined to make a full theatre program. Short plays are known from ancient times and are presented in nontraditional settings, such as lunchtime theatres, dramatic festivals, school assemblies, social gatherings, street entertainments, or cabaret performances. The shortest play on record is probably Samuel Beckett's *Breath,* which can be performed in one minute. But there are exceptionally long plays as well, particularly in Asia; for example, Chinese theatre traditionally lasts all day, and Indian dance-dramas last all night. In recent decades, six- to nine-hour productions have proven extremely popular in the West: *Nicholas Nickleby* in London, *Brothers and Sisters* in St. Petersburg, *The Mahabharata* in Paris, *The Oresteia* in Berlin, and both Robert Schenkkan's *The Kentucky Cycle* and Tony Kushner's *Angels in America* in New York. (Indeed, it has been reported that Robert Wilson's *Ka Mountain* was once performed over 168 continuous hours.) In short, a play does not have a precisely fixed duration.

Genre

"Genre" is a more subjective means of classifying plays than is duration, and the term brings with it certain critical perspectives. *Genre* is directly derived from the Old French word for "kind" (this is also our root word for *gender*); thus, to define a play's genre is to categorize it — to say "what kind of play" it is.

Editors and publishers have often identified plays by genre as a shorthand description — even as a sort of advertising. Early publications of Shakespeare's plays, for example, bore such generic classifications on their title pages (*The Most Excellent Conceited Tragedy of Romeo and Juliet; The Most Lamentable Roman Tragedy of Titus Andronicus*), and when the first collection of Shakespeare's plays was published (the First Folio of 1623), his plays were divided into three genre classifications: comedies, tragedies, and histories.

What defines a genre is not always absolute, however, and many critics, and even more authors, including Shakespeare, have bridled at this sort of categorization (see box). But an identification of genres can generate useful distinctions — not only for the student but also for the practitioner. Russian playwright Anton Chekhov certainly guided the principal director of his works, Konstantin Stanislavsky, by pointing out that his plays were intended as comedies, thereby agreeably blunting what he thought was Stanislavsky's excessively tragic

> ## GENRE-LY SPEAKING
>
> Shakespeare has brightly parodied the division of plays into genres, a practice that in his time was already becoming almost an affectation. In *Hamlet*, Polonius describes an acting company as "the best actors in the world, either for tragedy, comedy, history, pastoral, pastoral-comical, historical-pastoral, tragical-historical, tragical-comical-historical-pastoral, scene individable, or poem unlimited."

tone. And many an actor, hamstrung by considerations of psychological realism, has been freed to find a more vigorous theatricality when given to understand that the author meant the play as farce, thereby encouraging a rampaging and "over-the-top" comic style.

Two genres have dominated dramatic criticism since ancient times: tragedy and comedy. Aristotle, the ancient Greek philosopher and father of dramatic criticism, considered tragedy and comedy not as genres, however, but as wholly separate art forms, deriving from entirely unrelated sources. Tragedy, Aristotle believed, was an outgrowth of prehistoric religious rituals, whereas comedy was a secular entertainment developed out of bawdy skits and popular revels. In his monumental *Poetics* (c. 325 B.C.), Aristotle strove to define these dramatic forms and create standards for their perfection. Unfortunately, only his poetics for tragedy has survived.

Today, critics and scholars recognize a number of genre classifications by which both classic and modern plays can be roughly classified. In addition to the original tragedy and comedy (now more narrowly defined then in Aristotle's day), the interlude, mystery play, history play, tragicomedy, dark comedy, melodrama, farce, musical, and documentary have been identified as major genres into which modern plays (and, retroactively, older plays) can be classified.

A *tragedy* is a serious play (although not necessarily devoid of humorous episodes) with a topic of universal human import as its theme. Traditionally, the central character, often called the *protagonist,* is a person of high rank or stature. During the play, the protagonist undergoes a decline of fortune, leading to suffering and death. Integral to tragedy, according to Aristotle, is the protagonist's period of insightful *self-recognition* of some fundamental *hamartia* — error or sin — and a consequent reversal of his or her fortunes. The effect of a tragedy, Aristotle then claimed, is for the protagonist's self-recognition and reversal to elicit both pity and terror in the audience, which are then resolved in a *catharsis,* or purging, of those aroused emotions.

The recognition of the protagonist, his or her struggle against decline, and the consequent catharsis of the audience's aroused feelings are central to the tragic experience, which is not to be confused with a merely sad or pathetic experience. Tragedy is neither pathetic nor sentimental; it describes a bold, aggressive, human attack against huge, perhaps insurmountable, odds. Tragic protagonists are often flawed in some way (indeed, classical tragic theory insists that they must be flawed or at least acting in ignorance), but they are leaders, not victims, of the play's events. Indeed, their leadership of the play's action and their discoveries during the course of that action bring the audience to deep emotional and intellectual involvement.

The notion of *protagonist* (Greek: "carrier of the action") is complemented by the notion of *antagonist* ("opposer of the action"), which gives tragedy its fundamental conflict and character struggle. The protagonists of tragedy often go forth against superhuman antagonists: gods, ghosts, fate, or the hardest of human realities. Such protagonists are heroes — or tragic heroes — because their struggle, though doomed, takes on larger-than-life proportions. Then, through the heat of conflict, the tragic heroes assume superhuman force, drawing us into the full magnitude of their thoughts and actions. Thus, tragedy offers us a link with the divine and puts us at the apex of human destiny.

A tragedy should therefore ennoble, not sadden, us. Characters that we admire may fall but not before heroically challenging the elements, divinity, and death. Tragic heroes carry us to the brink of disaster — but, finally, it is their disaster and not ours, or at least not ours yet. Seeing a tragedy is to contemplate and perhaps rehearse in our minds the great conflicts we may still have ahead of us.

There are only a few universally acknowledged tragedies. Sophocles' *Oedipus Tyrannos,* from the fifth century B.C., was Aristotle's model of a great one. Most critics also class the same dramatist's *Electra* and *Antigone;* Aeschylus' *Oresteia* and *Prometheus Bound;* Euripides'

Above left: Tragedy, the oldest form of recorded drama, probes fundamental problems in the human condition. Aeschylus, Sophocles, and Euripides – the great Greek tragedians of the fifth century B.C. – each developed plays about the royal house (family) of Atreus, revealing ancient Greek thought (and disagreement) about the crucial issues of justice, revenge, and the often conflicting obligations of family, state, religion, and personal/sexual fulfillment. Contemporary French director Ariane Mnouchkine's compilation and reworking of several of these ancient plays, collectively retitled *Les Atrides,* toured Europe and North America in the late 1980s, demonstrating the permanence of these themes and the power of tragedy to animate and illuminate them for modern times.

Above: In one of the most horrific scenes in classical tragedy, the Earl of Gloucester has his eyes gouged out in Shakespeare's *King Lear.* The scene has echoes of Sophocles' *Oedipus Tyrannos,* except that the blinding in *King Lear* is done onstage. Here, Dudley Knight, as Gloucester, wanders away from the scene of his torture in the 1999 Utah Shakespearean Festival production of the play. Costume design by Dean Mogle.

"Comedy Tonight" is the apt title of the opening song from *A Funny Thing Happened on the Way to the Forum*, a Broadway musical by Stephen Sondheim based primarily on a 2,000-year-old Roman play by Plautus. Brilliant colors, wildly exaggerated expressions, and tightly choreographed staging characterize both classical and musical comedies. This 1995 Utah Shakespearean Festival production featured costumes by Bill Black.

The Trojan Women, Medea, and *The Bacchae;* Racine's *Phèdre;* and Shakespeare's *Hamlet, King Lear, Othello,* and *Macbeth* as among a handful of true tragic masterpieces. The question often arises as to whether a modern play can be termed a tragedy. Take, for example, Arthur Miller's *Death of a Salesman* (1947). Miller deliberately challenged the traditional notion of a high-ranking protagonist by naming his principal character Willy Loman (that is, low man). Further, the antagonists Willy challenges are not gods, fates, or ghosts, but rather faceless bureaucrats, insensitive children, and an impersonal capitalistic economic system. Most critics today, if they approach this question at all, deny Miller's play the classification as a tragedy on the grounds that the struggle is human, not superhuman, and that tragedy demands a larger-than-life context. If that is the case, tragedy probably belongs to an earlier world, a world in which audiences could be expected to accept without dissent the presence of divine forces mixing in with everyday human affairs.

Comedy began, according to Aristotle, in an entirely different way: as an improvised entertainment that combined satirical skits, bawdy jokes, erotic singing and dancing, and uninhibited revelry. The first known comedies were those of Aristophanes, a playwright of brilliantly funny wit and savagely penetrating political acumen. Writing in Athens a generation after Sophocles, Aristophanes set the general recipe, though not the structure, for comedies to come: interpersonal conflicts, topical issues, witty dialogue, physical buffoonery, and verbal and sexual playfulness.

Comedy is not a simple amusement, however, nor is comedy simply entertaining; comedy is always about a serious human conflict. The passionate pursuit of love, ambition, social status, and money are age-old comic themes. Indeed, the themes of many comedies are often hard to distinguish from those of tragedies; it is the plot of comedy, requiring a happy ending, and the comic style, providing human-scaled characters facing everyday — if exaggerated — problems, that allow the dramatic experience to avoid tragedy's sustained pity, terror, and cathartic shock. Gods, fate, suffering, and death rarely figure significantly in comedies, where the characters' problems are social rather than metaphysical.

The best comedies are often those in which characters foolishly overreach themselves and are hilariously shown up for their foolishness. Not only are Aristophanes' plays (*The Birds, The Frogs, The Clouds, Lysistrata,* for example) masterpieces of this format, but so are the great comedies of Shakespeare (*As You Like It, Twelfth Night, A Midsummer Night's Dream*) and Molière (*The Miser, The Bourgeois Gentleman, The Misanthrope, The School for Wives*). In these plays, excesses of romantic love, intellectual pretension, physical braggadocio, or financial greed are wittily shown up, to the delight of the spectators in the audience — who can also recognize the germs of such behaviors in themselves. In this fashion, comedy seeks to advise as well as to entertain. The Roman poet Horace coined the term *utile dulce,* or "sweet instruction," to denote this deeper purpose of the comic drama.

There are many modern authors of dramatic comedy: George Bernard Shaw, George S. Kaufman, Alan Ayckbourn, and Neil Simon are only a few of the twentieth-century playwrights who have succeeded brilliantly in this genre. Because they are topical, however, comedies are usually less enduring than tragedies. Because they generally probe less profoundly into the matter of human destiny, they offer less fertile ground to academic scholarship. Hence, relative to tragedies, comedies are usually less frequently published in play anthologies, less frequently examined in critical literature, and less frequently studied in most academic institutions. Nevertheless, comedy's place in the theatre is every bit as secure as is tragedy's, and its impact on audiences is as strong now as it was in Aristophanes' day.

Comedy and tragedy remained the two "official" dramatic genres through the seventeenth century, when neoclassic French critics attempted to formalize them into absolutely rigid classifications. But from the Renaissance onward, playwrights and critics began to develop new dramatic genres or to dispense with genres altogether. The medieval theatre, for example, brought to the stage *interludes* (from *inter,* "between," and *ludus,* "play"), comic entertainments presented between courses at state banquets, and *mystery plays,* short biblical plays performed in a series during the fourteenth and fifteenth centuries.

Shakespeare's editors employed a newly defined genre, the *history play,* which dramatizes the key events in the life of a king or head of state. Shakespeare himself seems to have invented this genre, and his great series of nine such plays, covering English royal history from 1377 to 1547 (inaccurate as they may be as historical documents) provides the bulk of what most people ever remember of the English kings Richard II, Henry IV, Henry V, Henry VI, and Richard III. Shakespeare's history plays combine serious scenes, brilliant poetry, battlefield pageants, and hilarious comic moments. None of the plays, however, seeks to attain the classical catharsis of tragedy or the sustained humor of comedy.

More enduring than the history play are two other mixed genres. *Tragicomedy,* as the name implies, is a form that deliberately attempts

Corliss Preston is Queen Margaret, surrounded by her knights in the 2000 Utah Shakespearean Festival production of *War of the Roses*, a three-hour adaptation by Howard Jenkins of all three parts of Shakespeare's nine-hour *Henry VI*. Costumes are by McKay Coble and lighting by Donna Ruzika.

to bridge the two original genres. It maintains a serious theme throughout but varies the approach from serious to humorous and relaxes tragedy's larger-than-life scale. The problems of tragicomedy are solvable, and the antagonists are not divinely insuperable; tragicomedies, despite their rousing speeches and sentiments, conclude without the violent catharsis that their audience has been led to expect. As such, tragicomedy has been called "tragedy that ends happily." *Amphitryon*, by the Roman playwright Plautus, is generally considered the first tragicomedy, and the play has been revised by subsequent authors — including Molière and Jean Giraudoux — into both tragic and comic versions. Many of Shakespeare's tragedies were in fact rewritten into tragicomedies

in the following century: Nahum Tate's 1687 revision of *King Lear*, for example, concludes with Lear and Gloucester retiring to "calm reflections on our fortunes past" and with Cordelia installed as Queen of England (all are dead at the close of Shakespeare's original).

Dark comedy is the obverse of tragicomedy: it is an often comic but finally disturbing play that ends darkly (or ironically), leaving the impression of an unresolved universe surrounding the play's characters — and perhaps surrounding the audience as well. Dark comedies are usually funny, at least at the beginning, but they don't aim to leave us laughing. There are dark themes and ironic endings to many of Shakespeare's later plays, including *The Tempest*, *Measure for Measure*, and *The Win-*

ter's Tale (these plays are also often classed as *romances*), and to many of the late-nineteenth- and early-twentieth-century plays of Anton Chekhov, Bertolt Brecht, and Luigi Pirandello. In more modern times, certainly after World War II, the dark comedy has come to dominate the theatre, particularly in the work of such playwrights as Harold Pinter, Samuel Beckett, Edward Albee, Joe Orton, Beth Henley, John Guare, Christopher Durang, and Caryl Churchill.

If histories, tragicomedies, and dark comedies are mixed genres, the next two forms are, conversely, extreme generic purifications. *Melodrama* describes plays that are outwardly serious but embellished with spectacular stagings, sentventious dialogue, and highly suspenseful — and contrived — plotting. Melodrama presents a simple and finite confrontation between good and evil rather than a complex exposition of universal human aspirations and sufferings; such plays cannot sustain unpleasant endings or generate catharsis but can indeed provoke a deeply emotional outpouring of audience sentiment — always a powerful theatrical response. A pure creation of the theatre, melodramas employ every possible theatrical device to generate audience emotion (the original name, "melo-drama," reveals the function music initially played in these works) and tend to reflect reality, or real human issues, only on the most superficial and sentimental level. Real melodramas are rarely performed today — when the melodramas we tend to see are usually played for laughs — but melodramatic elements frequently find their way into dramas of every sort.

Farce is similarly a pure creation of the theatre, where we expect to find a wildly hilarious treatment of a trivial theme — mistaken identity, illicit infatuation, physical dissolution, monetary scheming — that has been standard farce material since ancient times. Farcical plots are also drawn from stock situations and events: identical twins, lovers in closets or under tables, full-stage chases, switched potions,

The contemporary *Shockheaded Peter,* called by its creators a "junk opera," employs melodrama and Grand Guignol (a particularly sadistic nineteenth-century French melodramatic variation) in portraying its gruesome stories based on Heinrich Hoffman's savagely ironic "children's" tale, *Strewelpeter.* Here a maniacal tailor — portrayed by a shadow puppet — approaches a thumb-sucking boy in order to scissor off his fingers as punishment. The West Yorkshire Playhouse/London Lyric Hammersmith production toured America in 2000.

switched costumes (often involving transsexual dressing), misheard instructions, and various disrobings, discoveries, and disappearances. Elements of farce exist in almost all comedies, but pure farce makes no pretense toward Horace's *utile dulce;* the motto instead is "laugh 'til you cry," and in a well-written, well-staged farce the audience does just that. Michael Frayn's *Noises Off,* a pure farce set in a provincial English theatre, had audiences collapsed in hysteria on both sides of the Atlantic in the 1980s and again in the 2001–02 season. Every few years a new "laugh-riot"

Michael Frayn's *Noises Off* is perhaps the finest pure English-language farce of recent decades. A "backstage drama" in which we see a play being (badly) performed on stage, and then again from backstage, *Noises Off* hilariously spoofs everything that can go wrong in a play production. At the 2000 Utah Shakespearean Festival, with David Ivers as Garry and Gwyn Fawcett as Brooke.

tends to appear — just as we are beginning to lament the demise of this age-old yet perennially durable dramatic genre.

There are also some new genres in the theatre. The *musical* is a dramatic style that began in the late 1800s and has become immensely and increasingly popular right up to the present time, earning an entire chapter ("The Musical Theatre") in this book. The *documentary*, a much later genre, utilizes authentic evidence as its basis for portraying recent historical events. Plays written from actual courtroom transcripts — such as the trials of Oscar Wilde, J. Robert Oppenheimer, John Scopes, and Leopold and Loeb, for example — have proven successful in twentieth-century drama, and, in the twenty-first century, one play based

on the transcriptions of black-box cockpit recordings taken from downed airliners (*Charlie Victor Romeo*) and another drawn from news-clippings and personal interviews concerning various American presidents (Anna Deveare Smith's *House Arrest*) have taken the genre of documentary drama into newer territory yet.

Potentially, of course, there are as many theatrical genres as the diligent critic wishes to define. No system of classification should obscure the fact that each play is unique, and the grouping of any two or more plays into a common genre is only a convenience for purposes of comparison and analysis. We in the twenty-first century have learned that past formulations of tragedy and farce have had little bearing on the long-range assessment of

Moises Kaufman's Tectonic Theatre Project has pioneered in contemporary documentary dramas, beginning with a celebrated 1997 production, *Gross Indecency: The Three Trials of Oscar Wilde*, which premiered off-off-Broadway and successfully transferred to off-Broadway and then toured nationally. The trial is based on the official transcripts of Wilde's trials during the 1890s; in this presentational production, the transcripts are actually held up by cast members.

the importance, quality, or worth — on the staying power — of any individual play. Critics who today dwell inordinately on such questions as "Is *Death of a Salesman* a true tragedy?" are doubtless spending too much time deciding what box to put the artistic work in and too little time examining and revealing the work itself.

Nevertheless, genre distinctions can be useful if we keep their limitations in mind. They can help us to comprehend the broad spectrum of purposes to which plays may be put and to perceive important similarities and differences. For the theatre artist, an awareness of the possibilities inherent in each genre — together with a knowledge of the achievements that have been made in each — stimulates the imagination and aids in setting work standards and ambitions.

Structure

Plays can be analyzed structurally in two ways: by their components (that is, plot, characters, theme, and so on) and by their order of organization (exposition, development, climax, and so on). Both methods are used by most people who find it worthwhile to analyze dra-

matic art, and both will be used in this book. However, one thing must be clear from the outset: a drama that is taken apart in the classroom inevitably loses something. The individual components and the sequential aspects of any given play are never in fact isolated in the theatrical experience, and any truly useful dramatic analysis must end by putting the studied portions back into a living whole. The complexity of the theatrical experience and its emotional and sensual impact require that we see a play always as something greater than the mere sum of its parts.

The Components of a Play

The division of plays into components is an ancient analytical practice. Aristotle described the components of a tragedy as plot, characters, theme, diction, music, and spectacle — in that order, and, with some modification and elaboration, Aristotle's list still serves as an approximate breakdown of the major elements of all dramas, although the relative importance of each component has been a matter of continuing controversy.

PLOT   Although colloquially we may think of *plot* as synonymous with *story,* the two words

THE WELL-MADE PLAY

Pièce bien faite ("well-made play") was a term used to describe certain dramatic works, known for their complex and elegant plots, written by the popular French dramatists Eugène Scribe and Victorien Sardou (among others) during the latter part of the nineteenth century. The expression was originally complimentary but soon became a derisive reference to plays that were seen as merely mechanical, plot-heavy contrivances, holding their audience solely by a series of calculated dramatic effects. Arguing that drama should also be the vehicle for grand ideas and deep passions, playwright George Bernard Shaw coined the term "Sardoodledom" to express his contempt for Sardou's well-made, but shallowly felt, plays.

are quite different: *story* is simply a narrative of what is seen to happen in the play, as might be described by someone who has seen it, whereas *plot* refers to the *mechanics* of storytelling, including the sequence of the characters' comings and goings; the timetable of the play's events; and the specific order of revelations, reversals, quarrels, discoveries, and actions that take place on stage, as in "furthering the plot." (In London theatres of the sixteenth century, a written "platte" or "plotte" was hung on the wall backstage, reminding the actors of the play's order of major events, entrances, and exits.) Plot is a *structure of actions:* both outer actions (such as Romeo stabbing Tybalt) and inner ones (such as Romeo falling in love with Juliet). The specific sequence and arrangement of these actions are essentially what we take away from the play; they are usually the way we describe the play to someone who has not yet seen it. This is undoubtedly why Aristotle described plot first in his list of the elements of tragedy (drama). Creating a dramatically compelling plot is one of the most difficult and demanding tests of a playwright's skill.

Traditionally, the primary demands of plot are logic and suspense. To satisfy the demand for logic, the actions portrayed must be plausible, and events must follow one upon another in an organic rather than arbitrary fashion. To sustain suspense, the actions portrayed must set up expectations for further actions, drawing the audience along in a story that seems to move inexorably toward an ending that may be sensed but is never wholly predictable. Melodramas and farces tend to rely heavily on intricate and suspenseful plots. The "well-made plays" of the late nineteenth century reflect an attempt to elevate plot construction to the highest level of theatrical art; today, murder mysteries and "whodunits" are perhaps the most plot-intensive plays.

CHARACTERS   The characters of a play are the human figures — the impersonated presences — who undertake the actions of the plot. Their potency in the theatre is measured by our interest in them *as people*. The most brilliant plotting in the world cannot redeem a play if the audience remains indifferent to its characters; therefore, the fundamental demand of a play's characters is that they make the audience care. To this end, characters cannot be mere stick figures, no matter how elaborately detailed. The great dramatic characters of the past — Hamlet, Juliet, Peer Gynt, Phaedra, to name a few — bring to an experienced theatregoer's or playreader's mind personalities as vivid and memorable as those of good friends (and hated enemies); they are whole images, indelibly human, alive with the attributes, feelings, and expectations of real people. We can identify with them. We can sympathize with them.

Character depth is what gives a play its psychological complexity, its sensuality, and its warmth. Without it, we cannot experience love, hate, fear, joy, hope, despair — any of the emotions we expect to derive from theatre — and a theatre devoid of those emotions that stem from the humanness of the characters portrayed would be a theatre without an audience in a matter of days. For this reason, many playwrights have scoffed at the notion of primacy of plot and at the often mechanical contrivances of the well-made play. Indeed, several playwrights have fashioned plays that were arbitrarily plotted, with the story line designed simply to show various aspects of a fascinating character.

THEME The theme of a play is its abstracted intellectual content. It may be described as the play's overall statement: its topic, central idea, or message, as the case may be. Some plays have obvious themes, such as Euripides' *The Trojan Women* (the horrors of war) or Molière's *The Bourgeois Gentlemen* (the foolishness of social pretense). Other plays have less clearly defined themes, and the most provocative of these have given rise to much scholarly controversy. *Hamlet, Oedipus Tyrannos,* and *Waiting for Godot* all suggest many themes, and each has spawned a great many fierce debates about which of its themes is central.

Nothing demands that a play have a single theme, of course, or even that it be at all reducible to straightforward intellectual generalization. Indeed, plays that are too obviously theme-intensive are usually considered too propagandistic or too somberly academic for theatrical success: "If you want to send a message," one Broadway saying goes, "use a fax machine." Moreover, although the themes of plays address the central questions of society and humanity, a play's theatrical impact hinges always on the audience's engagement in its plot and characterization.

A play must have something to say, and that something — its theme — must seem *pertinent* to the audience. Further, the play must be sufficiently focused and limited to give the audience at least some insight into that something within its framework. Plays that try to say nothing or, conversely, plays that try to say everything, rarely have even a modest impact, no matter how entertaining or well plotted they may be. Thus, from the beginning, playwrights working in every genre, be it tragedy, comedy, melodrama, or farce, have recognized the merit of narrowing their field of intellectual investigation when crafting a play.

DICTION Aristotle's fourth component, diction, relates to the pronunciation of spoken dialogue; to the literary character of a play's text, including its tone, imagery, cadence, and articulation; and to its use of literary forms and figures such as verse, rhyme, metaphor, apostrophe, jest, and epigram.

The value of poetry has been well established from the theatre's beginning; until fairly recent times, as a matter of fact, most serious plays were written largely in verse. Today, comedies, as well as more serious plays, still make liberal use of carefully crafted dialogue, although the use of verse is relatively rare. Many plays succeed on the basis of brilliant repartee, stunning epigrams, poetic lyricism, witty arguments, and dazzling tirades. Other, quite different, sorts of plays feature a poetry of silences and inarticulate mutterings; these, as fashioned by Anton Chekhov or Harold Pinter, for example, can create a diction no less effective than the more ostentatiously crafted verbal pyrotechnics of a George Bernard Shaw or a Tom Stoppard (refer to the discussion later in this book on the modern theatre).

The diction of a play is by no means the creation of the playwright alone. It is very much the product of the actor as well, and for that reason throughout the history of Western theatre, an effective stage voice has been considered the prime asset of the actor. Even today, the study of voice is a primary and continuous obligation at most schools and conservatories of classical acting. The chief aim of such study is to create an acting voice capable of dealing in spectacular fashion with the broad palette of dramatic diction demanded by the works of the world's most noted playwrights.

MUSIC Any discussion of music, Aristotle's fifth component of theatre, forces us to remember that in Aristotle's time, plays were sung or chanted, not simply spoken. That mode of presentation has all but disappeared, and yet the musical component remains directly present in most plays performed today and indirectly present in the rest.

When it is directly present in a play, music can take many forms. Songs are common in the plays of Shakespeare, as well as in the works of modern writers (such as Bertolt Brecht) who employ presentational-performance techniques. Many naturalistic writers work familiar songs into their scripts, sometimes by having characters play recordings onstage. Chekhov and Tennessee Williams both make extensive use in their plays of offstage music — for example, a military marching band can be heard in Chekhov's *The Three Sisters,* and Williams provides for music from a nearby dance hall in *A Streetcar Named Desire* and from a cantina in *Night of the Iguana.* Directors also frequently add incidental music to play productions — sometimes to set a mood during intermissions or before the play begins, sometimes to underscore the play's action itself. The power of music directly present in the theatre is well known, and its effectiveness in moving an audience to ever-deeper feeling is one of its functions that few playwrights or directors wish to ignore.

Indirectly, music is present in every play. It is in the rhythm of sounds that, while not specifically tuneful, combine to create a different kind of "score" — the orchestration of sound rather than music. Vocal tones, footsteps, sighs, shouts, offstage railroad whistles, the shrilling of a telephone, muffled drumbeats, gunshots, animal cries, conversations in the next room, and amplified special effects (heartbeats, respiration, otherworldly noises, for instance) are frequently employed by authors, directors, and sound designers to create a theatrical symphony apart from, though supportive of, the plot, characters, dialogue, and theme. Moreover, the spoken word creates, in addition to its semantic impact (its

meaning and connotation), an aural impact: it is an integer of pure sound, and it can be appreciated as pure musical vibration. Under the guidance of a skilled director, all of a play's sounds can be orchestrated to produce a performance of such dramatic force that it can thrill even persons wholly unacquainted with the language of the dialogue.

SPECTACLE   Aristotle's last component, spectacle, encompasses the visual aspects of production: scenery, costumes, lighting, makeup, properties, and the overall *look* of the theatre and stage. It would be wrong to infer that *spectacle* is synonymous with *spectacular,* for some productions are quite restrained in their visual artistry. Rather, *spectacle* here refers to "something seen." Although this point may seem obvious, it is crucial. Theatre is as much a visual experience as it is an aural, emotional, and intellectual experience: the ancient Greeks clearly had this in mind when they chose the name *theatron* ("seeing place") to designate the site of their performances.

Much as the cinema has been called the art of moving pictures, so the theatre might be called the art of fluid sculpture. This sculpture is fashioned in part from the human body in motion and in part from still or moving scenery and props — natural and manufactured items of both dramatic and decorative importance, all illuminated by natural or artificially modulated light. It is a sculpture that moves in time as well as in space; and although it is generally considered to be primarily a support for the plot, characters, and theme of a play, it has an artistic appeal and an artistic heritage all its own. Certainly some ardent patrons of the theatre pay more attention to settings and costumes than to any other aspect of a play, and in many a successful production, dramatic visual effects have virtually carried the play.

Memorable visual elements can be both grand and prosaic, imposing and subtle.

Nineteenth-century romanticism, which survives today primarily in the form of grand opera, tends to favor mammoth stagings featuring processions, crowd scenes, palaces, animals, triumphal arches, and lavish costumes. In contrast, twentieth-century movements are more likely to go in for domestic environments and archetypal images: Jimmy and Cliff reading newspapers while Alison irons a shirt in John Osborne's *Look Back in Anger;* Laura playing with her glass animals in Tennessee Williams' *The Glass Menagerie;* Mother Courage pulling her wagon in Brecht's *Mother Courage;* and Nagg and Nell living in the ashcans of Samuel Beckett's *Endgame.* In the long run, conceptual richness and precision in a play's visual presentation are far more telling than grandeur for its own sake.

CONVENTION To these six components of every play we should add a seventh, discrete, item that Aristotle apparently never saw reason to consider: theatrical convention. The agreement between audience and actor entails a set of tacit understandings that form the context of playwatching — conventions that make us understand, for example, that when the stage lights fade out, the play (or the act) has ended. Over the years, other common conventions of the Western stage have included the following:

- When one actor turns directly from the others and speaks to the audience, the other characters are presumed not to hear him. This is the convention of the *aside* (to the audience).

- When the actors all leave the stage and then they or others reenter (particularly when the lights change), time has elapsed, and the locale may be changed.

- When the actors onstage freeze, we are seeing some sort of "dream state" (of one of the characters, presumably), and the words we hear are to be considered his or her thoughts, not anyone's speech.

We can see conventions more clearly in theatres unlike our own. In the *wayang kulit,* a shadow puppet theatre on the island of Bali, the play is over when the "tree of life" puppet, previously only seen in motion, finally comes to a standstill at the center of the stage. In the *nō* drama of Japan, the audience recognizes words sung by chorus members to be considered spoken by the actors who are dancing, and gestures of a fan to indicate wind, rain, or the rising moon. In the Chinese *xiqu,* or traditional opera, a character entering the bare stage while holding a boat paddle is understood to be rowing across a river. The conventions of theatre permit this sort of shorthand communication with the audience, without the encumbrance of extensive physical elaboration or acting out. If the locale can effectively be changed by the convention of a simple light shift, instead of by moving a half ton of scenery, the theatre saves money and the audience saves time. Stage violence is usually executed conventionally (that is, with little physical mayhem) rather than with lifelike (or cinematic) verisimilitude. The difficulty in realistically portraying severed torsos, rupturing intestines, and bleeding limbs onstage ordinarily outweighs any dramatic advantage in doing so; and the theatrical convention ("stab, grab, scream, collapse, and die") can be accepted fully if performed with emotional and psychological (though not physical) authenticity.

Each play sets up its own system of conventions, but in most cases they accord with the traditions of their times and therefore go largely unnoticed (doubtless that is why Aristotle, familiar with no drama other than his own, made no specific mention of them). In modern times, playwrights and directors have become increasingly aware of other traditions and possibilities; more and more play productions employ conventions of ancient times or foreign cultures and even establish new ones. Peter Shaffer's *Black Comedy,* which supposedly takes place in the dark, utilizes a convention that Shaffer attributes to the Chinese: when the lights are on they are "off," and when they are off they are "on." Eugene O'Neill's *Strange Interlude* and Steven Berkoff's *Kvetch* give us to understand that when the actors freeze and speak, we in the audience — but not the other characters in the play — hear their thoughts. Jean Anouilh's *Antigone* uses a variation on the Greek device of the chorus: a single man speaks with the author's voice as the characters onstage freeze in silence. Lanford Wilson, in *The Rimers of Eldritch,* presents a story in more than a hundred tiny scenes that jump back and forth in time; only at the play's end do we get any real sense of a story line. Arthur Miller's *After the Fall* places an imaginary psychiatrist in the midst of the audience, and the play's protagonist repeatedly interrupts the action of the drama to address his analyst in highly theatrical therapy sessions. And so it goes. There is no formal requirement for the establishment of theatrical conventions, except that the audience must "agree" to accept them (which it does, of course, unconsciously).

These seven components of every play — with the seventh framing Aristotle's six — are the raw material of drama. All are important. Indeed, the theatre could not afford to dispense with any one. Some plays are intensive in one or more components; most great productions show artistry in all. The balancing of these components in theatrical presentation is one of the primary challenges facing the director, who on one or another occasion may be called upon mainly to clarify and elaborate a theme, to find the visual mode of presentation that best supports the action, to develop and "flesh out" the characterizations in order to give strength and meaning to the plot, to heighten a musical tone in order to enhance sensual effect, or to develop the precise con-

vention — the relationship between play and audience — that will maximize the play's artistic impact. For as important as each of these components is to the theatrical experience, it is their combination and interaction, not their individual splendor, that is crucial to a production's success.

The Order of a Play

A play also has a temporal (time) structure. Here again, Aristotle affords some help. He tells us that drama has a beginning, a middle, and an end, and here and there in his *Poetics* he proffers a little detail about the nature of each of these elements. We can expand Aristotle's list somewhat, for by now some fairly consistent features have evolved in the orderly sequencing of a theatrical experience. These individual features can be divided into three major groupings: the preplay, the play proper, and the postplay.

The events that take place before the play proper begins are referred to as the *preplay.*

THE GATHERING OF THE AUDIENCE   Dramatic theorists often either ignore the audience in considering the crucial elements of theatre or dismiss it as a "paratheatrical" (*para* meaning "only somewhat") concern. The gathering of the audience is, however, an important consideration in the presentation of a play, entailing a process that is not without its artistic and cultural significance. The chief concerns in that process have to do with publicity, admission, and seating — concerns that have preoccupied theatre producers since ancient times.

For how does the theatre attract its audience in the first place? Theatregoing, after all, is not a human necessity per se; people do not spend half their waking hours trying to supply themselves with theatre in the same way they strive to secure food, shelter, and physical security. Therefore, if it is to survive, the theatre must go out and recruit attention.

As such, the goal of every theatre producer is to make his or her theatre accessible, inviting, and favorably known to the widest possible public — and also, in many eras, to the *richest* possible public — and to make theatre as an art form as thrilling and spiritually *necessary* as it can possibly be.

In every era, theatre has had the responsibility of gathering its audience. The procession is one of the oldest known ways of publicizing the theatre. The circus parade, which still takes place in some of the smaller towns of Europe and the United States, is a remnant of a once universal form of advertisement for the performing arts that probably began well in advance of recorded history. The Greeks of ancient Athens opened their great dramatic festivals with a *proagon* (literally, "pre-action"), in which both playwrights and actors were introduced at a huge public meeting and given a chance to speak about the plays they were to present on subsequent days. Today, similar conclaves — usually aired via television talk shows in this global village of ours — are often used to promote theatrical events to the public at large. The Elizabethans flew flags atop their playhouses on performance days, and the flags could be seen across the Thames in "downtown" London, enticing hundreds away from their commercial and religious activities. The lighted marquees of Broadway theatres around Times Square and of London theatres in the West End are a modern-day equivalent of the flags that waved over those first great English public theatres.

Developments in the printing and broadcast media have not only spurred the growth of theatre advertising but also made it into a major theatrical craft in its own right. Splendid posters, illustrated programs, multicolor subscription brochures, full-page newspaper advertisements, staged media events, articulate press releases, and flashy thirty-second television commercials summon patrons out of the comfort of their homes and into the theatre. For premieres or for openings of new playhouses, giant searchlights beckon the public to the theatrical location. Far from being an inconsequential aspect of theatre, publicity today occupies a place of fundamental importance in the thinking of theatrical producers and commands a major share of the budget for commercial theatrical ventures.

Now that the patrons have been attracted to the theatre, how should they be admitted and seated? Although procedures for admitting and seating the audience are usually straightforward and conventional, they can have important — and occasionally decisive — effects on the overall theatrical presentation.

Ordinarily, theatre is supported at least in part by its admission fees, otherwise known as the box-office revenue. For commercial theatres, box-office revenue provides the sole means of meeting production costs and providing a profit to investors. The admission charge dates from ancient Greek days, and since then only a few amateur or civic productions (such as the religious pageants of medieval England and the free Shakespeare performances in contemporary New York City) have managed to survive without it.

Seating is frequently determined by the price of admission: the best seats cost the most. What determines "best" and "poorest" seating, however, depends on many things. In modern Broadway and West End theatres, for example, the most costly seats are in the orchestra (known in the West End as the stalls), which is the ground-level seating area; balcony seats ordinarily cost less — the higher the balcony, the lower the price. In the public theatres of Elizabethan London, however, the ground level (which was standing room) was the cheapest space, and the "gentlemen's rooms" in the balcony — where one could be seen and visited — commanded up to twelve times as much. In the Restoration period, seats on the stage itself brought the highest prices of all, ensuring their purchasers the widest possible personal recognition (but affording a ridiculously poor view of the play's action).

Seating has not always been scaled according to price, however. In the drama festivals of ancient Athens, the front-row seats were reserved for priests, and members of the lay audience sat in sections of the theatron reserved for their particular tribe. In many noncommercial theatres today, the best seats go to the theatre company's most loyal — and longstanding — subscribers.

THE TRANSITION   Gathered, admitted, and seated, the audience remains a collection of individuals preoccupied with their daily concerns. Now the theatre must transform them into a community devoted to the concerns of the play and enmeshed in the actions of imaginary characters. The theatre, in other words, must shift the audience's awareness from real life to stage life, and it must do so in a smooth and agreeable fashion.

The written program is one modern device (modern in the sense that it dates from the eighteenth century) that helps to prepare the audience for the fiction they are about to see. It gives them the locale and time of the action and the names of the characters and of the actors who impersonate them; the program allows the audience to preview the play's spatial, temporal, and personal environment and to accept the actors as valid impersonators of the play's characters. Having read that Kevin Kline is playing Hamlet, for example, we don't spend playwatching time trying to determine who the lead actor is.

The contemporary theatre often uses music to set the mood or tone of a play, particularly when the action is set in a certain period in the past. For a musical production, an entire orchestral piece — called the overture — sometimes precedes the action onstage.

Lobby displays sometimes supplement the written programs, featuring either pictures of the actors or other pictures and documents relevant to the play, its period, its author, and its critical reception. Occasionally the seating area is altered to aid in this transition, sometimes by the addition of wall posters or other ornamentation. When no curtain is used, the scenery may be "warmed" by preshow lighting, which eases the audience into an expectation of the performance to follow — in some productions that "scenery" includes actors sitting, standing, or lying motionless on the set or engaging in quiet, understated movement. Sometimes slide presentations, songs, or improvised activities take place onstage before the play begins, and the patrons may be asked to participate in some manner as they find their way to their seats. Many of these transitional methods date from ancient times.

Finally, a swift new transition to stage life occurs: the play proper begins. Most often this is a shared moment. The houselights dim, and a curtain rises or stagelights come up to reveal a scene. Occasionally this transition is more subtle, and each member of the audience glides into the play at her or his own moment of discovery; a preshow improvisation begins to take on a more pronounced, attention-demanding character, or perhaps some small but seemingly significant alteration galvanizes the consciousness to full attention. Either way, the transition is complete. The thinking of the audience shifts from workaday concerns to the characters of the play and their story. This, to use a familiar theatrical term, is "magic time."

Almost all plays (as compared to most happenings, improvisations, and performance art pieces) contain a structured sequence of the following four identifiable dramatic elements in the *play proper:* exposition, conflict, climax, and denouement.

THE EXPOSITION   No important play has ever begun with a character dashing onstage and shouting, "The house is on fire!" At best, such a beginning could only confuse the audience, and at worst it could cause them to flee in panic. At that point they would have no way of knowing what house or why they should even care about it. Most plays, whatever their style or genre, begin with dialogue or action calculated to ease us, not shock us, into the concerns of the characters with whom we are to spend the next two hours or so.

Exposition is a word not much in favor now, coming as it does from an age when play structure was considered more scientific than it is today. But it is still a useful term, referring to the background information the audience must have in order to understand what's going on in the action of a play.

In the rather mechanical plotting of the "well-made plays," the exposition is handled with little fanfare, with a few characters — often servants (minor figures in the action to follow) — discussing something that is about to happen and enlightening each other (and, of course, the audience) about certain details around which the plot will turn. Consider these lines from the opening scene of Henrik Ibsen's 1884 classic, *The Wild Duck:*

PETTERSEN, *in livery, and* JENSEN, *the hired waiter, in black, are putting the study in order. From the dining room, the hum of conversation and laughter is heard.*

PETTERSEN: Listen to them, Jensen; the old man's got to his feet — he's giving a toast to Mrs. Sorby.

JENSEN: (*pushing forward an armchair*) Do you think it's true, then, what they've been saying, that there's something going on between them?

PETTERSEN: God knows.

JENSEN: He used to be quite the lady's man, I understand.

PETTERSEN: I suppose.

JENSEN: And he's giving this party in honor of his son, they say.

PETTERSEN: That's right. His son came home yesterday.

JENSEN: I never even knew old Werle had a son.

PETTERSEN: Oh, he has a son all right. But he's completely tied up at the Hoidal works. In all the years I've been here he's never come into town.

A WAITER: (*in the doorway of the other room*) Pettersen, there's an old fellow here . . .

PETTERSEN: (*mutters*) Damn. Who'd show up at this time of night?

After a few more lines, Pettersen, Jensen, and the waiter make their exits and are seen no more. Their function is purely expository — to pave the way for the principal characters. Their conversation is a contrivance intended simply to give us a framework for the action — and the information they impart is presented by means of a conversation only because a convention of realism decrees that words spoken in a play be addressed to characters, not to the audience.

In contrast, the exposition of nonrealistic plays can be handled more directly. It was the Greek custom to begin a play with a prologue preceding the entrance of the chorus and the major play episodes; the prologue was sometimes a scene and sometimes a simple speech to the audience. Shakespeare also used prologues in some of his plays. In one particularly interesting example, Shakespeare's *Henry V,* each of the five acts begins with a character called Chorus directly addressing the audience and setting the scene for the act:

CHORUS: O for a Muse of fire, that would ascend
The brightest heaven of invention!
A kingdom for a stage, princes to act,
And monarchs to behold the swelling scene!
Then should the warlike Harry, like himself,
Assume the port of Mars, and at his heels
(Leash'd in, like hounds) should famine, sword, and fire
Crouch for employment. But pardon, gentles all,
The flat unraised spirits that hath dar'd
On this unworthy scaffold to bring forth
So great an object. Can this cockpit hold
The vasty fields of France? Of may we cram
Within this wooden O the very casques
That did affright the air at Agincourt?
O, pardon! since a crooked figure may
Attest in little place a million,

And let us, ciphers to this great accompt,
On your imaginary forces work.
Suppose within the girdle of these walls
Are now confin'd two mighty monarchies,
Whose high, upreared, and abutting fronts
The perilous narrow ocean parts asunder.
Piece out our imperfections with your
    thoughts;
Into a thousand parts divide one man,
And make imaginary puissance;
Think, when we talk of horses, that you see
    them
Printing their proud hoofs i' th' receiving
    earth;
For 'tis your thoughts that now must deck
    our kings,
Carry them here and there, jumping o'er
    times,
Turning th' accomplishment of many years
Into an hour-glass: for the which supply,
Admit me Chorus to this history;
Who, Prologue-like, your humble patience
    pray,
Gently to hear, kindly to judge, our play.

This famous prologue establishes setting, characters, and audience expectation of plot in a straightforward manner, and it begs the audience's indulgence for the theatrical conventions they will be called upon to entertain.

THE CONFLICT Now is the time for the character to enter shouting, "The house is on fire!" It is a truism that drama requires conflict; in fact, the word *drama*, when used in daily life, implies a situation fraught with conflict. No one writes plays about characters who live every day in unimpaired serenity; no one would ever choose to watch such a play. Conflict and confrontation are the mechanisms by which a situation becomes dramatic.

Why is this so? Why is conflict so theatrically interesting? The reasons have to do with plot, theme, and character. Plot can hold suspense only when it involves alternatives and choices: Macbeth has strong reasons to murder King Duncan and strong reasons not to; if

he had only the former or only the latter, he would project no real conflict and we would not consider him such an interesting character. We are fascinated by such a character's actions largely in light of the actions he rejects and the stresses he has to endure in making his decisions. In other words, plot entails not only the actions of a play but also the inactions — the things that are narrowly rejected and do *not* happen. A character's decision must proceed from powerfully conflicting alternatives if we are to watch this behavior with empathy instead of mere curiosity. In watching a character act, the audience must also watch him *think*; a playwright gets him to think by putting him into conflict.

Conflict may be set up between characters as well as within them; it may be reducible to one central situation, or it may evolve out of many. Whatever the case, conflict throws characters into relief and permits the audience to see deeply into the human personality. To see a character at war with herself or in confrontation with another is to see how that character *works*, and this is the key to our caring.

The theme of a play is ordinarily a simple abstraction of its central conflict. In Sophocles' *Antigone*, for example, the theme is the conflict between divine law and civil law; in *Death of a Salesman*, it is the conflict between Willy's reality and his dreams. Conflicts are plentiful in farces and comedies as well; the conflicts inherent in the "eternal triangle," for example, have provided comic material for dramatists for the past two millennia. Many of the more abstract philosophical conflicts — independence versus duty, individuality versus conformity, idealism versus pragmatism, integrity versus efficiency, pleasure versus propriety, progress versus tradition, to name a few — suggest inexhaustible thematic conflicts that appear in various guises in both ancient and contemporary plays.

The playwright introduces conflict early in a play, often by means of an "inciting incident," in which one character poses a conflict or confrontation either to another character or to himself. For example:

FIRST WITCH: All hail, Macbeth, hail to thee, Thane of Glamis!

SECOND WITCH: All hail, Macbeth, hail to thee, Thane of Cawdor!

THIRD WITCH: All hail, Macbeth, that shalt be King hereafter!

BANQUO: (*to* MACBETH) Good sir, why do you start, and seem to fear
Things that do sound so fair?

In this, the inciting incident of Shakespeare's *Macbeth* (which follows two brief expository scenes), a witch confronts Macbeth with the prediction that he will be king, thereby posing an alternative that Macbeth has apparently already considered, judging from the startled response that elicits Banquo's comment.

Once established, conflict is intensified to crisis, usually by a series of incidents, investigations, revelations, and confrontations. Sometimes even nonevents serve to intensify a conflict, as in the modern classic *Waiting for Godot*, in which two characters simply wait, through two hour-long acts, for the arrival of a third who never comes. Indeed, with this play, Samuel Beckett virtually rewrote the book on playwriting technique by showing how time alone, when properly managed, can do the job of heightening and developing conflict in a dramatic situation.

THE CLIMAX   Conflict cannot be intensified indefinitely. In a play, as in life, when conflict becomes insupportable, something has to give. Thus every play, be it comic, tragic, farcical, or melodramatic, culminates in some sort of dramatic explosion.

As we have seen, Aristotle described that dramatic explosion, in tragedy, as a *catharsis*, a cleansing and/or purification. Aristotle's conception is susceptible to various interpretations, but it has been widely accepted and broadly influential for centuries. The catharsis releases the audience's pity and thereby permits the fullest experience of tragic pleasure, washing away the terror that has been mounting steadily during the play's tragic course. Such catharsis as accompanies Oedipus' gouging out his own eyes as he recognizes his true self illustrates the extreme theatrical explosion of which the classical Greek tragic form is capable.

For any dramatic form, the climax is the conflict of a play taken to its most extreme; it is the moment of maximum tension. At the climax, a continuation of the conflict becomes unbearable, impossible: some sort of change is mandated. Climaxes in modern plays do not, as a rule, involve death or disfiguration (although there are exceptions: Peter Shaffer's celebrated *Equus* reaches its climax with the blinding of six horses, and Edward Albee's *The Zoo Story* climaxes with one character's impaling himself on a knife held by another). However, climaxes inevitably contain elements of recognition and reversal if not of catharsis, and usually the major conflicts of a play are resolved by one or more of these elements.

THE DENOUEMENT   The climax is followed and the play is concluded by a denouement, or resolution, in which a final action or speech or even a single word or gesture indicates that the passions aroused by the play's action are now stilled and a new harmony or understanding has been reached. The tenor of the denouement tends to change with the times. In the American theatre of the 1950s and 1960s, for example, the sentimental and message-laden denouement was the rule: in Robert Anderson's *Tea and Sympathy*, a teacher's wife prepares to prove to a sensitive boy that he is not a homosexual; in Dore Schary's *Sunrise at Campobello*, a future American president makes his way on crippled legs to a convention platform. In the current theatre — in this existential age that looks with suspicion on tidy virtues and

The curtain call is not only a chance for the cast to take their bows; it is also an opportunity for a release of emotion. This is rarely truer than in the exuberant curtain call for Jonathan Larson's 1996 Broadway musical phenomenon, *Rent*.

happy endings — more ironic and ambiguous denouements prevail. The current theatre also provides less in the way of purgation than do more classical modes — perhaps because the conflicts raised by the best of contemporary drama are not amenable to wholesale relief. But a denouement still must provide at least some lucidity concerning the problems raised by the play, some vision or metaphor of a deeper and more permanent understanding. Perhaps the final lines of *Waiting for Godot* best represent the denouement of the current age:

ESTRAGON: Well, shall we go?
VLADIMIR: Yes, let's go.
They do not move.

Events that take place after the play ends are referred to as *postplay*.

THE CURTAIN CALL   The last staged element of a theatrical presentation is the curtain call, in which the actors bow and the audience applauds. This convention — customary in the theatre at least since the time of the Romans — plays an important but often overlooked role in the overall scope of theatrical presentation.

The curtain call is *not* simply a time for the actors to receive congratulations from the audience, although many actors today seem to think it is. Historically, it is a time in which the actors show their respect for the audience that patronizes them. And aesthetically, it is a time in which the audience allows itself to see the other side of the "paradox of the actor." The curtain call liberates the audience from the world of the play. Indeed, when there is no curtain call, audiences are palpably distressed and often disgruntled, for this convention fulfills the last provision, so to speak, in the mutual agreement that characterizes the theatre itself — the agreement by which the audience agrees to view the actors as the characters the actors have agreed to impersonate. It is at the curtain call that actors and audience can acknowledge their mutual belonging in the human society, can look each other in the eye and say, in effect, "We all know what it is to experience these things we've just seen performed. We must all try to understand life a little better. We have enjoyed coming this far together. We are with you. We like you." In the best theatre, this communication is a powerful experience.

THE AFTERMATH: CRITICISM   What follows the curtain call? The audience disperses, of course, but the individual audience members do not die. Through them the production enjoys an extended afterlife both in talk and — in print — in late-night postmortems at the theatre bar, in probing conversations and published reviews over the next few days, and sometimes in formal classroom discussions, television talk shows, letters to the editor in the local newspaper, and scholarly articles and books seen weeks, months, or years later. For the theatre is a place of public stimulation, both intellectual and emotional, and it should be expected that the stimulation provided by a provocative production would generate both animated discussions and illuminating commentaries.

Both of these we may call dramatic criticism, which is the audience's contribution to the theatre. Criticism is as ancient as Aristotle and as contemporary as the essays and lectures that are presented daily in newspapers, journals, books, and academies all over the world. But criticism is not solely an expert enterprise; criticism — which combines analysis and evaluation — is everybody's job. We will look further at this key aspect of the theatre's art in the final chapter of the book.

3

The Actor

She stands alone in the darkness, waiting in the wings, listening with one ear to the insistent rhythms of the dialogue played out upon the stage immediately beyond. Her heart races, and she bounces lightly on the balls of her feet, fighting the welling tension, exhilarated by the sense of something rushing toward her, about to engulf her.

The stage ahead of her is ablaze with light; dazzling colors pour on from all possible directions. The energy onstage is almost tangible: it is there in the eyes of the actors, the pace of the dialogue, the smell of the makeup, the sparkle of perspiration glittering in the lights, the bursts of audience laughter and applause, the sudden silence punctuated by a wild cry or a thundering retort.

She glances backward impatiently. Other actors wait in the backstage gloom. Some perform kneebends and roll their necks against the tension. Some gaze thoughtfully at the action of the play. Some stare at the walls. In one corner a stage manager, his head encased in electronic paraphernalia, his body hunched over a dimly lighted copy of the script, whispers commands into an intercom. The backstage shadows pulse with anticipation.

Suddenly the onstage pace quickens; the lines, all at once, take on a greater urgency and familiarity. It is the cue . . . if only there were time to go to the bathroom . . . it is the cue . . . she takes a deep breath, a deeper breath, a gasp . . . *it is the cue.* She bounds from the dimness into the dazzle: she is onstage, she is an actor!

Acting is perhaps the world's most bewildering profession. At the top, it can be extraordinarily rewarding. The thrill of delivering a great performance, the roar of validation from an enraptured audience, the glory of getting inside the skin of the likes of Hamlet, Harpagon, and Hecuba: these are excitements and satisfactions few careers can induce. Nor are the rewards purely artistic and intellectual; audience appreciation and the producer's eye for profit can catapult some actors to the highest income levels in the world, with salaries in the millions of dollars for actors achieving "star" status in films. And the celebrity that can follow is legendary. The private lives of the most universally admired actors become public property, their innermost thoughts the daily fare of television talk shows and fan magazines.

And yet, for all the splendor and glamor, the actor's life is more often than not depressingly anxious, beset by demands for sacrifice from every direction: psychological, financial, and even moral. Stage fright — the actor's nemesis — is an ever-present nightmare that often increases with experience and renown. Fear of failure, fear of competition, fear of forgetting lines, fear of losing emotional control, fear of losing one's looks, fear of losing one's audience — this list of concerns is endemic to acting as to no other profession.

Nor are the economic rewards in general particularly enticing. The six- and seven-figure salaries of the stars bear little relation to the scale pay for which most actors work: theirs is the lowest union-negotiated wage in the free market economy, and actors often realize less income than the janitors who clean the theatres. And although the stars billed "above the title" may be treated like celebrities or royalty, the common run of actors are freely bullied by directors, bossed about by stage managers, capriciously hired and fired by producers, dangled and deceived by agents, squeezed and corseted by costumers, pinched by wig dressers, poked and powdered by makeup artists, and traduced by press agents. Certainly no profession entails more numbing uncertainties than acting, none demands more sacrifices, and none measures its rewards in such extreme and contradictory dimensions.

What Is Acting?

But what is acting? The question is not as simple as it might seem. It is, of course, the oldest of the theatrical arts. It is older than playwriting, because actors began by improvising their texts. Thespis, the first known actor (and from whose name the word *thespian,* meaning "actor," derives), was the author of the dramas in which he appeared.

Acting is also the most public art of theatre, the most visible to — and recognized by — the audience. The average theatregoer today can probably name more actors than playwrights, designers, and directors put together. The average theatregoer also thinks he or she knows more about the art of acting than the other arts of the theatre as well, because acting seems relatively simple. But it isn't.

The Two Notions of Acting

Since the first discussions of acting, which date from Greek times, theatre artists have recognized two different and seemingly contradictory notions of what acting really is. The first notion is that acting is something that the actor "presents" to the audience — through vocal skill in phrasing and projection, through an ability to imitate different characters and their individual (and social) styles, and through a variety of associated talents, which may include singing, dancing, juggling, fencing, comic improvisation, oral interpretation, and the like. Such acting is sometimes called "presentational," "external," or "technical": the actor learns to "present" a role through a program of training that customarily originates externally — not from inside the actor but from an instructional process that includes formal analysis, technical lessons and drills, and often the imitation of teachers, well-known actors, and/or other students. Such actor training may cover technical skills in dramatic phrasing (learning rhetorical building, persuasive argumentation, and comic pointing), poetic scansion (learning to analyze and effectively accent metrical verse), vocal production (developing a multi-octave speaking range and sonorous resonance, and the ability to vocally project to large audiences), stage movement (learning and practicing period dances and various styles of physical combat), and both text and character analysis, from an acting standpoint, in a wide variety of dramatic styles. This list reflects the training curricula of many acting conservatories in the United States and abroad.

The second notion of acting, however, is that it emanates from somewhere *inside* the actor. By studying the role closely and entering — through her or his own imagination — the world of the play, the actor works to honestly and effectively "live the life of the character" within the play's situation. To do this, the actor must actually "feel" the emotions of the character portrayed and even feel that she or he "is" — during the moments of performance — the character. This is generally considered the "internal" or "representational" notion of acting; "internal" because it begins within the actor and "representational" because it asks the actor to represent all aspects — emotional as well as physical and intellectual — of the character portrayed. In the United States, this internal notion of acting is often called Method acting, or simply The Method, as it is derived from Russian actor-director Konstantin Stanislavsky's self-proclaimed System in the early years of the twentieth century. Stanislavsky's Method was made popular in America by the late Lee Strasberg at his Actors Studio in New York during the 1940s and 1950s.

The seeming opposition of these two notions of acting is still actively debated in act-

ALL CHARACTERS ARE ME

I think all the characters I play are basically me. I believe that under the right set of circumstances we're all capable of anything, and that acting allows the deepest part of your nature to surface – and you're protected by the fiction as it happens.

– Willem Dafoe

ing circles. American actors, for example, have often felt themselves torn between the "representational" notions of Stanislavsky and the "presentational" notions put forward by traditional English actors such as Laurence Olivier and John Gielgud. But the fact is that *both* of these notions of acting — when integrated — are vital to great acting wherever it takes place. All acting is both presentational and representational, both external and internal (and, we might say, both from the head and from the heart), and all great actors must learn, or somehow acquire, the ability to present their characters in a powerful and engaging manner and at the same time live their characters' lives fully and convincingly onstage.

The debate is by no means new. Indeed, the extent to which actors might be said to feel or not feel the emotions of their characters and believe or not believe they "are" the characters they play constitutes what Professor Joseph Roach has called "the historic, continuing, and apparently inexhaustible combat between technique and inspiration in performance theory." That actors connect emotionally with their parts was recognized in the most ancient of theatres. A Roman actor named Aesop, we are told, became so overwrought during a performance of *Orestes* that he ran his sword through a stagehand who unhappily strayed into his line of sight. Polus, another ancient actor, placed the ashes of his own dead son onstage in order to inspire himself while giving Electra's speech of lamentation. Socrates himself inquired of one Ion, a rhapsodist

Musicals, particularly in the current era, usually require acting as passionate as in other forms, even while singing into body microphones. Director Michael Greif expected no less of actors Adam Pascal (as Roger) and Daphne Rubin-Vega (as Mimi) as they sang their intense duet, "Without You," in the Broadway production of *Rent* ("The mind churns / The heart yearns / The tears dry / Without you / Life goes on / But I'm gone / 'Cause I die.").

(poetic reciter), as to the role of real emotion in his performances:

SOCRATES: Tell me, Ion, when you produce the greatest effect upon the audience . . . are you in your right mind? Or are you not carried out of yourself [and] . . . seem to be among the persons or the places of which you are speaking?

ION: Socrates, I must frankly confess that at the tale of pity my eyes are filled with tears, and when I speak of horrors, my hair stands on end and my heart throbs.

Obviously, Ion was "living the life" of his characters, feeling the emotions of his roles, and feeling himself as in the presence of the characters in his rhapsodic tales. But, as Socrates' inquiry soon reveals, Ion was also aware of the powerful effects his acting had upon his audience:

SOCRATES: . . . and are you aware that you produce similar effects on most of the spectators?

ION: Only too well; for I look down upon them from the stage, and behold the various emotions of pity, wonder, sternness, stamped upon their countenances when I am speaking.

Thus Ion considered his acting both representational (he felt himself among the characters of his story) and presentational (he was checking out the audience all the while.) It is a paradox, not an either/or debate, Socrates realized: Ion was both in the fiction of his recitation and at the same time outside of it.

Poets and actors ever since have deliberated on this paradox. The Roman poet Horace (65–8 B.C.) turned Ion's paradox into a famous maxim of the ancient world: In order to move the audience, you must first be moved yourself. Roman orator Quintilian (c. A.D. 35–c. 100) made this into a technique and by envisioning his wife's and children's imaginary deaths with "extreme vividness" while orating became "so moved" that he was brought to tears, turned pale, and exhibited "all the symptoms of genuine grief." True to acting's paradox, however, Quintilian also sought to present his characters according to appropriate stage conventions and for all his tears and passion urged his fellow actors to achieve the "regularity and discipline promised by calculation," cautioning, for example, that "it is never correct to employ the left hand alone in gesture" and that "the hand [may not] be raised above the level of the eyes."

Horace's notion extended right through the Renaissance; an eighteenth-century French critic even proposed that only actors who were truly in love could effectively play lovers onstage. The one great dissenter in acting theory, however, whose work remains startlingly provocative today, was also French: this was Denis Diderot, the famous encyclopedist who in 1773 directly confronted this issue in a brief but trenchant essay (in dialogue form) titled *The Paradox of Acting*. Diderot begins with the radical thesis that "a great actor . . . must [be] an unmoved and disinterested onlooker. . . . They say an actor is all the better for being excited, for being angry. I deny it. He is best when he imitates anger. Actors impress the public not when they are furious, but when they play fury well." By contrast, Diderot explained, "actors who play from the heart . . . are alternately strong and feeble, fiery and cold. . . . Tomorrow they will miss the point they have excelled in today." Thus, Diderot maintains, "the actor who plays from thought . . . will be always at his best; he has considered, combined, learned and arranged the whole thing in his head."

Diderot's view was rooted in his confidence that all knowledge, including art, was rational and could be categorized, analyzed, alphabetized, and (given his profession) "encyclopedized." Diderot's work typifies the Enlightenment, during which he lived, with its demystification of both medieval superstition and Renaissance idealism. The coming ages of romanticism and realism, however, particularly in the theatre, brought a strong rebellion against the "objective" rationalism of Enlightenment thinking.

Stanislavsky, already considered Russia's greatest actor by the time he founded the Moscow Art Theatre in 1898, attacked Diderot's thinking with great fervor. "Put life into all the imagined circumstances and actions," Stanislavsky said, "until you have completely satisfied your sense of truth, and until you have awakened a sense of faith in the reality of your sensations." By "life" Stanislavsky meant the ambiguity of emotion, the mystery of love and death, and the confusion of experience. To create this life onstage, Stanislavsky sought to identify the separate steps of the ac-

EMOTION IN ACTING

If emotion is a state, the actor should never take cognizance of it. In fact we can never take cognizance of an emotion when we are in its grip, but only when it has passed. Otherwise the emotion disappears. The actor lives uniquely in the present; he is continually jumping from one present to the next. In the course of these successive presents he executes a series of actions which deposit upon him a sort of sweat which is nothing else but the state of emotion. This sweat is to his acting what juice is to fruit. But once he starts perceiving and taking cognizance of his state of emotion, the sweat evaporates forthwith, the emotion disappears and the acting dries up. . . . We cannot think "I am moved" without at once ceasing to be so. [Therefore] . . . no one in a theatre should allude to the fragile phenomenon, emotion. Everyone, both players and audience alike, though under its influence, must concern themselves with actions.

— Jean-Louis Barrault

tor's preparation. Primary to his vision was that the actor must seek, in the act of performance, to resolve his or her "character's problem" (in Russian, *zadacha*), as opposed to his or her mere "actor's problem." Thus the actor playing Juliet concentrates on winning Romeo's love (or her father's respect, or her nurse's complicity) rather than showing the audience how romantic (or poetic, or young, or pretty) she is. By this means, according to Stanislavsky, the actor represents Juliet as a real and whole person rather than simply presenting Juliet as a fictional character of the Shakespearean tragic stage. The character's zadacha — somewhat mistranslated into English as "objective" by Elizabeth Hapgood, though her term has stuck — is Stanislavsky's key.

Stanislavsky was one of the first theatre artists to systematically investigate the notion of motivation in acting and to advance the concept that every move onstage must be seen to correspond to what the character (and not just the playwright or director) is striving to achieve. He also created the notion of "public solitude" to indicate the way in which an actor must focus her or his attention on the events of the play rather than simply on the play's impact on the audience. He established the notion that the play's text was accompanied by a "subtext" of meanings (unspoken and undescribed character goals) hidden beneath the lines. He hated all forms of empty theatricality, whereby the actor simply relies on theatrical gimmicks or conceits. He insisted that an "artistic communion" must exist among the actors into which actors must invest themselves deeply, drawing heavily, therefore, upon their own personal feelings in establishing a rapport with their characters, their fellow actors, and the fictional events of the play.

And Stanislavsky was deeply, almost obsessively, concerned with the actor's emotion. Discovering in the writings of French psychologist Théodule Armand Ribot that "all memories of past experiences are recorded by the nervous system and . . . may be evoked by an appropriate stimulus," Stanislavsky began to experiment with recalling his own past emotional states, eventually developing an acting technique known as "emotion memory" (or "emotional recall" or "affective memory"): by mentally substituting these remembered situations from his or her own life into the action of the play, the actor draws upon these memories so as to reach the emotional levels dramatically required. By this substitution of remembered emotion, Stanislavsky sought to make acting natural, truthful, and emotionally vivid for the performer and audience alike.

But emotion — and emotional memory — did not remain central to Stanislavsky's acting system for very long. True to acting's paradox, Stanislavsky was also greatly skilled and thoroughly trained in external theatre technique. Born to an affluent aristocratic family, he had performed in plays, operettas, and operas from the age of six, often in the large, fully equipped theatres his family had constructed

in both their Moscow home and country estate. A promising singer, he had studied with a major Bolshoi Opera star; Tchaikovsky had proposed writing an opera for him. Like Quintilian, Stanislavsky recognized the necessity for purely rational control in performance. "Feeling . . . does not replace an immense amount of work on the part of our intellects," he said. And so he studied elocution, dance, and phrasing as passionately as emotion. By the middle of his career, Stanislavsky had even discarded emotional memory in favor of physical actions as the key to stimulating truthful acting. He began to reproach his actors for excessive wallowing in private emotions: "What's false here? You're playing feelings, your own suffering, that's what's false. I need to see the event and how you react to that event, how you fight people — how you react, not suffer. . . . To take that line . . . is to be passive and sentimental. See everything in terms of action!"

No country — not even Russia — has been as influenced by Stanislavsky's teaching as the United States. By 1919, two of Stanislavsky's disciples, Richard Boleslavski and Maria Ouspenskaya, had moved to New York and founded the American Laboratory Theatre, bringing Stanislavsky's new System to the attention of American actors. Among their converts was Lee Strasberg, an Austrian immigrant who, with others, formed the Group Theatre in 1931 and the Actors Studio shortly thereafter. Strasberg's ensuing Method, derived from the early version of Stanislavsky's System and incorporating emotional recall as a principal technique, became the standard actor-training technique in America. Perhaps because it privileged actors over the script — making their own feelings as much the "subject" of the play as their characters' actions — American actors and not a few celebrities (such as Marilyn Monroe) flocked to his school. Other American acting teachers, some of whom (such as Stella Adler and Sonia Moore) studied with Stanislavsky at a later point in his career, preached

THE ACTORS STUDIO

The most influential school of acting in the United States has been New York's Actors Studio, which was founded by director Elia Kazan and others in 1947 and achieved prominence following the appointment of Lee Strasberg (1901–1982) as artistic director in 1951. Strasberg, an Austrian by birth and a New Yorker by upbringing, proved a magnetic teacher and acting theorist, and his classes revolutionized American acting.

Although the Studio added commercial acting classes to its activities in 1995, it is not primarily a school but an association of selected professional actors who gather at weekly sessions to work on acting problems. The methodology of the Studio derives in part from Stanislavsky and in part from the working methods of the Group Theatre – a pre-World War II acting ensemble that included Kazan, Strasberg, and playwright Clifford Odets. But Strasberg himself proved the key inspiration of Studio teaching and of the American love affair with Method acting attributed to the Studio work.

Strasberg's work is not reducible to simple formulas, for the Studio is a working laboratory and the Studio work is personal rather than theoretical, direct rather than general. Much of the mythology surrounding the Studio – that actors are encouraged to mumble their lines and scratch their jaws in the service of naturalness – is fallacious. Strasberg was a fierce exponent of firm performance discipline and well-studied acting technique; insofar as the Studio developed a reputation for producing actors that mumbled and fidgeted, this seems to have been only a response to the personal idiosyncrasies of Marlon Brando, the Studio's first celebrated "graduate."

Strasberg demanded great depths of character relationships from his actors, and he went to almost any length to get them. Explanation was only one of his tools, but it is the only one that can be made available to readers. The following quotes are from Strasberg himself:

> The human being who acts is the human being who lives. That is a terrifying circumstance. Essentially the actor acts a fiction, a dream; in life the stimuli to which we respond are always real. The actor must constantly respond to stimuli that are imaginary. And yet this must happen not only just as it happens in life, but actually more fully and more expressively. Although the actor can do things in life quite easily, when he has to do the same thing on the stage under fictitious conditions he has difficulty because he is not equipped as a human being merely to playact at imitating life. He must somehow believe. He must somehow be able to convince himself of the rightness of what he is doing in order to do things fully on the stage.
>
> When the actor explores fully the reality of any given object, he comes up with greater dramatic possibilities. These are so inherent in reality that we have a common phrase to describe them. We say, "Only in life could such things happen." We mean that those things are so genuinely dramatic that they could never be just made up. . . .
>
> The true meaning of "natural" or "nature" refers to a thing so fully lived and so fully experienced that only rarely does an actor permit himself that kind of experience on the stage. Only great actors do it on the stage, whereas in life every human being to some extent does it. On the stage it takes the peculiar mentality of the actor to give himself to imaginary things with the same kind of fullness that we ordinarily evince only in giving ourselves to real things. The actor has to evoke that reality on the stage in order to live fully in it and with it.

the Russian master's later emphasis on physical actions rather than emotional memory.

To this day, almost all American teachers of theatre pay homage to Stanislavsky, often framing the debate on acting theory as the opposition of his early teachings with his later ones. But most American stage actors agree that the technical aspects of acting are also critical to career success and that the best acting emanates from both the outside and the inside, with the two being fused in performance. Obviously a performance that failed to fulfill, in its external form, the expectations the text establishes (a performance, for example, that failed to show Prometheus as fiery, Juliet as romantic, Monsieur Jordain as comical) would prove unsatisfying. But equally unsatisfying would be a performance in which the characters' interactions, no matter how eloquently executed, seemed merely flat and mechanical, in which the passions seemed shallowly pasted on by the director, or in which no sparks flew and no romance kindled between the human beings represented onstage. Mere imitation without internal conviction ("living the part") rings hollow, but conviction without definition grows tiresome. The best acting synthesizes the two notions of acting into a comprehensive art.

Beyond these two main lines of the actor's art, there are two other aspects one always finds in the greatest performers: virtuosity of technique and the ineffable "magic" that defines the greatest artists in any field.

Virtuosity

Greatness in acting, like greatness in almost any endeavor, demands a superb set of skills. The characters of drama are rarely mundane; they are exemplary, and so must be the actors who portray them. Merely to impersonate — to imitate and embody — the genius of Hamlet, for example, one must deliver that genius oneself. Similar personal resources are needed to project the depth of Lear, the lyricism of Juliet, the fervor of St. Joan, the proud passion of Prometheus, the bravura of Mercutio, or the heroics of Hecuba. Outsized characters demand outsized abilities and the capacity to project them.

Moreover, it is ultimately insufficient for an actor merely to fulfill the audience's preconceptions of his or her character; finally, it is necessary that the actor strive to transcend those preconceptions and to create the character afresh, transporting the audience to an understanding of — and a compassion for —

Actors William Metzo and Jeannie Naughton play father and daughter – King Lear and Goneril – in the 1999 Utah Shakespearean Festival production of *King Lear.* While it is difficult for actors to learn to play kings and princesses, and to speak in seventeenth-century verse and wear seventeenth-century costume, the production will ultimately rise or fall mainly on the basis of how well the actors can capture the depth and intensity of something quite universal (and profound): the father-daughter relationship.

the character that they never would have achieved on their own.

Both of these demands require of the actor a considerable virtuosity of dramatic technique. Traditionally, the training of actors has concentrated on dramatic technique. Since Roman times (and probably before then), actors have spent most of their lifetime perfecting such performing skills as juggling, dancing, singing, versifying, declaiming, clowning, miming, stage fighting, acrobatics, and sleight of hand. Certainly no actor before the present century had any chance of success without several of these skills, and few actors today reach the top of their profession without fully mastering at least a few of them.

Whatever the individual skills required of an actor over time, the sought-after dramatic technique that is common to history and to our own times can be summed up in just two features: a magnificently expressive voice and a splendidly supple body. These are the tools every actor strives to attain, and when brilliantly honed they are valuable beyond measure.

The actor's voice has received the greatest attention throughout history. Greek tragic actors were awarded prizes for their vocal abilities alone, and many modern actors, such as James Earl Jones, Patrick Stewart, Glenn Close, and Maggie Smith, are celebrated for their distinctive use of the voice. The potential of the acting voice as an instrument of great theatre is immense. The voice can be thrilling, resonant, mellow, sharp, musical, stinging, poetic, seductive, compelling, lulling, and dominating; and an actor capable of drawing on many such "voices" clearly can command a spectrum of acting roles and lend them a splendor the less-gifted actor or the untrained amateur could scarcely imagine. A voice that can articulate, that can explain, that can rivet attention, that can convey the subtlest nuance, that can exult, dazzle, thunder with rage, and flow with compassion — when used in the service of dramatic impersonation — can hold an audience spellbound.

The actor's use of her or his body — the capacity for movement — is the other element of fundamental technique, the second basis for dramatic virtuosity. Most of the best actors are strong and supple; all are capable of great physical self-mastery and are artists of body language. The effects that can be achieved

A Thrilling Voice

Mr. [Richard] Burton happens to possess a vocal instrument that . . . is exactly what we expect to hear, and almost never do hear, on going to the theatre. The sounds produced in the living theatre are not meant to be the sounds produced in day-to-day life, though that is what actors have been giving us for years on end. We look for a "liveness" that has been intensified, as it is so often intensified in the control rooms of recording studios. Mr. Burton was his own control room, sending out sounds that swept the walls of the theatre clean with an apparently effortless power, magnifying the "natural" until we were caught up in its gale, left stunned and breathless. And yes, we said to ourselves, this is precisely the penetrating resonance all actors should possess, if the tonalities of the stage are to be differentiated from those of film. Not everyone, to be sure, can be born in Wales. But the sound, with all of its nuances and its pressures, can be acquired, as Irene Worth has acquired it. It is thrilling when heard, and the thrill is what playhouses are for.

— Walter Kerr

through stage movement are as numerous as those that can be achieved through voice. Subtly expressive movement in particular is the mark of the gifted actor, who can accomplish miracles of communication with an arched eyebrow, a toss of the head, a flick of the wrist, a whirl of the hem, or a shuffle of the feet. But bold movements, too, can produce indelible moments in the theatre: Helene Weigel's powerful chest-pounding when, as Mother Courage, she loses her son; Laurence Olivier's breathtaking fall from the tower as Coriolanus — these are sublime theatricalizations accomplished through the actors' sheer physical skill, strength, and dramatic audacity.

Virtuosity for its own sake can be appealing in the cabaret or lecture hall as well as in the theatre, but when coupled with the impersonation of character it can create dramatic performances of consummate depth, complexity, and theatrical power. We are always impressed

English actors Richard Briers and Geraldine McEwan have, between them, seventy years of professional experience, all of which was on display in their scintillating portrayals of the Old Man and his Wife in the 1998 Broadway revival of Eugène Ionesco's absurd tragicomedy *The Chairs*.

by skill — it is fascinating, for instance, to watch a skilled cobbler finishing a leather boot — but great skill in the service of dramatic action can be absolutely transporting. Of course, virtuosity is not easy to acquire, and indeed it will always remain beyond the reach of many people. Each of us possesses natural gifts, but not all are gifted to the same degree; some measure of dramatic talent must be inborn or at least learned early on. But the training beyond one's gifts, the shaping of talent into craft, is an unending process. "You never stop learning it," said actor James Stewart after nearly fifty years of stage and film successes, and virtually all actors would agree with him.

Traditional notions of virtuosity in acting went into a temporary eclipse in the middle of this century, owing mainly to the rise of realism, which required that acting conform to the behaviors of ordinary people leading ordinary lives. The *cinéma vérité* of the post–World War II era in particular fostered an "artless" acting style, to which virtuosity seemed intrusive rather than supportive. It is certainly true that the virtuosity of one age can seem mere affectation in the next and that modern times require modern skills, a contemporary virtuosity that accords with contemporary dramatic material. Yet even the traditional skills of the theatre have made a great comeback in recent decades: circus techniques, dance, and songs are now a part of many of the most experimental modern stagings; and multiskilled, multitalented performers are in demand as never before. The performer rich in talent and performing skills, capable not merely of depicting everyday life but of fashioning an artful and exciting theatrical expression of it as well, once again commands the central position in contemporary drama.

Magic

Beyond conviction and virtuosity (though incorporating them) remains a final acting ingredient that has been called "presence," "magnetism," "charisma," and many other terms. We shall call it "magic." It is a quality that is difficult to define but universally felt, a quality we cannot explain except to say we know it when we are under its spell.

We must always remember that the earliest actor was not a technician of the theatre but a priest — and that he embodied not ordinary men but gods. We may witness this function directly today in certain tribal dramas, in which a shaman or witch doctor is accepted by cocelebrants as the possessor of divine attributes — or as one possessed by them.

The modern secular actor also conveys at least a hint of this transcendent divinity. Elevated upon a stage and bathed in light for all to see, charged with creating an intensity of feeling, a vivid characterization, and a well-articulated eloquence of verbal and physical mastery, the actor at his or her finest becomes an almost extraterrestrial being, a "star," or, in the French expression, a *monstre sacré* ("sacred monster").

The actor's presence, the ability to project an aura of magic — does not come about as a direct result of skill at impersonation or technical virtuosity. It does, however, depend on the actor's inner confidence, which in turn can be bred from a mastery of the craft. Therefore, although "magic" cannot be directly acquired or produced, it can be approached, and its fundamental requisites can be established. For gifted individuals it might come quickly; for others, despite abundant skills and devoted

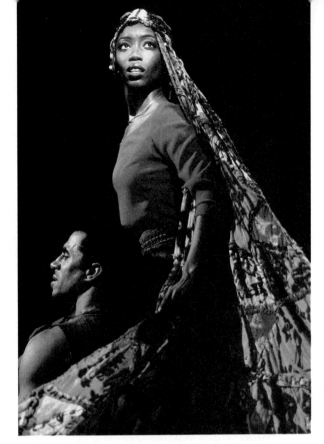

A truly great performance is occasionally said to "carry" a show, and certainly Heather Headley's sensational performance in the Broadway musical *Aida* (2000) was one of these; appearing in almost every scene and dazzling the audience with her vivacious musicality, Headley was, for many spectators (and critics), reason enough to adore the show.

training, it comes late or not at all, and they can never rise above pedestrian performances. It is perhaps frustrating to find that acting greatness depends so heavily on this elusive and inexplicable goal of magic, but it is also true that every art incorporates elements that must remain as mysteries. The best acting, like any art, ultimately transcends the reach of pure descriptive analysis; it cannot be acquired mechanically. The best acting strikes chords in the nonreasoning parts of our being; it rings with a resonance we do not fully understand, and it evokes a reality we no longer fully remember. We should extol, not lament, this fact.

Becoming an Actor

How does one become an actor? Many thousands ask this question every year; many thousands, indeed, *act* in one or more theatrical productions every year. The training of actors is now a major activity in hundreds of colleges, universities, conservatories, and private and commercial schools across the United States; and theories of actor training constitute a major branch of artistic pedagogy.

Essentially, actor training entails two distinct phases: development of the actor's instrument and development of the actor's method of approaching a role. There is no general agreement on the order in which these phases should occur, but there is a widespread understanding that both are necessary and that the two are interrelated.

The Actor's Instrument

The actor's instrument is the actor's self — mind, mettle, and metabolism are the materials of an acting performance. An actor's voice is the Stradivarius to be played; an actor's body is the sculpting clay to be molded. An actor is a portrait artist working from inside the self, creating characters with her or his own organs and physiological systems. It is obvious that a great artist requires first-rate equipment: for the actor this means a responsive *self*, disciplined yet uninhibited, capable of rising to the challenges of great roles.

The training of the actor's instrument is both physiological and psychological; for that reason it must be accomplished under the personal supervision of qualified instructors. In the past, acting instructors were invariably master actors who took on younger apprentices; even today, students of classical French and Japanese acting styles learn their art by relentless imitation of the actors they hope to succeed. In America, however, acting instruction has expanded to include a great many educational specialists who may or may not have had extensive professional acting experience themselves; indeed, some of the most celebrated and effective acting teachers today are play directors, theatrical innovators, and academicians.

No one, however, has yet discovered the art of training an actor's instrument simply by reading books or thinking about problems of craft. This point should be borne in mind while reading the rest of this chapter.

THE PHYSIOLOGICAL INSTRUMENT   Voice and speech, quite naturally, are the first elements of the actor's physiological instrument to be considered: "Voice, voice, and more voice" was the answer Tommaso Salvini, the famed nineteenth-century Italian tragedian, gave to the question "What are the three most important attributes of acting?" We already have discussed the importance of vocal skills in the acting profession: voice- and speech-training programs are aimed at acquainting the actor with a variety of means to achieve and enhance these skills.

The basic elements of voice (breathing, phonation, resonance) and of speech (articulation, pronunciation, phrasing) — as well as their final combination (projection) — are all separate aspects of an integrated voice-training program. Such a program ordinarily takes three years or longer, and many actors continue working on their voice and speech all their lives.

As devoted as teachers and scientists have been to the problems of perfecting voice and speech, however, a certain mystery still surrounds much of their work. Even the fundamental question of how the voice actually works is still a subject of fierce dispute among specialists in anatomy and physiology. Moreover, the processes involved in breathing and speaking have acquired a certain mystique; for example, the dual meaning of *inspiration* as both "inhalation" and "spirit stimulus" has

THE COMPONENTS OF VOICE AND SPEECH

Breathing pumps air through the vocal tract, providing a carrier for the voice. "Breath support," through the expansion of the rib cage and a lowering and controlling of the diaphragm, is a primary goal, as is natural, deep, free breathing that is sufficient to produce and sustain tone but not so forced as to create tension or artificial huffing and puffing.

Phonation is the process whereby vocal cord oscillations produce sound, a process that remains something of an anatomical and physiological mystery even today. Vocal warm-ups are essential for the actor to keep his or her vocal cords and other laryngeal (voice box) tissues supple and healthy; they also prevent strain and the growth of nodes that may cause raspiness and pain as well as phonic failure (laryngitis).

Resonance is the sympathetic vibration, or "resounding," of the voice as it is amplified in the throat, chest, and head. Resonance gives phonation its *timbre,* or tonal quality, its particular balance of bass and treble sounds. Open-throatedness — the lowering of the larynx within the neck, as by a yawn — increases the resonance in the pharynx (throat) and is a major goal in voice work. Keeping the mouth open while speaking and raising the soft palate also increase resonance and add to vocal quality.

Articulation is the shaping of vocal sound into recognizable *phonemes,* or language sounds, forty of which are easily distinguishable in the English language. Speech-training programs aim at improving the actor's capacity to articulate these sounds distinctly, naturally, and unaffectedly — that is, without slurring, ambiguous noise, or self-conscious maneuvering of the lip and tongue. A lazy tongue and slovenly speaking habits inhibit articulation and can be overcome only with persistent drilling and disciplined attention.

Pronunciation makes words both comprehensible and appropriate to the character and style of the play; clear standard pronunciation, unaffected by regional dialect, is a crucial part of the actor's instrument, as is the ability to learn regional dialects and foreign accents when required. Occasionally actors achieve prominence with the aid of a seemingly permanent dialect — Andy Griffith and Sissy Spacek are two examples — but such actors are likely to find their casting opportunities quite limited unless they can expand their speaking range.

Phrasing makes words meaningful and gives them sound patterns that are both rhythmic and logical. The great classical actors are masters of nuance in phrasing, capable of subtly varying their pitch, intensity, and rate of speech seemingly without effort from one syllable to the next. They rarely phrase consciously; rather, they apparently develop their phrasing through years of experience with classical works and a sustained awareness of the value of spontaneity, naturalness, and a commitment to the dramatized situation. Training programs in speech phrasing aim at enabling actors to expand the pitch range of their normal speech from the normal half-octave to two octaves or three, to double their clear-speaking capacity from 200 words a minute to 400, and to develop their ability to orchestrate prose and verse into effective and persuasive crescendos (where volume builds), diminuendos (where it diminishes), and sostenutos (where vowels are elongated for effect) just as if they were responding to a musical score.

Projection, which is the final element in the delivery of voice and speech to the audience, is what ultimately creates dramatic communication; it governs the force with which the character's mind is heard through the character's voice, and it determines the impact of all other components of the actor's voice on the audience. Anxiety and physical tension are the great enemies of projection because they cause shallow breathing, shrill resonance, and timid phrasing; therefore, relaxation and the development of self-confidence become crucial at this final stage of voice and speech development.

Martin Wuttke plays the title role, a savage but farcical parody of Adolf Hitler, in this 1999 Berliner Ensemble production of Bertolt Brecht's *Resistible Rise of Arturo Ui*, first by acting the part of Arturo's dog, snarling and panting wildly on all fours, and then by playing the demonic Arturo himself.

given rise to a number of exotic theoretical dictums that border on religiosity. Some of the fundamental practices of vocal and speech instruction, however, are generalized in the box on the components of voice and speech.

Movement is the second element of the actor's physiological instrument. Movement training typically involves exercises and instruction designed to create physical relaxation, muscular control, economy of action, and expressive rhythms and movement patterns. Dance, mime, fencing, and acrobatics are traditional training courses for actors; in addition, circus techniques and masked pantomime have become common courses in recent years.

Sheer physical strength is stressed by some actors. Laurence Olivier, for example, accorded it the highest importance because, he contended, it gives the actor the stamina needed to "hold stage" for several hours of performance and the basic resilience to accomplish the physical and psychological work of acting without strain or fatigue.

An actor's control of the body permits her or him to stand, sit, and move on the stage with alertness, energy, and seeming ease. Standing tall, walking boldly, turning on a dime at precisely the right moment, extending the limbs joyously, sobbing violently, springing about uproariously, and occupying a major share of stage space are among the capacities of the actor who has mastered body control through training and confidence. In the late days of the Greek theatre, known as the Hellenistic period, actors used elevated footwear, giant headdresses, and sweeping robes to take on a larger-than-life appearance; the modern actor has discovered that the same effect can be achieved simply by tapping the residual expansiveness of the body.

Economy of movement, which is taught primarily through the selectivity of mime, permits the conveyance of subtle detail by seemingly inconspicuous movement. The waggle of a fin-

ger, the flare of a nostril, the quiver of a lip can communicate volumes in a performance of controlled movement. The beginning actor is often recognized by uncontrolled behaviors — fidgeting, shuffling, aimless pacing, and nervous hand gestures — which draw unwanted audience attention. The professional understands the value of physical self-control and the explosive potential of a simple movement that follows a carefully prepared stillness. *Surprise,* which is one of the actor's greatest weapons, can be achieved only through the actor's mastery of the body.

One of America's most distinguished stage actors is Cherry Jones, who won the best actress Obie (off-Broadway) Award for *The Baltimore Waltz* in 1992 and the comparable Tony Award for *The Heiress* in 1995. Here (in her walker, accompanied by Monique Fowler) she is shown as Mabel Tidings Bigelow — at age 91 — in the 1997 Old Globe Theatre world premiere (directed by Jack O'Brien) of Tina Howe's *Pride's Crossing.* Later in the play, and without makeup changes of any sort, she played Mabel at 10, 13, 21, 36, and 56: a bravura performance.

Sean Campion and Conleth Hill play, among them, all sixteen male and female roles of Marie Jones's *Stones in His Pockets*.

THE PSYCHOLOGICAL INSTRUMENT Imagination, and the willingness and ability to use it in the service of art, is the major psychological component of the actor's instrument. At the first level, *an actress must use her imagination to make the artifice of the theatre real enough to herself* to convey that sense of reality to the audience: painted canvas flats must be imagined as brick walls, an offstage jangle must be imagined as a ringing onstage telephone, and a young actress must be imagined as a mother or grandmother.

At the second, far more important, level, *the actor must imagine himself in an interpersonal situation created by the play*: in love with Juliet, in awe of Zeus, in despair of his life. This imagination must be broad and all-encompassing: the successful actor is able to imagine himself performing and relishing the often unspeakable acts of his characters, who may be murder-

ers, despots, or monsters; insane or incestuous lovers; racial bigots, atheists, devils, perverts, or prudes. To the actor, nothing must be unimaginable; the actor's imagination must be a playground for expressive fantasy and darkly compelling motivations.

At the third, deepest, level, *the actor's imagination must go beyond the mere accommodation of an accepted role pattern to become a creative force* that makes characterization a high art. For each actor creates his or her role uniquely — each Romeo and Juliet are like no others before them, and each role can be uniquely fashioned with the aid of the actor's imaginative power. The final goal of creating a character is to make it fresh by filling it with the pulse of real blood and the animation of real on-the-spot thinking and doing. The actor's imagination, liberated from stage fright and mechanical worries, is the crucial ingredient in allowing the actor to transcend the pedestrian and soar toward the genuinely original.

The liberation of imagination is a continuing process in actor training; exercises and "theatre games" designed for that purpose are part of most beginning classes in acting, and many directors use the same exercises and games at the beginning of play rehearsal periods. Because the human imagination tends to rigidify in the course of maturation — the child's imagination is usually much richer than that of the adult — veteran professional actors often profit from periodic mind-expanding or imagination-freeing exercises and games.

Discipline is the fourth and final aspect of an actor's psychological instrument, and to a certain extent it is the one that rules them all. The imagination of the actor is by no means unlimited, nor should it be. It is restricted by the requirements of the play, by the director's staging and interpretation, and by certain established working conditions of the theatre. *The actor's artistic discipline keeps him or her within the established bounds and at the same time ensures artistic agility.*

The actor is not an independent artist, like a writer or a painter. The actor works in an ensemble and is but one employee (paid or unpaid) in a large enterprise that can succeed only as a collaboration. Therefore, although actors are sometimes thought to be universally temperamental and professionally difficult, the truth is exactly the opposite: actors are among the most disciplined of artists, and the more professional they are, the more disciplined they are.

The actor, after all, leads a vigorous and demanding life. Makeup calls at 5:30 in the morning for film actors and nightly and back-to-back weekend live performances for stage actors make for schedules that are difficult to maintain on a regular basis. Further, the physical and emotional demands of the acting process — the need for extreme concentration in rehearsal and performance, the need for phys-

ical health and psychological composure, the need for the actor to be both the instrument and the initiator of her or his performance, and the special demands of interacting with fellow performers at a deep level of mutual involvement — do not permit casual or capricious behavior among the members of a cast or company.

Truly professional actors practice the most rigorous discipline over their work habits. They make all calls (for rehearsal, costume fitting, photographs, makeup, audition, and performance) at the stated times, properly warmed up beforehand; they learn lines at or before stipulated deadlines, memorize stage movements as directed, collaborate with the other actors and theatre artists toward a successful and growing performance, and continually study their craft. If they do not do these things, they cease to be actors. Professional theatre producers have little sympathy or forgiveness for undisciplined performers, and this professional attitude now prevails in community and university theatres as well.

Being a disciplined actor does not mean being a slave, nor does it mean foregone capitulation to the director or the management. The disciplined actor is simply one who works rigorously to develop his or her physiological and psychological instrument, who meets all technical obligations unerringly and without reminder, and who works to the utmost to ensure the success of the entire production and the fruitful association of the whole acting ensemble. The disciplined actor asks questions, offers suggestions, invents stage business, and creates charactérization in harmony with the directorial pattern and the acting ensemble. When there is a serious disagreement between actor and director (a not uncommon occurrence), the disciplined actor seeks to work it out through discussion and compromise and will finally yield if the director cannot be persuaded otherwise. Persistent, willful disobedience has no place in the serious theatre and is not tolerated by it.

Above: Comedy requires a deep commitment to the passions of the characters; although the action is amusing to the audience, it is dead serious to the characters. Here Jeff Goldblum, as Malvolio, presses his unwanted attentions on Michelle Pfeiffer, Lady Olivia, in Shakespeare's comedy *Twelfth Night* at the New York Shakespeare Festival in 1989. This production played at the large, outdoor Delacorte Theatre in Central Park; both actors wore body microphones for electronic sound enhancement.

Above right: No one can say that sex appeal is not a vital part of theatre, which almost always centers on themes of erotic passion. Nicole Kidman is here the star, opposite Iain Glen, in English playwright David Hare's steamy *The Blue Room,* in the London premiere, 1998.

The Actor's Approach

As the dust clears from the last phases of the longstanding debate between external and internal acting techniques, certain elements of an integrated, or fusion, technique are nearly universal in actor training, at least in the West. The first element is Stanislavsky's primary principle: the actor creates her or his performance through the pursuit of the character's *zadacha,* or problem to be solved. Whether *zadacha* is further translated as "objective," "intention," "task," "victory," "want," or "goal" (this author's choice), the basic point — that the actor

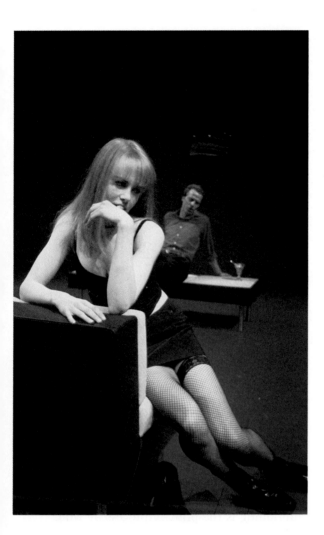

fect, "interacting with other people." Thus Juliet does not simply want "to marry" but "to marry Romeo," and Hamlet wants not just "to become king of Denmark" but "to replace Claudius." The acting thus becomes enlivened; it occurs in real time while onstage, with moment-to-moment interplay between all the actors involved.

The second element of the actor's approach is the identification of the tactics necessary to achieve goals and avoid defeats. Romeo woos Juliet by composing love poems to her and reciting them fetchingly; he silences Mercutio's jibes by wittily humoring him. Hamlet secures Horatio's aid by speaking kindly to him; he disorients Polonius by confusing him; and he steers Ophelia out of harm's way (he believes) by frightening her. These tactics are how Romeo and Hamlet try to make their goals come to fruition, and, for the actors who play them with committed vigor, their voices and bodies should pulse with excitement, anticipation, and alarm. Actors who play tactics boldly and with enthusiasm and who allow themselves to believe that they will win their goals (even if the play dictates that they will not) convey the theatre's greatest intangible: hope. Hope achieved — as when the young deaf and blind Helen Keller finally utters the word "wawa" as her teacher splashes water on her hands in the final moments of William Gibson's *The Miracle Worker* — can be overwhelmingly thrilling. Hope dashed — as when Jim O'Connor tells Laura he won't, in fact, be able to invite her on a date in Tennessee Williams's *The Glass Menagerie* — can be unbearably poignant. It is in the alternation of these sorts of climaxes that great theatrical impact is achieved.

The third and most complicated element of the actor's approach requires research into the style of the play and the mode of performance that will govern the production, in which each role is but a single integer. Some plays, and some productions, invite — indeed, require — a direct confrontation with the live

embodies the role by pursuing the character's goal (to marry Romeo, to displace the king of Denmark) rather than by pursuing the actor's own (to get a standing ovation, to get a better part in the next production) — is all but universally accepted. Pursuing the character's goal focuses the actor's energy, displaces stage fright, aligns the actor solidly with the character, and sets up the broadest and deepest foundation for employing all the technical skills at the actor's disposal.

It is usually best to identify the character's primary goal in relation to the other characters in the play so that acting becomes, in ef-

Frank Langella, in his masterful portrayal of the title role in August Strindberg's 1887 realistic masterpiece *The Father*, actually seemed to breathe real nineteenth-century air during the celebrated 1997 Broadway production of the play.

"Everybody Understands Frustration"

One time I had this scene where I was to walk into this actress' dressing room and say something like "I love you; will you marry me?" We managed to make it better by having the girl go into her bathroom and close the door and I had to say those lines to a closed door. I learned to work with counterpoint. To make the material more interesting I would find ways to create obstacles for the character – frustrate him in what he wants to accomplish. That makes the character more sympathetic, because everybody understands frustration.

– Jack Lemmon

audience. Some plays assume an environment in which the entire cast of characters expects and rewards refined speech; others assume an environment in which refined speech is ridiculed as pretentious. Some plays have several "worlds" of characters — the aristocrats, the laborers, and the fairies in Shakespeare's *A Midsummer Night's Dream*, for example — and the actor's approach must lead to an understanding of what the nature of each of the play's separate or inclusive worlds is.

The Actor's Routine

In essence, the actor's professional routine consists of three stages: the audition, the rehearsal, and the performance. The first is the way the actor gets a role, the second is the way the actor learns it, and the last is the way the actor produces it, either night after night on a stage or one time for filming or taping. Each of these stages merits independent consideration, for each imposes certain special demands on the actor's instrument and on his or her approach.

The Audition

For all but the most established professionals, auditioning is the primary process by which acting roles are awarded. A young actor may audition hundreds of times a year. In the film world, celebrated performers may be required to audition only if their careers are perceived to be declining: two of the more famous (and successful) auditions in American film history were undertaken by Frank Sinatra for *From Here to Eternity* and by Marlon Brando for *The Godfather*. Stage actors are customarily asked to audition no matter how experienced or famous they are.

In an audition the actor has an opportunity to demonstrate to the director (or producer or casting director) how well he or she can fulfill the role sought; in order to show

HOW TO AUDITION

Doubtless many readers of this book will wish to audition for a play at some time in their lives. It is a wonderful experience (provided one is prepared to deal with the chance of rejection), for it energizes the mind and body in a unique one-to-one relationship.

There can be no consensus as to what sort of audition will be successful in any given circumstance, since directors vary widely in what they are looking for – and what they are *not* looking for – and a certain amount of interpersonal chemistry inevitably influences the final decisions. However, the following general points about auditioning might prove useful to the beginner.

Audition pieces should always be selected from material suitable to the actor. For example, an inexperienced young person should not prepare a speech of King Lear's for audition purposes, for this role would almost surely be beyond his grasp; instead, it would be better to prepare a piece reasonably in concert with his own age and experience.

Similarly, audition pieces should be suited to the role sought or the play auditioned for. It would be foolish for even a veteran performer to prepare material from *King Lear* if the play being cast were a light comedy; only the most creative casting director could get any idea from the *Lear* audition of how the actor would come across if given a role in the play under consideration.

Auditions should evoke the actor's most theatrically interesting qualities. They should do something to grab the attention of the director; otherwise they fail, no matter how competently performed. An audition, after all, is not a classroom assignment: it is an appeal to the director that should say – should actually *scream* – "Look no further, you've found who you're looking for!" All auditions, whether of the prepared or the cold-reading variety, should be designed to bring out the actor's ability to concentrate on situational objectives and to employ engaging tactics,

thus giving evidence of the actor's range within the required context; only then can the director get a valid idea of the actor's potential contribution to the excitement of his or her planned theatrical experience.

Auditions should be given with confidence and without extensive preamble, apology, or explanation. Excessive nervousness or slavish deference to the director, even if they are due simply to shyness, can freeze the actor and ruin an audition; conversely, blustering in an attempt to cover shyness is likely to read as an attitude of superiority or defiance, which is rarely encouraged. Continual auditioning is the best single means of developing calm and powerful auditioning; every actor with professional ambitions should audition as often as possible and under as many sorts of circumstances as present themselves.

Auditions should be short. In some professional situations the actor has no control whatever over the amount of time allotted for auditions, and the audition is routinely cut off after just ten or fifteen seconds. Although most directors dislike cutting auditions off in midcourse, they do learn most of what they want to know in a few moments and allow the audition to continue only as a matter of courtesy. Thus the first few moments of an audition count enormously, and the best auditioners learn to get themselves across in a very short time.

Auditions can be practiced. Prepared auditions can be coached and rehearsed successfully, and cold-reading techniques can be developed. But nothing demonstrates a fine actor so much in an audition as the confidence, control, and authority that come with training and experience. No actor should concentrate exclusively on developing an "audition method," for the audition can afford only a glimpse of the performer's total capabilities. The best way an actor can prepare for auditions is to look to his or her whole development as an actor.

---

this, the actor presents either a prepared reading or a "cold reading" from the script whose production is planned. Every actor who is seriously planning for a career in the theatre will prepare several audition pieces to have at the ready in case an audition opportunity presents

itself. For the most part these pieces will be one- or two-minute monologues from plays, although sometimes short narrative cuttings from novels, short stories, and poems are used. Each audition piece must be carefully edited for timing and content (some alteration of the text, so as to make a continuous speech out of two or three shorter speeches, is generally permissible); the piece is then memorized and staged. The staging requirements should be flexible to permit adjustments to the size of the audition place (which might be a stage but could just as well be an agent's office) and should not rely on costuming or the use of particular pieces of furniture. Most actors prepare a variety of these pieces, for although auditions generally specify two contrasting selections (one verse and one prose, one serious and one comic, or one classical and one modern), an extra piece that fits a particular casting situation can often come in handy. An actor's audition pieces are as essential as calling cards in the professional theatre world and in many academies as well; they should be carefully developed, coached, and rehearsed, and they should be performed with assurance and poise.

The qualities a director looks for at an audition vary from one situation to another, but generally they include the actor's ease at handling the role; naturalness of delivery; physical, vocal, and emotional suitability for the part; and spontaneity, power, and charm. Most directors also look for an actor who is well trained and disciplined and capable of mastering the technical demands of the part, who will complement the company ensemble, and who can convey that intangible presence that makes for "theatre magic." In short, the audition can show the director that the actor not only knows her or his craft, but also will lend the production a special excitement.

The Rehearsal

Plays are ordinarily rehearsed in a matter of weeks: a normal period of rehearsal ranges from ten weeks for complex or experimental productions to just one week for many summer stock operations. Much longer rehearsal periods, however, are not unheard of; indeed, the productions of Stanislavsky and Brecht were frequently rehearsed for a year or more. Three to five weeks, however, is the customary re-

hearsal period for American professional productions — but these are forty-hour weeks, and they are usually followed by several days (or weeks) of previews and/or out-of-town tryouts, with additional rehearsals between performances.

During the rehearsal period the actor learns the role and investigates, among other things, the character's biography; the subtext (the unspoken communications) of the play; the character's thoughts, fears, and fantasies; the character's objectives; and the world envisioned by the play and the playwright. The director will lead discussions, offer opinions, and issue directives with respect to some or all of these matters; the director may also provide reading materials, pictures, and music to aid in the actor's research.

The actor must memorize lines, stage movements ("blocking"), and directed stage actions ("business," precisely scripted physical behaviors) during the rehearsal period. He or she must also be prepared to rememorize these if they are changed, as they frequently are: in the rehearsal of new plays it is not unusual for entire acts to be rewritten between rehearsals and for large segments to be changed, added, or written out overnight.

Memorization usually presents no great problem for young actors, to whom it tends to come naturally (children in plays frequently memorize not only their own lines but everyone else's, without even meaning to); however, it seems to become more difficult as one gets older. But at whatever age, memorization of lines remains one of the actor's easier problems to solve, contrary to what many naive audience members think. Adequate memorization merely provides the basis from which the actor learns a part; the actor's goal is not simply to get the lines down but to do it *fast* so that most of the rehearsal time can be devoted to concentrating on other things.

The rehearsal period is a time for experimentation and discovery. It is a time for the actor to get close to the character's beliefs and intentions, to steep in the internal aspects of characterization that lead to fully engaged physical, intellectual, and emotional performance. It is a time to search the play's text and the director's mind for clues as to how the character behaves and what results the character aims for in the play's situation. And it is a time to experiment, both alone and in rehearsal with other actors, with the possibilities of subtle interactions that these investigations develop.

Externally, rehearsal is a time for the actor to experiment with timing and delivery of both lines and business; to integrate the staged movements (given by the director) with the text (given by the playwright) and to meld these into a fluid series of actions that build and illuminate by the admixture of the actor's own personally initiated behavior. It is a time to suggest movement and business possibilities to the director (presuming the director is the sort who accepts suggestions, as virtually all do nowadays) and to work out details of complicated sequences with the other actors. It is also a time to "get secure" in both lines and business by constant repetition — in fact, the French word for rehearsal is *répétition*. And it affords an opportunity to explore all the possibilities of the role — to look for ways to improve the actor's original plan for its realization and to test various possibilities with the director.

Thus the rehearsal of a play is an extremely creative time for an actor; it is by no means a routine or boring work assignment — and indeed for this reason some actors enjoy the rehearsal process even more than the performance phase of production. At its best, a rehearsal is both spontaneous and disciplined, a combination of repetition and change, of trying and "setting," of making patterns and breaking them and then making them anew. It is an exciting time, no less so because it invariably includes many moments of distress, frustration, and despair; it is a time, above all, when the actor learns a great deal about acting and, ideally, about human interaction on many levels.

The Performance

Performing, finally, is what the theatre is about, and it is before an audience in a live performance that the actor's mettle is put to the ultimate test. Sometimes the results are quite startling. The actor who has been brilliant in rehearsal can crumble before an audience and completely lose the "edge" of his performance in the face of stage fright and apprehension. Or — and this is more likely — an actor who seemed fairly unexciting in rehearsal can suddenly take fire in performance and dazzle the audience with unexpected energy, subtlety, and depth: one celebrated example of this phenomenon was achieved by Lee J. Cobb in the original production of Arthur Miller's *Death of a Salesman,* in which Cobb had the title role. Roles rehearsed in all solemnity can suddenly turn comical in performance; conversely, roles developed for comic potential in rehearsal may be received soberly by an audience and lose their comedic aspect entirely.

Sudden and dramatic change, however, is not the norm as the performance phase replaces rehearsal: most actors cross over from final dress rehearsal to opening night with only the slightest shift; indeed, this is generally thought to be the goal of a disciplined and professional rehearsal schedule. "Holding back until opening night," an acting practice occasionally employed over the past century, is universally disavowed today, and opening-night recklessness is viewed as a sure sign of the amateur, who relies primarily on guts and adrenaline to get through the evening. Deliberate revision of a role in performance, in response to the first waves of laughter or applause, is similarly frowned upon in all but the most inartistic of theatres today.

Nevertheless, a fundamental shift does occur in the actor's awareness between rehearsal and performance, and this cannot and should not be denied; indeed, it is essential to the creation of theatre art. The shift is set up by an elementary feedback: the actor is inevitably aware, with at least a portion of her mind, of

England's most acclaimed actress, Judi Dench, playing the role of an acclaimed actress, here applies makeup in the 1999 Broadway production of David Hare's *Amy's View*, a story of broken relationships against a background of theatrical culture and an entertainment industry. Making-up and making up are both the literal and figurative topics. Design by Bob Crowley.

acter whom the actor portrays and the "self" of the actor who represents that character especially vibrant and "in the present" for the audience; it is the quality of an actor who takes the stage and acknowledges, in some inexplicable yet indelible manner, that he or she is there *to be seen*. Performance is not a one-way statement given from the stage to the house; it is a two-way, participatory communication between the actors and the audience members in which the former employ text and movement and the latter employ applause, laughter, silence, and attention.

Even when the audience is silent and invisible — and, owing to the brightness of stage lights, the audience is frequently invisible to the actor — the performer feels its presence. There is nothing extrasensory about this: the absence of sound is itself a signal, for when several hundred people sit without shuffling, coughing, or muttering, their silence betokens a level of attention for which the actor customarily strives. Laughter, gasps, sighs, and applause similarly feed back into the actor's consciousness — and unconsciousness — and spur (or sometimes, alas, distract) his efforts. The veteran actor can determine quickly how to ride the crest of audience laughter and how to hold the next line just long enough that it will pierce the lingering chuckles but not be overridden by them; he also knows how to vary his pace and/or redouble his energy when he senses restlessness or boredom on the other side of the curtain line. "Performance technique," or the art of "reading an audience," is more instinctual than learned. It is not dissimilar to the technique achieved by the effective classroom lecturer or TV talk-show host or even by the accomplished conversationalist. The timing it requires is of such complexity that no actor could master it rationally; he or she can develop it only out of experience — both on the stage and off.

Professional stage actors face a special problem unknown to their film counterparts and seldom experienced by amateurs in the theatre: the problem of maintaining a high level

the audience's reactions to her own performance and that of the other players; there is always, in any acting performance, a subtle adjustment to the audience that sees it. The outward manifestations of this adjustment are usually all but imperceptible: the split-second hold for a laugh to die down, the slight special projection of a certain line to ensure that it reaches the back row, the quick turn of a head to make a characterization or plot transition extra clear.

In addition, the best actors consistently radiate a quality known to the theatre world as "presence." It is a difficult quality to describe, but it has the effect of making both the charof spontaneity through many, many performances. Some professional play productions perform continuously for years, and actors may find themselves in the position — fortunately for their finances, awkwardly for their art — of performing the same part eight times a week, fifty-two weeks a year, with no end in sight. Of course the routine can vary with vacations and cast substitutions; and in fact very few actors ever play a role continuously for more than a year or two, but the problem becomes intense even after only a few weeks. How, as they say in the trade, does the actor "keep it fresh"?

Each actor has her or his own way of addressing this problem. Some rely on their total immersion in the role and contend that by "living the life of the character" they can keep themselves equally alert from first performance to last. Others turn to technical experiments — reworking their delivery and trying constantly to find better ways of saying their lines, expressing their characters, and achieving their objectives. Still others concentrate on the relationships within the play and try with every performance to "find something new" in each relationship as it unfolds onstage. Some actors, it must be admitted, resort to childish measures, rewriting dialogue as they go or trying to break the concentration of the other actors; this sort of behavior is abhorrent, but it is indicative of the seriousness of the actor's problems of combating boredom in a long-running production and the lengths to which some actors will go to solve them.

The actor's performance does not end with the play, for it certainly extends into the paratheatrical moments of the curtain call — in which the actor-audience communion is direct and unmistakable — and it can even be said to extend to the dressing-room postmortem, in which the actor reflects upon what was done today and how it might be done better tomorrow. Sometimes the postmortem of a play is handled quite specifically by the director, who may give notes to the cast; more typically, in professional situations, the actor simply relies on self-criticism, often measured against comments from friends and fellow cast members, from the stage manager, and from reviews in the press. For there is no performer who leaves the stage in the spirit of a factory worker leaving the plant. If there has been a shift up from the rehearsal phase to the performance phase, there is now a shift down (or a letdown) that follows the curtain call — a reentry into a world in which actions and reactions are likely to be a little calmer. There would be no stage fright if there were nothing to be frightened *about,* and the conquering of one's own anxiety — sometimes translated as conquering of the audience: "I really killed them tonight" — fills the actor at the final curtain with a sense of awe, elation . . . and emptiness. It is perhaps this feeling that draws the actor ever more deeply into the profession, for it is a feeling known to the rankest amateur in a high school pageant as well as to the most experienced professional in a Broadway or West End run. It is the theatre's "high," and because it is a high that accompanies an inexpressible void, it leads to addiction.

The Actor in Life

Acting is an art. It can also be a disease. Actors are privileged people. They get to live the lives of some of the world's greatest and best-known characters: Romeo, Juliet, Phèdre, Cyrano, St. Joan, and Willy Loman. They get to fight for honor, hunger for salvation, battle for justice, die for love, kill for passion. They get to die many times before their deaths, to duel fabulous enemies, to love magnificent lovers, and to live through an infinite variety of human experiences that, though imaginary, are publicly engaged. They get to reenter the innocence of childhood without suffering its consequences and to participate in every sort of adult villainy without reckoning its responsibility. They get to fantasize freely and be seen doing so — and they get paid for it.

Stage and film acting have their differences, but most American actors today hope to do both. McCauley Caulkin's first professional stage role, after starring as a child in several films, was as an adolescent student seduced by his teacher – and defying his father – in Richard Nelson's *Madame Melville*, which the author also directed off-Broadway in 2001.

Millions of people want to be actors. It looks easy, and, at least for some people, it *is* easy. It looks exciting, and there can be no question that it is exciting, very exciting; in fact, amateurs act in theatres all over the world without any hope of getting paid merely to experience that excitement. Acting addicts, as a consequence, are common. People who will not wait ten minutes at a supermarket checkout stand will wait ten years to get a role in a Hollywood film or a Broadway play. The acting unions are the only unions in the world that have ever negotiated a *lower* wage for some of their members in order to allow them to perform at substandard salaries. To the true acting addict there is nothing else; acting becomes the sole preoccupation.

The addicted actor — the actor obsessed with acting for its own sake — is probably not a very good actor, for fine acting demands an open mind, a mind capable of taking in stimuli from all sorts of directions, not merely from the theatrical environment. An actor who knows nothing but acting has no range. First and foremost, actors must represent human beings, and to do that they must know something about humankind. Thus the proper study of acting is life, abetted but not supplanted by the craft of the trade. Common sense, acute powers of observation and perception, tolerance and understanding for all human beings, and a sound general knowledge of one's own society and culture are prime requisites for the actor — as well as training, business acumen, and a realistic vision of one's own potential.

A lifetime professional career in acting is the goal of many but the accomplishment of very few. Statistically, one's chances of developing a long-standing acting career are quite small; only those individuals possessed of great talent, skill, persistence, and personal fortitude stand any chance of succeeding — and even then it is only a chance. But the excitement of acting is not the exclusive preserve of those who attain lifetime professional careers; on the contrary, it may be argued that the happiest and most artistically fulfilled actors are those for whom performance is only an avocation. The excitement of acting, finally, is not dependent on monetary reward, a billing above the title, or the size of one's roles, but on the actor's engagement with drama and with dramatized situations — in short, on a personal synchronization with the theatre itself, of which acting is the very evanescent but still solid center.

4

The Playwright

He is an anomalous figure in the theatre. In his home he is the master of the stage, the initiator of all theatrical art. Facing his writing paper, he is profoundly in control: actions cascade through his head, characters populate his imagination, great scenes parade across his vision, words and speeches pour from his pen. It is to be *his* play, *his* thoughts, *his* people, and *his* words that will resound through the theatres of the world, that will be praised in the press, immortalized in handsomely bound volumes, and scrutinized by scholars. It is he, the playwright, who will win the Pulitzer Prize and the Critics Circle citation and who will one day sit next to some contemporary Einstein or Schweitzer, his fellow Nobel laureates, at the Stockholm awards ceremony.

In the theatre, however, he is the lonely figure who huddles uncomfortably over a legal pad, in a back row, scarcely noticed by the actors and director who are rehearsing his play, certain in the back of his mind that the theatre is nothing more than an instrument for diluting his ideas and massacring his manuscript.

Has there ever been such an anomaly? For the playwright is both the most central and the most peripheral figure in the theatrical event.

The playwright is central in the most obvious ways. She or he provides the point of origin for virtually every play production — the script, which is the rallying point around which the director or producer gathers the troops. And yet that point of origin is also a point of departure. The days when a Shakespeare or a Molière would gather actors around, read his text to them, and then coach them in its proper execution are long gone. What we have today is a more specialized theatrical hierarchy in which the director is interposed as the playwright's representative to the theatrical enterprise and its constituent members. More and more, the playwright's function is to write the play and then disappear, for once the script has been typed, duplicated, and distributed, the playwright's physical participation is relegated mainly to serving as the director's sounding board and rewrite person. Indeed, the playwright's mere physical presence in the rehearsal hall can become an embarrassment, more tolerated than welcomed and sometimes not even tolerated.

Fundamentally, the playwright today is considered an independent artist, whose work, like that of the novelist or poet, is executed primarily, if not exclusively, in isolation. There are exceptions, of course: some playwrights work from actors' improvisations, and others participate quite fully in rehearsals, even to the point of serving as the initial director of their plays (as Edward Albee, Sam Shepard, and George C. Wolfe often do) or, more extraordinarily, by acting in them (as Tennessee Williams and Michael Christofer have done).

But the exceptions do not, in this case, disprove the rule; since the age of romanticism, the image of the playwright has turned increasingly from that of theatre coworker and mentor to that of isolated observer and social critic. In the long run, this change should occasion no lamentation; for if theatre production now demands collaboration and compromise, the art of the theatre still requires individuality, clarity of vision, sharpness of approach, original sensitivity, and a devotion to personal truth if it is to challenge the artists who are called upon to fulfill it and the audiences who will pay money to experience it.

It is often said that Shakespeare and Molière wrote great plays because they could tailor their parts to the talents of actors whom they knew well. It seems far more likely that they wrote great plays in spite of this, for at the hands of lesser writers, that sort of enterprise produces sheer hack work that simply combines the limitations of the actors with those of the author. Whether writing from inside an acting company or in submission to one, the playwright strives to give life to a unique vision, to create material that transcends what has gone before, both in writing and in performance.

Therefore, the *independence* of the playwright is perhaps her or his most important characteristic. Playwrights must seek from life, from their own lives — and not from the theatrical establishment — the material that will translate into exciting and meaningful and entertaining theatre; and their views must be intensely personal, grounded in their own perceptions and philosophy, in order to ring true. We look to the theatre for a measure of leadership, for personal enlightenment derived from another's experience, for fresh perspectives, new visions. In other words, simple mastery of certain conventional techniques will not suffice to enable the playwright to expand our lives.

We Are All Playwrights

Playwriting is not just something we learn. It's something we already do. All of us. Every day — or night.

Every night, dreams come to us in our sleep. Or, rather, they *seem* to come to us: in fact, we create them. For each of us has our own "playwright-in-residence" somewhere in the back of our minds, churning out a nightly mixture of vivid, believable, and sometimes terrifying fantasies that create half-real, half-imagined characters, idealized settings and surprising plot complications, nostalgic visions and often nightmarish climaxes and reversals. The situations and characters of our dreams are our own creations, drawn from our careful observations, colored by our unconscious phobias and fancies, stylized into associations of words, scenes, and "stagings" that ring with deep resonance of our innermost plans, fears, and secrets. We all know what it is to create a play out of our imaginations: we do it every night.

It is no wonder, then, that there is little conformity among playwrights. There are no easily identified "schools" of associated writers, nor have "rules" of playwriting been laid down with any demonstrable sustained success. Playwrights can come from anywhere.

The Playwright's Career

How does a person become a playwright? Writing plays, naturally, is the first (and most important) step. But getting that original play produced is almost as challenging.

There are hundreds of "break-in" opportunities for playwrights to develop their scripts in open rehearsals or in developmental workshop productions or staged readings. And sometimes a playwright can realize (or can produce herself or himself) a fully staged production. Many of these developmental opportunities are available through colleges and universities. David Henry Hwang's *FOB* was first presented at his college dormitory at Stanford University, and Wendy Wasserstein's *Uncommon Women and Others* was first presented at the Yale Drama School.

Virtually all regional professional theatres present new plays from time to time, and many — if not most of them — actively solicit new works, usually presenting them first in script-in-hand readings or special workshops, where the works are presented and critiqued by other writers and company artists. Many prize-winning plays have premiered, for example, at the Humana New Play Festival at the Actors Theatre of Louisville and at South Coast Repertory Theatre's NewSCRipts

AMERICAN WOMEN PLAYWRIGHTS

Two of America's leading women playwrights talk about the start of their careers:

[The women's movement] enabled me to leave New York and give up that whole careerism business — the man's world of career stuff. I was always acting as the woman behind a man anyway, I was giving my energies to male careers. That's what the women's movement freed me from, and it also made me see really clearly that there's a necessity to write about very strong women so women can know that there have been strong women in the past.

— Megan Terry
author of *Viet Rock* with the Open Theatre,
*Calm Down Mother, Keep Tightly Closed in a
Cool Dry Place*, and *Approaching Simone*

In one of my early conversations about writing plays, before I had ever written one, that is, Jon Jory, of Actors Theatre of Louisville, told me, "Go back at least ten years and write about some time when you were really scared."

Getting Out, my first play, was the result of that advice. The scary time was the two years I spent teaching in the children's unit of a state mental hospital. . . . The most frightening thing was the realization that once a violent child got into the system, there was no way out for her. The children were also aware of this, and consequently ran away as often as they could. . . . Later, when I sat down to write, I wondered what would happen if one of our girls ever found herself some place she couldn't get out of. Like solitary confinement in federal prison.

— Marsha Norman
author of *Getting Out, 'Night, Mother,*
and *The Secret Garden*

and play commission programs. Indeed, most important American plays of the 1980s and beyond were first presented in readings or workshops at theatres like these, although the competition for workshop slots at these premier theatres is, naturally, quite fierce. The annual publication *Dramatists Sourcebook* (published by Theatre Communications Group in

Marsha Norman's *'Night, Mother* is one of the most searing, most touching depictions ever written of the relationship between a mother and a daughter. The play is here shown in its 1986 production at the Alliance Theatre of Atlanta, Georgia.

New York) lists all theatres that solicit new works and identifies any special areas of interest they might have (such as a theatre dedicated to Spanish-speaking plays).

There are also certain "developmental" theatre companies totally devoted to finding and developing new scripts. The National Playwrights Conference (at the Eugene O'Neill Center in Waterford, Connecticut, with year-round offices in New York) receives hundreds of applications each year — and selects nine to twelve plays to present, in staged readings, each summer. August Wilson first came to prominence through his "discovery" at the Playwrights Conference.

Finally, aspiring playwrights might consider dramatic contests, fellowship and grant opportunities, commercial reading and critique services, and literary/dramatic agents as they try to build a career in this field; the *Dramatists Sourcebook* is a useful guide to all of these areas. It should be borne in mind, however, that playwriting is an extraordinarily competitive field and that the quality of the work — not the number of contacts — is far and away the critical factor.

Literary and Nonliterary Aspects of Playwriting

Because drama is often thought of as a form of literature (and is taught in departments of literature) and because many dramatic authors begin (or double) as poets or novelists, it may seem as if playwriting is primarily a literary activity. It is not. Etymology helps here: *playwright* is not *playwrite*. Writing for the theatre entails considerations not common to other literary forms. Although by coincidence the words *write* and *wright* are homonyms, a "playwright" is a person who *makes* plays, just as a wheelwright is a person who makes wheels. This distinction is particularly important, because some plays, or portions of plays, are never written at all. Improvisational plays, certain rituals, whole scenes of comic business, subtextual behaviors, and many documentary dramas are created largely or entirely in performance or are learned simply through oral improvisation and repetition. Some are created with a tape recorder and the collaboration of multiple imaginations and may or may not be committed to writing after the performance is concluded. And others, although dramatic in structure, are entirely nonverbal; that is, they include no dialogue, no words, and very little that is written other than an outline of mimetic effects.

So drama is a branch of literature, but it is a special and distinctive branch. It is not merely an arrangement of words on a page; it is a conceptualization of the interactions of myriad elements in the theatrical medium: movement, speech, scenery, costume, staging, music, spectacle, and silence. It is a literature whose impact depends on a collective endeavor and whose appreciation must be, in large part, spontaneous and immediate.

A play attains its finished form only in performance upon the stage: the written script is not the final play but the *blueprint* for the play, the written foundation for the production that is the play's complete realization. Some of a play's most effective writing may look very clumsy as it appears in print; take, for example, the following lines from Shakespeare:

> Oh! Oh! Oh!   — *Othello*
>
> Howl, howl, howl, howl!   — *King Lear*
>
> No, no, the drink, the drink. O my dear Hamlet,
> The drink, the drink! I am poisoned.
>   — *Hamlet*

These apparently unsophisticated lines of dialogue in fact provide great dramatic climaxes in an impassioned performance; they are *pretexts for great acting,* the creation of which is far more crucial than literary eloquence to the art of playwriting.

Of course some formal literary values are as important to the theatre as they are to other branches of literature: allusional complexity, descriptive precision, poetic imagery, metaphoric implication, and a careful crafting of verbal rhythms, cadences, and textures all contribute powerfully to dramatic effect. But they are effective only insofar as they are fully integrated with the whole of the theatrical medium, as they stimulate action and behavior through stage space and stage time in a way that commands audience attention and involvement. Mere literary brilliance is insufficient as theatre, as a great many successful novelists and poets have learned to their chagrin when they attempted to write plays.

Playwriting as Event Writing

The core of every play is action. In contrast to other literary forms, the inner structure of a play is never a series of abstract observations or a collage of descriptions and moralizings; it is an ordering of observable, dramatizable *events*. These events are the basic building blocks of the play, regardless of its style or genre or theme.

Fundamentally, the playwright works with two tools, both representing the externals of human behavior: dialogue and physical action. The inner story and theme of a play — the psychology of the characters, the viewpoint of the author, the impact of the social environment — must be inferred, by the audience, from outward appearances, from the play's events as the audience sees them. Whatever the playwright's intended message and whatever the playwright's perspective on the function and process of playwriting itself, the play cannot be put together until the playwright has conceived of an event — and then a series of related events — designed to be enacted on a stage. It is this series of related events that constitutes the play's scenario or, more formally, its plot.

The events of drama are, by their nature, compelling. Some are bold and unusual, such as the scene in which Prometheus — in Aeschylus' tragedy — is chained to his rock. Some are subdued, as when the military regiment in Chekhov's *The Three Sisters* leaves town at the play's end. Some are quite ordinary, as in the domestic sequences depicted in most modern realist plays. But they are always aimed at creating a memorable impression. To begin playwriting, one must first conceptualize events and envision them enacted in such a way as to hold the attention of an audience.

The events of a play can be connected to each other in a strict chronological, cause-effect continuity. This has been a goal of the realistic theatre, in which dramatic events are arranged to convey a lifelike progression of experiences in time. Such plays are said to be *continuous* in structure and *linear* in chronology, and they can be analyzed like sociological events: the audience simply watches them unfold as it might watch a family quarrel in progress in an apartment across the way.

Continuous linearity, however, is by no means a requirement for play construction. Many plays are discontinuous and/or nonlinear. The surviving plays of ancient Greece are highly discontinuous, with odes alternating with episodes in the tragedies and a whole host of nonlinear theatrical inventions popping in and out during the comedies. Shakespeare's plays are structured in a highly complex arrangement of time shifts, place shifts, style shifts, songs, and subplots ingeniously integrated around a basic theme or investigation of character. And many contemporary plays break with chronological linearity altogether, flashing instantly backward and forward through time to incorporate character memories, character fantasies, direct expressions of the playwright's social manifesto, historical exposition, comic relief, or any other ingredient the playwright can successfully work in.

Linear, point-to-point storytelling still has not disappeared from the theatre — indeed, it remains the basic architecture of most popular and serious plays — but modern (and postmodern) audiences have proven increasingly

Not all plays are written by individual playwrights; increasingly common in the current era are plays written by the theatre companies that perform them. *Above:* Despite its French name, Complicite (formerly Theatre de Complicite) is a British company specializing in startling productions of new and contemporary dramatic works; the company's group-authored *Mnemonic* (2001) concerns the "Iceman" – a 5,300-year-old corpse that was found frozen and mummified in the Italian Alps in 1991. Complicite's play, conceived and directed by company founder Simon McBurney (also pictured here as the Iceman), explores our cultural memory (as the title suggests) and the continuum of humanity from our archeological past and our current preoccupations. "It is hard to think of another company that makes such persuasive, ambitious, and varied cases for the singular powers of theater," said the *New York Times* of the show's New York premiere. Pictured studying McBurney's Iceman (in the London premiere production) are Katrin Cartlidge, Richard Katz, Tim McMullan, Catherine Schuab Abkarian, and Daniel Wahl. *Below:* The Tectonic Theatre Company of New York, under Moisés Kaufman, created *The Laramie Project* by interviewing townspeople in Laramie, Wyoming, as they responded to the 1998 murder of gay college student Matthew Shepard; the company then transcribed, adapted, and performed the interviews in a highly successful production staged in several cities, shown here in its off-Broadway 2000 staging.

receptive to less-conventional structures: the exuberance of the music hall, for instance, inspired the structuring of Joan Littlewood's *Oh, What a Lovely War!;* the minstrel show served as a structure for George C. Wolfe's *The Colored Museum;* and the didacticism of the lecture hall underlay much of the theatre of Bertolt Brecht. Nonlinear, discontinuous, and even stream-of-consciousness structures can provide powerful and sustained dramatic impact in the theatre, provided they are based in the dramatization of events that the audience can put together in some sort of meaningful and satisfying fashion.

The Qualities of a Fine Play

As with any art form, the qualities that make up a good play can be discussed individually, but it is only in their combination, only in their interaction — only in ways that cannot be dissected or measured — that these qualities have meaning.

Credibility and Intrigue

To say that a play must be credible is not at all to say that it has to be lifelike, for fantasy, ritual, and absurdity have all proven to be enduringly popular theatrical modes. The demand of *credibility* is an audience-imposed demand, and it has to do with the play's internal consistency: the actions must flow logically from the characters, the situation, and the theatrical context the playwright provides. In other words, credibility is the audience's demand that what happens in act 2 makes sense in terms of what happened in act 1.

Credibility demands, for example, that the characters in a play appear to act out of their own individual interests, instincts, and intentions rather than serving as mere pawns for the development of theatrical plot or effect, as empty disseminators of propaganda. Credibility means that characters must maintain consistency within themselves: that their thoughts, feelings, hopes, fears, and plans must appear to flow from human needs rather than purely theatrical ones. Credibility also demands that human characters appear to act and think like human beings (even in humanly impossible situations) and not purely as thematic automatons. Credibility, in essence, is a contract between author and audience, whereby the audience agrees to view the characters as "people" as long as the author agrees not to shatter that belief in order to accomplish other purposes.

Thus James Barrie's famous play *Peter Pan,* although undeniably fantastical, creates a cast of characters wholly appropriate to their highly imaginary situation and internally consistent in their actions within the context of their developing experience. All of their aspirations (including those of the dog!) are human ones, and their urgencies are so believable that when Tinkerbell steps out of the play's context to ask the audience to demonstrate its belief in fairies, the audience is willing to applaud its approval. At that moment, the world of the play becomes more credible, more "real," than that of the audience. So much for the power — and consequently the necessity — of dramatic credibility.

Intrigue is that quality of a play that makes us curious (sometimes fervently so) to see "what happens next." Sheer plot intrigue — which is sometimes called "suspense" in that it leaves us suspended (that is, "hanging") — is one of the most powerful of dramatic approaches. Whole plays can be based on little more than artfully contrived plotting designed to keep the audience in a continual state of anticipation and wonder. Plot, however, is only one of the elements of a play that can support intrigue. Most plays that aspire to deeper insights than whodunits or farces develop intrigue in character as well and even in theme. Most of the great plays, in fact, demand that we ask not so much "What will happen?" as "What does this mean?" Most

Two English Playwrights

The two leading English playwrights of the last thirty years exhibit radically different styles. The plays of Harold Pinter, which are filled with abrupt, almost inexplicable transitions, intense pauses and glances, and elliptical dialogue that seems to contain innuendos we don't fully comprehend, create an almost palpable sense of foreboding and spookiness that plunges the audience deeper and deeper into Pinter-esque moods and reveries. The plays of Tom Stoppard, by contrast, race glibly through brilliant rhetorical flights of language that always manage to stay one step ahead of the audience's capability to follow, keeping the audience breathless while forcing them to remain intellectually alert.

BATES: (*moves to* ELLEN) Will we meet tonight?

ELLEN: I don't know. (*Pause*)

BATES: Come with me tonight.

ELLEN: Where?

BATES: Anywhere. For a walk. (*Pause*)

ELLEN: I don't want to walk.

BATES: Why not? (*Pause*)

ELLEN: I want to go somewhere else. (*Pause*)

BATES: Where?

ELLEN: I don't know. (*Pause*)

BATES: What's wrong with a walk?

ELLEN: I don't want to walk. (*Pause*)

BATES: What do you want to do?

ELLEN: I don't know. (*Pause*)

BATES: Do you want to go somewhere else?

ELLEN: Yes.

BATES: Where?

ELLEN: I don't know. (*Pause*)

— From Pinter's *Silence* (1969)

COCKLEBURY-SMYTHE: May I be the first to welcome you to Room 3B. You will find the working conditions primitive, the hours antisocial, the amenities non-existent and the catering beneath contempt. On top of that the people are for the most part very boring, with interests either so generalized as to mimic wholesale ignorance or so particular as to be lunatic obsessions. Their level of conversation would pass without comment in the lavatory of a mixed comprehensive and the lavatories, by the way, are few and far between.

— From Stoppard's *Dirty Linen* (1976)

great plays, in other words, make us care about the characters and invite us to probe the mysteries of the human condition.

Look, for example, at this dialogue from David Mamet's *Glengarry Glen Ross*, in which a disgruntled real-estate salesman proposes to a colleague that they rob their front office, stealing some real-estate "leads" (names of potential customers) which they can then sell to a competitor.

MOSS: I want to tell you something.

AARONOW: What?

MOSS: I want to tell you what somebody should do.

AARONOW: What?

MOSS: Someone should stand up and strike back.

AARONOW: What do you mean?

MOSS: *Somebody* . . .

AARONOW: Yes . . . ?

MOSS: Should do something to *them*.

AARONOW: What?

MOSS: Something. To pay them back. (*Pause*) Someone, someone should hurt them. Murray and Mich.

AARONOW: Somebody should hurt them.

MOSS: Yes.

AARONOW: (*Pause*) How?

MOSS: How? Do something to hurt them. Where they live.

AARONOW: What? (*Pause*)

MOSS: Someone should rob the office.

AARONOW: Huh.

MOSS: That's what I'm *saying*. We were, if we were that kind of guys, to knock it off, and *trash* the joint, it looks like a robbery, and *take* the fuckin' leads out of the files . . . [. . .] (*Pause*)

Above: Surprise! Steven Berkoff's dark comedy *Kvetch* is filled with sudden discoveries; it was written in part out of experiences from his childhood. Shown here is the 1986 Odyssey Theatre Ensemble production.

Above right: Few dramatic moments are as suspenseful as a pointed gun – if the acting is sufficiently credible and intense. In Lee Kalcheim's seriocomic *Defiled,* Jason Alexander plays the bibliomaniacal librarian, Harry Mendelssohn, threatening to blow up the town library – and shoot the detective (played by Peter Falk) who's trying to prevent him. Geffen (Los Angeles) Theater premiere, 2000.

AARONOW: Are you actually *talking* about this or are we just . . .

MOSS: No, we're just . . .

AARONOW: We're just *"talking"* about it.

MOSS: We're just *speaking* about it. (*Pause*) As an *idea.*

AARONOW: As an idea.

MOSS: Yes.

AARONOW: We're not actually *talking* about it.

MOSS: No.

AARONOW: Talking about it as a . . .

MOSS: No.

AARONOW: As a *robbery.*

MOSS: As a "robbery"?! No.

AARONOW: *Well.* Well . . .

The basic action of this scene could be expressed in just two or three lines of dialogue, but since a conspiracy is being proposed each character must proceed with extreme caution — as his colleague could turn him in at any time. As each of the thirty-two short lines takes the conspiracy one tiny — but precise — step forward, the credibility is exacting while the intrigue builds to an increasingly higher level of tension.

Intrigue draws us into the world of a play; credibility keeps us there. In the best plays the two are sustained in a fine tension of opposites: intrigue demanding surprise, credibility demanding consistency. Combined, they generate a kind of "believable wonder," which is the fundamental state of drama. Credibility alone will not suffice to make a play interesting, and no level of intrigue can make a noncredible play palatable. The integration of the two must be created by the play-

wright in order to establish that shared ground that transcends our expectations but not our credulity.

Speakability, Stageability, and Flow

The dialogue of drama is written upon the page, but it must be spoken by actors and staged by directors. Thus the goal of the dramatist is to fabricate dialogue that is actable and stageable and that flows in a progression leading to theatrical impact.

One of the most common faults of beginning playwrights — even when the playwright may be an established novelist or poet — is that the lines lack *speakability*. This is not to say that dramatic dialogue must resemble ordinary speech. No one imagines people in life speaking like characters out of the works of

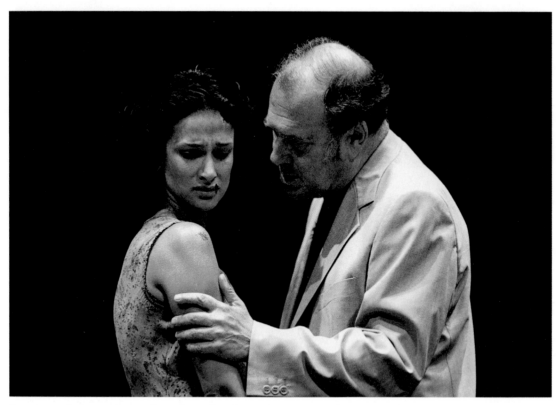

Since actors do the speaking in plays, playwrights who are also actors — including Aeschylus, Shakespeare, and Molière — usually excel in the speakability of their dialogue. Harold Pinter, one of Britain's greatest dramatists, began his career as an actor and has continued to perform; he is shown here as Nicholas, a torturer in an unnamed country, in his play *One for the Road*, performed by the Gate Theater of Ireland at Lincoln Center (New York City) in 2001. Indira Varma plays one of his victims.

Aeschylus, Shakespeare, or Shaw, or even contemporary writers like Harold Pinter or Edward Albee. A brilliantly styled language is a feature of most of the great plays in theatre history, and lifelikeness is not, by itself, a dramatic virtue — nor is its absence a dramatic fault.

Rather, speakability means that a line of dialogue should be so written that it achieves its maximum impact when spoken. In order to accomplish this, the playwright must be closely attuned to the *audial shape* of dialogue: the rhythm of sound that creates emphasis, meaning, focus, and power. Verbal lullabies and climaxes, fast punch lines, sonorous lam-

entations, sparkling epigrams, devastating expletives, significant pauses, and electrifying whispers — these are some of the devices of dialogue that impart audial shape to great plays written by master dramatists. Look, for example, at Andrew Undershaft's chiding of his pretentious son, Stephen, in George Bernard Shaw's *Major Barbara,* where Stephen has just said that he knows "the difference between right and wrong."

UNDERSHAFT: You don't say so! What! no capacity for business, no knowledge of law, no sympathy with art, no pretension to philosophy; only a simple knowledge of the secret that has puzzled all the philosophers, baffled all the lawyers, muddled all the men of business, and ruined most of the artists: the secret of right and wrong. Why, man, you're a genius, a master of masters, a god! At twentyfour, too!

No one would call this "everyday speech" as in the David Mamet dialogue quoted earlier, but it is immensely speakable and its cascading sarcasm develops a fiercely intimidating momentum, leaving Stephen speechless and, with a great actor playing it, the audience breathless.

Speakability also requires that the spoken line appear to realistically emanate from the character who utters it and that it contain — in its syntax, vocabulary, and mode of expression — the marks of that character's milieu and his or her personality. The spoken line is not merely an expression of the author's perspective; it is the basis from which the actor develops characterization and the acting ensemble creates a play's style. Thus the mastery of dramatic dialogue writing demands more than mere semantic skills; it requires a constant awareness of the purposes and tactics underlying human communication, as well as of the multiple psychological and aesthetic properties of language.

Stageability, of course, requires that dialogue be written so that it can be spoken effectively upon a stage, but it requires something more: dialogue must be conceived as an integral element of a particular staged situation, in which setting, physical acting, and spoken dialogue are inextricably combined. A stageable script is one in which staging and stage business — as well as design and the acting demands — are neither adornments for the dialogue nor sugarcoating for the writer's opinions but are intrinsic to the very nature of the play.

Both speakability and stageability are contingent upon human limitations: those of the actors and directors as well as those of the audience. Speakability must take into account that the actor must breathe from time to time, for example, and that the audience can take in only so many metaphors in a single spoken sentence. Stageability must reckon with the forces of gravity and inertia, which both the poet and the novelist may conveniently ignore. The playwright need not simply succumb to the common denominator — all the great playwrights strive to extend the capacities of actors and audience alike — but still must not forget that the theatre is fundamentally a human event that cannot transcend human capabilities.

A speakable and stageable script flows rather than stumbles; this is true for nonlinear plays as well as for more straightforwardly structured ones. *Flow* requires a continual stream of information, and a play that flows is one that is continually saying something, doing something, and meaning something to the audience. To serve this end, the playwright should address such technical problems as scene shifting, entrances and exits, and act breaks (intermissions) as early as possible in the scriptwriting process. Furthermore, in drafting scenes, the writer should be aware that needless waits, arid expositions (no matter how "necessary" to the plot), and incomprehensible plot developments can sink the sturdiest script in a sea of audience apathy.

Richness

Depth, subtlety, fineness, quality, wholeness, and *inevitability* — these are words often used in reference to plays that we like. They are fundamentally subjective terms, easier to apply than to define or defend, for the fact is that when a play pleases us, when it "works," the feelings of pleasure and stimulation it affords are beyond the verbal level. Certainly *richness* is one of the qualities common to plays that leave us with this sense of satisfaction — richness of *detail* and richness of *dimension*.

A play that is rich with detail is not necessarily one that is rife with detail; it is simply one whose every detail fortifies our insight into the world of the play. For going to a play is in part a matter of paying a visit to the playwright's world, and the more vividly created that world, the greater the play's final impact. In Margaret Edson's *Wit,* for example, Vivian, a terminally ill English professor, addresses the audience from her hospital bed. Her tone is professorial, and her vocabulary is currently filled with medical terminology, little of which the average audience member will understand, but in the context of an intellectual woman struggling against a fatal disease, Edson's dialogue creates an immensely compelling and affectingly detailed portrait:

VIVIAN: I don't mean to complain, but I am becoming very sick. Very, very sick. Ultimately sick, as it were.

In everything I have done, I have been steadfast, resolute — some would say in the extreme. Now, as you can see, I am distinguishing myself in illness.

I have survived eight treatments of Hexamethophosphacil and Vinplatin at the *full* dose, ladies and gentlemen. I have broken the record. I have become something of a celebrity. Kelekian and Jason [her doctors] are simply delighted. I think they foresee celebrity status for themselves upon the appearance of the journal article they will no doubt write about me.

But I flatter myself. The article will not be about *me,* it will be about my ovaries. It will be about my peritoneal cavity, which, despite their best intentions, is now crawling with cancer. What we have come to think of as *me* is, in fact, just the specimen jar, just the dust jacket, just the white piece of paper that bears the little black marks.

Vivian's free use of seven-syllable words, refining her words on the spot (from "very sick" to "very, very sick" to "ultimately sick," from "steadfast" to "resolute"), her public style of presentation ("ladies and gentlemen"), parellel phrases ("I have . . . I have . . . I have . . . ," "just the . . . just the . . . just the . . ."), allit-eration of consonants ("just . . . jar . . . just . . . jacket, just"), and use of antithesis ("white piece of paper . . . little black marks") tell us volumes about her character and how she is "distinguishing" herself in illness. Richness of linguistic detail lends a play authority, an aura of sureness. It surrounds the play's characters as a city surrounds homes and gives them a cultural context in which to exist. It lends a play specificity: specific people are engaged in specific tasks in a specific place. Going to (or even reading) a play rich with texture is like taking a trip to another world — it is an adventure no travel agent could possible book.

Richness is not an easy quality to develop in writing. It demands of its author a gift for close observation, an uninhibited imagination, and an astute sense of what to leave out as well as what to include. A person who can recollect personal experiences in great detail; who can conjure up convincing situations, peoples, locales, and conversations; and who is closely attuned to nuance can perhaps work these talents into the writing of plays.

Depth of Characterization

Depth of characterization probably presents perhaps the greatest single stumbling block for novice playwrights, who tend either to write all characters "in the same voice" (normally the author's own) or to divide them into two camps: good characters and bad. But capturing the depth, complexities, and uniqueness of real human beings, even seemingly ordinary human beings, is a more difficult task.

Depth of characterization requires that every character possess an independence of intention, expression, and motivation; moreover, these characteristics must appear sensible in the light of our general knowledge of psychology and human behavior. In plays as in life, all characters must act from motives that appear reasonable to *them* (if not to those watching them or those affected by them).

"CONSIDER THE ACTOR"

If this is the dramatist's day, he will be wise to consider the actor, not as a mere appendage to his work, but as its very life-giver. Let him realize that the more he can learn to ask of the actor the more he will gain for his play. But asking is giving. He must give opportunity.

– Harley Granville-Barker

Moreover, the writer should bear in mind that every character is, *to himself or herself,* an important and worthwhile person, regardless of what other people think. Thus even the great villains of drama — Shakespeare's Richard III, Claudius, and Iago for example — must be seen to believe in themselves and in the fundamental "rightness" of their cause. Even if we never completely understand their deepest motivations (as we can't fully understand the motives of real villains such as Hitler, Caligula, or John Wilkes Booth), we should be able to sense at the bottom of any character's behavior a validity of purpose, however twisted or perverse we may find it.

The realistic theatre — Chekhov, Williams, Miller, and the like — has provided many works in which the psychological dimensions of the characters dominate all other aspects of the theatrical experience. Look, for example, at this speech of Big Mama in Tennessee Williams's *Cat on a Hot Tin Roof:*

BIG MAMA [*outraged that her son-in-law, Gooper, is offering her a written trusteeship plan which would give him and his wife control over the estate of Big Daddy, Mama's ailing husband*]: Now you listen to me, all of you, you listen here! They's not goin' to be any more catty talk in my house! And Gooper, you put that away before I grab it out of your hand and tear it right up! I don't know what the hell's in it, and I don't want to know what the hell's in it. I'm talkin' in Big Daddy's language now; I'm his *wife,* not his *widow,* I'm still his *wife!* And I'm talkin' to you in his language an' —

Williams has brilliantly crafted Big Mama's rage with aggressive verbs ("grab," "tear"), local vernacular usage ("they's"), clause repetitions ("I'm his wife . . . I'm still his wife"), loaded adjectives ("catty"), profanities rare for a southern woman ("hell's"), dialectical contractions ("goin'", "talkin'"), and individual word emphases as marked by italics. But he has also undermined her rage by having her admit to assuming her husband's vocabulary — so that while she states that she's not Big Daddy's widow, her language indicates that she knows, even if only unconsciously, that it shall soon be otherwise.

Modern dramatists have even made psychotherapy part of their dramatic scheme in many cases: psychiatrist characters may be seen (or are addressed) in plays such as Williams's *Suddenly, Last Summer,* Miller's *After the Fall,* Peter Shaffer's *Equus,* and the 1941 American musical *Lady in the Dark,* each of which portrays a principal character undergoing psychotherapy and discussing what he or she learns. Certainly the psychological sophistication of modern theatre audiences has afforded playwrights expanded opportunities to explore and dramatize characters' psyches, and it has helped to make the "case study" drama a major genre of the current theatre.

Gravity and Pertinence

Gravity and *pertinence* are terms used to describe the importance of a play's theme and its overall relevance to the concerns of the intended audience. To say that a play has *gravity* is to say simply that its central theme is one of serious and lasting significance in humanity's spiritual, moral, or intellectual life. The greatest dramas — comedies as well as tragedies — are always somehow concerned with what is sometimes called the human predicament: those universal problems — aging, discord, love, insecurity, ambition, loss — for which we continually seek greater lucidity. Gravity does not mean somberness, however;

it requires only a confrontation with the most elemental tasks of living. When an audience truly understands and identifies with a play's experiences, even the darkest tragedy radiates power and illumination.

Look, for example, at Bynum's speech in August Wilson's *Joe Turner's Come and Gone.* Bynum is what Wilson calls a rootworker (conjuror). A younger man, Jeremy, has just praised a woman as knowing "how to treat a fellow," and Bynum chastises him for his shallowness:

> You just can't look at it like that. You got to look at the whole thing. Now, you take a fellow go out there, grab hold to a woman and think he got something 'cause she sweet and soft to the touch. It's in the world like everything else. Touching's nice. It feels good. But you can lay your hand upside a horse or a cat, and that feels good too. What's the difference? When you grab hold to a woman, you got something there. You got a whole world there. You got a way of life kicking up under your hand. That woman can take and make you feel like something. I ain't just talking about in the way of jumping off into bed together and rolling around with each other. Anybody can do that. When you grab hold to that woman and look at the whole thing and see what you got . . . why she can take and make something of you. Your mother was a woman. That's enough right there to show you what a woman is. Enough to show you what she can do. She made something out of you.

Using only simple words (compare, for instance, Vivian's speech in *Wit*), Wilson's Bynum probes at the heart of a profound subject: the most meaningful relationship between a man and a woman. When well acted, the import of these lines will stay with us long after we have left the theatre.

Pertinence refers to the play's touching on current audience concerns, both of-the-moment and timeless. Plays about current political situations or personalities are clearly pertinent; they may, however, quickly become outdated.

Plays whose concerns are both ephemeral and universal, however, such as Miller's *The Crucible* — which, in treating the Salem witch trials of 1692 pertains as well to the McCarthy trials of the 1950s as well as to corrupt investigations in all eras — will have a more enduring relevance. The greatest plays are not merely pertinent to a given moment, but also serve as archetypes for all time.

Compression, Economy, and Intensity

Compression, economy, and intensity are also aspects of the finest plays. *Compression* refers to the playwright's skill in condensing a story (which may span many days, even years, of chronological time) into a theatrical time frame; *economy* relates to an author's skill in eliminating or consolidating characters, events, locales, and words in the service of compression. Unlike other literary or visual art forms that can be examined in private and at the leisure of the observer, a play must be structured to unfold in a public setting and at a predetermined pace.

Many beginning playwrights attempt to convert a story to a play in the most obvious way: by writing a separate scene for every event described in the story (and sometimes including a different setting and supporting cast for each scene). Economy and compression, however, require that most stories be restructured in order to be dramatically viable. If the play is to be basically realistic, the playwright has traditionally reworked the story so as to have all the events occur in one location, or perhaps in two locations with an act break between to allow for scenery changes. Events that are integral to the story but cannot be shown within the devised settings can simply be reported (as in Shaw's *Misalliance,* for example, in which an airplane crash occurs offstage as the onstage characters gawk and exclaim). More common today is the use of theatricalist techniques that permit an integration of settings so that events occurring in

Athol Fugard's *My Children! My Africa!* ends tragically; but before it does, South African township teacher Mr. M. (played here by Brock Peters) and his visiting pupil Isabel (Nancy Travis) share an exquisite moment of triumph, which makes the resulting tragedy all the more poignant and insupportable. This photograph comes from the 1990 La Jolla Playhouse production.

various places can be presented on the same set without intermission. Similarly, economy and compression commonly dictate the deletion or combination of characters and the reduction of expository passages to a few lines of dialogue.

The effects of economy and compression are both financial and aesthetic. Obviously, when scenery changes and the number of characters are held to a minimum, the costs of production are minimized as well. But beyond

that, compression and economy in playwriting serve to stimulate intrigue and focus audience expectation: a tightly written play gives us the feeling that we are on the trail of something important and that our quarry is right around the next bend. Thus, economy and compression actually lead to *intensity*, which is one of the theatre's most powerful attributes.

Dramatic intensity can take many forms. It can be harsh, abrasive, explosive, eminently physical, or overtly calm. It can be ruminative, tender, or comic. But whenever intensity occurs and in whatever mood or context, it conveys to the audience an ineradicable feeling that this moment in theatre is unique and its revelations are profound. Intensity does not come about by happy accident, obviously, but neither can it be simply injected at the whim of the playwright. It must evolve out of a careful development of issues, through the increasing urgency of character goals and intentions and the focused actions and interactions of the plot that draw characters and their conflicts ever closer to some sort of climactic confrontation. A play must spiral inward toward its core; that is, its compression must increase and its mood must intensify as it circles toward its climax and denouement. Too many tangential diversions can deflect a play from this course, rendering it formless and devoid of apparent purpose.

Celebration

Finally, a fine play celebrates life; it does not merely depict or analyze or criticize it. The first plays were presented at festivals that — though perhaps haunted by angry or capricious gods — were essentially joyful celebrations. Even the darkest of the ancient Greek tragedies sought to transcend the more negative aspects of existence and to exalt the human spirit, for the whole of Greek theatre was informed by the positive (and therapeutic) elements of the Dionysian festival: spring, fertility, the gaiety and solidarity of public communion.

The theatre can never successfully venture too far from this source. A purely didactic theatre has never satisfied either critics or public, and a merely grim depiction of ordinary life has little to offer this art form. Although the word *theatrical* usually suggests something like "glittery" or "showy," it better accords with the theatre's most fundamental aspirations: to extend our known experience, to illumi-

nate life, and to raise existence to the level of art: the art of theatre.

This celebration can easily be perverted. Dramas intended to be merely "uplifting" — with a reliance on happy endings and strictly noble sentiments — or written in self-consciously "elevated" tones do not celebrate life, they merely whitewash it. The truest and most exciting theatre has always been created out of a passionate, personal vision of reality and a deep devotion to expressing life's struggles and splendors. For the theatre is fundamentally an affirmation. Writing, producing, and attending plays are also acts of affirmation: attesting to the desire to share and communicate, celebrating human existence, participation, and communion. Purely bitter plays, no matter how justly based or how well grounded in history or experience, remain incomplete and unsatisfying as theater, which simply is not an effective medium for nihilistic conveyance. Even the bleakest of modern plays radiates a persistent hopefulness — even joyousness — as represented archetypally by Samuel Beckett's two old men singing, punning, and pantomiming so engagingly in the forlorn shadow of their leafless tree as they wait for Godot.

The Playwright's Process

How does one go about writing a play? It is important to know the elements of a play (as discussed in Chapter 2) and the characteristics of the best plays — credibility, intrigue, speakability, stageability, flow, richness, depth of characterization, gravity, pertinence, compression, economy, intensity, and celebration — as discussed in the preceding sections. But that is not enough; one must still confront the practical task of writing.

The blank sheet of paper is the writer's nemesis. It is the accuser, the goad and critic that coldly commands action even as it threatens humiliation. There is no consensus among writers as to where to begin. Some prefer to begin with a story line or a plot outline. Some begin with a real event and write the play to explain why that event occurred. Some begin with a real character or set of characters and develop a plot around them. Some begin with a setting and try to animate it with characters and actions. Some begin with a theatrical effect or an idea for a new form of theatrical expression. Some write entirely from personal experience. Some adapt a story or a legend, others a biography of a famous person, others a play by an earlier playwright; others simply expand upon a remembered dream.

A documentary might begin with a transcript of a trial or a committee hearing. Other documentary forms might begin with a tape recorder and a situation contrived by the playwright. Some plays are created out of actors' improvisations or acting-class exercises. Some are compilations of material written over the course of many years or collected from many sources.

The fact is, writers tend to begin with whatever works for *them* and accords with their immediate aims. Because playwrights usually work alone, at least in the initial stages, they can do as they please whenever they want: there is no norm. On the other hand, certain steps can be followed as introductory exercises to playwriting, and these may in fact lead to the creation of an entire play.

Dialogue

Transcription of dialogue from previous observation and experience — that is, the writing down of *remembered dialogue* from overheard conversations or from conversations in which the author has participated — is a fundamental playwriting exercise; probably most finished plays contain such scenes. Because we remember conversations only selectively and subjectively, a certain amount of fictionalizing and shading inevitably creeps into these transcriptions; and often without even meaning to do so, authors also transform people in their memory into characters in their scenes.

Writing scenes of *imagined dialogue* is the logical next step in this exercise, for all the author need do now is to extend the situation beyond its remembered reality into the area of "what might have happened." The dialogue then constructed will be essentially original yet in keeping with the personalized "characters" developed in the earlier transcription. The characters now react and respond as dramatic figures, interacting with each other freshly and under the control of the author. Many fine plays have resulted from the author's working out, in plot and dialogue, hypothetical relations between real people who never confronted each other in life; indeed, many plays are inspired by the author's notion of what *should* have happened among people who never met. In this way, the theatre has often been used as a form of psychotherapy, with the patient-playwright simply acting out — in imagination or with words on paper — certain obligatory scenes in life that never occurred.

Conflict

Writing scenes of *forced conflict* accelerates the exercise and becomes a third step toward the creation of a play. Scenes of separation, loss, crucial decision, rejection, or emotional breakthrough are climactic scenes in a play and usually help enormously to define its structure. If a writer can create a convincing scene of high conflict that gets inside *each* of the characters involved and not merely one of them, then there is a good chance of making that scene the core of an exciting play — especially if it incorporates some subtlety and is not dependent entirely on shouting and denunciation. What is more, such a scene will be highly actable in its own right and thus can serve as a valuable tool for demonstrating the writer's potential.

Exercises that result in scripted scenes — even if the scenes are just a page or two in length — have the advantage of allowing the writer to test her or his work as it progresses. For a short scene is easily producible: all it requires is a group of agreeable actors and a modest investment of time, and the playwright can quickly assess the total impact. The costs and difficulties of testing a complete play, on the other hand, may prove insurmountable for the inexperienced playwright. Moreover, the performance of a short original scene can sometimes generate enthusiasm for the theatrical collaboration needed for a fuller theatrical experience.

Structure

Developing a complete play demands more than stringing together a number of scenes, of course, and at some point in the scene-writing process the playwright inevitably confronts the need for structure. Many playwrights develop outlines for their plays after writing a scene or two; some have an outline ready before any scenes are written or even thought of. Other playwrights never write down anything except dialogue and stage directions yet find an overall structure asserting itself almost unconsciously as the writing progresses. But the beginning playwright should bear in mind that intrigue, thematic development, compression, and even credibility depend on

a carefully built structure and that it is an axiom of theatre that most playwriting is in fact *rewriting* — rewriting aimed principally at organizing and reorganizing the play's staged actions and events.

A strong dramatic structure compels interest and attention. It creates intrigue by establishing certain expectations — both in the characters and in the audience — and then by creating new and bigger expectations out of the fulfillment of the first ones. A good dramatic structure keeps us always wanting more until the final curtain call, and at the end it leaves us with a sense of the inevitability of the play's conclusion, a sense that what happened onstage was precisely as it had to be. A great structure makes us comfortable and receptive; we feel in good hands, expertly led through whatever terrain the play may take us. And we are willing, therefore, to abandon ourselves to a celebration of vital and ineffable matters.

The Playwright's Rewards

There will always be a need for playwrights, for the theatre never abandons its clamor for new and better dramatic works. Hundreds of producers today are so anxious to discover new authors and new scripts that they will read (or instruct an associate to read) everything that comes their way; thus a truly fine play need not go unnoticed for long. Moreover, playwrights are the only artists in the theatre who can bring their work to the first stage of completion without any outside professional help at all; they do not need to be auditioned, interviewed, hired, cast, or contracted to an agent in order to come up with the world's greatest dramatic manuscript.

The rewards that await the successful playwright are absolutely staggering: they are the most fully celebrated artists of the theatre, for not only do they receive remuneration commensurate with their success, but they also acquire enormous influence and prestige on the basis of their personal vision. The public may adore an actor or admire a director or designer, but it *listens* to the playwright, who in Western culture has always assumed the role of prophet. Playwriting at its best is more than a profession, and it is more than a component of the theatrical machine. It is a creative act that enlarges human experience and enriches our awe and appreciation of life.

Contemporary American Playwrights

America was the site of some of the most exciting playwriting in the twentieth century. Eugene O'Neill was America's first internationally celebrated dramatist, both for his realistic works (most notably his autobiographical *Long Day's Journey into Night*) and his experiments in antirealism (such as the expressionist *Hairy Ape,* about workers in a boiler room). Tennessee Williams and Arthur Miller followed, energizing the American theatre beginning in the 1940s with their blend of realism, poetry (Williams's forte), and political insight (most notably in Miller). At the turn of the century, literally dozens of American playwrights — including the still-active Miller — are currently defining their society to a worldwide theatre audience. Among them, seventeen are listed here, in the order of their birth dates.

Arthur Miller

Arthur Miller (born 1915), author of the world-famous modern classics *All My Sons* (1947), *Death of a Salesman* (1949), *The Crucible* (1953), and *A View from the Bridge* (1955), is clearly America's premier living dramatist, as exemplified by major London and New York revivals of virtually all of his works — capped by a wondrously successful *Death of a Salesman* with Brian Dennehy that reached Broadway (from Chicago's Goodman Theatre) in

1999, and Richard Eyre's 2002 Broadway production of *The Crucible* with Liam Neeson and Laura Linney. Even Miller's first play, *The Man Who Had All the Luck,* quickly dismissed in its 1944 Broadway premiere, returned to Broadway (at the American Airlines Theatre) in 2002.

But Miller is hardly a relic and remains, even in his late eighties, a contemporary playwright who cannot be ignored. In four new plays of the 1990s, all dealing with a blend of late-twentieth-century social and medical themes, Miller continues to explore and criticize the American body politic. *The Ride Down Mount Morgan,* which had its Broadway premiere in 2000, covers almost every topic Miller has written about before — and much more. Centered on themes of bigamy and generational dissonance, *Mount Morgan* is also concerned with American views of pleasure, guilt, marriage, money, children, race, sex, death, business, Jewishness, non-Jewishness, socialism, Christianity, suicide, political and sexual betrayal, men versus women, humans versus animals, the Reagan-Bush administration versus Arthur Miller, and, almost as an afterthought, capital-T Truth — all delivered in exquisitely Millerish agony: "Only the truth is sacred," Miller's male protagonist declares to one of his two wives at the play's end. *The Last Yankee* (1992) also mines many of these themes in a play set, in part, in a hospital waiting room where two middle-aged couples experience America's brusquely competitive society. *Broken Glass,* produced on Broadway in 1994, examines the sexual, social, psychological, and political reactions to Nazism during the 1930s with Miller's typically caustic and lively penetration. And *Mr. Peters' Connections,* an impressionistic memory play written in the author's eighty-third year (1998) and set in a seeming nightclub of the dead, recycles and deconstructs many of the author's preoccupations — both political and marital — in the contemporary climate of political disillusion and penile implants. No other playwright in the current theatre has so aggressively called society to task

Neil Simon's award-winning *Lost in Yonkers* (1990) is one of his most serious and moving plays. Here, Irene Worth (*seated*) plays an embittered Holocaust survivor, and Mercedes Reuhl plays her slightly retarded daughter.

for its failures nor so passionately told the audience to pay attention to the world around them.

Neil Simon

It can be argued that Neil Simon (born 1927 and, like Miller, a New York native) is not only America's most successful commercial playwright but also the most successful playwright in the entire history of theatre. Beginning as a TV comic writer in the early 1950s, Simon quickly spun off a staggering series of hit Broadway comedies in the 60s and 70s, including consistently revived works such as *Barefoot in the Park, The Odd Couple, Plaza Suite, The Last of the Red Hot Lovers, The Sunshine Boys,* and *California Suite,* not to mention the books for musicals such as *Little Me, Sweet Charity* and the screenplays for dozens of films. Virtually all of his plays "work," at least in the sense that they make the audience laugh, and they have made Simon, among other things, enormously rich.

In the late 1980s, Simon turned decidedly more serious, however, and his deeply felt trilogy of autobiographical plays, *Brighton Beach Memoirs, Biloxi Blues,* and *Broadway Bound,* have proved astute and compassionate works that have attracted a more sober appreciation of Simon's gifts. Since that time, he has continued writing semi-autobiographical works, including the highly unconventional *Jake's Women,* a revisitation of various women in the author's life and mind; *Laughter on the 23rd Floor,* recalling the experiences of Simon and his colleagues as gag writers for the 1950s TV comic Sid Caesar; and *Lost in Yonkers,* a profoundly powerful work about a Holocaust survivor and her family, for which Simon has received the Pulitzer Prize and the widespread critical acclaim that, for the most part, had previously eluded him. But the prolific Simon has also continued to write straight comedies as well, including the pure farce *Rumors,* another "hotel play," *London Suite* (which for the first time in Simon's career was premiered off-Broadway rather than on), the rather gloomy *Proposals,* which deals with illness, death, race relations, and family breakup, and the somewhat more buoyant *The Dinner Party,* concerning three divorced couples at a mysterious dinner party in Paris, which opened on Broadway in 2000.

Simon is a consummate playwright, whose work is also popular in dinner and community theatres. His work is rarely performed in regional theatres, however; it is almost a mark of pride for such theatres to say "we don't do Neil Simon" as a shorthand way of saying that they don't produce conventional, commercial, or well-made comedies. Simon probably has more fans and more detractors than any other living playwright, but his early comedies are unmatched in their craftsmanship and easygoing humor, and his recent work shows evidence of a deep and lasting theatrical achievement.

Edward Albee

The Zoo Story, a one-act, two-character play set in New York's Central Park, brought Edward Albee (born 1928) to prominence in 1959. The play concerns a chance meeting between a married publisher (Peter) and a young drifter (Jerry), both male; at play's end, Jerry impales himself on a knife he has given to Peter. The odd story, its electrifying dialogue, its gingerly oblique treatment of homosexuality, and, par-

ticularly, its initial pairing on a double bill with Samuel Beckett's *Krapp's Last Tape* gave Albee immediate national attention that would be almost impossible to achieve today. And with his first full-length play, *Who's Afraid of Virginia Woolf?,* premiering on Broadway in 1962, Albee quickly assumed the mantle of America's leading new playwright in the early 1960s.

Subsequent Albee plays have had both great success — *A Delicate Balance* (What happens when a married couple mysteriously gets frightened and moves in with their best friends?) and *Seascape* (What happens when a pair of lizards pop in on a married couple at the beach?) won the Pulitzer Prizes in 1967 and 1975 — and failure (*Tiny Alice* provoked outrage along with mild admiration in its Broadway debut, and *The Man with Three Arms* was scathingly attacked by New York critics and has not been performed since). But Albee's trenchant and autobiographical *Three Tall Women* in 1994 thrust the author squarely back into the limelight, winning him his third Pulitzer and a chance to laugh at his critics once again. This two-act disquisition on Albee's own mother, as a person and as a spirit, tempers anger with compassion as Albee had not previously done and places its author back in the front ranks of American dramatists. Albee's newest work, *The Play about the Baby,* wittily recapitulates some of Albee's earlier themes and techniques (an older couple sarcastically taunting a younger one; a baby that may or may not exist), adding doses of quite postmodern nudity and self-referential disjunction (including the title). After its very successful 1998 London premiere, *The Play about the Baby* played at the Alley Theatre in Houston and opened off-Broadway in 2000–01. And with two completely new plays opening in New York in 2002 (*The Goat, or Who Is Sylvia?* on Broadway and *The Occupant* off-Broadway), we can be assured that this gifted and prolific dramatist will continue to both captivate and consternate the American stage.

Edward Albee's *The Play about the Baby*, an ascerbic dialogue ("endlessly disturbing and surprising," said *Variety*) on childhood and parenthood between a young couple (David Burtka and Kathleen Early) and an older couple (the exceptional Marian Seldes and Brian Murray), proved a sophisticated off-Broadway hit in 2001. Postmodern set design by John Arnone; costumes by Michael Krass.

Lanford Wilson

Lanford Wilson (born 1937) emerged as a pioneer playwright in the heady days of New York experimental theatre in the 1960s. His first plays, many produced at the Cafe La MaMa and Caffé Cino theatre bars, were evocative and sometimes profound studies of male homosexuality (*The Madness of Lady Bright*), interracial marriage (*The Gingham Dog*), and small-town small-mindedness (*The Rimers of Eldritch*). Joining with director Marshall Mason and other Caffé Cino colleagues, Wilson helped create the Circle Repertory Theatre in New York, which produced his finely crafted *The Hot l Baltimore*, about the comings and goings of a down-and-out hotel (the missing

e in the title indicates a burnt-out letter in the hotel's neon sign), and a series of emotionally affecting plays about the fictional midwestern Talley family: *The Fifth of July, Talley's Folly* (which won the 1980 Pulitzer Prize), and *A Tale Told*.

When the Circle Repertory Theatre disbanded in the late 1980s, Wilson opened his newer plays at regional theatres around the country, with *Burn This* at the Los Angeles Mark Taper Forum and *Redwood Curtain* at the Seattle Repertory Theatre; both plays subsequently went on to Broadway. Remaining loyal to his former Circle Rep collaborators, however, Wilson gave his *Sympathetic Magic* to Marshall Mason for its premiere at New York's Second Stage in 1997 and his *Book of Days*, which Wilson calls "a mystery with a sort of *Our Town* feel" to actor Jeff Daniels, who produced it at his Purple Rose Theatre in Chelsea, Michigan, in 1998. In 2002–03, the Signature Theatre in Manhattan will devote its entire season to a Lanford Wilson repertory.

Wilson is an extraordinarily prolific playwright, having written, thus far, eighteen full-length and twenty one-act plays. His writing for the most part (*Burn This* is an exception) is gentle, poetic, natural, and wise; increasingly, his works focus on the larger social and philosophical contexts of contemporary life. And although he is dramaturgically innovative, his plays rarely call attention to their structures or to the author's subtle stylistic departures.

John Guare

Following graduate school (Yale), John Guare (born 1938) became widely known in the Cafe La MaMa–Caffé Cino avant-garde circle in the early 1960s for his series of mildly surrealistic and "wacky" plays, such as *Muzeeka* in 1968 and *The House of Blue Leaves* in 1970, laced with social and cultural satire. He continued to mine the same vein, securing a small but loyal New York audience through the 1970s and 80s. In 1981, Guare won a Tony Award for his libretto for a musical adaptation of Shakespeare's *Two Gentlemen of Verona*.

In the 90s, Guare has again burst onto the national scene with the masterful satire *Six*

John Guare's whimsical and poetic *Four Baboons Adoring the Sun* alternates between realism and surrealism as it portrays an American couple and their two sets of children meeting ancient mythic forces on an archeological dig. Shown here is the 1992 Lincoln Center production directed by Peter Hall, with settings by Tony Walton.

Degrees of Separation, which explores and acidly reveals racial stereotyping, contemporary parenting and misparenting, and the cultural dissonances in contemporary adult America. *Six Degrees,* which opened at Lincoln Center in 1990, was widely produced by America's regional theatres shortly thereafter; Guare's title (and its global implications) have even attained a national mythic status.

Guare's subsequent work returned him to the wacky: *Four Baboons Adoring the Sun* (an even more ambitious allegory about a his-kids-and-her-kids family on an archeological dig in Sicily) and his *Moon under Miami Collides with Chicago! Seer Predicts Audiences Stunned! Outraged! Delighted!* (a tale of political bribery and tropical shenanigans) are as audacious and offbeat as their titles. And his *Chaucer in Rome* (2001), about a painter who gets skin cancer from the toxins in his oil paints, is a madcap mélange that satirizes contemporary art, religion, and gay pride with equal delight. Guare is an eternal experimenter on the stage, always provocative, always challenging norms.

Terrence McNally

The first produced play of Terrence McNally (born 1939), the angry and nightmarish *And Things That Go Bump in the Night,* was virtually booed off its Broadway stage when it premiered in 1965 — with the theatre management reduced to loudly hawking tickets for $1 apiece on New York streetcorners to passersby who "wanted to see a Broadway play." McNally was quickly pigeonholed as a raging young avant-gardist, having little in common with the audiences of his time. Both time and McNally changed. A series of hilarious and provocative comedies, often on sexual themes, followed in the 1970s (*Next* and *The Ritz* became widely popular), yielding to a more deft and delicate comic collection in the 1980s and 90s. *The Lisbon Traviata* (1989) explores a gay male couple's relationship in which their passion for opera masks a fundamental void in their capacity for affection. *Lips Together, Teeth*

Apart (1992) explores the relationships of and between two married couples summering in a beach house where a relative of one of them has just died of AIDS; it is a comedy with a poisonous snake under the pretty terrace.

Subsequently, *Kiss of the Spider Woman* (1993) got McNally — who wrote the book — his first Tony Award, and *Love! Valour! Compassion!* (1994) got him his second. The first is a darkly brilliant musical about sexual and political betrayal in a South American prison, and the second is a wicked and sensitive portrayal of eight gay men — bright, urban, and urbane — weekending in the country, occasionally in the buff.

Much of McNally's recent work has been, like *Lisbon Traviata* and *Kiss of the Spider Woman,* involved with music. *Master Class* (1995), portraying a music lesson by Maria Callas, won McNally a third Tony in 1996, and his book for the musical *Ragtime* (1998) won him his fourth, while his books for musicals *The Full Monty* (2000) and *The Visit* (2001) and the opera *Dead Man Walking* (2000), have earned him even further acclaim. Yet McNally's highly controversial *Corpus Christi* (1998) about a contemporary Christ-like figure (see under "A Dangerous Theatre" in the Theatre Today chapter) has made clear that the much-lauded author retains the capacity, and probably also the desire, to shock as well as to entertain.

McNally has the gift of blending passion with humor and tracking the universal emotions within a variety of lifestyles and belief systems. No longer just an angry young playwright, McNally has become a superb theatrical craftsman and a powerful innovator of new dramatic idioms without compromising his investigation of controversial and immensely provocative subjects.

Sam Shepard

Like Guare, Sam Shepard (born 1943) came to prominence in the coffeehouses of Greenwich Village in the 1960s. He then received great acclaim in the 1970s and 80s for his successful full-length plays *The Tooth of Crime, The Curse of the Starving Class, Buried Child* (which won the Pulitzer Prize), *True West, Fool for Love,* and *A Lie of the Mind.*

Shepard's plays are basically prose poems; the language is musical, and the subject matter, which is generally contemporary and American, suggests modern myth more than everyday reality. His plays, which invariably involve sex and violence, create arresting (and often inexplicable) images and tantalize the audience with moments of extreme surface realism that ultimately open into something more abstract. His early plays are wildly surreal and dreamlike, but these qualities have diminished in his more realistic plays of the late 1980s, during which period Shepard also became well known for his acting performances in films such as *The Right Stuff, Frances,* and his own *Fool for Love.* Shepard has continued to both act and write for the theatre over the past decade and has scored significant playwriting successes in recent years for his Broadway revision of *Buried Child* as well as for his new plays *Simpatico* (1995), *Eyes for Consuela* (1998), and *States of Shock* (1998). Shepard's newest drama, *The Late Henry Moss,* will be opening (with Ethan Hawke in the central role) at the Signature Theatre in New York as this book goes to press.

August Wilson

August Wilson (born 1945) has received no less than seven Tony Award nominations and two Pulitzer Prizes, and his amazing work — a decalogy of ten full-length plays, which when complete will represent a decade-by-decade history of the lives and struggles of African Americans in the twentieth century — has elevated him to the very highest rank of dramatic importance, virtually redefining the nature of American theatre. There can be little question but that Wilson is, at the moment, America's greatest active playwright.

Born to an interracial couple in Pittsburgh, Wilson began his rise as a dramatist there

when, in 1968, he founded the Black Horizons on the Hill Theatre, creating, as he remembers, "an explosion of poetry and black art that made the Harlem Renaissance look like a tea party. . . . Suffice it to say, we were *bad.*" When, soon after, Wilson submitted a dramatic manuscript to the Eugene O'Neill Theatre Center in Waterford, Connecticut, in 1981, it came to the attention of the center's director, Lloyd Richards. Already a major figure in the American theatre (he had directed the major African American play of the postwar era, Lorraine Hansberry's *A Raisin in the Sun,* in 1959), Richards was quick to see Wilson's writing potential. In the ensuing years, Richards encouraged and directed a series of five brilliant Wilson plays that form the heart of the Wilsonian decalogy: *Ma Rainey's Black Bottom, Fences, Joe Turner's Come and Gone, The Piano Lesson,* and *Two Trains Running.* Each of these works was first produced at the Yale Repertory Theatre (which Richards also headed at the time), and each went on to regional theatre tours and prize-winning Broadway runs.

Wilson's dramaturgy takes many forms. *Fences* (set in the 1950s) and *Jitney* (the 70s) are in the mainstream of American realism (*Fences* is indeed in many ways a black *Death of a Salesman*); while *Ma Rainey* (set in the 20s), the story of a black jazz singer, and *Seven Guitars* (the 40s), concerning a black singer-guitarist, blend musical, racial, tragic, and romantic themes. By contrast, *The Piano Lesson* (set in the 30s) and *Joe Turner's Come and Gone* (set in the 10s, and Wilson's masterpiece) are profoundly emotive family dramas that draw deeply upon black American history and ancient African roots. Wilson's most recent play, *King Hedley II* (set in the 80s), playing on Broadway in 2001, is the first of these works to incorporate characters from the earlier plays: *Hedley* tracks people first seen in *Seven Guitars* and reports the death — at age 366! — of a mythic "Aunt Esther," who appeared in the 60s-set *Two Trains Running.* Thus Wilson seems to be weaving together the human and time threads of his epic-like vision,

August Wilson's *King Hedley II* tells the story of an idealist young black man, scarred by both life and a hellacious knife fight, who seeks to escape from his petty criminality, open a video rental store, and raise vegetables. Here, Brian Stokes Mitchell plays the title role in the 2001 Broadway production, which followed a long regional tour. David Gallo designed the scenery, and Toni-Leslie James the costumes.

which is expected to be completed in the first decade of the twenty-first century.

Wilson's commitment to exploring African American culture is both broadly political and deeply aesthetic. He glories, though not always uncritically, in black life, and is not at all interested in synthesizing races or glossing over cultural differences. A poet still, Wilson blends drama with profound observation and glorious, though disturbing, humanity.

David Mamet

David Mamet (born 1947) is called a Chicago playwright because Chicago is his birthplace, his home, the setting of most of his plays, and the city where his plays have most often been premiered; moreover, Mamet served for some time as an associate artistic director of Chicago's Goodman Theatre. He is, however, a truly national figure. Mamet's plays, like some of Shepard's, employ at least fragments of intensely realistic writing and feature rhythmic language patterns that, though brutal, seem almost musical. Indeed, Mamet's dialogue is often strung out of mere language fragments: the tortured syntax of everyday speech rather than the turned phrases of eloquent discourse, often consisting of a series of frustrated stammerings, grunts, curses, repetitions, trail-offs, and the hemmings and hawings of nervous conversation. In all, there might not be but one or two complete sentences in an entire Mamet play. *Sexual Perversity in Chicago* brought Mamet broad attention in 1974, and *American Buffalo* (1977), *A Life in the Theatre* (1977), and the Pulitzer Prize–winning *Glengarry Glen Ross* (1984) solidified it. All four of these plays were written to be performed with all-male casts, however, confronting Mamet with questions as to whether he could write women's roles as well — questions to which he responded with a new play, *Speed-the-Plow,* which featured the actress Madonna in its 1988 Broadway premiere.

In the 1990s, Mamet (like Shepard) has turned much of his attention to the cinema, with screenplays such as *Hannibal, Wag The Dog, Whistle, Heist,* and *The Spanish Prisoner.* But in 1992 Mamet strongly returned to the theatre with the scorching play *Oleanna,* a masterful and intense drama about a charge of sexual (and academic) harassment brought by a college student (female) against her professor (male). And in 1994 he premiered a gripping new autobiographical work, *The Cryptogram,* and not long after another autobiographical play, *The Old Neighborhood,* which enjoyed a Broadway and touring success in 1998. Mamet's latest work, which premiered in London in 2001, is *Boston Marriage* (the term describes, according to the program, "a long-term monogamous relationship between two otherwise unmarried women"), marking yet another departure for Mamet: it is a period play with an all-female cast and high-toned epigrammatic language more in the vein of Oscar Wilde than the Chicago Bulls. Clearly, David Mamet is not going to be easily categorized or limited as he continues to play a major role in the coming era of American theatre and film.

Wendy Wasserstein

After receiving her bachelor's and master's degrees from Mount Holyoke College and City College of New York, respectively, Wendy Wasserstein (born 1950) wrote her first important play, *Uncommon Women and Others,* while a graduate student at the Yale Drama School (1976). Since then she has been highly admired for her successful off-Broadway play *Isn't It Romantic?* and subsequently *The Heidi Chronicles,* which won both the Tony Award and Pulitzer Prize for 1989.

Wasserstein is concerned with the situation of the American woman, particularly those

One of America's finest playwrights at the turn of the century is Wendy Wasserstein, who won the 1989 Pulitzer Prize and Tony Award for *The Heidi Chronicles* and enjoyed long-running Broadway and regional-theatre success with *The Sisters Rosensweig* three years later. While not considering herself a strict feminist, Wasserstein elegantly – and often comically – limns the contemporary struggle between feminist and traditional ideals. Shown here is the Alabama Shakespeare Festival production of *The Sisters Rosensweig.*

struggling with what they see as the dialectics of marriage and career, romance and politics, activism and traditionally passive "feminine" roles. Though her characters mostly come from the upper-middle-class Jewish intelligentsia from which the author herself springs, her writing aims at universality; there are no easy answers in Wasserstein's work, but there is a deep level of investigation and a powerful dramatic momentum.

Wasserstein's 1993 play *The Sisters Rosensweig* is in some ways her most accomplished: a neo-Chekhovian comedy about three sisters who meet in London (where one of them lives) and compare their ongoing lives and loves. Themes of Jewishness, feminism, career versus home, and the theatricalization of everyday life are melded into a brilliant comic stew. With triumphant performances by Jane Alexander and the late Madeline Kahn, *Rosensweig* was a Broadway hit and has moved into regional theatre with considerable success. In more recent years, Wasserstein has begun to move into films, television, magazine essays, and, notably, motherhood, but she has continued writing for the stage, providing recent audiences with *An American Daughter* (1997), about women and status in public life, and *Old Money* (2000) satirizing the values of two New York socialite families who live in the same house — but a century apart. Like Neil Simon, Wasserstein writes comfortable and accessible dramas, always wise, funny, and compassionate. Whether she will continue in this trend or expand her dramaturgical horizons (which *Old Money* seems to attempt) is one of the questions that makes current theatregoing an always-fascinating adventure.

Paula Vogel

Paula Vogel (born 1951) is one of America's outstanding newer playwrights, winning the 1998 Pulitzer Prize for drama with her powerful and unnerving *How I Learned to Drive,* which excoriates the implications of a long-

standing incestuous relationship between a young Maryland girl, L'il Bit, and her adult uncle, Peck. L'il Bit, it turns out, learned to drive while sitting on her uncle's lap, her hands on the steering wheel and his hands on her. Prior to her Pulitzer, Vogel had earned a strong playwriting reputation with *Hot 'n' Throbbing, Desdemona, And Baby Makes Seven, The Oldest Profession,* and, her own favorite, *The Baltimore Waltz,* each of which has been produced at close to a hundred regional and foreign theatres. More recently, her *Mineola Twins* — a story about two identical (but emotionally and politically dissimilar) sisters set over the course of three Republican administrations — has had wide visibility.

Vogel's plays delve into profoundly disturbing social and cultural issues, including AIDS, incest, eroticism, betrayal, and mental disturbance, but her tones and techniques include broad satire and whimsy; sudden juxtapositions of popular music, signs, and slide projections; and bold theatricalizations of her characters' unconscious thoughts. *Baltimore Waltz, Hot and Throbbing* (which concerns a female pornographer), and *Mineola Twins* all include dream sequences in which the characters' fantasies become, for a time, the core of the play's present action. *How I Learned to Drive* is written for two characters plus a three-person "Greek chorus" whose members play all the subsidiary roles and make announcements; one of the chorus even speaks for L'il Bit herself at the play's conclusion.

Able to sustain audience interest without step-by-step linear plot construction, Vogel's plays seem to circle their subjects gingerly at first, then spiral sharply inward to propel the audience into a shocking, deeply unsettling, and extraordinarily powerful conclusion. A master at her craft, Vogel also heads a master's-level playwriting program at Brown University and has taught in a women's prison as well. Her most recent public work, *A Friend of Dorothy,* was produced on Showtime television (as part of three gay-themed works, collec-

Paula Vogel won the 1998 Pulitzer Prize for her extraordinary dramatization of sexual abuse in childhood, *How I Learned to Drive.* Shown here are Mary Louise Parker as the seventeen-year-old L'il Bit and David Morse as her Uncle Peck, who teaches L'il Bit how to drive – and a few other things as well. This sometimes funny, sometimes searing play premiered at the off-Broadway Vineyard Theatre in 1997 and has quickly become a staple of the international repertoire.

Beth Henley

For her first play, *Crimes of the Heart,* Beth Henley (born 1952) was awarded the 1981 Pulitzer Prize. Initially produced at Louisville's Humana New Play Festival before going to Broadway, *Crimes* is a wildly irreverent comedy about three young Mississippi sisters coming together at the joint crises of their individual lives. The play, though not directly feminist in its themes, was one of the first mainstream American plays to focus primarily on women's problems and women's issues.

Henley's subsequent work has stayed true to this focus: *The Miss Firecracker Contest* is another Mississippi family drama in which two cousins vie for first place in a beauty contest, and *Abundance* is the story of two mail-order brides in chauvinist nineteenth-century Wyoming; both plays remain in regional repertories as, in the words of one critic, "Henley has an unmistakable talent for making human desperation seem funny, complex, and unpredictable." Henley's most recent plays, usually described by both admirers and critics as eccentric and bizarre, include *The Impossible Marriage* (1998), which Henley calls an absurdist comedy; *Signature* (1999), a play set in a future Los Angeles where, because of global warming, the shoreline has retreated to the Hollywood Hills; *Family Week* (2000), in which the play's time passages are identified by electronic supertitles flashing above the stage; and *Sisters of the Winter Madrigal* (2001), a tale of male lust in a medieval village. It must be said, however, that none of Henley's recent plays have attracted the critical or popular attention of her earlier work.

George C. Wolfe

Widespread distinction came to George C. Wolfe (born 1954) with his satirical musical play *The Colored Museum* in 1986 and then *Spunk,* a musical and dramatic adaptation of tales by Zora Neale Hurston, in 1989. Both

tively titled *Common Ground*) by Vogel, Terrence McNally, and Harvey Fierstein) in 2000; set in the 1950s, *Dorothy* treats a young woman discharged from the navy for being caught in a gay bar during a police raid. As current playwright-in-residence for Washington's Arena Stage, Vogel is certain to provide fascinating drama in the years to come.

were initially produced at the Crossroads The-atre of New Brunswick, New Jersey, and sub-sequently at the Public Theatre in New York, where Wolfe became artistic director in 1993, and where he remains.

Wolfe, a Kentucky-born African American, uses humor and music as wedges to explore deeply painful subjects; as a result, his plays are hilarious and unsettling — even scath-ing — at the same time. "Once we reach the desired altitude, the Captain will turn off the 'Fasten Your Shackle' sign," says the stew-ardess of the "Celebrity Slaveship" at the be-ginning of *The Colored Museum.*

Wolfe's genius is to skewer hoary clichés and persistent stereotypes of the "colored" world that emanate from both white and African American subgroups — and, at the same time, to embed his societal critique of racism in a theatricality that is enthusiastic, accessible, and celebratory. With his *Jelly's Last Jam* in 1992, a Broadway musical about the African Ameri-can jazz musician Jelly Roll Morton, Wolfe went mainstream, winning Tony nominations for both writing and directing as well as win-ning a worldwide audience of admirers. Since that time, Wolfe has devoted himself to di-recting the New York Public Theatre, and many of its productions, but in May 2002 he is scheduled to open a new original review, "Harlem Song," which he is writing around the music of Duke Ellington and James Brown, and which he will direct for an opening at the Apollo Theatre on New York's 125th Street.

Tony Kushner

Surely no play has burst upon the contempo-rary American theatre scene with such thrill-ing panache as the seven-hour, two-part *Angels in America* by Tony Kushner (born 1956). Ini-tially commissioned by the Eureka Theatre in San Francisco, *Angels* was subsequently de-veloped at the Mark Taper Forum in Los Angeles and (part one only) at the Royal Na-tional Theatre in London. The two parts had

Tony Kushner's brilliant, two-part *Angels in America* is thought by many critics to be the finest American play in years or even decades. A complex work of comedy, sagacity, and fantasy, it casts a wicked eye on American politics, reli-gion, economics, medicine, and racial and sexual bigotry — but it is also a moving story of human affection and alien-ation. In this 1993 Broadway production, an angel visits Prior Walter, who is dying of AIDS.

separate openings on Broadway in 1993 (un-der the direction of George C. Wolfe) and re-ceived rapturous critical acclaim. Part one, *Millennium Approaches,* took the Tony Award and Pulitzer Prize in 1993, and part two, *Pere-stroika,* itself took the Tony in 1994 — an un-precedented achievement. By 1995 the play had fully entered the international repertoire and was featured in major productions in theatre capitals and drama festivals through-out the world.

Angels fully merits this extraordinary atten-tion: it is a true masterpiece of modern drama; many critics consider it the finest American play of the present generation. Dealing un-stintingly with the AIDS crisis, Kushner has laid bare still-unsettled issues in American culture that touch upon race, religion, gender, politics, economics, and sexual orientation. Pairing a heterosexual couple (Joe and Harper Pitt, Mormons from Utah) with a homosexual couple (Louis Ironson, a New York Jew, and Prior Walter, afflicted with both AIDS and a lineage that goes back to the *Mayflower*), Kushner interweaves their stories and shakes up their lives within a vast medical-political "America," which is run in Kushner's imagination by Roy Cohn — the (real) self-hating, self-baiting, one-time gay Jewish lawyer in raging self-denial right up to his awful AIDS-ravished demise. A black nurse (male) and a white angel (female) also play sustained roles in this adventure, which is additionally peopled with another twenty-five characters, real and imagined and all played by the eight actors in the cast: a rabbi, an Eskimo, a travel agent, a real-estate saleswoman, the ghost of Ethel Rosenberg, various doctors, nurses, angels, and a man we are told is "the world's oldest Bolshevik." What is astonishing about Kushner's work is its explosive humor; this is one of the funniest American plays of the twentieth century. But it's also one of the saddest. Though not meant for all audiences (rejected by many theatre producers in conservative cities, the play includes frontal nudity, grisly depictions of AIDS suffering, savage religious satire, the blatant miming of homosexual acts, and a good deal of in-your-face hurling of loathing invectives), *Angels* has a transporting and trans-forming effect on spectators who are attuned to its rhythms and subject. Most claim to come out of the seven-hour performance ennobled.

And just who is this Tony Kushner? Born in New York City and raised in Louisiana, Kushner had been known, pre-*Angels,* almost entirely for his clever adaptation of Pierre Corneille's French classic *The Illusion.* Since *Angels* he has resurfaced with a brilliant short play on a Russian theme, *Slavs! Thinking about the Longstanding Problems of Virtue and Happiness;* a new translation of S. Ansky's Yiddish classic *The Dybbuk;* and a revision of an earlier un-produced manuscript, *Hydriotaphia or the Death of Dr. Browne* (which Kushner calls "An Epic Farce about Death and Primitive Capital Accumulation in Five Scenes") in 1998. None of these works have received the acclaim of *Angels in America,* but what could? Will Kushner again reach the pinnacle of international dramatic acclaim? Perhaps his newest play, *Homebody/Kabul,* which opened off-Broadway at the end of 2001, will answer this question. *Homebody,* written well before the September 11 attacks on New York and Washington, D.C., is a chilling and amazingly prescient account — written in English, French, Farsi, and Pashto — of Afghanistan as an arena for East-West global confrontation, where Osama bin Laden, the Taliban, a worldwide heroin trade, and the religions of East and West, past and present, come clashingly into focus. "Don't worry, they're coming to New York!" a suffering Afghan woman tells her foreign visitors regarding Taliban extremists, making Kushner both playwright and visionary. *Homebody/ Kabul,* which has already scored highly promising initial reviews and has been scheduled for future productions in the United States and abroad, will surely help keep Tony Kushner's name ranked among the world's leading dramatists well into the third millennium.

David Henry Hwang

Growing up in San Gabriel, California, David Henry Hwang (born 1957) began writing — "on a lark," he says — while an undergraduate at Stanford University. His first play, *FOB* (for "Fresh Off the Boat"), is a biting, honest, angry reaction to hidden (and not-so-hidden) American racism; it was first produced at Stanford and subsequently at the Eugene O'Neill Center in Connecticut and at the New York Public Theatre winning the "Obie" (off-Broadway) award.

David Henry Hwang's completely overhauled book for Rodgers and Hammerstein's *Flower Drum Song* has given new life to this 1958 musical drama of Mei-Li, a young Chinese woman emigrating to San Francisco's Chinatown. Whereas the original script concerned Mei-Li's buoyant assimilation to American culture ("I Enjoy Being a Girl" is the show's best-known song), Hwang's version begins with the tragic events of her leaving China (as pictured, as played by Lea Salonga, *center*) and portrays Asian-American relations with substantially greater irony and complexity. The 2001 premiere was mounted at the Mark Taper Forum in Los Angeles. Costumes by Gregg Barnes; lighting by Brian Nason.

Hwang's subsequent *M. Butterfly* (1988), his most celebrated work, explores the bizarre (and apparently true) relationship between a French diplomat and his Chinese mistress: bizarre because the mistress is revealed, during the play, to be — unbeknown to the diplomat — a male in disguise. Hwang's main subject is "Orientalism," the ingrained sense of deprecation with which Western culture views the East. In *Butterfly*, Hwang, of Chinese heritage, brilliantly interweaves gritty Western romanticism (including portions of the Puccini opera that gives the play its name) with Asian theatre and Chinese Opera technique, lending it current-political and timeless-mythic proportions. *Butterfly* won Hwang the Tony Award in 1988 and international fame. His subsequent *Golden Child* (1998), a play about a traditional Chinese family assimilating to Westernizing influences after World War I, was also a Broadway critical success, earning its author another Tony nomination for best play. Hwang's prominence continues into the twenty-first century, as the author of the librettos for Disney's popular Broadway production of *Aida*, as translator of Ibsen's *Peer Gynt* ("Peer is very reflective of the modern condition as well as the issues of assimilation and cultural identity," Hwang says), as writer and producer of television's 2001 miniseries *The Lost Empire*, and, perhaps most significantly, as the adapter of Rodgers and Hammerstein's *Flower Drum Song*, which opened to great acclaim at the Mark Taper Forum in Los Angeles in 2001 and will appear on Broadway in the season to follow.

Margaret Edson

Born in 1961, Margaret Edson is currently a kindergarten teacher in Atlanta, Georgia. She has written only one play in her entire life, which was rejected by all but one of the dozens of theatre companies she sent it to. Why, then, is she mentioned in this listing? Simply because her only play, *Wit,* was indeed produced by the one theatre — South Coast Repertory, in Costa Mesa, California — that saw merit in it. And because *Wit,* produced in New Haven and New York, soon went on to earn Edson the 1999 Pulitzer Prize, America's most prestigious playwriting award.

Wit, in fact, turns out to be one of the most searing and affecting plays of its time. Set in the cancer ward of a university research hospital — and moving back and forth among other locales remembered (or possibly in some cases dreamed up) by its main character — the play describes the last days of the fictional Vivian Bearing, a witty, often caustic English professor specializing in the seventeenth-century poetry of John Donne. Bearing is now dying of ovarian cancer. She faces her imminent death with courage but cannot hide her scorn for the impersonality of her doctors, who treat her not as a human patient but as so much research data. And it is particularly galling to her that among her doctors — actually medical researchers in training — is a former student from her English class, who, she realizes, now treats her with the same sort of casual disdain as she once treated him.

What makes *Wit* transcend its seeming movie-of-the-week genre is the dramatist's outstanding mastery of details — Edson was the manager of the AIDS and cancer inpatient unit of a research hospital and, before that, a Smith college student of Renaissance history — plus her brilliant decision to allow Professor Bearing to engage the audience directly, which the character does with a spectacular flamboyance. Wearing her hospital gown and bright red baseball cap, Bearing rises from her bed to lecture us variously on Donne, literature, medicine, metaphysics, and even the play she's in, at one point complaining (as if to the author) about the play's necessary brevity: "If *I* were writing this scene, it would take fifteen minutes!" she exclaims. For *Wit* is basically about language (as the title suggests); words, and the way they're used, are Bearing's tools

Margaret Edson's *Wit* portrays English Professor Vivian Bearing facing her death with courage and, yes, wit, in this powerfully affecting, Pulitzer Prize–winning play. Bearing is here played by Kathleen Chalfant, with Walter Charles as one of her doctors, in the Geffen Theatre's 2000 production.

for survival. "My only defense is the acquisition of vocabulary," Vivian Bearing proclaims. (See also discussion on page 92.)

What is dramatist Edson doing now? She's back teaching kindergarten. "If there's something else I want to say in ten years, then I'll think about it, but I'm not interested in leaving teaching for anything," Edson explains. The theatre world will take her at her word but certainly hopes she finds something else she wants to say.

Suzan-Lori Parks

In the summer of 2001, *New York Times* drama critic Ben Brantley declared Suzan-Lori Parks "ferociously talented," while ranking the first act of her *Topdog/Underdog* "as exciting as any new play from a young American since Tony Kushner's *Angels in America."* Donald Lyons in the *New York Post,* on the other hand, called the same play "clumsy" and "glib," a mix of "incredible and pretentious ideas." Such fiercely mixed reaction is highly characteristic of Parks's work, which typically meets with both angry walkouts and standing ovations.

Born in 1964, and raised in both the United States and Germany, Parks studied with the great American writer James Baldwin, at Mount Holyoke College; it was Baldwin who, hearing Parks read her stories aloud in class, first suggested she write for the stage. Parks's first play, *The Sinners' Place,* earned her cum laude honors in English — but was turned down for production by Holyoke's theatre department on the grounds that "you can't put dirt onstage! That's not a play!" Her next play, however, *Imperceptible Mutabilities in the Third Kingdom* (1989), won her a coveted "Obie" (off-Broadway) award, leading to subsequent positions as resident dramatist at both the Yale Repertory Theatre and the New York Public Theatre, each of which has produced several of her plays.

Parks's plays are not easy to read, however, and it is easy to sympathize with her theatre department not immediately seeing their merit. Writing about the black experience in America — slavery, lynchings, poverty, discrimination, minstrelsy, and racism are common themes — she rejects both realism and easy polemics, preferring a savagely comic irony and freshly minted language to diatribes or bald recountings. With the speech of Mrs. Aretha Saxon from *Mutabilities,* for example,

> Six seven eight nine. Thupp. Ten eleven twelve thirteen fourteen fifteen sixteen. Thupp. Seventeen. Eighteen nineteen twenty twenty-one. And uh little bit. Thuuup. Thuup. Gotta know thuh size. Thup. Gotta know thuh size exact. Thup. Got people comin. Hole house full. They gonna be kin? Could be strangers. How many kin kin I hold. Whole hold full. How many strangers. Depends on thuh size. Thup. Size of thuh space. Thuup. Depends on thuh size of thuh kin. Pendin on thuh size of thuh strangers. Get more mens than womens ssgonana be one number more womens then mens ssgonna be uhnother get animals thuup get animals we kin pack em thuup. Tight. Thuuup. Thuuuup. Mmmmm. Thuuup.

Parks vividly — but in an indelible style — describes the process of packing human cargo into an English slave ship.

Two subsequent Parks plays, both set in nineteenth-century sideshows, have created startling themes that have continued in her work. In *America Play* (1993), her main character, "The Foundling Father," is so obsessed with Abraham Lincoln that he leaves his family to play the role of America's sixteenth president in a sort of traveling carnival, soliciting spectators to come up on stage and, for a fee, pick up a prop gun and, as John Wilkes Booth, shoot him. And *Venus* (1996) portrays a nineteenth-century African woman, Saartjie Baartman, who, because of her enormous buttocks, was displayed throughout America as a freak. The basic situations — as well as Parks's savagely comic and ironic style — of both plays have been transmuted to current times in

Suzan-Lori Parks's *Topdog/Underdog* (2001) returns to a common Parks's theme, the reenactment of Abraham Lincoln's assassination as a public amusement. Jeffrey Wright (*right*) is a contemporary "Lincoln," who also plays the role of Lincoln in a sideshow, and Don Cheadle is his brother "Booth," who also plays Booth. Con games and crooked gambling (the sidewalk "three-card monte" ruse) are the brothers' preoccupations and escape from wretched conditions. Sets designed by Riccardo Hernandez; costumes by Emilio Sosa. New York Public Theatre production.

two of Parks's more recent works. *Fucking A,* which Parks directed in Houston in 2000, is a present-day *Venus,* though the character is now an abortionist. And *Topdog/Underdog,* staged by playwright/director George C. Wolfe at the Public Theatre in 2001, while set in present-day America, concerns a violently contentious pair of brothers named Lincoln and Booth, and once again Lincoln, now a retired master of three-card monte, New York's sidewalk con game, is playing President Lincoln in an arcade show, while Booth, a shoplifter, is his assassin in a fugue of sibling and status rivalry.

Inner identities, outer roles, and status levels all continuously shift and jostle in these newest Parks plays, which are more generally accessible than her earlier work (she is currently working on a new Disney musical about the Harlem Globetrotters basketball team), but no less controversial in their reception than her earlier work. And the 2002 restaging of Parks's *Topdog/Underdog* on Broadway coincided with her winning the coveted Pulitzer Prize for Drama for that same work, crowning her playwriting accomplishments with broad public and critical acceptance.

5

Designers and Technicians

The actor and the playscript may be at the core of the theatrical experience, but they are by no means the sum of it. Indeed, in the view of many spectators and participants, the primacy of acting and playwriting is extremely debatable. For acting and textual brilliance are not isolated components capable of full expression in and by themselves. In even the most primitive of dramas the theatrical experience always has a look and a sound and a shape — a visual and aural impact — that can be achieved only through *design*. And the execution of that design always entails a measure of *technology*. In many ways and at many times, the theatre has had occasion to celebrate the artistic talent of its designers and the engineering capability of its technicians, for many of the world's great aesthetic and technological innovations have been made public primarily through theatrical exploitation.

Therefore, in examining a play it is hardly sufficient to inquire, What is it about? We must also ask, How does it look? How does it sound? How is it built? How does it run? These questions bring us face to face with an army of backstage personnel: the artists and technicians who create and make possible what Aristotle called the spectacle of theatre, the individuals responsible for the overall appearance, orchestration, and management of the theatrical experience.

It is customary for purposes of discussion to divide design functions into a series of components — scenery, lighting, costume,

George Maxwell's setting, Bill Black's costumes, Linda Essig's lighting, and the well-balanced stage composition by director Charles Morey presented a vivid portrait of Edwardian society, which is the starting context for Noel Coward's *Relative Values*, as produced by the Utah Shakespearean Festival in 1998.

makeup, and so forth — and to a certain extent this categorization is appropriate; most productions involve separate "departments" of design, each with its own designers, assistants, and crews. Yet in fact all design functions of a production are closely interrelated: the appearance of scenery, for example, is heavily dependent on the light that falls upon it, and the look of a costume is greatly affected by the actor's makeup and hairstyle, to say nothing of his or her acting and bearing. Designers tend, therefore, to work as a design "team," in close collaboration with each other and with the director, from the outset of the production process. In the following listing of the various contributing "arts" of theatrical design, therefore, we must recognize that in examining each function separately we are attempting only to clarify certain traditional practices and that no single design art can be fully realized in isolation. Similarly, the ordering of these sep-

arate arts can only be arbitrary, for no fundamental hierarchy exists among them. We will begin with the theatre's architecture, scenery, and lighting and then move on to costuming, makeup, sound design, special effects, and the new computer technologies that affect all of them. Finally, we will discuss the many and varied theatre technicians who, jointly, play a crucial role in every theatrical production.

Theatre Architecture

Theatre architecture has long been one of the glories of the Western world. The Greek theatres, which evolved out of a pagan rite celebrated on a hillside, rank high among the magnificent relics of antiquity: the surviving theatre at Epidaurus is only one of many from the fourth century B.C. that still resound from time to time with revivals of the same great plays that thrilled audiences in the Hellenistic age. The theatres of ancient Rome were so grandiose in conception and execution that only hyperbole, it appears, could convey their proper character. For example, can we believe Pliny's account of an 80,000-seat theatre built in three stories, one each of marble, glass, and gilt? or of the two theatres built back-to-back that, filled with spectators, rotated on a pivot to join in a huge amphitheater that was then flooded for sea battle scenes?

Later times have given us many more fine theatres. Of Peter Street, the architect of Shakespeare's Globe and Henslowe's Fortune the-atres, historical documentation unfortunately tells us little more than that his theatres were provocative of the best in dramatic art. The Teatro Olimpico in Vicenza, Italy, was designed by the famed Andrea Palladio; built in 1584, it not only survives intact but is still occasionally used for dramatic presentations. Other theatres surviving from earlier eras, such as the elegant eighteenth-century court theatre at Drottningholm, Sweden, and the opulent nineteenth-century romantic structure built for the Paris Opera, are cultural landmarks as well as theatrically significant sites of contemporary production.

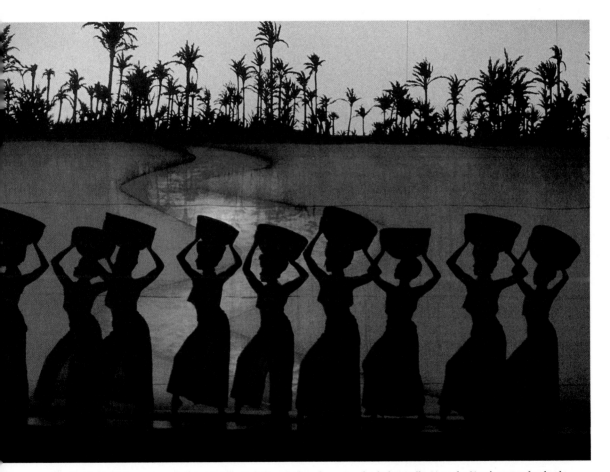

Gloriously exotic scenery and costumes (by Bob Crowley) and spectacular lighting (by Natasha Katz) create the throbbingly colorful North African panorama that is fundamental to the 2000 Disney musical, *Aida.*

The last half of the twentieth century experienced an explosion of theatre construction that began just after the end of World War II. Since that time, theatres and performing arts centers have sprung up in virtually every major city in North America, Europe, and Asia. Indeed, the last half-century may well be considered a golden age of theatrical architecture. It is an age marked by a growing public willingness to lend financial support to the theatre and by a greatly increased understanding of the need for extensive collaboration between theatre artists and architects in order to reconcile the needs for theatrical "tone" and atmosphere with those of practical flexibility and operational ease.

Staging Formats

The two principal types of modern theatre building are the "proscenium" stage design and the "thrust" stage design. These two basic types, and their various combinations, account for more than 95 percent of the professional theatres in Europe and America today and for the bulk of amateur stages as well. The *proscenium* theatre is essentially a rectangular room, with the audience on one side facing the stage on the other; separating the two areas is an arch (the "proscenium arch") through which the audience peers. This creates the well-known "picture-frame" stage, with the arch serving as the frame for the action going on within. The proscenium format was developed in Italy during the Renaissance as a mode of presenting elaborate masques and other court entertainments; because it put the audience on but one side of the action, it allowed extensive hidden areas backstage for the scene shifting and trickery involved in creating the illusions and fantasies so admired at the time. The proscenium theatre achieved its fullest realization in the baroque era, and some of the surviving court theatres and opera houses of Europe testify eloquently to the splendor of that age. Modern proscenium theatres have proven particularly serviceable for the use of realistic scenery and for the presentation of scenic spectaculars. Virtually all Broadway theatres feature the proscenium format.

The *thrust* design, pioneered in North America by Tyrone Guthrie, was in fact the favored format in ancient Greece and Elizabethan England. Because it places much of the action in the midst of the audience, the thrust stage is a more actor-centered (rather than scenery-centered) theatre configuration. In the thrust format the members of the audience are more aware of each other than they are in a darkened proscenium "fan," and their viewing perspectives differ radically, depending on their seating locations. When the acting platform, or thrust, can be accessed from tunnels (*vomitoria*) that come up through the audience, the stage can be flooded by actors in a matter of seconds, creating a whirlwind of movement that is dazzling and immediate — the thrust stage's alternative to elaborate stage machinery and painted scenes. That is not at all to say that there can be no scenery on a thrust stage but merely that scenic pieces tend to be placed behind the action rather than surrounding it to leave a relatively unencumbered acting space that projects into the center of the audience. In a thrust stage, the treatment given to the stage floor may in fact become the dominant scenic element.

Combined proscenium and thrust stage theatres, which can be converted from one format to another depending on the nature of the production, have increasingly come into fashion since the 1960s, particularly in academic-based theatre structures such as the Loeb Drama Center at Harvard and the Loretto-Hilton Center at Webster College. In these cases, mechanical lifts raise a thrust stage into the midst of the audience or lower it for an orchestra pit or additional seating in the proscenium mode.

A third theatrical configuration is the *arena* format (also known as "theatre-in-the-round"), in which the audience surrounds the action

The Loeb Drama Center at Harvard University (1960) can be configured, at the behest of a director, either in a proscenium-stage format (*above*) or – with the first seven rows of seats moved to the side and the orchestra floor raised – in a thrust-stage format (*below*); thus the theatre can accommodate a variety of production styles. The theatre was designed by Hugh Stubbins and Associates, with George C. Izenour as theatre consultant.

The Guthrie Theatre in Minneapolis is a modified thrust stage, loosely modeled after the outdoor theatres of Shakespeare's time. Designed by Ralph Rapson, with director Tyrone Guthrie and stage designer Tanya Moisewitsch as theatre consultants, the Guthrie Theatre was widely influential in establishing the thrust stage as a viable stage format – in addition to the proscenium stage – in the American theatre.

on all sides. One American regional theatre, the Arena Stage in Washington, D.C., has presented an arena season regularly since 1950. Arena staging dispenses with all scenery except floor treatments, furniture, and out-of-the-way hanging or standing pieces, and it focuses audience attention sharply and simply on the actors. The long-standing success of the Arena Stage — as well as the Alley Theatre in the Round (Houston), the Cassius Carter theatre at the Old Globe (San Diego), and the North Shore Music Festival (Beverly, Massachusetts) — testifies to the continuing viability of this format.

A final staging alternative is the so-called *black box* theatre, a formatless space that can be adjusted to any desired arrangement and is therefore particularly useful in experimental, environmental, or academic stagings. Usually painted black (hence the name), this type of theatre consists of a bare room fitted with omniflexible overhead lighting; in this room, the stage and seating can normally be set up in a variety of ways — proscenium, thrust, arena, or two-sided "alley" configuration — or the action can be staged *environmentally,* so as to occur at several locales interspersed variously throughout the room and perhaps above or below the audience as well. The black-box theatre allows the director/creator to develop a near-infinite variety of actor-audience interactions and to make use of highly unusual scenic designs and mechanisms. Performance art, participatory dramas and rituals, and seminar plays — all of which demand active audience involvement — are well suited to these sorts of spaces.

Other Architectural Considerations

Designing a theatre involves a great deal more than choosing a staging format. It involves creating a seating space that is suited to the requirements of the expected audience; this may mean one thing in a sophisticated urban area, another in a rural setting, and yet another on a college campus. It involves providing for effective communication systems, sightlines, and stage mechanisms for the sorts of productions the theatre will handle. This means there must be adequate wiring, soundproofing, and rigging, as well as a good use of backstage and onstage spaces, both open and enclosed — often that means calling in a consultant to ascertain the most practical design for the widest variety of uses.

Architectural design also involves principles of acoustics, which can determine whether actors' voices will be heard, given a normal volume level, in all parts of the house and whether singers' voices can be heard when the orchestra is playing. As a science, acoustics is maddeningly inexact; the best results come only after much experience and testing. Theatre architecture also involves the art of lighting, for no lighting designer can possibly overcome the limitations imposed by poorly located, permanently installed lighting fixtures. One of the sadder sights in many older theatres is the snarls of exposed pipes and lighting instruments awkwardly strapped to gilded cupids in a latter-day attempt to make up for antiquated lighting systems.

And finally, designing a theatre building involves a love of theatre, an emotional and aesthetic understanding that a theatre is not merely a room, a hall, or an institutional building with certain features but a permanent home for the portrayal of human concerns and a repository of 2,500 years of glorious tradition. Such a place must be functional and flexible, to be sure, but it should also be a welcoming environment — for both artists and audiences — and a place that inspires us to focus our attention on the concerns of the dramatic production. Whether that implies the cushy velvet seats of a Broadway playhouse, the hard, backless wooden benches of Peter Brook's Bouffes du Nord in Paris, or the standing-room pit of the newly restored Globe

Illustrated here are the four basic staging formats: proscenium, thrust, arena, and black box. Deciding where to locate the stage in relation to the audience is the architect's first consideration in theatre design.

Theatre in London, the theatre's architectural structure powerfully orients us toward our ultimate perception of the play.

Scenery

Scenery is often the first thing we think of under the general category of theatrical design. It is usually what we first see of a play, either at the rise of the curtain in a traditional proscenium production or as we enter the theatre where there is no curtain. The scene designer is usually listed first among designers in a theatre poster or program. But scenery is a relatively new design area, historically speaking. Costume, makeup, and masks are far more ancient; scenery was not needed at all in the *Abydos Passion Play* or the Greek dithyramb, and it probably played little part in early Greek or Roman drama, save to afford entry, exit, and sometimes expanded acting space for actors (such as rotating prisms and rolling platforms) or to provide a decorative backdrop later in the period. In much Asian theatre, scenery remains rare or even nonexistent; this is the case in most Chinese Opera and — apart from the elaborate stagehouse itself — in nō drama as well. Nor was scenery of paramount importance in the outdoor medieval or public Elizabethan theatres — apart from a few painted set pieces made to resemble walls, trees, caves, thrones, tombs, porches, and the occasional "Hellmouth" — for virtually all visual aspects of staging prior to the seventeenth century were dictated by the architecture of the theatre structure itself.

It was the development of European indoor stages, artificially illuminated, that fostered the first great phase of scene design: the period of painted, flat scenery. Working indoors, protected from rain and wind, the scenic designers of Renaissance court masques and public spectacles were free for the first time to erect painted canvases and temporary wooden structures without fear of having the colors run

and the supports rot out or blow away. And with the advent of controllable indoor lighting, designers could illuminate their settings and acting areas as they wished, leaving other parts of the theatre building, such as the audience, in the dark. Designers could, in short, create realistic illusion and extravagant visual spectacle and have the audience focus on this work in decent comfort.

The result was a series of scene-design revelations that brought the names of a new class of theatre artists to public consciousness: designers such as the Italians Sebastiano Serlio (1475–1554), Aristotile de Sangallo (1481–1551), and Giacomo Torelli (1604–1678); the Englishman Inigo Jones (1573–1652); and the Frenchman Jean Bérain (c. 1637–1711). By the beginning of the eighteenth century, the scene designer's art had attained a prominence equal to (or perhaps greater than) the playwright's; and for almost two hundred years thereafter, flat scenery, painted in exquisite perspective, took on even greater sophistication under the brilliant artists of the theatre's baroque, rococo, and romantic epochs. The proscenium format, which was developed primarily to show off elegant settings, dominated theatre architecture for two hundred years,

---

THE HIDDEN ENERGY

A stage setting has no independent life of its own. Its emphasis is directed toward the performance. In the absence of the actor it does not exist. Strange as it may seem, this simple and fundamental principle of stage design still seems to be widely misunderstood.... A scene on the stage is ... like a mixture of chemical elements held in solution. The actor adds the one element that releases the hidden energy of the whole. Meanwhile, wanting the actor, the various elements which go into the setting remain suspended, as it were, in an indefinable tension. To create this suspense, this tension, is the essence of ... stage designing.

– Robert Edmund Jones

Eighteenth-century Venetian playwright Carlo Gozzi blended medieval fantasy, a florid commedia dell'arte style, and his own aristocratic sensibility to create visually spectacular productions in the late Royal era. Here, Andrei Serban's eye-popping production of *The Serpent Woman* at the American Repertory Theatre of Cambridge, Massachusetts, featured scenery and costumes by Setsu Asakura and lighting by Victor En Yu Tan.

and it remains the most widely used theatre format in the world. But the painted flat scenery that the proscenium gave rise to has been only one of many competing scenic formats in the modern era, which began at the end of the nineteenth century.

Modern scenery is generally either realistic or metaphoric — or (most often these days) a combination of both. Realistic scenery attempts to depict, often in great detail, a specific time and place in the real world where the play's events are presumed to take place. Metaphoric scenery favors, instead, visual images that seek to evoke (or to suggest, abstract, or make a visual statement about) the production's intended theme, mood, or social/political implications. Metaphoric scenery tends to remind us — at least when we first see it — that we are in a theatre, not in a bedroom or

butcher shop; generally its intention is to draw us more deeply into the play's larger issues and concerns. And although stage design today most often combines realism with metaphor — these terms are better described as end points on a continuum rather than purely exclusive categories — these complementary design goals have each contributed mightily to the important position of scenery in the theatrical experience today.

Realistic settings carry on the tradition of illusionism established in eighteenth-century painted scenery; at that time, an ingeniously arranged assembly of "wings" (vertical, flat scenery pieces standing left and right of the stage), "borders" (horizontal, flat scenery pieces hung above the stage), and "drops" (short for *backdrops:* large, flat scenery pieces at the rear of the stage), painted in perspective, created

Ming Cho Lee's great realistic setting for Patrick Meyer's adventure drama *K-2* portrays a ledge in the Himalaya Mountains. It even feels cold.

the lifelike illusion of drawing rooms, conservatories, ballrooms, reception halls, parlors, libraries, servants' quarters, professional offices, and factory yards of many a dramatist's imagination. By the nineteenth century, this "wing-and-drop set," as it was known, yielded to the "box set": a three-dimensional construction of interconnected hard-covered "flats" (representing the walls and ceilings of a real room), which was then filled with real furniture and real properties taken from ordinary real-world environments. The box set is very much alive today and is indeed the major scenic format for the contemporary domestic drama (particularly comedy) of New York's Broadway, London's West End, and most community and college theatres across America. Although no longer particularly voguish (the box set rarely wins design awards), it admirably fulfills the staging requirements of a great many domestic comedies, thrillers, and serious linearly structured dramas, particularly those requiring interior settings. Advances in scenic construction and technology have made the box set a marvel of lifelike appearance and detail.

Box sets do more than merely designate a play's locale. By adding three-dimensional features, they allow for acting and playwriting opportunities previously unachievable: staircases to descend, doors to slam, windows to climb through, bookcases to hide revolvers in, and grandfather clocks to hide characters in. The public fascination with realistic scenery reached its high-water mark in the ultrarealistic "theatre of the fourth wall removed," in which the box set was used to such advantage that it helped to foster a uniquely architectural theory of theatre — that it should represent life as it is normally lived but with one wall removed so that the audience could look in upon it.

Metaphoric scenic design, however, tends to be more conceptual than literal, more kinetic than stable, more theatrical than photographic. The use of scenic metaphor is hardly new; in the *Abydos Passion Play,* two maces rep-

QUINCE'S SIGNIFICANT MOON

Shakespeare understood and at times apologized for the pictorial limitations of the scenery of his time ("Piece out our imperfections with your thoughts," he advised the audience in the prologue to *Henry V*), but he also appreciated its capacity to signify – rather than merely depict realistically – the world of his plays. In Shakespeare's *A Midsummer Night's Dream*, the character of Peter Quince is seen directing a play of *Pyramus and Thisbe* with a group of amateur actors and pondering the "hard things" that this *Pyramus* requires, mainly the effect of moonshine in a bedroom chamber. One actor, finding that the moon will be shining on the night of performance, suggests they simply open the window and let the real moon shine in. Quince, however, prefers that an actor hold up a lantern to "disfigure, or to present" the moon. The created "scenic" moon is preferred to the real one because it *signifies* moonshine; it is intentional and consequently meaningful rather than accidental and meaningless. To indicate a "wall" in the same play – the other "hard thing" – Quince abjures bringing in a real wall and instead has another actor put on "some plaster or some loam" so as "to signify wall." Life may be a tale, as Shakespeare's Macbeth says, "full of sound and fury, signifying nothing," but the theatre tells tales that signify a great many things. Thus scenery's function is not merely to depict but to signify – to "make a sign," to be "significant."

resent Set's testicles and a red stone, the Eye of Horus. Shakespeare, in his prologue to *Henry V,* apologizes for the "unworthy scaffold" of his stage and begs his audience to use their "imaginary forces" to complete the scenic picture; for example, with the help of two or three scaling ladders placed against the stage balcony the audience could imagine the English army storming a castle wall in France. These are scenic "abstractions" in the most elemental sense: they present reality by a sign rather than *trompe-l'oeil* ("eye-deceiving") realism. But the modern sense of metaphoric scenery began with the theoretical (and occasionally practical) works of designers Adolphe Appia

(1862–1928) and Gordon Craig (1872–1966), both of whom urged the fluid use of space, form, and light as the fundamental principle of dramatic design. Today, aided by technological advances in motorized, computer-controlled lighting and scene shifting, the movement toward a more conceptual, abstract, and kinetic scenography has inspired impressive stylizations around the world. Shafts and walls of light, transparent "scrims," sculptural configurations, wall-sized photo reproductions, mirrored and burlapped surfaces, "floating" walls and rising staircases, and "found" or "surreal" environments have all become major scenic media over the past fifty years.

Metaphoric settings can of course establish locales (as with Quince's "wall," mentioned in the accompanying box), but they are even more effective in establishing moods and styles. Of course, a play's mood can be established by realistic scenery as well: by creating a theatrical space that is tall and airy, for example, or cramped and squat, by using certain colors or shapes, the designer can create an environment in any mode so that the play's action delivers a strikingly defined tone. But with a determined metaphoric extension, the designer can greatly elaborate upon this tone and translate it into a highly specific sensory impact.

The dark walls and cobwebby interiors designed by Edward Gorey for the Broadway production of *Dracula* (1977), for example, were a significant factor in the play's communication of fascinating horror. The bare but shiny white walls and lacy black catwalks designed by Sally Jacobs for the 1970 Peter Brook production of *A Midsummer Night's Dream* focused all attention on the poetry of the human relationships in that famous Shakespearean revival. The remarkable "found object" — a complete nineteenth-century iron foundry — that served as the surround for Eugene Lee's basic set in the original Harold Prince production of *Sweeney Todd* (1979) indelibly conveyed the underlying theme of industrial oppression.

Eiko Ishioka's stunning set for David Henry Hwang's *M. Butterfly* employed minimal details: a soaring white ramp, a black floor, glossy, Chinese-red chairs, and a red surround contrasting purity and passion in this 1987 Broadway play of East-West cultural (and male-female sexual) tensions.

Designer Eiko Ishioka's soaring white ramp arcing through a brilliant Chinese-red background epitomized the racial conflict and the psychosexual theme of David Henry Hwang's *M. Butterfly* in 1988. Tony Walton's boldly colorful, brashly cartoonish street scenes for the 1992 Broadway revival of *Guys and Dolls* animated the play's New York City setting with a giddy, unworldly, and unthinking nostalgia, allowing current audiences to bask in Runyon's fantasy Manhattan — while just outside the door, on real New York City streets, contemporary urban agony and despair dominated the scene. And Robin Wagner's spectacular collapsing ceiling provided the most unearthly possible entrance of the grandly descending angel in Tony Kushner's *Angels in America: Millennium Approaches* in 1996.

Specifically postmodern design elements, too, have made their appearance in the theatre of the 1980s and 1990s. Because the postmodern emphasizes disharmonies and associations, it travels in a somewhat different path from the departures of modernist innovators Craig and Appia; postmodern design is identifiable by its conscious disruption of "unifying" stylistic themes, replacing them with what may at first seem random assemblages of different and unrelated styles, some "quoting" other historical periods or intellectual sources and others disrupting the linear flow of consistent imagery or effect. Postmodern design also tends to reconfigure, or refer to, the theatre facility itself with (for example) painted scenery made to look specifically scenic, particularly in contrast to seemingly arbitrary found objects strewn about the set, and with designed units meant to comment on — and to mock — their own "theatricality." Richard Hudson's setting and costumes for David Hirson's 1990 *La Bête,* a play set in 1654, ironically juxtaposes classical, neoclassical, baroque, and contem-

LIGHT AS MUSIC

Light and shadow in the course of the drama achieve the same significance as a musical motif which, once stated and developed, has an infinite range of variation. Tristan's agony is sufficient motivation for carrying this kind of lighting to its greatest degree of expressiveness, and the audience, overwhelmed vicariously by the spiritual tragedy of the hero and heroine, would be disturbed by any form of stage setting which did not incorporate this element of design. The audience would really suffer for lack of the kind of staging I have indicated, because it needs to get through its eyes a kind of impression which, up to a given point, can equal the unexampled emotional power of the score. Light is the only medium which can continuously create this impression and its use is motivated and justified by the score itself.

— Adolphe Appia

porary images with superbly ironic and hilarious effect. And Richard Hudson's 1997 *The Lion King* fills Broadway's New Amsterdam Theater — stage and house alike — with multiple and ingenious recapitulations of African, Asian, and American avant-garde design in a joyous celebration of the theatre's truly global virtuosity.

The best scenic design today is so much more than mere "backing" for the action of a play; it is instead the visual and spatial architecture of the play's performance, an architecture that when fully realized is *intrinsic to the play's action:* it is the place *where* the play exists; it also determines exactly *how* the play exists and, along with other factors, helps reveal the play's deepest meanings. Consider, for example, the multilevel, multiroomed setting designed by Jo Mielziner for the original production of Arthur Miller's 1949 American classic *Death of a Salesman:* Mielziner's set provided a cutaway view of both floors of the salesman's house, permitting the simultaneous staging of activity in the kitchen and in

the upstairs bedrooms; as a result, playwright Miller (and director Elia Kazan) restructured the play so that events originally planned to evolve sequentially could be performed simultaneously, thereby tremendously increasing the intensity and impact of the action.

The many brilliant designs of Joseph Svoboda, who is certainly Europe's most celebrated twentieth-century "scenographer" (his own term), are nothing short of dramatic architecture in action. Svoboda has made highly imaginative use of a whole array of contemporary technologies — including laser beams, computerized slide and film projections, power-driven mirrors, low-voltage lighting instruments, aerosol sprays, and innovative stage machinery — to create a body of scenic design unrivaled for theatrical impact and expressive dramaturgy. Speaking of "dramatic space" as "psychoplastic," Svoboda has said: "The goal of a designer can no longer be a description of a copy of actuality, but the creation of its multidimensional model." And for Svoboda — as for most contemporary designers — that multidimensional model is a dynamic one, flowing through time as well as space and responding to the rhythms of both actors and dramatic actions.

Thus the functions of scenery design are both practical and metaphoric, both concrete and imaginative. And although a latecomer to theatre history, scenery has occasionally overwhelmed the drama itself: in Paris in the 1730s, entire performances were arranged with nothing but scene designs, lighting, music, and posed actors, in so-called mute spectacles created by Jean-Nicholas Servandoni. Svoboda's *Diapolyekran* and *Lanterna Magika* have accomplished the same effects in more modern times.

Scenic Materials

Scene designers work, most fundamentally, with space, time, and images. The traditional materials with which these have been created over the past four centuries — wood, canvas, and paint — have in the twentieth century been extended to include virtually every form of matter known to (or created by) human-kind: metals, plastics, masonry, and fabrics; earth, stone, fire, and water; fog, smoke, rain, and light projections. Designing scenic components that employ any or all of these materials is the first area of training for every scene designer.

Platforms, flats, and draperies are the traditional building blocks of fixed stage scenery, and no changes in aesthetics or technology have in any way diminished their importance in the contemporary theatre. *Platforming* serves the all-important function of giving the actor an elevated space from which to perform, making her or him visible over the heads of other actors and stage furniture. A stage setting that utilizes several artfully arranged platforming levels (normally of increasing height toward the back of the stage), together with appropriate connecting staircases and ramps or "raked" platform units, can permit dozens of actors to be seen simultaneously. Platforms can be created in any size and shape; moreover, with the growing use of steel in stage-platform construction, platform support can be fairly open, allowing for huge but still "lacy" settings of great structural stability.

Flats, which today are normally sturdy wooden frames covered in various hard surfaces (such as plywood) and then painted or otherwise treated, are generally used to indicate vertical walls and to define space. In a realistic design, such flats can be pierced with windows, doors, and open archways; adorned with moldings, paintings, hangings, bookcases, or fireplaces; and turned horizontally to serve as ceilings. They can be "tracked" onto the stage in grooves, as they were in the eighteenth century, or "flown" down from the overhead "flies" (rope-and-pulley or counterweight systems for moving hanging scenery),

as they often still are in repertory theatres that store many different settings. The flat is an immensely versatile workhorse that until recently had almost become a symbol of the theatre itself.

Drapery, on the other hand, is widely used as the great neutral stuff of stage scenery. Black hanging drapery is conventionally used to mask (hide) the backstage areas and the lighting instruments; in such cases it is not formally considered part of the scenic picture. Sometimes, in fact, a full set of neutral black drapery — which is standard equipment in most proscenium theatres — can be employed as the entire surround for a staged reading or chamber production. The stage curtain of the proscenium theatre is another form of conventional hanging drapery. When the curtain rises vertically or parts horizontally or is pulled diagonally upward (the "opera drape") at the beginning of a play, it normally signals the drama's first engagement of the audience.

A final type of drapery found in most well-equipped theatres is the "cyclorama," a hanging fabric stretched taut between upper and lower pipes and curved to surround the rear and sides of the stage. Colored white, gray, or gray-blue, the "cyc" can be lighted with stronger colors to represent a variety of "sky-scapes" with great effectiveness; it can also be used for abstract backgrounds and projections.

In addition to the three primary components of stage settings, many productions make use of the special objects, or *set pieces,* which frequently become focal points for an overall setting design or even for the action of a whole play. The tree in *Waiting for Godot,* for example, is the primary scenic feature of that play's setting, symbolizing both life and death. The moment when Vladimir and Estragon "do the tree" — a calisthenic exercise in which each man stands on one leg and tries to assume the shape of the tree — is a profound moment of theatre in which set piece and actors coalesce in a single image echoing the triple crucifixion on Calvary, where two thieves died alongside Christ. Similarly, the massive supply wagon hauled by Mother Courage in Bertolt Brecht's epic play of the same name gives rise to a powerful visual impression of struggle and travail that may last long after the words of the characters are forgotten. And what would *Prometheus Bound* be without its striking set piece, which represents Prometheus' rock and chains? No matter how stylized this element may have been in its original realization, it must have radiated to the Athenian audience a visual poetry every bit as eloquent as the verbal poetry with which Aeschylus supported it. Individual set pieces indeed tax the imagination of author, director, designer, and scene technician alike, and the masterpieces of scenic invention can long outlive their makers in the memory of the audience.

A host of modern materials and technological inventions add to the primary components and set pieces from which scenery is created. *Light* as scenery (as opposed to stage lighting, discussed later) can create walls, images, even (with laser holography) three-dimensional visualizations. Banks of sharply focused light sent through dense atmospheres (enhanced by smoke or dust or fog) can create trenches of light that have the appearance of massive solidity and yet can be made to disappear at the flick of a switch. Carefully controlled slide projections can provide images either realistic or abstract, fixed or fluid, precise or indefinite.

Scrim has been a staple of theatre "magic" for years. This loosely woven, gauzy fabric looks opaque when lit from the front (the audience side) and transparent when lit from behind, allowing actors and even whole sets to suddenly appear or disappear simply by a shift in the lighting.

Stage machinery — turntables, elevators, hoists, rolling carts and wagons, and the like — can be used to create a veritable dance of scenic elements to accompany and support dramatic action. The ancient Greeks apparently

The scenic elements are central in Nicky Silver's *Pterodactyls.* This funny-sad contemporary American drama concerns a dysfunctional modern American family posed against a paleontological reconstruction of ancient times (and values). The scenery for this 1994 South Coast Repertory Theatre production was designed by Michael Vaughn Sims.

understood the importance of mechanical devices quite well, as did Shakespeare, with his winched thrones and disappearing witches. Tricks and sleight of hand (called in the medieval theatre "trucs" and "feynts") have always imparted a certain sparkle of mystery to the theatre and hence will always play a part in the designer's art.

Sound also must be taken into consideration by the designer, who must plan for the

For Patrick Marber's *Closer*, a contemporary British drama about adult couplings and decouplings, designer Vicki Mortimer designed a candle-lit mausoleum backdrop that framed the disquieting drama with its incipient mortality. Liza Walker plays Alice and Clive Owen is Dan in the 1997 English National Theatre Cottesloe production, directed by the author.

actors' footfalls as well as for the visual elements behind, around, and underneath them. The floor of a Japanese nō stage, for example, has a characteristic look and produces a characteristic sound; it is meant to be stamped upon, and it must sound just so. Joseph Svoboda has designed a stage floor for *Faust* that can be either resonant or silent depending on the arrangement of certain mechanisms concealed underneath; when Faust walks upstage his steps reverberate; when he turns and walks downstage his steps are silent — and from this we know that Mephistopheles has taken his body.

Properties and furniture, which are often handled by separate artists working under the guidance of the scene designer, are crucial not only in establishing realism but also in en-

hancing mood and style. Although furniture often functions in the theatre as it does in real life — to sit upon, lie upon, and so forth — it also has a crucial stylistic importance; often stage furniture is designed and built in highly imaginative ways in coordination with the setting to convey a special visual impact. Properties such as ashtrays, telephones, letters, and tableware are often functional in realistic plays, but they can also have aesthetic importance and are therefore carefully selected — or else specially designed. Frequently, furniture pieces or properties have considerable symbolic significance, as in the case of the thrones in Shakespeare's *Richard III* or the glass figurines in Tennessee Williams's *Glass Menagerie;* indeed, on occasion they are raised to titular metaphoric importance (in which cases their design may be enhanced), as in Elmer Rice's expressionistic play *The Adding Machine*.

The Scene Designer at Work

The scene designer's work inevitably begins with a reading and rereading of the play, normally followed by research on the play and its original period (and the periods in which it may be set), a consideration of the type of theatre in which the play is to be produced, and extensive discussions with the director and other members of the design and production team. It is usually by a mutual, collaborative process — among the director, other designers, and the technical staff — that scenic design proceeds in the modern professional and academic theatre. (We'll examine this process in more detail in the next chapter.)

This discussion phase normally proceeds, almost simultaneously, with the designer's preparation of a series of visualizations, which may begin with collected illustrations (for example, clippings from magazines, notations from historical sources, color ideas, spatial concepts) and move on to sketches, color renderings, and/or three-dimensional models. Eventually, this process results in a full set of working drawings or other materials, approved by the director and producer, that will serve as a guide for construction. Throughout the process, of course, the designer must reckon with budgetary constraints and the skills of the construction staff available to execute and install the finished design. Part architect, part engineer, part accountant, and part interpretive genius, the scene designer today is one of the theatre's premier artists/craftspeople.

Douglas-Scott Goheen's ingenious setting for the medieval York play of *Noah* (for the Focused Program in Medieval Drama in California) used the theatre's counterweight hoisting machinery to suspend Noah's ark, thus allowing it to float up as the "water" rose around it, and to sway back and forth to suggest the pitch and roll of a boat at sea.

PHOTO ESSAY: BROADWAY DESIGNER TONY WALTON

1.

British-born Tony Walton has become, over a forty-plus-year career, one of America's premier theatre designers. In addition to his extraordinary design accomplishments in stage scenery (for which he has won three Broadway Tony Awards), Walton is noted for his work in stage costumes as well as innumerable designs for films, ballets, operas, posters, books, and record albums.

Born in Surrey in 1934, he found his way to classically oriented Radley College (a prep school near Oxford), London's Slade School of Fine Art, and, at age twenty-one, the hard-knocks post of assistant designer at a provincial theatre in Wimbledon, where he was expected to design, assistant design, and paint scenery for a new production every week. British military service took him to Canada the following year, and upon his discharge Walton settled in New York, earning his living by designing caricatures and illustrations for *Harpers* and *Vogue* magazines. He subse-

quently passed the exam — in all three areas of scenery, costumes, and lighting — for admission to the United Scenic Artists, America's sole professional union for theatre designers.

By 1957 Walton had designed his first New York play, Noel Coward's *Conversation Piece,* and by 1999 he had designed sets for more than forty New York productions, plus many more in London, Los Angeles, Seattle, New Haven, Washington, and other cities. Among his most celebrated stage designs have been the Broadway or Lincoln Center premiere productions

2.

3.

4.

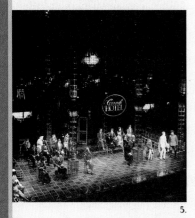

5.

of *A Funny Thing Happened on the Way to the Forum* (for which he also designed the 1996 revival), *Pippin* (for which he received his first Tony), *Chicago, Streamers, The Real Thing, Hurlyburly, I'm Not Rappaport, Lend Me a Tenor, Grand Hotel, Six Degrees of Separation, Death and the Maiden, Laughter on the 23rd Floor, Waiting for Godot, Four Baboons Adoring the Sun, Steel Pier, Conversations with My Father, The Beauty Queen of Leenane,* and Broadway revivals of *Anything Goes, Guys and Dolls, She Loves Me, Company,* and *1776.*

On a 1998 visit to his labyrinthine upper West Side (New York) home and studio — a virtual beehive of constant activity — this author asked Walton what he was working on at the moment. Having prepared himself for this question at a Chinese restaurant the night before, Walton pulled from his pocket a chopsticks wrapper on which he had listed his current projects. "Let's see," he began. "At the moment I'm designing a production of *Noel and Gertie* for the Bay Street Theatre on Long Island, plus an off-Broadway production of a new play by Terrence McNally and Jon Robin Baitz called *House,* plus a production of Harold Pinter's *Ashes to Ashes* for Broadway." While catching his breath, he turned over the wrapper. "Then of course I'm also redesigning this

1. Tony Walton is shown here in his New York studio, with one of his design assistants. The model for his 1998 revival of *1776,* for which he is preparing to unroll a set of plans, is to the left.

2. Walton's drawing of the wedding scene for his 1992 Broadway revival of *Guy and Dolls* is complete with characters as he imagines them in the show's finale.

3. Here is the actual wedding scene from that production of *Guys and Dolls,* directed by Jerry Zaks. (Walton won the Tony Award for this design.)

4. Walton's set model for *Grand Hotel* shows the orchestra's position above the play's action.

5. Here is the actual set of the play as realized in this 1989 production, directed by Tommy Tune.

6. Walton's set design for Martin McDonagh's 1998 Irish-themed off-Broadway hit, *The Cripple of Inishman,* beautifully captured the dank chill of rural Irish mudplaster.

6.

7.

8.

completed projects: the Broadway sets for *Leenane* and *1776*. The workmanship for the latter production was admirable, and one of Walton's assistants said that the ceiling moldings, which had to be precisely carved to account for the forced perspective of the illusion, had been hand-shaped by a team of specialist woodsmiths from Germany. "Getting it right in the model saves countless hours in the shops," Walton explained.

One looks in vain for a "signature style" in Walton's many works, and Walton himself agrees: "For me it is preferable to try and start out as a blank slate — completely available to the special nature of the piece. I hope to let the piece itself — via the director's approach to it — dictate the design," he says in his entry in *Contemporary Designers*. His amazing virtuosity over a wide range of dramatic and aesthetic styles, as well as the sureness of his technique, is illustrated in the designs in the portfolio of photographs shown here.

massive *Christmas Carol* for Madison Square Garden again, plus designing the interior of the Roundabout Theatre company's new 42nd Street stagehouse. Also I'm directing a production of my wife, Gen's, new play, *Missing Footage*. I think there's more, but I ran out of room here."

In the studio wing of Walton's apartment, two design assistants — both professional designers themselves — were busily at work. One was touching up the *Ashes* model; another was carefully cutting out some simulated tile squares to use on the model for *House*. Around the room, in addition to stacks of books, drawings, photos, scripts, and material samples, were the models of just-

Lighting

The very word *theatre,* meaning "seeing place," implies the crucial function of light. Light is the basic condition for theatrical appearance. Without light, nothing can be seen.

The use of light for dramatic effect, as distinct from pure illumination, can be traced back to the earliest surviving plays: *Agamemnon,* by Aeschylus, was staged so that the watchman's spotting of the signal fire heralding Agamemnon's return to Argos coincided with the actual sunrise over the Athenian skene (stagehouse); it is also probable that the burning of Troy at the conclusion of Euripides' *Trojan Women* was staged to coincide with the sunset that reddened the Attic sky. Modern plays commonly use light in metaphoric and symbolic ways: the blinking neon light that intermittently reddens Blanche's quarters in Williams's *A Streetcar Named Desire* and the searching follow-spot (a swivel-mounted lighting instrument that can be pointed in any direction by an operator) demanded by Samuel Beckett to train upon the hapless, trapped characters in his *Play.*

Although it is customary to think of theatre lighting as dating from the invention of electricity, nothing could be more misleading. Lighting has always been a major theatrical consideration. In addition to coordinating the timing of their plays to the sunrise and sunset, the ancient Greeks paid a great deal of attention to the proper orientation of their theatres to take best advantage of the sun's rays. The medieval outdoor theatre, although as dependent on sunlight as was the Greek theatre, made use of several devices to redirect sunlight, including halos made of reflective metal to surround Jesus and his disciples with a focused and intensified illumination; in one production a brightly polished metal basin was held over Jesus' head to concentrate the sun's rays — and surviving instructions indicate that medieval stagehands substituted torches for the bowl in the case of cloudy skies!

It was in indoor stagings as early as the Middle Ages, however, that lighting technology attained its first significant sophistication. In a 1439 production of the *Annunciation* in Florence, one thousand oil lamps were used for illumination, plus a host of candles that were lighted by a "ray of fire" that shot through the cathedral. One can imagine the spectacle. Leonardo da Vinci designed a 1490 production of *Paradise* with twinkling stars and backlit zodiac signs on colored glass. And by the sixteenth century the great festival lighting of indoor theatres, located in manor houses and public halls, would serve as a symbol of the intellectual and artistic achievements of the Renaissance itself, a mark of the luxury, technical wizardry, and ostentatious, exuberant humanism of the times. People went to the theatres in those times simply to revel in light and escape the outside gloom — in rather the same way that Americans, earlier in the twentieth century, populated air-conditioned movie theatres largely to escape the heat of summer days.

By the Renaissance, the sheer opulence of illumination was astonishing — though the entire effect was created simply from tallow, wax, and fireworks. Raphael "painted" the name of his patron, Pope Leo X, with thirteen lighted chandeliers in a 1519 dramatic production; Sebastiano Serlio inserted sparkling panes of colored glass, illuminated from behind, into his flat painted scenery to create glistening and seductive scenic effects. And, as the Renaissance spirit gave way to the lavish Royal theatre of the age of the Sun King, Louis XIV, artificial illumination — calculated to match Louis's presumed incendiary brilliance — developed apace: one 1664 presentation at Versailles featured 20,000 colored lanterns, hundreds of transparent veils and bowls of colored water, and a massive display of fireworks.

It was the invention of the gaslight in the nineteenth century and the development of electricity shortly thereafter — first in carbon arc and "limelight" electrical lighting and then in incandescence — that brought stage lighting into its modern phase and made it less strictly showy and more pertinent to individual works and dramatic action. Ease and flexibility of control are the cardinal virtues of both gas and electric lighting. By adjusting a valve, a single operator at a "gas table" could raise or dim the intensity of any individual light or of a preselected "gang" of lights — just as easily as we can raise or lower the fire on a gas range with the turn of a knob today. And, of course, with electricity — which was introduced in American theatres in 1879 and in European theatres the following year — the great fire hazard of a live flame (a danger that had plagued the theatre for centuries and claimed three buildings a year on average, including Shakespeare's Globe) was at last over. The fire crews, which were round-the-clock staff members of every major theatre in the early nineteenth century, were dismissed; and the deterioration of scenery and costumes from the heat, smoke, and carbon pollution similarly came to a halt. Incandescent lighting also had the great advantage of being fully self-starting — it did not need to be relit or kept alive by pilot lights — and it could easily be switched off, dimmed up and down, and re-ganged or reconnected simply by fastening and unfastening flexible wires. Within a few years of its introduction, electricity became the primary medium of stage lighting in the Western world, and great dynamo generators — for electricity was used in the theatre long before it was commercially available from municipal power supplies — were installed as essential equipment in the basements of theatres from Vienna to San Francisco.

Electricity provides an enormously flexible form of lighting. The incandescent filament is a reasonably small, reasonably cool point of light that can be focused, reflected, aimed, shaped, and colored by a great variety of devices invented and adapted for those purposes; and electric light can be trained in innumer-

In this 1991 Adrian Hall production of *King Lear* at the American Repertory Theatre, Natasha Katz's intense downlighting keeps our attention on Edmund (Jonathan Fried), his sword drawn before his duel with Edgar (*deep background*).

able ways upon actors, scenery, audiences, or a combination of these to create realistic and/or atmospheric effects through dimensionality, focus, animation, distortion, diffusion, and overwhelming radiance. Today, thanks to the added sophistication of computer technology and microelectronics, it is not uncommon to see theatres with nearly a thousand lighting instruments all under the complete control of a single technician seated in a comfortable booth above the audience.

Modern Lighting Design

Today, the lighting for most productions is conceived and directly supervised by a professional lighting designer, a species of theatre artist who has appeared as a principal member of the production team only since the mid-twentieth century. By skillfully working with lighting instruments, hanging positions, angles, colors, shadows, and moment-to-moment adjustments of intensity and directionality, the lighting designer can illuminate a dramatic production in a great variety of subtle and complex ways. The manner in which the lighting designer uses the medium to blend the more rigid design elements (architecture and scenery) with the evolving patterns of the movements of the actors and the meanings of the play is normally a crucial factor in a production's artistic and theatrical success.

Visibility and *focus* are the primary considerations of lighting design: visibility ensures that the audience sees what it wants to see, and focus ensures that it sees what it is supposed to see without undue distraction. Visibility, then, is the passive accomplishment of lighting design, and focus is its active accomplishment. The spotlight, a development of the twentieth century, has fostered something akin to a revolution in staging. Contemporary productions now routinely feature a darkened auditorium (a rarity prior to the 1880s) and a deliberate effort to illuminate certain characters (or props or set pieces) more than others — in other words, to direct the audience's

Individual pools of light illuminate the parasols and costumes — and the isolation — of ladies waiting for the soldiers' return at the beginning of *Much Ado about Nothing*. This 1994 Indiana Repertory Theatre production was directed by Libby Appel, with lighting design by Robert Peterson.

attention toward those visual elements that are dramatically the most significant.

Realism and *atmosphere* also are common goals of the lighting designer, and both can be achieved largely through the color and direction of lighting. Realistic lighting can be created to appear as if emanating from familiar sources: from the sun, for example, from "practical" (real) lamps on the stage, or from moonlight, fire, streetlights, neon signs, or the headlights of moving automobiles. Atmospheric lighting, which may or may not suggest a familiar source, can be used to evoke a mood appropriate to a play's action: sparkly, for example, or gloomy, oppressive, nightmarish, austere, verdant, smoky, funereal, or regal.

Sharp, bold lighting designs are frequently employed to create highly theatrical effects — from the glittery entertainments of the Broadway musical tradition to harsher experimental stagings like those often associated with the plays and theories of Bertolt Brecht. Brecht's concept of a "didactic" theatre favors lighting that is bright, cold (uncolored), and specifically "unmagical." Brecht suggested, in fact, that the lighting instruments themselves be made part of the setting, placed in full view of the audience; this "theatricalist" use of the lighting instruments themselves is now widespread even in nondidactic plays. Moodier plays may employ dense or unnatural colors, "gobo" filters that break light beams into shadowy fragments (such as leaf patterns), or atmospheric "fog" effects that make light appear misty, gloomy, or mysterious. The Broadway-type musical, on the other hand, often makes splashy use of banks of colored footlights and border lights, high-intensity follow-spots that track actors around the stage, "chaser" lights that flash on and off in sequence, and a near fuse-busting incandescence that makes a finale seem to burn up the stage; in fact, this traditional exploitation of light has done as much to give Broadway the name Great White Way as have the famous billboards and marquees that line the street.

Stylized lighting effects are often used to express radical changes of mood or event; indeed, the use of lighting alone to signal a complete change of scene is an increasingly common theatrical expedient. Merely by switching from full front to full overhead lighting, for example, a technician can throw a character into silhouette and make her or his figure appear suddenly ominous, grotesque, or isolated. The illumination of an actor with odd lighting colors, such as green, or from odd lighting positions, such as from below, can create mysterious, unsettling effects. The use of follow-spots can metaphorically put a character "on the spot" and convey a specific sense of unspeakable terror. Highly expressive lighting and projections, when applied to a production utilizing only a cyclorama, a set piece, sculpture, or stage mechanism and neutrally clad actors, can create an infinite variety of convincing theatrical environments for all but the most resolutely realistic of plays; it is here, in the area of stylization and expressive theatricality, that the modern lighting designer has made the most significant mark.

The Lighting Designer at Work

The lighting designer ordinarily conceives a lighting design out of a synthesis of many discrete elements: the play, discussions with the director and other members of the design team as to the approach or concept of the production, the characteristics of the theatre building (lighting positions, control facilities, and wiring system), the scenery and costume designs, the movements and behavior of the actors, and the available lighting instruments. Occasionally the availability of an experienced lighting crew must also be a consideration. Because not all of these variables can be known from the outset (the stage movement, for example, may change from one day to the next right up to the final dress rehearsal), the lighting designer must be skilled at making adjustments and must have the opportunity to exercise a certain amount of control, or at least to voice concerns with regard to areas affecting lighting problems.

Ordinarily, the two major preparations required of the lighting designer are the light plot and the cue sheet. A *light plot* is a plan or series of plans showing the placement of each lighting instrument; its type, wattage, and size; its wiring and connection to an appropriate dimmer; its color; and sometimes its movement, as lighting instruments are increasingly being programmed to pan, tilt, or change color by remote, motorized control. A *cue sheet* is a list of the occasions, referred to by number and keyed to the script of the play (or, in final form, the more full annotated stage manager's script), when lights change in intensity or color or move. The light plot and cue sheet are developed in consultation with the director and other members of the design team, who may take major or minor roles in the consultation, depending on their interests and expertise. Inasmuch as some productions use hundreds of lighting instruments and require thousands of individual cues, the complexity of these two documents can be extraordinary; weeks and months may go into their preparation.

The lighting designer works with a number of different sorts of lighting instruments and must know the properties of each instrument well enough to anticipate fully how it will perform when hung and focused on the stage. Few theatres have the time or space flexibility to permit much on-site experimentation in lighting design; thus the development of the light plot and cue sheet takes place primarily in the imagination and, where possible, in workshop or free experimentation apart from the working facility. This requirement places a premium on the designer's ability to predict instrument performance from various distances and angles and with various color elements installed; it also demands a sharp awareness of how various lights will reflect off different surfaces.

Once the light plot is complete, the lights are mounted (hung) in appropriate positions,

Above: The ellipsoidal reflector spotlight (sometimes called "leko" after its two inventors, Joe Levy and Ed Kook) is the lighting designer's workhorse instrument, offering an intense and precisely focused circular light beam that is easily reconfigured by shutters (which make straight-line cuts "shuttering" the beam), irises (which diminish the beam's diameter), gobos (which create silhouette patterns of any type), and color media. The ETC (Electronic Theatre Control) company's "Source Four" model is an outstanding example of such an instrument, with interchangeable lens tubes and a rotating barrel. *Below:* Lights are controlled by a board which can turn individual instruments – or hundreds at a time – on, off, or to any mid-level in between with a simple button or lever. ETC's Obsession II control board, with its ergonomic lines and Pentium processor, is a leader among such devices, with which a single operator can control literally tens of thousands of individual lighting changes during a production.

1.

Chris Parry's interest in lighting began in his native England where, as a talented physics student, he was tapped to run the lighting for his high school's plays, and then for several amateur theatre groups. "I had no idea at the time that you could do this for a living, though," Parry recalls, and so he began his professional life as an apprentice telephone repairman. The theatre still beckoned, however, and, while still in his early twenties, he wrote to the distinguished lighting designer Richard Pilbrow inquiring how one might start a professional lighting career. Pilbrow suggested applying for an apprenticeship at a regional British theatre, and before long Parry had landed an electrician's post "at the very bottom rung" of the Royal Shakespeare Company's lighting department. Hanging and focusing lights for the company's many resident and guest designers was "an incredible learning experience," and working the daily changeovers from one show to another in the company's rotating repertory schedule gave him a sure command of his craft. By the late 70s, Parry was beginning to freelance as a designer outside the company, and by the early 80s as an RSC resident designer himself, creating the lighting for major productions of the classics (*Othello, King Lear, The Plantagenets, Macbeth, Hamlet, The Winter's Tale*) as well as modern plays (*The Master Builder, Les Liaisons Dangereuses, The Blue Angel, The Crucible*) at England's two greatest theatre companies: the RSC and the Royal National Theatre.

It was the RSC *Les Liaisons* that brought Parry to the United States; when the production came to the Music Box Theatre in 1987, he received a Tony Award nomination for his lighting and a few years later moved permanently to America, where

2.

3.

he continues to reside while designing widely in both countries. Among Parry's internationally visible productions since moving to the United States have been *The Who's Tommy* (1995), which won him the Tony Award, *Not About Nightingales* (1999), winning him another Tony nomination, and *Translations* (1995), all on Broadway, plus *Jane Eyre* in Toronto, and London productions of *The Secret Garden* (RSC, 2000) and *The Way of the World* (Royal National Theatre, 1995). And for America's regional market, the very busy Parry has designed more than sixty productions for companies including the Seattle Repertory, Hartford Stage, Geffen Playhouse (Los Angeles), South Coast Repertory, La Jolla Playhouse, Milwaukee Repertory, Mark Taper Forum, Pasadena Playhouse, Oregon Shakespeare Festival, Shakespeare Theatre (Washington), Guthrie Theatre, and Yale Repertory, plus operas in Los Angeles, Houston, Lucca (Italy), and Buxton

(UK). He also heads the graduate lighting program at the University of California, San Diego, and teaches master classes in New York City.

Parry considers himself half artist and half craftsman, remarking that "I still struggle as to where the art actually comes from; I was always told I wasn't 'artistic' in school . . . !" Working in his Beverly Hills, California, studio, decorated with posters from his productions and, discreetly tucked into a bookshelf, his Tony Award, he drafts detailed and comprehensive lighting plots for shows opening in London, Seattle, and San Diego. "Sometimes it's an agonizing process," he admits, "and then sometimes it comes almost immediately." Three elements figure prominently in Parry's design process: the script, the director, and the set. As to the latter, "I try to make it look like the scenery and lighting were designed by the same person," he explains, aiming at a seamless integration of scenic objects and their illumination. I'm always interested in any lighting ideas the scenic designer has too — after all, he's the one who designed it, and who presumably sees the set already illuminated in his mind's eye." Parry acknowledges, however, that audiences and critics are not quick to "see" the lighting. "The curtain

4.

1. Parry lives and works in a pleasant, contemporary apartment in Beverly Hills, California, which is decorated with, among other things, posters and award certificates from the many shows he has designed in his career — which marked its twenty-fifth anniversary at the time of this 2001 interview.

2. At his drafting table in the studio of his apartment, Parry, using a plastic template (in green), inks a new instrument into the light plot for an upcoming production of *A Little Night Music* for Seattle's Fifth Street Theatre. On the left side of the plot, Parry has taped swatches of the basic colors he intends to use in the final plot.

3. Parry searches for an additional color from one of the several manufacturer's swatch books he keeps in his studio.

4. On the wall opposite his drafting table, Parry has taped up samples of the colors used in the costume and set designs, and samples of wallpaper used in the set.

5.

goes up and they say 'what a beautiful set.' But what would it look like just under work lights?" Not much.

As for the script, Parry tries to be guided by the director's vision, seeking to arrange early conversations with his directors. "Of course, some di-

rectors have very little time to give you. With Trevor Nunn or Adrian Noble [artistic directors of the Royal National and Royal Shakespeare Companies] you might just get fifteen minutes. But then fifteen minutes with Trevor or Adrian can get you everything you need, whereas two hours with someone else might leave you wondering if you have anything at all!" Parry relishes directors that can make concrete assessments of how they see a scene, and provide him with images as opposed to abstractions. "To say that the lighting should be 'optimistic' doesn't really help very much, does it?" he inquires, answering his own question with a wry grimace. "But tell me it should look like cotton candy — well, I can do something with that. I know what that looks like, feels like, and what it means."

6.

Parry frequently speaks of lighting as painting ("I can't actually paint or draw, and so this is how I do it . . .") referring to lighting instruments as "light paintbrushes." And, like a painter, he enjoys having a wide array of different brushes to work with. Designers in England, he explains, have a greater variety of instruments at their disposal than do their American counterparts, and he is often

5. In a separate office, Parry, like most designers today, works out many details of his lighting design on CAD (computer-aided-design) programs on his computer.

6. Chris Parry won the coveted Tony Award for his brilliantly florid and tightly focused lighting — emphasizing the electronic atmosphere and the lighting instruments themselves — in the 1993 Broadway production of *The Who's Tommy*, a rock musical set in and around a somewhat mythical pinball parlor. Stage settings by John Arnone; costumes by David C. Woolard.

7. Toplighting — focusing lights from directly overhead — isolates the prisoners and guards, leaving some in sight and some in shadow, in Parry's lighting design for the 1999 Royal Shakespeare Production of Tennessee Williams's recently rediscovered *Not About Nightingales*.

7.

hard-pressed to find some of the specialty lights he wants, such as the supersized 2000-watt or even 5000-watt fresnels (a lamp with a broad beam) which he prefers to the banks of the more tightly focused

8. Parry's low lighting instruments are angled upward to create colorful and expressive shadows on both the walls and the ceiling of Ming Cho Lee's grotesquely skewed set in South Coast Repertory's 2000 world premiere production of Howard Korder's *The Hollow Lands*. The play, directed by David Chambers and with costumes by Shigeru Yaji, fantasizes America's western expansion in the nineteenth century; Mark Harelik, standing on the bed, plays a spellbinding pioneer who projects his distorted visions to others – as underlined by all aspects of the production's design.

lekos or PAR lamps most American designers use. "A large single-source instrument focused on an actor on a big stage gives one single shadow. It can feel very 'lonely,' and that's beautiful," he points out, while dozens of smaller instruments "give you dozens of smaller shadows that wash each other out." Shadows figure prominently in many Parry designs, as in his Broadway/Royal National Theatre production of *Not About Nightingales,* a recently rediscovered Tennessee Williams play set in a prison for which Parry relied, at times exclusively, on selective but intense toplighting (lighting from directly above the stage), with dark spaces between the lighted ones to convey the isolation and control of a prison environment.

And while Parry's lighting is normally quite subtle, underlining but — from the audience's viewpoint — seeming to disappear underneath the action, there are times when a production calls for big, splashy, and dominant lighting, as in his Tony-winning *The Who's Tommy*, which centers on a pinball game — a garishly illuminated object in its own right. For shows like this one, Parry designs more aggressively and enjoys having "a lot of toys" with which to work. "Light curtains" — of low-voltage, high-intensity instruments (originally invented by Josef Svoboda, whose transition to the United States Parry attributes to colleague David Hersey) — and intense light that penetrates through the wispy smoke he uses in battle

8.

9. Contrasting colors from floodlights, spotlights, and direct sources provide the distinctive design elements in Parry's Olivier-nominated 1994 production of *A Midsummer Night's Dream* at the Royal Shakespeare Company, with settings and costumes by Anthony Ward.

10. In this Old Globe (San Diego) 2000 production of *Love's Labor's Lost*, directed by Roger Rees, the patterns of James Joy's setting are created by Parry's "gobos" — filters placed in the lighting instruments to scatter and variegate the light — creating a romantically dappled effect. The ominous figure in black silhouette at bottom center is Mercade, not yet discovered by the others on stage, who will shortly prove a messenger of death.

9.

10.

scenes are among his particular favorites.

Above all, Parry considers himself an essentially intuitive designer. When your craft is secure, "lots of things play into your creativity." He prefers setting cues during technical rehearsals rather than working them all out on paper beforehand, believing that the lighting designer needs to see and hear all the elements of the scene — actors, set, costumes, sound — before deciding what must be created to complete the picture. "You have to work fast, but it's so instinctual that you don't get time to second-guess yourself. Your first response is usually the best," he says. Of course, it helps that he is at a point in his work where he has sufficient confidence to trust those instincts. "I'm a great believer in intuition," Parry asserts. "But when that fails, your craft is still there to support you."

attached to the theatre's wiring system (or wired separately), "patched" to proper dimmers, focused (aimed) in the desired directions, and colored by the attachment of frames containing plastic color media. Ideally, the stage setting is finished and in position when all of this occurs, but it rarely works this way, particularly on Broadway, where theatres are often rented only a short time before the opening performance. Once the instruments are in place and functioning, the lighting designer begins setting the intensities of each instrument for each cue, a painstaking process involving the recording of thousands of precise numerical directions on a series of track sheets (or charts) for the technicians who must effect the cues. Computer technology has vastly simplified this process for most theatres; with or without computers, however, much time and care inevitably go into this process, which is vital to the development and execution of a fully satisfying lighting design. Finally, the lighting designer presides over the working and timing of the cues, making certain that in actual operation the lights shift as subtly or as boldly, as grandly or as imperceptibly, as is appropriate for the play's action and for the design aesthetic.

It is out of thousands of details, most of which are pulled together in a single final week, that great lighting design springs. Gradations of light, difficult to measure in isolation, can have vastly differing impacts in the moment-to-moment focus and feel of a play. Because light is a medium rather than an object, audience members are rarely if ever directly aware of it; they are aware only of its illuminated target. Therefore, the lighting designer's work is poorly understood by the theatregoing public at large. But everyone who works professionally in the theatre — from the set and costume designers to the director to the actor — knows what a crucial role lighting plays in the success of the theatre venture. As the Old Actor says as he departs the stage in off-Broadway's longest-running hit, *The Fan-*

tasticks: "Remember me — in light!" The light that illuminates the theatre also glorifies it; it is a symbol of revelation — of knowledge and humanity — upon which the theatrical impulse finally rests.

Costume

Costume has always been a major element in the theatrical experience; it is a vehicle for the "dressing up" that actors and audiences alike have always considered a requirement for the fullest degree of theatrical satisfaction. Costume serves both ceremonial and illustrative functions.

The Functions of Costume

The first theatrical costumes were essentially ceremonial vestments. The *himation* (a gownlike costume) of the early Aeschylean actor was derived from the garment worn by the priest-chanter of the dithyramb; the comic and satyr costumes, with their use of phalluses and goatskins, were likewise derived from more primitive god-centered rites. The priests who first enacted the *Quem Queritis* trope (liturgical text) in medieval Europe simply wore their sacred albs, hooded to indicate an outdoor scene but otherwise unaltered. And the actors of the classic Japanese nō drama even today wear costumes that relate more to spiritual sources than to secular life. Ancient and original uses of costuming have served primarily to separate the actor from the audience, to "elevate" the actor to a quasi-divine status. The thick-soled footwear (*kothurnoi*) worn by Greek actors in the fourth century B.C. were calculated to enhance this ceremonial effect by greatly increasing the height of the wearers, thereby "dressing them up" both figuratively and literally.

The shift of stress in costuming from a "dressing up" of the actor to a defining of the character came about gradually in the theatre's history. In the Elizabethan theatre, the costumes often had an almost regal, ceremonial quality because the acting companies frequently solicited the cast-off raiment of the nobility; English theatre of this time was known throughout Europe for the splendor of its costuming, but apparently little effort was made to suit costume to characterization. Moreover, it was not unusual in Shakespeare's time for some actors to wear contemporary garb onstage while others wore costumes expressive of the period of the play. In Renaissance Italy, costuming developed a high degree of stylization in the commedia dell'arte, in which each of the recurring characters wore a distinctive and arresting costume that instantly signified a particular age, intelligence, and disposition. The same characters and the same costumes can be seen today in contemporary commedia productions, and they are still as eloquent and entertaining as they were four hundred years ago.

Modern costuming acquired much of its present character during the eighteenth and nineteenth centuries, when certain realistic considerations took control of the Western theatre. These centuries witnessed a great deal of radical social change that led to, among other things, the widespread acceptance of science and its methods and a great fascination with detail and accuracy. These trends coalesced in the European (and eventually the American) theatre with a series of productions in which historical accuracy served as the guiding principle. For the first time, painstaking effort ensured that the design of every costume in a play (and every prop and every set piece as well) accorded with an authentic "period" source. Thus a production of *Julius Caesar* would be intensively researched to re-create the clothing worn in Rome in the first century A.D., a *Hamlet* would be designed to mirror the records of medieval Denmark, and a *Romeo and Juliet* would seek to re-create, in detail, the world of Renaissance Verona.

The movement towards historical accuracy and the devotion with which it was pursued led ultimately to a widespread change in the philosophy of costume design that persists to this day. For although historical accuracy itself is no longer the ultimate goal of costume design, stylistic consistency and overall design control have proven to be lasting principles. Costuming today stresses an imaginative aesthetic creativity as well as a coordinated dramatic suitability; thus the influence of realism, with its attendant emphasis on historical accuracy, has fostered coherent and principled design in place of the near anarchy that once prevailed.

Modern costume design might then be said to serve four separate functions. First, in concert with its ancient origins, it retains at least a hint of that ceremonial magic once conjured by ancient priests and shamans. Costume, even today, bespeaks a primordial theatricality. As Theoni Aldredge said of the costumes for *A Chorus Line,* they "had to look real and yet theatrical enough for an audience to say, 'Okay, I'm in the theatre now.'"

Second, in aggregate, the costumes of a play show us what sort of world we are asked to enter, not only by its historical place and period but by implication its social and cultural values as well. The word *costume* has the same root as *custom* and *customary;* as such it indicates the "customary" wearing apparel (or the "habitual habit") of persons living in a particular world. For example, the Mexican

PSYCHODRAMA IN THE FITTING ROOM

The distinguished costume designer William Ivey Long was initially trained as a scene designer but turned to costumes at the start of his career. In Long's words, "I feel I need psychodrama in my life. I found that there's more interaction with people in costume design than in set design.... I think it's how I work out my own insecurities, by helping people discover and solve theirs. And there's nothing more basic and more right on the line than the fitting room. There's the mirror and there's the actor and there you are."

American characters in Luis Valdez's *Zoot Suit,* set in the 1940s, are seen as virtual extensions of their overly long pegged trousers and looping watch chains. Tennessee Williams, in *A Streetcar Named Desire,* specifically directed the poker players to wear shirts of "bright primary colors," to contrast their primary sexuality with Blanche du Bois's dead (and sexually ambivalent) husband, whom the dramatist had named "Allan Grey." The ensemble of costumes in a play production generally reveals the production's style, at least as it emanates from the play's characters.

Third, the individual costumes can express the specific individuality of each character's role; they reveal at a glance, for example, the character's profession, wealth, age, class status, tastes, and self-image. More subtly, costume can suggest the character's vices, virtues, and hidden hopes — or fears. By the judicious use of color, shape, fabric, and even the *sound* a fabric makes, costume designers can imbue every character with individual distinctiveness, particularly in contrast to the standard dress in which other characters of his or her class are seen. When Hamlet insists on wearing his "inky cloak" in his uncle's presence, he silently signifies his refusal to accept his uncle's authority; he refuses to "fit" into the world of the Danish court, which becomes both a mark of Hamlet's character and a significant action in the play. When Monsieur Jourdain in Molière's *The Bourgeois Gentleman* dons his fancy suit with the upside-down flowers and, later, his Turkish gown and grotesque turban, he is proclaiming (foolishly) to his peers that he is a person of elegance and refinement. And Estragon's unlaced shoes in *Waiting for Godot* represent — pathetically to be sure — his great wish to be unfettered, not "tied to Godot" but simply free, fed, and happy.

Finally, the costume serves as wearable clothing for the actor! For a costume, of course, is indeed clothing; it must be functional as well as meaningful and aesthetic. The actor

IMPORTANCE OF SMALL DETAILS

The task of subtly distorting uniformity, without destroying the desired illusion, is a difficult one. Anton Chekhov's play *The Three Sisters* presents a case in point. The characters of the male players are clearly defined in Chekhov's writing, but because the men are all wearing military uniforms they are theoretically similar in appearance. One of the few ways in which the designer can help to differentiate between characters is by the alteration of proportion; alterations such as these, which do not show enough from the "front" to make the uniforms seem strange to the audience, can be extremely effective, as well as helpful to the actor. In a London production of *The Three Sisters*, Sir Michael Redgrave wore a coat with a collar that was too low; Sir John Gielgud one that was too high. No one in the audience was unaware of the characters' individuality, the talents of these actors being what they are, but the small details added to the scope of their performances.

– Motley

does not model his costume; he walks in it, sits in it, duels in it, dances in it, tumbles downstairs in it. Indeed, unless the character is a prisoner or a pauper, we are supposed to believe that he chose the costume himself and really *wants* to wear it! The costume designer thus cannot be content merely to draw pictures on paper but must also design workable, danceable, *actable* clothing, for which cutting, stitching, fitting, and quick changing are as important considerations as color coordination and historical context. Thus costume designers generally collaborate very closely with the actors they dress.

The Costume Designer at Work

The costume designer works primarily with fabric, which comes in a variety of materials and weaves and can be cut, shaped, stitched, colored, and draped in innumerable ways. Aside from fabric, jewels, armor, feathers, fur,

Costume and scenic elements need not necessarily be designed on paper and crafted in a shop. Found objects, such as those woven into the costumes of these two wonderful French street performers (collectively known as Groudeck), in *Le Temps Immobile*, can also have special visual impact.

hair (real or simulated), and metallic ornamentation commonly figure into costume design. The costume designer both selects and oversees the acquiring or building of costume elements, usually in combination. The costumes for some plays are assembled entirely out of items ready at hand. For contemporary plays with modern settings, the costumes are often selected from the actors' own wardrobes or from department store racks. Sometimes a costume designer will acquire clothing from thrift shops and used-clothing stores, particularly for plays set in the recent past; indeed, this is not unusual even for high-budget professional productions. In one celebrated instance, Louis Jouvet appealed to the citizens of Paris to donate costumes for the post-

humous premiere of Jean Giraudoux's *The Madwoman of Chaillot,* and the clothing that poured into the Athénée theatre for that brilliant 1945 Parisian production signaled to the world that France had survived the scourge of the Nazi Occupation with its devotion to the theatre intact.

Even in a "fully designed, fully built" production, some costume elements are usually purchased, rented, or taken from costume storage; shoes, for example, are not ordinarily built from scratch for theatrical productions. Nonetheless, it is those productions that are designed and built for a given set of performances that test the full measure of the costume designer's imagination and ability. In these productions, the costume designer can

Costume designs are normally drawn on paper or canvas before being built, and they are often annotated by the designer with construction details or actual fabric swatches. Many such drawings have come down to us through history, though the costumes (and swatches) have long disappeared. Jean Bérain (c. 1637–1711) has left us many colorful renderings, including this one of a costume for the character of Pluton in the 1680 "lyrical tragedy" (what we would today call an opera) of *Prosperine* by Jean-Baptiste Lully.

create a top-to-toe originality. The comprehensive design for such a production begins with a series of sketches and material choices — these usually proceed hand in hand — based on a thorough knowledge of the play, a clear agreement with the director on interpretation and style, research into necessary historical sources, and a firm understanding of the production monies and "build time" available to the costume shop. Generally, a separate costume sketch is made for each character, although choruses and extras are sometimes represented in a single sketch. Once approved, the sketches are developed into full-color renderings with sample fabric swatches attached. Construction details are frequently included on the rendering itself so that a single document conveys both the general look and specific construction of each costume.

The purchase of fabric is of course a crucial stage in costuming, for fabric is the basic medium of the costumer's art. Texture, weight, color, suppleness, and response to draping, dying, folding, crushing, twirling, and twisting are all considerations. Velvet and velveteen, silks and woolens are the costumer's luxury fabrics; cottons, felt, burlap, and even painted canvas are less expensive and often appropriate for theatrical use. Coloring, "aging" (making a new fabric appear old and used), and detailing are often achieved with dyes, appliqués, and embroidery and sometimes with paint, glues, and other special treatments (for example, the costume designers Motley — three women working under a single professional name — simulate leather by rubbing thick felt with moist yellow soap and spraying it down with brown paints). Frequently, of course, fabrics with designs printed, embossed, or woven in are purchased for women's costumes or for male period attire.

The cutting, fitting, draping, and stitching of original costumes are equally important steps in costume design. Most designers are very involved with all these procedures, for the cutting of a fabric determines the manner in which it drapes and moves, and the fitting and draping of a costume determines its shape and silhouette. Needless to say, cutters, stitchers, and drapers are full-time professionals in the theatre, and the designer must work in close collaboration with them to achieve worthy results. Fitting and stitching (as well as re-fitting, restitching, and often re-refitting and re-restitching) are part of the obligatory and time-consuming backstage process by which the costume becomes a wearable garment for the actor and the actor "grows into" the theatrically costumed characterization.

Finally, the accessories of costume can greatly affect the impact of the basic design; occasionally they may even stand out in such a way as to "make" the costume or to obliterate it. Hairstyles (including beards and mustaches) and headdresses, because they frame the actor's face, will convey a visual message every time the actor speaks a line; they are obviously of paramount importance. Jewelry, sashes, purses, muffs, and other adornments and badges of various sorts have considerable dramatic impact insofar as they "read" from the audience — that is, insofar as the audience can see them clearly and understand what they may signify about the character. The lowly shoe, if unwisely chosen, can de-

> ## The Third Dimension
>
> The great thing is the collaboration between the artist putting something down on paper, and the people who turn it into the third dimension.... who pick up the sketches and run with them. A costume sketch has to excite the people who are going to make the clothes. Also, it has to excite the people who are going to wear them. They're going to bring the character to life, and you give them the blocks to start the race with.
>
> — Jane Greenwood

stroy the artistry of a production, either by being unsuitable for the character or style of the play or by being so badly fitted (or so unwieldy) that the actor exhibits poor posture or even stumbles about the stage.

Whether arrived at through design and fabrication or through careful selection from the Army surplus store, good costume design creates a sense of character, period, style, and theatricality out of wearable garments. In

Left: Costumes are not always created from ordinary fabrics. Here, Janet Swenson has designed a garment of fishnet and flesh-colored latex, augmented by seashells, flotsam and jetsam, mottle-dyed spandex stretched over pieces of plastic, and hand-crocheted pieces of "hairy yarn" to created the blistered, bee-stung, and "fishified" flesh of the monstrous Caliban, as performed (and in part co-designed) by David Ivers for the 2001 Utah Shakespearean production of Shakespeare's *The Tempest.*

Above right: Costumes do not merely hang and cling; they move, sometimes spectacularly. In this 1997 English National Theatre production of the American musical *Lady in the Dark,* Maria Friedman plays the title role of Liza Elliot, a fashion editor who reenacts her dreams with a psychiatrist, revealing her suppressed desires. The costume, designed by Nicky Gillibrand (who won an Olivier nomination for this show), soars with her spirit – though her body remains grounded on earth.

Below right: When we first see Perdita, in Shakespeare's *The Winter's Tale,* she is disguised as Flora, the queen of a boisterous, rural sheep-shearing festival. In this 1997 production at London's Globe Theatre, Anna-Livia Ryan sports a spectacularly floral headdress and garlands of flowers, all designed by Tom Phillips.

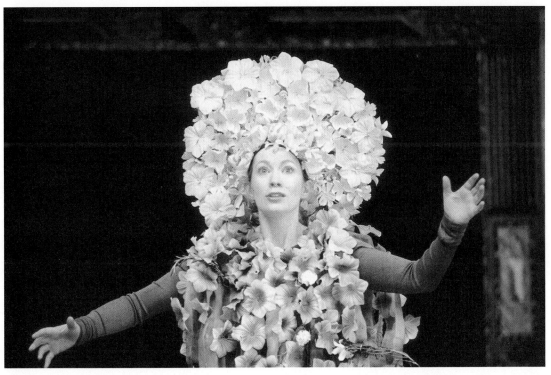

PHOTO ESSAY: BROADWAY DESIGNER PATRICIA ZIPPRODT

1.

For more than forty years, Patricia Zipprodt — working mainly in the sunny Greenwich Village penthouse apartment pictured on these pages — designed award-winning costumes for New York and regional theatres as well as opera and ballet companies, winning Tony Awards in design for the original Broadway production of *Fiddler on the Roof, Cabaret,* and *Sweet Charity.* She also received dozens of other awards and nominations for her fifty-five Broadway productions, including the world or American premieres of *Sunday in the Park with George, The Blacks, Plaza Suite, Shogun, Pippin, Chicago, Alice in Wonderland, Fools, Brighton Beach Memoirs, The Little Foxes, Mack and Mabel, 1776, Zorba, King of Hearts,* and *Picasso at the Lapin Agile* and revivals of *My Fair Lady* and her own *Cabaret* and *Fiddler on the Roof.* Additionally, she found time to design for films, television, ballet, opera, and ice skating spectaculars; to head the MFA costume program at Brandeis University; and to help found the National Theatre of the Deaf. Sadly, Ms. Zipprodt died in the summer of 1998, just as this photo essay was published (in the previous edition of this book), and within months of what turned out to be her final design, the Wilshire theatre (Los Angeles) production of *Picasso at the Lapin Agile* that the *Variety* critic praised as "evoking a wonderful sense of being in another time and place." The essay that follows is unchanged from the previous edition.

Born in Chicago, where she studied painting as a high school student at an annex of the famous Art Institute, Zipprodt headed for Wellesley College for premedical studies. After graduation, however, she moved to New York rather than going on to medical school. There she waited on

2.

3.

tables at Schrafft's and ushered at Carnegie Hall to pay the rent; at the same time, she resumed her painting studies at the Art Students League. But ballet and theatre soon competed for her attention, and discovering that "a play is a painting that moves," Zipprodt changed her medium from paint to fabric. After taking some classes at the Fashion Institute of Technology, she embarked on what was to become a legendary career. Beginning right at the top, she started her career by designing the highly successful Broadway production of Gore Vidal's *Visit to a Small Planet* in 1957, then two more Broadway shows the same year (*The Potting Shed* and *The Rope Dancers*), but all of these were small-cast, realistic modern plays, which Zipprodt termed "go to Macy's" jobs.

4.

Her original talent more fully emerged in the celebrated off-Broadway production of Jean Genet's *The Blacks* in 1962, which let to increasingly important assignments, ranging

from avant-garde theatre to major Broadway musicals — particularly those directed and choreographed by Bob Fosse, for whom she became an inextricable professional partner.

ZIPPRODT AT WORK: 1957–98

Zipprodt's achievements span virtually every dramatic style, but she is best known for

1. Shown here is costume designer Patricia Zipprodt in her New York studio. Behind her are masks and posters from her breakthrough production of Jean Genet's *The Blacks*, which she designed off-Broadway in 1962.

2. One of Zipprodt's most masterful designs was the Broadway *Sunday in the Park with George*, the first half of which details the life and, in part, the work of French artist Georges Seurat.

3. The rich textures of Zipprodt's costumes, shown in this detail, brought to life not only the play's period but Seurat's painting – the subject of the act – *La Grande Jatte*.

4. In 1998, forty-one years after her Broadway design debut, Zipprodt designed three productions for Washington's Arena Stage, including the one pictured here: Kaufman and Hart's classic and eccentric American comedy, *You Can't Take It With You*, directed by Douglas C. Wager.

5. Zipprodt's collection of fabrics includes literally thousands of swatches, which she keeps organized in a wall-sized color-coded "card catalogue" that forms the heart of her New York design studio.

5.

6.

7.

highly textured fabrics, aesthetically harmonious color balances, and meticulous research. Her working method begins with an assemblage of a huge "bible" of preliminary drawings and fabric swatches ("I think I must have done at least eighteen different sketches of the Tevye family [in *Fiddler on the Roof*], just to get going on them and find out who they were," she says). Zipprodt selects her fabrics — which may include cottons, rayons, silks, gold-threaded brocades, tie-dyes, muslins, leather — from the thousands she keeps on file in a wall cabinet in her studio. For color palettes, Zipprodt assembles onto a single sheet of black construction paper the major color swatches in each scene, to assess their harmony and avoid color clashes. Considering the number of costumes involved in a major production — her *Shogun* had over 350 — helps explain the importance of these steps.

Zipprodt finds that costume construction shops — which handle the cutting, stitching, dyeing, and assemblage of costumes — are better now than at any time in memory: "What we're having now is a renaissance of skilled artisans." And she appreciates the ensemble work that theatre artistry provides. "I love the process. I think we are very privileged people . . . to be able to start something every time and not know what we are going to do . . . [to] put a whole new network of people together and start again on the process. It is thrilling to work constantly and collaboratively in that kind of newness and fresh discovery, because who else has that opportunity, except those of us in the theatre?"

6. Zipprodt collects swatches and paint samples on a single "color palette" for each scene in the plays she designs so that she can keep track of color complementarity and balance for each one. This example is from *Shogun.*

7. For the Broadway musical *Shogun,* Zipprodt designed over 350 costumes, many with fabrics purchased in Japan. This sketch is one of hundreds in her collection.

harmony with scenery, makeup, and lighting and with the play's interpretation and performance, costuming can have its maximum impact in a subtle way — by underlining the play's meaning and the characters' personalities — or it can scream for attention and sometimes even become the "star of the show." Not a few musicals have succeeded primarily because the audience "came out whistling the costumes," as a Shubert Alley phrase reminds us. Certainly the magnificently attired principals of Chinese Opera, the gloriously patchworked Arlecchino of the commedia dell'arte, and the stunningly garbed black-and-white mannequins of Cecil Beaton's creation in *My Fair Lady* have dominated stages past and present. But even in the most naturalistic drama, well-designed and well-chosen costumes can exert a magical theatrical force, lending a special magnitude to the actor's and the playwright's art.

Makeup

Makeup, which is essentially the design of the actor's face, occupies a curiously paradoxical position in the theatre. In much modern production, certainly in the realistic theatre, makeup seems sorely neglected. It tends to be the last design technology to be considered; indeed, it is often applied for the first time at the final dress rehearsal — and sometimes not until just before the opening performance. Indeed, makeup is the only major design element whose planning and execution are often left entirely to the actor's discretion. And yet, ironically, makeup is one of the archetypal arts of the theatre, absolutely fundamental to the origins of drama. The earliest chanters of the dithyramb, like the spiritual leaders of primitive tribes today, invariably made themselves up — probably by smearing their faces with blood or the dregs of wine — in preparation for the performance of their holy rites: their resulting makeup subsequently inspired the Greek tragic and comic masks that are today the universal symbols of theatre itself. The ancient art of face painting remains crucial to the Chinese Opera as well as to other traditional Asian, African, and Native American theatre forms.

The reason for this paradox resides in the changing emphasis of theatre aims. Makeup, like costuming, serves both ceremonial and illustrative functions. The illustrative function of makeup is unquestionably the more obvious one today — so much so that we often forget its ceremonial role entirely. Illustrative makeup is the means by which the actor changes her or his appearance to resemble that of the character — or at least the appearance of the character as author, director, and actor imagine it. Makeup of this sort is particularly useful in helping to make a young actor look older or an old one look younger and in making an actor of any age resemble a known historical figure or a fictitious character whose appearance is already set in the public imagination. Makeup gives Cyrano his great nose and Bardolph his red one; it reddens *Macbeth*'s "bleeding captain" and blackens Laurence Olivier's Othello; it turns the college sophomore into the aged Prospero, the Broadway dancer into one of T. S. Eliot's cats, and Miss Cathy Rigby into Master Peter Pan. Artificial scars, deformities, bruises, beards, wigs, sunburn, frostbite, and scores of other facial embellishments, textures, and shadings can contribute significantly to realistic stage-craft when needed or desired.

A subtler use of makeup, but still within the realistic mode, is aimed at the evocation of psychological traits through physiognomic clues: the modern makeup artist may try to suggest character by exaggerating or distort-ing the actor's natural eye placement, the size and shape of her mouth, the angularity of her nose, or the tilt of her eyebrows. There can be no question that we do form impressions of a character's inner state on the basis of observ-able physical characteristics — as Caesar no-tices and interprets Cassius's "lean and hungry look," so do we. And the skilled makeup artist can go far in enhancing the psychological texture of a play by the imaginative use of fa-cial shapings and shadings.

Still another use of makeup, also within the realistic and practical spectrum, seeks merely to simplify and embolden the actor's features in order to make them distinct and expres-sive to every member of the audience. Using a theatre term mentioned earlier, this is known as creating a face that "reads" to the house — a face that conveys its fullest expression over a great distance. To achieve this effect the makeup artist exaggerates highlights and shad-ows and sharply defines specific features such as wrinkles, eyelashes, eyebrows, and jawlines. Such simplified, emboldened, and subtly exag-gerated makeup, combined with stage light-ing, creates an impression of realism far greater than any that could be achieved by makeup or lighting alone; in fact, most directors and actors consider a minimum level of makeup to be a necessity, if only to prevent the actor from looking washed out in the glare of the stage lights.

Yet none of these realistic or practical uses of makeup truly touches upon its original the-

atrical use, which was aimed at announcing the actor as a performer and at establishing a milieu for acting that was neither realistic nor practical but rather supernatural, mysteri-ous, and calculatedly theatrical. For it was the ritual makeup of the chanters of the dithy-ramb — and the face painting of the ancient Chinese actor — that endowed them with the same aspect of spiritual transcendence that warpaint provides for the celebrant of tribal rituals: by making himself "up," the actor was preparing to ascend to a higher world; he was self-consciously assuming something of the power and divinity of the gods, and he was

Above left: Dionysis Fotopoulos' costumes for Peter Hall's extraordinary ten-hour production of John Barton's Greek-themed *Tantalus,* premiering at the Denver Center Theatre in 2000, combined ancient and modern designs in enacting the myriad myths of Odysseus and his followers. Behind the full-face masks of Aegisthus and Clytemnestra are Robert Petkoff and Annalee Jefferies.

Above: Glenn Close's makeup and costume define the character of Norma Desmond as living in her past, as a star of the silent screen, though the play – Broadway's 1994 production of *Sunset Boulevard* – is set in much more recent times.

Below: A makeup artist carefully applies luxuriant eye makeup to a stage performer.

THE MAKEUP KIT

Basic makeup consists of a foundation, color shadings, and various special applications. The foundation is a basic color that is applied thinly and evenly to the face and neck and sometimes to other parts of the body as well. Creme makeup, formerly (and still commonly) known as grease-paint, is a traditional foundation material; a highly opaque and relatively inexpensive skin paint, it comes in a variety of colors. Cake makeup, or "pancake" as it is also known, is another type of foundation; it is less messy than creme but also less flexible. Cake makeup comes in small plastic cases and is applied with a damp sponge. Most theatrical foundation colors are richer and deeper than the actor's normal skin color so as to counteract the white and blue tones of stage lights.

Color shading defines the facial structure and exaggerates its dimensions so as to give the face a sculptured appearance from a distance; ordinarily, the least imposing characteristics of the face are put in shadow and the prominent features are highlighted. Shading colors – universally called "liners" – come in both creme and cake form and are usually chosen to harmonize with the foundation color, as well as with the color of the actor's costume and the color of the lighting. Shadows are made with darker colors and highlights with lighter ones; both are applied with small brushes and blended into the foundation. Rouge, a special color application used to redden lips and cheeks, is usually applied along with the shading colors. When greasepaints are used, the makeup must be dusted with makeup powder to "set" it and prevent running. A makeup pencil is regularly used to darken eyebrows and also to accentuate eyes and facial wrinkles.

Special applications may include false eyelashes or heavy mascara, facial hair (beards and mustaches, ordinarily made from crepe wool), nose putty and various other prosthetic materials, and various treatments for aging, wrinkling, scarring, and otherwise disfiguring the skin. A well-equipped actor has a makeup kit stocked with glue (spirit gum and liquid latex), solvents, synthetic hair, wax (to mask eyebrows), and hair whiteners – in addition to the standard foundation and shading colors – to create a wide variety of makeup effects.

Dean Mogle's witty costuming for the Fool in the 1999 Utah Shakespearean Festival production of *King Lear* employs masklike makeup, as well as masklike "knee pads," to capture the highly performative role of this almost metatheatrical character, portrayed by Jered Tanner.

an even wider spectrum for the circus clown. Avant-garde and expressionist playwrights also frequently utilize similar sorts of abstracted makeup, as does French dramatist Jean Genet in *The Blacks* (which features black actors in clownish white-face) and German playwright Peter Handke (whose *Kaspar* features stylized facial painting similar to Genet's conception). And Asian theatre has always relied on the often dazzling facial coloring (and manelike wigs and beards) of certain characters in Japanese kabuki, Indian kathakali, and Chinese Opera — not to mention the violently expressive makeup often seen in contemporary avant-garde productions in Tokyo. The American theatre, which so far has witnessed only a small sampling of stylized makeup, is perhaps due for an awakening to this fascinating approach to theatrical design.

In most cases, makeup and hairstyle design fall to the costume designer, whose final renderings include all aspects of the character's appearance. But because the actual makeup is normally applied night-by-night by each actor, the costume designer, director, and actor often collaborate on the precise makeup details. In the Broadway production of *Cats,* for example, John Napier designed the makeup for each "cat" along with its costume and worked with each actor to "tweak" that design for maximum individual expression. For highly complicated makeup, however, specialist designers may be employed, such as Jon Dodd, who designed the beast's prosthetics in *Beauty and the Beast* in collaboration with costume designer Ann Hould-Ward, and Jean Begin, who designed the highly stylized makeup of the Cirque du Soleil's *Saltimbanco.* Specialists in hair and wig design are also engaged for major Broadway productions, such as David H. Lawrence for *Guys and Dolls,* Angela Gari for *Carousel,* and Paul Huntley for *Once upon a Mattress* and *Laughter on the 23rd Floor.* Still, makeup, because it must be reapplied for every performance, also relies in most

moreover offering to guide the audience on a divine adventure.

Today one still sees some obvious examples of such traditional makeup and "making up," particularly in European and Asian theatre. The makeup of the circus and the classic mime, two formats that developed in Europe out of the masked commedia dell'arte of centuries past, both use bold colors: white, black, and sometimes red for the mimist and cases on the actor's ability to execute the design — and the makeup kit is a fundamental part of each actor's professional equipment.

The realistic and symbolic functions of makeup are probably always combined to some extent in the theatre, for even the most stylized makeup is ultimately based on the human form and even the most realistic makeup conveys an obvious theatricality. The theatre, after all, is never very far from human concerns, nor is it ever so immersed in the ordinary that it is completely mistaken for such. When the American actor sits at a makeup table opening little bottles and tubes, moistening Chinese brushes, and sharpening eyebrow pencils, more is going on than simple, practical face-making: atavistic forces are at work, linking the actor not merely to the imagined physiognomy of his or her character or to the demands of facial projection in a large arena but also, and more fundamentally, to the primitive celebrants who in ages past painted their faces to assure the world that they were leaving their temporal bodies and boldly venturing into the exalted domain of gods.

Sound Design

Music and sound effects have been in use in the theatre since ancient times; Aristotle considered music one of the six essential components of tragedy, and offstage thunder, trumpet "flourishes" and "tuckets," and "a strange hollow and confused noise" are all called for in Shakespeare's original stage directions. Since at least the Renaissance, theatres have been equipped routinely with such devices as rain drums (axis-mounted barrels that, partly filled with pebbles or dried seeds, made rain sounds when revolved), thundersheets (hanging sheets of tin that rumbled ominously when rattled), and thunder runs (sloping wooden troughs down which cannonballs rolled and eventually crashed). Since 1900, most theatres have

also used an electric telephone ringer (a battery-powered bell mounted on a piece of wood) and a door slammer (a miniature doorframe and door, complete with latch) to simulate the sounds of domestic life. All of these "sound effects" were ordinarily created by an assistant stage manager, among many other duties. But the development of audio recording and playback technologies in the 1970s and 80s has led to a virtual revolution in the area of sound design and the emergence of an officially designated sound designer in theatres around the world. As with musical underscoring in cinema and sound balancing and enhancement in rock concerts, theatre sound is now almost entirely an electronic art.

Augmented sound is now routinely used in theatrical performances. Musical theatre and larger theatres increasingly employ electronic sound enhancement to reinforce the actors' voices and create a "louder than life" sonic ambiance for certain plays; usually, in such cases, the actors wear miniature wireless microphones (ordinarily concealed in their hair). The use of live or recorded offstage sounds may establish locale (such as foghorns), time of day (midnight chimes), time of year (birdsong), weather conditions (thunder and rain), and onstage or offstage events in the play (a ringing telephone, an arriving taxi, an angel crashing through the ceiling). Music, as well as sound, is often used to evoke a mood, support an emotion, intensify an action, or provide a transition into or between scenes. Stage sounds can be realistic (an ambulance siren), stylized (an increasingly amplified heartbeat), stereophonically localized (an airplane crossing overhead from one side of the stage to another), or pervasive and "in-your-head" (a buzzing mosquito). Music accompanying a play can be composed for the production and played "live" during the performance or derived from (legally acquired and paid-for) copyrighted recordings, which are then played back through a theatre's sound system (or, sometimes, through onstage "prop" boom boxes). Naturally, many combinations are possible. The sound designer designs and oversees the implementation of all of these elements, and, particularly if she or he is also the play's musical composer, this work may be of immense importance in the overall production.

Sound design has rapidly escalated in importance over the past two decades as playwrights and directors have sought to incorporate the new sound technologies that have swiftly expanded the theatrical potential, first with audio tape recording, which permitted accurate recording and playback; then with audio cartridges, which provided exact cuing of individual sounds; and most recently with digital samplers, which permit an operator to program dozens of individually recorded sounds onto a control keyboard, where each can be instantly recalled and played, individually or in any combination, simply by pressing the appropriate keys, which are, moreover, volume responsive, as are those on a piano. Almost any sound can be programmed into a sampler, except for gunshots — which are usually performed "live," with blanks, because they are too loud for most sound systems and all but impossible to synchronize with the necessarily simultaneous fireflash.[1]

Contemporary sound design is not without its detractors. The electronic amplification of speaking and singing voices in most Broadway musicals, and many nonmusical plays as well, is often derided by critics who prefer — or claim to prefer — the more natural unamplified sound. The sound mixing board, which is now commonplace in the back orchestra rows of most Broadway and larger regional theatres, is a visual reminder of the modern technology that some feel mediates the "liveness" of "live theatre." Extended musical underscoring in some plays raises objections that

---

[1]*Note:* Any stage gunshot, even with blanks, must meet precise conditions specified by authorized fire and safety officers.

it turns drama into cinema and suffuses the articulation of ideas in the syrup of generalized emotion. Nonetheless, sound design — as well as original music composition — is definitely here to stay.

Special Effects

Theatre "magic" implies special effects not easily described as simply lighting or sound, such as fire, explosions, sudden apparitions, mysterious disappearances ("Witches vanish," Shakespeare writes in a stage direction in *Macbeth*), fog, smoke, wind, rain, snow, lightning, and a whole host of blood effects — all of which must be accomplished, of course, without burning down the theatre or puncturing the actors. (For it was the firing-off of an offstage cannon that burned down Shakespeare's Globe Theatre in 1613!) Commercial devices can achieve all of these effects, but each requires its own on-the-spot ingenuity to be both credible and effective. There are also one-of-a-kind tricks, such as having Hans's armor suddenly fall off his body in Jean Giraudoux's *Ondine*, that must be individually designed and perfected. Effects designers are not universally employed in the theatre, but their day may not be long off.

Computer Technologies in Theatre Design

Designers — like other visual artists — have always used the technologies available to them. For centuries, designers have worked with such basic drawing implements as charcoal, colored paints, rulers, squares, and drafting tables. Complicated "drawing machines" came into play during the Renaissance: Leonardo da Vinci invented a "perspectograph" to help artists transform their perceived earthly realities into two-dimensional sketches and engravings in the early 1500s, and Caneletto's

Theatrical smoke is commonly used with stage lighting to provide atmospheric and supernatural effects, and also to create a level of stylization that permits a suspension of realism – as in a battle scene which would be dangerous to stage with greater physical authenticity. Here, smoke and lighting combine to create the chaos and violence of battle in the Utah Shakespearean Festival production of *War of the Roses*, a compilation by Howard Jensen of Shakespeare's three plays of *Henry VI*. Lighting by Donna Ruzika.

the mid-1980s, computer-aided design (CAD) and computer-aided manufacture (CAM) had become securely established by the 1990s as the fastest growing technology of the current stage.

What do computers offer over pencil and paper? Computers don't think and can't create. Nor can they analyze a text, imagine an environment, suggest a costume, conceive a style, or even make an audience laugh. But what they can do is aid those artists who can do these things. In its capacity for combining and configuring (and then reconfiguring) ideas, angles, shapes, colors, spaces, perspectives, and measurements, which designers uncover through research or create through imagination, the computer consolidates a vast realm of experimental possibilities with the technical assurance of a mathematician or an engineer. Perhaps no "machine" of any era has so successfully counterpoised reality's hard facts with the artist's free-floating imagination.

Computers are useful — and becoming invaluable — to the contemporary designer on a variety of levels. First, they can assist with or even replace much of the drudgery of sheer drawing mechanics. With a click of the mouse, straight lines, angles, circles, shapes, colors, and typefaces can be selected from a menu of choices and placed where desired. Moreover, all of these design elements can be reconfigured in an instant: colors can be changed, lines lengthened, walls thickened, floors raised, furniture moved, sightlines adjusted, dimensions measured, and texts edited and resized. Individual design elements can be instantly replicated: an elaborately drawn banister post can become a dozen such posts in a matter of seconds. Indeed, whole drawings can be rescaled, zoomed in or out on, printed and reprinted. Whole designs — or designated portions of them — can be rotated or relocated freely about the page. And working designs can be instantly sent around the world by digital electronic transmission. Instant and virtually unlimited "clean" revisions and

detailed paintings of eighteenth-century Venice were executed with the aid of a room-sized "camera obscura." The computer of today is only the most recent in a long list of technological tools used by visual artists, but it is a tool of far-reaching potential for the theatre. Becoming widespread in industry in instantaneous communications are the hallmarks of the computer revolution, in art as well as in text processing.

Second, computers enable designers to draw upon vast visual databases: virtual libraries of art that can be found in commercial clip-art palettes or on CD-ROMs; designers themselves may create such libraries and store them for later use. These libraries give instant access to thousands of existing drawings and photos — such as "virtual catalogues" of eighteenth-century chandeliers, Victorian drapery, or Roman statuary — which have been digitized for computer retrieval and can be, subject to legal copyright considerations, incorporated into stage designs. Computerized data banks have already revolutionized costume management in theatre shops and film studios, permitting designers to access pictures of, for example, hundreds of blouses currently available in various wardrobe collections. Computerized libraries are also replacing the plastic templates used by scenic and lighting designers to configure furniture on the set or lighting instruments on the light pipes, saving many hours of painstaking pencil and plastic copywork, particularly when multiple revisions are necessary. Yet far more advanced computing capabilities are now coming into the art and craft of theatre design.

Third, computerized cutting and pasting allow the designer to combine visual forms on the screen; for example, a costume designer can "virtually sew" the sleeves of one garment onto another without requiring a single stitch; a wig designer can have an actor "virtually try on" wigs by combining a photo of the actor with drawings of wigs of different colors and styles — all without having to buy a single strand of hair or calling the actor in for a fitting. Actors, indeed, can be "virtually dressed" in entire costume designs long before any fabric is purchased.

Fourth, computerized scenographic modeling supplements traditional ground-plan and elevation drawings by creating, on a computer screen, three-dimensional models of the stage set that can demonstrate perspectives from any vantage: from the left, right, and center of the house or from a bird's-eye position that may clarify lighting and offstage storage positions. With sufficient computing power and memory, designers, directors, and actors can then "walk through" the designed set, which at that point exists only as a "virtual reality," not as a hard construction of steel, wood, and fabric. Although computing equipment for such modeling is expensive, it is surely — in the long run — much cheaper than building and rebuilding stage scenery until it's just right. And integrated computer design — which might enable a design team to design a scenic model, inhabit it with actors wearing designed costumes, and throw colored light upon the scene from precisely calibrated lighting positions — is already with us in some places and is likely to become a regular part of design conferences in many new theatres over the coming decade. The opportunity to "storyboard" scenery, costumes, and lighting, together with text and music and sound, is an extraordinary advance in the art of production planning wherever time and money are involved, as they almost always are.

Finally, dedicated database programs permit lighting and sound technicians to save innumerable hours in storing, sorting, and printing the dozens of dimmer schedules, cue sheets, and loudspeaker assignments needed in multiproduction repertory assignments.

Will computer-aided design reduce the creativity and imagination that go into the designer's art? Veteran designers often voice this concern, apprehensive about the encroachment of binary numbers and microelectronics on what has generally been considered a more freehand, soul-expressive art. But there is little question that by the arrival of the twenty-first century most young designers are trained in — and employ — a wide variety of CAD techniques, and many senior designers are switching over to them as well. Imagination, most designers now believe, is not a function of one's tools — pen and paper or keyboard and screen — but of the mind that guides them.

Computer adherents are resoundingly supportive of the computer revolution. To its professional devotees, computers are tools — superpencils, really — not ends in themselves; they provoke experimentation and innovation as well as (or even in lieu of) mere craft precision and mechanics. The computer age has, of course, long since arrived in all major areas of commerce and culture, and it already has a substantial history in the theatre; indeed, one of the first commercial uses of computing was in theatrical lighting, which has been largely computerized since at least the mid-1960s. And the theatre has been one of the testing places for many of the world's emerging technologies, including hydraulic elevators, gas lighting, electricity, and air conditioning. It seems inevitable that the computer screen will become a principal conveyor of design creativity and communication in the immediate years to come.

Technical Production

We shall end this chapter with a discussion of theatre technicians. Far outnumbering all the others — actors, designers, writers, and directors put together — they are the artisans or "technologists" who get the production organized, built, installed, lit, and ready to open, and who then make it run.

Because of their numbers, theatrical technicians are ordinarily marshaled into a hierarchical structure, headed by stage, house, and production managers, technical directors, and shop supervisors, all of whom are charged with guiding and supervising the work of a virtual army of craftspersons. A typical breakdown of these functions — which you might find detailed in the theatre program of any major theatre — could be something like this:

The production manager (PM) is a position that has grown mightily in importance over the past two decades. The PM coordinates the scheduling, staffing, and budgeting of every element of the production, from the acting rehearsals to the building, installation ("load-in"), and operation ("running") of all the design and technical elements. Expert in legal codes, safety procedures, and accounting policies and sensitive to the varying artistic needs of actors, directors, designers, and technicians, the PM wrestles with the complex problems of integrating the play's disparate elements, determining, for example, whether the lights should be hung and focused before or after the scenery is installed (there can be reasons for going either way on this), and anticipating how long it will take to train the stage crew or set the light cues.

The stage manager (SM), now often called the production stage manager (PSM), has the highly responsible position of coordinating the director's work with that of the actors and the technical and design departments. At the beginning of rehearsals, the SM is involved primarily in organizational work: scheduling calls and appointments, recording the blocking of actors, anticipating technical problems of quick costume changes, set shifts, and the like, and organizing the basic "calling" of the show — that is, the system by which lighting, sound, and scene-shift cues are initiated. During performance, the SM actually runs the show, having final authority over the entire onstage and backstage operation; moreover, it is the SM who ordinarily conducts understudy and replacement rehearsals in a professional run and who assumes the functions of the director when the director is absent or no longer employed by the production.

Working for the stage manager are normally one or more assistant stage managers. In rehearsals, ASMs typically will set out props, follow the script and prompt actors who are "off book" (no longer rehearsing with script in hand) if they forget their lines, take line notes when actors say lines incorrectly, and substitute for actors who may be temporarily away, as at costume fittings. During performance, with the stage manager normally calling the show from a booth above the audience, ASMs — on their two-way headset connections — implement the SM's calls by transmitting them as visual "go" signs for scene shifts, actor entrances, and effect cues. ASMs also serve as the backstage eyes and ears of the SM, who is out front, watching the stage.

The technical director (TD) is generally in charge of the building and operation of scenery and stage machinery and is often in charge of the lighting crews as well. The TD must oversee the moving of scenery into and out of the theatre; ensure that all technical departments have adequate "stage time" to do their jobs; establish policies and directives for scene shifting, special effects, and "strike" (the final removal of scenery from the theatre after a run); and, most important, make certain that everything is ready on time — no small order considering the massive technical complexities of theatre today.

Working in the scene shop, normally under the TD, a shop foreman, or a scenery supervisor, are carpenters (and master carpenters) and scenic artists (painters), with welders required when steel — commonly used today for weight-bearing constructions — is to be joined. In the costume shop, a wider array of specialists are required (though many costume designers and technologists assume more than one of these roles):

- the costume director (or costume shop manager), who coordinates the entire operation, supervising personnel, work spaces, and schedules.

- dyers, who dye fabrics to the color specified by the design and may also be skilled at fabric painting, aging, distressing, and other fabric modifications.

- drapers, who drape fabrics on an actor, or a dummy, testing and choosing the way the fabric falls — either with the grain or on the bias — to create the desired look of the eventual garment both at rest and on a moving (and possibly dancing, tumbling, or fencing) actor.

- cutters, who cut the fabric according to the selected grain direction, either from a flat paper pattern or with no pattern at all, often first on a cheap muslin prototype. (Most often today, draping and cutting are performed by the same person: a draper/cutter).

- first hands, who, working directly for the cutter, correct the pattern after the muslin prototype has been fitted to the actor and then "hand off" the work to the stitchers.

- stitchers, who sew the garment.

- craft specialists, who make costumes or costume elements involving more than fabric — such as armor, belts, masks, and so forth. Specific specialists as milliners may be added to make hats, and cobblers to make shoes. Other specialists may also be involved in distressing costume elements (making them look older and well-used) or adding decorations — badges, military ribbons, gold braid, and the like.

- hairstylists and wigmakers, who coif the actors as the designers specify.

- wardrobe supervisors ensure that costumes are delivered to the appropriate backstage areas during dress rehearsals and performances, and that costumes are cleaned and maintained during the run of a show. Wardrobe (or storage) supervisors and technicians also oversee the costume storage area, and help determine which existing costumes can be taken from storage and rebuilt to serve a new design.

- dressers, who work backstage during dress rehearsals and performances, helping the actors when necessary with quick-changes between the scenes.

In the area of lighting, master electricians and electricians hang, focus, and gel (put color media in) lights prior and during technical rehearsals, and maintain the lighting technology during the run of a show, while trained lighting-board and follow-spot operators execute the lighting cues called by the stage manager. For the sound department, one or more sound engineers works with the sound designer in recording the sound cues and placing the speakers, and a sound-board operator executes the cues during technical and dress rehearsals and performances. And in the makeup room, makeup artists may provide assistance to actors requiring it, or they may indeed apply full makeup to the actors as specified by the designers.

Each of these "backstage" technicians plays an absolutely crucial role in theatrical presentation — and the "stage fright" of the actor playing Hamlet is not necessarily any greater than that of the stagehand who must pull the curtain. For backstage work, though technical, is never simply mechanical, and every stage production poses a host of problems and situations in each area that are new to the people who deal with them and, sometimes, new to the theatre itself. Technological innovation takes place when a sound knowledge of craft combines with creative imagination in the face of unanticipated problems. The technical artists of the theatre have always manifested an impressive ingenuity at meeting unprecedented challenges in creative ways. Each of the theatre's shops — scene shop, costume shop, prop shop, and makeup room — is therefore a creative artistic studio, and a teaching laboratory for all its members, as well as a theatrical support unit.

Indeed, in contemporary theatre, particularly under the influences of Bertolt Brecht and then postmodernism, the theatre's technology — such as lighting instruments and sound-enhancing devices — has increasingly been taken out of hiding and placed right on the stage itself. And, with follow-spot operators (and sometimes stage managers) often placed in direct public view, sound operators plopped right in the midst of the audience, and *Lion King* puppeteers visibly manipulating their animals right on the stage, the theatre's technicians themselves have increasingly been drawn into direct public awareness — in some cases, with the "backstage" crew taking onstage curtain calls with the rest of the cast. A popular fascination with technology, together with a diminishing interest in stage "magic" or naturalistic illusion, has led to a scenography that deliberately incorporates technology as a visible aesthetic component of the theatre itself. Given this trend and the theatre's increasing use of the most recent technical innovations — lasers and holograms, air casters, large-screen video, motorized lights and projections, to name but a few — the theatre technologist is becoming widely recognized (as cinematographers are in cinema) as not merely implementers but as full-fledged stage artists and creators.

Throughout history, theatrical crafts have been learned through apprenticeship; even today, although beginning theatre technologists are often trained in universities before their first employment, much of their learning is necessarily on the job, as each job is somewhat unique to the play that prompts it. And although written and unwritten "textbooks" of stage practice can illustrate the traditional means of building a flat, cutting a pattern, organizing a rehearsal, laying out a prop table, and painting a prop, it is artistic sensitivity that ultimately determines the technical quality of a production, and it is artistic imagination that brings about the technical and technological advances that furthers theatrical creativity.

6

The Director

The room is already filled with people when she enters, a bit fussily, with a bundle of books and papers under her arm. Expectation, tension, and even a hint of panic can be sensed behind the muffled greetings, loose laughter, and choked conversation that greet her arrival.

She sits, and an assistant arranges chairs. Gradually, starting at the other end of what has suddenly become "her" table, the others seat themselves. An edgy silence descends. Where are they going? What experiences lie ahead? What risks, what challenges, are to be demanded? What feelings, in the coming weeks and months, are going to be stirred to poignant reality?

Only she knows — and if she doesn't, no one does. It is in this silence, tender with hope and fear, that the director breaks ground for the production. It is here that plan begins to become work and idea begins to become art. It is the peak moment of directing and of the director.

This is an idealized picture, to be sure. There are many directors who deliberately avoid invoking an impression of "mystique" and whose primary efforts are directed toward dispelling awe, dread, or any form of personal tension among their associates. Nonetheless, the picture holds a measure of truth for every theatrical production, for the art of directing is an exercise in leadership, imagination, and control; in the director's hands, finally, rest

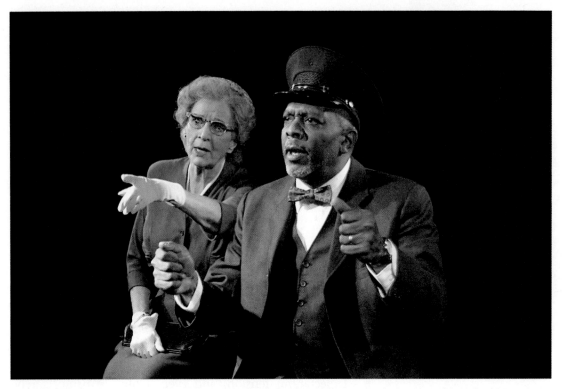

Directing is often a job of suggestion. In *Driving Miss Daisy,* the playwright portrays the growing relationship between an elderly southern Jewish woman and her African American chauffeur; director J. R. Sullivan here stages their developing affection as well as the car in which they're driving and what they're seeing outside their windshield. Patricia Fraser plays Daisy and Ernest Perry, Jr., plays the chauffeur, Hoke, in this 2000 Utah Shakespearean Festival production.

the aspirations, neuroses, skills, and ideas of the entire theatrical company.

Directing is an art whose product is the most ambiguous, perhaps the most mysterious, in the theatre. The direction of a play is not visible like scenery or costumes; and unlike the actor's voice or the sound designer's score, it cannot be directly heard or sensed. And yet direction underlies everything we see and hear in the theatre. Utterly absorbed by the final theatrical experience, direction animates and defines that experience. A whole class of theatrical artists in our time have reached international eminence in this particular art. But what, exactly, is involved?

At the *technical* level, the director is the person who organizes the production. This involves scheduling the work process and supervising the acting, designing, staging, and technical operation of the play. This is the easiest part of the directorial function.

At the more fundamental, *artistic,* level, the director inspires a creation of theatre with each production. He or she conceptualizes the play, gives it vision and purpose — both social and aesthetic — and inspires the company of artists to join together in collaboration.

It is in the conjunction of these levels, the technical and the artistic, that each director defines the directorial function anew. And it is with one foot in each that the director creates — through an adroit synthesis of text, materials, and available talent — a unique and vivid theatrical experience.

The Arrival of the Director: A Historical Overview

Directing has been going on ever since theatre began, but there has not always been a director — that is, there has not always been a sole individual specifically charged with directorial functions and responsibilities. The evolution of the director as an independent theatre artist, less than a century ago, has had as much to do with the development of modern theatre as has any dramatic innovation. The gradual process of this evolution can be roughly divided into three phases.

Phase One: The Teacher-Directors

In the earliest days of the theatre and for some time thereafter, directing was considered a form of teaching. The Greeks called the director the *didaskalos,* which means "teacher," and in medieval times the director's designation, in all the various European languages, was "master." The underlying assumption of teaching, of course, is that the teacher already knows and understands the subject; the teacher's task is simply to transmit that knowledge to others. The earliest directors, therefore, were simply asked to pass along the accumulated wisdom and techniques of "correct" performance within a "given" convention. Often the playwrights themselves served as directors, for who would be better qualified to "teach" a play than the person who wrote it? In one famous dramatic scene, Molière delightfully depicts himself directing one of his own plays; this is surely an effective model of the author-teacher-director for the seventeenth century and indeed for much of the theatre's history.

The teacher-director reached a pinnacle of influence, albeit anonymously, during the late Enlightenment and the Victorian era — during the eighteenth and nineteenth centuries — partly in response to the remarkable fascination of those times with science, scientific method, and humanistic research: the same dedication to rationalism that fostered a profusion of libraries, museums, and historic preservation also emphasized accuracy, consistency, and precision in the arts. The temper of the times led to major directorial changes in the theatre. For on the one hand audiences were demanding revivals of classic plays — whose authors were no longer around to direct them — and on the other hand they were demanding that these revivals be historically edifying, that they have a museumlike authenticity. All of this required research, organization, and comprehensive coordination; in other words, it demanded an independent director.

Most of the directors of this time — virtually all of them until the latter part of the nineteenth century — received no more recognition for their efforts than the museum director who created historical dioramas. Sometimes the directing was attributed to a famous acting star, such as the Englishman Charles Kean or the American Edwin Booth, when in fact the work was done by a lesser functionary; in Booth's case, for example, one D. W. Waller was the true director, but his name was all but buried in the program and never appeared in the reviews or publicity. Nevertheless, these teacher-directors who labored largely in the shadows began the art of directing as we know it today. They organized their productions around specific concepts, independently arrived at, and they dedicated themselves to creating unified and coherent theatrical works by "directing" an ensemble of actors, designers, and technicians toward established ends.

Phase Two: The Realistic Directors

The second stage in the development of modern-day directing began toward the end of the nineteenth century and brought to the fore a group of directors who restudied the conventions of theatrical presentation and strove in various ways to make them more lifelike. George II, Duke of Saxe-Meiningen, was the first of this breed and is generally regarded as the first modern director. The duke, who headed a provincial troupe of actors in his rural duchy, presented a series of premieres and classical revivals throughout Europe during the late 1870s and 1880s that were dazzling in their harmonized acting, staging, and scenery. Although still historically "correct," the duke's productions featured an ensemble of performances rather than a hierarchy of "star, support, and supernumerary." All of his performers were vigorously rehearsed toward the development of individual, realistically conceived roles — which were then played out in highly organic, even volatile, patterns of dramatic action. The stodgy lineup of spear carriers that had traditionally looked on while the star recited center stage was conspicuously absent from the Meiningen productions; so was the "super" who was customarily hired on the afternoon of performance, squeezed into a costume, and set upon the stage like so much living scenery. The totality of the Meiningen theatre aesthetic, embracing acting, interpretation, and design, was acclaimed throughout Europe: when the Meiningen troupe ceased touring in 1890, the position of a director who would organize and rehearse an entire company toward a complexly and comprehensively fashioned theatrical presentation was firmly established.

In 1887 André Antoine began a movement of greater realism in Paris with his Théâtre Libre, and Konstantin Stanislavsky initiated his even more celebrated Moscow Art Theatre in 1898. Both of these directors, amateurs like the duke of Saxe-Meiningen at the start of their careers, went on to develop wholly innovative techniques in acting and actor-coaching based on the staging concepts of the duke; both also theorized and worked pragmatically at the organizing of theatre companies, the development of a dramatic repertory, the re-education of theatregoing audiences, and the re-creation of an overall aesthetic of the theatre. Although both Antoine and Stanislavsky

were known primarily as naturalists — somewhat to their disadvantage, perhaps, for they had many other interests as well — they were above all idealists who sought to make the theatre a powerful social and artistic instrument for the expression of truth. Their ideals and their commitment virtually forced them to expand the directorial function into an all-encompassing and inspirational art.

The importance of these directors — and of certain other pioneers of the same spirit, including Harley Granville-Barker in England, David Belasco in America, and Otto Brahm in Germany — was not merely that they fostered the developing realist and naturalist drama but also that they opened up the theatre to the almost infinite possibilities of psychological interpretation. Once the psychology of the human individual became crucial to the analysis and acting of plays, directors became more than teachers: they became part analyst, part therapist, and even part mystic; their *creative* function in play production increased substantially. The rise of realism in the theatre of the late nineteenth and early twentieth centuries and the rise of directors capable of bringing out realistic nuances and patterning them into highly theatrical productions brought about an irreversible theatrical renovation that in turn irrevocably established the importance of the director.

Phase Three: The Stylizing Directors

Right on the heels of the realist phase of direction came a third phase — one that brought the director to the present position of power and recognition. This phase arrived with the directors who joined forces with nonrealist playwrights to create the modern antirealistic theatre. Their forces are still growing. They are the ones who demand of directing that it aim primarily at the creation of originality, theatricality, and style. The stylizing directors are unrestrained by rigid formulas with respect to verisimilitude or realistic behavior; their goal

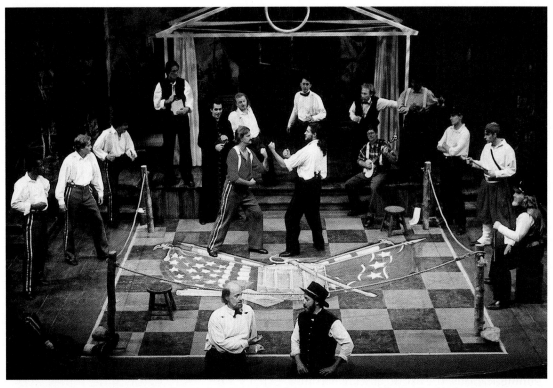

Updates of Shakespeare's plays can point out their relevance to later issues, as exemplified by Tom Markus's provocative production of *Troilus and Cressida*, here set in the American Civil War. In this 1997 Colorado Shakespeare Festival production, the scenery was conceived by Joseph Varga and the nineteenth-century costumes were designed by Linda Sarver.

is to create sheer theatrical brilliance, beauty, and excitement and to lead their collaborators in explorations of pure theatre and pure theatrical imagination.

Paul Fort, one of the first of these third-phase directors, launched his Théâtre d'Art in Paris in 1890 as a direct assault upon the realist principles espoused by Antoine. Similarly, Vsevolod Meyerhold, a one-time disciple of Stanislavsky, began his theatre of "biomechanical constructivism" (an acting method characterized by bold gestures and rapid, near-acrobatic movement) in Moscow to combat the master's realism. The movement toward stylized directing occasioned by these innovators and others like them introduced a lyricism and symbolism, an expressive and abstract use of design, an explosive theatricality, and certain

intentionally contrived methods of acting that continue to the present day to have a profound effect on the theatre and its drama.

Perhaps the most influential proponent of this third-phase position of the director, however, was not himself a director at all but an eminent designer and theorist: Gordon Craig. In a seminal essay titled "The Art of the Theatre" (1905), Craig compared the director of a play to the captain of a ship: an absolutely indispensable leader whose rule, maintained by strict discipline, extends over every last facet of the enterprise. "Until discipline is understood in a theatre to be willing and reliant obedience to the manager [director] or captain," wrote Craig, "no supreme achievement can be accomplished." Craig's essay was aimed at a full-scale "Renaissance of the Art of the

Theatre," in which a "systematic progression" of reform would overtake all the theatre arts — "acting, scenery, costuming, lighting, carpentering, singing, dancing, etc." — under the complete control and organizing genius of this newcomer to the ranks of theatrical artistry, the independent director.

The Contemporary Director

Craig's renaissance has surely arrived: this indeed is the "age of the director," an age in which the directorial function is fully established as the art of synthesizing script, design, and performance into a unique and splendid theatrical event that creates its own harmony and its own ineffable yet memorable distinction. If, as J. L. Styan says, "the theatre persists in communicating by a simultaneity of sensory impressions," it is above all the director who is charged with inspiring these impressions and ensuring this simultaneity.

Today, in a world of mass travel and mass communications, the exotic quickly becomes familiar and the familiar just as quickly becomes trite. Nothing is binding; the directorial function has shifted from teaching what is "proper" to creating what is stimulating and wondrous. At the beginning of a production, the director faces a blank canvas but has at hand a generous palette. At his or her disposal are not only the underlying conventions of the time but also all those of the past, which can be revived for novel effects and stunning juxtapositions: our conglomerate theatre of today allows Shakespeare in modern dress, Greek tragedy à la kabuki spectacle, theatre of the absurd as vaudevillian buffoonery, and romantic melodrama as campy satire. Thus, at the conception of a theatrical idea today — in the first moments of imagining a specific production — no question can be answered automatically, no style is obligatory, no interpretation is definitive. Jean-Paul Sartre has said about the whole of modern life that "man is condemned to be free"; in the theatre the director's freedom in the face of almost limitless possibilities leads to a certain existential anxiety that is both chilling and thrilling in its challenge.

Directorial Functions

Directing is not simply a craft; it is *directing* in the dictionary as well as in the theatrical sense: it is to lead, to supervise, to instruct, to give shape. In other words, it is to do what is necessary to make things "work." The director has final responsibility for *everything* that happens in a production; as such the "function" of a director must be, at least in part, subject to day-to-day demands and continuous improvisation.

"ALWAYS AN IMPOSTOR"

When I hear a director speaking glibly of serving the author, of letting a play speak for itself, my suspicions are aroused, because this is the hardest job of all. If you just let a play speak, it may not make a sound. If what you want is for the play to be heard, then you must conjure its sound from it. This demands many deliberate actions and the result may have great simplicity. However, setting out to "be simple" can be quite negative, an easy evasion of the exacting steps to the simple answer.

It is a strange role, that of the director: he does not ask to be God and yet his role implies it. He wants to be fallible, and yet an instinctive conspiracy of the actors is to make him the arbiter, because an arbiter is so desperately wanted all the time. In a sense the director is always an impostor, a guide at night who does not know the territory, and yet he has no choice — he must guide, learning the route as he goes. Deadliness often lies in wait when he does not recognize this situation, and hopes for the best, when it is the worst that he needs to face.

– Peter Brook

Lev Dodin is the artistic director of the Maly Theatre in St. Petersburg, Russia, and one of his signature productions is surely his stately, six-hour, forty-actor *Brothers and Sisters*, which has twice toured the United States. The play concerns a Russian village during and after World War II, a devastating event in the life of citizens of what was then the Soviet Union. Dodin's realistic staging vividly projects his vision of both Russia's collective suffering and the agony of individual peasants caught in war's clutches. From the 2000 New York tour.

Producer and Director

Part of what the director does in any given production is determined by the possible existence of a *producer*. The producer is the person (or the institution) responsible for the financial support of the production: the producer may be a resident theatre, a university theatre, or, as in Broadway or off-Broadway productions, an independent individual or partnership of individuals. In the regional theatre, the artistic director normally serves as the producer of each production in the theatre's season as well as the director of one or more plays; associate and/or freelance directors may be hired to direct other individual productions.

Where there is an active producer, separate from the director, it is the producer who is generally responsible for hiring the director, for establishing the production budget, and for determining the theatre facility and the production dates. The producer also normally plays an important role (if not *the* dominant role) in selecting the play, engaging the artistic staff (designers and technicians), and possibly even casting the actors.

As a result, functions listed below as "directorial" may in fact be divided between the director and the producer. They remain directorial functions, however, inasmuch as they "direct" the artistic product that will finally appear on the stage.

Directorial Vision

Principally, the directorial function is one of *envisioning* the main lines of the production and providing the artistic *leadership* necessary to realize that vision. Envisioning, however, does not mean plotting out every detail in advance, nor does leadership mean dictatorship or tyranny. Directing means, quite literally, "giving direction," which implies choosing a point of focus and guiding everyone to face the same way. The talents of the play director are, in this regard, not unlike those of the bank director or the director of a research team: to provide goals, establish procedures, facilitate communication, drive the schedule, monitor the progress, encourage the timid, rein in the errant, heighten the stakes, refine the objectives, build the morale, and inspire absolute excellence from every participant. No two individuals will fulfill each of these functions in the same way nor to the same degree. Directing clearly involves a confident and natural way of working with other people, as well as learned directorial technique. Artistic sensitivity, interpersonal skills, and an eagerness to accept responsibility (and exercise authority) should always be expected of the professional play director.

For purposes of discussion, individual directorial functions can be viewed as so many separate steps in the process of play production. The process, in fact, takes place over a period of weeks and sometimes years and is at no time as orderly as a schematic listing might suggest. Nonetheless, such a listing can help us to see the basic architecture of the directorial process and the progression of decisions and actions that bear upon the final production.

The steps divide easily into phases: a preparatory phase, which involves play selection, concept, designer selection, designing, and casting; and an implementation phase, which involves staging, actor-coaching, pacing, coordinating, and presenting. All of these steps are continuous rather than segmented — a director conceptualizes the production right up to the last minute and begins pacing it from the instant the play is chosen — but they are generally centered in a time frame of relatively set order and organization.

Preparatory Phase

The preparatory phase of a production may take days or months or years; it is the director's dreamworld, wherein ideas germinate and begin to flower. Most directors are "in preparation" for several productions at once: even as one production is in rehearsal, others are taking shape in her or his mind. At various times these preparatory phases move from fancy to plain and from the world of dreams to the conference room, the rehearsal hall, and the scene shop.

PLAY SELECTION   The selection of a script is unquestionably the most critical act of any director. The play is the essential theatrical product, so to speak: it is the basic element to which the audience responds — or thinks it responds — and it is universally perceived as the core of the theatrical experience. For this reason, play selection is the one directorial decision over which the producer — the provider of a production's financial support — invariably reserves the right of review.

Three basic considerations go into play selection: the director's interest, the interest of the intended audience, and the capability of the director and producer to acquire, conceptualize, and produce the play. The director's interest is important because no director, save by chance, can create theatrical excitement from a script he or she finds dull and uninteresting. Nonetheless, it is also the director's job to seek the excitement latent in a script and to imagine its various theatrical possibilities. Often a director who can envision the improvements to be gained by script revision, adaptation, or reinterpretation can discover plays that otherwise would be ignored; indeed, one of the marks of a great director is the ability to make us recognize the brilliance or beauty of a script we have unwittingly passed over.

The audience's interest is of even greater importance. It is the audience, after all, that makes the theatre possible; and the ability to assess an audience's needs and wants is absolutely fundamental to directing, both for pragmatic reasons (to ensure that an audience turns out to see the play) and for artistic reasons (to ensure that the play is satisfying and pertinent to those who come to see it). For a director directs not only the actors and designers but the audience members as well, by giving direction to their feelings and perceptions through the intellectual focus of the production. A director who discounts or ignores the interests — and the intelligence — of the audience stands little chance of creating any genuine theatrical impact.

Play selection that considers audience interest does not necessarily mean a reliance on the tried and true; quite the contrary, it means providing the audience with theatrical work that is fresh, fascinating, vigorous, and exciting. For some audiences, these ingredients can be provided by musicals, thrillers, and domestic comedies, for others by works of the European avant-garde, for others by plays of social protest and reform, for still others by new plays hot off the laptops of yet unknown authors. There is an audience for every sort of good play, and it is the director's job to find that audience and attract it to the theatre. The audience demands to be challenged as well as confirmed — and, in the long run, directors who lead their audiences are far more likely to gain artistic recognition than are those who either follow the audience or ignore them completely.

The capability of the director to produce the play adequately with available resources is the final requisite for sound play selection. Can the production rights to the play be acquired? Can a cast be brought together? a production staff? a theatre? Is there enough money? Interest alone — the director's and the audience's — will not buy the scripts, rent the theatre, pay for the electricity, or perform the roles. Considerations of quality must also be factored in: Are the available actors experienced enough to master the play's style? Is the costume budget adequate for the size of the cast and the period of the play? And, finally, does the director understand this play well enough to bring out its ideas? A realistic consideration of one's own capabilities, together with an ability to assess the potential of one's expected collaborators, must be a significant factor in the critical decisions of play selection.

CONCEPT   More has been written in modern times about the director's role in conceptualizing a play than about any other directorial tasks; entire books have been devoted to the "directorial image," or the creation of the central concept that focuses and informs an entire production. Particularly through those concepts that give unexpected and fresh insights into character, story, or style, the modern director has seized the imagination of the public. Like it or not (and there are many who do not), audiences and critics today are much more likely to admire (and remember) "high-concept" productions like Peter Brook's staging of *A Midsummer Night's Dream* than they are "traditional" stagings of this sixteenth-century play.[1] Although the director runs a considerable risk with this kind of undertaking — for indeed Wild West Romeos, homosexual Hamlets, and Watergate Macbeths have more often been laughable than laudable — a brilliantly appropriate concept can completely captivate an audience by focusing a play production with such pertinence and meaning that it transcends time, place, and stylistic artifice to create profound, moving, and illuminating theatricalization.

The formation of a directorial concept takes place at both the conscious and the unconscious level; it takes place, in fact, whether

---

[1] Indeed, what *is* a "traditional" staging of Shakespeare? We don't really know how the play was staged in Shakespeare's own time; what people call traditional staging is generally nineteenth-century staging, which is far removed from whatever Shakespeare intended. In truth, *all* stagings of Shakespeare and of other authors of his era are speculative and creative, governed by imaginative concepts as much as by historical research.

The Taming of the Shrew poses interesting problems for modern audiences, as the early Shakespeare comedy seems to promote male dominance in marriage, particularly in the final scene, in which Katherine (the "tamed shrew") urges wives to "place your hands below your husband's foot." Contemporary directorial approaches may, in various ways, seek to explore possible ironies or contradictions in this message, or, conversely, to make the play a "noisy, politically incorrect, irresistibly funny romp," as was Andrei Serban's intention in this 1998 American Repertory Theatre production, with settings by Christine Jones.

the director wants it to or not. There is no avoiding it: it begins when the director first hears of a certain play, and it grows and develops as she or he reads the play, considers producing it, imagines its effects on an audience, and mentally experiments with possible modes of staging. The directorial concept is a product not only of the director's personal intelligence and vision but also of the director's personal experiences that relate to the matters portrayed by the play, as well as personal likes and lusts, appreciations and philosophical leanings, and desires concerning audience reaction to the final directorial product. The thought processes by which the concept develops are both deductive and inductive, and they are set in motion with the first impressions the director receives from a play.

Concepts can be expressed in many ways. Often they are social statements ("this is a play about tyranny") or philosophical ones ("this is a play about self-knowledge"). Often they involve specific interpretations ("this is a play about a man who cannot make up his mind"), and often they invoke a particular genre of theatricality ("this is a revenge melodrama"). Frequently a director will state the concept psychodramatically ("this is a primitive ritual of puberty"), and frequently the concept is predominantly historical ("this is a play about fratricide in the Middle Ages") or imagistic ("this is a play about swords, sables, and skulls") or metatheatrical ("this is a play about playing"). Often the conception of a play includes a basic tone ("sad," "heroic," "royal"), often a basic texture ("rich," "cerebral," "stark"). Diverse as these examples may seem, they all fall within the range of possibility in conceptualizing a single play: indeed, any one of them could be applied to Shakespeare's *Hamlet,* and probably at one time or another every one of them has been, as have hundreds of others besides.

The concept is the director's creation, and to a certain extent it remains primarily his or her own concern. It constitutes a personal organizing focus, the means of keeping the production aimed in a *specific* direction and impervious to deflection by tempting possibilities that might come to mind over the course of a production period. Therefore the concept, expressed succinctly but comprehensive in its implications, becomes the director's starting point in choosing designers and actors, in initiating design discussions, and in setting the direction for the first rehearsals. Directing, of course, means giving *direction,* and the concept is the first and most decisive step in getting a particular production under way.

A great directorial concept has many qualities. It is specific, appropriate, evocative, visual, theatrical, concrete, and original, as well as a bit mysterious and a bit amusing. It *leads* the actors and the designers; and if it is truly inspired, it leads the director as well. Doubtless some play productions manage to attain a measure of success without the benefit of much conceptualization or with concepts flying in and out of the production process like so many blackbirds, but in today's multimedia, future-shocked world, theatrical excellence increasingly requires that the director have a strong and persistent conceptual vision.

DESIGNER SELECTION   Although normally falling to the producer, the selection of production designers constitutes a vital step in

Nudity, in one fashion or another, has increasingly been employed in contemporary theatre. Jerôme Savary, once a director of Parisian follies-type reviews, has over the past two decades increasingly turned his interests – and skills – to racy stagings of classic plays, such as this 1989 production of Molière's *The Bourgeois Gentleman* at the Théâtre du Chaillot in Paris. Here, Savary employs breast-baring attendants to illustrate bourgeois society's exploitation of women and menial workers. Or is it only the audience's prurience that Savary is exploiting?

the directorial process simply because both the playwright's script and the director's concept must ultimately be translated into concrete visual effects by a group of human beings of individual temperament, sensibility, and vision. The concept is the director's own creation, but its refinement and realization finally rest in the hands of collaborators whose personal artistry and inclinations will inevitably play an enormous role in the shape and impact of the final product. Hence the selection of these individuals is by no means a mechanical or arbitrary task; it is a central directorial concern of great artistic consequence.

Director-designer teams are common in the theatre; some run for years, encompassing dozens of productions. Resident companies, whether national, regional, or community, often keep a core staff of directors and designers on the payroll year after year to facilitate continuing team relationships; most university theatre groups establish similar long-standing collaborations among faculty artists. Even the more fractious Broadway stage has its collaborations that span years and decades, although these teams work on a show-to-show basis rather than under continuing contract; Broadway directors frequently demand to work with certain designers whose work has proven sympathetic to their own in the past.

Ordinarily directors make every effort to find designers with whom they feel not only a personal compatibility but also a mutual respect and a synchrony of artistic and intellectual vision. Like all true collaborations, the most effective director-designer relationships result in a give-and-take of ideas, plans, feelings, and hypotheses — a sense of sharing and complementary support.

Apart from these general considerations in designer selection, the director must look more specifically for the designers most appropriate for the play at hand: those whose abilities are best suited to the demands of the script and the director's conception of the production. Sometimes these specific considerations lead in a direction different from that generally indicated — away from the designer with whom the director feels most comfortable and toward the one who promises to be more helpful in narrowing and clarifying the director's concept. A designer's interest in a certain kind of scenic technology, for example, or in historical aestheticism or light cuing, can often help in many ways to sharpen the conceptual focus and provide insights through the design that will inspire the production itself.

Designer selection, then, is a subtle and complicated process. The director chooses *people,* not colors or fabrics or instruments; he or she must select those people based on an estimate of their ultimate potential in the working conditions provided for them. Naturally the director will be interested in knowing something about the designer's previous work — and most designers can show prospec-tive directors a résumé of experience and a portfolio of completed designs — but the director will also be interested in sounding out the designer's thinking and artistic sensibility. Like all decisions made in the preparatory phase of production, the choice of designers will affect the entire production process; it is a choice that is difficult to retract, and the moment it is made it automatically closes certain directorial options and opens others that could prove either brilliant or catastrophic.

DESIGNING   The design phase of production marks the first step toward transforming vision into actuality: at this stage, people turn ideas into concrete visual realizations. The director's work in designing a production is generally suggestive and corrective; how well she or he succeeds in this delicate task is highly dependent on the personalities and predilections of the individuals involved. In theory, the director's and designer's goals in this phase are identical: actable space, wearable costumes, and an evocative, memorable, and meaningful appearance of the whole. In practice, each of the principals will have an independent perspective on what is actable, what is memorable, and what is evocative; moreover, each may have a different sense of the importance of sometimes contradictory values. A costume designer, for example, may place a higher value on the appearance of a garment than will the director, who may be more concerned with the actor's ability to move in it. A lighting designer may be greatly interested in the aesthetics of murkiness whereas the director may be more concerned that an actor's face be clearly seen at a particular moment. These are the sorts of artistic perspectives that must be reconciled in the design phase, which is essentially a collaboration whose decisions are acknowledged to be subjective rather than right or wrong; it is a phase that demands qualities of leadership and artistic inspiration that are as sensitive as any the director may ever be called upon to exercise.

The design phase normally takes place in a series of personal conferences between director and designers, sometimes on a one-on-one basis and sometimes in group meetings. These are give-and-take affairs, for the most part, with the director doing most of the giving at the beginning and the designers taking over shortly thereafter. Often the first step is a collective meeting — the first design conference — at which the director discusses his or her concept in detail and suggests some possibilities for its visual realization: colors, images, spaces, textures, and technological implementations.

In the ensuing conferences, which are often conducted one-on-one and sometimes on an ad hoc basis, designers normally present their own conceptions and eventually provide the director with a progressive series of concrete visualizations: sketches (roughs), drawings, renderings, models, ground plans, working drawings, fabrics, technical details, and devices. During these conferences the design evolves through a collaborative sharing, in which the director's involvement may range from minimal to maximal depending on how well the initial concept and the developing design seem to be cohering. Periodically — whenever the overall design effort reaches a stage requiring coordinated planning — full design conferences are called to review and compare current plans for scenery, costume, lighting, and properties; these conferences afford opportunities for the designers to collaborate with each other instead of simply with the director.

The director's function at this stage of design is to approve or reject, as well as to suggest. As the person who sits at the top of the artistic hierarchy, the director has the last word on design matters, but that does not mean she or he can simply command the show into being: theatre design, like any creative process, cannot be summoned forth like an obedient servant. Moreover, wholesale rejection of a designer's work after the initial stages inevitably involves serious time loss and budgetary waste — not to mention the risk of provoking some important staff resignations. For these reasons, the directorial effort must be committed from the outset to sound collaborative principles. Once under way, the director-designer collaboration must take the form of shared responsibility in a developing enterprise, not confrontation between warring artists attempting to seize the reins of aesthetic control.

CASTING   The cliché "Casting is 90 percent of directing" undeniably contains more than a germ of truth. The people in a play — the actors — not only attract more audience attention than any other aspect of the play but also represent what the audience *cares* about and will remember the next day. They garner about 90 percent of all the interest an audience expends on a play, and if they squander that interest they can destroy the effectiveness of any theatrical presentation.

The theatre as a medium has many individual elements that are standardized and predictable: flats are made according to formula, lighting instruments are factory-calibrated to conform to precise specifications, color media are mathematically measured and numbered, and one theatre's black velours are identical to those of another. But the one unique ingredient of the theatre — as the audience sees it — is the actor. Actors are people, and as people they are exquisitely individual; moreover, the audience, being human itself, is particularly attuned to the actor's human and idiosyncratic uniqueness. We would never mistake the Hamlet of Kevin Kline with the Hamlets of Kenneth Branagh, Ralph Fiennes, Roger Rees, Mel Gibson, or Val Kilmer. The actor's personality, physical and vocal characteristics, technical abilities, and sheer talent and "presence" weigh mightily in the final realization of every individual performance and in every ensemble of performances. A miscast or untalented or untrained actor can mar the effectiveness of any production, even in a minor

Theatre is an art that people make out of themselves. But that art doesn't simply arise out of thin air; it must be created, afresh, in every instance. That creation requires both inspiration and organization, which together turn ideas and wishes into an actual dramatic production, comprising many separate ingredients.

THE FOUR INGREDIENTS OF THEATRE . . .

To make theatre — that is, to produce a play — two ingredients are absolutely required: *space* and *people*. Two additional ingredients are almost certainly needed: a *text* and various *materials,* such as scenery, costumes, and props. Of course, It's nice to have money as well, but money, after all, is only useful for acquiring the previously mentioned ingredients; indeed, great productions have been created by unpaid volunteers who improvised their texts in available spaces, using materials already in their possession. So money facilitates but is not an absolute requirement of theatrical art.

AND A FIFTH . . .

But there is one vital, intangible component of theatrical art that animates and drives the other four: *purpose*. Purpose asks the question, *Why* do you want to make theatre? to create a work of art? to entertain an audience? to convey a message? to ritualize a sacred belief? to build a community? to investigate drama more deeply? or, for more personal and social reasons, to meet new people? to impress your friends? to build a dramatic career? All productions are driven by an individual mix of such purposes, some idealistic, some social, and some career-centered. Any and all of these purposes can motivate and anchor a play's production, and none of them are inimical to theatre art.

PUTTING IT TOGETHER

Putting a play production together is an art in itself. Although the end product may appear to be seamlessly assembled, the ingredients are many, and the process of bringing them all to individual excellence — and then fusing them into an integrated artistic whole — takes time, experience, and skill.

SEQUENCE OF ASSEMBLY

There is no "normal" order in which a play's text, space, people, and materials are brought together. In what we might call the twentieth-century European model, a director might simply choose a play and begin rehearsing it with a company of actors, designers, and technicians, all of whom would work simultaneously and collaboratively towards an ultimate production. Staging possibilities are suggested, explored, and tested in rehearsal, and designs are developed to support the emerging stage action. When (and if) a viable production appears, an opening performance date is announced, and eventually the production is placed in the theatre's repertory. This European model was standard for directors Konstantin Stanislavsky at the Moscow Art Theatre and Bertolt Brecht at the Berliner Ensemble, each of whom spent up to a year rehearsing his individual productions; it is still common in many state-subsidized European theatre companies. But this model is dependent on a number of factors rarely available outside of those state-run theatres that maintain a large company of permanent artists (on year-round salaries) and enjoy a budget unconstrained by commercial (box-office) pressures. Even in Europe, such theatres are becoming increasingly rare.

In the much more common model, virtually universal in America, productions are largely assembled on paper and in meetings well before rehearsals even begin. Plays are selected with production schedules (and opening dates) already determined; they are often designed before the roles have been cast. Rehearsal and construction periods, in the professional American theatre, are often as short as three weeks or less. This

American model, as we'll call it here, is obviously more efficient with regard to up-front costs, as the great bulk of theatre workers (actors and most technicians) need only be hired for a few weeks of concentrated work prior to the opening performance, when box-office receipts start coming in to cover expenses. But many theatre artists lament the decreased opportunity to make creative decisions — and changes — that arise from discoveries in rehearsal. This is the trade-off in the American model.

Notwithstanding its limitations, however, the American model generates brilliant and amazing productions while redundant making ever-increasing demands for exhaustive preparation. Today, far more than at any time in the past, those leading the theatrical production process — directors, designers, production managers, and stage managers — are expected to be visionaries: to create in their heads, to communicate quickly and easily in writing (and sketching), to organize productively, to anticipate wisely and surely, and to inspire in a void.

Using the American model, then, we will examine the play production process by dividing it into two parts: *conception* and *execution*. Because the former is essentially done in the minds of the leadership team (the producer, director, and designers), we will discuss this process in general terms. For the latter, however, we will examine through photographs an actual play production.

Conception

The conception phase is generally headed by a producer, who ordinarily has final responsibility for choosing a script, securing the financing and the theatre facility, hiring the staff, and overseeing all aspects of the production.

Once a director and design team are in place, however, these individuals become a fundamental part of the conceptualizing process. They are the ones responsible for making — and integrating — the initial decisions about the bringing in and bringing together of the first four ingredients of play production. We'll look at these ingredients separately, keeping in mind, however, that they are only meaningful in their eventual combination.

Text Unless you are hoping to present a totally improvised play, making the words up as you go along (and such works have existed since the beginning of theatre history, though not always labeled as plays), your drama will be built around a specific dramatic text: perhaps a recognized classic, a play from the modern repertoire, a new play — an original script to be seen for the first time — or an adaptation or translation of any of these. What questions should you, as a potential producer-director, consider when selecting a text?

- Who is the potential audience for this play? Are there enough people in the community who would be interested in seeing it?
- Does the play have meaning for a contemporary audience? Does it have relevance to contemporary issues? Will the play entertain the audience, not only in the comedic sense but also in the root sense of the word (in French, *entretenir*); that is, will the play hold the audience's attention?
- Can I — and the staff I can attract — pull it off? Do I understand this play, and can I imagine its theatrical possibilities well enough to make the play a "success" with the resources available to me?
- Can I get *performance rights* to the play? If it's an original play, you will need the author's written permission. If it's a published play and still protected by copyright, you will need the permission of the author's legal representative. Published plays and play translations written before 1978 are protected for seventy-five years from the date of publication. Plays published after that date are protected for seventy years following the author's

death. Thus if the play you want to produce was written within the past seventy-five years, it's probably covered by copyright. Fortunately, play leasing companies — such as Samuel French, Inc., and Dramatists' Play Service — normally make rights available for such plays, at a reasonable cost, after their initial professional runs have been completed.

Space Where might the play be staged? In a school auditorium? an outdoor amphitheater? a leased theatre in the city? a public plaza? a back room in a restaurant? or a "site-specific" venue, such as a train station or a woody grove? Whatever location you choose will have profound influence on the way the play will be staged, seen, and received. You should certainly consider the following:

- How large an audience do I anticipate? The number of seats times the number of performances will determine the theatre's maximum capacity for this play; you will certainly want a seating area large enough to accommodate those who come, but you won't want a house so large as to leave a sea of empty seats.
- What *scale* and *style* of production am I considering? A bustling farce with several sets and a huge cast would overwhelm a small theatre; conversely, an intimate play would get lost if staged in a cavernous dining hall.
- How do I want to stage the play? If you want to use flying scenery, you'll obviously need a theatre with the appropriate equipment. If you want to stage the play throughout the audience space, you might look for a theatre without a fixed seating area.
- Is the theatre available for rehearsal time? for loading in scenery? Is the theatre heated? air-conditioned? reasonably free from traffic noise? too expensive?

People How many people does it take to put on a play? Consider the original program for Claudia Shear's semi-autobiographical drama, *Blown Sideways through Life*. This one-woman, one-set, one-act play was written and performed by Shear at the Cherry Lane Theatre in New York in the late 1990s. What might amaze you is the number of persons listed in that program: there were eight producers, two assistants to the producers, a director, an assistant director, four designers (set, costumes, lighting, and sound), two assistant designers, a composer, a choreographer, a production stage manager, an assistant stage manager, two general managers, one assistant to the general managers, three press representatives, a company manager, a production manager, a technical director, an assistant technical director, three painters, a production electrician, a production photographer, a legal counsel, an accountant, a comptroller, and two management interns. Then there was Cherry Lane Theatre's general manager, plus its house manager, box-office treasurer, assistant treasurer, and house carpenter. Finally, there were six business firms (general management, insurance, advertising, banking, payroll service, press representation) plus three production firms (scenery, lighting, and sound). And after all of this, the program gave "special thanks" to fifteen additional persons and institutions.

So this small, off-Broadway "one-woman" show required no less than seventy named individuals and nine firms — in addition to the author-performer — to make its way to the public. And that figure doesn't even include the ushers, the ticket takers, the concession personnel, or the maintenance crew. It actually took over a hundred people to put on this "one-woman" show. And if it takes a hundred people to mount *Blown Sideways through Life,* you can imagine what it takes to mount the Broadway *Phantom of the Opera.* Here are some things you'd want to consider before assembling the people who will help to put the play together:

- How many people (and in what roles: actors, stage managers, carpenters, running crew, and so on — perhaps all of those job titles listed in the program just mentioned, plus some others unique to your play) will I actually need? Where can I find them?
- What sort of a company do I want to assemble? Professionals? students? amateur enthusiasts? family members? There are pros and cons for each choice.
- Will they be able to work together? Will they be able to work with me? Putting on a play necessarily involves collaboration; all the people engaged must work in close harmony for the play to succeed. Will the people I want, individually, prove compatible with each other in their respective roles?
- Do the people I want (whom I believe I have access to) have the skills I need for the play? Will they be available for rehearsals, work calls, and performances? Can I afford their services — that is, will they work for free, or, if not, will I be able to hire them within my budget? Are there legal or union provisions governing such hirings?

Materials Most play productions include manufactured items such as scenery, costumes, props, and lighting. Many productions also include music and/or sound, which can be recorded or played "live" on instruments or other implements. Some of these materials can be purchased, rented, or built. If materials are to be built, you may also need shop space for building, painting, and assembling. Some considerations include the following:

- *Style:* What kind of look do I want for this production? Elegant? lavish? shocking? experimental? naturalistic? political? Every look should be reflected in the mix of materials you choose.
- *Cost:* Can I afford what I'm looking for? What are my resources for creating it — from purchasing to renting to building? If I build, do I have the people, the space, the funds, and the time to do it the way I want?
- *Safety:* What safety measures do I need to take? Anything an actor or audience member walks on (or under or near) or sits on must meet all local codes for structural soundness and fireproofing. Aisles and exits must be kept clear at all times.

Execution

To illustrate the execution part of a play's production process, we will look at the 1998 production of *Measure for Measure*, directed by the author of this book at the Colorado Shakespeare Festival. The *CSF*, which has operated continuously on the campus of the University of Colorado in Boulder since 1957, employs about 175 persons each summer, mounting four productions in two theatres, including the outdoor Mary Rippon Theatre, where *Measure for Measure* was staged.

The production process lasts roughly a year, with initial staff hirings (directors and designers) occurring in the previous summer, consultations (generally by mail or e-mail) between directors and designers beginning in the fall, full-scale and on-site design and production meetings in January and March, casting and rehearsals beginning in mid-May, and a seven-week performance season beginning at the end of June — when the whole process begins all over again for the following year.

The *CSF* is considered a "semiprofessional" theatre company because the directors, designers, and many of the senior managers and technicians are professionals (members of professional stage unions and/or academic theatre faculties) and a number of the actors (two in 1998) are members of Actors Equity Association; the remaining company members are selected in a national search, including exhaustive auditions, from current students and recent graduates of leading American graduate theatre programs.

1.

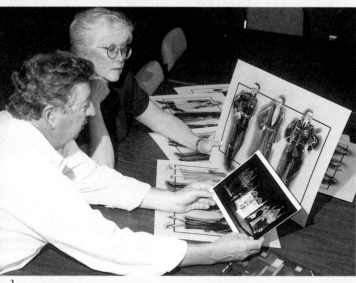

2.

1. Planning meetings. We get started as the director meets regularly with the designers and staff — beginning nearly six months before rehearsals begin — to create the basic production concepts, designs, staging plans, and building/rehearsal schedules that will bring the production into being.

2. Design meeting. Continuing design "minimeetings" are essential to make certain that design and directorial goals are integrated and consistent. Here, scene designer William Forrester and costume designer Madeline Kozlowski compare their individual renderings to ensure that the colors harmonize effectively.

3.   4.

5.

3. Auditions. Actors in the company first present prepared monologues and then are asked to "read for" (that is, read aloud from) roles in each play. The site shown here is the outdoor stage where the play will ultimately be presented; Tyler Layton and Andrew Shulman audition for the roles of Isabella and Angelo, which they will get.

4. First reading. When the play is cast, the director gathers the actors around a table, introduces them to the design staff and each other, explains the initial production concepts that have already been developed, and invites the designers to show their designs to the company. Then, still around the table, the actors read the play aloud. Layton, having highlighted her character's lines in green, reads aloud from her text as designer Forrester looks on and Courtney Peterson — who will play five different roles in this production (Francesca, Marianna, a dancer, a prisoner, a whore) — highlights lines she is assigned at this reading.

5. Scene shop. Designer Forrester, using the three-dimensional model he has developed, explains its mechanics to master carpenter Michael Dombroski.

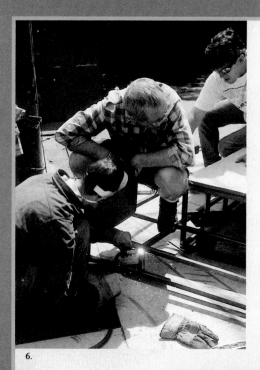

6.

6. Set construction. On the stage, technical director Stancil Campbell oversees the welding together of structural pieces in the central scenic unit.

7. Set detail. In the scene shop, property artisan Janelle Baarspul sculpts and sands the statuary that is to be part of the scenic architecture.

7.

8.

8. Costume shop. Here, designer Kozlowski arranges the sash on the duke's costume while cutter Andrea Johnson works on a garment. Behind Kozlowski are the renderings (colored drawings) that guide the shop in creating each costume.

9. Fittings. With Kozlowski looking on, Layton is fitted into a preliminary costume, made with an inexpensive fabric but on the pattern of the final garment; this will serve as a model for the actual costume.

9.

10. Checking the callboard. Because four plays are rehearsing simultaneously in this company, rehearsal schedules are extremely complicated. Actor Greg Ungar checks the callboard, where all schedules are posted at least twenty-four hours in advance.

11. Blocking. One of the most fundamental directorial functions is to "block" the actors' movements — to determine from which side of the stage they enter; where, when, and how they sit, stand, walk, fall down, or leave the stage; and, in general, how they create the physical action of the play. Here, at an early rehearsal on the outdoor stage — with the yet-unbuilt scenery indicated by lines taped onto the stage floor — the director blocks a scene between Mikel McDonald, playing the duke, and Layton; both are still carrying and reading from their scripts, into which they will also write down their blocking.

10.

11.

12. Rehearsing. Once the actors are "off book" (have memorized their lines and basic moves), they can begin to fully embody their roles, filling them with passion and intensity. Wearing rehearsal costumes (that is, clothing that approximates the shape — though not necessarily the look — of their costumes), and working in an indoor rehearsal hall (with the lines of the set again taped onto the floor), Layton and Shulman rehearse one of their confrontations. Shulman is wearing prop eyeglasses in order to get used to them. This rehearsal is just for a single scene; subsequent rehearsals will run whole acts at a time, and, eventually, "runthrough" rehearsals will be called for the whole play.

13. Choreography. Directors call in specialist directors when required. Here, in a dance studio, choreographer David Capps (*center*) stages the Viennese waltz with which the production will begin.

12.

13.

14. Hanging lights. On and around the stage, technicians hang and mount the hundreds of lighting instruments that will be used in the production. Here, master electrician Kevin Feig mounts an ellipsoidal reflector at the side of the stage.

15. Cabling. Atop the "diving board," apprentice technician Tiffany Williams wires up a string of overhead lights twenty-four feet above the ground.

16. Prop shop. The director has requested a stand-up desk for the play; it will hold the papers, pens, official stamping devices, sealing wax, envelopes, and several other items to be used during performance. But it also must stand straight on a raked (tilted) stage floor and have a device that will hold props steady in a high wind — the production will be staged in an outdoor theatre! Scenic designer Forrester has designed the unit; it remains for property master Jolene Obertin and master property artisan Sean McArdle to determine exactly how it will be used onstage and to make and paint it accordingly.

15.

14.

16.

17.

18.

17. **Craft shop.** The area of crafts encompasses everything that falls between props and costumes, particularly nonfabric items that are worn, such as shoes, armor, and insignia. Here, crafts artisan Abbey Rayburn glues together the leather epaulets that will be part of Angelo's costume.

18. **Sound studio.** Sound design creates all the non-actor-generated music and sound effects — prerecorded or performed live — heard by the audience. In this production, Strauss waltzes, 1930s jazz, medieval religious chants both male and female, coarse German drinking songs, gloomy "prison music," an extended royal trumpet fanfare, amplified door knockings and key-lock turnings, and the sound of a 1930s propeller airplane flying across the stage will be heard. Sound designer Kevin Dunayer must acquire, record, and establish the cuing (timing) of all these effects and determine how they will emanate from his various tape decks and amplifiers to the myriad of speakers on and around the stage.

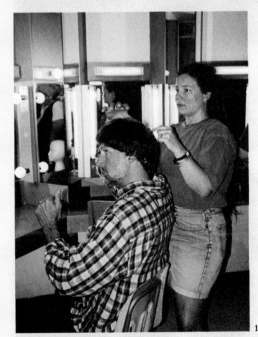

19.

19. **Wig shop.** For part of the play, the duke disguises himself as a friar, and so McDonald must be fitted for a friar's wig, complete with "baldpate" in the center, by wig shop manager Lee Barnette-Dombrowski.

20.

21.

22.

20. Paper tech. To this point the show has been created in separate spaces: acting in the rehearsal room, choreography in the dance studio, lighting on the stage, and scenery, costumes, props, wigs, crafts, and sound in their separate shops and studios. Now it is time to start putting them together and under the control of the stage manager, Richard Ballering (*second from left*), who will "call" the show moment-by-moment. At the "paper tech," every light and sound event, every scenery and prop move, and every actor entrance and exit is precisely identified and written into the stage manager's production book. These are the "cues" that the stage manager will time and call — ordinarily through headsets — during every performance.

21. Tech table. At the subsequent technical rehearsal (known as "tech" — of which there may be many more than one), acting is finally combined with the technical elements of scenery, lighting, props, and sound. For tech, a special table is set up in the back of the audience; there, stage manager Ballering and the lighting and sound designers can communicate over headsets, write notes about what must be corrected, and still watch every second of what is happening onstage.

22. Tech rehearsal is under way. Onstage, actors rehearse the play on the basic set and under stagelights; they are still in rehearsal clothes, though some actors wear pieces of their actual costumes. The set is not yet fully completed or painted, but enough elements are in place that the lighting and sound can be roughly established — and later perfected during the two dress rehearsals and preview that are to follow.

23.

24.

23. Scene painting. Charge artist Heidi Hoffer gives the set its final coats of paint and texture.

24. "Quick-change" rehearsal. Because some actors must change costumes in a matter of seconds without having time to get back to the dressing room, offstage clothing changes are carefully choreographed and rehearsed before full dress rehearsals. A team of backstage "dressers" are essential to the process. Here, Alex Ward and his dressers rehearse one of his quick changes — from Antonio to Barnardine.

25. Stage manager's booth. In preparation for dress rehearsal, stage manager Ballering moves from the tech table to his hidden perch above the audience where he will call the show. His headset connects him with the sound and light operators and to the assistant stage manager backstage who will coordinate the cuing of actors and scenery shifters.

25.

26.

26. Makeup room. Readying for dress rehearsal, actors Laurie G. Lapides and Layton share a makeup mirror; behind them actor Robert May, playing old Escalus, has just put on his baldpate.

27. First dress rehearsal. "First dress" is where costumes and (usually) makeup are added to the mix. Everything is coming together, in fact, except for the audience. Here, backstage, as Francesca (*far right, facing us*) leaves the stage proper, the provost (*his back to us*) prepares to make his entrance, while assistant stage manager Stephanie Dulaney cues a stagehand to rotate the "office wall" into position. Not everything will work perfectly tonight: one quick change won't get completed on time, and Isabella's veil will come off prematurely. But this is what tech and dress rehearsals are for: to find the problems and then fix them.

27.

28.

28. Director's notes. From run-throughs on, the director (*standing at right*) meets with the cast after every rehearsal to suggest how the production can be improved. Do we need faster pacing? clearer diction? heightened intensity? revised blocking? Because rehearsal time is quite limited in a repertory company as opening night nears (the actors are preparing another production simultaneously with this one), almost all of these changes will have to be made in such a note session, held in the theatre's rehearsal hall, rather than in a full re-rehearsal. Actors write down their notes. Because tomorrow is opening night, there will be no further chance to get everything right before facing the audience — and the critics.

29.

29. The house manager. It's time to open. In the final act of preparation, one of the house managers instructs the ushers how to seat the patrons. The actors are in the dressing rooms, the stage manager is in his perch, the technicians are at their booths and offstage positions, and the director (typically) is nervously pacing at the back of the house. The show is just about to begin.

30.

30. and 31. These are photographs of the final production. *At left,* a waiter and three patrons drink, smoke, and argue about the day's events in an outdoor cafe early in the first act; *below,* Viennese prostitutes are rounded up in act 2.

31.

role; in a major role a poor performance simply ruins the play. Casting may not, in the end, account for 90 percent of the director's contribution, but there can be no doubt that bad casting renders all other efforts immaterial.

Most casting takes place in auditions, where the actor can be seen and heard by the director and associates either in a "cold reading" of material from the play to be produced or in a prepared presentation of previously developed material not necessarily related to the production at hand. Although "star" performers are often cast apart from auditions, owing to their known ability to attract audiences to any production, most veteran professional actors regularly submit to auditioning. The director's ability to detect an incipiently brilliant performance in the contrived audition format is a critical factor in effective casting.

Depending on the specific demands of the play and the rehearsal situation, the director may pay special attention to any or all of the following characteristics: the actor's training and experience, physical characteristics and vocal technique, suitability for the style of the play, perceived ability to impersonate a specific character in the play, personality traits that seem fitted to the material at hand, ability to understand the play and its milieu, personal liveliness and apparent stage "presence," past record of achievement, general deportment and attitude, apparent cooperativeness and "directability" in the context of an ensemble of actors in a collaborative enterprise, and overall attractiveness as a person with whom one must work closely over the next four to ten weeks. And the director might well be looking for a great many other things besides.

What is ultimately astonishing about the casting process is that most of the decisions based on these complex criteria are made not in agonizing conferences but in two- to four-minute auditions among perfect strangers! Indeed, this practice is often looked upon as a regrettable theatrical fact, but its very persistence indicates that a great many valid casting judgments can be made in a very short time — provided that time is used with wisdom and sensitivity.

Most of the decisions that are made in the two- to four-minute initial audition are "no" decisions; that is, those actors who are immediately perceived as wrong for the play, wrong for the part, or lacking in the desired level of proficiency are winnowed out. Others may be winnowed out on the subjective ground of apparent attitude — a dangerous ground, because the director might mistake shyness for hostility or "audition jitters" for an exaggerated reserve.

Actors who survive the first audition are then "read" again, sometimes several times, and at this stage the director is involved more and more in the audition process, often coaching the actors to determine how rapidly they can acquire the qualities needed. Such "callbacks" can go on for days and even weeks in the professional theatre, limited only by the union requirement that actors receive pay after a certain point; the frequency with which such payments are made amply attests to the care that attends final casting decisions in the professional theatre.

There is good casting and bad casting, of course, and there is also inspired casting. Many of the greatest performances in theatre history have been achieved by actors who at first glance appeared unsuited to their roles: gangly Janet McTeer seemed to many an odd choice to play Nora, whose husband calls her his "little lovebird" in Ibsen's *A Doll's House,* but her dazzling performance in that role received an enthusiastic reception in London and New York and won her the 1997 Broadway Tony Award for best actress; and diminutive Michael Emerson was more than a foot shy of Oscar Wilde's stature but played him to sensational acclaim in Moises Kaufman's award-winning 1997 play *Gross Indecency.* The ability to perceive an actor's unique and unexpected relationship to a specific role — and to chance

Above: One of the goals of a director's staging is to place important characters where the audience can see their expressions at key moments and to focus audience attention on certain individual characters at critical times. Although they appear entirely natural onstage, eight ordinary people truly sequestered in an Amsterdam attic would, in real life, never find themselves in such a carefully composed physical relationship – with each one's expression clearly defined and focused – as we see in this moment of director James Lapine's staging of the 1997 Broadway revival of *Diary of Anne Frank*. Notice the variety of character positions – standing, bending over, sitting down, and sitting up – and exactly who is looking at whom and why.

Above right: In Robert Egan's premier production of *The Poison Tree*, at the Mark Taper Forum in Los Angeles, Bob Gunton expresses mock dismay at a dinner gathering – while we see the differing reactions of the play's other characters. Setting by David Jenkins, costumes by Salvatore Salamone, lighting by Michael Gilliam.

that casting in place of a "safer" and more traditional choice — has always been the mark of the most daring and most successful film and play directors.

Implementation Phase

With the play selected and conceptualized, with the designers chosen and the designs under way, and with the actors auditioned and cast, the production moves from its preparatory phase to its implementation. It is here that the meeting described at the beginning of this chapter occurs; it is here in the silence between the completion of a plan and its execution that the blood begins to flow in a *corpus dramaticus* that heretofore lived only in the form of conversation and ink on paper.

The time structure of a production is a variable affair, but its direction is inevitably toward greater and greater tautness; that is, time becomes more and more precious as the play draws nearer and nearer to its opening performance. At the juncture between a production's preparatory phase and its implementation, the schedule that was relatively leisurely during the conceptual stage now becomes accelerated and intense. The pressure is on. Now the director's ability to maintain both leadership and creative inspiration under pressure — always an important element of professional skill — becomes crucial.

From the time of that first company meeting, the director controls the focus and consciousness of the entire cast and staff. As head of an ambitious and emotionally consuming enterprise, the director will be the repository of the company's collective artistic hopes — the focal point for the company's collective frustration, its anxiety, and, on occasion, its despair. The company's shield against the intrusions of an outside world, the director is also the spokesperson for the enterprise to which the company has collectively dedicated itself. Directorial power or influence cannot be substantially altered by any attempt the director may make to cultivate or repudiate it — it simply comes with the job and with the need for every theatrical company to have a head, a focus, a direction. The manner in which the director uses that power, and the sensitivity with which she or he now brings the production into being, determines the nature of each director's individual brand of artistry.

STAGING   Staging — which essentially involves positioning actors on the set and moving them about in a theatrically effective manner — is certainly the most obvious of directorial functions. It is the one thing directors are always expected to do and to do well, and it is the one they are most often *seen* doing; it is no wonder that traditional textbooks on directing tend to be largely devoted to this function.

The medium of staging is the actor in space and time — with the space defined by the acting area and the settings and the time defined by the duration of the theatrical event and the dynamics of its dramatic structure. The goals of staging are multiple and complementary: to create focus for the play's themes, to lend credibility to the play's characters, to generate interest in the play's action, to impart an aesthetic wholeness to the play's appearance, to provoke suspenseful involvement in the play's events, and, in general, to stimulate a fulfilling theatricality for the entire production.

The basic architecture of staging is called "blocking," which refers to the timing and placement of a character's entrances, exits, rises, crosses, embraces, and other major movements of all sorts. The "blocking pattern" that results from the interaction of characters in motion provides the framework of an overall staging; it is also the physical foundation of the actors' performance — and many actors have difficulty memorizing their lines until they know the blocking that will be associated with them.

The director may block a play either by preplanning the movements ("preblocking") on paper or by allowing the actors to improvise movement on a rehearsal set and then "fixing" the blocking sometime before the first performance. Often a combination of these methods is employed, with the director favoring one method or the other depending on the specific demands of the play, the rehearsal schedule, rapport with the acting company, or the director's own stage of preparation: complex or stylized plays and settings and short rehearsal periods usually dictate a great deal of preblocking; simple domestic plays and experienced acting ensembles are often accorded more room for improvisation. Each method can produce highly commendable results in the right hands and at the right time; both can present serious problems if misapplied or ineptly handled.

For the most part, the blocking of a play is hidden in the play's action; it tends to be effective insofar as it is *not* noticed and insofar as it simply brings other values into play and focuses the audience's attention on significant aspects of the drama. By physically enhancing the dramatic action and lending variety to the play's visual presentation, a good blocking pattern can play a large role in creating theatrical life and excitement. But beyond this, there are moments when inspired blocking choices can create astonishing theatrical effects — effects that are not hidden at all but are so surprising and shocking that they compel intense consideration of specific dramatic moments and their implications. Such a *coup de théâtre* was achieved, for example, by director Peter Brook in his celebrated 1962 production of *King Lear,* when Paul Scofield, as Lear, suddenly rose and, with one violent sweep of his arm, overturned the huge oak dining table at which he had been seated, sending pewter mugs crashing to the floor as he raged at his daughter Goneril's treachery. This stunning action led to a reevaluation of the character of both Lear and Goneril and of the relationship between this tempestuous and sporadically vulgar father and his socially ambitious daughter.

Some plays require specialized blocking for certain scenes — for duels, for example, or dances. Such scenes demand more than nuts-and-bolts blocking and are frequently directed by specialists, such as dueling masters or fight choreographers, working with the director. These specialized situations are not at all rare in the theatre — almost every play that was written before the nineteenth century includes a duel or a dance or both — and the ability to stage an effective fight scene or choreographic interlude (or at least to supervise the staging of one) is certainly a requisite for any director who aspires to work beyond the strictly realistic theatre.

"Business" is a theatre term that refers to the small-scale movements a character performs within the larger pattern of entrances and crosses and exits. Mixing a cocktail, answering a telephone, adjusting a tie, shaking hands, fiddling with a pencil, winking an eye, and drumming on a tabletop are all "bits of business" that can lend a character credibility, depth, and fascination. Much of the stage business in a performance is originated by the actor — usually spontaneously over the course of rehearsal — although it may be stimulated by a directorial suggestion or command. The director ultimately must select from among the rehearsal inventions and determine what business will become a part of the finished performance; when this determination is made, bits of business become part of the blocking plan.

Staging, then, in the largest sense, includes both hidden and bold blocking effects, specialized movements, and small idiosyncratic behaviors, all combined into a complex pattern that creates meaning, impact, and style. Skillful staging unites the design elements of a production with the acting, creating an omnidynamic spatial interaction between actors, costumes, scenery, and audience, infusing the stage with life. Getting a play "on its feet," as the theatrical jargon puts it, is usually the first step in making it breathe; and the best staging is that which gives the actors the chance to breathe the air of the playwright's world and to awaken to the true vitality of the playwright's characters.

ACTOR-COACHING   The director is the actor's coach, and in practice the director is likely to spend the largest share of her or his time exercising this particular function. The coaching begins at the first meeting with the cast.

Initially, it is the director who conveys the direction the production is expected to take: the concept, the interpretation, the intended "look" and style of the theatrical product. It is also the director who determines the schedule and process of work that will lead up to that final product. The director is the rehearsal leader and decides what activities — discussions, improvisations, games, exercises, lectures, research, blocking, or polishing —

"THIS IS HOW IT'S DONE!"

Publicity photographs taken in rehearsal frequently show a director onstage with a few actors, demonstrating a bit of business and "showing them how it's done." This kind of publicity has probably fostered a certain misunderstanding of the director's role among the general public, for demonstration is only a part of directing, and a distinctly small part at that. Indeed, some directors scrupulously avoid it altogether.

Demonstration as a way of teaching an actor a role has a long history in the theatre and was a particularly common practice in those periods when directing was carried out chiefly by retired actors. Even today, young actors rehearsing for classical plays at the Comédie Française (founded in 1680) are expected to learn their parts by mimicking the performance of their elders down to the last detail of inflection, tone, gesture, and timing. And, of course, many contemporary American directors occasionally give "line readings" to an actor or demonstrate the precise manner of gesturing, moving, sitting, or handling a prop if they perceive that a specific desired behavior might not come naturally from the actor himself.

But demonstration as an *exclusive* method of coaching an actor in a role is very much a thing of the past. Most contemporary directors make far greater use of discussion, suggestion, and improvisation. These methods seek to address the inner actor and to encourage him to distill his performance out of self-motivated passions and enthusiasms. Because they know that a purely imitative performance is all too likely to be a mechanical performance, today's directors tend to rely on more creative methods than "getting up there and showing how it's done."

---

will occupy each rehearsal period; the director leads such activities with an eye to their ultimate goal.

Further, like the manager of an athletic team, the director is responsible for stimulating the best efforts of the cast and for instilling in them a high regard for teamwork (which in the theatre is called "ensemble") as well as for individual craft excellence and artistry. And, because the work of the theatre inevitably demands of the actor a good measure of emotional, psychological, even irrational investment, the director has an opportunity (if not an obligation) to provide an atmosphere in which actors can feel free to liberate their powers of sensitivity and creativity. Good directors lead their cast; great directors inspire them.

The ways in which directors go about coaching actors are various and probably more dependent on personality than on planning. Some directors are largely passive; they either "block and run," in the jargon of commercial theatre, or function primarily as a sounding board for actors' decisions about intention, action, or business. Conversely, there are directors closer to the popular stereotype, mercurial directors whose approaches at times verge on the despotic: they cajole, bully, plead, storm, and rage at their actors; involve themselves in every detail of motive and characterization; and turn every rehearsal into a mixture of acting class, group therapy session, and religious experience. Both methods, as experience teaches, can produce theatrical wizardry, and both can fail utterly; probably the determining factors either way are the strength of the director's ideas and the extent to which the cast is willing to accept his or her directorial authority.

Too little direction, of course, can be as stultifying to an actor as too much; the passive director runs the risk of defeating an actor's performance by failing to confirm it, that is, by withholding constructive response. Similarly, the extremely active director may, in a whirlwind of passion, overwhelm the actor's own creativity and squelch his efforts to build a sensitive performance, thereby condemning the production to oppressive dullness. For these and other reasons, most directors today strive to find a middle ground, somewhere between task mastery and suggestion, from which they can provide the actor with both a goal and a disciplined path toward it while maintaining an atmosphere of creative freedom.

Directors need not be actors themselves, but they must understand the paradoxes and ambiguities inherent in that art if they are to help the actor to fashion a solid and powerful performance. The greatest acting braves the unknown and flirts continuously with danger (the danger of exposure, of failure, of transparency, of artifice); the director must give the actor a careful balance of freedom and guidance in order to foster the confidence that leads to that kind of acting. Directors who are insensitive to this requirement — no matter how colorful their stormings and coaxings or how rational their discussions of the playwright's vision — are virtually certain to forfeit the performance rewards that arise from the great actor-director collaborations.

PACING   Despite all the director's responsibilities, pace is perhaps the only aspect of a theatrical production for which general audiences and theatre critics alike are certain to hold the director accountable. Frequently, newspaper reviews of productions devote whole paragraphs of praise or blame to the actors and designers and evaluate the director's contribution solely in terms of the play's pace: "well paced" and "well directed" are almost interchangeable plaudits in the theatre critic's lexicon; and when a critic pronounces a play "slow" or "dragging," everyone understands he or she is firing a barrage at the director.

To the novice director (or critic), pace appears to be primarily a function of the rate at which lines are said; hence a great many beginning directors attempt to make their productions more lively simply by instructing everyone to speak and move at a lively clip: "Give it more energy!" "Make it happen faster!" But pace is fundamentally determined by a complex and composite time structure that must be developed to accommodate many variables, such as credibility, suspense, mood, style, and the natural rhythms of life: heartbeat, respiration, the duration of a spontaneous sob or an unexpected laugh. How much

Director Susan Stroman creates a wonderful farcical moment in *The Producers* as "theatre queen" director Roger De Bris (played in drag by Gary Beach) desperately tries to keep his wig on. Facial expressions around the room focus the action and intensify the hilarity. Matthew Broderick and Nathan Lane, the "producers" of the musical's title, are at left; De Bris' hangers-on (with Roger Bart, as his "common-law assistant," Carmen Ghia) are perfectly arranged on the stairs by director Stroman to capture every possible droll expression. Scenic design by Robin Wagner, costumes by William Ivey Long, and lighting by Peter Kaczorowski.

time is properly consumed, for example, by a moment of panic? a pregnant pause? a flash of remembrance? an agonized glance? a quick retort? These are the ingredients of pace, and they are not subject to the generalized "hurry-up" of the director who has not first discovered the pattern of rhythms inherent in a play.

The pace of a play should be determined largely by the quantity and quality of the information it conveys to the audience, and the director must decide how much time the audience requires to assimilate that information. In a farce, of course, the audience needs almost no time to synthesize information — therefore,

According to Temperament

It is most important that the individuality of the actor, whatever be the character he is to interpret, be preserved, for individuality is an essential qualification of a great artist. So, at the outset, I suggest little to my people, in order to make them suggest more. I appeal to their imagination, emotion, and intelligence, and draw from them all I can. When I can get no more from them I then give them all there is in me. I coax and cajole, or bulldoze and torment, according to the temperament with which I have to deal.

– David Belasco

A two-character play, such as David Mamet's *Oleanna* — concerning a male professor and a female college student — demands continuous and intense interaction between the characters to propel the story forward. The director has a profound responsibility to pace and vary the action so that it has both sharp detail and a continuous momentum, as Michael Canavan and Lynsey Mcleod developed in this 1998 South Coast Repertory production directed by Martin Benson.

farce generally is propelled rapidly, with information coming as fast as the actors can get it out. A psychological drama, on the other hand, may require a slower pace to convey a deeper understanding of its characters and issues; sympathy is engendered when audience members have an opportunity to compare the characters' lives with their own, to put themselves in the characters' situations, and to engage in introspection even as they observe the action onstage. Similarly, political drama commonly demands of us a critical inquiry into our own societies and our own lives as part of our understanding of what is happening onstage; this form, too, demands time to linger over certain perfectly poised questions — and the pace of a production must give us that time.

Just as a symphony is composed of several movements, so a well-paced theatrical production will inevitably have its adagio, andante, and allegro tempos. Faster tempos tend to excite, to bedazzle, and to sharpen audience attention; slower ones give audience members a chance to consider and to augment the play's actions and ideas with their own reflections. Often directors speak in terms of "setting up" an audience with a rapid pace and then delivering a "payoff" with a powerful, more deliberately paced dramatic catharsis. The sheer mechanics of theatrical pacing demand the greatest skill and concentration on the part of both actor and director, and for both the perfection of dramatic timing (and most notably comic timing) is a mark of great theatrical artistry.

Directors vary in their manner of pacing plays, of course. Some wait until final rehearsals and then, martinetlike, stamp out rhythms on the stage floor with a stick or clap their hands in the back of the house. Some work out intricate timing patterns in the early rehearsals and explore them in great detail with the actors as to motivation, inner monologue, and interpersonal effect. Directorial intervention of some sort is almost always present in the achievement of an excellent dramatic pace; it rarely occurs spontaneously. Actors trained to the realist manner often tend to work through material slowly and to savor certain moments all out of proportion to the information they convey; actors trained in a more technical manner just as often are "off to the races" with dialogue, leaving the audience somewhat at sea about the meaning or importance of the matters at hand. And when a variety of actors, trained in different schools, come together in production for the first time, they can create such an arrhythmic pace that the play becomes unintelligible until the director steps in to guide and control the tempo.

COORDINATING   In the final rehearsals the director's responsibility becomes more and more one of coordination: of bringing together the concept and the designs, the acting and the staging, the pace and the performance. Now all the production elements that were developed separately must be judged, adjusted, polished, and perfected in their fuller context. Costumes must be seen under lights, staging must be seen against scenery, pacing must include the shifting of sets, acting must coalesce with sound amplification, and the original concept must be reexamined in light of its emerging realization. Is the theme coming across? Are the actions coming across? Can the voices be heard and understood? Do the costumes read? Is the play focused? Is the play interesting? Do we care about the characters? about the themes? about anything? Does the production seem to *work?*

Timing and wholeness are governing concepts in this final coordinating phase of production. In assessing the play's overall timing, the director must be prepared to judge the play's effectiveness against its duration and to modify or even eliminate those parts of the production that overextend the play's potential for communicating information, feelings, or ideas. Last-minute cutting is always a painful process — much labor and creative spirit have gone into those parts that will be cut — but many a production has been vastly improved by judicious pruning at this time. And in the interest of providing wholeness — that quality which unifies a play and gives it the stamp of taste and aesthetic assurance — the best and bravest directors are willing in these final moments to eliminate those elements that fail to cohere with the play's overall appearance and significance. Often these elements hold a special meaning for the director; they may even have figured into his or her earliest conception of the production. But now, in the cold light of disciplined analysis, they look painfully like directorial indulgence or extraneous showing off. The best directors are those who can be most rigorous with themselves at this stage, for they are the ones who are capable not only of generating ideas but also of refining and focusing artistic form.

In the final rehearsals — the "technical rehearsals," when scenery, lighting, and sound are added, and the "dress rehearsals," when the actors don costumes and makeup for the first time — the director arrives at a crossroads: although remaining fundamentally responsible for every final decision about the timing and balance of theatrical elements, she or he must now "give over" the production to the actors and technicians who will execute it. Beyond this junction the director will be consumed by the production and will disappear within it in a matter of days: it will reflect the director's personal conceptions and directorial skills without reflecting the director's own persona. After contributing to everything that appears upon the stage and initiating much of it, the director must accept the fact that he or she will not be recognized in any single moment, any single act, any single costume or lighting cue. In these final rehearsals the director's presence normally becomes more a force for organization than a source of inspiration — clipboard in hand, she or he delivers hundreds of last-minute notes to actors, technicians, and stage managers in an effort to give the production that extra finesse that distinguishes the outstanding from the mediocre.

What an extraordinary exchange of power has taken place between the first meeting of the cast and director and these final days! Whereas earlier the entire production was in the director's head and the cast waited in awe and expectation, now the actors hold the play in their heads and everyone confronts the unknowns of the play's reception. The actors have a new master now: the audience. It is in these days that even the most experienced actors confront their fundamental nakedness in performance: they must face the audience, and they must do it without benefit of directorial protection, with nothing to shield them save their costumes, characters, and lines. To the actor, the director is no longer a leader but a partner, no longer a parent but a friend. Actors may indeed experience a certain feeling of betrayal; the director, after all, has abandoned them to face the audience alone, just as in the medieval play Good Deeds accompanied Everyman only to the brink of the grave. But then acting, like death, is a trial that cannot be shared.

PRESENTING   It is an axiom of the theatre that nobody is more useless on opening night than the director. If all has progressed without major catastrophe and the production has successfully been "given over" to those who will run it and perform in it, the director's task on opening night consists chiefly in seeing and evaluating the production and gauging the audience response. This night may,

of course, prove to be nothing but a calm between storms: in the professional theatre it may simply be the first of a series of opening nights, one calculated to serve as a guide to future rehearsals, rewritings, and rethinkings. Still, at this time the major work has reached a stopping point, and the director must shift perspectives accordingly.

The director in this last phase sometimes takes on certain responsibilities of a paratheatrical nature, such as writing directorial notes for use in newspaper stories and interviews and overseeing the house management, the dress of the ushers, the lobby decorations, the concession stands, or the "dressing of the house" (the spacing of audience members in a less than full house). The director may also play an active role as audience member by greeting patrons, chatting with critics, or leading the laughter and applause — although all of these activities are more common in community theatres than in professional ones.

More central to the directorial function in this final stage is the director's continuing evaluation of every production element in an effort to improve the audience impact. This may lead to changes at any time during the run of a play. In the professional theatre, new productions commonly go through a tryout period of two weeks or more — up to a year in a few cases — when the play is rehearsed and re-rehearsed daily between performances and material is deleted, revised, restaged, and freshly created in response to audience reception. Some quite famous plays have succeeded only because of such "doctoring" during tryout periods, and it is not at all uncommon in the contemporary commercial theatre for a director to be replaced during this phase in order to accelerate revision.

Even after the final opening, however, and throughout the run of a play, most directors attend performances periodically and follow up their visits with notes to the actors — either to encourage them to maintain spontaneity or to discourage them from revising the original directorial plan. One perhaps apocryphal show-business story has it that the American director George Abbott once posted a rehearsal call late in a play's run in order to "take out the improvements."

Just as the actor might feel alone and somewhat betrayed in those empty moments prior to opening performance, so might the director feel a twinge of isolation at the ovation that follows the first performance. For it is in that curtain-call ovation that the audience takes over the director's critic-mentor function and the director is consigned to anonymity. The actors, heady with the applause, suddenly remember that it is they who provide the essential ingredient of theatre, while the director, cheering the ensemble from the back of the house, suddenly realizes he or she is now just one of the crowd, one witness among many to the realization of his or her own intangible and now remote plans and ideas. In the professional theatre, it is at this moment that the director's contract expires — a fitting reminder of the "giving over" that occurs in the direction of all plays. Only those directors who can derive genuine satisfaction from creating out of the medium of others' performance will thrive and prosper in directorial pursuits; those who aspire to public acclaim and adulation will most likely face perpetual frustration as practitioners of this all-encompassing and yet all-consuming art.

The Training of a Director

Traditionally, directors have come to their craft from a great many areas, usually after achieving distinction in another theatrical discipline: for example, Elia Kazan was first an actor, Gower Champion was a choreographer, Harold Prince was a producer, Peter Hunt was a lighting designer, Franco Zeffirelli was a scene designer, Robert Brustein was a drama critic, Harold Pinter was a playwright, Mike Nichols was an improvisational comedian, and Rob-

ert Wilson was an architectural student. Still, in addition to a specialty, most of these directors have brought to their art a comprehensive knowledge of the theatre in its various aspects. Having distinction in one field is important chiefly insofar as it gives directors a certain confidence and authority — and it gives others a confidence in their exercise of that authority. But it is comprehensive knowledge that enables directors to collaborate successfully with actors, designers, managers, playwrights, and technicians with facility and enthusiasm.

New directors entering the profession today are more likely than not to have been trained in a dramatic graduate program or conservatory — and often they have supplemented this training with an apprenticeship at a repertory theatre. One of the most remarkable recent developments in the American theatre has been the emergence of a cadre of expertly trained directors: men and women with a broad understanding of the theatre and a disciplined approach to directorial creativity.

Well-trained directors will possess — in addition to the craft mastery of staging, actor-coaching, pacing, and production coordinating — a strong literary imagination and an ability to conceptualize intellectually and visually. They will be sensitive to interpersonal relationships, which will play an important role in both the onstage and offstage activities under their control. They will have a sound working knowledge of the history of the theatre, the various styles and masterworks of dramatic literature, the potential of various theatre technologies, and the design possibilities inherent in the use of theatrical space. They will have at their command resources in music, art, literature, and history; they will be able to research plays and investigate production possibilities without starting at absolute zero; and they will be able to base ideas and conceptions on sound social, psychological, and aesthetic understandings.

All of these advanced skills can be effectively taught in a first-rate drama program, and for that reason today's top-flight theatre directors, more than any other group of stage artists, are likely to have studied in one or another of the rigorous drama programs now in place across the country. The accomplished director is perhaps the one all-around "expert" of the theatre; this is not to deride the director's function as a creative and imaginative force but to emphasize her or his responsibility over a broad and highly complex enterprise. Nothing is truly irrelevant to the training of a director, for virtually every field of knowledge can be brought to bear upon theatre production. The distinctiveness of any production of the contemporary theatre is largely a reflection of the unique but comprehensive training of its director, who is responsible not only for the overall initiative and corrective authority that infuse the production but also for the personal vision that inspires its singular direction.

7

Theatre Traditions: East and West

Theatre, which consists of live actors who perform in real time before live audiences, is a unique art form because it exists "in the present." Theatre, however, is also deeply rooted in its past; plays seen today are often revivals, adaptations, or parodies of earlier ones. Even when they're wholly original, new plays will inevitably be compared to earlier works. Likewise, contemporary actors — like contemporary baseball players — will also be compared to their predecessors. Theatre is a living art but also a living tradition.

Some plays travel through time effortlessly, reappearing in new guises at dozens of points throughout history. A fourth-century-B.C. Greek comedy named *The Lot Drawers,* by Diphilis, concerning an old man foolishly in love with a young girl, was revised more than a hundred years later by the Roman comic dramatist Plautus under the title of *Sorientes;* another Roman dramatist revised it some years later into a play called *Casina;* and more than a thousand years later this play became the basis for a fifteenth-century Italian comedy by Niccolò Machiavelli entitled *Clizia.* Thereafter, major elements of the plot appeared in early-sixteenth-century Italian *commedia dell'arte* farces, in the sixteenth- and seventeenth-century plays of Shakespeare and Molière, and more recently in American comedies on stage, film, and television.

Indeed, many of the world's greatest plays — in both the East and the West — are closely based on preceding ones. Dozens of eighteenth-century Japanese *kabuki* dramas are based on fourteenth-century Japanese *nō* scripts (often bearing the same titles), and

211

most traditional Indian and Chinese plays are based on dramas from prior millennia. French neoclassic tragedies of the seventeenth century, as well as French comedies of the twentieth century, were often based on Greek and Roman models more than two thousand years old. At least three of William Shakespeare's best-known plays — *King Lear, Hamlet,* and *The Taming of the Shrew* — were revisions of earlier English plays of virtually the same names by other authors. And Shakespeare's plays, in turn, have been a source for literally hundreds of modern dramas, including Tom Stoppard's *Rosencrantz and Guildenstern Are Dead,* Lee Blessing's *Fortinbras,* Paul Rudnik's *I Hate Hamlet,* Richard Nelson's *Two Shakespearean Actors,* Ann-Marie McDonald's *Goodnight Desdemona (Good Morning Juliet),* Amy Freed's *The Beard of Avon,* Stephen Sondheim's *West Side Story,* and Neil Simon's *The Goodbye Girl* and *Laughter on the 23rd Floor,* all of which parody or creatively extend portions of Shakespeare's plays. Indeed, the theatre continually resurrects its past traditions, just as it always seeks to extend and surpass them.

Therefore it is helpful, in looking at the theatre of today, to look to the traditions of the theatre in the past, from both the East (Asia and the subcontinent) and the West (Europe and the Americas). What follows is a capsule history of eleven important theatre traditions, from both East and West, that together outline the major world developments prior to the start of the modern theatre in the nineteenth century.[1]

The Origins of Theatre

Drama is probably a more recent art than painting or singing because of its complexity:

it is an activity that requires many people (often in the hundreds) with different skills, all working together — not to mention the large group of people who gather at one place at one time to witness it. Drama is a public art, requiring, in addition to the inspiration and skill demanded of all artistic creation, a sophistication of social organization. But drama is, nonetheless, very old, perhaps ten (and possibly twenty or thirty) thousand years old.

The fact is, we don't know exactly when drama first appeared. Unlike painting, drama leaves no permanent record of its existence. Drama is "something that is done" (see Chapter 1), and after it is done it simply disappears. We do have dramatic scripts that date back more than 4,500 — or possibly 5,330 — years, and we have some indication as to where such drama was performed. That period (about 2500–3330 B.C.) is the known beginning of dramatic art. However, the actual origin of drama, which dates well before that time, is shrouded in mystery.

Although we don't know exactly how drama was created, we do know that it derives from very ancient sources, two of which — storytelling and ritual — are clearly dominant. Both of these deserve our serious attention. Ever since humans developed phrased and coherent speech, the act (if not the art) of *storytelling* has been practiced: the public relating of daily adventures, stories of the hunt and conquest, and histories of the family and the tribe. Indeed, such storytelling probably went hand in glove with the development of speech itself, for why invent such words as *glorious, brave,* and *beautiful* if not to augment a story being told?

Doubtless, storytelling soon developed elements of character impersonation as well — specifically, the imitation of voices, gestures, and facial expressions and, more important, the imitation or representation of emotion. There is ample evidence of this in the storytelling practices of tribal cultures today. Storytelling remains a vibrant art form in urbanized culture as well; festivals dedicated to spoken

---

[1]Readers searching for expanded information on the theatre's past should consult the long edition of this book or, for a detailed accounting of the theatre's history, surveys and guides such as those by Martin Banham and Oscar Brockett (see the Selected Bibliography at the back of this book).

Storytelling, an art more ancient than theatre, is still practiced as a public performance form, nowhere more successfully than at the annual Jamestown, Tennessee, storytelling festival.

narratives, both factual and fictional, are growing in popularity around the world.

The second, equally important, source of drama is *ritual,* a ceremonial act performed for religious or cultural reasons, either to summon gods and influence nature (as with rain dances or healing ceremonies) or to dignify and memorialize an important social, political, or mythic event. Collective cultural rituals may celebrate, for example, the changing of the seasons, or they may provide social witness and cultural authentication for one of life's passages; take, for example, the Christian baptism, the Jewish *bar mitzvah* (coming of age) ceremony, or the funeral practices of virtually all cultures. Other rituals may reenact defining moments of a culture's presumed history — such as the birth, death, or resurrection of a divine being — which can serve to unite adherents in a shared passion of sacred events and to educate and evangelize the general public as well.

Unlike storytelling, rituals normally involve elements of staging — costume, music, formalized speech, and props — often with totemic properties crucial to the staged event. Wholly secular rituals, which are as ancient as social behavior itself, continue in contemporary life and give mundane events a spiritual dimension: there are, for example, ritual elements in the black robes of courtroom judges, in the precisely choreographed changing of the guard ceremony at the Tomb of the Unknown Soldier, and even in the lowering of the ball in Times Square on New Year's Eve. Perhaps the most common ritual in American life is the wedding ceremony, with its formal costumes (lace or tie-dye), its elevated language (psalm or sonnet), its traditional music (Mendelssohn or McCartney), and its gravely cadenced "march" down the aisle transmitting the ancient symbolism — a bride being handed from father to groom — wholly intact.

Drama arises from both of these sources, particularly from their combination. Storytelling provides drama with a plotted structure, which makes a play's events both interesting and compelling to an audience. And ritual provides drama with the corporeal reality and the emotional intensity of participant-performers who commit, body and soul, to the truthful reenactment of real (or real-seeming) events, sometimes with a believed reliance on supernatural powers. Even in the earliest, prehistoric dramas, storytelling and ritual became inextricably merged in the dramatic act.

Recorded Drama

In general, dramatic art is divided into two grand traditions: Eastern and Western. Since the time of the first-known playwrights — around 500 B.C. — drama seems to have developed in each hemisphere quite separately, with little cross-fertilization until the past 150 years. But such categorization is misleading. The truth is that drama began in neither the East nor the West but in the Middle East, in Mesopotamia, Canaan, and, most notably, Egypt.

The first recorded drama was the *Abydos Passion Play*. Discovered in 1896, this play dates back at least as far as 2500 B.C. and quite possibly eight hundred years before that. This "coronation drama," as it is called, was staged each spring in a boating procession along the Nile, with performances taking place at several stations along the way. The play tells the story of the murder of the wheat god, Osiris, by his enemy, Set. Scenes of lamentation by the priestesses Isis and Neptys, the tearing asunder of Osiris's body (which is then thrown into the Nile), Osiris's eventual "resurrection" in the person of the god Horus, and a ritual combat between the resurrected Horus and Set are the ingredients of this drama, portrayed through dialogue, dancing, the wailing of dirges, animal sacrifice, a ceremony of royal

investiture, a communal feast, and the performance of sacred fertility rites. Bold effects were created to complement the play's symbolic actions: beads of carnelian (a translucent red stone) represented the great Eye of Horus, which was bloodied when Set plucked it out in the combat between the two demigods. Two maces represented Set's testicles, which Horus tore off and engrafted upon his own body to become stronger. The lowering and raising of ceremonial pillars into the Nile represented the burial and resurrection of Osiris.

Modern anthropology has concluded that this Egyptian springtime drama — and other similar ancient Middle Eastern texts dealing with the same plot elements, such as the Canaanite play *Baal* and the Hittite play *Snaring of the Dragon*, coming from what are now Syria and Turkey, respectively — derives from even more ancient ritualized reenactments of the coming of spring that celebrated the rebirth of vegetation in the fields. The death of Osiris, like the death of the wheat sheaf he represents, is not permanent; when his body is torn apart and thrown into the river, he is resurrected — as is the wheat sheaf when its seeds are scattered by the wind and irrigated by the annual springtime flooding of the Nile. The tragedy of death, therefore, yields life, and the tears of tragic lamentation become nourishment for the seeds of life's renewal. Such tragedy, therefore, however painful, brings with it rejuvenation and hope. To emphasize the connection between drama and nature, the Abydos play was performed at temples that were oriented so their doorways faced the sun's rising on the day the play was staged, on the vernal equinox.

Drama did not flourish continuously in the Middle East, however; much of the ancient theatre tradition had disappeared by the third century B.C., and the religion of Islam, which originated early in the seventh century A.D., viewed depictions of humans — in both the visual and performing arts — as irreligious. The dramatic instinct was thus stifled in that

Euripides' *The Trojan Women*, shown here in Matthias Langhoff's 1998 production at the French National Theatre of Rennes, Brittany, is the all-time masterpiece of war's horror and ruin. Hecuba, here played by Evelyne Didi, cries out against her country's destruction from an ancient Trojan theatre laid to waste by Greek armies. Thus, Langhoff employs a "stage theatre" to face the real one in which the audience sits. Certainly, no one in the French audience will fail to grasp the parallels to contemporary struggles elsewhere in Europe.

region for more than a thousand years. But the dramatic art form itself was not stifled: from its Middle Eastern origins, it spread rapidly both east and west. In both India and Attica (now Greece), cultic rituals were performed well before the first millennium B.C.

Theatre in the West

By the middle of the first millennium B.C., there arose in the West a spectacular theatre in the city-state of Athens, which, over the course of 150 years, produced four of the greatest playwrights and the most important dramatic theorist of the theatre's long history. Greek drama

ushered in the Western strain of theatre, establishing its major modes of tragedy and comedy and characters and plot lines that underlie much of Western drama as we know it today.

Greek Drama

The drama of Athens in the fifth century B.C. still stands as one of the greatest — some would say *the* greatest — body of theatrical creation of all time. A magnificent and vigorous blend of myth, legend, philosophy, social commentary, poetry, dance, music, public participation, and visual splendor, Athenian drama created the forms of both tragedy and comedy, peopling them with characters that have become

The Greek theatre of Priene, in modern-day Turkey, dates from about 300 B.C. Unlike most Greek theatres, Priene was never rebuilt by the Romans and thus remains one of the best examples of a hillside Greek *theatron*. The standing row of columns and connecting lintel once made up the front of the stone *skene*, or stagehouse.

cultural archetypes in successive eras and laying thereby the foundation not only of future Western drama but also of continuing debates as to how — and to what purposes — life should be lived.

Aristotle and later scholars tell us that Greek tragedy derived from ancient, orgiastic rites, filled with wine drinking, phallus worshipping, and the chanting of ancient poems, called *dithyrambs,* in honor of the Greek demigod Dionysus (the Greek god of fertility and wine and, eventually, the god of theatre as well). Thought to have come to Greece by way of the Middle East, Dionysus was the counterpart of Egypt's Osiris and, like the Egyptian wheat god, was believed to have been dismembered in the winter and resurrected in the spring, proving a demi-divine analogue to the rebirth

of vegetation on the Attic peninsula. And when classic Greek dramas came to be staged on the Athenian acropolis by the latter part of the sixth century B.C., it was at the Great Theatre of Dionysus, during the annual springtime festival known as the City Dionysia (or Great Dionysia), that the demigod's apparent rebirth was celebrated. Dionysus has, ever since, been considered the founding deity of Western drama.

Although the transition from orgiastic celebrations to tragic drama is decidedly obscure, we do know that by the end of the fifth century three great tragedians — Aeschylus, Sophocles, and Euripides — had written and produced close to three hundred plays, of which thirty-three have come down to us, most of which are on every theatre scholar's list of the world's greatest dramatic master-pieces. Furthermore, there was a brilliant author of comic dramas — Aristophanes — from whom eleven plays survive, one of which (*The Frogs*) is a biting and vastly informative satire about the three great tragedians who shared his times. Other authors of Greek comedy, including Menander, and literary theorists, including Aristotle (with his *Poetics,* a treatise on tragedy), plied their trades in the century that followed, making for one of the richest bodies of dramatic work ever created.

Greek tragedies explored the social, psychological, and religious meanings of the ancient gods and heroes of Greek history and myth, as well as current events; the comedies presented contemporary issues affecting all Atheni-ans. Both types of drama were first staged in a simple wheat-threshing circle on the ground (the *orchestra*), with a dressing hut (*skene*) behind it; the audience was seated on an adjacent hillside (the *theatron*). As Greek culture expanded, however, huge amphitheaters — the largest of which sat upwards of 15,000 people — were built in Athens and subsequently throughout the growing Greek empire. Many of those later theatres remain today, in various stages of ruin and renovation, in parts of Greece, Italy, and Turkey; and of course the terms *orchestra, scene,* and *theatre* remained to define the theatre of future eras.

Ancient Greek actors were all male. They performed in masks, partly to indicate the age, gender, personality, and social standing of

In the earliest days of Greek tragedy, choruses numbered fifty performers. Romanian director Silviu Purcărete, at the National Theatre of Craiova, actually employed a chorus of double that number – with fifty men and fifty women – in his innovative production of *Les Danaïdes*, adapted from Aeschylus' war tetralogy, *The Suppliants*. Purcărete's highly stylized production, performed (in French) in Manhattan's Damrosch Park as part of the Lincoln Center Festival in 1997, had clear overtones of current problems in eastern Europe and the Balkans and a strong emphasis on political terrorism, sexual assault, and the ambiguity of gender and cultural identity.

Fanciful modern costumes by Shigeru Yagi and boisterous performances by the Hispanic American group Culture Clash brought this 1997 South Coast Repertory (Costa Mesa, California) production of Aristophanes' ancient comedy *The Birds* rousingly and sagely into the present era.

the characters they were playing and partly to amplify their voices. (The word *person,* which derives from the Latin *per son,* or "for sound," originally referred to the amplification provided by an actor's mask, as used in the phrase *dramatis personae,* or "cast of characters.") Each tragic actor wore elevated shoes (*kothurnoi*), an elaborate headdress (*onkos*), and a long, usually colorful gown (*himation*) with a tunic over it (*chlamys*) to enhance the larger-than-life struggles between royal heroes, gods, and demigods. Plays were performed with only two (later three) principal actors, who, by changing masks, could play several parts each during the course of a play. The actors were supported by a Greek invention, a chorus of twelve or fifteen singer-dancers (usually representing the local populace) who chanted their lines in uni-

son or through a single chorus leader. When the skene became an elevated stage for the principal actors, the chorus members remained in the orchestra below, separating them from the main interactions of the principals.

Greek tragedy was chanted and/or sung, not spoken; unfortunately, the music has not survived. And the chorus danced, as it did in the dithyrambic ceremonies, sometimes formally, sometimes with wild abandon. Greek tragedy, therefore, is not merely the foundation of Western drama but of Western musical theatre, including opera, as well. Greek comedy, by contrast, is the foundation of burlesque, satire, and television sitcoms. The plays of Aristophanes, referred to as Old Comedy, are filled with broad physical humor, gross sexual gags and innuendos, and brilliant wordplay and repartee, often at the expense of contemporary politicians and celebrities. The later plays of Menander, known as New Comedy, gave rise to "stock characters" (such as the bumbling suitor and the timid warrior) and comic plot devices (such as mistaken identity), both of which are recurrent elements of thirty-minute network television.

The City Dionysia was a weeklong festival of celebrations and dramatic competitions. On the first day, introductory ceremonies were held; at these ceremonies, each playwright (selected in advance by civic authorities) introduced his cast and announced the theme of his work. The second day featured processions, sacrifices, and the presentation of ten dithyrambs; and on the third day, five comedies were played. On the fourth, fifth, and sixth days, the three competing playwrights presented — each on a separate day — three related tragedies (a *trilogy*), followed by a comic variation or parody (a *satyr play*) on the same theme. The authors served as the directors of their works. On the seventh, and final, day, judging took place, and prizes for the best play and best leading actor were awarded. It appears that the entire population of freeborn males, and perhaps of freeborn females (we don't know this for certain), attended these performances and rooted for their favorites; judging by later commentaries, outstanding dramatists and actors were as famous then as are today's best-known film directors and movie stars. Clearly the City Dionysia of fifth-century Athens was a monumental and glorious undertaking, which led to some of the most thrilling dramas and theatrical spectacles in history.

Roman Drama

Greek civilization, battered by internal wars, had lost its leading edge by the end of the fifth century B.C., and the power balance in the Mediterranean shifted, in succeeding centuries, to the growing Roman Empire. Excelling in architecture and engineering, more than in dramatic creativity, the Romans created some astonishing stage buildings, of which more than two hundred (most dating from the first centuries A.D.) survive to the present day. Roman architects dispensed with the Greek hillside theatron and threshing-circle orchestra and designed a theatre that was an entirely integrated structure set on a level plain. They also cut the orchestra in half and created tunnel entrances to it (*vomitoria*) on both sides. The simple Greek skene had become a very elaborate, three-story wall (the *frons scaenae*), which was decorated by dozens of statues.

Roman dramatists, however, were rarely as impressive as Roman architects and almost always drew upon Greek sources for their work; indeed, most Roman plays are about Greek characters and Greek struggles. The Roman comic playwrights Plautus and Terence were quite popular in their time, however, and many of their works survive and are performed occasionally today, as are (albeit more rarely) the chamber tragedies of Seneca, a protégé (and victim) of Emperor Nero. All three of these Roman dramatists, in fact, were very popular and much admired by writers and audiences during the European Renaissance. Roman theatre, however, degenerated into sheer spectacle and decadence by the end of the empire, as many theatres were converted into arenas for gladiatorial combat, pitched sea battles, and gruesome public massacres. Together, Greek and Roman drama form a "classical theatre" tradition that has been referenced over and over in Western drama since the Renaissance and right up to the present day.

Medieval Drama

The Fall of Rome (around the middle of the first millennium A.D.) brought to an end the classical era of theatre, and both the early Christian and new-founded Islamic religions of those times banned theatrical representation altogether, partly in reaction to the excesses

Left: In July 1994, for the first time in 335 years, the city of York, in northern England, mounted a procession of medieval wagon performances through city streets. Nine cycle plays, each on its own wagon, were presented sequentially at five different stations, under the overall direction of Jane Oakshott. Shown here is the play of the Annunciation and Visitation, performed in front of a restaurant on Jubbergate.

Right: Adam (Iain Page) and Eve (Joanna Page) are expelled from Eden, while Satan writhes away on his belly, in *The Mysteries*, Tony Harrison's adaptation of the English medieval cycle plays directed by Bill Bryden at the Royal National Theatre in London, 1999.

of late Roman theatre. And when Western drama reappeared, as it did in Europe shortly before the year 1000, it was an altogether different product, sponsored by the same Christian Church that had once banned it. The earliest known dramatization of that period was not a play in the ordinary sense but rather a brief moment in the church's Easter service, when officiating monks reenacted the biblical story of the Virgin Mary and her two companions (also named Mary) as they visit the tomb of Jesus. "Whom seek ye?" (*Quem queri-*

tis?) an angel asks. "Jesus of Nazareth," reply the Marys, whereupon they are told, "He is not here, He has risen." They then break into a chorus of Hallelujahs. It is fascinating, of course, that European drama of the Christian era, like the drama of ancient Egypt and ancient Greece, began with the springtime celebration of a divine resurrection. This simple liturgical playlet, now known as the *Quem Queritis,* became the first of literally hundreds of church-sponsored dramatizations depicting and celebrating the Judeo-Christian story of

MEDIEVAL VERSE — AND A SHAKESPEAREAN PARODY

Medieval English drama was written in verse employing irregular line lengths, an extensive use of alliteration (neighboring words that begin with the same consonant), and rhymes that were seemingly forced into place. This excerpt (with archaic words but modernized spellings) is from the anonymous Fall of Lucifer cycle play, written and performed in York, England, in the fourteenth century. It exemplifies early English dramatic verse:

LUCIFER: (*in Heaven*) Oh, certain, how I am worthily
      wrought with worship, iwis!
  For in glorious glee, my glittering gleams!
  I am so mightily made, my mirth may not miss —
  E'er shall I bide in this bliss through brightness
      of beams!
  Me needs no annoyance to neven,
  All wealth in my world I am wielding!
  Above yet shall I make by building
  Oh high in the highest of heaven!
      (*Lucifer falls into Hell.*)
  Ow! Deuce! All goes down!
  My might and my main all is marring.
  Help, fellows! In faith, I am falling!
  Out! Out! Harrow! Helpless, such heat is there here

This is a dungeon of dole in which I can't delight!
What has my kind become, so comely and clear?
Now I am loathsome, alas who was light.
My brightness is blackest and blue now,
My bale is e'er beating and burning.
I hie me a-howling and churning.
Out! Ay, welaway! I wallow in woe now!

Shakespeare parodied this style of writing two centuries later in *A Midsummer Night's Dream*, in which a group of village craftsmen write and produce a play called "Pyramus and Thisbe," which includes such lines as:

PYRAMUS: Sween moon, I thank thee for thy sunny
      beams.
  I thank thee, moon, for shining now so bright;
  For by thy gracious, golden, glittering gleams,
  I trust to take of truest Thisbe sight.
      But stay, O spite!
      But mark, poor knight,
  What dreadful dole is here!
      Eyes, do you see?
      How can it be?
  O dainty duck! O dear!

humankind — from the Creation of the Universe and Adam and Eve to Doomsday and the Harrowing of Hell.

Medieval drama remained in church liturgy for nearly two centuries, but by about 1250, Bible-based drama had moved outdoors into the churchyards and then into the public streets of every country in Europe. By this time the medieval "mystery plays," as they were then called, were performed in the emerging modern languages of French, English, Spanish, German, and Italian rather than Latin and included scenes that were more secular than purely religious, often with contemporary political overtones. The actors were no longer monks but ordinary citizens, some of whom — those who had mastered the leading parts — were well paid for their efforts. The authors, though anonymous to us, were highly prized

by their communities, as they converted the formal prose of the Bible to comic interplay, jesting repartee, swashbuckling bluster, and intricate versification.

Entire festivals of such plays, numbering in the dozens, were presented in hundreds of European towns every spring, dominating city life where and when they were played and attracting rural audiences from all around. On the European continent, such drama festivals lasted for many days or even weeks, with huge casts performing on a series of stages (known as *mansions*) set up next to each other in the town plaza or marketplace; audiences could stroll from one play to the next, as the plays were performed in sequence. In England, however, the plays were performed on wagon-mounted stages, one for each playlet, that wheeled from one audience site to another

French artist Jacomo Callot's engravings, published in his *Balli di Sfessania* around 1618–20, provide a marvelous, if somewhat fanciful, version of early commedia dell'arte performers, many of whom – for the first time in professional theatre history – were women. The commedia character of Fracischina, pictured here, is a female servant, often seen singing, dancing, and/or flirting, as with a young, gallant Gian Farina. In the background, one sees the ever guileful and acrobatic Arlecchino, standing on his hands.

Fracischina.   *Gian Farina*

during a daylong springtime festival known as *Corpus Christi.*

At first glance, these mystery plays may appear stylistically primitive (see box on previous page), at least in contrast to the splendor of the classic Greek tragedies, but twentieth-century productions have demonstrated their tremendous dramatic impact, even to a religiously diverse contemporary audience. And the scale of medieval theatre production — with its mansions, rolling stages, and casts of hundreds — was simply astonishing. Like the great Gothic cathedrals — also created anonymously and at roughly the same time — the Bible-based medieval theatre was a monumental enterprise that affected the lives of the entire culture that created and experienced it.

Renaissance Drama

Medieval drama was created in ignorance of its classical predecessors, but when, in the High Middle Ages, Roman and then Greek texts began to be translated and published, their influence — on all arts and culture, not merely the theatre — proved overwhelming. We call this the Renaissance: the period when ancient culture was "reborn" and fused — sometimes uneasily — with the medieval and Gothic forms that had been dominant for centuries.

The Renaissance began, by most reckonings, in Italy, where the plays of Plautus and Seneca were first translated in the 1470s. Amateur productions of these Italian translations soon became popular, giving rise to freer adaptations, which are now known as *commedia erudita,* or "learned comedies." By the 1520s, the Florentine diplomat and essayist Niccolò Machiavelli was famous throughout Italy for his learned comedies based on — and taking off from — Roman forebears, and by the middle of the sixteenth century a semi-improvised variation of that comedy, known as *commedia dell'arte,* was performed by itinerant professional actors throughout the Italian peninsula and even beyond. Soon both commedia dell'arte and scripted plays in modern European languages — based on classic or current themes, not biblical ones — were common throughout Europe.

Above: Shakespeare's original theatres were built with an upper staging level, which has been copied by many Shakespeare festival theatres. In this 1997 Utah Shakespeare Festival production, Macbeth and his lady prepare to descend from their upper chamber to the joint (and suggestively twisted) throne they have attained through murder.

Right: It is occasionally argued – though no evidence supports it – that the plays of Shakespeare were written by another writer, with most revisionists favoring one Edward de Vere, the seventeenth Earl of Oxford. Virtually all Shakespearean scholars find this theory absurd, but it remains a piquant issue to the public, which Amy Freed's *The Beard of Avon* exploits in its hilarious South Coast Repertory 2001 premiere. Douglas Weston (left) plays Shakespeare and Mark Harelik the more elegant Earl. Costumes by Walker Hicklin; lighting by Chris Parry.

It was in England that the Renaissance brought forth the greatest dramatic masterpieces of that (or perhaps any) era, in the works of William Shakespeare. Coming of age during the reign of Queen Elizabeth I, Shakespeare began his career in a vibrant theatre world of palatial court theatres, freestanding outdoor "public theatres" that dominated the London skyline, and companies of professional actors who entertained court and public at home and on tour. This "Elizabethan" theatre featured dozens of playwrights whose works

DID SHAKESPEARE WRITE SHAKESPEARE?

Students occasionally wonder about the so-called "authorship question," which challenges the commonly held belief that Shakespeare's plays were written by Shakespeare. Yet while several books have argued against Shakespeare's authorship, and some distinguished thinkers (among them Mark Twain and Sigmund Freud) have shared their doubts as well, there is simply no question to be posed: the evidence that Shakespeare wrote Shakespeare's plays is absolutely overwhelming. Nor has a shred of evidence appeared thus far to indicate that anyone else wrote them. Not a single prominent Elizabethan scholar has accepted the "anti-Stratfordian" (as proponents of other authors are called) argument, which America's most noted Shakespearean scholar, Harold Bloom, simply dismisses as "lunacy."

How can there be a question? Shakespeare is named as author on the title page of seventeen separate publications during his lifetime and is cited as the author of eleven known plays in a book published when he was thirty-four. He is credited as the author of the First Folio in its title, *Mr. William Shakespeare's Comedies, Histories, and Tragedies*, published just seven years after his death; the Folio's editors were his acting colleagues, who describe Shakespeare as fellow actor, author, and friend, and their preface also includes four poems – one by dramatist Ben Jonson – each unequivocally referring to Shakespeare as the author of plays. Surviving records show him performing in his plays at the courts of both Queen Elizabeth and King James, and he was buried, along with his wife, daughter, and son-in-law (and no one else), in the place of greatest honor in his hometown church. An inscribed funeral monument, mentioned in the Folio and showing him with pen in hand, looks down on Shakespeare's grave and was regularly visited in the coming years by persons wishing to see, as one wrote, the last resting place of "the wittiest poet in the world." Birth, marriage, death, heraldic, and other legal records, plus dozens of citations during and shortly after his life tell us more about dramatist William Shakespeare than we have collected for all but a few common-born citizens of his era.

So, what is left to argue? Anti-Stratfordians maintain that the evidence doesn't paint the picture we should expect of such a magnificent playwright: He apparently didn't go to college; his name was spelled in several different ways and sometimes hyphenated; his signatures indicate poor handwriting; his wife and daughters were probably illiterate; he didn't leave any books in his will; no ceremony marked his death; he never traveled to Italy, where many of his plays were set; and an early engraving of the Stratford monument looks different – lacking its pen – than the monument does now.

Little of this is provable, and none of it is remotely convincing even if true. Aeschylus, Euripides, and George Bernard Shaw didn't go to college, either.

remain popular today; Christopher Marlowe, Ben Jonson, and John Webster are three of Shakespeare's most prominent contemporaries, but none, however, was fully comparable to Shakespeare himself. Alone among the world's great authors, Shakespeare was equally adept at producing exemplary postclassical masterpieces of both comedy and tragedy. Four centuries after they were written (approximately 1580–1610), his plays are the most-produced dramas in literally thousands of theatres around the world; they are, indeed, the primary repertoire of over a hundred theatre companies named after him.

Shakespeare was not only an author; he was also an actor and part owner of his own theatre company, the King's Men, and of The Globe theatre in London, which his company built and operated; a new Globe, in fact, has been built near the original site and, since its 1997 opening, has been used for the presentation of Shakespearean-era (and occasionally other)

Right: Like its predecessor, the modern Globe Theater replica in London schedules performances by daylight, come rain or shine. As in Shakespeare's day, a sizable portion of the audience (the groundlings, as they were called in Elizabethan times) observes from a standing-room pit in front of the stage; everyone else sits on hard wooden benches in the surrounding galleries. Shown here, the concluding dance of the Globe's 1998 *As You Like It* – as staged by Lucy Bailey – enchants the audience on all sides.

Shakespeare's knowledge of Italy is nothing an intelligent person couldn't have picked up in an afternoon's conversation – and it wasn't that accurate, either (Shakespeare writes of one who could "lose the tide" facilitating a trip from Verona to Milan – where no water route exists). Many people have unreadable signatures, and in Shakespeare' day neither spelling nor hyphenation was standardized, nor was literacy a norm among country women. That we don't know of a memorial ceremony doesn't mean there wasn't one, and evidence clearly indicates the engraving of a pen-less monument was simply one of many errors in a too-hastily-prepared book. And if Shakespeare maintained a library, he could simply have given it to his son-in-law (a doctor) before his death, or left it to be passed on to his wife along with his house and furnishings, or perhaps he kept books in a private office at the Globe Theater in London, which burned to the ground three years before his death. And who actually knows that he didn't travel to Italy or even study at a university for that matter? We know absolutely nothing about Shakespeare between his ages of twenty-one and twenty-eight; he could have been anywhere and done anything.

But we do know he was a man of the theatre. And obviously an genius. What else need we know? Why must we insist that he have good handwriting? Or literate relatives? Because we do? But we're not Shakespeare, and Shakespeare doesn't have to be like us.

And absolutely no evidence exists that anyone else wrote any of the plays – which explains why there are nearly a half-dozen claimants to this phantom position of the "real" Shakespeare.

It is impossible to represent the entirety of either argument in a few paragraphs (one of the books, proposing the Earl of Oxford, runs over 900 pages), but the entire anti-Stratfordian case, diverting as it may be, is painstakingly and effectively refuted in Irvin Leigh Matus's relentlessly straightforward *Shakespeare, IN FACT* (1994).

It is, of course, possible that all the evidence we now have – *all* of it – has somehow been fabricated. This would mean Shakespeare managed to fool – or buy off – virtually everyone in his town, everyone in his church, everyone in his theatre company, everyone at two royal courts, everyone in the London theatre world, most of the printers and booksellers in England, and everyone they talked to. We would be asked to believe that this gigantic lie (for which we have not a trace of evidence) *never* got out, not through the revival of his plays after his death and then later during the Restoration era. It would have been the most stupendous hoax in human history, incomparable to the insignificant hoax proffered to us by anti-Stratfordians today.

Above: Shakespeare has long been popular in Germany (indeed, *Englische Komödianten* – English actors – toured Germany during Shakespeare's lifetime, effectively inaugurating the German professional theatre), and Shakespearean productions – often radically reconceived – are common throughout Germany today. In this 2001 Berliner Ensemble production of Shakespeare's *Richard II*, directed by the company's celebrated artistic director Claus Peymann, Michael Rothmann plays Richard and Katja Danowski plays his queen, in an environment tattered with the assaults of political corruption and social turmoil not unlike Europe of the 1930s.

Above right: Shakespeare's theatre can be both sexual and brutal, as exemplified by many productions: here, Agamemnon (Richard Elmore) assaults Cressida (Tyler Layton) in the 2001 Oregon Shakespeare Festival production of *Troilus and Cressida*, directed by Kenneth Albers, with costumes by Susan E. Mickey.

plays. With its "thrust stage" and standing-room "pit" open to the sky and surrounded by thatch-roofed seating galleries on three levels, the modern Globe may not — because of modern fire regulations — seat the three thousand people accommodated by the original building, but its restoration helps us better understand the vigor of Shakespearean-era staging and the potential of the drama to electrify a large and diverse audience with profound intelligence and passion, as well as comically expressive hijinks. Shakespeare's plays are well known to literary scholars for their poetic brilliance, relentless investigation of the human condition, and deeply penetrating character portrayals, but they are also filled with music, dancing, ribaldry, puns, satire, pageantry, and humor, which only performance brings to life. They are both great dramatic art and magnificent theatrical entertainment.

The Royal Theatre

If the Renaissance was the rebirth of classical civilization, the age that followed was a vast consolidation and refinement of what had come before; it was an era organized intellectually by the then-emerging empirical sciences and rational philosophies and politically by the increasing importance of European royalty. The seventeenth-century theatre of this so-called Royal era featured the dramas of Pedro Calderón de la Barca at the court of King Philip IV in Spain, the tragedies of Jean Racine and Pierre Corneille and the comedies of Molière under King Louis XIV in France, and the Restoration comedies of William Wycherley and William Congreve under English King Charles II, who was crowned when the royal family was restored to the throne after eighteen years of English civil war and Puritan rule.

Plays of the Royal era were generally aimed more at the aristocracy than at the general populace and reflected the gentility of the seemingly refined taste of courtly patrons. Rational sensibility dominated the times: theories of drama, adapted from Aristotle and hence called "neoclassic," sought to regularize plays within "reasonable" frameworks of time and place, establish strictly measured structures for dramatic verse, unify styles around set genres, and eliminate onstage depictions of physical violence. Indoor theatres, lit by candles instead of sunlight, replaced the outdoor public theatres of earlier times, providing more intimate and comfortable surroundings for an increasingly well dressed audience. Furthermore,

Priest and playwright Pedro Calderón de la Barca (1600–1681) was Spain's great court dramatist, whose philosophical and theological plays were deemed more elegant and refined than his Renaissance predecessors, Lope de Vega and Miguel Cervantes. Calderón's masterpiece, *Life Is a Dream* (c. 1638), treats moral responsibility in a royal (courtly) context; this scene is from the Denver Theatre Center's 1998 production, staged as part of a summer festival of Spanish golden-age drama.

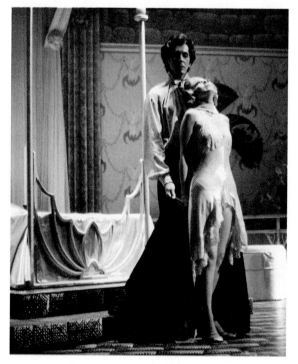

Above: Shown here is the dinner-party scene, in full Louis XIV period setting and costume, from Molière's *The Bourgeois Gentleman* at San Francisco's American Conservatory Theatre (1977). William Ball directed, and Charles Hallahan played Monsieur Jourdain.

Left: Romanticism is in full sway in this stage adaptation reviving Bram Stoker's gothic novel *Dracula*. This Broadway production, starring Frank Langella as the fifteenth-century Transylvanian vampire, featured horrifically luscious scenery and costumes by Edward Gorey.

protection from wind and weather permitted elaborately painted scenery and stage machinery. Several of these theatres are architectural gems that have remained in continuous use to the present day. Style, wit, grace, and class distinction became not merely the framework of drama but its chief subject, and the fan and the snuffbox became signature props. This was also the Western world's first era of extensive theatrical commentary and thus the first from which we have detailed commentaries and evidence — both textual and visual — of the era's dramatic repertoires, acting styles, artists' lives, and the manifestos and controversies that continue to define, in sum, the art of drama.

The Romantic Theatre

Every era in theatre is, to some extent, a rebellion against the previous one, and the romantic theatre of the eighteenth and nineteenth centuries was, in the main, a bold rejection of the rational decorum of the preceding Royal era and its spirit of ordered, elegant, and enlightened debate. Romanticism, by contrast, was florid, exotic, grotesque, sprawling, and imbued with the free-flowing spirit of the individual rather than the social organization of class, court, or scientific or aesthetic academy. Compassion, rather than style and wit, was central to the romantic creed, and authors, such as Johann Wolfgang von Goethe and Friedrich von Schiller in Germany and Victor Hugo in France, intrigued audiences with their deep humanitarian concerns in plays that dealt with devils and monsters, robbers and priests, hunchbacks and heroes.

Romanticism gave rise to melodrama and grand opera and much of the anarchic passion and sprawling sentiment of modern realism as well. Moreover, the romantic quest for the foreign and exotic represented Western drama's first serious re-engagement with the theatre of the East. This, then, is a good point at which to return to drama's earlier years — to the Eastern strain of theatre that sprang from Egyptian and Canaanite beginnings and soon resurfaced on the Indian subcontinent and thereafter throughout Asia.

Theatre in the East

It is misleading to refer to *an* "Asian theatre," for drama in Asia is as rich and diverse as — if not more so than — theatre in the West. Asia, after all — with three-fifths of the world's population — comprises dozens of countries, hundreds of languages, and thousands of identified theatre forms. Nevertheless, although Asian dramatic forms differ markedly from each other, they generally adhere to many fundamental principles, mostly in strong contrast to Western traditions:

- Asian drama is almost never just "spoken"; rather, it is danced, chanted, mimed, and very often sung. Mere spoken drama, when it does occur in the East, is generally recognized as Western in origin or influence.

- Asian dramatic language is invariably rhythmic and melodic; it is appreciated for its sound as much as (or more than) for its meaning. Alliteration, imagery, rhyme, and verbal juxtaposition are often as important in Asian dramatic dialogue as logic, persuasive rhetoric, and realism are in Western drama; and the sonic value of words is as valued by an Asian audience as their semantic value is by a Western audience.

- Asian theatre is ordinarily more visual and sensual than literary or intellectual. Although some Asian dramatists are known for their literary gifts (and several are mentioned in the following discussion), few Asian plays have been widely circulated for general reading or academic study. Most Asians would consider the act of reading a play — separate from seeing it in performance — a rather odd pastime.

Circus-style acrobatics have always been a great feature of the stylized battle scenes in Chinese xiqu, as shown here by the brilliant leaps and back flips of the *wu sheng* (acrobat warrior) performers of China's Hebei Opera Company during their 1998 international tour.

Rather, Asian drama is inextricable from the arts of performance that bring it to life: dance, song, mime, gesture, acrobatics, puppetry, music, sound, costume, and makeup.

- Asian theatre has a strong emphasis on storytelling and myth, yet it is not tightly plotted, as Western drama is, and rarely leads to escalating incidents, stunning reversals, crescendoing climaxes, or elaborate plot closures. Asian theatre, whose metaphysical roots lie in those timeless meditations on human existence that are at the very heart of Hindu and Buddhist cultures, instead may seem, to Western tastes, leisurely and almost wandering. Certainly, Asian theatre's dramatic appeal is more continuous and rapturous than cathartic or arresting.

- Asian theatre is broadly stylized. As one might expect of a dramatic form imbued with music and dance, slice-of-life realism is virtually unknown. Brilliantly colored costumes and makeup, long and obviously artificial beards, elegantly danced battle scenes, and live instrumental accompaniment are virtually standard in traditional Asian theatre.

- Actors train in traditional Asian dramatic forms through an intense apprentice system beginning in early childhood and lasting into early middle age. Most Asian actors, indeed, are born or adopted into their trade.

- The Asian theatre is deeply traditional. Although there are modern and avant-garde theatre movements in most Asian countries — and some Western influence is evident in many of them — what is most remarkable about Eastern theatre is its near-universal consonance with folk history, ancient religions, and cultural myths.

Indian Sanskrit Drama

Asian drama begins in India, where it sprang from the same Middle Eastern roots as its Western counterpart; some scholars even believe that the Greek Dionysus had an Indian heritage. Indeed, there are tantalizing connections between ancient India and Greece, which, one scholar argues, suggests an "Indo-Greek theatre" of the first millennium B.C.; these include fragments of Indian archeological remains that seem to be based on Greek dramatic texts and intriguing anecdotes of Greek theatre productions mounted by officers of Alexander the Great during his Indian invasion in 326 B.C.

Despite its connections to Greek theatre, Indian theatre is very much an independent Asiatic creation, which is first known to us in the form of a native Sanskrit dance-theatre that achieved a solid foothold in the subcontinent somewhere around 200 B.C. and remained popular for more than a thousand years thereafter.[2] Sanskrit plays survive from about A.D. 100, and a comprehensive book of dramatic theory, the *Natyasastra,* or "treatise on theatre," ascribed to Bharata Muni, dates from somewhere between 200 B.C. and A.D. 200. The *Natyasastra,* the most comprehensive study of theatre surviving from the ancient world, contains detailed analyses of Sanskrit dramatic texts, theatre buildings, acting, staging, music, gesture, dance, and even theatre-company organization. The treatise describes ten major genres of Sanskrit drama, including two primary ones: the *nataka,* which was based on well-known heroic stories of kings or sages,

and the *prakarana,* based on the theme of love. The greatest Sanskrit poet, Kalidasa, wrote his masterpiece, *Sakuntala and the Ring of Recognition,* in the nataka style somewhere around the fifth century A.D. *The Little Clay Cart,* attributed to Sudraka, is the best known of two surviving examples of prakarana.

Sanskrit theatre, as far as we can tell (no ruins or drawings survive), was performed indoors, within a roofed building. Rectangular in structure and fitted with a stage of about forty-eight by twenty-four feet, these buildings could seat somewhere between two hundred and five hundred spectators. Two doors, with an onstage orchestra between them, provided access to the dressing area behind the stage, and four columns held up the roof or an upper pavilion. Carved wooden elephants, tigers, and snakes adorned the pillars and perhaps the ceiling. The performance of Sanskrit drama was danced and acted with an onstage instrumental and percussion accompaniment. Performers, all from priestly castes and trained from very early childhood, were absolute virtuosos of their particularly demanding art.

Sanskrit drama died out around the tenth century, as the broad-based Hindu court culture fragmented in the wake of repeated Mongol invasions and the peoples of India fell back into preexisting regional cultures and languages. In succeeding centuries, dozens — even hundreds — of provincial theatre forms became popular throughout the subcontinent, a vast number of which remain to the present day. Despite their many differences, all Indian drama forms share many of the fundamental theatre aesthetics of their Sanskrit predecessors and the doctrines of the ancient *Natyasastra.*

Indian Kathakali

Today the most widely known of these regional dance-drama forms is the *kathakali* ("story play"), which originated in rural villages in the province of Kerala in the seventeenth century; it currently plays in many urban centers in the

---

[2]All dates in early Indian drama are extremely approximate, within a plus-or-minus margin of sometimes up to four or five *centuries.*

In the Indian kathakali dance-drama, royal characters wear an elaborate *kiritam*, or crown, which frames the actor's eye movements – one of the most intensively studied skills of kathakali performers. Kalamandalam Gopi, a senior kathakali maestro, is shown here in the role of King Rugmangada in *Rugmangadacharitam*, performed in Trichur, Kerala (India) in 1993.

province and often abroad. Kathakali is a drama based on any of thousands of stories from the two great Indian epics, the *Ramayana* and the *Mahabharata*. Kathakali performance itself is somewhat of an epic as well, with its outdoor performances lasting from about ten at night until well beyond dawn the next day. Traditionally, audience members are free to leave, take naps, and eat during the performance; today, however, kathakali is more often performed in the three-hour evening time blocks common to Western theatre.

In kathakali, the text is sung — to a percussion accompaniment of gongs, drums, and cymbals — by two singers seated at the side. Actors dance and pantomime the dramatic action; by employing precise and elaborate hand gestures, footwork patterns, distinctive eye and eyebrow movements, and postural contortions, they reveal subtleties of meaning and characterization that are barely suggested by the text. Consequently, actors train rigorously for kathakali performance from early childhood, achieving mastery — if at all — only by about age forty. Highly stylized makeup and costuming also convey characterization and attitude; red- or black-bearded characters represent evil, and white-bearded ones the divine. No scenery is used in kathakali, as plays are presented in arbitrary sites, with four simple poles defining the acting area.

Japanese Nō

The island nation of Japan has created two great theatre forms, *nō* and *kabuki.* Each is virtually a living museum of centuries-old theatre practice — nō and kabuki are performed today in very much the same fashion as in earlier times — yet each is also an immensely satisfying theatre experience for modern audiences attuned to the Japanese culture.

Nō is Japan's most revered and cerebral theatre. It is also the oldest continuously performed drama in the world. Perfected in the fourteenth and fifteenth centuries almost solely by a single father-son team (Kan'ami and Zeami), who between them wrote and produced approximately 240 of the surviving plays, nō is a highly ceremonial drama, mysterious and tragic, that almost always portrays supernatural events and characters. All nō plays center on a single character, known as the *shite* (the "doer"), who is interrogated, prompted, and challenged by a secondary character, called the *waki.* Whereas waki characters are always living male humans — usually ministers, commoners, or priests — shite characters may be gods, ghosts, women, animals, or warriors; the shite role, unlike the waki, is played in a mask. Nō actors — all of whom are male — train for only one of these role types, which they normally perform throughout their careers. Long training provides actors with the precise choreography and the musical notations required of their danced and chanted performance.

The actual nō stage is a precisely measured square of highly polished Japanese cypress flooring, about eighteen feet across, supported from below by large earthenware jars that resonate with the actors' foot-stompings. A bridgelike runway (*hashigakari*) provides stage access from stage right; it is used for the solemn entrances and exits particularly characteristic of nō. An ornate, curved roof covers the stage and is reminiscent of the time when the stage was housed in a separate building, which the audience observed from a distance; the nō roof is supported by four wooden pillars, each with its own name and historic dramatic function. A wooden "mirror wall" at the rear of the stage bounces back the sounds of music and singing to the audience; on the wall, a painted pine tree, delicately gnarled and highly stylized, provides the only scenery. A four-man orchestra — whose instruments include a flute, small and large hand drums, and a stick drum — provides continuous musical accompaniment at the rear of the stage, and a chorus of six to ten singer-chanters is positioned on a platform addition at stage left. The absolute precision of the theatre design and the stately performance choreography and musicality give nō a ceremonial quality that is unique in world drama.

Nō has never been a theatre of mass entertainment, and first-time patrons today — including many Japanese — often find it bewildering. Plotting, even in comparison to other Asian forms, is weak or virtually nonexistent. The language is medieval, elliptical, and often forbiddingly obscure. The cast is small, the action relatively static, and the pace,

This nō theatre mask, worn by the *shite* (doer) character, dates from the eighteenth century, although its design dates from nearly half a millennium earlier.

by modern standards, virtually glacial: the basic nō walk, said to be derived from tramping through rice paddies, is an agonizingly deliberate slip-slide shuffle, with the feet barely leaving the ground. Even when unmasked, the actors are trained to keep their faces immobile and expressionless at all times. Certainly nō is produced today more for enthusiasts than for the general public, but it is notable that the number of such enthusiasts — at least in Japan — is currently growing not falling; in fact, one scholar claims that "performances are at their most popular level in the history of the art." Like the study of martial arts, flower arranging, and the tea ceremony, nō remains as a Japanese national passion. Its sublime

The most famous kabuki dance-drama is the 1753 *Musume Dōjōji* ("The maiden at Dōjō Temple"), in which the wronged, fire-breathing serpent Kiyohime, masquerading as the beautiful young lady Hanako, dances for the monks of Dōjō Temple only in order to seize the temple's new gong and melt it down in vengeance. Nakamura Jakuemon IV plays the *onnagata* ("women-type") role of Kiyohime/Hanako; the kneeling chanters and musicians upstage perform the accompanying "long song" music.

mystery and serenity — reflective of deep Buddhist and Shinto values — resonate profoundly in contemporary Japanese life and have proven increasingly influential to Japanese as well as Western dramatists of the current era.

Japanese Kabuki

Created two hundred years after nō, kabuki has always been a more spectacular and accessible form of theatrical entertainment. Whereas nō is refined, dignified, and designed for small, studious audiences, kabuki is gaudy and exhilarating; from its earliest days, it was created to delight large crowds of merchants, traders, courtesans, and ordinary city dwellers. Whereas nō is sober and ascetic and staged on a relatively small, bare platform, kabuki is a theatrical extravaganza of dazzling colors, flamboyant dance and recitation, passionate emotion, and elaborate stage machinery and

effects. Japanese audiences often respond by shouting their favorite actors' names or other words of encouragement at key moments in the play.

Kabuki was created in Kyoto around 1600 by the legendary shrine maiden Izumo Okuni, whose flamboyant and dramatic style of dancing became hugely popular in Kyoto's brothels and teahouses. The outlandish extravagance of Okuni's costumes and the fact that women performed both male and female characters invited the term *kabuku*, meaning "askew" (we might translate it today as "punk"). This fast-developing and exotic entertainment was transformed by midcentury — in a series of government edicts — from an all-female to an all-male performing art. More complex dramatic storytelling — with themes based on traditional myths, historical incidents, local sex scandals and suicides, and already-ancient nō drama — was adapted into the evolving format, which was by then renamed *kabuki,* a term comprising three Chinese characters: *ka* ("song"), *bu* ("dance"), and *ki* ("skill"), the three major ingredients of kabuki.

By the century's end, kabuki staging had incorporated curtains and scenery, playwrights' names were being printed in kabuki programs, and star actors had emerged, creating the two principal kabuki acting styles: *wagoto* (the elegant and naturalistic "soft style" of actor Sakata Tōjūrō I, from Kyoto) and *aragoto* (the thundering "rough style" of Ichikawa Danjūrō I, from Edo, now Tokyo). The traditions of both these actors remain central to kabuki to the present day, as all kabuki actors are members of but eleven famous families and all

can trace their lineage — familial and professional — back to their kabuki-performing ancestors. The current star Ichikawa Danjūrō XII, for example, is the great-great-great-great-great-great-great-great-grandson of Ichikawa Danjūrō I, born in 1660; the celebrated Danjūrō style has been directly passed, father to son, down through the centuries.

There are many types of kabuki dramas, but the major works fall generally under two categories: history plays (*jidaimono*, or "period things") and domestic plays (*sewamono*, or "common things"). The history plays dramatize — usually in spectacular fashion — major political events of the remote past; often, however, the historical distance was little more

In kabuki's famous dance-drama *Kagami Jishi* ("The lion dance"), the lion (played by Nakamura Kankuro V) is teased by butterflies (played by his sons Nakamura Kantaro II and Nakamuro Schichinosuki II).

Chikamatsu Hanji's *Mount Imose* (1771) is a kabuki tragedy in which, as in *Romeo and Juliet,* children of rival families fall in love. Here, Princess Hinadori (*at left*, played by Nakamura Senjaku III) is in her house, and the nobleman Kaganosuki (*at right*, played by Nakamura Baigyoku IV) laments their separation. The houses, backed by blossoming cherry trees, are separated by the Yoshino River, represented by rolling cylinders painted in wavy stripes.

than a protective cover for past playwrights and actors, who were in fact reflecting — under the guise of an apparently historical depiction — various controversial issues of nobles and political officials of their own time. Domestic plays, by contrast, deal with the affairs of the townspeople, merchants, lovers, and courtesans of the playwright's own era, often focusing on the conflicts — intense throughout Japanese culture — between affairs of the heart and the call of duty. A great many domestic plays end in suicide (many, in fact, end in double suicides), with the lovers vowing to meet again in the world to come; such plays have been the subject of attempted bannings, as they have led to real suicides in consequence.

Kabuki is mainly an actor's theatre; many of its plays are of unknown authorship and have been augmented over the centuries by actors' additions. One notable exception, however, is the kabuki author Chikamatsu Monzaemon (1653–1724). Considered the greatest Japanese dramatist of all time, Chikamatsu was also a famous playwright of the Japanese puppet theatre *bunraku*.

Chinese Xiqu

China, Asia's largest nation, is Asia's oldest continuous culture, as well as the home of Asia's oldest continuous theatre tradition. As with all Asian drama, Chinese theatre is more sung than spoken, but since even Chinese speech is itself semimusical — as it is based on tonal changes as well as syllabic pronunciation — all traditional Chinese theatre is known by the Chinese term *xiqu* ("tuneful theatre"), which we translate as "Chinese Opera."

Although forms of xiqu existed in China before the first century, the first well-defined Chinese Opera form, known as *zaju* ("various plays"), appeared in China during the Song dynasty in the tenth century, reaching its golden age in the thirteenth century under the Mongol Emperor Kublai Khan. Zaju was a comedic music-dance-drama, with acrobatics and clowning; it was so popular that a single amusement park in thirteenth-century Keifeng (then China's northern capital) featured at least fifty indoor zaju theatres, the largest holding several thousand people.

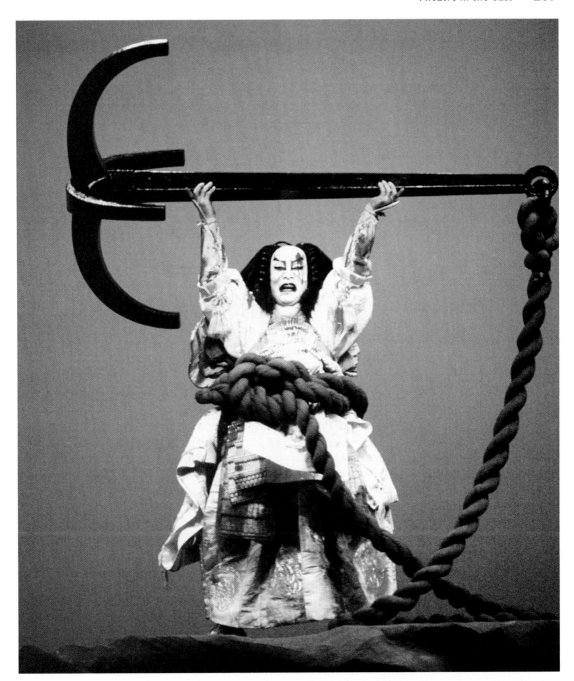

One of kabuki's most celebrated moments is Tomomori's suicide, which ends the 1747 history play *Yoshitsune Sembon Zakura* ("Yoshitsune and the thousand cherry trees"). Tomomori, a defeated Heike warlord, ties a ship's anchor to his waist and throws it back over his head, following it overboard to a watery death. The role is performed here by Ichikawa Danjūrō XII.

SPEAKING THEATRICAL CHINESE

There are several Chinese words referring to the theatrical arts. *Xi* (pronounced "shee") refers to theatrical entertainments of all sorts. *Qu* ("chyoo") denotes tune, or music. Their combination, *xiqu* (pronounced "shee-chyoo" and meaning "tuneful theatre"), is the most common term by which we refer to all varieties of traditional Chinese theatre, commonly known in the West as Chinese Opera. *Ju* is a more limited Chinese word for theatre, and *xiju* can be used to refer to modern as well as Chinese theatre. Unfortunately, Western ears have difficulty distinguishing the pronunciation of *qu* and *ju*, both of which are phonetically transcribed into English as "chyoo" but are aspirated differently in spoken Mandarin. *Jing* (pronounced "jean") means "capital"; therefore *jingju* (pronounced "jean-chyoo" and meaning "theatre of the capital") refers specifically to Beijing Opera, the most popular form of xiqu. (Beijing literally means "northern capital.")

By current convention, these and other generic Asian theatre terms such as *kathakali*, *kabuki*, and *nō* are normally uncapitalized in English.

By the end of the Ming dynasty, in 1644, zaju had been succeeded by a more stately, poetic, and aristocratic opera known as *kunqu,* originating from the town of Kunshan; soon thereafter kunqu became the favored theatre entertainment of the Chinese court. Kunqu is still performed today. More popular theatre developed around the same time in the form of a more boisterous "clapper opera," characterized by the furious rhythmic beating of drumsticks on a hardwood block. And in subsequent years, many regional theatre styles, influenced by the zaju, kunqu, and clapper opera forms, arose throughout the country. Today there are as many as 360 variations of Chinese Opera in the People's Republic, most of them — such as Cantonese Opera, Sichuan Opera, Hui Opera — known by their regional origins.

The most famous Chinese Opera in modern times, however, is the Beijing (Peking) Opera, which is known in Chinese as *jingju,* or "theatre of the capital." Jingju was founded in 1790, when, in celebration of the emperor's eightieth birthday, a group of actors from the mountains of Anhui — led by one Cheng Chang-geng — came to Beijing and amazed the court with their brilliant and innovative style of singing, music, and (in particular) acrobatics and martial arts. As local actors assimilated the Anhui style with their own, a new "capital" style was developed, reaching its current form by about 1850, by which time it had become the dominant popular theatre of all China. Beijing Opera remains not just one of the great glories of the world's traditional performing arts but — after a nearly thirteen-year hiatus occasioned by the Chinese Cultural Revolution in the 1960s and 1970s — a highly popular national entertainment in China and around the world.

Because the stories and plots of Chinese Opera are normally ancient and well known, the actual staging of such works becomes, above all, a celebration of the performers' individual skills (*gong*); in particular, actors must master the classic fourfold combination of singing (*chong*), speech (*nian*), acting and movement (*zuo*), and martial arts and acrobatics (*da*). Virtually all Chinese Opera performers are proficient in all four of these arts;

Above right: The seventeenth-century *Peony Pavilion* is one of the best-known plays in the traditional Chinese theatre. This 1998 Shanghai production, directed by Chen Shi-Zheng, demonstrates the extraordinarily detailed *jing* ("painted-face") roles, together with the brilliantly colored costumes and weaponry characteristic of xiqu. The twenty-hour production was scheduled to perform at Lincoln Center in New York, but the tour was prevented at the last minute by Shanghai authorities (see the chapter titled "Theatre Today").

Below right: The Monkey King — a ferocious scamp, not dissimilar to the Italian Arlecchino — is the most enduring character in xiqu; he is always dressed in yellow, as shown here in this Shanghai Jingju Theatre production of *Pansi Cave.*

No boat and no water! As with most Asian theatre forms, xiqu achieves its greatest effects by simple and stylized means. Here, in a 1997 production of the Chinese classic *The Meeting by the Lake*, the famed Shanghai performer Liu Yilong portrays a boatman ferrying passengers across the lake simply (but it's not so simple) by standing and waving a paddle behind him on the bare stage.

"water-sleeves," which fall all the way to the floor. Chinese Opera singing, much of which is in an extreme falsetto (originally employed so that actors could be heard over the din of people talking during the performance), is accompanied by the near-constant clanging of gongs and cymbals, clapper claps, drumbeats, and the furious strumming of various two-stringed fiddles. Movement skills include a rapid heel-to-toe walk, contortionist bendings and swayings, sudden jerks and freezes, and thrilling displays of full-stage acrobatics: continuously back-springing performers bound across the stage in a literal blur, and in battle scenes combatants repel spear thrusts — eight at a time, all in different directions — with both hands and both feet. Chinese Opera has never been dependent on scenery — an actor who enters holding a paddle behind him is assumed to be on a boat; an actor entering with a riding crop is assumed to be on horseback — but its storytelling conventions and its spectacular musical, visual, and acrobatic displays offer audiences one of the world's most thrilling and magnificent theatrical experiences.

The Theatrical Tradition Today: East and West

These eleven great theatre traditions of the past — Greek, Roman, medieval, Renaissance, Royal, and romantic in the Western world; Sanskrit, kathakali, nō, kabuki, and xiqu in the East — are all alive today, either in the form of regular and careful revivals or, happier yet in the case of the last four (and, to some extent, the plays of the Royal and romantic eras as well), by a continuous tradition of performance. All of these traditions have influenced the modern theatre, as we will see in the next chapter. Increasingly, that influence crosses and recrosses the East-West divide that has existed in theatre history since the decline of the Egyptian coronation dramas two thousand years ago.

the greatest performing artists — who are famous throughout China — have mastered each of them to virtuoso standards. Indeed, it might be said that the equivalent of a great Chinese actor in the West would be someone who could perform for the American Ballet Theatre, La Scala Opera, the Royal Shakespeare Company, the Ringling Brothers Circus, and the French Foreign Legion — all on the same evening.

Chinese Opera is a spectacular visual feast, with dazzling costumes, huge glittery headdresses, and brilliantly colorful face painting. Actors of both sexes wear multilayered gowns in bold primary colors, many of which have

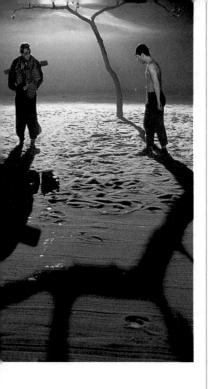

8

The Modern Theatre

The theatre has experienced many great periods, as we have seen, but one of its greatest is still going on. This is the period we call the modern, to which can be added the onrush of avant-garde movements we call (for the time being) the postmodern. Together, these make up the theatre of our times, a theatre that will likely be heralded for *all* times.

Modern drama can be said to date back to about 1875, and its roots lie deep in the social and political upheavals that developed in the eighteenth and nineteenth centuries, a time characterized by revolution. Political revolution in the United States (1776) and France (1789) irrevocably changed the political structure of the Western world, and industrial-technological revolution cataclysmically overhauled the economic and social systems of most of the world. In the wake of these developments came an explosion of public communication and transportation, a tremendous expansion of literacy, democracy, and public and private wealth, and a universal demographic shift from country to town. These forces combined to create in Europe, the United States, and elsewhere mass urban populations hungering for social communion and stimulation: a fertile ground for the citified and civilized theatre of our times.

Simultaneously, an intellectual revolution — in philosophy, in science, in social understanding, and in religion — was altering human consciousness in ways far transcending the effects of revolutionary muskets and industrial consolidation. The intellectual

241

certainty of Louis XIV, whose divine right to rule was unquestioned in the seventeenth and early eighteenth centuries, appeared ludicrous in an age governed by secular scientific investigation. The clear-sightedness of a playwright such as Molière seemed simplistic in an age of existentialism signaled by the soul-searching, self-doubting analyses of Søren Kierkegaard. The intellectual revolution was an exceedingly complex phenomenon that occurred in many spheres of thought and was to gain momentum with each passing decade. It continues to this day.

The Copernican theory had already made clear that human beings do not stand at the geographic center of the universe but rather that our world, indeed our universe, is swept up in a multiplicity of interstellar movements. Later scientists would press further than that, until eventually the revelations of Albert Einstein, Werner Heisenberg, and others would remove all of our "hitching posts in space" and establish the human animal as little more than a transformation of kinetic energy, wobbling shiftily in a multigravitational atomic field marked by galaxies and black holes, neutrinos and quarks, matter and antimatter, all in a vast dance of inexplicable origin and doubtful destiny.

Nor was that "human animal" so vastly privileged over other species, it would seem. Darwin would argue that we *homo sapiens* are directly linked to other mammals — descended not from Adam and Eve nor pre-Hellenic demigods but from primal apes and prehistoric orangutans. Our morals and religions, anthropologist Ruth Benedict would argue, were not handed down to all humanity from a single source but are instead a ranging complex of laws and traditions, wholly relative to the climes and cultures we inhabit. The work of Freud would disclose the existence of the unconscious, a dark and lurking inner self aswarm with infantile urges, primordial fantasies, and suppressed fears and rages. The writings of Karl Marx would contend that all social behavior has its basis in economic greed, class struggle, and primal amorality. "Everlasting uncertainty and agitation" is the nature of human intercourse, according to Marx, and society comprises "two great hostile camps" continually engaged in civil war.

These and scores of other serious challenges to traditional thinking were accompanied everywhere by public debate and dispute. By the turn of the twentieth century, an investigative ferment had seized Western civilization: data were being collected on every conceivable topic, and scientific questioning and testing replaced intuition and dogma as the accepted avenues to truth. Experimentation, exploration, documentation, and challenge became the marching orders of the artist and intellectual alike.

The modern theatre has its roots in these political, social, and intellectual revolutions. Ever since its outset it has been a theatre of challenge, a theatre of experimentation. It has never been a theatre of rules or simple messages, nor has it been a theatre of demigods or of absolute heroes and villains. It has reflected, to a certain degree, the confusions of its times, but it has also struggled to clarify and to illuminate, to document and explore human destiny in a complex and uneasy universe.

Realism

Thus far, the movement that has had the most pervasive and long-lived effect on modern theatre is, beyond question, realism. Realism has sought to create a drama without conventions or abstractions. *Likeness to life* is realism's goal, and in pursuit of that goal it has renounced, among other things, idealized or prettified settings, versifications, contrived endings, and stylized costumes and performances.

Realism is a beguiling aesthetic philosophy. Indeed, the theatre has *always* taken "real life" as its fundamental subject, and so realism seems at first glance to be an appropriate

Tennessee Williams is perhaps America's most enduring twentieth-century playwright. His timeless work *A Streetcar Named Desire* presents a poetic and theatrical realism that grows even more meaningful over the years. Company cofounder (and now film actor) Gary Sinese played Stanley in this 1997 production at Chicago's Steppenwolf Theatre.

style with which to approach the reality of existence. Instead of having actors represent characters, the realists would say, let us have the actors *be* those characters; instead of having dialogue stand for conversation, let us have dialogue that *is* conversation; instead of having scenery and costumes that convey a sense of time and place and atmosphere, let us have scenery that is genuinely inhabitable and costumes that are real clothes.

But, of course, realism has its limits: any dramatic piece must inevitably involve a certain shaping and stylization, no matter how lifelike its effect; the advocates of theatrical realism are well aware of this inevitability. Nevertheless, the ideology of realism was tested, during the last years of the nineteenth century and the first years of the twentieth,

in every aspect of theatre — acting, directing, design, and playwriting — and the results of those tests form a body of theatre that is both valid and meaningful and a style that remains enormously significant.

A Laboratory

In essence, the realistic theatre is conceived to be a laboratory in which the nature of relationships, the ills of society, the symptoms of a dysfunctional family are "objectively" set down for the final judgment of an audience of impartial observers. Every aspect of realistic theatre should strictly adhere to the "scientific method" of the laboratory; nothing must ring false. The setting is to resemble the prescribed locale of the play as closely as possible;

indeed, it is not unusual for much of the scenery to be acquired from a real-life environment and transported to the theatre. Costumes worn by characters in the realistic theatre follow the dress of "real" people of similar societal status; dialogue re-creates the cadences and expressions of daily life.

Early on in the realist movement, the proscenium stage was modified to accommodate scenery constructed in box sets, with the walls given full dimension and with real bookcases, windows, fireplaces, swinging doors, and so forth built into the walls just as they are in a house interior. In the same vein, realistic acting was judged effective insofar as it was drawn from the behavior of life and insofar as the actors seemed to be genuinely speaking to each other instead of playing to the audience. A new aesthetic principle was spawned: the "theatre of the fourth wall removed," in which the life onstage was conceived to be the same as life in a real-world setting, except that, in the case of the stage, one wall — the proscenium opening — had been removed. Thus the theatre was like a laboratory telescope and the stage like a microbiologist's slide: a living environment set up for judicious inspection by neutral observers.

And so realism presents its audience with an abundance of seemingly real-life "evidence" and permits each spectator to arrive at his or her own conclusions. There is some shaping of this evidence by author and performer alike, to be sure, but much of the excitement of the realistic theatre is occasioned by the genuine interpretive freedom it allows the audience and by the accessibility of its characters, whose behaviors are familiar enough to the average spectator that they may be easily assimilated and identified.

Moreover, in presenting its evidence from the surface of life, realism encourages us to delve into the mystery that lies beneath — for the exploration of life's mystery is the true, if unspoken, purpose of every realistic play. Realism's characters, like people in life, are defined by detail rather than by symbol or abstract idealization: like people we know, they are ultimately unpredictable, humanly complex rather than ideologically absolute.

The success of realism is well established; indeed, realism remains one of the dominant modes of drama to this day. At its most profound, when crafted and performed by consummately skilled artists, realistic theatre can generate extremely powerful audience empathy by virtue of the insight and clarity it brings to real-world moments. In giving us characters, the realist playwright gives us *friends:* fellow travelers on the voyage of human discovery with whom we can compare thoughts and feelings. In the uncertainties and trepidations, the wistfulness, the halting eloquence and conversational syntax of these characters we recognize ourselves, and in that recognition we gain an understanding of our own struggles and a compassion for all human endeavors.

Pioneers of Realism

The realistic theatre had its beginnings in the four-year period that saw the premieres of three shocking plays by Norwegian playwright Henrik Ibsen: *A Doll's House* (1867), *Ghosts* (1881), and *An Enemy of the People* (1882). Already famous for historical and poetic dramas, including the magnificent *Peer Gynt* (1867), Ibsen (1828–1906), soon to be known as the "father of dramatic realism," had in these works turned his attention to more contemporary and day-to-day themes: woman's role in society, hereditary disease and mercy killing, and political hypocrisy. Ordinary people populate Ibsen's realistic world, and the issues addressed in these dramas affect ordinary husband-wife, mother-son, and brother-brother relationships and are played out in the interiors of ordinary homes. Controversial beyond measure in their own time, these plays retain their edge of pertinence even today and still have the power to inform, move, and even shock. The reason for their lasting impact lies in Ibsen's choice of issues and his skill at showing both sides through brilliantly captured psychological detail.

The realistic theatre spread rapidly throughout Europe as the controversy surrounding Ibsen's plays and themes stimulated other writers to follow suit. The result was a proliferation of "problem plays," as they were sometimes called, which focused genuine social concern through realistic dramatic portrayal. In Germany, Gerhart Hauptmann (1862–1946) explored the plight of the middle and proletarian classes in several works, most notably in his masterpiece *The Weavers* (1892). In England, Irish-born George Bernard Shaw (1856–1950) created a comedic realism through which he addressed issues such as slum landlordism (in *Widowers' Houses,* 1892), prostitution (in *Mrs. Warren's Profession,* 1902), and urban poverty (in *Major Barbara,* 1905). In France, under the encouragement of innovative director André Antoine, Eugène Brieux (1858–1938) wrote a series of realistic problem plays that included *Damaged Goods* (1902), which deals with syphilis, and *Maternity* (1903), which deals with birth control. By the turn of the century, realism was virtually the standard dramatic form in Europe.

If the realistic theatre came to prominence with the plays of Henrik Ibsen, it attained its stylistic apogee in the major works of Anton Chekhov (1860–1904). Chekhov was a physician by training and a writer of fiction by vocation. Toward the end of his career, in association with realist director Konstantin Stanislavsky (1863–1938) and the Moscow Art Theatre, he also achieved success as a playwright through a set of plays that portray the end of the czarist era in Russia with astonishing force and subtlety: *The Seagull* (1896), *Uncle Vanya* (1899), *The Three Sisters* (1901), and *The Cherry Orchard* (1904). The intricate craftsmanship of these plays has never been surpassed; even the minor characters seem to breathe the same air we do.

Chekhov's technique was to create deeply complex relationships among his characters and to develop his plots and themes more or

"CRAPULOUS STUFF"

"This mass of vulgarity, egotism, coarseness, and absurdity . . . This disgusting representation . . . An open drain; a loathsome sore unbandaged; a dirty act done publicly . . . Absolutely loathsome and fetid . . . Crapulous stuff." These were the *London Daily Telegraph*'s comments on the 1891 English premiere of what they described as "Ibsen's positively abominable play entitled *Ghosts.*"

The *Telegraph* was hardly alone. "Unutterably offensive . . . Abominable . . . Scandalous," said the *Standard.* "Naked loathsomeness . . . Most dismal and repulsive," said the *Daily News.* "Revoltingly suggestive and blasphemous," said the *Daily Chronicle.* "Morbid, unhealthy, unwholesome, and disgusting," said *Lloyds.* "Most loathsome of Ibsen's plays . . . Garbage and offal," said *Truth.* "Putrid," said *Academy.* "A wicked nightmare," said *Gentlewoman.* "As foul and filthy a concoction as has ever been allowed to disgrace the boards of an English theatre," said *Era.*

Why such outrage? What offense, precisely, did *Ghosts* commit? This is a play without a single obscene word, without a single undraped bosom, without a single sexual act, and without a single double entendre.

What *Ghosts* does is to explore ruthlessly, honestly, and *realistically* the fullest implications of a hypocritical Victorian marriage, one behind whose seeming serenity exists a chaotic history of promiscuity, incest, disease, and deceit. In the play, Mrs. Alving maintains the outward shell of her marriage, thought by society to be an "ideal" one, despite the profligacy of her husband. When her son, Oswald, loses his mind at the end of the play – a mind destroyed by the syphilitic spirochetes (the literal "ghosts" of the play) inherited from his father's sins – the high spirit of European romanticism was forcibly retired in favor of a more searching, more demanding, ground-level analysis of contemporary life in a postindustrial age.

less between the lines. Every Chekhovian character is filled with secrets that are never fully revealed by the dialogue.

As an example of Chekhov's realist style, examine particularly the dialogue in the following scene from *The Three Sisters.* In this scene,

Vershinin, an army colonel, meets Masha and her sisters, Irina and Olga, whom Vershinin dimly remembers from past years in Moscow:

VERSHININ: I have the honor to introduce myself, my name is Vershinin. I am very, very glad to be in your house at last. How you have grown up! Aie-aie!

IRINA: Please sit down. We are delighted to see you.

VERSHININ: (*with animation*) How glad I am, how glad I am! But there are three of you sisters. I remember — three little girls. I don't remember your faces, but that your father, Colonel Prozorov, had three little girls I remember perfectly. How time passes! Hey-ho, how it passes! . . .

IRINA: From Moscow? You have come from Moscow?

VERSHININ: Yes. Your father was in command of a battery there, and I was an officer in the same brigade. (*To* MASHA) Your face, now, I seem to remember.

MASHA: I don't remember you.

VERSHININ: So you are Olga, the eldest — and you are Masha — and you are Irina, the youngest —

OLGA: You come from Moscow?

VERSHININ: Yes. I studied in Moscow. . . . I used to visit you in Moscow.

Masha and Vershinin are destined to become lovers; their deepening, largely unspoken communion will provide one of the most haunting strains in the play. And how lifelike is the awkwardness of their first encounter! Vershinin's enthusiastic clichés ("how time passes") and interjections ("Aie-aie!") are the stuff of everyday discourse; the news that he comes from Moscow is repeated so that it becomes amusing rather than informative, a revelation of character rather than of plot.

Masha's first exchange with Vershinin gives no direct indication of the future of their relationship; it is a crossed communication in which one character refuses to share in the other's memory. Is this a personal repudiation, or is it a teasing provocation? The acting, not simply the text, must establish their developing rapport. The love between Vershinin and Masha will tax to the maximum the capabilities of the actors who play their parts to express deep feeling through subtle nuance, through the gestures, the glances, the tones of voice, and the shared understandings and sympathetic rhythms that distinguish lovers everywhere. It is a theme that strongly affects the mood of the play but is rarely explicit in the dialogue.

Naturalism

Naturalism, a movement whose development paralleled but was essentially independent of realism, represents an even more extreme attempt to dramatize human reality without the appearance of dramaturgical shaping. The naturalists, who flourished primarily in France during the late nineteenth century (Émile Zola, 1840–1902, was their chief theoretician), based their aesthetics on nature, particularly humanity's place in the natural (Darwinian) environment. To the naturalist, the human being was merely a biological phenomenon whose behavior was determined entirely by genetic and social circumstances. To portray a character as a hero, or even as a credible force for change in society, was anathema to the naturalist, who similarly eschewed dramatic conclusions or climaxes. Whereas realist plays at that time tended to deal with well-defined social issues — women's rights, inheritance laws, worker's pensions, and the like — naturalist plays offered nothing more than a "slice of life," in which the characters of the play were the play's entire subject; any topical issues that arose served merely to facilitate the interplay of personalities and highlight the characters' situations, frustrations, and hopes.

The naturalists sought to eliminate every vestige of dramatic convention: "All the great successes of the stage are triumphs over con-

Arthur Miller's *Death of a Salesman* is often considered America's finest tragedy. In this memory scene from the distinguished 1999 Goodman Theatre (Chicago) production – which subsequently moved to Broadway – Brian Dennehy (*center*) is Willy Loman, reliving his happier days with sons Biff (Kevin Anderson, the former high-school sports hero) and ironically-named Happy (Ted Koch).

vention," declared Zola. Their efforts in this direction are exemplified by August Strindberg's elimination of the time-passing intermission in *Miss Julie* (instead, a group of peasants, otherwise irrelevant to the plot, enter the kitchen setting between acts and dance to fill the time Miss Julie is spending in Jean's offstage bedroom) and by Arthur Schnitzler's elimination of conventional scene beginnings, endings, and climaxes in the interlocking series of cyclical love affairs that constitute the action of *La Ronde*.

Inasmuch as sheer verisimilitude, presented as "artlessly" as humanly possible, is the primary goal of the naturalist, the term *naturalism* is often applied to those realistic plays that seem most effectively lifelike. This is not

a particularly felicitous use of the term, however, because it ignores the fundamental precept of naturalism — that the human being is a mere figure in the natural environment. Naturalism is not merely a matter of style; it is a philosophical concept concerning the nature of the human animal. And naturalist theatre represents a purposeful attempt to explore that concept, using extreme realism as its basic dramaturgy.

Eugene O'Neill, America's first great playwright, pioneered an earthy naturalistic style in his early plays, returning to that style in his autobiographical masterpiece, *Long Day's Journey into Night* — a play so true to life that O'Neill forbade its production or publication until many years after his death. In our times, the dramas of Arthur Miller, Tennessee Williams, Robert Anderson, William Inge, David Mamet, Lorraine Hansberry, and William Gibson are all strongly influenced by both realism and naturalism, which continue to have a commanding presence on the American stage.

Antirealism

Realism and naturalism were not the only new movements of the late nineteenth century to make themselves strongly felt in the modern theatre. A counterforce, equally powerful, was to emerge. First manifest in the movement known as symbolism, this counterforce evolved and expanded into what we will call antirealistic theatre, which moved across Europe and quickly began contesting the advances of realism step-by-step.

The Symbolist Rebellion

The symbolist movement began in Paris during the 1880s as a joint venture of artists, playwrights, essayists, critics, sculptors, and poets. If realism was the art of depicting reality as ordinary men and women might see it, symbolism would explore — by means of images and metaphors — the *inner* realities that cannot be directly or literally perceived. "Symbolic" characters, therefore, would not represent real human beings but instead would symbolize philosophical ideals or warring internal forces in the human (or the artist's) soul.

Symbolism had another goal as well: to crush what its adherents deemed to be a spiritually bankrupt realism and to replace it with traditional aesthetic values — poetry, imagery, novelty, fantasy, extravagance, profundity, audacity, charm, and superhuman magnitude. United in their hatred for literal detail and for all that they considered mundane or ordinary, the symbolists demanded abstraction, enlargement, and innovation; the symbolist spirit soared in poetic encapsulations, outsized

REALISM AS BLINDNESS: CRAIG'S VIEW

Realism is a vulgar means of expression bestowed upon the blind. Thus we have the clear-sighted singing: "Beauty is Truth, Truth Beauty — that is all ye know on earth, and all ye need to know." The blind are heard croaking: "Beauty is Realism, Realism Beauty — that is all I know on earth, and all I care to know — don't 'ya know!" The difference is all a matter of love. He who loves the earth sees beauty everywhere: he is a god transforming by knowledge the incomplete into the complete. He can heal the lame and the sick, can blow courage into the weary, and he can even learn how to make the blind see. The power has always been possessed by the artist, who, in my opinion, rules the earth. . . .

The limited section of playgoers who love beauty and detest Realism is a small minority of about six million souls. They are scattered here and there over the earth. They seldom, if ever, go to the modern theatre. That is why I love them, and intend to unite them.

– Gordon Craig

dramatic presences, fantastical visual effects, shocking structural departures, and grandiloquent speech. Purity of vision, rather than accuracy of observation, was the symbolists' aim, and self-conscious creative innovation was to be their primary accomplishment.

The first symbolist theatre, founded in 1890 by Parisian poet Paul Fort (1872–1960), was intended as a direct attack on the naturalistic Théâtre Libre of André Antoine (1858–1943), founded three years earlier. Fort's theatre, the Théâtre d'Art, was proposed as "a theatre for Symbolist poets only, where every production would cause a battle." In some ways, Antoine's and Fort's theatres had much in common: both were amateur, both gained considerable notoriety, and each served as a center for a "school" of artistic ideology that attracted as much attention and controversy as any of its theatrical offerings.

But the two theatres were openly, deliberately, at war. While Antoine was presenting

This 1990 production of George Bernard Shaw's 1903 play, *Man and Superman,* employs costumes and props of Shaw's time but has a thoroughly modern (or postmodern) spirit. This South Coast Repertory (Costa Mesa, California) production was directed by Martin Benson and designed by Cliff Faulkner (scenery) and Shigeru Yaji (costumes).

premieres of naturalistic and realistic dramas by August Strindberg, Émile Zola, and Henrik Ibsen, Fort presented the staged poems and poetic plays of both contemporary and earlier writers such as the French Arthur Rimbaud (1854–1891) and Paul Verlaine (1844–1896), the Belgian Maurice Maeterlinck (1862–1949), and the American Edgar Allan Poe (1809–1849). Whereas Antoine would go to great lengths to create realistic scenery for his plays (for example, he displayed real sides of beef hung from meathooks for his presentation of *The Butchers*), Fort would prevail upon leading impressionist easel painters — including Pierre Bonnard, Maurice Denis, and Odilon Redon — to dress his stylized stage. Silver angels, translucent veils, and sheets of crumpled wrapping paper were among the decors that backed the symbolist works at the Théâtre d'Art.

Fort's theatre created an immediate sensation in Paris. With the stunning success in 1890 of *The Intruder,* a mysterious and poetic fantasy by Maeterlinck, the antirealist movement was fully engaged and, as Fort recalled in his memoirs, "the cries and applause of the students, poets, and artists overwhelmed the huge disapproval of the bourgeoisie."

The movement spread quickly as authors and designers alike awakened to the possibilities of a theatre wholly freed from the constraints of verisimilitude. Realism, more and more critics concluded, would never raise the commonplace to the level of art; it would only drag art down into the muck of the mundane. It ran counter to all that the theatre had stood for in the past; it throttled the potential of artistic creativity. In fact, such naturalistic and realistic authors as Henrik Ibsen, August Strindberg, Gerhart Hauptmann, and George Bernard Shaw soon came under the symbolist influence and abandoned their social preoccupations and environmental exactitude to seek

Above: Robert Wilson (the director) and John Conklin (the costume designer) co-designed the scenery for this dreamlike American Repertory Theatre production of Ibsen's *When We Dead Awaken* in 1991.

Left: "Think lovely, wonderful thoughts, and up you'll go!" Cathy Rigby flies away — as the title character in *Peter Pan* (the role is traditionally played by a woman). Chase Kniffen, Drake English, and Elisa Sagardia appeared as the Darling children in the 1998 American tour.

new languages and more universal themes. As an added element, at about this time Sigmund Freud's research was being published and discussed, and his theories concerning dream images and the worlds of the unconscious provided new source material for the stage.

By the turn of the century, the counterforce of theatrical stylization set in motion by the symbolists was established on all fronts; indeed, the half decade on either side of 1900 represents one of the richest periods of experimentation in the history of dramatic writing. Out of that decade came Hauptmann's archetypal fairy tale *The Sunken Bell* (Germany, 1896), Alfred Jarry's outrageously cartoonish and scatological *Ubu Roi* (France, 1898), Ibsen's haunting ode to individualism *When We Dead Awaken* (Norway, 1899), Strindberg's metaphoric and imagistic *The Dream Play* (Sweden, 1902), William Butler Yeats's evocative poetic fable *Cathleen ni Houlihan* (Ireland, 1903), Shaw's philosophical allegory *Man and Superman* (England, 1903), and James Barrie's whimsical, buoyant fantasy *Peter Pan* (England, 1904). Almost every dramatic innovation that has followed since that time has been at least in part prefigured by one or more of these seminal works for the nonrealist theatre.

The realist-versus-symbolist confrontation affected every aspect of theatre production. Symbolist-inspired directors and designers, side by side with the playwrights, were drastically altering the arts of staging and decor to accommodate the new dramaturgies that surged into the theatre. Realist directors such as Antoine and Stanislavsky suddenly found themselves challenged by scores of adversaries and renegades: a school of symbolist and poetic directors rose in France, and a former disciple of Stanislavsky, the "constructivist" Vsevolod Meyerhold, broke with the Russian master to create a nonrealist "biomechanical" style of acting and directing in sharp contrast to that established at the Moscow Art Theatre; by 1904 Stanislavsky himself was producing the impressionistic plays of Maeterlinck at the Moscow Art Theatre. With the advent of elec-

trical stage lighting, opportunities for stylizing were vastly expanded: the new technology enabled the modern director to create vivid stage effects, starkly unrealistic in appearance, through the judicious use of spotlighting, shadowing, and shading. Technology, plus trends in postimpressionist art that were well established in Europe by 1900, led to scenery and costume designs that departed radically from realism. Exoticism, fantasy, sheer sensual delight, symbolic meaning, and aesthetic purity became the prime objectives of designers who joined the antirealist rebellion.

In some respects, the symbolist aim succeeded perhaps beyond the dreams of its originators. Paul Fort's Théâtre d'Art, although it lasted but a year, now has spiritual descendants in every city in the Western world where theatre is performed.

The Era of "Isms"

The symbolist movement itself was short-lived, at least under that name. *Symbolism,* after all, was coined primarily as a direct contradiction of *realism,* and movements named for their oppositional qualities — called for what they are not — are quickly seen as artistically limited, as critiques of art rather than as art itself.

Within months of the symbolist advances, therefore, symbolism *as a movement* was deserted by founders and followers alike. Where did they go? Off to found newer movements: avant-gardism, futurism, Dadaism, idealism, aestheticism, impressionism, expressionism, constructivism, surrealism, formalism, theatricalism, and perhaps a hundred other "isms" now lost to time.

The first third of this century, indeed, was an era of theatrical isms, an era rich with continued experimentation by movements self-consciously seeking to redefine theatrical art. Ism theatres sprang up like mushrooms, each with its own fully articulated credo and manifesto, each promising a better art — if not, indeed, a better world. It was a vibrant era for the theatre, for out of this welter of isms the aesthetics of dramatic art took on a new social and political significance in the cultural capitals of Europe and America. A successful play was not merely a play but rather the forum for a *cause,* and behind that cause was a body of zealous supporters and adherents who shared a deep aesthetic commitment.

Nothing quite like that ism spirit exists today, for we have lost the social involvement that can turn an aesthetic movement into a profound collective belief. But the experiments and discoveries of those early days of the twentieth century and the nonrealistic spirit of symbolism itself survive and flourish under a variety of formats: ritual theatre, poetic theatre, holy theatre, theatre of cruelty, existentialist theatre, art theatre, avant-garde theatre, theatre of the absurd, and theatre of alienation. These present-day groupings, unlike the isms, are critic-defined rather than artist-defined; indeed, most theatre artists today reject any "grouping" nomenclature whatever. However, the formats these groupings pursue can be shown to reflect the general approach to structure, style, and experimentation that began with the symbolists in the late nineteenth century.

Stylized Theatre

We have chosen the rather loose term *antirealistic theatre* or, occasionally, the *stylized theatre* to embrace the entire spectrum of nonrealistic modern theatre, which, although disparate in its individual manifestations, exhibits a universal insistence on *consciously stylizing reality* into larger-than-life theatrical experience. Any theatre mode in any era, of course, has its distinctive style, but in past eras that style was always largely *imposed* by current convention and technological limitations. Modern dramatists, by contrast, have consciously *selected and created* styles to satisfy their aesthetic theories, their social principles, or simply their desire for novelty and innovation.

Antirealistic theatre attempts to create new theatrical formats, not merely to enhance the portrayal of human existence but also to disclose fundamental patterns underlying that existence: patterns of perception, patterns of association, patterns of personal and environmental interaction. The styles employed by this modern theatre come from anywhere and everywhere: from the past, from exotic cultures, and from present and futuristic technologies. The modern theatre artist has an unprecedented reservoir of sources to draw upon and is generally unconstrained in their application by political edict, religious prohibition, or mandated artistic tradition. The modern stylized theatre is undoubtedly the freest in history: the dramatist, director, actor, or designer is limited only by physical resources and individual imagination. Virtually anything can be put upon a stage, and in the twentieth century it seems that virtually everything was.

Antirealistic theatre does not altogether dispense with reality but wields it in often unexpected ways and freely enhances it with symbol and metaphor, striving to elucidate by parable and allegory, to deconstruct and reconstruct by language, scenery, and lighting. Further, it makes explicit use of the theatre's very theatricality, frequently reminding its audience members, directly or indirectly, that they are watching a performance, not an episode in somebody's daily life. Stylization inevitably reaches for universality. It tends to treat problems of psychology as problems of philosophy and problems in human relations as problems of the human condition. Stylization reaches for patterns, not particulars; it explores abstractions and aims for sharp thematic focus and bold intellectual impact.

In the stylized theatre, characters usually represent more than individual persons or personality types. Like the medieval allegories, modern stylized plays often involve characters who represent forces of nature, moral positions, human instincts, and the like — entities such as death, fate, idealism, the life force, the earth mother, the tyrant father, and the prodigal son. And the conflicts associated with these forces, unlike the conflicts of realism, are not responsive to any human agency; they are, more often than not, represented as permanent discords inherent in the human condition. The stylized theatre resonates with tension and human frustration in the face of irreconcilable demands.

But that is not to say the antirealistic theatre is necessarily grim; to the contrary, it often uses whimsy and mordant wit as its dominant mode. Although the themes of the antirealistic theatre are anxious ones — for example, the alienation of humanity, the futility of communication, the loss of innocence, the intransigence of despair — it is not on the whole a theatre of pessimism or of nihilistic outrage. Indeed, the glory of the stylized theatre is that, at its best, it refuses to be swamped by its themes; it transcends frustration; it is the victory of poetry over alienation, comedy over noncommunication, and artistry over despair. The antirealistic theatre aims at lifting its audience, not saddling them; and even if it proffers no solutions to life's inevitable discords, it can provide considerable lucidity concerning the totality of the human adventure.

The diversity of stylized theatrical works precludes further generalization about their shared characteristics. To help us understand this diversity, however, we will examine eleven brief examples from plays written over the past hundred years that serve to establish the main lines of the antirealistic theatre.

THE FRENCH AVANT-GARDE: *UBU ROI* The opening of Alfred Jarry's *Ubu Roi* (King Ubu) at the Théâtre Nouveau in Paris on December 11, 1896, was perhaps the most violent dramatic premiere in theatre history: the audience shouted, whistled, hooted, cheered, threw things, and shook their fists at the stage. Duels were even fought after subsequent performances. The *avant-garde* was born.

The term *avant-garde* comes from the military, where it refers to the advance battalion, or the "shock troops" that initiate a major assault. In France the term initially described the wave of French playwrights and directors who openly and boldly assaulted realism in the first four decades of the twentieth century. Today the term is used worldwide to describe any adventurous, experimental, and nontraditional artistic effort.

Jarry (1873–1907), a diminutive iconoclast ("eccentric to the point of mania and lucid to the point of hallucination," says critic Roger Shattuck), unleashed his radical shock troops from the moment the curtain rose. Jarry had called for an outrageously antirealistic stage — painted scenery depicting a bed, a bare tree at its foot; palm trees, a coiled boa constrictor around one of them; a gallows with a skeleton hanging from it, and falling snow. Characters entered through a painted fireplace. Costumes, in Jarry's words, were "divorced as far as possible from [realistic] color or chronology." And the title character stepped forward to begin the play with a word that quickly became immortal: *"Merdre!"* or "Shrit!"

This *mot d'Ubu* ("Ubu's word") occasioned scandal more than anything else, for although Ibsen had broken barriers of propriety in subject matter, no one had tested the language barriers of the Victorian age. Vulgar epithets, common enough in the works of Aristophanes and Shakespeare, had been pruned from the theatre in the Royal era and abolished entirely in the lofty spirit of romanticism; far from trying to sneak them back in, Jarry simply threw them up, schoolboy-like, in the face of the astonished audience. The added "r" in *merdre*, far from "cleansing" the offending obscenity, only called more attention to it and to its deliberate intrusion onto the Parisian stage.

Ubu Roi was, in fact, a schoolboy play; Jarry wrote the first version at the age of fifteen as a satire of his high school physics teacher. Jarry was only twenty-three years old when the play astounded its Parisian audiences, and the juvenile aspects of the play's origins were evident throughout the finished product, which proved to be Jarry's sole masterwork.

Ubu Roi is a savage and often ludicrous satire on the theme of power, in which Father

Mother Ubu pokes her strikingly made-up face through an abstractly colored backdrop in Babette Masson's 1993 French production of Jarry's *Ubu Roi*.

(later King) Ubu — a fat, foul-mouthed, venal, amoral, and pompous Polish assassin — proves one of the stage's greatest creations. The play sprawls; its thirty-three scenes are often just crude skits barely linked by plot, but the interplay of farce and violence is inspired, as in the famous eating scene:

FATHER UBU, MOTHER UBU, CAPTAIN BORDURE *and his followers.*

MOTHER UBU: Good day, gentlemen; we've been anxiously awaiting you.

CAPTAIN BORDURE: Good day, madam. Where's Father Ubu?

FATHER UBU: Here I am, here I am! Good lord, by my green candle, I'm fat enough, aren't I?

CAPTAIN BORDURE: Good day, Father Ubu. Sit down boys. (*They all sit.*)

FATHER UBU: Oof, a little more, and I'd have bust my chair.

CAPTAIN BORDURE: Well, Mother Ubu! What have you got that's good today?

MOTHER UBU: Here's the menu.

FATHER UBU: Oh! That interests me.

MOTHER UBU: Polish soup, roast ram, veal, chicken, chopped dog's liver, turkey's ass, charlotte russe . . .

FATHER UBU: Hey, that's plenty, I should think. You mean there's more?

MOTHER UBU: (*continuing*) Frozen pudding, salad, fruits, dessert, boiled beef, Jerusalem artichokes, cauliflower à la shrit.

FATHER UBU: Hey! Do you think I'm the Emperor of China, to give all that away?

MOTHER UBU: Don't listen to him, he's feeble-minded.

FATHER UBU: Ah! I'll sharpen my teeth on your shanks.

MOTHER UBU: Try this instead, Father Ubu. Here's the Polish soup.

FATHER UBU: Crap, is that lousy!

CAPTAIN BORDURE: Hmm — it isn't very good, at that.

MOTHER UBU: What do you want, you bunch of crooks!

FATHER UBU: (*striking his forehead*) Wait, I've got an idea. I'll be right back. (*He leaves.*)

MOTHER UBU: Let's try the veal now, gentlemen.

CAPTAIN BORDURE: It's very good — I'm through.

MOTHER UBU: To the turkey's ass, next.

CAPTAIN BORDURE: Delicious, delicious! Long live Mother Ubu!

ALL: Long live Mother Ubu!

FATHER UBU: (*returning*) And you will soon be shouting, "Long live Father Ubu." (*He has a toilet brush in his hand, and he throws it on the festive board.*)

MOTHER UBU: Miserable creature, what are you up to now?

FATHER UBU: Try a little. (*Several try it, and fall, poisoned.*) Mother Ubu, pass me the roast ram chops, so that I can serve them.

MOTHER UBU: Here they are.

FATHER UBU: Everyone out! Captain Bordure, I want to talk to you.

THE OTHERS: But we haven't eaten yet.

FATHER UBU: What's that, you haven't eaten yet? Out, out, everyone out! Stay here, Bordure. (*Nobody moves.*) You haven't gone yet? By my green candle, I'll give you your ram chops. (*He begins to throw them.*)

ALL: Oh! Ouch! Help! Woe! Help! Misery! I'm dead!

FATHER UBU: Shrit, shrit, shrit! Outside! I want my way!

ALL: Everyone for himself! Miserable Father Ubu! Traitor! Meanie!

FATHER UBU: Ah! They've gone. I can breathe again — but I've had a rotten dinner. Come on, Bordure.

They go out with MOTHER UBU.

The elements of deliberate scatology, toilet humor, juvenile satire, and a full-stage food fight make clear that *Ubu Roi* is a precursor of American teen films such as *Dumb and Dumber;* it is a little more difficult, however, to see the play as a precursor of a serious art and literary movement like surrealism, but such is the case. *Surrealism,* a word that means "beyond realism" or "superrealism," was officially inaugurated by André Breton in 1924 but can be said to date from this play — which, its advocates claim, reaches a superior level of reality by tracing the unconscious processes of the mind rather than the literal depictions of observable life.

EXPRESSIONISM: *THE HAIRY APE* Of all the isms, expressionism is the one that has given rise to the most significant body of modern theatre, probably because of its broad definition and its seeming alliance with ex-pressionism in the visual arts. The theatrical expressionism that was much in vogue in Germany during the first decades of the twentieth century (particularly in the 1920s) featured shocking and gutsy dialogue, boldly exaggerated scenery, piercing sounds, bright lights, an abundance of primary colors, a not very subtle use of symbols, and a structure of short, stark, jabbing scenes that built to a powerful (and usually deafening) climax.

In America, Eugene O'Neill (1888–1953) came under the influence of the expressionists after his earlier ventures into naturalism, and in the 1920s O'Neill wrote a series of explosive plays concerning human nature in an industrial landscape. *The Hairy Ape,* produced in 1921, is almost a textbook case of expressionist writing and well illustrates the extreme stylization popular with ism writers. It is a one-act play featuring eight scenes. Its workingman-hero Yank meets and is rebuffed by the genteel daughter of a captain of industry. Enraged, Yank becomes violent and eventually crazed; he dies at play's end in the monkey cage of a zoo. Scene 3 illustrates the tenor of the writing:

The stokehold. In the rear, the dimly outlined bulks of the furnaces and boilers. High overhead one hanging electric bulb sheds just enough light through the murky air laden with coal dust to pile up masses of shadows everywhere. A line of men, stripped to the waist, is before the furnace doors. They bend over, looking neither to right nor left, handling their shovels as if they were part of their bodies, with a strange, awkward, swinging rhythm. They use the shovels to throw open the furnace doors. Then from these fiery round holes in the back a flood of terrific light and heat pours full upon the men who are outlined in silhouette in the crouching, inhuman attitudes of chained gorillas. The men shovel with a rhythmic motion, swinging as on a pivot from the coal which lies in heaps on the floor behind to hurl it into the flaming mouths before them. There is a tumult of noise — the brazen clang of the furnace doors as they are flung open or slammed shut, the grating, teeth-gritting grind of steel against steel, of crunching coal.

O'NEILL'S EXPRESSIONISM

In the scene [in *The Hairy Ape*] where the bell rings for the stokers to go on duty, you remember that they all stand up, come to attention, then go out in a lockstep file. Some people think even that is an actual custom aboard ship! But it is only symbolic of the regimentation of men who are the slaves of machinery. In a larger sense, it applies to all of us, because we all are more or less the slaves of convention, or of discipline, or of a rigid formula of some sort.

The whole play is expressionistic. The coal shoveling in the furnace room, for instance. Stokers do not really shovel coal that way. But it is done in the play in order to contribute to the rhythm. For rhythm is a powerful factor in making anything expressive. You can actually produce and control emotions by that means alone.

– Eugene O'Neill

This clash of sounds stuns one's ears with its rending dissonance. But there is order in it, rhythm, a mechanical regulated recurrence, a tempo. And rising above all, making the air hum with the quiver of liberated energy, the roar of leaping flames in the furnaces, the monotonous throbbing beat of the engines.

As the curtain rises, the furnace doors are shut. The men are taking a breathing spell. One or two are arranging the coal behind them, pulling it into more accessible heaps. The others can be dimly made out leaning on their shovels in relaxed attitudes of exhaustion.

PADDY: (*from somewhere in the line — plaintively*) Yerra, will this divil's own watch nivir end? Me back is broke. I'm destroyed entirely.

YANK: (*from the center of the line — with exuberant scorn*) Aw, yuh make me sick! Lie down and croak, why don't yuh? Always beefin', dat's you! Say, dis is a cinch! Dis was made for me! It's my meat, get me! (*A whistle is blown — a thin, shrill note from somewhere overhead in the darkness.* YANK *curses without resentment.*) Dere's de damn engineer crackin' de whip. He tinks we're loafin'.

PADDY: (*vindictively*) God stiffen him!

YANK: (*in an exultant tone of command*) Come on, youse guys! Git into de game! She's

gettin' hungry! Pile some grub in her. Trow it into her belly! Come on now, all of youse! Open her up! (*At this last all the men, who have followed his movements of getting into position, throw open their furnace doors with a deafening clang. The fiery light floods over their shoulders as they bend round for the coal. Rivulets of sooty sweat have traced maps on their backs. The enlarged muscles form bunches of highlight and shadow.*)

YANK: (*chanting a count as he shovels without seeming effort*) One — two — tree — (*His voice rising exultantly in the joy of battle*) Dat's de stuff! Let her have it! All togedder now! Sling it into her! Let her ride! Shoot de piece now! Call de toin on her! Drive her into it! Feel her move. Watch her smoke! Speed, dat's her middle name! Give her coal, youse guys! Coal, dat's her booze! Drink it up, baby! Let's see yuh sprint! Dig in and gain a lap! Dere she go-o-es! (*This last in the chanting formula of the galley gods at the six-day bike race. He slams his furnace door shut. The others do likewise with as much unison as their wearied bodies will permit. The effect is of one fiery eye after another being blotted out with a series of accompanying bangs.*)

PADDY: (*groaning*) Me back is broke. I'm bate out — bate — (*There is a pause. Then the inexorable whistle sounds again from the dim regions above the electric light. There is a growl of cursing rage from all sides.*)

YANK: (*shaking his fist upward — contemptuously*) Take it easy dere, you! Who d'yuh tink's runnin' dis game, me or you? When I git ready, we move. Not before! When I git ready, get me!

VOICES: (*approvingly*) That's the stuff!
Yank tal him, py golly!
Yank ain't affeerd.
Goot poy, Yank!
Give him hell!
Tell 'im 'e's a bloody swine!
Bloody slave-driver!

YANK: (*contemptuously*) He ain't got no noive. He's yellow, get me? All de engineers is yellow. Dey got streaks a mile wide. Aw, to hell wit him! Let's move, youse guys. We had a rest. Come on, she needs it! Give her pep!

It ain't for him. Him and his whistle, dey don't belong. But we belong, see! We gotter feed de baby! Come on! (*He turns and flings his furnace door open. They all follow his lead. At this instant the* SECOND *and* FOURTH ENGINEERS *enter from the darkness on the left with* MILDRED *between them. She starts, turns paler, her pose is crumbling, she shivers with fright in spite of the blazing heat, but forces herself to leave the* ENGINEERS *and take a few steps nearer the men. She is right behind* YANK. *All this happens quickly while the men have their backs turned.*)

YANK: Come on, youse guys! (*He is turning to get coal when the whistle sounds again in a peremptory, irritating note. This drives* YANK *into a sudden fury. While the other men have turned full around and stopped dumbfounded by the spectacle of* MILDRED *standing there in her white dress,* YANK *does not turn far enough to see her. Besides, his head is thrown back, he blinks upward through the murk trying to find the owner of the whistle, he brandishes his shovel murderously over his head in one hand, pounding on his chest, gorilla-like, with the other, shouting.*) Toin off dat whistle! Come down outa dere, yuh yellow, brass-buttoned, Belfast bum, yuh! Come down and I'll knock yer brains out! Yuh lousy, stinkin', yellow mut of a Catholic-moiderin' bastard! Come down and I'll moider yuh! Pullin' dat whistle on me, huh? I'll show yuh! I'll crash yer skull in! I'll drive yer teet' down yer troat! I'll slam yer nose trou de back to yer head! I'll cut yer guts out for a nickel, yuh lousy boob, yuh dirty, crummy, muck-eatin' son ofa — (*Suddenly he becomes conscious of all the other men staring at something directly behind his back. He whirls defensively with a snarling, murderous growl, crouching to spring, his lips drawn back over his teeth, his small eyes gleaming ferociously. He sees* MILDRED, *like a white apparition in the full light from the open furnace doors. He glares into her eyes, turned to stone. As for her, during his speech she has listened, paralyzed with horror, terror, her whole personality crushed, beaten in, collapsed, by the terrific impact of this unknown, abysmal brutality, naked and shameless. As she looks at his gorilla face, as his eyes bore into hers, she utters a low, choking cry and shrinks away from him, putting* both hands up before her eyes to shut out the sight of his face, to protect her own. This startles YANK to a reaction. His mouth falls open, his eyes grow bewildered.*)

MILDRED: (*about to faint — to the* ENGINEERS, *who now have her one by each arm — whimperingly*) Take me away! Oh, the filthy beast! (*She faints. They carry her quickly back, disappearing in the darkness at the left, rear. An iron door clangs shut. Rage and bewildered fury rush back on* YANK. *He feels himself insulted in some unknown fashion in the very heart of his pride. He roars.*) God damn yuh! (*And hurls his shovel after them at the door which has just closed. It hits the steel bulkhead with a clang and falls clattering on the steel floor. From overhead the whistle sounds again in a long, angry, insistent command.*)

Curtain

O'Neill's forceful combination of visual and auditory effects lends this expressionistic play a crude, almost superhuman power. The use of silhouette in the staging and lighting, the "masses of shadows everywhere," the "tumult of noise," the "monotonous throbbing beat of the engines," the "fiery light," the "rivulets of sooty sweat," the massed chanting and the movements in unison, the "peremptory, irritating note" of the "inexorable whistle," the shouting of curses and bold ejaculations, the animal imagery, and the "horror, terror . . . of . . . unknown, abysmal brutality, naked and shameless," are all typical of the extreme stylization of early-twentieth-century expressionism. The scene also demonstrates how O'Neill and his followers in the American theatre turned away from realism and romanticism in their effort to arrive at a direct presentation of social ideology and cultural criticism.

THEATRICALISM: *SIX CHARACTERS IN SEARCH OF AN AUTHOR* First produced in 1921, *Six Characters in Search of an Author* expresses from its famous title onward a "theatricalist" motif in which the theatre itself becomes part of the content of play production, not merely the vehicle. "All the world's a stage," said

Shakespeare; but in this play Luigi Pirandello (1867–1936) explores how the stage is also a world — and how the stage and the world, illusion and reality, relate to each other. In this still-stunning play, a family of dramatic "characters" — a father, his stepdaughter, a mother, and her children — appear as if by magic on the "stage" of a provincial theatre where a "new play" by Pirandello is being rehearsed. The "characters," claiming they have an unfinished play in them, beg the director to stage their lives in order that they may bring a satisfactory climax to their "drama." This fantasy treats the audience to continually shifting perceptions, for clearly a play-within-the-play is involved, but which is the real play and which the real life? There are actors playing actors, actors playing "characters," and actors playing actors-playing-"characters"; there are also scenes when the actors playing "characters" are making fun of the actors playing actors-playing-"characters." It is no wonder that most audiences give up trying to untangle the planes of reality Pirandello creates in this play; they are simply too difficult to comprehend except as a dazzle of suggestive theatricality.

Pirandello contrasts the passionate story of the "characters" — whose "drama" concerns a broken family, adultery, and a suggestion of incest — with the artifice of the stage and its simulations; in the course of this exposition Pirandello's performers discuss the theatricality of life, the life of theatricality, and the eternal confusions between appearance and reality:

THE FATHER: What I'm inviting you to do is to quit this foolish playing at art — this acting and pretending — and seriously answer my question: WHO ARE YOU?

THE DIRECTOR: (*amazed but irritated, to his actors*) What extraordinary impudence! This so-called character wants to know who I am?

THE FATHER: (*with calm dignity*) Signore, a character may always ask a "man" who he is. For a character has a true life, defined by his characteristics — he is always, at the least, a

---

> ## PIRANDELLO: THE PLANE OF REALITY TRANSFORMED
>
> A stage which accommodates the fantastical reality of these six characters is not, itself, a fixed or immutable space, nor are the events of the play preconceived in a fixed formula. On the contrary, everything in this play is created freshly as it happens; it is fluid, it is improvised. As the story and the characters take shape, so the stage itself evolves, and the plane of reality is organically transformed.
>
> — Luigi Pirandello

"somebody." But a man — now, don't take this personally — A man is generalized beyond identity — he's a nobody!

THE DIRECTOR: Ah, but me, me — I am the Director! The Producer! You understand?

THE FATHER: Signore — Think of how you used to feel about yourself, long ago, all the illusions you used to have about the world, and about your place in it: those illusions were real for you then, they were *quite* real — But now, with hindsight, they prove to be nothing, they are nothing to you now but an embarrassment. Well, signore, that is what your present reality is today — just a set of illusions that you will discard tomorrow. Can't you feel it? I'm not speaking of the planks of this stage we stand on, I'm speaking of the very earth under our feet. It's sinking under you — by tomorrow, today's entire reality will have become just one more illusion. You see?

THE DIRECTOR: (*confused but amazed*) Well? So what? What does all that prove?

THE FATHER: Ah, nothing, signore. Only to show that if, beyond our illusions (*indicating the other characters*), we have no ultimate reality, so your reality as well — your reality that touches and feels and breathes today — will be unmasked tomorrow as nothing but yesterday's illusion!

These lines illustrate Pirandello's use of paradox, irony, and the theatre as metaphor to create a whimsical drama about human identity and human destiny. By contrasting the passion of his "characters" and the frequent frivolity of his "actors," Pirandello establishes a provocative juxtaposition of human behavior and its theatricalization — and the whole fantastical style is nothing but an exploitation of the theatrical format itself.

THEATRE OF CRUELTY: *JET OF BLOOD*   Antonin Artaud (1896–1948) is one of drama's greatest revolutionaries, although his importance lies more in his ideas and influence than in his actual theatrical achievements. A stage and film actor in Paris during the 1920s, he founded the Théâtre Alfred Jarry in 1926, producing, among other works, Strindberg's surrealist *A Dream Play* and, in 1935, an adaptation of Shelley's dramatic poem *The Cenci*. His essays, profoundly influential in the theatre today, were collected and published in 1938 in a book titled *The Theatre and Its Double*.

The theatre envisaged by Artaud was a self-declared theatre of cruelty, for, in his words, "Without an element of cruelty at the root of every performance, the theatre is not possible." The "cruel" theatre would flourish, Artaud predicted, by "providing the spectator with the true sources of his dreams, in which his taste for crime, his erotic obsessions, his savagery, his illusions, his utopian ideals, even his cannibalism, would surge forth."

In Artaud's vision, ordinary plays were to be abolished; there should be, in his words, "no more masterpieces." In place of written plays there should be

cries, groans, apparitions, surprises, theatricalities of all kinds, magic beauty of costumes taken from certain ritual models; resplendent lighting, the incantation of beautiful voices, the charms of harmony, rare notes of music, colors of objects, physical rhythm of movements whose crescendo and decrescendo will accord exactly with the pulsation of familiar movements, concrete appearances of new and surprising objects, masks, effigies yards high, sudden changes of light, the

physical action of light which arouses sensations of heat and cold . . . evocative gestures, emotive or arbitrary attitudes, excited pounding out of rhythms and sounds . . . [and] all the abortive attitudes, all the lapses of mind and tongue, by which are revealed what might be called the impotences of speech.

Language in Artaud's theatre was an impotent force, drowned out by the more "sensational" (as in sensory) aspects of sonic vibrations and visual extravagance continuously assaulting all the senses. But this was not to be simply a theatre of stage effects; it was, for Artaud, a theatre of profound meaning:

Even light can have a precise intellectual meaning, light in waves, in sheets, in fusillades of fiery arrows. . . . Paroxysms will suddenly burst forth, will fire up like fires in different spots. . . . The varied lighting of a performance will fall upon the public as much as upon the actors — and to the several simultaneous actions or several phases of an identical action in which the characters, swarming over each other like bees, will endure all the onslaughts of the situations and the external assaults of the tempestuous elements.

In a famous metaphor, Artaud compared the theatre to the great medieval plague, noting that both plague and theatre had the capacity to liberate human possibilities and illuminate the human potential:

The theatre is like the plague . . . because like the plague it is the revelation, the bringing forth, the exteriorization of a depth of latent cruelty by means of which all the perverse possibilities of the mind, whether of an individual or a people, are localized. . . .

In the theatre as in the plague there is a kind of strange sun, a light of abnormal intensity by which it seems that the difficult and even the impossible suddenly become our normal element.

One cannot imagine, save in an atmosphere of carnage, torture, and bloodshed, all the magnificent Fables which recount to the multitudes the first sexual division and the first carnage of essences that appeared in creation. The theatre, like the plague, is in the image of this carnage and this essential separation. It releases conflicts, disengages powers, liberates possibilities, and if these possibilities and these powers are dark, it is the fault not of the plague nor of the theatre, but of life.

Artaud's ideas were radical, and his essays were incendiary; his power to shock and inspire is undiminished today, and many contemporary theatre artists claim an Artaudian heritage. It is not at all clear, however, what final form the "theatre of cruelty" should actually take in performance, and it is readily apparent even to the casual reader that the theatre Artaud speaks of is much easier to realize on paper than on an actual stage. Artaud's own productions were in fact failures; he was formally "expelled" from the surrealist movement, and he spent most of his later life abroad in mental institutions. His one published play, *Jet of Blood* (1925), illustrates both the radically antirealistic nature of his dramaturgy and the difficulties that would be encountered in its production. This is the opening of the play:

THE YOUNG MAN: I love you, and everything is beautiful.

THE YOUNG GIRL: (*with a strong tremolo in her voice*) You love me, and everything is beautiful.

THE YOUNG MAN: (*in a very deep voice*) I love you, and everything is beautiful.

THE YOUNG GIRL: (*in an even deeper voice than his*) You love me, and everything is beautiful.

THE YOUNG MAN: (*leaving her abruptly*) I love you. (*Pause*) Turn around and face me.

THE YOUNG GIRL: (*she turns to face him*) There!

THE YOUNG MAN: (*in a shrill and exalted voice*) I love you, I am big, I am shining, I am full, I am solid.

THE YOUNG GIRL: (*in the same shrill tone*) We love each other.

THE YOUNG MAN: We are intense. Ah, how well ordered this world is!

A pause. Something that sounds like an immense wheel turning and blowing out air is heard. A hurricane separates the two. At this moment two stars crash into each other, and we see a number of live pieces of human bodies falling down: hands, feet, scalps, masks, colonnades, porches, temples, and alembics, which, however, fall more and more slowly, as if they were falling in a vacuum. Three scorpions fall down, one after the other, and finally a frog and a beetle, which sets itself down with a maddening, vomit-inducing slowness . . .

Enter a knight of the Middle Ages in an enormous suit of armor, followed by a nurse holding her breasts in both hands and puffing and wheezing because they are both very swollen.

Artaud's apocalyptic vision has stimulated many subsequent theatre directors, including Jean-Louis Barrault and Roger Blin in France, Peter Brook in England, Jerzy Grotowski in Poland, and André Gregory in America; his influence can also be seen in the plays of Jean Genet and the productions of Robert Wilson. His notion of a theatre of cruelty, although not fully realized onstage in his lifetime, has been more closely approached by each of these artists and may still be achieved.

PHILOSOPHICAL MELODRAMA: *NO EXIT*   *No Exit* is one of the most compelling short plays ever written. In this one-act fantasy written in 1944, Jean-Paul Sartre (1905–1980), the well-known French existentialist philosopher, establishes a unique "Hell," which is a room without windows or mirrors. Into it come three people, lately deceased, all condemned to this netherworld because of their earthly sins. The three are brilliantly ill matched: Garcin, the sole man, tends toward homosexuality, as does Inez, one of the two women; Estelle, the final occupant of this bizarre inferno, tends toward heterosexual nymphomania. Estelle pursues Garcin, Garcin pursues his fellow spirit, Inez, and Inez pursues the beautiful Estelle in a triangle of misdirected affection that, one presumes, will continue maddeningly through all eternity. The infinite bleakness of this play's fantastical situation

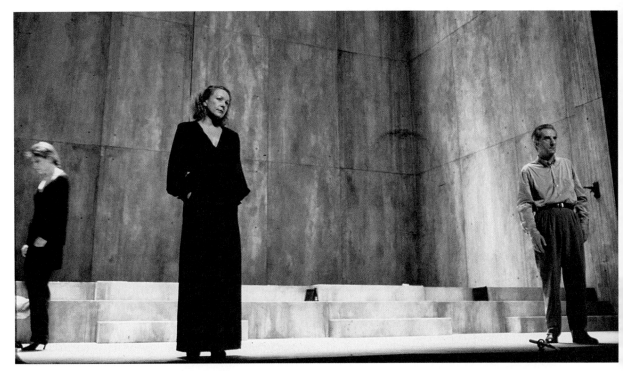

Jean-Paul Sartre's *No Exit* is a philosophical study of three characters locked together in "Hell" – which is discovered to be "other people." Shown here is the 1993 Comédie Française production.

and the numbing futility of each character's aspirations provoke Garcin to beg for some good old-fashioned torture — but nothing quite so simple is forthcoming. Instead, he is forced to conclude: "Hell is other people." And the play ends with a curtain line that is characteristic of the modern stylized theatre:

GARCIN: Well, well, let's get on with it.

This line suggests that although the play concludes, the situation continues, eternally, behind the drawn curtain.

No Exit is a classic dramatic statement of existentialism, of which Sartre was the twentieth century's leading exponent. Remove the fantastical elements — that this is Hell and the characters are ghosts — and we have Sartre's vision of human interaction: every individual forever seeks affirmation and self-realization in the eyes of the Other. Each character in the play carries with him or her a baggage of guilt

and expectation, each seeks from another some certification of final personal worth, and each is endlessly thwarted in this quest. We are all condemned to revolve around each other in frustratingly incomplete accord, suggests Sartre; we are all forced to reckon with the impossibility of finding meaning in the unrelated events that constitute life.

One can accept or reject Sartre's view — which is perhaps more than usually pessimistic for having been written during the Nazi Occupation of Sartre's Paris — but no one can dispute the brilliance of his dramatic stylization: the fantastical Hell, an amusing "valet" who brings each character onto the stage, and the highly contrived assemblage of mismatched characters all serve to focus the intellectual argument precisely. Sartre's characters are philosophically representative rather than psychologically whole; there is no intention on Sartre's part to portray individual people

ALBEE ON THE ABSURD

As I get it, The Theatre of the Absurd is an absorption-in-art of certain existentialist and post-existentialist philosophical concepts having to do, in the main, with man's attempts to make sense for himself out of his senseless position in a world which makes no sense — which makes no sense because the moral, religious, political, and social structures man has erected to "illusion" himself have collapsed.

— Edward Albee

with interesting idiosyncracies, and there is no feeling on our part that the characters have a personal life beyond what we see in the play. Biographical character analysis would be useless for an actor assigned to play one of these

roles, and the interlock of psychological motivation, even in this sexually charged atmosphere, is deliberately ignored by the author. What Sartre presents instead is a general understanding of human affairs: a philosophy of interpersonal relations.

THEATRE OF THE ABSURD: *WAITING FOR GODOT*　The name *theatre of the absurd* applies to a grouping of plays that share certain common structures and styles and are tied together by a common philosophical thread: the theory of the absurd as formulated by French essayist and playwright Albert Camus (1913–1960). Camus likened the human condition to that of the mythological Corinthian King Sisyphus, who because of his cruelty was condemned forever to roll a stone up a hill in Hades only to have it roll down again upon

Vladimir and Estragon are still waiting for Godot in this eloquent 1993 Paris production at the Théâtre de la Tempête, directed by Philippe Adrien.

EXISTENTIALISM, ABSURDISM, AND WORLD WAR II

Both Jean-Paul Sartre's existentialism and Albert Camus's philosophy of the absurd were forged largely in the outrages of World War II, when both men were leading figures in the French Resistance movement. A hellish world that affords "no exit" and in which human activity is as meaningless as Sisyphus' torment seems perfectly credible during such desperate times, times of national occupation and genocidal slaughter. After the war, Jean-Paul Sartre, who was France's foremost exponent of existentialism and one of that country's leading dramatists during the 1940s and 1950s, spoke eloquently of his first experience as playwright and director, which occurred when he was a prisoner of war:

> My first experience in the theatre was especially fortunate. When I was a prisoner in Germany in 1940, I wrote, staged and acted in a Christmas play which, while pulling the wool over the eyes of the German censor by means of simple symbols, was addressed to my fellow prisoners. This drama, biblical in appearance only, was written and put on by a prisoner, was acted by prisoners in scenery painted by prisoners; it was aimed exclusively at prisoners (so much so that I have never since then

permitted it to be staged or even printed) and it addressed them on the subject of their concerns as prisoners. No doubt it was neither a good play nor well acted: the work of an amateur, the critics would say, a product of special circumstances. Nevertheless, on this occasion, as I addressed my comrades across the footlights, speaking to them of their state as prisoners, when I suddenly saw them so remarkably silent and attentive, I realized what theatre ought to be — a great collective, religious phenomenon.

To be sure, I was, in this case, favored by special circumstances; it does not happen every day that your public is drawn together by one great common interest, a great loss or a great hope. As a rule, an audience is made up of the most diverse elements: a big business man sits beside a traveling salesman or a professor, a man next to a woman, and each is subject to his own particular preoccupations. Yet this situation is a challenge to the playwright: he must create his public, he must fuse all the disparate elements in the auditorium into a single unity by awakening in the recesses of their spirits the things which all men of a given epoch and community care about.

---

nearing the top. Camus saw the modern individual as similarly engaged in an eternally futile task: the absurdity of searching for some meaning or purpose or order in human life. To Camus, the immutable irrationality of the universe is what makes this task absurd. On the one hand, human beings yearn for a "lost" unity and lasting truth; on the other hand, the world can only be seen as irrecoverably fragmented — chaotic, unsummable, permanently unorganized, and permanently unorganizable.

The plays that constitute the theatre of the absurd are obsessed with the futility of all action and the pointlessness of all direction. These themes are developed theatrically through a deliberate and self-conscious flaunting of the "absurd" — in the sense of the ridiculous. Going beyond the use of symbols and the fantasy and poetry of other nonrealists, the absurdists

have distinguished themselves by employing in their dramas, for example, clocks that clang incessantly, characters that eat pap in ashcans, corpses that grow by the minute, and personal interactions that are belligerently noncredible.

The theatre of the absurd can be said to include mid-twentieth-century works by Jean Genet (French), Eugène Ionesco (Romanian), Friedrich Dürrenmatt (Swiss), Arthur Adamov (Russian), Slawomir Mrozek (Polish), Harold Pinter (English), Edward Albee (American), Fernando Arrabal (Spanish), and the Irish poet, playwright, and novelist Samuel Beckett. And although Paris is the center of this theatre — so much so that the works of Ionesco, Adamov, Arrabal, and Beckett are all written in French rather than in their native tongues — its influence is felt worldwide.

Samuel Beckett (1906–1989), the unquestioned leader of the absurdist writers, eschews all realism, romanticism, and rationalism to create works that are relentlessly unenlightening, that are indeed committed to a final obscurity. "Art has nothing to do with clarity, does not dabble in the clear, and does not make clear," argues Beckett in one of his earliest works, and his theatre is based on the thesis that man is and will remain ignorant regarding all matters of importance.

Born in Dublin, Beckett emigrated in 1928 to Paris, where he joined a literary circle centered on another Irish émigré, James Joyce. Beckett's life before World War II was an artistic vagabondage, during which he wrote several poems, short stories, and a novel; following the war and his seclusion in the south of France during the Occupation, he produced the masterworks for which he is justly famous: the novels *Molloy, Moran Dies,* and *The Unnamable* and the plays *Waiting for Godot* and *Endgame.* By the time of his death in 1989, Beckett had received the Nobel Prize in literature, and his works had become the subject of hundreds of critical books and essays. It was *Godot* that first brought Beckett to worldwide attention: the play's premiere in Paris in 1953 occasioned a great stir among French authors and critics, and its subsequent openings in London and New York had the same effect there.

Waiting for Godot is a parable without a message. On a small mound at the base of a tree, beside a country road, two elderly men in bowler hats wait for a "Mr. Godot," with whom they have presumably made an appointment. They believe that when Godot comes they will be "saved"; however, they are not at all certain that Godot has agreed to meet with them or if this is the right place or the right day or whether they will even recognize him if he comes. During each of the two acts, which seem to be set in late afternoon on two successive days (although nobody can be sure of that), the men are visited by passersby — first by two men calling themselves Pozzo and Lucky and subsequently by a young boy who tells them that Mr. Godot "cannot

come today but surely tomorrow." The two old men continue to wait as the curtain falls. Although there are substantial references in the play to Christian symbols and beliefs, it is not clear whether these imply positive or negative associations. The only development in the play is that the characters seem to undergo a certain loss of adeptness while the setting blossoms in rebirth (the tree sprouts leaves between the acts).

What Beckett has drawn here is clearly a paradigm of the human condition: an ongoing life cycle of vegetation serving as the background to human decay, hope, and ignorance. Beckett's tone is whimsical: the characters play enchanting word games with each other, they amuse each other with songs, accounts of dreams, exercises, and vaudevillian antics, and in general they make the best of a basically hopeless situation. Beckett's paradigm affords a field day for critical investigators: *Waiting for Godot* has already generated a veritable library of brilliantly evocative discussions, and few plays from any era have been so variously analyzed, interpreted, and explored for symbolic meaning and content. Owing largely to the international critical acceptance of this play and its eventual public success, absurdist drama, as well as the whole of modern stylized theatre, was able to move out of the esoteric "art theatre" of the world capitals and onto the stages of popular theatres everywhere.

THEATRE OF ALIENATION: *THE GOOD PERSON OF SEZUAN*   Contrasting vividly with the theatre of the absurd is the theatre of alienation (or of distancing). Whereas the hermetic, self-contained absurdist plays highlight the essential futility of human endeavors, the sprawling, socially engaged "epic" theatre of alienation concentrates on humanity's potential for growth and society's capacity to effect change.

The guiding genius of the theatre of alienation was Bertolt Brecht (1898–1956): theorist, dramatist, and director. No single individual has had a greater impact on post–World War II theatre than Brecht. This impact has been felt in two ways. First, Brecht introduced theatre practices that are, at least on the surface, utterly at variance with those in use since the time of Aristotle; second, his accomplishments invigorated the theatre with an abrasive humanism that reawakened its sense of social responsibility and its awareness of the capacity of theatre to mold public issues and events.

Brecht, who was born in Germany, emerged from World War I a dedicated Marxist and pacifist. Using poems, songs, and eventually the theatre to promote his ideals following the German defeat, Brecht vividly portrayed his country during the Weimar Republic as caught in the grips of four giant vises: the military, capitalism, industrialization, and imperialism. His *Rise and Fall of the City of Mahagonny,* for example, an "epic opera" of 1930, proved an immensely popular blending of satire and propaganda, music and expressionist theatricality, social idealism and lyric poetry; it was produced all over Germany and throughout most of Europe in the early 1930s as a depiction of a rapacious international capitalism evolving toward fascism.

Brecht was forced to flee his country upon Hitler's accession to the chancellorship. Thereafter he moved about Europe for a time and then, for much of the 1940s, settled in America. Following World War II he returned in triumph to East Berlin, where the East German government established for him the Berliner Ensemble Theatre; there Brecht was allowed to consolidate his theories in a body of productions developed out of his earlier plays and the pieces he had written while in exile.

Brecht's theatre draws upon a potpourri of theatrical conventions, some derived from the ancients, some from Eastern drama, and some from the German expressionist movement in which Brecht himself played a part in his early years. Masks, songs, verse, exotic settings, satire, and direct rhetorical address are fundamental conventions that Brecht adopted from other theatre forms. In addition, he developed many conventions of his own: lantern-slide projections with printed "captions," asides and invocations directed to the audience to encourage them to develop an objective point of view, and a variety of procedures aimed at demystifying theatrical techniques (for example, lowering the lights so that the pipes and wires would be displayed) became the characteristics of Brecht's theatre.

Brecht deplored the use of sentimentality and the notion of audience empathy for characters and attempted instead to create a performance style that was openly "didactic": the actor was asked to alienate himself, or distance himself, from the character he played — to "demonstrate" his character rather than to embody that character in a realistic manner. In Brecht's view, the ideal actor was one who could establish a *critical objectivity* toward his or her character that would make clear the character's social function and political commitment. In attempting to repudiate the "magic" of the theatre, he demanded that it be made to seem nothing more than a place for workers to present a meaningful "parable" of life, and he in no way wished to disguise the fact that the stage personnel — actors and stagehands — were merely workers doing their jobs. In every way possible, Brecht attempted to prevent the audience from becoming swept up in an emotional, sentimental bath of feelings: his goal was to keep the audience "alienated" or "distanced" from the literal events depicted by the play so that they would be free to concentrate on the larger social and political issues that the play generated and reflected. Brecht considered this theatre to be an "epic" one because it attempted, around the framework of a parable or an archetypal event, to create a whole new perspective on human history and to indicate the direction that political dialogue should take to foster social betterment.

Brecht's theories were to have a staggering impact on the modern theatre. In his wholesale renunciation of Aristotelian catharsis, which depends on audience empathy with a noble character, and his denial of Stanislavsky's basic principles concerning the aims of acting, Brecht provided a new dramaturgy that encouraged playwrights, directors, and designers to tackle social issues directly rather than through the implications of contrived dramatic situations. Combining the technologies and aesthetics of other media — the lecture hall, the slide show, the public meeting, the cinema, the cabaret, the rehearsal — Brecht fashioned a vastly expanded arena for his *dialectics:* his social arguments that sought to engender truth through the confrontation of conflicting interests. These ideas were played out, in Brecht's own works and in countless other works inspired by him, with a bold theatricality, an open-handed dealing with the audience, a proletarian vigor, and a stridently entertaining, intelligently satirical, and charmingly bawdy theatre. This theatre has proven even more popular today than it was in Brecht's time, because since then the world seems to have grown even more fragmented, more individualistic, and more suspicious of collective emotions and sentimentality.

No play better illustrates Brecht's dramatic theory and method than *The Good Person of Sezuan* (1943). This play, set in western China (of which Brecht knew virtually nothing, thus adding to the "distancing" of the story), concerns a kindhearted prostitute, Shen Te, who is astounded to receive a gift of money from three itinerant gods. Elated by her good fortune, Shen Te uses the money to start a tobacco business. She is, however, quickly beset by petty officials seeking to impose local regulations, self-proclaimed creditors demanding payment, and a host of hangers-on who simply prey upon her good nature. At the point of financial ruin, Shen Te leaves her tobacco shop to enlist the aid of her male cousin Shui Ta, who strides imperiously into the tobacco shop and rousts the predators, making it safe for Shen Te to return. But the predators come back, and Shen Te again has to call on the tyrannical Shui Ta to save her. A simple story — but Brecht's stroke of genius is to make Shui Ta and Shen Te the same character: Shui Ta is simply Shen Te in disguise! The aim of the play is not to show that there are kindhearted people and successful people but that a person must choose to be one or the other. What kind of society is it, Brecht asks, that forces us to make this sort of choice?

Brecht is no mere propagandist, and his epic theatre is not one of simple messages or easy conclusions. At the end of *The Good Person of Sezuan*, Shen Te asks the gods for help, but they simply float off into the air reciting inane platitudes as the curtain falls. The gods do not have the answer — so the audience must provide it. In the play's epilogue, a character comes forward and addresses us:

Hey, honorable folks, don't be dismayed
That we can't seem to end this play! You've stayed
To see our shining, all-concluding moral,
And what we've given you has been this bitter quarrel.
We know, we know — we're angry too,
To see the curtain down and everything askew.
We'd love to see you stand and cheer — and say
How wonderful you find our charming play!
But we won't put our heads into the sand.
We know your wish is ever our command,
We know you ask for *more:* a firm conclusion
To this alarming more-than-mass confusion.
But what is it? Who knows? Not all your cash
Could buy your way — or ours — from this mishmash.
Do we need heroes? Dreams? New Gods? Or None?
Well, tell us — else we're hopelessly undone.
The only thing that we can think to say
Is simply that it's *you* must end this play.
Tell us how our own good woman of Sezuan
Can come to a good ending — if she can!

Honorable folks: you search, and we will
trust
That you will find the way. You must, must,
must!

Brecht's parables epitomize the conflicts between social classes; they do not presume to
solve these conflicts. Indeed, the social problems he addresses are not to be solved on the
stage but in the world itself: the audience
must find the appropriate balance between
morality and greed, between individualism
and social responsibility. Brecht's plays reenact the basic intellectual dichotomy posed by
Marx's dialectical materialism; thus they are,
in a sense, Marxist plays, but they certainly
are not Leninist, much less Stalinist. They radiate a faith in the human potential. Yet although they are both socially engaged and
theatrically eclectic — qualities not particularly noticeable in the theatre of the absurd —
they still resound with the fundamental human uncertainty that pervades all of modern
stylized theatre.

COMEDY OF CONTEMPORARY MANNERS:
BEDROOM FARCE   Comedy has always been
one of the greatest staples of the theatre; since
the days of Aristophanes in ancient Greece and
Plautus in Rome, comedians have entertained
the public with puns, antics, lighthearted social commentaries, and a host of other amusing reflections on the human struggle. It is
an axiom of the theatre that "comedy is serious business," and the true comedian is understood to be as inspired an artist as any
who labors under the lights. Yet comedy is
rarely accorded its fair share of academic consideration, partly because comedy tends to be
topical and therefore less than universal and
partly because the very thing that makes comedy popular — its accessibility — also makes
it relatively simple, and academicians adore
complexity. But simple does not mean simple-
minded, and the relative scarcity of fine comic

Shown here is the opening scene from the 1997 National
Theatre (London) production of Alan Ayckbourn's *Bedroom Farce*.

plays originating in any generation attests to
the enormous talent it takes to write, direct,
and act comedically.

In America, Neil Simon (born 1927) has for
four decades exhibited enormous talent and
success as a writer of light comedy for the stage
(and film), and in England, Alan Ayckbourn
(born 1939) has demonstrated a comparable
skill at the form. Ayckbourn's *Bedroom Farce*
was first produced in 1975 by the Library
Theatre in Scarborough, England, with which
Ayckbourn is associated; the play was subsequently produced by the National Theatre in

London in 1977 and came to Broadway and various other American cities shortly thereafter.

Like all of Ayckbourn's works, *Bedroom Farce* is an ingenious comedy of current manners, novel in its dramatic structure and reasonably true to life in its concerns. The setting for *Bedroom Farce* is three bedrooms, all in view simultaneously; the characters consist of four couples who, for reasons cleverly worked out in the plot, find themselves in one bedroom after another by turns. Although the innuendos of this play are highly sexual, the action consists primarily of animated verbal exchanges and comic business and pratfalls; thus the play lives up to the farcical structure promised by its title.

The opening scene of *Bedroom Farce,* an exchange of dialogue between Ernest and Delia, the oldest couple in the play, typifies the witty and very British repartee mastered by Ayckbourn. The scene takes place in a bedroom described as a "large Victorian" room "in need of redecoration":

. . . DELIA *sits in her bedroom at her dressing table mirror. She is going out. She is in her slip and finishing her make-up. An elaborate operation.* ERNEST *wanders in. Birdlike, bumbling, nearly sixty. He is in evening dress. He stares at* DELIA. *They are obviously going to be late but* ERNEST *has learnt that impatience gets him nowhere.*

DELIA: It would appear that things between Susannah and Trevor are coming to a head.

ERNEST: Ah.

DELIA: He was always a difficult boy. I sometimes think if you hadn't ignored him quite as much —

ERNEST: I did?

DELIA: Of course you did. You hardly said a word to him all the time he was growing up.

ERNEST: I seem to remember chatting away to him for hours.

DELIA: Well. Chatting. I meant conversation. Conversation about important things. A father should converse with his son. About things that matter deeply.

ERNEST: Doesn't really leave them much to talk about then, does it?

DELIA: And that if I may say so is typical. No. Let's admit it. We weren't good parents. You did nothing and I tried to make up for it, and that's why he's like he is today. I mean if he'd had a stable childhood, he'd never have completely lost his sense of proportion and married Susannah. I mean, I sometimes feel on the rare occasions one does see them together that she's not really — awful thing to say but — not really resilient enough for Trevor. He wants somebody more phlegmatic. That Jan girl for instance would have been ideal. Do you remember her?

ERNEST: Jan? Jan? Jan?

DELIA: Nice little thing. Beautifully normal. She came to tea, do you remember? You got on very well with her.

ERNEST: Oh yes. She was jolly, wasn't she? She was very interested in my stamps. What happened to her?

DELIA: Oh, she married — someone else, I think. She still writes occasionally.

ERNEST: I must say I preferred her to Susannah. Never really hit it off with her, I'm afraid.

DELIA: Well, she's a very complex sort of girl, isn't she? Hasn't really made up her mind. About herself. I mean, I think a woman sooner or later has simply got to make up her mind about herself. I mean, even if she's someone like Carolyn — you know, Mrs. Brightman's Carolyn — who looks at herself and says, right, I'm a lump. I'm going to be a lump but then at least everyone can accept her as a lump. So much simpler.

ERNEST: I think he should have married this other one.

DELIA: Jan? I don't think she was that keen.

ERNEST: She was altogether much jollier.

DELIA: Well, we're saddled with Susannah as a daughter-in-law — at least temporarily. We'd better make the best of it — I think I've put these eyes on crooked — we'd better make the best of it.

ERNEST: It's their bed. They can lie on it.

DELIA: Yes. I think that's one of the problems.

ERNEST: Eh?

DELIA: B — E — D.

ERNEST: B — E — D? Bed?

DELIA: Enough said.

ERNEST: Good lord. How do you know?

DELIA: One reads between the lines, darling. I've had a little look around their house. You can tell a great deal from people's bedrooms.

ERNEST: Can you? Good heavens. (*He looks about.*)

DELIA: If you know what to look for.

There is nothing obscure or difficult in *Bedroom Farce,* which stands out in the contemporary theatre mainly for its capacity to entertain, to titillate, and to dazzle with cleverness. Indeed, Ayckbourn makes clear his purely comedic intentions in the selection of his title, which suggests an even more frivolous diversion than Ayckbourn actually provides. For what the author has created in *Bedroom Farce* is, ultimately, something more than just another series of hijinks, physical incongruities, and dramatic clichés: it is a wry combination of social satire, middle-class insights, and boisterous good fun. The modern stylization can be seen in the intricacy of the plot design, which is echoed if not exceeded in Ayckbourn's other plays (*Absurd Person Singular* takes place, successively, in the kitchens of three married couples; *The Norman Conquests* consists of three interlocking plays, occurring simultaneously, involving the same cast of characters in three parts of the same house) and reflects a skill at construction that borders on pure genius. This kind of craftsmanship alone would suffice to elevate any comedy far beyond the usual level of television skit or sitcom; in Ayckbourn's case, it enables his stage works to reach the heights of inspired farce.

SUPRAREALISM: *BURIED CHILD* *Buried Child,* a play by American actor-author Sam Shepard (born 1943), was originally produced at the Magic Theatre of San Francisco in 1978 and moved to New York's off-Broadway stage the following year. Shepard established himself as an American avant-garde playwright in the 1960s and 1970s with such works as *The Tooth of Crime, Operation Sidewinder, Angel City,* and *Curse of the Starving Class.* All of his plays have the characteristic of *suprarealism;* that is, they are ostensibly realistic but actually suffused with menacing obscurity and mythic symbolism, steadily seeking out patterns beneath everyday surfaces and meanings in the silences that punctuate ordinary conversation.

Buried Child is set in a decaying farmhouse in the American Middle West; the degenerate condition of the house is echoed by that of the family who inhabit it. The setting is realized in wholly realistic detail, down to the "pale, frayed carpet," the "upright lamp with a faded yellow shade," and the "large, old-fashioned brown TV" that is left on during much of the play. The dialogue, too, is of the everyday variety, but the incidents, the interactions, and the involvements of the play are just enough removed from the familiar to create an atmosphere of mystery, menace, and doom.

The following scene, which comes near the beginning of the play, conveys something of the overriding spirit of *Buried Child.* In it, the aged, irascible Dodge — who sits on a sofa watching the TV — calls in his middle-aged son, Tilden, over shouted objections of his offstage wife, Halie. Inexplicably, Tilden enters with an armload of freshly picked, unshucked corn:

DODGE: (*yelling off left*) Tilden!

HALIE'S VOICE: Dodge, what are you trying to do?

DODGE: (*yelling off left*) Tilden, get in here!

HALIE'S VOICE: Why do you enjoy stirring things up?

DODGE: I don't enjoy anything!

HALIE'S VOICE: That's a terrible thing to say.

DODGE: Tilden!

HALIE'S VOICE: That's the kind of statement that leads people right to the end of their rope.

DODGE: Tilden!

HALIE'S VOICE: It's no wonder people turn to Christ!

DODGE: TILDEN!!

HALIE'S VOICE: It's no wonder the messengers of God's word are shouted down in public places!

DODGE: TILDEN!!!!

DODGE *goes into a violent, spasmodic coughing attack as* TILDEN *enters from stage left, his arms loaded with fresh ears of corn.* TILDEN *is* DODGE's *oldest son, late forties, wears heavy construction boots, covered with mud, dark green work pants, a plaid shirt and a faded brown windbreaker. He has a butch haircut, wet from the rain. Something about him is profoundly burned out and displaced. He stops center stage with the ears of corn in his arms and just stares at* DODGE *until he slowly finishes his coughing attack.* DODGE *looks up at him slowly. He stares at the corn. Long pause as they watch each other.*

HALIE'S VOICE: Dodge, if you don't take that pill nobody's going to force you.

The two men ignore the voice.

DODGE: (*to* TILDEN) Where'd you get that?

TILDEN: Picked it.

DODGE: You picked all that?

TILDEN *nods.*

DODGE: You expecting company?

TILDEN: No.

DODGE: Where'd you pick it from?

TILDEN: Right out back.

DODGE: Out back where?

TILDEN: Right out in back.

DODGE: There's nothing out there!

TILDEN: There's corn.

DODGE: There hasn't been corn out there since about nineteen thirty-five! That's the last time I planted corn out there!

TILDEN: It's out there now.

DODGE: (*yelling at stairs*) Halie!

HALIE'S VOICE: Yes dear!

DODGE: Tilden's brought a whole bunch of corn in here! There's no corn out in back is there?

TILDEN: (*to himself*) There's tons of corn.

HALIE'S VOICE: Not that I know of!

DODGE: That's what I thought.

HALIE'S VOICE: Not since about nineteen thirty-five!

DODGE: (*to* TILDEN) That's right. Nineteen thirty-five.

TILDEN: It's out there now.

DODGE: You go and take that corn back to wherever you got it from!

TILDEN: (*after pause, staring at* DODGE) It's picked. I picked it all in the rain. Once it's picked you can't put it back.

DODGE: I haven't had trouble with neighbors here for fifty-seven years. I don't even know who the neighbors are! And I don't wanna know! Now go put that corn back where it came from!

TILDEN *stares at* DODGE *then walks slowly over to him and dumps all the corn on* DODGE's *lap and steps back.* DODGE *stares at the corn then back to* TILDEN. *Long pause.*

DODGE: Are you having trouble here, Tilden? Are you in some kind of trouble?

TILDEN: I'm not in any trouble.

DODGE: You can tell me if you are. I'm still your father.

TILDEN: I know you're still my father.

DODGE: I know you had a little trouble back in New Mexico. That's why you came out here.

TILDEN: I never had any trouble.

DODGE: Tilden, your mother told me all about it.

TILDEN: What'd she tell you?

TILDEN *pulls some chewing tobacco out of his jacket and bites off a plug.*

DODGE: I don't have to repeat what she told me! She told me all about it!

TILDEN: Can I bring my chair in from the kitchen?

DODGE: What?

TILDEN: Can I bring my chair in from the kitchen?

DODGE: Sure. Bring your chair in.

TILDEN *exits left.* DODGE *pushes all the corn off his lap onto the floor.* . . .

Where did the corn come from? Why does Tilden bring it in? Why does he drop it on Dodge's lap? What was the "trouble" in New Mexico? We will never receive overt answers to these questions. *Buried Child* is a play that radiates implication and never becomes explicit. It creates the impression of a theme not by rational plot development or logical moral positioning but rather by a pattern of seeming non sequiturs, abrupt transitions, and bizarre, enigmatic actions.

There was, we find out over the course of the play, a baby that was killed many years ago and buried by Dodge out in back; this is the "buried child" of the title, a metaphorical fertilizer for Tilden's corn and a symbolic seminalization for middle America, which the play gives us to understand was established by acts of murder and built by successive cover-ups. A series of demented children — there is also a crazed amputee, Bradley, and Tilden's shell-shocked and psychotic son, Vince — uncover the family's horrific past in the play's ambiguous (but curiously cathartic) conclusion.

Shepard plays upon our natural fascination with — and fear of — the unexpected and the unusual. The contrast between Dodge's violent spasm of coughing and Tilden's silent, corn-laden entrance exemplifies the theatricality of Shepard's technique: it is a wholly unforgettable — if inexplicable — moment of theatre. So also is Tilden's act of throwing the corn on Dodge's lap. The repetition of the following line seems at first a simple mimicry of humdrum conversation:

TILDEN: Can I bring my chair in from the kitchen?

DODGE: What?

TILDEN: Can I bring my chair in from the kitchen?

As part of an overall pattern of dialogue, however, the repetition enhances rhythms of uncertainty and confusion: unanswered questions about the possibilities of communication between these characters in their insistent attempts to get through to . . . something.

Shepard's suprarealism, with its highly theatrical use of rhythms and juxtapositions, creates an electrified surface intensity around an obscure center, which has increasing resonance in postmodern culture. The revival of a somewhat revised *Buried Child* was a stunning Broadway success in 1996. Similar suprarealist techniques may be seen in the plays of British author Harold Pinter (*The Homecoming*) and American authors Edward Albee (*Who's Afraid of Virginia Woolf?*, *A Delicate Balance*, *Three Tall Women*) and David Mamet (*American Buffalo*, *Glengarry Glen Ross*, and *Oleanna*).

THE CASE STUDY: *WINGS*   *Wings*, by American author Arthur Kopit (born 1937; previously known for his intriguingly titled *Oh Dad, Poor Dad, Mama's Hung You in the Closet and I'm Feeling So Sad*), was originally written as a play for radio. It was subsequently revised for the stage and premiered in 1968 at the Yale Repertory Theatre in New Haven, Connecticut, whence it eventually moved to Broadway for a limited run. In 1992 a musical version of the play was staged at the Goodman Studio Theatre in Chicago, bringing Kopit's provocative work to new audiences.

The play is one of a growing number of dramatic works that present "case studies" of individuals in medical distress: other plays with similar themes include Bernard Pomerance's *The Elephant Man* (American, 1979), dealing with extreme disfigurement; Albert Innaurato's *The Transfiguration of Benno Blimpie* (American, 1978), dealing with obesity; Peter Shaffer's *Equus* (British, 1973), dealing with schizophrenic behavior; and Brian Clark's *Whose Life Is It Anyway?* (British, 1978), dealing with total paralysis. Medical issues are not the dominant concern of these plays, of course,

Constance Cummings plays Mrs. Stilson in this original (1968) production of *Wings* by the Yale Repertory Theatre, directed by John Madden. Cummings is attended by Marianne Owen as Amy.

but in each case a medical problem furnishes a perspective for the playwright's philosophical investigations.

Wings takes place in a setting that is nothing but "a system of black scrim panels that can move silently and easily, creating the impression of featureless, labyrinthine corridors." The setting, therefore, represents both a hospital and the inside of a patient's mind — the patient being a Mrs. Stilson, former aviatrix, now a victim of a stroke. Mrs. Stilson sits in a chair downstage of the panels, and what we in the audience see and hear is a confusion of images, sounds, words, and illusions that represent Mrs. Stilson's "inner self," where "time and space are without definition" and "information is coming in too scrambled and too fast to be properly decoded." "Were her head a pinball game," Kopit says, "it would register TILT."

Kopit achieves this scrambled effect through a brilliant dramaturgical design that conveys onstage what the stroke victim perceives herself: in other words, by his stylization of the dramatic dialogue and imagery, Kopit gives his audience the opportunity not merely to observe a stroke but also to experience it. The first scene, titled "Catastrophe," illustrates his technique:

IMAGES	SOUNDS OUTSIDE HERSELF	MRS. STILSON'S VOICE
	(SOUNDS *live or on tape, altered or unadorned*)	(VOICE *live or on tape, altered or unadorned*)
Mostly, it is whiteness. Dazzling, blinding.	*Of wind.*	
	Of someone breathing with effort, unevenly.	Oh my God oh my God oh my God —
	Of something ripping, like a sheet.	— trees clouds houses mostly planes flashing past, images
Occasionally, there are brief rhombs of color, explosions of color, the color red being dominant.	*Of something flapping, the sound suggestive of an old screen door perhaps, or a sheet or sail in the wind. It is a rapid fibrillation. And it is used mostly to mark transitions.*	without words, utter disarray disbelief, never seen this kind of thing before!

Where am I? How'd I get here? |

IMAGES

The mirrors, of course, reflect infinitely. Sense of endless space, endless corridors.

Nothing seen that is not a fragment. Every aspect of her world has been shattered.

Utter isolation.

In this vast whiteness, like apparitions, partial glimpses of doctors and nurses can be seen. They appear and disappear like a pulse. They are never in one place for long.

The mirrors multiply their incomprehensibility.

Sometimes the dark panels are opaque, sometimes transparent.

Always, they convey a sense of layers, multiplicity, separation.

Sense constantly of doors opening, closing, opening, closing.

Fragments of hospital equipment appear out of nowhere and disappear just as suddenly. Glimpse always too brief to enable us to identify what this equipment is, or what its purpose.

SOUNDS OUTSIDE HERSELF

It can seem ominous or not.

Of a woman's scream (though this sound should be altered by filters so it resembles other things, such as sirens).

Of random noises recorded in a busy city hospital, then altered so as to be only minimally recognizable.

Of a car's engine at full speed.

Of a siren (altered to resemble a woman screaming).

Of an airplane coming closer, thundering overhead, then zooming off into silence.

Of random crowd noises, the crowd greatly agitated. In the crowd, people can be heard calling for help, a doctor, an ambulance. But all the sounds are garbled.

Of people whispering.

Of many people asking questions simultaneously, no question comprehensible.

Of doors opening, closing, opening, closing.

Of someone breathing oxygen through a mask.

VOICES: (*garbled*) Just relax. / No one's going to hurt you. / Can you hear us? / Be careful! / You're hurting her! / No, we're not. / Don't lift her, leave her where she is! / Someone call an ambulance! / I don't think she can hear.

MALE VOICE: Have you any idea —

MRS. STILSON'S VOICE

My leg (What's my leg?) feels wet arms . . . wet too, belly same chin nose everything (Where are they taking me?) something sticky (What has happened to my plane?) feel something sticky.

Doors! Too many doors!

Must have . . . fallen cannot . . . move at all sky . . . (Gliding!) dark cannot . . . talk (Feel as if I'm gliding!).

Yes, feels cool, nice . . . Yes, this is the life all right!

My plane! What has happened to my plane!

Help . . .

— all around faces of which nothing known no sense ever all wiped out blank like ice I think saw it once flying over something some place all was white sky and sea clouds ice almost crashed couldn't tell

where I was heading right side up topsy-turvy under over I was flying actually if I can I do yes do recall was upside down can you believe it almost scraped my head on the ice caps couldn't tell which way was up wasn't even dizzy strange things happen to me that they do!

What's my name? I don't know my name!

IMAGES	SOUNDS OUTSIDE HERSELF	MRS. STILSON'S VOICE
	OTHER VOICES: (*garbled*) Do you know your name? / Do you know where you are? / What year is this? / If I say the tiger has been killed by the lion, which animal is dead?	Where's my arm? I don't have an arm!
Mrs. Stilson's movements seem random. She is a person wandering through space, lost.		
	A hospital paging system heard.	What's an arm?
Finally, Mrs. Stilson is led by attendants downstage, to a chair. Then left alone.	*Equipment being moved through stone corridors, vast vaulting space. Endless echoing.*	AB-ABC-ABC123DE451212 what? 123 — 12345678972357 better yes no problem I'm okay soon be out soon be over storm . . . will pass I'm sure. Always has.

By an ingenious combination of voices, non-verbal sounds, colors, and movements with an intricate interplay of actors, hospital equipment, and panels, Kopit captures the intellectual dislocation caused by brain trauma and compels his audience to partake of the victim's fear, bewilderment, and sense of helplessness. *Wings* is a disturbing play, but it is also extremely thought-provoking. Beyond the purely medical issues, it explores a whole range of philosophical and epistemological questions: What is communication? What is emotional support? What is learning? What are words, and what are they worth? Finally, the play is inspiring as a portrait of a human being whose struggle to control her inner world has intense meaning for every sensitive person.

POLITICAL SATIRE: *SERIOUS MONEY*   Since at least the time of Aristophanes, playwrights have used the theatre as a broad public platform to criticize the social world of their times — most often in a way that is both caustic and entertaining. Causticity gives such criticism its necessary bite, but a playful or whimsical tone renders even the harshest criticism palatable — and, in exceptionally dangerous times, may also protect a playwright from political retribution. We use the term *satire* to distinguish such works, which have been popular in the theatre of most cultures.

British playwright Caryl Churchill (born 1938) has been a unique exemplar of socially conscious dramatic satire since the 1970s, with trenchant and brilliantly innovative works on a wide variety of issues: sexual orientations and their attendant prejudices and hypocrisies (*Cloud 9*), gender discrimination throughout history (*Top Girls*), British-American attractions and antipathies (*Ice Cream*), and the post-cold-war chaos in eastern Europe (*Mad Forest*). In each of these works, Churchill has reinvestigated — and in some cases reinvented — the dramaturgical format itself: in *Cloud 9*, for example, she double-casts actors in both male and female — and youthful and elderly — roles, putting a wholly new slant on the complex perspectives that gender and age cast on our notions of personal identity. And in all of her plays, Churchill reexamines the syntaxes of stage dialogue, often creating new conversational punctuation systems to identify just how characters — like people in real life — frequently overlap, interrupt, and self-abort their own and each other's speeches.

In *Serious Money* (1987), Churchill employs a racy rhyming verse — in an exceptional glib patter that lies somewhere between e. e. cummings and gangsta rap — to explore the va-

The trading action in Caryl Churchill's *Serious Money* is continuous and rambunctious, as shown here in this 1987 New York Public Theatre production.

garies of arbitrage stock trading on the London market and of international finance:

ZACKERMAN [an international banker in
    London]:
  There's some enterprising guys around and
      here's an example.
  You know how if you want to get a job in the
      states you have to give a urine sample?
          (This is to show you're not on
              drugs.)
  There's a company now for a fifty dollar fee
  They'll provide you with a guaranteed pure,
      donated by a churchgoer, bottle of pee.
          (They also plan to market it dehydrated
          in a packet and you just add water.)
  And AIDS is making advertisers perplexed
  Because it's no longer too good to have your
      product associated with sex.
  But it's a great marketing opportunity.
  Like the guys opening up blood banks
      where you pay to store your own blood
      in case of an accident and so be guaran-
      teed immunity.
          (It's also a great time to buy into
          rubber.)

Anyone who can buy oranges for ten and
    sell at eleven in a souk or bazaar
Has the same human nature and can go
    equally far.
The so-called third world doesn't want our
    charity or aid.
All they need is the chance to sit down in
    front of some green screens and trade.

The witty rhymes, punctuated by paren-thetical "ad libs," and the complicated frenzy of *Serious Money*'s plot and staging (much of the play takes place on a stock brokerage's trading floor, bursting with stock monitors, telephone banks, and continuous, shouted deal-making) create a mesmerizing enchant-ment. Yet Churchill's views of economic ex-ploitation on an international level beam through loud and clear. Satire is a topical dra-matic form that often does not outlive its top-ics, but when the content is compelling and the form brilliant — as it was with Aristoph-anes and is with Churchill — the play usually survives its merely political utility and makes its way into the lasting theatrical repertoire.

9

The Musical Theatre

M usical theatre — a theatre that employs a full singing score, usually accompanied by an orchestra and often dance as well — would generally have to be considered "antirealistic" in the most obvious sense. Nonetheless, its particularity derives not from a rebellion against verisimilitude (thus it does not fit into the category "antirealistic theatre," as described in the preceding chapter) but rather from its basis in an aesthetics unique to its performance. Hence we will treat musical theatre in a chapter of its own.

It could actually be argued that most drama throughout theatre's history has been in fact musical, that musical theatre is, indeed, the dominant — not merely an alternative — mode of dramatic art. Classic Greek tragedy was sung and danced; it was accompanied by the *aulis* (flute) and other instruments, and Aeschylus, who directed his plays, was particularly noted for his choreography in the choral entrance of *The Eumenides*. Most Renaissance and commedia dell'arte plays included songs and instrumental music, and twenty-five of Shakespeare's thirty-eight plays contain at least some singing (*The Tempest* alone has nine scripted songs). Moreover, Shakespeare's comedies, as well as those of his contemporaries, seem to have each ended with a full-stage company dance. In the seventeenth century, English dramatist Ben Jonson wrote musical masques (dance-dramas) for the court of King James I, and in France, Molière wrote *comédie ballets* for King Louis XIV, such as *The Bourgeois Gentleman*, whose five acts each end with a fully orchestrated and choreographed mini-opera. And, of course, all major Asian dramatic forms involve singing, dancing, and instrumental music — sometimes continuously throughout the performance.

And while a spoken text predominates in modern Western drama, singing and dancing make frequent appearances, certainly in the antirealistic theatre. Most of Bertolt Brecht's theatre of alienation plays involve songs (his *The Threepenny Opera, Happy End,* and *The Rise and Fall of the City of Mahagonny* are indeed fully orchestrated musical works), and brief songs also are included in the texts of Samuel Beckett's theatre of the absurd plays *Waiting for Godot* and *Happy Days* and Peter Weiss's *Marat/Sade.*

Still, musical theatre has become a specific genre of its own over the past 150 years of Western drama, not so much as a reaction to (or against) prevailing theatre traditions but as a medium calculated, at first anyway, to provoke audience merriment. Absorbing elements of light opera and ballet and, even more significantly, of popular nineteenth-century entertainments such as the English music hall and American minstrel and variety shows, the modern musical theatre brings to the contemporary dramatic repertory a proven and widely enjoyed form of entertainment with a global commercial appeal.

Nowhere is that commercial and entertainment success better known than in New York, which remains the international capital of the world's musical theatre — although London, Toronto, and even Sydney are currently hot competitors. In New York, during the past decade, as much as 80 percent of Broadway's box-office income has derived from musicals alone, several of which (*Phantom of the Opera, Les Misérables,* and *The Producers*) seem all but permanently installed in the theatres where they play eight times a week. At the time of this writing, eighteen full-scale musicals are performing on Broadway, and more are waiting in the wings. And the income from "road" (touring) versions of these shows attests to an

even greater dominance of musicals in larger performing halls around the country. Furthermore, New York's less-capitalized off-Broadway theatres are also home to musicals, many of them smaller musical theatre pieces with simpler stagings, reduced casts, and less-than-complete orchestras. *The Fantasticks,* with an eight-member cast and an "orchestra" of piano and harp, opened in 1960 and ran for 42 years, closing (in 2002) after 17,162 performances.

Not-for-profit regional theatres are increasingly drawn to musicals, too, as are universities, community and dinner theatres, and even Shakespeare festivals. And musical theatre is also now a staple of major theatres abroad, including government-subsidized houses such as the Royal National Theatre of England, which in the past decade has become a major producer of American musicals (*Guys and Dolls, Carousel, Oklahoma!, Lady in the Dark, My Fair Lady, South Pacific*). Indeed, up to a third of the main theatres in Berlin, Budapest, London, Tokyo, Sydney, and Stockholm (many of them government subsidized) are at any given time hosting engagements of such world-popular musicals as *Phantom of the Opera, Rent, Chicago, Jekyll and Hyde, The Lion King, Les Misérables,* and *The Sound of Music.* Such musical theatre engagements, often (but not always) spectacularly produced, can form the commercial backbone of an entire theatre community's offerings.

But commercial appeal is hardly the sum of musical theatre's international importance. Musical theatre is a dramatic form of great variety, vitality, and — on many occasions — artistic significance. The Pulitzer Prize has been awarded to numerous musical dramas (*Of Thee I Sing, South Pacific, Fiorello!, How to Succeed in Business without Really Trying, A Chorus Line, Sunday in the Park with George*); using techniques as old as Greek tragedy and as inspired as those of Mozart and Wagner, musical theatre authors and artists have created both aesthetic innovations and social impact through brilliantly integrated disciplines of melody, cadence, choreography, and rhyme.

The nineteenth-century operettas of Gilbert and Sullivan gave rise to musical theatre traditions in both England and America, where they often premiered, as with *Pirates of Penzance* in 1877, simultaneously. As these works were highly satirical to begin with, present-day directors often redirect the authors' original barbs at more currently topical subjects. In Russell Treyz's wonderfully tongue-in-cheek production for the 2001 Utah Shakespearean Festival, Glenn Seven Allen plays an Elvis-like Frederic, an apprentice pirate who has renounced his profession upon turning twenty-one, in search of a bride from among Major General Stanley's eager daughters.

The Development of the Broadway Musical: America's Contribution

America didn't invent musical theatre, and it no longer dominates the genre the way it did in the middle decades of the twentieth century, but there is no doubt that the Broadway musical — even in its current international form — is America's best-known contribution to world theatre. Moreover, the Broadway musical, in the beginning of the twenty-first century, seems to be in a renewed period of ascendancy. But the "Broadway musical" is not a purely American product; as we shall see, it is created today by artists from all over the world.

The Broadway musical dates back to the staging of *The Black Crook* at Niblo's Garden in New York City in 1866; this play was in fact a rather ordinary melodrama, but when a French dance company stranded in the city was added to the show to give it some extra spice, *Crook* became a rather sexy spectacle, with dances, songs, and a bevy of scantily clad young women. The popularity of staged musical entertainments featuring a wide diversity of performers grew by leaps during the nineteenth and early twentieth centuries. Challenging the old custom of white actors' "blacking up" (with burnt-cork makeup) for minstrel shows, a new black musical comedy arose, employing the emerging ragtime musical syncopations of earlier black vaudeville reviews. Bob Cole's 1898 *A Trip to Coontown*, ("coon" was, at the time, a common and generally offensive term for blacks) was one of the most successful: a full-length black musical comedy written and performed by African Americans (some in whiteface!), it played to large mixed-race audiences in New York. Though an unapologetic farce — with ethnic humor, girlie numbers, and neo-operatic inserts — Cole's play included at least one song of direct social protest: "No Coons Allowed!" tells of a young man unable to bring his date to the "swellest place in town" on account of the club's racist policy.

New York also proved a hospitable site for sophisticated musical theatre works from abroad at the end of the nineteenth century. The sensational and still-popular satirical light operas of the English duo W. S. Gilbert and Arthur Sullivan (*HMS Pinafore, The Pirates of Penzance,* and *The Mikado*), the *opéra bouffe* (satirical comic opera) of French composer Jacques Offenbach (*La Perichole, La Belle Hélène, Orpheus in the Underworld* — which introduced the cancan), and the Viennese operetta of Franz Lehar (*The Merry Widow*) all demonstrated that musical theatre could tell a story in a delightfully appealing way. Audiences flocked to these musicals, and American writers and composers emerged to create homegrown products that could compete with these imports. Irish-born Victor Herbert, an émigré to the United States at twenty-seven, became America's first great composer for the stage; Herbert's major hits, *Babes in Toyland* (1903) and *Naughty Marietta* (1910), proved immensely successful, introducing songs such as "Ah, Sweet Mystery of Life" to America's popular music repertoire. More prominent still was Rhode Island–born vaudevillian George M. Cohan, whose *Little Johnny Jones* (1904), in which Cohan also starred, provided what became his — and some of his country's — signature songs: "I'm a Yankee Doodle Dandy" and "Give My Regards to Broadway." By the first decade of the new century, American musical theatre was entering what was to prove a golden age.

The First Phase of the Golden Age: Musical Comedy

We refer to the first two-thirds of the twentieth century as a "golden age" for the American musical with some reservation, not only

AUTHORSHIP IN MUSICAL THEATRE

A musical generally has three creators: an author for the *book* (the spoken text), another for the lyrics (the words in the songs), and a composer for the music. It is not unusual, however, for a single person to perform two or even three of these tasks: Cole Porter and Stephen Sondheim have written lyrics and music to most of their musicals, and with his 1997 *Rent,* Jonathan Larson added his name to the several triple-threats who have written the book, lyrics, and music for a single show. When working in collaboration, lyricists and composers tend to work in teams, such as the famous pairings of Gilbert and Sullivan, Rodgers and Hammerstein, and Lerner and Loewe. Generally the composer is named first (as in the cases of Richard Rodgers and Alan Jay Lerner), but occasionally the lyricist gets the top billing (as in the case of W. S. Gilbert).

because such encomia are always fairly arbitrary but also because the era has two fairly distinct phases. The first, from about 1900 to the late 1920s, was the great age of *musical comedy* — a genre that, of course, emphasized comedy as well as singing but also youthful romance; it featured sexy (and lightly clad) girl choruses, liberal doses of patriotic jingoism, and, in response to the "dance craze" of the early 1900s, spectacular dancing — including the show-offy "tap" — to a jazzy or ragtime beat.

By the 1920s and 30s, American musical comedy had dozens of starring composers, lyricists, and performers. Tourists from all over the country flocked to midtown Manhattan to see such musical works as the brothers George (music) and Ira (lyrics) Gershwin's cool and still-memorable *Lady Be Good, O Kay!, Funny Face,* and *Girl Crazy;* Vincent Youmans's sweetly romantic *Hit the Deck* and *No, No, Nanette* (with "Tea for Two"); Jerome Kern's bouncy *Very Good Eddie* and *Sunny;* Cole Porter's wittily engaging *Anything Goes* and *DuBarry was a Lady;* and a series of especially droll and delightful musical comedies by Richard Rodgers (music) and Lorenz Hart (lyrics), including *A Connecticut Yankee, On Your Toes,* and *Babes in Arms.* What all these works had in common were a laughably simple plot, a cast composed strictly of romantic and comedic characters, a wholly unchallenging theme, lots of pretty girls in revealing costumes, and abundantly cheerful singing and dancing that had little or no connection to the plot. And although these works were often silly as dramas, there can be no mistaking the musical glories of the best of them, with music that remains enchanting to the present day. The Gershwin songs ("Embraceable You," "'S Wonderful," and "The Man That Got Away") and those of Rodgers and Hart ("The Lady Is a Tramp," "Small Hotel," and "Bewitched, Bothered and Bewildered") and the shows they came from have been regularly revived; the songs themselves have become a staple of the repertories of literally hundreds of modern jazz singers.

Up in Harlem, meanwhile, Bert Williams and J. Leubrie Hill drew large mixed-race audiences for their *Darktown Follies of 1914* (introducing the hit number "After the Ball"), and in 1921 a black musical dominated a full Broadway season for the first time, with composer Eubie Blake's and lyricist Noble Sissle's wildly successful *Shuffle Along,* which ran more than 500 performances and introduced such songs as "In Honeysuckle Time" and "I'm Just Wild about Harry." Popular high-stepping, side-slapping "black-bottom" dancing was a feature of many black musicals of the 1920s, as was the epoch-defining dance known as "the Charleston," which, introduced in the 1923 black musical *How Come?* (composed by Maceo Pinkard), started a national craze in the hit show *Runnin' Wild* (by James P. Johnson and Cecil Mack) later that year.

The Second Phase of the Golden Age: Musical Drama

Toward the middle of the twentieth century, the second phase of the golden age of Broadway musicals began. This phase ushered in a new genre — musical drama — characterized by increasingly serious plots and sophisticated musical treatments. *Show Boat,* written by Jerome Kern (book) and Oscar Hammerstein II (lyrics) in 1927, was an early masterpiece of musical drama (though its authors insisted on calling it a musical comedy). It represents one of the great pieces of fully acted — and not just sung — vocal literature in the American theatre. Adapted from a gritty novel by Edna Ferber, *Show Boat* has a complex plot that is carried by the music and dancing as well as by the work's spoken dialogue; the musical touches significantly on race relations in America. Indeed, the famous "Ol' Man River" aria (though viewed by some as patronizing at the time of its successful 1993 revival) referred pointedly to the then-current racial divisions as sung by a black actor in front of the show's (largely white) 1927 audience:

> Colored folks work on de Mississippi,
> Colored folks work while de white folks play,
> Pullin' dem boats from de dawn to sunset,
> Gittin' no rest till de Judgment Day —
> Don' look up
> An' don' look down —
> You don' dast make
> De white boss frown.
> Bend your knees
> An' bow your head,
> An' pull dat rope
> Until yo' dead.

Meanwhile, the Gershwin brothers' *Strike Up the Band* and *Of Thee I Sing* moved this fraternal team into the arena of political satire and proved so successful that the latter production received the 1932 Pulitzer Prize in drama — the first musical to do so. The Gershwins followed with the full-out folk opera *Porgy and Bess* (1935), which remains a staple of international opera companies today.

The second, serious, phase of the musical's golden age came into full flower with Rodgers and Hart's startling *Pal Joey* (1940), adapted from grimly ironic and sophisticated *New Yorker* stories by John O'Hara and featuring an amoral gigolo and his often unsavory companions in a musical pastiche of the contemporary urban nightclub scene. Tame by today's standards, *Joey* shocked prewar audiences with its blithely suggestive lyrics about sexual infidelity and shady business ethics and with a show-stopping song ("Zip!") belted out by an intellectual stripteaser — who sang out her thoughts while doing her act.

Many serious musicals followed, straining the word *comedy* wholly out of the musical's nomenclature. Marc Blitzstein's *The Cradle Will Rock* (1938), concerning the struggle to organize a union of steelworkers in "Steeltown" against the opposition of one Mr. Mister, the town's leading capitalist, was canceled an hour before its New York opening by government officials who objected to the play's "left-wing propaganda" (the government provided funding for the sponsoring theatre). The play was performed later that night across the street, oratorio-style and without scenery or costumes, to tremendous enthusiasm — as memorialized in Tim Robbins's film, *Cradle Will Rock*, in 1999. *Lady in the Dark* (1941) — with a book by dramatist Moss Hart, lyrics by Ira Gershwin, and music by Kurt Weill (Brecht's colleague, who, like Brecht, had fled to America from Nazi rule in Germany) — concerned itself with psychoanalysis and dream analysis and the perilous situation of a career woman (Liza Elliott) in a world dominated by old-fashioned ideas of marriage and women's roles; the musical numbers were all contained in Liza's three long dream sequences. *Oklahoma!* (1943), with music by Richard Rodgers and lyrics by Oscar Hammerstein II, dealt with social and sexual tensions in the opening of the western states. Dispensing with the accepted convention of decorative dancing girls, *Oklahoma!* featured content-laden balletic choreography by Agnes de Mille to advance the plot and treated its historical subject — which included an onstage killing and the quick dispensing of frontier justice — with romantic passion and a new level of social intensity.

During the late 1940s and the 1950s, seriously themed Broadway musicals dominated the commercial American theatre. Rodgers and Hammerstein followed *Oklahoma!* with one success after another: *Carousel* (dealing with spousal abuse), *South Pacific* (racial prejudice), *The King and I* (gender prejudice and ethnocentricity), *Flower Drum Song* (East-West assimilation), and *The Sound of Music* (Nazism), all marked with social and intercultural conflict, richly romantic settings and songs, beautiful solo numbers and love duets, and thrilling choral, choreographic, and orchestral ensembles. Leonard Bernstein, one of America's leading orchestral conductors and composers, left a considerable mark on the musical's golden age with his *On the Town*, about World War II sailors on leave in Manhattan, and *West Side Story* (with lyrics by Stephen Sondheim), a powerfully emotional retelling of the *Romeo and Juliet* story, with a contemporary Polish American (Tony) as his Romeo and a Puerto Rican American (Maria) as Juliet. And Jerry Bock and Sheldon Harnick conveyed a profoundly moving version of Jewish shtetl life in czarist Russia with *Fiddler on the Roof*.

Not all musicals were deeply sober and serious, of course. More-lighthearted and satirical musicals of the 1940s and 1950s — first-rate works that still featured well-integrated plots, characters, themes, and musical styles — included Frank Loesser's *Guys and Dolls*, based on the idiosyncratic urban stories of Damon Runyon; Cole Porter's *Kiss Me Kate*, based on a backstage romance during a tour of Shakespeare's *Taming of the Shrew*; and Irving Berlin's *Annie Get Your Gun*, based on the life of American folk heroine Annie Oakley. Richard Adler and Jerry Ross's *Pajama Game* (about union organizing in a pajama factory) and *Damn Yankees* (a Faustian tale about baseball) featured superlative jazz dancing choreographed by Bob Fosse. Alan Jay Lerner (book and lyrics) and Frederick Loewe (music) first successfully collaborated on the fantasy *Brigadoon*, about a mythical Scottish village, and

Left: Voted the "greatest musical of the century" by the American Drama League, Rodgers and Hammerstein's 1943 *Oklahoma!* integrated dance, music, and realistic drama as rarely seen on a theatre stage. Adapted from Lynn Riggs's *Green Grow the Lilacs* (1931), the musical sought to tell, in Riggs's words, "a *kind of truth* about people who happen to be living in Oklahoma.... Gamblers, traders, vagabonds, adventurers, daredevils, fools." Beyond the jollity of *Oklahoma!*'s merrier moments, we can see the hardworking, hardliving, and often agonizing rural life of territorial America. The Royal National Theater revival of 1998, directed by Trevor Nunn, was remounted on Broadway in 2002. Hugh Jackman is Curly and Josefina Gabrielle is Laurey.

Above: The stunning 1994 Broadway revival of Rodgers and Hammerstein's 1945 *Carousel* showed what a powerful impact the golden-age Broadway musicals can still deliver. Although elements of the script — adapted from Ferenc Molnar's Hungarian classic, *Liliom* (1909) — are clearly dated, brilliant design and a contemporary staging and sensitivity bring out the play's still-valid insights and premises, along with Rodgers's glorious musical score. This production, directed by Nicholas Hytner, featured scenery and costumes by Bob Crowley.

then followed up with their brilliant musical revision of George Bernard Shaw's *Pygmalion*, renamed *My Fair Lady*, which wittily explores and exploits heroine Liza Doolittle's proper and improper pronunciation of spoken English.

The best of these musicals during Broadway's golden age were commercially successful beyond anything in the theatre's previous history. Hit plays ran not for weeks or months, as before, but for years. They were, indeed, more than just "plays"; they were world-renowned cultural phenomena. For the first time, theatre tickets were sold as far as six months in advance, and business travelers returning from Manhattan were expected to provide a full report on "the new musicals in town." Touring companies brought the best

Musical Lyrics through the Eras

A brief sampling of the lyrics from different eras clearly indicates the changing styles of musical theatre popular in America:

W. S. Gilbert's lyrics tend toward lighthearted satire and revel in their own cleverness and literary showmanship. With multisyllable rhymes and a mocking attitude toward all pomposity, Gilbert amusingly skewers official British pretension, as in the Major General's self-explanatory "patter song" (so called because its singing requires rapid enunciation) from *The Pirates of Penzance* (1879):

STANLEY: I am the very model of a modern major
    general,
    I've information animal and vegetable and
    mineral,
    I know the kings of England and I quote the
    fights historical,
    From Marathon to Waterloo in order
    categorical.
    I'm very well acquainted too with matters
    mathematical,
    I understand equations both the simple and
    quadratical,
    About binomial theorems I am teaming with a lot
    of news,
    With many cheerful facts about the square of the
    hypotenuse!...

Ira Gershwin's lyrics are openly romantic and tender; rather than call attention to the lyricist's own wit, the clever wordplay is more hidden within the feelings of the characters. The following excerpt from "'S Wonderful" was coauthored by Ira and his brother George (music) for the musical *Funny Face* (1927). Like most songs, it is divided into a verse, which sets up the situation, and a refrain, which is the musical (and emotional) heart of the song:

PETER: Life has just begun:
    Jack has found his Jill.
    Don't know what you've done,
    But I'm all a-thrill.
    How can words express
    Your divine appeal?
    You could never guess
    All the love I feel.
    From now on, lady, I insist,
    For me no other girls exist.

(Refrain)

    'S wonderful! 'S marvelous
    You should care for me!
    'S awful nice! 'S Paradise –
    'S what I love to see!
    You've made my life so glamorous
    You can't blame me for feeling amorous.
    Oh, 'S wonderful! 'S marvelous –
    That you should care for me!...

Perhaps no lyricist in the field has conveyed thwarted love and ironic longing as well as Lorenz Hart, the first partner of Richard Rodgers. In "Bewitched, Bothered and Bewildered" (*Pal Joey,* 1940), Vera, a society lady, drunkenly sings of her going-nowhere affair with a sexy but good-for-nothing nightclub owner:

VERA: After one whole quart of brandy,
    Like a daisy I awake.
    With no Bromo Seltzer handy.
    I don't even shake.
    Men are not a new sensation;
    I've done pretty well, I think.
    But this half-pint imitation's
    Put me on the blink.

(Refrain)

    I'm wild again,
    Beguiled again,
    A simpering, whimpering child again –
    Bewitched, bothered and bewildered am I.
    Couldn't sleep
    And wouldn't sleep
    Until I could sleep where I shouldn't sleep –
    Bewitched, bothered and bewildered am I.
    Lost my heart, but what of it?
    My mistake, I agree.
    He's a laugh, but I love it
    Because the laugh's on me...

By the time of Hart's death in 1943, Rodgers had begun a new partnership, with Oscar Hammerstein II, already the lyricist for Jerome Kern's *Show Boat* and many other musicals. Hammerstein wrote that he barely dared "place a timid encroaching foot on the territory" of the "masters" Gilbert and Hart and sought to write instead what he himself termed "a more primitive type of lyric... expressing my own true convictions and feelings." His lyrics for the opening song in *Oklahoma!* (1943) clearly convey this:

CURLEY: There's a bright, golden haze on the meadow,
There's a bright, golden haze on the meadow.
The corn is as high as an elephant's eye,
An' it looks like it's climbin' clear up to the sky.

(*Refrain*)

Oh, what a beautiful mornin'!
Oh, what a beautiful day!
I got a beautiful feelin'
Ev'rythin's goin' my way...

Hammerstein derived the verse of this song from a written stage description in Lynn Riggs's *Green Grow the Lilacs*, the source play for *Oklahoma!* Riggs had described the scene as "a radiant summer morning... cattle in the meadow, blades of the young corn... their images giving off a visible golden emanation that is partly true and partly a trick of imagination...." Deciding it was a shame to waste Riggs's images on the reading audience only, Hammerstein made them the source of his famous opening lyric.

Stephen Sondheim, who enlarged the musical's palette more profoundly, perhaps, than any artist in the field, is most noted for a deeply ironic and anti-romantic tone that, nonetheless, remains amusing and surprisingly good-spirited; somehow he has managed to leaven his gloomy message with buoyant music, penetrating observation, and fiendishly clever rhymes and rhythm breaks. In "The Little Things You Do Together" (*Company*, 1970), Sondheim mocks the too-easy sentimentality of marital "relationships":

JOANNE: It's the little things you share together,
Swear together,
Wear together,
That make perfect relationships.
The concerts you enjoy together,
Neighbors you annoy together,
Children you destroy together,
That keep marriage intact.

(*Refrain*)

It's not so hard to be married
When two maneuver as one
It's not so hard to be married,
And, Jesus Christ, is it fun.

Finally, Jonathan Larson in *Rent* has brought a new style to lyric writing altogether and, with it, a new audience for the Broadway musical. With a rock and rap beat (Larson wrote his own music) and with a script and staging that derived in part from cast improvisations, the musical scored an enormous success. "Contact" is one of the show's closing songs. Because it does not easily divide into verse and refrain stanzas, none are noted here:

ROGER, MARK, JOANNE, & BENNY: Hot-hot-hot-sweat-sweet
Wet-wet-wet-red-heat
Hot-hot-hot-sweat-sweet
Wet-wet-wet-red-heat
Please don't stop please
Please don't stop stop
Stop stop stop don't
Please please please please
Hot-hot-hot-sweat-sweet
Wet-wet-wet-red-heat
Stick-licky-trickle-tickle
Steamy-creamy-stroking-soaking

COLLINS: Touch!

MAUREEN: Taste!

MIMI: Deep!

COLLINS: Dark!

MAUREEN: Kiss!

COLLINS: Beg!

MIMI: Slap!

MIMI, MAUREEN, & COLLINS: Fear!

COLLINS: Thick!

COLLINS, MIMI, & MAUREEN: Red, red
Red, red
Red, red – please

MAUREEN: Harder!

ANGEL: Faster!

MAUREEN: Wetter!

MIMI: Bastard!

COLLINS: You whore

MAUREEN: You animal

MIMI & ANGEL: More

MAUREEN, COLLINS, & MIMI: Fluid no fluid no contact
yes no contact

ALL: Fire fire burn – burn yes!
No latex rubber rubber
Fire latex rubber latex bummer lover bummer

of these shows to the rest of the country: first-class national tours, with the Broadway stars intact, and, subsequently, "bus and truck" tours, with less-familiar performers — nonetheless advertising "straight from Broadway!" — traveled around the nation. It is likely that most Americans during these years first experienced live theatre in the form of a road version of a Broadway musical, as did the author of the book you are reading. Songs from the best musicals — and even some mediocre ones — routinely made the radio "hit parade" (forerunner of the "top ten" or "top forty" listings of today) and gained an instant national audience. Film versions of many musicals — *Oklahoma!, Carousel, My Fair Lady, Guys and Dolls, The Sound of Music* — were also widely popular. For a couple of decades, at least, it seemed as if everyone in America was whistling the latest creation from the tunesmiths of Broadway. And the stars of Broadway mu-

sicals past and present — Jimmy Durante, Eddie Cantor, Mary Martin, Ethel Merman, Julie Andrews, Carol Channing, Pearl Bailey, Bob Hope, and John Raitt — achieved national celebrity status; many became the pioneer performers on America's new entertainment medium, television. It is certain that the theatre had never played such a central role in American popular culture before; it is questionable if it ever will again.

The Contemporary Musical

No golden age lasts forever, and in retrospect no such age is unquestionably remembered as golden; the glittery epithet may in fact become little more than a quaint historical milepost. It is unquestionable, however, that the bulk of musicals produced in America today, not just by amateur groups but on Broadway as well, are revivals of the great musicals of the American mid-century. In the ten years immediately prior to this book's publication, Broadway has been host to long-running productions of such golden-age hits (often in revised formats) as *The Music Man, Oklahoma!, Annie Get Your Gun, Cabaret, Show Boat, Gypsy, Guys and Dolls, Carousel, Grease, How to Succeed in Business without Really Trying, The Sound of Music,* and *Girl Crazy.* Nonetheless, a new and more contemporary musical theatre, at once less sentimental and more ironic, has come onto the scene.

The Emergence of Choreographer-Directors: Jerome Robbins, Gower Champion, Bob Fosse, Tommy Tune, Michael Bennett

The last fifty years have seen a tremendous escalation in the importance of choreography in American musicals. Agnes de Mille was

Above left: Many of the musicals on Broadway at present are revivals of shows from Broadway's golden age. For the 1998 New York revival of John Kander and Fred Ebb's 1966 musical *Cabaret,* the Roundabout Theatre was turned into a cabaret of its own, with the audience seated at cafe tables instead of orchestra seats, thus emphasizing the participatory decadence and salaciousness of Nazi-era entertainment. Alan Cumming won the Tony Award for his performance as the MC; here we see him surrounded by his cabaret's "Kit Kat" girls.

Above: A musical about musicals – that describes *42nd Street,* along with several other American musicals of the past decades. Here, in the Tony Award–winning 2001 Broadway revival, the chorus tap-dances down a giant staircase, against a background of illuminated theatre marquees (the "Great White Way"). Scenery by Douglas W. Schmidt; costumes by Roger Kirk; lighting by Paul Gallo.

instrumental in initiating this movement, with her plot-advancing dance numbers, already mentioned, in Rodgers and Hammerstein's *Oklahoma!* But the coming years saw the emergence of several choreographers who became more widely known than the directors they worked with — indeed, who *became* their productions' directors.

Jerome Robbins (1918–1998) was the first of these; trained both in ballet and acting, his "Small House of Uncle Thomas" ballet — a deliberately quaint, Siamese-themed version of Uncle Tom's Cabin — in *The King and I,* and his vigorous teenage "street rumble" dances in *West Side Story* earned him national critical fame, leading to his combining directorial and choreographic chores in the seriocomic Broadway musicals *Gypsy,* about the life of striptease artist Gypsy Rose Lee and her mother, and *Fiddler on the Roof,* about Jewish life in pre-revolutionary Russia. In 1989 Robbins put together a retrospective collection of his dances in *Jerome Robbins' Broadway,* winning him the Tony Award for best musical.

Gower Champion (1921–1980) and Bob Fosse (1927–1987) were of Robbins's generation but utterly unalike. Champion, a veteran dancer (with his wife, Marge) in many Broadway shows and Hollywood films, returned to the stage in 1960 to both stage and choreograph the energetic, crowd-pleasing *Bye Bye Birdie,* and followed this up with the romantic *Carnival* (1961) and the brashly presentational *Hello, Dolly!* (1964), in each case placing dance at the center of his dramatic entertainment. Champion's final show — he died tragically on its opening night — was *42nd Street* (1980), a virtual valentine to the Broadway theatre, and particularly to tap dancing; the show enjoyed a long run and was brought back in a Tony Award–winning revival in 2000–01. Fosse, also a golden-age choreographer (*Pajama Game* and *Damn Yankees,* 1954 and 1955), went on to develop, in the coming years, a highly idiosyncratic style — quick, jerky moves that suddenly segue to slow, sinuous come-ons;

bumps and grinds from the striptease; white gloves and black bowler hats from minstrel and vaudeville; dance-as-sex and sex-as-dance — in, particularly, *Chicago* (1975) and *Dancin'* (1978), as well as in the film of *Cabaret* and his own filmed autobiography, *All That Jazz.* A posthumous retrospective of Fosse's dances, simply titled *Fosse,* opened on Broadway in 1999, running two years and winning the Tony Award for best musical.

Tommy Tune (born 1939) and Michael Bennett (1943–1987) are of a later generation. The lanky Tune, a brilliant tap dancer, even performs in some of the productions he also choreographs and/or directs; indeed, he is the only person to have won Tony Awards in four categories — director, choreographer, leading and featured actor. Tune's *My One and Only* (1988), in which he also starred, *Grand Hotel* (1989), and *Will Rogers Follies* (1991) were virtually celebrations of dance entertainment. Bennett's artistic goals are somewhat more conceptual: his masterwork (after choreographing and co-directing Stephen Sondheim's *Company* and *Follies*) was *A Chorus Line* (1975), a musical which, conceived, staged, and choreographed by Bennett, takes place in a dance audition and consists largely of dances interspersed with "interviews" with the auditioning dancers; it was initially developed off-Broadway using improvisations with performers, many of whom landed in the show itself. *A Chorus Line* was, for many years, Broadway's longest-running show.

This list could not possibly be complete without mentioning Susan Stroman, director-choreographer of *Contact* and *The Producers,* but her work is covered more fully later in the next chapter, "Theatre Today."

Stephen Sondheim

No one has been more influential in the modern musical than the composer and lyricist Stephen Sondheim (born 1930), whose first important work, mentioned earlier, was the composition of lyrics for Leonard Bernstein's 1957 *West Side Story*. After one more assignment as a golden-age lyricist (for Jule Styne's *Gypsy*), Sondheim turned composer as well, winning high praise and success for both the lyrics and music to the songs in the highly novel *A Funny Thing Happened on the Way to the Forum,* drawn from the Roman comedies of Plautus.

But in his work from 1970 onward, Sondheim departed from the standard formats of those early shows to develop a new style, marked by a disturbing plot, an ironic and sometimes even cynical tone, a brutal skepticism about conventional morality, and highly sophisticated, adult, intricately rhymed lyrics that are integrated with a score that brings surprising new rhythms to popular music. Sondheim's first works in this style include *Company* (1970), a devilishly clever and incisive look at sexual pairings and partings in the Manhattan of the time; *Follies* (1971; Broadway revival 2001), set at an onstage reunion of able but aging musical theatre performers, also set in Manhattan ("I'm Still Here!" is the famous number from this show); and *A Little Night Music* (1973), adapted from an Ingmar Bergman film about summer sexual dalliances on a country estate in Sweden. These works were widely heralded for their brilliantly acerbic but always entertaining portrayal of the inevitable and eternal conflicts between social mores and romantic idealism (or, more bluntly, between laws and lust). Furthermore, they established Sondheim's supremacy in the American musical form for the entire generation that followed.

Sondheim continued to break new boundaries in three amazing creations. His *Pacific Overtures* (1976) employs kabuki-inspired music and stage techniques to trace the history of relations between Japan and the United States since Commodore Perry's "opening" of Japan in 1853. Sondheim's *Sweeney Todd* (1979) integrates Brechtian alienation techniques and blends elements from Italian grand opera, the

Sondheim's *Passion* is a profound, intense musical examination of irrational sexual attraction, set in a nineteenth-century military camp – and in a woman's bedroom. This photograph comes from the 1994 Broadway production.

English music hall, and Victorian melodrama in a wildly morbid story of a barber's revenge: having murdered his customers while shaving them, the barber shuttles the bodies to the basement through an ingenious trapdoor beneath his barbering chair, whereupon his long-devoted lady friend (Mrs. Lovett) serves up their flesh in meat pies sold to the public. *Sweeney*'s score is so powerful and its actions and images so compelling that the work has been staged by several European opera companies. Conversely, Sondheim's *Sunday in the Park with George* (1984) is an elegant musical play about the pointillist painter Georges Seurat; for this production, Sondheim invented a "pointillist" style of music to echo Seurat's painting style.

Sondheim's most controversial new works are *Assassins* (1991) and *Passion* (1993). *Assassins* is a musical review of presidential assassinations (and assassination attempts), which cascades through two centuries, portraying the quirks and oddities of John Wilkes Booth, Lee Harvey Oswald, Squeaky Fromm, and John Hinckley, Jr., among other unlikely musical theatre protagonists (if not heroes). *Assassins* was so unconventional and, to some, so alarming that it did not open on Broadway after its limited (and sold-out) off-Broadway premiere, and the show has reached an international audience only through its cast recording and subsequent successful runs in London and Los Angeles and frequent college productions. (A Broadway opening was finally scheduled for November 2001, but the terrorist attacks of September 11 deferred the production for at least a year.)

In contrast, *Passion* opened on Broadway and despite mixed reviews won four Tony Awards in 1994, including best musical. An intermissionless nineteenth-century gothic tragedy — "one long love song," according to Sondheim — *Passion* tells the strange story of Giorgio, a handsome Italian army officer who is deeply in love with the beautiful Clara but is relentlessly pursued by his commanding officer's cousin, Fosca, a homely, ailing, and pathetically obsessional woman. The initial attractiveness of Giorgio and Clara's love (they begin the play in bed together, totally naked, singing in duet, "I'm so happy, / I'm afraid I'll die / Here in your arms") gradually gives way against its own limitations (Giorgio's assignment to the provinces, Clara's nondivorceable marriage) and to the intensity of Fosca's amorous fixations, to which Giorgio ultimately yields — to Clara's despair and to that of most of the audience as well. As there is little to admire or "root for" in this romantic tangle, *Passion*'s success was somewhat limited, but its achievements and innovations are exhilarating nonetheless; it is a profound, intense musical examination of irrational sexual at-

traction and will again be before audiences, along with five other Sondheim shows, in a Sondheim Celebration at Washington's Kennedy Center in 2002.

European Musicals

But several of the most successful new musicals running on Broadway and around the world at the turn of the century are not American at all: the megahits of Englishman Andrew Lloyd Webber (particularly *Cats* and *Phantom of the Opera* but also *Jesus Christ Superstar, Evita, Starlight Express, Aspects of Love,* and *Sunset Boulevard*) and of Frenchmen Alain Boublil and Claude-Michel Schönberg (*Les Misérables* and *Miss Saigon*). These works, usually sung-through (that is, entirely sung, without any spoken words at all), are known for their lush musical scores more than either their book (if there is any) or lyrics, which in part explains their international popularity (because they have less of a language barrier to surmount). They are also generally presented in an exceptionally spectacular manner: *Starlight Express* features a cast on roller skates and a roller racetrack encircling the audience; in *Phantom of the Opera,* a chandelier all but falls in the midst of the audience, and the extraordinarily magical second act is set on a fiery lake beneath the Paris Opera; and in *Miss Saigon* a "helicopter" descends to rescue American and Vietnamese citizens fleeing the U.S. Embassy in the last days of the Saigon regime. Webber's music-dominant works, combined with the rapid technological advances in audio enhancement, have also inspired gifted sound designers to work their special magic into the acoustics of musical theatre; wireless microphones on the performers and superpotent electronic amplification between performers and house speakers (computer-delayed to reach every seat in the house simultaneously) are now commonplace — to the chagrin of many purists and critics — in musical theatre stagings from Broadway to Bangkok.

Though not (yet) a commercial success, Andrew Lloyd Webber's most recent work has found great favor with many critics, including the author of this book, and is currently headed for international showings. *The Beautiful Game*, centered on an English school's football (soccer) team, depicts young love and sporting excitement against the background of apparently ceaseless violence between Protestants and Catholics in Northern Ireland. David Shannon is John (*holding the cup*) and Frank Grimes is Father O'Donnell in the 2000 production at London's Cambridge Theatre.

Some of the Webber and Boublil-Schönberg works will likely run well into the twenty-first century, but the era of lushly sung-through musicals might soon be reaching its end. Despite a series of tryout runs, Boublil and Schönberg's *Martin Guerre* has not yet proven successful, leaving them without a hit since 1991. And Webber's *Cats,* though displacing *A Chorus Line* as Broadway's longest-running show, failed to live up to its "Now and Forever" slogan, closing in 2000, while his *Whistle Down the Wind* met with only tepid response in Washington (1996) and a subsequent London reworking (1998). Webber has, in fact, seriously switched gears for his more recent and very powerful *The Beautiful Game* (2000), a brutal, realistic, and non-sung-through musical about a Belfast, Ireland, school football (i.e., soccer) team and their girl and boy friends, during a deeply troubled recent period of the Irish troubles. Though running but a single London season, *The Beautiful Game* developed, with its powerful themes, athletic dancing, and engaging, youthful characters, tremendous audience enthusiasm and will almost certainly soon be seen in North America.

Mel Brooks: The Producers

Mel Brooks has had a long career in show business, beginning in the 1950s and 60s as a writer of review sketches and musical librettos

Left: Nathan Lane plays the fictional Broadway producer "Max Bialystock" in Mel Brooks's 2001 *The Producers,* an outrageously satirical musical farce which, though neither subtle nor particularly innovative, is certainly the biggest American musical hit of the past two decades.

Below: George C. Wolfe's *Jelly's Last Jam* brilliantly pairs the "black musical" entertainment format with a serious and avant-garde exploration of African American life. The play portrays the life and times of Creole jazz composer-performer Jelly Roll Morton. Wolfe's staging employs both traditional musical-comedy elements and neo-Brechtian stylizations.

for the Broadway stage (*New Faces of 1952, Shinbone Alley*), as well as award-winning records (*The 2000 Year Old Man*), television shows (Sid Caesar's *Your Show of Shows*), and feature films (*The Producers*), and in the latter field he continued in the 1980s and 90s with *Blazing Saddles, Young Frankenstein,* and *Robin Hood: Men in Tights.* But Brooks has almost certainly climaxed his amazing career with his stage version of *The Producers,* which opened in 2001 and won a record-shattering twelve Tony Awards, Brooks himself sharing in three of them: for best book, best score, and (as the show's producer) best musical — and would doubtless also have won a fourth, for best musical lyrics, except that there is no such award. For *The Producers* has clearly turned out to be the most spectacular success the Broadway theatre has enjoyed in at least a generation, with performances sold out up to a year in advance, and premium tickets being legally sold at a record-shattering $480 apiece — and a few others "scalped" (illegally resold) for up to $1,800.

The Producers is neither novel nor innovative; indeed, much of the script was taken directly from Brooks's own 1968 screenplay which had already won him an Academy Award. Rather, it is an unapologetic return to classic musical comedy of the 1930s, with corny jokes, a "dumb blonde" secretary, scantily clad chorus girls (two of whom are named Like-me Bite-me and Kiss-me Feel-me), and a vaudeville style reminiscent of the Marx Brothers and Harold Lloyd. What makes the show work so brilliantly are the show's outrageously offensive story (two Broadway producers, trying to create an enormous flop so as to bilk unwary investors, present a musical about Adolf Hitler which turns out to be a giant success, landing them in bankruptcy and jail), its absolutely delicious, over-the-top performances (by Nathan Lane and Matthew Broderick as the corrupt producers, Cady Huffman as the dumb blond, and Gary Beach caricaturing a gay director who, at the last moment, steps into the role of Hitler), the exuberant direction and choreography (culminating in the "Springtime for Hitler" showstopper) by Susan Stroman, and the very funny scenery and costumes by, respectively, Robin Wagner and William Ivey Long. *The Producers* is a production that, by virtually universal agreement, shows conventional theatrical craft at the absolute top of its form, and the immense entertainment potential that musical theatre can offer.

Directions in the Modern Musical

Modern musicals — *The Producers* excepted — have increasingly tackled serious subjects. Gang violence in *The Beautiful Game,* unemployment in *The Full Monty* (2001), Nazism in *Cabaret* and *Grand Hotel,* homosexuality in *A Chorus Line, Falsettos, Kiss of the Spider Woman,* and *La Cage aux Folles,* environmental degradation in *Urinetown,* and race-ethnic relations in *Big River, Jelly's Last Jam, Zoot Suit,* and *Ragtime* have been explored in many musical dramas with sharp, even brutal, insight and penetration. A nightmarish seagoing disaster and the ensuing physical and class struggle for survival were the focus of *Titanic,* which preceded by more than a year — and exceeded in social insight — the notable film of the same name.

More than a dozen major "black musicals" (musicals largely by, about, and performed by African Americans), including *Bubbling Brown Sugar* and *Eubie* (both based on the music of Eubie Blake), *Ain't Misbehavin'* and *Sophisticated Ladies* (featuring, respectively, the music of Fats Waller and Duke Ellington), *Dreamgirls* (celebrating a Supremes-like singing group), and *Bring in 'Da Noise, Bring in 'Da Funk* (a capsule history of racial injustice in America, conceived and directed by George C. Wolfe and choreographed by Savion Glover, who also performs), have explored African American culture and cultural issues, often passionately, through the medium (among others) of

Above: Ain't Misbehavin' – a musical celebrating the life and career of African American jazz pianist-composer Fats Waller – won the 1978 Tony Award for best Broadway musical and has since become popular in America's regional theatres. Seen here are Cynthia Thomas, Fuschia Walker, and Kyme in the 1995 production by the Alabama Shakespeare Festival.

Above right: One of the most innovative and popular musicals of the past decade is Jonathan Larson's *Rent;* using a contemporary pop musical vernacular, this musical takes the youthful bohemianism of Puccini's nineteenth-century opera *La Bohème* to New York's East Village in the late 1990s. "How do you measure the life / of a woman or a man?" Larson asks, in an urban environment filled with street crime, homelessness, and HIV? The play premiered at the downtown New York Theatre Workshop; cast with relative unknowns, it rose to international stature (and received a Tony Award) at its subsequent 1996 Broadway opening. Tragically, author-composer Larson died of an aneurysm just prior to the Broadway reopening. Actor Anthony Rapp (*facing front*) plays the role of Marc Cohen, perhaps Larson's alter ego.

black performance culture. *It Ain't Necessarily the Blues* (1999) was the latest of this genre, premiering in Denver then heading around the country before landing at Lincoln Center in New York.

Rock and other forms of music particularly popular with American youth were introduced into the mainstream first in the 1968 Broadway musical *Hair* (which also introduced full frontal nudity to the genre) and then in more recent musicals such as *The Who's Tommy* and the 1997 sensation (and winner of that year's Tony Award for best musical) *Rent*. And family musicals were pioneered in the late 1990s by none other than the Disney Corporation, which constructed and renovated Broadway theatres to present stage adaptations of their animated films *Beauty and the Beast* and *The Lion King*. The latter, fabulously successful and winner of the 1998 Tony Award for best musical, was directed by avant-garde director-designer Julie Taymor (see the following chapter) and brilliantly recaptures both African jungle and universal myth, creating a magnificent and unique blend of African, Asian, and American performance styles.

In any event, the musical theatre is alive and well in the cities that can afford to mount and present such works, and the stage musical continues to reinvent itself in both subject matter and style of presentation. *Rent, The Producers,* and *The Lion King* are unique not merely because of their forms but also because of their audience appeal; the first draws huge numbers of young people in their teens, twenties, and thirties, and the latter two attract audience members ages five to ninety-five. The musical's only drawback, in the minds of many, is its very success; musicals so dominate the Broadway theatre that straight plays tend to play a secondary role. But of course straight theatre has its solid base in America's not-for-profit theatres, including those in New York, and need not compete at every level of the mass-market economy. Moreover, playwrights of the nonmusical stage, such as Terrence McNally (author of *Ragtime, Kiss of the Spider Woman,* and *The Full Monty*), Marsha Norman (*The Secret Garden*), and David Henry Hwang (*Aida*), are increasingly tapped for new musical-theatre assignments, as are literally hundreds of actors, directors, and designers who work in both spoken and sung dramas. It appears that at the dawning of the twenty-first century, the Broadway musical is the commercial leader of a vibrant all-genre American theatrical establishment.

10

Theatre Today: What, Who, and Where?

The theatre of today exists onstage, not in the pages of this or any other book. The theatre of today is being performed right now, in the multimillion-dollar theatres of the world's great cities as well as on the simpler stages at schools, community theatres, nightclubs, roadhouses, and experimental theatre clubs everywhere.

The theatre of today is all around us, simply waiting to be discovered, seen, heard, felt, and experienced. The easiest and best way to apprehend its fundamental impulse is to go out and see it firsthand.

What's Happening?

What's happening in the theatre today? It's not easy to say. We cannot evaluate the current theatre with the same objectivity that we can the theatre of the past — even the recent past. Theatre is a business as well as an art, and the flurry of promotion, publicity, and puffery that surrounds each current theatrical success makes a cool perspective difficult. Whereas poets and painters are often ignored until years following their deaths, the opposite is more often true of theatre artists: they are frequently lionized in their own time, only to be forgotten a few years later. A permanent place in the repertory of world theatre is the achievement of very few indeed; among the playwrights once deemed equal to Shakespeare

are such now-dimly remembered figures as John Fletcher, Joseph Addison, Edward George Bulwer-Lytton, August Friedrich, von Kotzebue, Eugène Brieux, and Maxwell Anderson. Which of our present-day writers and actors and other theatre artists will achieve more than ephemeral glory? Which, if any, will leave a mark on future generations? No one can answer either question with any certainty. But there are some directions in today's theatre that show signs of becoming established, and these are worthy of examination.

The Modern and the Postmodern

From a practical point of view — looking at stage practice rather than theory — theatre is a fairly conservative institution. Certainly, theatre companies the world over will continue to present plays from the past as well as from our own time — and will also conserve (the root of "conservative") many of the theatre's traditional ways of working. In fact, virtually all the plays mentioned in the previous chapters are being performed somewhere in the world today, and the vigorous debates among today's actors and directors often repeat, almost verbatim, dialogues from the days of Aristophanes, Shakespeare, and Stanislavsky.

Nevertheless, as we begin the twenty-first century, a new era seems to be emerging. The twentieth century was a particularly violent one: two world wars and one cold one, assassinations of great political and cultural leaders (Martin Luther King, Jr., John and Robert Kennedy, Mohandas Gandhi, Anwar Sadat, Yitzhak Rabin, John Lennon), both Nazi and nuclear holocausts, the proliferation of alluring but dangerous drugs and sex-linked diseases, and the threatened destruction of our planet's vital resources. The arts responded to these social changes with an artistic freedom that was frightening in its extremity — nowhere more so than in the theatre, where, by the 1970s, Dionysian ecstasy had returned to the stage with a force almost equal to that

The Company Theatre of Los Angeles was only one of many theatre companies in the 1960s and 70s to experiment with total nudity and participatory improvisation onstage. This original production, titled *The Emergence*, was one of the finest and most visually eloquent productions of the turbulent times.

of the dithyramb. As play-licensing laws fell in England and legal censorship became locally unenforceable in America, profanity, nudity, copulation, violence, and libelous accusation — all unknown on the legitimate stage since ancient times — became almost commonplace. Plays popular in America in the last third of the century included one accusing the sitting president of murder (*MacBird*), another accusing a recent pope of genocide (*The Deputy*), another featuring a farm boy copulating with his pig (*Futz*), another of teenage boys stoning a baby to death in its crib (*Saved*), and another that concluded with the actors and some of the audience undressing and marching naked out into the street (*Paradise Now*). Most of this reached right into the theatre's mainstream when the rock Broadway musical *Hair* (1968) concluded with the actors — who had already sung rapturously about sodomy, fellatio, and cunnilingus — brazenly stripped off their clothes and grinningly faced the audience. Nor were theatre audiences themselves immune from such changes in theatrical convention; often in the 1970s and 80s, spectators found themselves physically sat upon, fondled, assaulted, hurled about, handed lit joints (of marijuana), and, in at least one case (in Finland), urinated upon. These and other extreme behaviors had become part of the license claimed by a theatre purportedly trying to make itself heard above the societal din of war, riots, and corruption. Or, many asked, were its adherents only clamoring for personal attention? In any event, it was an era of dramaturgical violence and abandon that brought the age of "modernism" to a crisis, if not to a conclusion.

The Directions of Today's Theatre

Well before the century's end, however, this mood of violent protest was largely spent. The novelty of stage sex and profanity had mostly passed, much of it being filtered into more mainstream artistic forms, and the latent voyeurism of the audience had been more than satisfied; an increasingly serious and sober public soon began demanding a more focused response to major issues than the theatre had been providing. And many artists (and critics) were beginning to freshly examine and reveal the hidden prejudices and privileges — in terms of gender, race, class, and sexual orientation — that continued to undermine even modernism's seeming freedom and fairness.

At the same time, the end of the twentieth century brought with it an explosion of new social and political alignments, and a sometimes overwhelming spectrum of new technologies. With the cold war ended, and its empires and military alliances dissolved or reconfigured, a newly globalized economy challenged local cultures with enhanced but often troubling prospects, while astonishing advances in telecommunications — e-mail, mobile phones, satellite television broadcasting, broadband webcasting — revolutionized the way global citizens connect with each other. Theatre has found, and capitalized on, a vast store of new subjects and fresh opportunities. Once again the live stage has surfaced as an arena where new thoughts, fashions, feelings, morals, theologies, and aesthetics could be enacted, and new technologies explored, in order to bring lucidity and structure to the confusions that beset us all.

Although generalizations about an era still upon us must be tentative, there are clearly three major movements, or themes, in the current theatre, the theatre of the age we increasingly call "postmodern." These movements might be categorized as a theatre of postmodern experiment, an open theatre, and a theatre of revival. (Because these terms are not at all in general use, they are preceded by the indefinite article *a* rather than the definite *the*.)

A Theatre of Postmodern Experiment

The notion of a postmodern era is not as historically defined as the name suggests. As the term has developed since the 1970s, *postmodernism* indicates a way of thinking, or even of nonthinking, more than it defines a particular period in time.

The postmodern defies complete analysis, because postmodernism literally defies (repudiates) the act of analyzing. A postmodern approach essentially dismisses logic and cause-and-effect determinism, replacing both with more parallel, almost random, reflections. These reflections are of two sorts: self-reflections, whereby a work of art pays homage to itself, and reflections of the past, whereby the art pays homage to past texts and models.

One can see postmodernism, therefore, in Andy Warhol's repeated and repainted images (of Campbell soup cans, head shots of Marilyn Monroe, electric chairs), each of which emphasizes the artist's redefining an existing artifact as an independent work of "art." One may see it also in Philip Johnson's AT&T building in New York (1984), with its neo-Renaissance facade and "Chippendale highboy" roofline. Whereas modernism repudiated the past, postmodernism gaily embraces it, quotes it, and even recycles it.

A postmodernist work of art, therefore, is not about "something" so much as it is about itself — about "art." Moreover, a postmodern work might also be said to "deconstruct" itself, so as to make us think about ourselves as much as what we're seeing. Indeed, postmodern art is about us as well as it is about art. How do we view art? And, we might say, how does art view us? Are there any hidden assumptions about "what art is" that exclude us from enjoying it — or that "privilege" other audiences? Inasmuch as a postmodern work is self-referential (refers to itself), it also contains its own critique; it parodies itself; it throws us back, sometimes in amusement and sometimes in irritation, upon our own thoughts.

Postmodern artists — and postmodern critics — are as deeply concerned with the social orders from which art springs, with the processes of creating art, and with the open or hidden assumptions that inform art as with the art products themselves. Such definitions of the postmodern are admittedly complex, probably humorous (if not bewildering) to a first-time reader, and are themselves subject to parody — which is itself a postmodern approach!

In theatre, which is a practical art, the notion of postmodernism can be understood concretely. Postmodern drama springs directly from the antirealistic theatre, but un-like most antirealistic theatres, it has little, if any, of the modernist's aesthetic or social optimism. Whereas the symbolists and surrealists were working to reveal inner truths, a "higher order" of reality, and whereas the Brechtian epic theatre was struggling to change (or save) the world and to create a higher level of society, none of these goals are deemed within the reach of the postmodernist, who presupposes no higher levels of reality or social order. Because there is no higher reality to symbolize, the postmodernist abjures symbols (the postmodern is the art, one critic suggests, of the *métaphore manquée,* or "missing metaphor"). Because social progress is impossible (and social decline possibly inevitable), the postmodernist can only contemplate the future warily, if at all.

The postmodern writer or director, therefore, is more likely to explore the discontinuity of observable reality rather than attempt to find any integrated synthesis or meaning. Postmodern art celebrates the apparent randomness of arbitrary juxtaposition, and it prides itself not on logic and conviction but, rather, on delightful surprise, even shock, and tantalizing (if bewildering) irrelevancies. Students of the postmodern find its salient features, for example, in the action painting of Jackson Pollock, who randomly dripped paint from buckets with holes in their bottoms; in break dancing, which is improvised, haphazard, and disjunctive; and in the music (or, as some say, cacophony) of John Cage, which consists of apparently indiscriminate sounds, few of which come from conventional "musical" instruments. Television, with its night-and-day agglomeration of dramatic fragments intermixed with commercials, promos, newsbreaks, announcements, station identifications, and old film clips, is a perfectly postmodern creation, made all the more discontinuous by a technology that permits the viewing of two or more agglomerations (split-screen, or picture-in-picture) simultaneously and remote-control shuttling between a hundred-odd channels at lightning speed.

The first great postmodern theatre (although its creators refused to call it "theatre," and the term *postmodern* had yet to be invented) was the short-lived arts phenomenon called *Dada,* which flourished, beginning at the Cabaret Voltaire, in Zurich, Switzerland, in 1916, in the years immediately following World War I. As critic Mel Gordon describes it, Dada was a "chaotic mix of balalaika music, Wedekind poems, dance numbers, cabaret singing, recitations from Voltaire, and shouting in a kaleidoscopic environment of paintings." So-called chance poetry, created by Dada poet Tristan Tzara by pulling words out of a hat, led to cabaret performances of chance drama. The Dadaists — as they came to be called (the name was chosen at random from an unabridged dictionary) — found themselves the artistic darlings of Berlin and Paris in the early 1920s. And while Dada was short-lived, it clearly stimulated the experimentalism of the theatre of the absurd, which was its longer-lasting successor.

Today's theatrical postmodernism follows in the wake of the absurd. The late plays of Samuel Beckett best exemplify the pessimism and flight from meaning characteristic of the postmodern. Although Beckett explored meaninglessness from his earliest writings, by the 1980s his vision had become grim, if not completely nihilistic. In his very short play *Rockabye* (1981), Beckett's sole visible character is an old lady with "huge eyes in white expressionless face." On a dark stage she rocks alone, dimly lit in a rocking chair; during the play she says but one word ("More") in what is apparently a beyond-the-grave dialogue with her prerecorded voice. The play ends with the recorded voice saying:

> rock her off
> stop her eyes
> fuck life
> stop her eyes
> rock her off
> rock her off

And the rocking stops as the lights fade out.

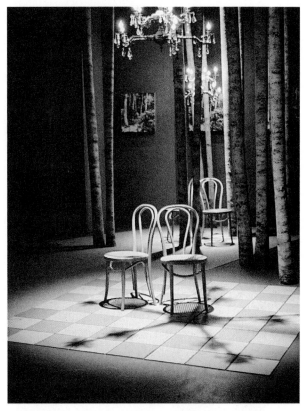

At Theatre 40 in Beverly Hills, California, Douglas-Scott Goheen's 1991 set for *Much Ado about Nothing* intermixed outdoors and indoors, putting chandeliers in the "forest" and placing "real" birch trees in front of replicated photos of more birches. The set gave a sense of location but also, in postmodernist fashion, suggested its own "setting" on the stage.

But contemporary postmodernism also owes a debt to the other mainstream of antirealistic theatre, the theatre of alienation as created and promoted by Bertolt Brecht. If Beckett's theatre stimulates the postmodern's intellectual pessimism, Brecht's theatre stimulates its parodic delight, as his plays deconstruct themselves into storytelling lectures and seek to disconnect the actor from his or her character in order to toss the play's issues directly into the audience. Postmodern directors and dramatists who are influenced by Brecht therefore openly — and even gaily — employ the theatre as an ironic metaphor, jumping back

Above: The Full Monty is a mainstream musical about male striptease. With a book by Terrence McNally (see the chapter titled "The Playwright"), the concept was adapted from the 1996 British film of the same name and transposed to Buffalo, New York, where a group of laid-off steelworkers seek to regain some of their financial independence — and restore their personal dignity — by creating a male strip show and going "the full monty," in their final number. Composed by David Yazbek, his first attempt at a stage musical, *Monte* was a great success at the Old Globe Theatre of San Diego, California, and subsequently on Broadway. Here, Patrick Wilson as Jerry Bukatinsky leads the blue-collar chorus as they prepare for their final disrobing — which was, however, lighted only from behind so as to silhouette rather than fully reveal the actors.

Left: Pidgin Macbeth, directed by Ken Campbell at the English National Theatre (1998), sets Shakespeare's play in the New Hebrides Islands and changes the language to *Wol Wantok,* or Pidgin, a 400-word simplified language used throughout the South Pacific. Roddy McDevitt plays "Makbed" in this production, which, while exuberantly comic, also includes a Polish mime artist and a didgeridoo player, as it has been Campbell's effort to further the development of an international dramatic language.

and forth between simulations of reality (realism) and comments on that very simulation. Many post-Brechtian and postmodern theatrical techniques stem from this: Deliberate cross-gender casting — as for, example, actors switching roles as well as genders between the first and second acts of Caryl Churchill's *Cloud Nine* (1983), or a young actress with an obviously fake beard playing the old Jewish rabbi at the opening of Tony Kushner's *Angels in America* (1993) — forces us to confront a profound separation between the actor and his or her role. This was taken a step further in Matthew von Waaden's off-Broadway production of *Eat the Runt* in 2001, where the theatre spectators actually cast the eight roles — regardless of gender — from among the actors who presented themselves on stage right before the play began.

Increasingly, the raw mechanics of theatrical practice have come into play in even mainstream plays and productions; clearly visible microphones, worn on the actor's body, are increasingly employed in musicals and even some straight plays, for example, making us continually aware that the characters are played by technologically augmented actors, while the sound mixer that adjusts their volume levels is no longer hidden away backstage, but plunked right in the midst of the audience. (In the Broadway musical *The Full Monty*, the conductor — who dances to the music she conducts — is fully visible from every seat in the house and is illuminated by a spotlight during much of show).

Plays increasingly comment on their own dramatization. A character asks another, "Why did you just walk downstage right?" during *The Producers* (2001), and in *Urinetown* (2001) a character asks another, "Is this where you tell the audience about the water shortage?" and the other replies, "Everything in its time . . . nothing can kill a show like too much exposition."

And today's plays have more and more frequently adopted the theatre as their primary setting and subject: in one of the classic postmodern deconstructions of theatrical "real-ity," the opening scene of Tom Stoppard's *The Real Thing* (1982) is revealed to have been a staged play when, at the beginning of scene two, we see the "characters" of scene one appear as the actors that played them. Shakespeare is fodder for many deconstructed variations: Amy Freed's *The Beard of Avon* (2001) shows Shakespeare writing — or perhaps not writing — the plays attributed to him; Paul Rudnick's *I Hate Hamlet* (1992) shows actors rehearsing and presenting a production of *Hamlet;* Lee Blessing's 1992 *Fortinbras* (as well as Tom Stoppard's seminal 1967 *Rosencrantz and Guildenstern Are Dead*) expand on previously untold stories of the same play; Anne-Marie McDonald's *Good Night Desdemona (Good Morning Juliet)* deconstructs and then recombines two Shakespearean tragedies. Even Neil Simon's *Laughter on the 23rd Floor* and musical stage version of *The Goodbye Girl* include scenes parodying performances of Shakespeare — *Julius Caesar* and *Richard III*, respectively. And musicals, particularly in the postmodern era, are almost all about show business: *The Producers, Tick, Tick . . . Boom! George Gershwin Alone*, and *A Class Act* (all 2001) are Broadway musicals about Broadway musicals, as are recent revivals of *Follies, Crazy for You*, and *42nd Street*, while *Urinetown* and *Forbidden Broadway* (also 2001) are off-Broadway parodies of Broadway musicals. It is certainly clear that in the twenty-first century, postmodernism has long transcended its experimental roots.

Two of the most noted postmodern dramatic themes are its rejection of linear storytelling and its enhanced appeal to the senses — particularly visual and aural (but also, in some cases, tactile and olfactory). These, together with some of their applications, are worth specific discussion.

A Nonlinear Theatre

Aristotle proposed that plays should contain a "beginning, middle, and end," and they generally still do — but no longer always in that

Above: Mel Brooks's *The Producers* is a Broadway musical about Broadway musicals, where Leo Bloom, a midlevel New York accountant, fantasizes about becoming a producer on the Great White Way – with his name in lights and surrounded by beautiful chorus girls. Matthew Broderick is Bloom, and costumes are by William Ivey Long.

Above right: Relative newcomer David Auburn won the 2001 Pulitzer Prize for *Proof,* a play about an awkward young woman who has inherited the mathematical genius of her late father – but is accused only of plagiarizing his work. Mary Louise Parker won the Tony Award for her portrayal of the woman; she is shown here with Larry Bryggman as her dad in the Manhattan Theatre Club production that subsequently transferred to Broadway. Set design by John Lee Beatty; costumes by Jess Goldstein.

order. For the conventional development of plot — from an inciting incident through intensifying action, climax, and denouement — is no longer uniformly presented in linear fashion. Temporary "flashbacks," of course, have been used in drama, as well as film, for several decades (they appear prominently in Arthur Miller's *Death of a Salesman,* for example, and the action of Tennessee Williams's *The Glass Menagerie* is, in effect, almost entirely a flashback), but flashbacks are generally framed as such, as by a narrative or musical transition, or, in film, a blurry cross-dissolve, which makes clear that the story is now shifting to an earlier time period.

In postmodern drama, however, shuttling from one time zone to another is usually in-

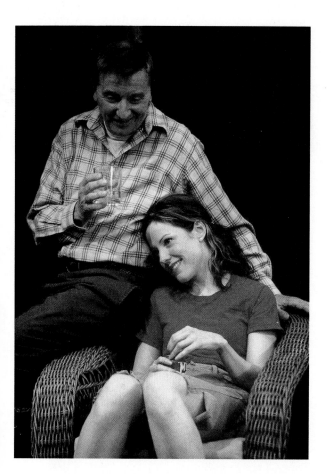

ing man in act two), virtually no reviewer thought this reordering of events even worth mentioning; indeed, the *New York Times* theatre critic called the play "as accessible and compelling as a detective story." Postmodern plays are therefore freed from the necessity to align themselves with a forward-moving arrow of time, and even from the need to explain when the arrow reverses direction.

A few other examples of postmodern nonlinear theatre: In Tom Stoppard's 1998 *The Invention of Love,* the principal character, poet and scholar A. E. Housman is divided into a younger and an older self, each played by a different actor; the play's scenes alternate back and forth between Housman's student days, professorial years, and boat-borne journey to purgatory after death, with both the younger and elder Housmans even crossing paths for conversation as the eras of their lives intertwine. In Canadian dramatist David Young's 1992 *Glenn,* the dramatist divides his principal character, pianist Glenn Gould, into four separate characters, each played by different actors representing different eras in Gould's career, and each character speaks — to the audience or to one of the other "Glenns" — from his own era. In Margaret Edson's 1999 Pulitzer Prize–winning *Wit,* the action moves freely backward and forward from the central character's medical ward, where she is being treated for a terminal illness, to her earlier school years, to events in her professional career, and to her postdeath ascension. And in Tony Kushner's Pulitzer Prize–Winning 1993 *Angels in America,* the action makes quantum moves in time — between previous centuries, the present, and the afterlife — with never so much as a program note, while actors jump back and forth between different roles and occasionally between different genders as well. None of these nonlinear shifts represent sheer dramaturgical novelty; rather, each indicates a theatre — and an audience — prepared for instant cross-association, able to keep several ideas and chronologies in mind at the same

stant and unnarrated: the audience is simply expected to figure it out. Moreover, we are not necessarily "returned" to the present when a postmodern flashback concludes; a play can proceed, in the current theatre, in almost any order the playwright wishes to construct. Such time-warping is no longer surprising. When Harold Pinter, in *Betrayal* (1978), organized his play's nine scenes in mostly reverse chronological order, it was considered revolutionary and reviewers talked of little else; when David Auburn, in his 2001 Pulitzer Prize–winning *Proof,* began his second act with a scene chronologically four years earlier than the first (requiring that a ghost in act 1 be instantly seen — with no change of costume or makeup and without explanation — as a liv-

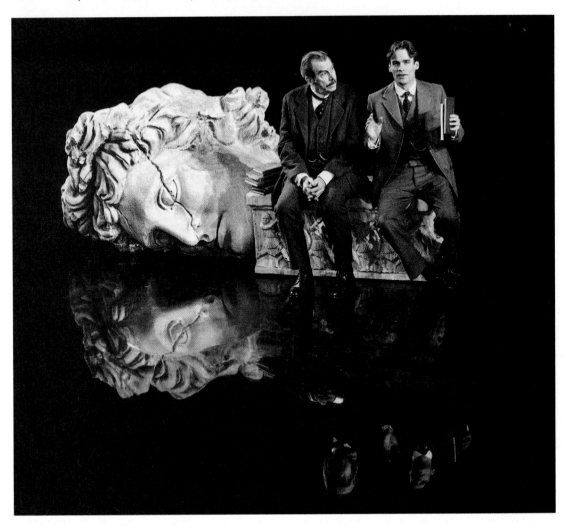

Tom Stoppard's *The Invention of Love* portrays various events in the life of the English classical scholar and poet A. E. Housman from age eighteen to seventy-seven, not only by jumping backward and forward in time but also through intriguing same-time conversations between the young Housman (played by Robert Sean Leonard, *right*) and Housman as a just-deceased old man (played by Richard Easton, *left*), here shown – along with their reflections – sitting on a fallen antique monument (another postmodern touch) on the River Styx in Hades (the land of the dead). Both Leonard and Easton won Tony Awards for their Housman portrayals in the 2001 Broadway season. Sets and costumes by Bob Crowly; lighting by Brian MacDevitt.

time, and meld them into a satisfying dramatic experience.

A Theatre of the Senses

Theatre has always appealed to the senses as well as the intellect, certainly since Sophocles introduced painted scenery in ancient Greece and Aeschylus choreographed his Furies with such whirling passion that audiences fainted and had miscarriages, but the visual, aural, and generally sensory role of theatrical performance has been profoundly enhanced in the current era. Certainly the theatre's scenic design has expanded in the past decades from a primary focus on identifying locales and underlining dramatic themes to making bold, flamboyant, semi-autonomous statements, often in an analogous juxtaposition, or even at a (presumably clarifying) dissonance, from the play's actions. And stage lighting, never wholly realistic to begin with, has become even more directly expressive in making its presence crucial to the intellectual, as well as the mere physical, illumination that a play provides — perhaps in part a technological response to Antonin Artaud's hyperbolic call (see Chapter 9) for "light in waves, in sheets, in fusillades of fiery arrows." The use of scenery and lighting simply as scenery and lighting — as contrasted to its use to depict "a living room in Manhattan during late afternoon" — has now become fundamental to the theatre, leading to design innovations that create bold surprises, provocative, meaningful imagery, and a deeply sensual impact. Thus design has become self-consciously "sensational" in the best sense of that term, creating sensory impact — rather than mere realistic or historical detail — at every moment of the production.

Such postmodern designs may make references to elements wholly outside the play and outside the play's historical period; they may employ vivid colors, written texts, mythic or religious or erotic images; they may take the form of wall-sized photographs, surrounding projections and illuminations, kinetic sculptures, or video images (sometimes of the play's actions and sometimes extraneous to them). Any or all of these design elements create a structure of meaning meant to be viewed as integral to — not merely background to — the performance of the actors.

Sound design has been particularly enhanced in the postmodern era. Virtually unknown by anything resembling that name a generation ago, sound design has become a fundamental partner of the theatrical design team in the last decade, expanding from

sound effects to sound surround, employing at various points continuous underscoring, live stage orchestras, rock-concert-level amplification, and body microphones for the actors. And increasing use of theatrical smoke, fog, wind, and even rain (in, for example, De La Guarda's 1998 *Villa Villa* and GAle GAtes's 2001 *So Long Ago I Can't Remember,* described later in the chapter), often sent directly into or onto the audience, has profoundly increased the all-sensory impact of contemporary theatre stagings.

Much of today's drama has become sexually sensual as well. Total nudity, introduced to drama mainly as a risqué novelty in the 1960s, swiftly entered the theatre's mainstream of serious works in the succeeding decades. Coming of age with Peter Shaffer's Tony Award–winning 1973 *Equus* (in which a young boy and girl strip to make love in a stable), wholly unclothed actors subsequently appeared in such mainstream plays as David Storey's 1973 *The Changing Room* (quarrels in the locker room of an English rugby team), David Henry Hwang's 1988 *M. Butterfly* (a transvestite proves his real gender by disrobing), Terrence McNally's 1994 *Love! Valour! Compassion!* (gay men sunbathe in a country retreat), and Stephen Sondheim's 1994 musical, *Passion* (which begins with a postcoital man and woman in bed, totally nude but for their body microphones, singing about their relationship). Theatrical nudity has now in fact become all but commonplace, appearing, in 2000–01 alone, in widely acclaimed productions of David Hare's *The Blue Room,* Rebecca Gilman's *Blue Surge,* Margaret Edson's *Wit,* Edward Albee's *The Play about the Baby,* Charles Mee's *The Big Love,* John Patrick Shanley's *Cellini,* John Barton's *Tantalus,* and two musicals for which nudity is the title subject: *Naked Boys Singing!* and *The Full Monty.*

Nudity is not specific only to postmodernism, of course. But it creates a postmodern shock wave: though not necessarily (and in some cases not remotely) used for erotic

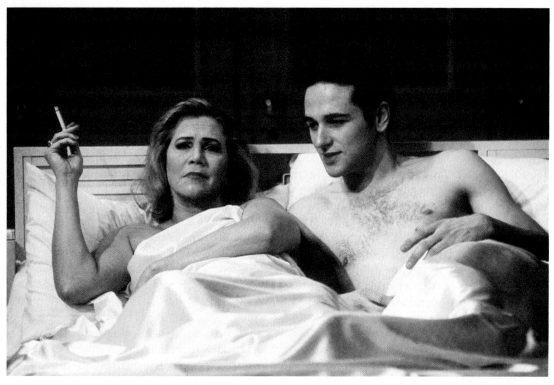

Nudity is increasingly a feature of mainstream theatre in many countries, including England and the United States. In this famous postcoital scene from *The Graduate*, adapted from the Charles Webb novel, Kathleen Turner (here partially covered up) plays Mrs. Robinson to Matthew Rice's Benjamin in the completely-sold-out London production of 2000.

reasons, on-stage nudity creates a sudden jolt in which, for a moment at least, time seems to stop, logic and analysis are temporarily suspended, and the fiction of drama is forced to contend with the blatancy of sheer naked humanity — the "bare forked animal" that Shakespeare wrote of in *King Lear* but was unable to show. Nudity forces us to confront the reality within the theatrical fiction: that within the construct of a dramatic character lies the exposed and defenseless reality of a live and very naked actor.

An Open Theatre

It is safe to say that the theatre of the twenty-first century will be open to an infinitely wider range of interests, cultures, and individuals than has been any other period in the theatre's history. The deconstruction of the theatre, promoted by its most stellar luminaries — Beckett and Brecht among them — made us painfully conscious of the theatre's challenge to fully reflect the humanity inside us and the society around us. For although Shakespeare (for example) was certainly able to create magnificent female and ethnic characters (Beatrice and Cleopatra, Othello and Shylock) and his acting company was clearly able to bring them vividly to life, the notion of an all-white (not to mention all-male) theatre company claiming to hold "a mirror up to nature" has proven generally unsustainable.[1] For how could an exclusively male or exclusively white or even a single-ethnic company wholly mirror the hopes and concerns of women as well as men, Asians and blacks as well as whites? Postmodern authors and directors, therefore, have increasingly sought to open the theatre to all comers. Using the deconstructed disconnect between actor and character, the postmodern theatre shows roles as "roles" rather than characters indissolubly linked to the physical characteristics of the actors who play them. Thus, casting considerations have broadened to bend gender distinctions, cross racial lines, and span age ranges, as will be detailed below.

A brilliantly innovative American company named The Open Theatre, created by Joseph Chaikin in 1963, happily gives a name to this theatrical movement. For a decade, Chaikin's Open Theatre combined social improvisation with Brechtian techniques, developing plays in which performers glided into and out of the characters they played (they also played scenery and props; often they played themselves), and using story and character merely as vehicles for direct interactions with audiences. These plays, including Megan Terry's *Viet Rock*, Susan Yankowitz's *Terminal*, and the company-authored *Mutation Show*, were continually evolving workshop performances that addressed immediate audience concerns. The company toured Europe — as well as American cities, campuses, and prisons. They made fraternal and sororal alliances with the New Lafayette Theatre in Harlem, El Teatro Campesino in California, and the Women's Collective Theatre. The Open Theatre ended its existence in 1973, but its influence has been extraordinary, and its name may well stand to represent the larger "opening" of our contemporary stage.

For today's newest and most provocative theatre is truly open, or is at least opening, to voices heretofore shut out or severely limited in the largely Western, white, and male-dominated theatre of yesterday and even of

"modern" yesterday. And that opening is occurring on all levels.

A Theatre By and About Women

Save for rare exceptions such as in the commedia dell'arte, women were virtually unrepresented in the theatre until the seventeenth century, and from then until the 1950s they had been largely relegated to acting, copying scripts, and building costumes. Today, however, women are a major force in every one of the theatrical arts. Five different American women — Paula Vogel, Beth Henley, Marsha Norman, Wendy Wasserstein, and Margaret Edson — received the esteemed Pulitzer Prize for playwriting during the 1980s and 90s, and many critics accord Ntozake Shange and Tina Howe similar stature. In England, no dramatic writer of the 1990s has been more respected than Caryl Churchill, nor none in the 2000s more promising than Charlotte Jones. And women directors had dramatically moved to the forefront by 1998, when Julie Taymor and Garry Hynes became the first and second women in history to win Broadway's Tony Award in directing, topped only by 2001, when Susan Stroman, for *The Producers*, won Tony Awards for both best directing and best choreography. At the same time, women are increasingly assuming the artistic directorships at major American repertory companies: fully one-third of America's 200-plus professional regional theatres are currently headed by women, an astounding record of achievement in a field in which women were all but invisible three or four decades ago.

Meanwhile, over one hundred separate feminist theatre ensembles — groups of women presenting plays by, about, and for women — have been founded in the United States since 1970. The goal of each is to present plays about sex-role stereotyping, abortion, pregnancy, motherhood, rape, the mother-daughter relationship, lesbianism, domestic violence, historically important women, battered women, and women in prison. "The content of almost

---

[1]Shakespeare himself seems to have been frustrated at the convention of his day that disallowed women on the stage, judging by Cleopatra's complaint that, upon capture, the Romans' "quick comedians . . . will stage us . . . , and I shall see some squeaking Cleopatra boy my greatness . . ." (*Antony and Cleopatra*, 5, ii, 222–23).

all feminist drama," says Elizabeth J. Natalle, "comes out of the personal lives of the theatre group members. Feminist theatre groups write their own drama, and the reality they depict comes from their own experience" — and from the experience of the audience as well. Natalle explains: "In feminist theatre the audience is more than just a passive body viewing the action on stage. . . . Audience members [play] an active role in the creation of a total theatre experience." Natalle goes on to show how, in a play about rape, for example, the audience is invited "to stop the play at any moment and give witness to their own rapes, both literal and metaphoric."

A Theatre of Ethnic Diversity

It is a typically postmodern phenomenon that the leading American playwright of the current era is certainly August Wilson, of mixed racial heritage and generally identified as African American. Wilson's *Ma Rainey's Black Bottom, Fences, The Piano Lesson, Joe Turner's Come and Gone, Two Trains Running, Seven Guitars, Jitney,* and *King Hedley II* are among the most powerful and evocative dramas of our times, concerning, as they do, an entire twentieth-century history of black America. Significantly, Wilson's plays have been commercial as well as artistic hits, playing to huge audiences of all races both on Broadway and in a great many American regional theatres. Wilson is certainly the most honored playwright of recent years (see the chapter titled "The Playwright"), yet he is but one of a number of minority voices that are surfacing in the theatre of the 1990s and beyond.

AN AFRICAN AMERICAN THEATRE   African American theatre has existed since the earliest American times, and black-themed, black-authored drama made particularly strong creative inroads in the earlier years of the twentieth century (Langston Hughes's *Mulatto* in the 1930s and Lorraine Hansberry's *A Raisin in the Sun* in the late 1950s), becoming a truly revolutionary force with the plays of Amiri Baraka (then LeRoi Jones) in the early 1960s. With his boldly defiant *Dutchman* and *The Toilet,* Baraka confronted American racism head-on, not shrinking from its potentially violent ramifications. In light of the 1965 Watts riots, Baraka's voice proved prophetic; in light of the 1992 Los Angeles uprisings, we can understand that the problems he revealed have still not been solved.

The Negro Ensemble Company, created by Douglas Turner Ward, and the New Lafayette Theatre in Harlem, with Ed Bullins as chief playwright-in-residence, soon followed Baraka's successes, inching the African American experience into the global arts marketplace. In 1970 Charles Gordone's *No Place to Be Somebody,* produced by Joseph Papp at the New York Public Theatre, won the Pulitzer Prize in drama, at once putting black and minority playwrights into the American forefront. Black authors achieving national success in subsequent years included Lonne Elder III (*Ceremonies in Dark Old Men*), Adrienne Kennedy (*Funnyhouse of a Negro*), and Ntozake Shange (*for colored girls who have considered suicide/ when the rainbow is enuf*). Meanwhile, in Africa, black Nigerian dramatist Wole Soyinka received the Nobel Prize for literature in 1986.

Beginning in the 1970s, Broadway inaugurated an era of lavishly produced black (or largely black) musicals, including *Purlie, Bubbling Brown Sugar, The Wiz, Ain't Misbehavin',*

Above right: Jean Genet's *The Blacks* was one of the first plays to treat the oppression and exploitation of Africans and their descendants. This French play was given a German staging by Peter Stein in 1983; the production emphasizes the international political reality of contemporary Africa and its peoples.

Below right: Umbatha, the "Zulu Macbeth," transports Shakespeare's play to the nineteenth-century Zulu rebellion, using African masks, dance, ritual, and language to augment the action. The 1997 production at London's Shakespearean replica Globe Theatre was directed by Msosi.

One of the most influential black-themed American plays is Ntozake Shange's "choreopoem" titled *for colored girls who have considered suicide / when the rainbow is enuf*, which received Tony, Drama Desk, and Obie Awards at its 1976 premiere and spurred a new growth in black theatre – especially black female theatre; it has also been accounted as the beginning of hip-hop. This photo, from the twenty-fifth anniversary production in 2001 at the (New York) American Place Theatre, features Eleanor McCoy (*in red*), Katherine J. Smith (*in orange*), and J. Ieasha Prome (*in yellow*), as directed and choreographed by George Faison.

Sophisticated Ladies, Dreamgirls, Raisin, Timbuktu, Five Guys Named Moe, and *Bring in 'Da Noise, Bring in 'Da Funk,* with substantial black casting in *The Life, Rent,* and *Ragtime* as well (not to mention African American Brian Stokes Mitchell starring in — and receiving a Tony for — the 2000 revival of *Kiss Me Kate*). In the first full season of the twenty-first century, Charles Randolph-Wright's *Blue,* about a family of black morticians in South Carolina, Suzan-Lori Parks's *Topdog/Underdog* (see "The Playwright" chapter), Regina Taylor's *Urban Zulu Mambo* about black female rage, and Kia Corthron's *Breath, Boom* and *Force Continuum,*

about girl gangs and police brutality, joined August Wilson's *Jitney* and *King Hedley II* as important black-written and black-themed plays in New York alone, most of them attracting huge crossover (black and white) audiences. Indeed, over the past three decades, African American performers have constituted up to a third of the theatre artists on Broadway and, at least for *Blue,* a third of the theatre audience as well.

No one should suppose, however, that an African American theatre exists to universal satisfaction. In the 1990s, August Wilson publicly lamented the decline of black-specific theatres that flourished in the 1960s, demanding that African American theatre artists come "face to face" with each other to create a truly postcolonial black theatre. To that end, Wilson premiered *Jitney* at the black-run Crossroads Theatre of New Jersey instead of the Yale Repertory Theatre, his former premiere site. Wilson's ideas, still debated furiously, provide a brilliant departure point for any discussion as to how theatre best represents the concerns of the community for which it is intended.

A LATINO THEATRE   A Spanish-speaking theatre has existed in North America since the late sixteenth century; indeed, the first play ever staged in what is now the United States was *Los Moros Y Los Cristianos* (*The Moors and the Christians*) at the San Juan Pueblo outside of Santa Fe, then part of Mexico. By the mid-nineteenth century, serious and talented professional Mexican touring companies had established residence in Los Angeles and San Francisco and were touring to Texas, Arizona, and New Mexico. On the East Coast, Spanish-speaking theatre — largely imported from Spain and Cuba — had become established in New York and Tampa well before 1900, with stable Spanish-language companies presenting the classical plays of Pedro Calderón de la Barca and Lope de Vega, mixed with melodramas and zarzuelas (light operettas). Spanish-speaking theatre of this time largely served a community function, preserving traditional Latino culture in Anglo-dominated environments.

With the founding of El Teatro Campesino by Luis Valdez in 1965, however, a contemporary Chicano theatre with a powerful creative and political thrust burst into prominence in California and ultimately won national acclaim. Valdez, a Mexican American, created his Teatro with and for migrant farmworkers in rural California. "In a Mexican way," wrote Valdez in 1966, "we have discovered what Brecht is all about. If you want unbourgeois theatre, find unbourgeois people to do it." Valdez's short, didactic *actos* of the farm-

workers' situation have been performed — in English and in Spanish — on farms, in city squares, and, eventually, in theatres all over California and on national and European tours as well; his full-length plays *Zoot Suit* and *I Don't Have to Show You No Stinking Badges* have been performed for major metropolitan audiences; and his film *La Bamba* has brought his Teatro to international acclaim (and some financial stability). "Our theatre work is simple, direct, complex and profound, but it works," Valdez explains. Other noted Latina and Latino dramatists include Cuban-born Maria Irene Fornés (whose *Fefu and Her*

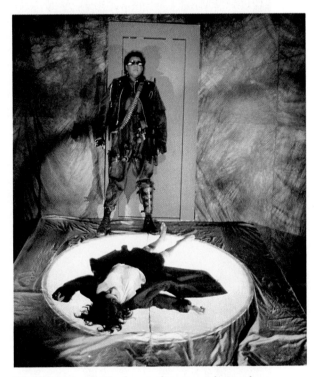

"We all think magically when we sleep; in our dreams there are monsters and angels," says Puerto Rican–born José Rivera, whose play *Marisol* exemplifies the "magic realism" of several Latino and Latin American writers. The title character, a young female copy editor, is set upon in her bedroom by a band of guerrilla angels who are trying to assassinate God. *Marisol* premiered at London's Royal Court Theatre and subsequently (as pictured here) at the Humana New Play Festival at the Actors Theatre of Louisville.

Above: David Henry Hwang's 1998 *Golden Child* centers on Eng Ahn, a young girl of about twelve (played by the remarkable Julyana Soelistyo, *kneeling*) who lives with her father and his three wives in prerevolutionary China. Eng, as well as the China she inhabits, is torn between disparate ideals of Eastern traditionalism and Western "progress." Like most of Hwang's work, *Golden Child* reflects the conflicts of Asian assimilation into a cultural melting pot. This South Coast Repertory production was directed by James Lapine; it also played at the Public Theatre in New York and subsequently on Broadway.

Left: Japanese American (third-generation) playwright Philip Kan Gotanda has been exploring social and psychological aspects of Asian American assimilation for more than twenty years. His *Ballad of Yachiyo* concerns Japanese working families in prestatehood Hawaii and, more specifically, the title character, a seventeen-year-old girl (played by Sala Iwamatsu) who leaves her family to apprentice with an Old World potter. Gotanda employs bunraku-style puppets to help further his ultimately tragic storyline. Emily Kuroda plays Okusan, in this 1996 Berkeley Repertory Theatre premiere directed by Sharon Ott.

Friends, 1977, is an often-produced appraisal of friendship and women's roles), Puerto Rican–born José Rivera (*Marisol,* 1992), and Chicano authors Josefina López (*Real Women Have Curves,* 1990) and Carlos Morton (*The Miser of Mexico,* 1989).

AN EAST-WEST THEATRE   The Eastern voice stunned American drama in the late 1980s with David Henry Hwang's *M. Butterfly,* which boldly reinterpreted the Madame Butterfly myth, effectively exploding narrow and deprecatory "Orientalist" stereotypes and misperceptions of Asian culture. Hwang's incorporation of Beijing Opera technique into Western drama draws on a tradition that predates postmodernism — Ezra Pound, Bertolt Brecht, W. S. Gilbert, and Antonin Artaud all drew heavily on Asian dramatic styles in their antirealistic works of the modernist period. But Hwang, who is of Asian (Chinese) background himself (see the chapter titled "The Playwright"), employs Asian and Western performers in this deliberately confrontational play, which poses East against West (and maleness against femaleness) in a continually informing, continually surprising way. Hwang's play brought postmodernism into Broadway commercialism — as a certified Broadway hit spectacle. Hwang returned to Broadway in 1998 with the Chinese family drama *Golden Child,* which was nominated for a best-play Tony Award, and authored the book for the Disney musical *Aida,* treating African legends. Other Asian American authors, such as Philip Kan Gotanda, whose *Ballad of Yachiyo* was a 1998 success in California and New York, Han Ong (*L.A. Stories*), and Elizabeth Wong (*The Monkey King, The Student Revolutionary*), have risen to prominence over the past decade, with the help of such nurturing companies as the East-West Players in Los Angeles and the Pan Asian Repertory Theatre in New York.

Asian performance techniques have also broadly influenced Western theatre, even for Western plays. French director Ariane Mnouch-kine (also see later discussion) introduced Japanese kabuki music and movement to her production of Shakespeare's *Richard II,* Indian kathakali technique to her *Twelfth Night,* and Middle Eastern music and dancing to her production of Molière's *Tartuffe,* thereby setting each play's Western orientation in bold relief and universalizing many of the play's themes. English director Peter Brook (also see later discussion) directed a 2001 production of *Hamlet* that included a continuous score played live by Japanese composer Toshi Tsuchitori, who had also contributed the Indian-inspired orchestration for Brook's celebrated production — with an international cast — of the Indian Sanskrit epic, *The Mahabharata.* Japanese director Tadashi Suzuki's acting theories and teachings, as well as his bilingual productions, have broadly influenced acting and actor training in both Europe and America. And the late Jerzy Grotowski completed his life's work by training an international group of performers in prehistoric performance techniques drawn largely from Asia and Africa, attempting to create an "objective drama" that sought to dissolve the unconsciously applied linguistic and cultural codes separating human beings from their true biological (and, some might say, spiritual) selves. These east-west movements have occasioned lively debate in recent years: proponents of such "fusion art" applaud the integration of disparate cultural and aesthetic values; dissenters, however, criticize this as a neocolonialist appropriation of one culture by another. The debate — as well as that led by August Wilson, mentioned earlier — bespeaks the vital social and ethical complexity of today's theatre.

A Theatre of Difference

Gender and ethnicity are not the only bases for the new voices that have entered the mainstream of postmodern theatre. The issue of sexual preference had been buried deeply in the closet during most of the theatre's history,

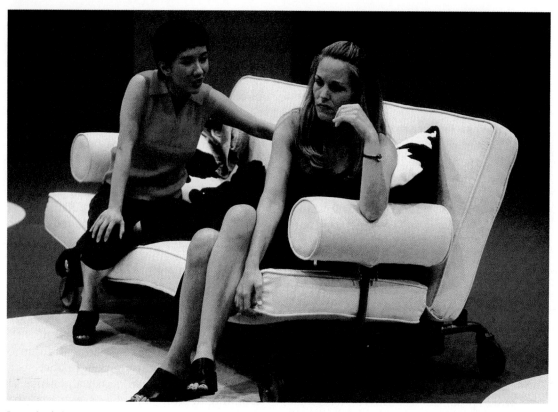

Diana Son's *Stop Kiss* is a contemporary drama about two women who discover their repressed sexuality – and homophobia – at the same moment. Julie Oda (*left*) and Tyler Layton play the pair in Loretta Greco's 2000 production at the Oregon Shakespeare Festival. The geometric scenic design, which serves the play's multiple settings, is by Robert Brill.

and as late as 1958 the representation of homosexuality was actually illegal in England and widely (if not legally) suppressed in America. The love that "dared not speak its name" came to the stage in those eras only through authors' implications and audiences' inferences, and gay playwrights, such as Oscar Wilde, Tennessee Williams, Gertrude Stein, Edward Albee, William Inge, and Gore Vidal, were forced to speak — at certain critical moments in their work — only by innuendo and through oblique code words.

All of this changed dramatically in the late 1960s, when gay and lesbian life — and gay and lesbian issues — began to be treated as serious dramatic subjects, most notably by Mart Crowley in his groundbreaking American comedy *The Boys in the Band* (1968). Since that time, sexual-preference issues have become principal or secondary topics in hundreds of plays, including mainstream Broadway musicals (*La Cage aux Folles, Falsettos, Aspects of Love, Kiss of the Spider Woman*), popular comedies (*Love! Valour! Compassion!, Party, Jeffrey, The Lisbon Traviata*), and serious dramas (*Bent, M. Butterfly, Gross Indecency, The Invention of Love, Breaking the Code, The Laramie Project*). Gay actors came out of the closet (most of them theatrically) to advocate gay rights worldwide, as did the British classical star Sir Ian McKellen in his one-man performance "A Knight Out" at the Gay Games in New York

Left: Deaf West is a nonprofit professional sign language theatre in Los Angeles. Shown here is the celebrated 1996 production of Peter Shaffer's *Equus*, with Aaron Kubey signing as he rides the horse of the play's title.

Above: Handicapped actors proved no barrier whatsoever to director Philippe Adrien, whose production of Molière's *The Imaginary Invalid*, which premiered at France's Avignon Festival in 2001, featured blind actors (Bruno Netter and Oiuza Oyed) as the title character (*center*) and his wife, and a dwarf (Jean-Luc Orofino, *right*) as their lawyer. Meanwhile, Toinette (*not pictured*) was played by a deaf and mute actress. The production proved a great success and was subsequently performed at the Théâtre de l'Aquarium in Paris.

in 1994. In the wake of a new and terrible illness, a growing genre of AIDS plays (*The Normal Heart, As Is*) addressed the tragic human consequences of this disease, whose initial victims in the United States and Europe were predominantly gay. And in 1992, Tony Kushner's extraordinary "gay fantasia on national themes," titled *Angels in America,* proved one of the most celebrated stage productions of the decade in both England and the United States. Sexual preference has emerged over the past decade as a defining issue for many theatre groups, theatre festivals, and theatre publications, each seeking to examine the political, cultural, and aesthetic implications of gay- and lesbian-themed drama.

Persons differently abled are also represented in new theatre companies created specifically for these voices and for expanding audiences. Theatre by the Blind, in New York, employs sightless actors for all of its productions, and the National Theatre of the Deaf is only one of four American companies (Deaf West, Sign Rise Theatre, and the Fairmount Theatre of the Deaf are the others) that create theatre of and for the hearing-impaired, employing American Sign Language (ASL) as the primary verbal dramatic medium. With Mark Medoff's play *Children of a Lesser God,* the hearing-impaired found a broad popular audience, and a number of hearing-impaired actors and actresses found national recognition. In 2001 the opening at the Mark Taper Forum of John Belluso's *The Body of [Randolph] Bourne,* which treats the esteemed cultural critic's physical disfiguration, was wisely accompanied by a quadrupling of the Taper's wheelchair-accessible seating and a renovation of the theatre's backstage area to better accommodate performers with disabilities. The Coalition for Inclusive Performing Arts (CIPA), based in the National Arts and Disability Center at UCLA (http://nadc.ucla.edu), is currently devoted to full inclusion of children and adults with disabilities into the theatre community.

A Theatre of Nontraditional Casting

Across the country, color-blind casting — once thought of as daring — has become almost routine, particularly in the classics. African Americans are playing roles once thought to be reserved for whites — while, conversely, the white Patrick Stewart has played the black Othello (without makeup!) opposite a black Desdemona. The New York Shakespeare Festival has been a leader in such alternative casting, choosing Angela Bassett as their 1998 Lady Macbeth, Morgan Freeman as their Petruchio, and Denzel Washington as their Richard III. But such nontraditional casting is not limited to large metropolitan venues: the Oregon Shakespeare Festival, in a state with less than 4 percent African Americans and Asian Americans *combined,* has, under the leadership of Libby Appel, routinely assembled acting companies of whom fully a third are non-Caucasian and prominently features nonwhite actors as English royalty, Renaissance Italian lovers, and, indeed, whatever roles the company has to offer. The Nontraditional Casting Project (http://www.ntcp.org), with headquarters in New York, coordinates a national oversight of this color-blind casting process.

Cross-gendered casting is also commonplace in the postmodern age. The New York Shakespeare Festival was also a pioneer in this area, featuring New York's first female Hamlet in modern times, and by now female Hamlets,

In Shakespeare's *Othello,* the title character is black and the society in which he lives is white. In this noteworthy Shakespeare Theatre (Washington, D.C.) production in 1998, Patrick Stewart played Othello; everyone else in the cast was black. The goal, mainly achieved, was to put racial discrimination into bold, even shocking, relief.

Prosperos, Lears, and Richard IIs are everywhere apparent — as are male Cleopatras and Rosalinds. Indeed, on mainstream Broadway in 2001, the males Sean Campion and Conleth Hill played, between them, all sixteen male and female roles in Marie Jones's *Stones in his Pockets,* and female Lily Tomlin played all seventeen male and female roles in her revival of Jane Wagner's *The Search for Intelligent Signs in the Universe.*

Multiculturalism extends, of course, to play selection. The canon of past dramatic works is now being exhumed and expanded to "discover" women and minority voices that were suppressed or ignored in the past; revivals today are likely to focus on previously unheralded female authors, such as Aphra Behn (one of the most prolific Restoration dramatists), Alice Brown, Rachel Crothers, Sophie Treadwell,

Susan Glaspell, and Zoe Atkins, demonstrating how women and minorities have often been neglected and marginalized in past cultural undertakings. Theatres devoted to the exploration of minority voices are likewise expanding the standard canon with new works. The Black Repertory Company of St. Louis, the Penumbra Theatre of St. Paul, the Crossroads Theatre Company of New Brunswick, the Mixed Blood Theatre of Minneapolis, Jomandi Productions in Atlanta, Latino Chicago and Teatro Vista in Chicago, El Teatro Campesino and the East-West Players in California, the National Jewish and Travelling Jewish Theatres, and, in New York, the Pan Asian Repertory Theatre, the New Federal Theatre, INTAR Hispanic American Arts Center, Repertorio Español, and the New Federal Theatre are only some of a long list of professional theatre companies seeking to make minority voices competitive in the American theatre world.

And for each professional company, there are a dozen amateur and university companies now forming. It is abundantly clear, as the new millennium begins, that the theatre will never again revert to the protected confines of a privileged elite. Nor can it live successfully in social isolation in some "underprivileged" ghetto. Isolation, at the top or bottom, has no place in the postmodern — or post-postmodern — culture. One of the great achievements of the current era has been the relentless (if still incomplete) democratization of art and the multiplicity (if not the integration) of struggling, and often competing, voices.

A Dangerous Theatre

Late modern and postmodern theatre has increasingly been seen as dangerous. The nudity and sensory assault of much contemporary drama has caused consternation in many quarters; subjects such as political torture (*Death and the Maiden*), the Nazi Holocaust (*Ghetto, The Deputy*), prison atrocities (*Bent, The Island*), and urban mayhem (*Aven "U" Boys*) have also proliferated in today's theatre.

Simulated homosexual intercourse in *Angels in America* has caused the play to be banned in many communities; vulgar language in, for example, David Mamet's 1983 *Glengarry Glen Ross* ("*Fuck* marshalling the leads. What the fuck talk is that? What the fuck talk is that?") and the very title of Mark Ravenhill's *Shopping and Fucking* have occasioned barrages of angry letters to theatre producers and the editorial pages of many newspapers. Accusations of religious defamation led to bomb threats at the 1998 New York opening of Terrence McNally's *Corpus Christi*, which concerns

One of the most gripping contemporary plays about urban British violence is Mark Ravenhill's shockingly titled *Shopping and Fucking*. Andrew Clover is the besieged actor in this photo of the original London production, at the Royal Court Theatre, in 1996.

a Jesus-like character who has sexual relations with his disciples, and more recently legal threats, put forth by twenty-one members of the Indiana legislature in the summer of 2001, prevented Purdue University from producing the same play. And producers of Christopher Durang's bitingly satirical *Sister Mary Ignatius Explains It All For You* were threatened, also in 2001, with boycotts and reprisals by outraged groups in several parts of the country. The theatre continually treads on toes — and sometimes the toes kick back.

Political censorship and even judicial intervention have, of course, been with the theatre since its inception. The ancient Greek playwright Phyrynicus was heavily fined for producing his *Capture of Miletus,* which offended sixth-century (B.C.) Athenian officers by vividly portraying a Greek military defeat. Shakespeare seems to have deleted several oaths from his manuscript of *Othello* because they were deemed sacrilegious by authorities; and his contemporaries Ben Jonson, John Marston, and John Chapman were all jailed for writing satirical plays. Molière rewrote *Tartuffe* at least three times to get it past the king's aunt's religious scruples. Almost every country has regulated what can and cannot be seen on the stage, right up to modern times: in twentieth-century England, for example, authorities temporarily suppressed such nonclassic plays as August Strindberg's *Miss Julie,* Eugene O'Neill's *Desire under the Elms,* Luigi Pirandello's *Six Characters in Search of an Author,* and Arthur Miller's *A View from the Bridge.* Samuel Beckett's *Endgame* was officially censored (for disputing the existence of God) as late as 1958. Even W. S. Gilbert and Arthur Sullivan's *The Mikado* was suppressed by the British so that it would not offend the visiting crown prince of Japan in 1907. Nor is such outright censorship, even now, wholly in the past. Many Asian countries maintain censorship boards; in fact, the Chinese government initiated a huge international uproar in 1998 by canceling a planned American tour of the Shanghai-

based production of *The Peony Pavilion* — a 22-hour xiqu (Chinese Opera) directed by an American of Chinese descent. According to Chinese officials, the production did not give a truthful representation of the xiqu form and was too "erotic" by Chinese standards.

There is no outright artistic censorship in the United States, owing to the First Amendment of the U.S. Constitution. But of course government funding is subject to approval by local and national legislators, who often balk at the works of artists of whom they disapprove. Thus performance artist Karen Finley (who in her most famous one-woman show smears her naked body with chocolate — see later discussion) was engaged in a decade-long battle to reinstate her NEA grant, canceled following vigorous complaints from local and national government officials who disapproved of her performance — or of what they had heard about that performance, since few if any had seen it. The argument against *Corpus Christi* at Purdue was not about censorship but money: raising the issue of a state university using public funds to present a play that outraged members of the community — and not a few state legislators. No one can fully respond to the facts of any of these cases without a more complete understanding of them than one gets from the newspapers (or this book). Certainly a government, especially one democratically elected and proceeding according to recognized law, has the right as well as the responsibility to make well-considered funding decisions — for the arts as well as for everything else. But one certainly hopes that such legislators will not assume the roles of sole arbiters of artistic merit and propriety. And surely no one believes that bomb threats should determine what sort of dramatic material adults should be permitted to produce — and to see — on any American or world theatre stage.

The good news from these contemporary episodes, one might say, is that even in a world that continually blasts us with high-

What is and is not permissible in the theatre varies widely from culture to culture. Chen Shi-Zheng's Shanghai production of the sixteenth-century Chinese masterpiece *The Peony Pavilion* had to cancel its 1998 tour to New York when Chinese authorities complained that certain scenes, perhaps this one, were so nontraditional and "sexually provocative" that they would give a false impression of the xiqu form to foreign audiences.

tech media and mega-information — through our ubiquitous TVs, films, magazines, computers, video games, talk radio, and CDs — the theatre remains a forum that is both provocative and perilous, still daring enough to provoke outrage and outrageous enough to be thought a danger. This — the theatre's leading edge — is worth protecting fiercely, though it may give many theatre artists, and legislators, a few sleepless nights.

A Theatre of Revival

Not all current theatre is at the cutting edge of postmodernity, however. Indeed, the postmodern vogue for quoting the past, seen in contemporary architecture which includes Greek pediments and paintings which "quote" designs of classical masters, has a parallel in a theatre that revives — sometimes ironically, sometimes satirically, and sometimes in a straightforward, probing, and thoughtful way — masterpieces of the past. Indeed, the discontinuities and sensationalism of some postmodern art have reminded others of the sublime harmonies (and hopefulness) created by artists of an earlier age, and occasioned the revival of past theatrical masterpieces that seek nothing but to bring fresh life (the literal meaning of revival) to dramatic classics from the world's theatre history.

Shakespearean festivals are only one visible national indication of a theatre of revival: at last count, there were over a hundred theatre companies, in virtually every state in America, devoted at least in part to producing the 400-year-old works of England's most celebrated dramatist. Meanwhile, on Broadway, new stagings of old American musicals have threatened to dominate the street, with new productions of *Follies, Forty-Second Street, The Music Man, Kiss Me Kate, Cabaret, Chicago, Annie Get Your Gun, Oklahoma!,* and *The Rocky Horror Show* running on the New York's Great White Way in 2001. Nor are America's classic dramas ignored, with Arthur Miller's *Death of a Salesman,* Eugene O'Neill's *The Iceman Cometh,* and Tennessee Williams's *Not About Nightingales* also appearing in major twenty-first-century productions. Restagings of modern world classics, indeed, constitute roughly half to two-thirds of the offerings among America's regional, community, and academic theatres at any given time. And new plays mimicking these modernist classics — serious dramas as well as comedies — might in any year make up another quarter of the bill.

Kevin Spacey starred in this very successful 2001 Broadway revival (following an initial London showing) of Eugene O'Neill's profoundly realistic barroom drama, *The Iceman Cometh*, directed by Howard Davies.

One might even call the most successful of our new century's productions thus far, Mel Brooks's musical *The Producers,* a revival, as it is not only based on Brooks's 1968 movie but also revives (and quotes) well over a hundred gags, techniques, and themes of American musical comedies since the 1938 Olson and Johnson *Hellzapoppin!*

The theatre of revival — including new plays mimicking earlier forms — has broad and legitimate appeal. For most audiences, it is familiar, entertaining, and aesthetically satisfying; on the best occasions, it profoundly addresses serious and tangible problems that face humanity around the world. The theatre of revival is not merely a theatre of nostalgia; at its best it can be a forum for insight, infor-

mation, ideas, empathy, catharsis, wit, rapture, virtuosity, and laugh-'til-you-cry comedy. The tears of audiences emerging from the recent *Death of a Salesman* are real tears, and the laughs from the *Kiss Me Kate* revival virtually shake theatre seats. Finely crafted revivals also provide a box-office and public-relations lift to the whole theatre world, providing both employment for veteran artists and training for beginners, while raising the visibility and importance of dramatic art throughout national and world cultures. Though not at the cutting edge of innovation, and therefore easily derided by many avant-gardists, the traditional (or derrière-garde) theatre of revival needs no apologists; it is a vital, vibrant, thriving glory of the current stage.

Who's Doing Today's Theatre?

No book can tell you what's happening, or who's doing it, in the theatre right now — for by the time you read about it, it's already happened. The artist who sprang to prominence last year may sink to total obscurity next month. No one can safely predict the theatre of tomorrow.

What we can do, however, is list a few promising artists and artistic trends that may be at the forefront of theatrical life during the first years of the new century. Even if the list is less than prophetic, it should give a general picture of the diversity of the theatre of our times and of the sorts of dramatic possibilities that theatre artists and enthusiasts are currently anticipating.

Robert Wilson, Michael Counts, and Performance Art

Performance art is used to distinguish certain types of performances that, while generally lacking plot structures or character impersonation, and frequently staged as installations in nontheatrical facilities (such as art galleries), nonetheless provide highly provocative performance events, normally featuring spoken text, movement, and music, and always dominated by a powerful design contribution. First initiated and named by visual artists in the 1970s, and dominated by visual and sound aesthetics, extreme originality, and often improvisation, performance art recognizes none of the usual theatre conventions. Generally featuring performers without specific theatrical training (and, in some cases, openly proud of it — as they are "playing themselves" rather than representing characters), performance art dispenses with both suspense and catharsis, providing, in return, a provocative and stirring association of vivid, unexpected impressions organized around a given theme. The Dada experiments in the early years of the twentieth

Laurie Anderson is a long-recognized performance artist, specializing in the integration of visual excitement and electronic sound perturbations. In her "techno-opera" of *Moby Dick*, as presented at the Brooklyn Academy of Music in 1999, Anderson serves as singer, speaker (in many voices), composer, violinist, keyboardist, guitarist, and operator of an electronic, sound-generating Talking Stick, mostly while perched on a supersized chair of her own invention.

century (mentioned earlier) were certainly forerunners of this contemporary art form, which seems if anything to be gaining recognition and importance since the turn of the century.

Lines between the arts are not absolute, however, and many early performance artists, at least some of their work, may now be regarded as theatre artists as well. And vice versa. Since the 1980s, Americans Richard Foreman, Laurie Anderson, and Robert Wilson have made significant contributions jointly in both

performance and theatre art. Wilson, in particular, has enjoyed high visibility both here and overseas.

Born in Texas in 1941, Wilson first came to prominence in Germany, where his highly original collages of poetic texts recited against brilliantly evocative *tableaux vivants* ("living pictures") gained serious attention from enthusiasts of the avant-garde. The extraordinary length of these pieces, which Wilson both wrote and directed, earned him early notoriety: *The Life and Times of Joseph Stalin* (1973) lasted twelve hours; *Ka Mountain* (1972) lasted twenty-three. Wilson became a world figure when he was invited to create the central performance work of the 1984 Los Angeles Olympic Arts Festival, for which he composed *The CIVIL warS*, a massive piece to be rehearsed in several countries around the world; funds could not be raised for the performance, however, and only fragments of the work were ever performed. Since then, however, Wilson's work has stayed within more practical time and space limits, as he has begun to direct — however unconventionally — more conventional works, including operas, and original pieces of mixed genre.

Wilson's work is not performance art in the strictest sense: his pieces have a theme, they are not improvised, and the performers usually (but not always) play characters other than themselves. But he shares with performance art a disdain for logical language and plot construction and a corresponding preference for combining music, movement, sculpture, video, painting, lighting, poetry, and human expressiveness. "I hate ideas," Wilson has said,

Left: Robert Wilson's production of *Time Rocker*, an experimental musical work by Lou Reed and Darryl Pinckney, was originally created in Hamburg before its 1997 opening at the Paris Odeon – the Theatre of Europe. Wilson served, as he customarily does, as director and designer; his startlingly original theatrical visualizations, exemplified by these production photographs, have become celebrated worldwide.

and in their place he presents visions, dreams, and impressions. Frequent collaborators like nō and kabuki specialist Suzushi Hanayagi and the autistic poet Christopher Knowles — a longtime Wilson friend—make non-Western and nontraditional contributions to most of Wilson's work, as do overscale props, ideographic and kinetic scenery, free intermixing of humans and puppets, utterly nontraditional casting, and, most characteristically, stage movements in extremely slow motion, as if the characters are wholly under water. Everything — even the sheer duration — of Wilson's work forces a reexamination of the nature of performance and the relationship of audience and art, meaning and aesthetics, making us question the very foundations of dramaturgy: Why do we watch theatre? What are we looking for? What do we care about?

Wilson now directs plays. Starting with Euripides' *Alcestis*, a visually stunning and magical production (featuring a mountain falling down in slow motion) at the American Repertory Theatre in Cambridge, Massachusetts, Wilson now works with professional actors, often in normal proscenium theatres. His 1995 adaptation of *Hamlet,* with Wilson himself playing the title and various other roles, was set in a minimalist construction of black slabs against a horizon shifting from white to blue to red according to the prince's mood, presenting Shakespeare's text as a deathbed meditation on the play's confounding events and discoveries. His 1999 *The Days Before: Death, Destruction and Detroit III,* based on the Apocalypse and accompanied by seemingly unrelated texts by Italian philosopher Umberto Eco, seeks to create a "celebration of humanity" out of the grim Eco texts (read by actors Tony Randall and Fiona Shaw), nō dance, baboonlike "soldiers," Tibetan chanting, costumes parading across the stage (with no actors in them), a wing-flapping owl, and a rapacious red rooster. "If I had studied theatre," Wilson has said, "I would never make the work I do." Though it may not be theatre,

Above: The Days Before: Death, Destruction and Detroit III, according to creator/director/designer Robert Wilson, "explores the process of destruction and reconstruction, drawing from apocalyptic history, thought, and imagination." Based loosely on Umberto Eco's novel *The Island of the Day Before* and with music composed by Ryuichi Sakamoto, the work creates a "moving tableau of stories," in which The Rooster (in red, *at left*) is a "prophet who sees the Apocalypse" and The Owl (flying, *at right*) doubts the Apocalypse will ever happen. From the 1999 world premiere at Lincoln Center, New York.

Above right and far right: Michael Counts's production of *So Long Ago I Can't Remember,* as staged by his GAle GAtes et.al. in their Brooklyn warehouse-stage in 2001, is an intensely theatrical walk-through performance (the audience being led through thirteen different staging areas in the group's 40,000-square-foot staging space), roughly based on Dante's *Divine Comedy. Above:* Here, in Purgatory, spirits (and eventually the audience) wander through a forest of ethereal trees and chanting fellow-wanderers. *Right:* The dead float through the audience on the River Styx.

virtually everyone working in the contemporary theatre world knows of Wilson's work, and a great many are deeply influenced by it.

Wilson's successor may well be Michael Counts. Born in 1970, Counts has, since the late 1990s, been mounting performances — called "epic installations," "hallucinatory art," "postmodern fantasy," or "extreme theatre" by reviewers searching for an appropriate description — in a huge renovated warehouse in Brooklyn, New York, operated under the company name of GAle GAtes et. al. Counts, who describes his theatre aesthetic as "mystery and surprise" and his works as "chaotic," creates magnificently detailed, highly surrealistic dreamscapes that occupy his vast (40,000-square-foot) workspace, with the audience guided through several fully designed spaces throughout the cavernous structure. His *1839,* receiving wide acclaim in 1999, was described by reviewer Jason Zinoman as "a constantly shifting languorous dreamscape, filled with naked archers, giant fruit and masked ancient Greek characters with phallic noses." Even more astonishing was his *So Long Ago I Can't Remember* (2001), based loosely on Dante's *Divine Comedy,* which takes place in thirteen isolated and individual settings that recede into the depths of the warehouse space, with the theatre's forty-odd spectators, guided by a female Virgil, making their way through dense smoke and collapsing walls through nine circles of Hell, then Purgatory, and finally Paradise. Amazing images characterize this work: a boat of wide-eyed corpses glides across the River Styx; angels — nude but for their white fluffy wings — redeem Christian martyrs; a wheezing pope confronts a red-garbed virgin as his monks chortle; a man sways on a rope after hanging himself; gangsters stage a hit in a Waldorf-Astoria hallway while a maid cleans the rooms behind them; purgatorial denizens

chant woefully while wandering through a vast forest of giant trees; Nazi commandants argue in German (and a Pushkin lover poetizes in Russian) as a young girl soars on a swing across the room. In the last minutes, the audience is led on catwalks in heaven — above clouds so dense no floor can be seen beneath them — before being sent out into the street a block from where they first came in. This piece is accompanied throughout by a nearly continuous musical score, often ear-splitting, which is composed by longtime company member (and Counts collaborator) Joseph Diebes, together with a recorded spoken text to which the performers lip-synch with surprising precision. Nothing of GAle GAtes et. al.'s work is easily or cheaply accomplished; the apparent arbitrariness is obviously a result of taut discipline as well as startling imagination. While not everyone in the theatre world is ready for Counts's creations, and his story-less art certainly frustrates many, he clearly is not only the heir of Robert Wilson's achievement but also a current leader of a vigorous new performance and theatre art that may well have a greater importance in years to come.

Susan Stroman, Matthew Bourne: Dance Theatre and Dance Play

Choreographers — and choreographer-directors — have become increasingly important in the musical theatre (see the previous chapter), but two of today's younger choreographer-directors have reconfigured the nature of theatre itself. They have also helped a new field, dance-theatre, emerge into American consciousness.

Susan Stroman, by the first year of the new millennium, had virtually seized at least temporary control of the Broadway musical stage, winning every award in sight for her extraordinary choreography and direction of the hit Broadway productions of *The Producers, Contact,* and *The Music Man,* plus her choreography for the London (and then Broadway) revivals of Rodgers and Hammerstein's great 1943 classic, *Oklahoma!* — all within a three-year period! No overnight sensation, the Delaware native had arrived in New York back in the mid-1970s, dancing in road companies of *Chicago* and *Sugar Babies,* and receiving her

first choreographic assignment in the 1987 off-Broadway production of *Flora, the Red Menace.* She gained worldwide attention, and her first Tony Award, with her 1995 *Crazy for You* — a Broadway adaptation of George Gershwin's earlier *Girl Crazy* — which she followed with Broadway productions of *Show Boat, Big,* and *Steel Pier,* plus dance works for the New York City Ballet and the Martha Graham Company, before her meteoric four-show ascendancy of 1999–2001. What is remarkable about Stroman's choreography is its great humor, exuberance, inventiveness, and down-to-earth accessibility — across an enormously wide-ranging stylistic palette. A brilliantly clever deployment of props is as close as Stroman comes to having a trademark: dozens of farm implements in the country dance of *Crazy for You,* trays filled with dishes in the restaurant scene of *Contact,* eye-popping rope tricks in *Oklahoma!,* and old ladies "tap dancing" with metal walkers in *The Producers,* where pigeons also flap in comic unison and chorus girls pop out of file cabinets. But trademarks are not really what Stroman offers: rather, her work seems less about herself and more about a clever integration of choreography with storytelling. In her revival of *Music Man,* for example, she had Harold Hill, the title character, "teach" other characters the dance steps that eventually figured into the "Shipoopi" number, thus making what was previously strictly a dance interlude an integral part of the plotline. Now the *Music Man* characters "really have a musical journey," Stroman notes.

Contact has perhaps been Stroman's most important production to date. Billed as a "dance play" (with no singing, no original music, and only minimal speaking), it was nonetheless classified, by the Tony Awards committee among others, as musical theatre on the sheer strength of its vivid storytelling and the implicit passion of its characters. *Contact* consists of three separate pieces linked only by the theme of romantic linkups: *Swing-*

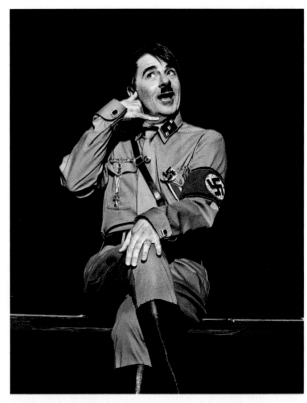

Susan Stroman has directed and choreographed two of the biggest Broadway musical hits of the current century, but they are radically different from each other. *Left:* In *Contact*, Debra Yates is the dazzling dancer in the yellow dress who attracts the life-changing attention of Boyd Gaines (spotlighted behind her), who plays a burnt-out advertising exec. *Right:* In *The Producers*, however, outrageous farce is the order of the day; here, Gary Beach plays the "title role" of a producer of a satirical play-within-a-play ("Springtime for Hitler") meant by its corrupt producers to be a deliberate failure so that they can walk off with their duped investors' money. Costumes for both productions by William Ivey Long.

ing, in which Fragonard's famous eighteenth-century French painting of a girl on a swing comes to life as a three-way sex romp; *Did You Move?,* a housewife's seriocomic fantasy in a chaotic, outer-borough, 1950s New York restaurant; and the title piece, *Contact,* in which an alcoholic and burnt-out advertising executive tries to commit suicide — after failing to make contact, in a high-voltage dance club, with a supersexy lady dazzlingly dressed in brilliant yellow. Opening in the small downstairs theatre in New York's Lincoln Center, *Contact* quickly moved to the larger upstairs

space and subsequently to a national tour, thrilling its audiences with the complexity, conviction, and intensity of its acting — rare for musical theatre of any sort, and exceptionally rare for a theatre piece based principally on movement.

Stroman's 2001 successes included *The Producers* (see the previous chapter) and the Harry Connick, Jr., musical, *Thou Shalt Not,* which is based on the Zola novel *Thérèse Raquin,* both of which she directed as well as choreographed. Supremacy in the theatre never lasts forever, and very little lasts even for more than

Matthew Bourne achieved international acclaim with his intensely theatrical reconception of the familiar *Swan Lake* ballet, which Bourne reinterpreted as a homosexual fantasy. Though using the original Tchaikovsky score and adding no dialogue, the resulting work was so dramatically powerful – and well acted – that Bourne received a Tony Award for its staging in 1999. Adam Cooper and Scott Amber are the principals in the legendary – but radically reconceived – pas de dux.

a few years, but Susan Stroman will almost surely be making important theatre works for a generation or more to come.

English-born Matthew Bourne has been choreographing for the stage since the late 1980s, with assignments at the London Palladium (*Oliver!*), Royal Shakespeare Company (*As You Like It*), Malmo (Sweden) City Theatre (*Show Boat*), and Los Angeles Ahmahn-son (*Cinderella*), but his move into innovative dance theatre began with a series of radical adaptations of classical nineteenth-century ballets, including *Cinderella, La Sylphide,* the *Nutcracker,* and, most notably, *Swan Lake,* for which Bourne replaces the airy and delicate swan-ballerinas with bare-chested, buzz-cut men, muscular but amply feathered around the loins. "See it, or live to regret it!" said the *London Independent* after the British opening. Bourne's beautifully danced and beautifully acted version of this classic — possibly the world's best-known ballet, with music by Tchaikovsky — presents a young prince alternately coddled by his parents and servants (parodying current English royalty), seduced in a dream-fantasy by a flock of male swans, both brutal and tender; the famous pas de deux then becomes a homoerotic opus turning romanticism on its head — and then back on its feet. *Swan Lake* won Bourne Tony Awards for both choreography and direction in 1999, an extraordinary achievement for a work that consists of nothing but dance.

Bourne has followed *Swan Lake* with *Car Man: An Auto-Erotic Thriller* in 2000, restaging Bizet's opera *Carmen* and moving it from Spain to a diner/auto repair shop in a mythic 1960s "Harmony, USA." *Car Man* is flagrantly sexual, violent, and raw; characters copulate on kitchen tables and bloody fights redden the stage. Bizet's music is reorchestrated for a percussion-heavy score, which blares forth (presumably) from an onstage jukebox, while the title role is now divided in two: one male and one female. Opening in London, *Car Man* toured the United States in 2001–02.

Bourne's and Stroman's work have brought dance theatre squarely into the American dramatic mainstream. They did not, however, invent it: Pina Bausch defined such a form with her Tanztheater Wuppertal in Germany during the 1970s with works that were both playful and experimental but always underlaid with strains of contemporary human anguish. Recent glorious revivals of her *Sacre du*

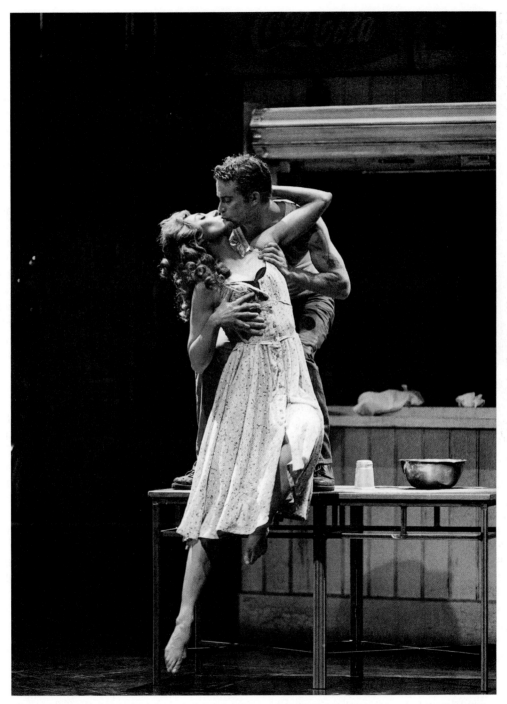

Matthew Bourne's *Car Man*, a sexy, powerful, dance adaptation of Bizet's opera *Carmen*, is set in a diner that doubles as an auto repair shop (hence "car" man) in a mythic "Harmony, USA" of the 1960s. The original role of Carmen is split in two: Michaela Meazza plays Lena and Wean Wardrop is Luca in the 2000 London premiere.

The Garden of Earthly Delights, a highly innovative dance-drama conceived and directed by Martha Clarke, is a brilliantly evocative staging – with music, mime, dance (on the ground and in the air), and stunning stage effects – of the great Hieronymus Bosch painting of the same name (c. 1510). Adam and Eve are seen here in the 1987 New York off-Broadway revival, with lighting by Paul Gallo, costumes by Jane Greenwood, and flying effects by Peter Foy.

Printemps (about youthful sexual desire) and *Café Müller* (about troubled sexual relationships) added further luster to her legend, maintaining her at the forefront of the avant-garde, and her *Only You* (1997) and *The Window Washer* (1998) continue to dazzle audiences and influence stage directors around the world. Martha Clarke, a veteran of the Pilobolus dance troupe, created two stunning dance-theatre pieces in the late 1980s: *The Garden of Earthly Delights*, based on a painting by Hieronymus Bosch, and *Vienna Lusthaus*, evoking the artistic and sexual ferment of Vienna at the time of painter/designer Gustav Klimt. Dance theatre now has both history and Tony-certified

prominence in the United States, and we can expect its achievement and influence to grow in the coming years.

Stomp, Blue Man Group, De La Guarda: *Movement Art*

Somewhere between performance art and dance theatre is a group performance based primarily on surprising movement techniques, where rhythm, sound, color, and pure athleticism reign over plot, character, and language. Many of these groups enjoy enormous popularity.

Stomp was created in England by Luke Cresswell, a percussionist and composer, and Steve McNicholas, an actor and writer. Collaborators since the early 1980s, Cresswell and McNicholas created *Stomp,* a purely percussive and choreographic performance piece, in 1991; it proved a great success in both London and New York, and has run ever since in those cities and many others around the world. *Stomp* employs, instead of drums, an assortment of garbage-can lids, pipes, brooms, and other everyday objects; its rhythms are furious, its choreography explosive, and its intensity relentless — and often comic. There is no story, no characters, and no dramatic impact, but the performers are young, diverse, and exciting and the sheer theatricality is captivating.

Blue Man Group is a similar, storyless, percussion enterprise but which also employs riotous clowning, interaction with the audience, and amazing food fights; it is performed by three head-shaved actors covered from the neck up in superglossy blue makeup. Created in New York City by former school pals Chris Wink, Matt Goldman, and Phil Stanton, first as improvised street theatre and then as staged performance art, the group's opening of their first full show, *Tubes,* at the small, off-Broadway Astor Place Theatre in 1991 made the group a near-permanent fixture in the New York theatre scene — and a few years later the Boston and Chicago scenes as well. Now with television appearances (on *The Tonight Show,* at the

Grammy Awards, and in frequent Intel commercials) and an expanded show, *Live at Luxor*, at a 1,200-seat Las Vegas showroom, the avant-garde troupe has become a very big business, with an annual budget of $28 million and a reported staff of 473. Blue Man Group revels in low technology: actors bang on homemade instruments, hurl marshmallows at each other (catching them in their mouths), and hold printed cards up to the audience to convey verbal thoughts or admonitions; they also invite audience members onstage — on some occasions to be hung upside down and pelted with various substances. Both of their shows, however, are continuously evolving, according to BMG's founders, and therefore anything you read about the shows may have changed before you see them.

De La Guarda, the most recent of these three groups, opened their *Villa Villa* in New York's Daryl Roth Theatre in 1998; it is, at the moment of writing, still running and like Blue Man has opened another version in Las Vegas. *Villa Villa* combines dazzling elements of disco rock, rave parties, soaring arial acrobatics, and all-weather immersion for cast and audience alike. This textless, intermissionless, ninety-minute wonder, which takes place largely above and sometimes amidst the audience — who are penned into a standing-room-only boxlike space — is most notable for its actors whizzing around overhead, first atop a translucent "cloud" of theatrical scrim, where only their angel-like silhouettes are glimpsed, and then plunging down through the "clouds" to grab audience members (presumably by prearrangement) and carry them up into the sky. Such soaring performers combine and re-combine like swarming bees, hurling themselves into each other and the walls, often with orgasmic intensity (and accompanying gasps), all to pounding rock music played from above, fierce winds, and very wet rain that fills the room. The total effect is a vividly sensual kinetic surround; while there is no plot, there are implicit real-life interactions — flirtations, couplings, and dissolutions — among the cast,

De La Guarda is an avant-garde performance group from Buenos Aires, Argentina, which, in its signature piece, *Villa Villa*, plucks audience members from the ground (presumably by prearrangement) and carries them aloft.

all costumed in ordinary street clothes. Created by unemployed recent theatre graduates from Buenos Aires, Argentina, De La Guarda's *Villa Villa* is destined, like the other groups in this section, for a long run and major influence in world theatrical movements.

Sherry Glaser, John Leguizamo, Karen Finley, Spaulding Gray, Eric Bogosian, Anna Deveare Smith, Danny Hoch: Solo Performance

Although Anton Chekhov wrote a short play for a single actor (*On the Harmfulness of Tobacco,* in which the character is a lecturer addressing his audience), it has only been in recent times that authors have seriously entertained the possibilities of full-length plays employing a single actor. Sometimes these are little more than star vehicles or extended monologues, often based on historical characters, as, for example, Hal Holbrook's long-running portrayal of America's great writer in *Mark Twain Tonight,* James Whitmore's rendition of America's feisty thirty-third president in *Give 'Em Hell, Harry!,* and Julie Harris's recurrent tours as Emily Dickinson in *The Belle of Amherst.* More fully dramatized works followed in the 1990s, when Jay Presson Allen wrote two intriguing and generally successful Broadway plays for solo actors: *Tru,* about novelist and society darling Truman Capote in his despairing last days, performed by Robert Morse; and *The Big Love,* about the mother of Errol Flynn's mistress, played by Tracey Ullman. Also noteworthy in the 90s was Willy Russell's *Shirley Valentine,* in which a frustrated middle-aged housewife tells us of leaving her English husband for a boatman on a Greek island, Lily Tomlin's portrayal of all seventeen characters in Jane Wagner's previously mentioned *Search for Signs* (reprised on Broadway in 2001), and Patrick Stewart's one-man presentation of Charles Dickens's *A Christmas Carol,* in which the celebrated Shakespearean actor (and *Star Trek* star) played all the roles.

The most recent strain of one-person shows, however, makes serious attempts at complex (and often comic) dramaturgy, often with an autobiographical basis. Sherry Glaser's seemingly plain but dramatically astonishing *Family Secrets,* for example, recounts the author's family story through the lively and racy monologues of five characters: Glaser, her mother, her sister, her father, and her grandmother — all played by Glaser, who transforms herself onstage, often in midsentence, with simple costume and makeup changes. Glaser's family secrets — some hilarious, some painful, and all poignant and provocative — revolve around sexual identity and ambiguity, religious absorp-

tion and assimilation, mental illness, menstruation, and childbirth.

Colombian-born John Leguizamo has become one of America's leading solo writer-performers; his *Freak,* set in Leguizamo's childhood borough of Queens (New York), is a hugely comic and often deeply poignant autobiographical journey in which Leguizamo plays at least a dozen entirely distinct — and indelibly memorable — roles. The play was nominated for a 1998 Broadway Tony Award, and his solo follow-up, *Sexaholix . . . A Love Story,* received wide praise at its Broadway premiere in 2001.

Karen Finley's 1990 solo performance, *We Keep Our Victims Ready,* in which the artist smeared her naked body with chocolate to represent the exploitation and sexual abasement of women, earned unwanted notoriety when national columnists portrayed her performance as indecent. The ensuing furor cost Finley future grants and even occasioned congressional threats, fortunately short-lived, to terminate the National Endowment for the Arts that had supported her work. But Finley has prevailed over many of her detractors, with subsequent performances that expand upon the themes of self-exposure and self-degradation, presenting human eroticism together with its inherent ironies. In a 1999 performance of *Shut Up and Love Me* (and Finley's performances are never the same from night to night or year to year), the artist again smeared herself with chocolate, this time inviting audience members to lick it off her (at $20 a lick, to compensate for the loss of her funding); in a 2001 performance of the same work, she covered herself entirely in honey, turning herself into what one reviewer called "the ultimate objectified woman." By confronting viewers with their own lust — and consequent disgust — Finley rarely fails to create a vividly memorable unease.

Spaulding Gray's impressionistic and personal storytellings, seemingly casual ruminations that develop a subtly enchanting momentum, became avant-garde classics in the 1980s (*Swimming to Cambodia*) and mainstream successes by the early 1990s (*Monster in a Box*). In his *Morning, Noon and Night* (2000), Gray reflects on his new domesticity as a stay-at-home dad, from waking with baby Theo's foot in his face, to ventures out with his five-year-old son for an afternoon ice cream. "My life is much more balanced now with the family, and I hadn't expected that. The character of Spaulding Gray is more grounded than he's ever been," Gray reports.

Eric Bogosian's series of intensely and penetrating performances, savage and comic by turns, has created an indelible cast of American low-life characters — pimps and whores, addicts and agents, executives and rock stars, panhandlers and jocks — in his increasingly brilliant collection of solo evenings, variously titled *Drinking in America, Sex, Drugs, and Rock & Roll, Pounding Nails in the Floor with My Forehead,* and *Wake Up and Smell the Coffee.*

Anna Deveare Smith, in two works, *Fires in the Mirror* and *Twilight: Los Angeles 1992,* has taken the personal one-woman play to new levels altogether, with performances of the latter play moving from the Mark Taper Forum in Los Angeles (which commissioned it) to the New York Public Theatre and then to Broadway, where it was nominated for two Tony Awards and the Pulitzer Prize. Smith — who when not performing is a professor at Stanford University — writes of and performs specific urban events that focus on fundamental problems of contemporary American society, particularly racism. *Fires* centers on the many days of rage in Crown Heights, Brooklyn, that followed the violent deaths of Gavin Cato (an African American) and Yankel Rosenbaum (a Hasidic Jew). *Twilight* concerns the Los Angeles riots that followed the acquittal of white police officers charged with the beating of a black motorist, Rodney King. In both pieces, Smith excerpted personal interviews with hundreds of individuals who lived through these city-defining events. Using minimal props and costume elements, Smith transforms herself into an entire cast of characters for each social upheaval, creating, in one critic's words, "pure, unbiased, tumultuous symphonies." Smith's most recent performance reaches further back into history. Premiered as a solo work at New York's Public Theatre in 2000 (although earlier staged by Smith elsewhere with a cast of actors), *House Arrest* concerns American presidents (notably Jefferson, Lincoln, F. D. Roosevelt, Kennedy, and Clinton), amidst a host of cultural and media celebrities (Walt Whitman, Studs Terkel, Arianna Huffington) who expose the presidents' contradictions. Smith limits herself to dramatizing actual historical documents and verbatim transcriptions in this solo work, which powerfully illumines darker corners of American thoughts and practices concerning the interfaces of race, sex, politics, idealism, and democracy over the past hundred and fifty years.

Danny Hoch is sort of a young Bogosian, and the ten monologues he presents in *Jails, Hospitals & Hip-Hop* come from the mouths of those unraveling around our cultural fringes, conveying an underclass ire and wit we rarely see on the legitimate stage or even in stand-up comedy. Hoch's characters in this 1998 piece include seventeen-year-old Flip-Dogg, a burger-flipper at a small town fast-food joint in Montana who, dressing for work, fantasizes that he's the number one black rapper in the world ("I'm the baddest motherfuckin' thug-ass dogg, straight up," he imagines himself telling a late-night television interviewer; "the fans, Jay, they won't leave me alone, man!"). Flip-Dogg pathetically imagines his white skin comes from a rare skin disease and that "even though I live in Montana, I still got the ghetto in my heart." Other exceptional Hoch characters are Andy, a dying drug addict and new-age Vietnam vet ("I was shootin' heroin, but I was eatin' organic"), and the endearing Peter, a Cuban engineering student who sells rapping sticks to American tourists in downtown Havana.

Danny Hoch, the writer and solo performer of *Jails, Hospitals & Hip-Hop*, is one of the newest entries in the solo performance genre.

Two of the most commercially popular solo shows of the late 90s and into the twenty-first century are about sexual roles in America. Rob Becker's *Defending the Caveman* (1995), satirizing male defensiveness in what he considers an increasingly feminized culture, was an enormous success on Broadway and on national tour. And in what is perhaps a new variation of the one-woman performance, *The Vagina Monologues* (1998), dramatist Eve Ensler has compiled a series of short narratives — mini-solos — initially performed by their authors (of which Ensler is one) on women and their sex organs. Included among the original contributors were Whoopi Goldberg ("My Angry Vagina"), Lily Tomlin, Marisa Tomei, Glenn Close, Rosie Perez, and Gloria Steinem;

however, the play is now regularly performed, on both coasts and around the country, by rotating female performers. "People long to talk about their vaginas. It's like a secret code between women," Ensler says.

Two American Directors: Julie Taymor and Mary Zimmerman

Nothing really prepared the theatre world for the colossal triumph of Julie Taymor's Disney-produced *The Lion King* in 1998. Taymor, born in Newton, Massachusetts, in 1953, was known at the time strictly as an avant-garde director, designer, and choreographer, who, having studied in Paris and Indonesia, had developed a professional reputation for cutting-edge productions of classical plays (*Titus Andronicus, The Tempest, The Taming of the Shrew, King Stag*), primarily at off-Broadway's Theatre for a New Audience and the American Repertory Theatre in Cambridge, Massachusetts. *The Lion King*, with its giant corporate producer, far exceeded any scale on which Taymor had previously operated; its production budget ($20 million — an all-time Broadway record) was doubtless more than the budgets for all her previous productions combined. But *Lion King* turned the commercial and avant-garde American theatre upside-down.

With *The Lion King*, Taymor animated the vast African plain, employing more than 50 performers and 100 puppets to represent 25 species of animals, birds, fish, and insects. In the spectacular opening scene, 26-foot giraffes lope soulfully across the stage, gazelles leap in staggered unison, and a 13-foot-long elephant, more than 11 feet high, makes an astonishing entrance down the auditorium aisle — while birds fly and court in midair, warthogs wobble close to the ground, wildebeests stampede, grasses spring from the soil, flowered vines descend from the trees, and an enormous, latticed sun rises to reveal the radiant African dawn.

In this glorious work, Taymor ingeniously mixes Javanese rod puppetry, Balinese headdresses, African masks, American and British music (much of it written by Elton John), and the Disney style of family entertainment; she also incorporates South African music and lyrics in various African languages — particularly the click language of Xhosa (performed by Tsidii Le Loka from South Africa, as Rafiki the baboon sorceress) — with the confidence that a literal understanding of a musical's libretto (text) is not at all times strictly necessary. But the individual signature of Taymor in *The Lion King* is how she openly reveals the theatricality of the puppetry and the musicality of the production rather than hiding them to maintain a realistic illusion. Her puppets' heads are located well above the faces of the actors who wear them so that the audience is continually aware of the actors manipulating (and often speaking for) each animal; all of the strings, wheels, and sticks of the puppetry mechanics are in full sight of the audience. And the orchestra is not wholly buried in a pit below the stage but, rather, extends to costumed African drummers and chanters in the audience boxes that frame the action.

The Lion King opened to rapturous reviews from even the most hardened New York critics — winning for Taymor Tony Awards for both directing and costume design. At the time of this writing, it is running in several cities on three continents, including two theatres in Japan. "I think *The Lion King* bridges the divide between Broadway and avant-garde theatre," Taymor has said, "and I am delighted that my work, which has been characterized as 'too downtown' or 'too sophisticated,' is now going to be seen by the widest possible

Julie Taymor's *The Lion King* forges a profound alliance between experimental theatre, African ritual, Asian dance and puppetry, and American mass-market entertainment (namely, the Disney Corporation and Broadway). Here, South African vocalist Tsidii Le Loka plays the role of Rafiki, the singer-narrator, amidst leaping gazelles and a menagerie of other animals.

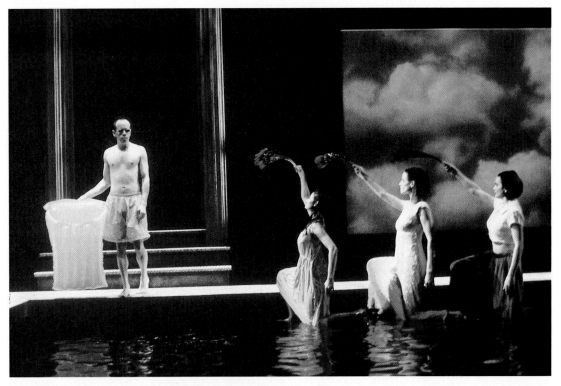

Phaeton, who wanly proposes to set the world on fire, gazes at walking-on-water sea maidens in Mary Zimmerman's Ovidian dramatization of *Metamorphoses* at the Mark Taper Forum in Los Angeles. His yellow plastic raft is a lighthearted, contemporary touch.

audience." Most in the theatre world are equally delighted at (if not a little nervous because of) this merger of experimental and intercultural innovation with broad public appeal and international corporate financing.

Mary Zimmerman's most unique theatre works are theatrical adaptations of nondramatic texts, including, so far, *The Notebooks of Leonardo da Vinci, The Odyssey,* and Ovid's *Metamorphoses.* A professor of performance studies (not drama) at Northwestern University, Zimmerman follows that program's emphasis (made famous by Frank Galati) of adapting narrative texts for theatrical performance, while lending them an exceptionally striking visual and choreographic presence. *Metamorphoses* is perhaps her most impressive work to date, in which Ovid's famous (and

some not-so-famous) stories are staged on, in, and around a square-bordered pool of water that — backed by a stately door, horizontal screen of painted clouds, and towering waterfall — occupies virtually the entire stage. In Zimmerman's pool, Ovid's legendary and often fantastical characters do everything: swim, float, splash, thrash, drown, paddle, bathe, fight, make love, wash their clothes, study their reflections, and, in general, get sopping wet. Yet Zimmerman does not simply rely on theatrical novelty or physical sensationalism; in *Metamorphoses* the despair of Alcyon for her drowned lover, Ceyx, is heartbreaking, while their resurrection as a pair of seabirds is ethereally lovely. And the passionate carnality of Eros and Psyche, and of Myrrha and her father Cinyras, contains lusty fires that mere water cannot douse. *Metamorphoses* came to New York in 2001–02 after its Chicago premiere and a year touring in the United States. Also known for her imaginative direction of conventional plays, including a 2001 production of Shakespeare's *Measure for Measure* in New York's Central Park, Zimmerman's narrative adaptations have visual poetry galore, creating stories of genuinely mythic poignancy.

Four European Directors: Peter Brook, Ariane Mnouchkine, Frank Castorf, Christoph Marthaler

Today's European theatre is generally more highly subsidized by government support than is American theatre, and it is likewise more responsive to cultural (as opposed to commercial) expectations from its audience. For these and other reasons, most European stage directors have greater opportunity (and perhaps desire) than their American counterparts to create radical staging innovations in working with — and often deconstructing — classical dramatic texts.

Four such directors, each at the helm of a permanent company of actors and designers and thus able to expend greater sums over a much larger rehearsal/preparation period than exists in the United States, have among them created an immensely original body of startling theatre works that tour internationally. Peter Brook and Ariane Mnouchkine, born in 1925 and 1939 respectively, are the elders of this group, each making their longtime headquarters in Paris where they work with international casts in unconventional performing spaces. The younger Frank Castorf and Christoph Marthaler, both born in 1951, make their bases in Berlin and Zurich respectively and represent a new wave of German-language directors noted for radically reconfiguring classic dramatic texts and/or crisscrossing the boundaries of artistic and literary disciplines in the creation of both wholly new works and adaptations.

PETER BROOK: THE INTERNATIONAL CENTER OF THEATRE RESEARCH   No director was more influential in the latter half of the twentieth century or is more provocative in the current theatre than the English-born Peter Brook. Brook began his directorial career with freshly conceived experimental productions of Shakespeare, Marlowe, Sartre, and Jean Cocteau, receiving sufficient attention to be appointed, at the age of twenty, to direct at the Shakespeare Memorial Theatre at Stratford-upon-Avon, where his 1955 *Hamlet* was the first English play to tour the Soviet Union. Within a short time, Brook was staging classics, plays, a Broadway musical (*House of Flowers*) and operas at the major performing venues — Covent Garden, Broadway, the Metropolitan Opera — of London and New York.

Brook's heart remained in experimental theatre, however, and in three landmark productions with the newly founded Royal Shakespeare Company at Stratford in the 1960s, he received immense international acclaim. These productions — Shakespeare's *King Lear* (1962), deeply influenced by Beckett and the theatre of the absurd; Peter Weiss's *Marat/Sade* (1964), a production blending Artaud's notion of a theatre of cruelty with Brecht's theatre of alienation; and (1966) *US*, a company-improvised documentary commenting on American (i.e., "U.S." as "us") involvement in Vietnam — toured widely, and both *Lear* and *Marat/Sade* were subsequently filmed, thereby receiving even wider exposure.

Brook's subsequent publication of *The Empty Space,* in 1968, extended his reputation to theory, presenting a brilliant analysis of modern drama. Brook divides the current theatre into three categories: "deadly, holy, and rough" (corresponding, more or less, to conventional, Artaudian, and Brechtian). Rejecting all three, he culminates his study with a manifesto on behalf of an "immediate" theatre, one not preplanned by the director but developed through a creative and improvisational process, "a harrowing collective experience" rather than a dispassionate assemblage of the separate contributions of cast and designers. Brook then proved his point with an amazingly comic, penetrating, original, and "immediate" production of Shakespeare's *A Midsummer Night's Dream* in 1970, a production that — staged without sentimentality on a bare white set — combined circus techniques with uninhibited sexual farce, creating fresh interactions between the play's very familiar (though often shallowly realized) characters. Brook's *Dream* captivated critics and audiences throughout Europe and America during the early 1970s, further establishing him as one of the most creative and talented theorist-theatrical practitioners of all time.

Brook walked away from all of this, however, in 1971, moving to Paris and creating the International Center of Theatre Research, which he continues to head. Engaging a company of actors from every continent, and performing, mostly in French, in a long-abandoned, dirt-floored theatre (the Bouffes du Nord, located in the African quarter of Paris), Brook has produced a series of intercultural works of extraordinary interest, including *The Iks* (about a northern Ugandan tribe), *The Conference of the Birds* (based on a twelfth-century Persian poem), Alfred Jarry's *Ubu Roi*, Georges Bizet's opera *Carmen*, a production of Shakespeare's *The Tempest,* and, most remarkably, *The Mahabharata,* which opened in Paris in 1986 and which Brook filmed for worldwide audiences in 1991. *The Mahabharata* is the national novel of India, ancient, archetypal, and immense (it is the longest single work of world literature); Brook had it adapted into a nine-hour play, which he initially staged with an international cast in a rock quarry in the south of France, and subsequently at his Bouffes du Nord. Brook blends the text with a myriad of natural (but not naturalistic) elements: actors wade in pools and rivers of real water trapped by circles of real fire; chariot wheels are mired in the real mud of the Bouffes du Nord stage; armies clash by torchlight, and candles float in the pond. The multifaceted reality of this

Indian epic — directed by an Englishman, in French, with an intercontinental cast — lends a universality to the production that leaves the audience fulfilled in ways previously unrealized in the theatre's history.

Brook's most recent work studies the individual human mind and includes notable productions of such works as *The Man Who,* a 1994 adaptation of Dr. Oliver Sacks's study of neurological illness; an English staging — in French — of Beckett's *Happy Days,* starring Brook's wife, Natasha Parry, as Winnie; a 1998 Parisian staging of a new play, *I Am a Phenomenon,* concerning a Russian man with a wizard-like memory; and *Le Costume,* a South African play by Can Themba about a ménage à trois that consists of a man, his wife, and her lover's suit of clothes!

Brook's most recent production, an abridged and intermissionless *Hamlet* which toured to Seattle and New York in 2001, is his first production in English in decades. It is also a mental journey, during which actor Adrian Lester in the title role brilliantly guides us, by precise modulations of voice, gesture, and highly expressive mime, through the ethics and logistics of Hamlet's predicament, all but asking us to participate in cerebral adventure. *Hamlet,* however, also furthers Brook's interculturalism, with the Jamaican-born Lester playing opposite the Indian Shantala Shivalingappa as Ophelia and the English Natasha Parry as Gertrude, all of whom are accompanied by a subtle string and percussion score composed and performed onstage by Japanese musician Toshi Tsuchitori. Brook's memoir, *Threads of Time* (1998), explores his goals: "The theatre is like a small restaurant whose responsibility is to nourish its customers. There is only one test: Do the spectators leave the playhouse with slightly more courage, more strength than when they came in? If the answer is yes, the food is healthy."

ARIANE MNOUCHKINE: THÉÂTRE DE SOLEIL
Like Brook, director Ariane Mnouchkine (born 1939) disdains conventional theatres, and her

Above: Peter Brook's production of *The Maha-bharata,* India's great epic poem, featured an international cast and toured widely in Europe and America prior to filming. It is shown here in Brook's Paris headquarters, the decrepit and long-abandoned Bouffes du Nord theatre, which Brook has resolutely declined to paint or renovate.

Rigth: Peter Brook's *Hamlet,* with Jamaican-born and English-trained Adrian Lester in the title role, was co-produced by Brook's International Center of Theatre Research and the Vienna *Festwochen* with an international cast, and toured widely in 2001, including stops in Seattle and New York. Design by Chloé Obolensky.

Ariane Mnouchkine, artistic director of the Théâtre de Soleil, has been considered one of France's — and Europe's — greatest directors since the 1970s. She is known particularly for melding Eastern and Western theatrical forms. Her 1995 production of Molière's *Tartuffe* transported the play to an Algerian setting and unmistakably referenced current French concerns over the rising tide of Islamic fundamentalism in that country and in France as well. Tartuffe was played by a Turkish actor, and Elmire by an East Indian. The setting (by Guy-Claude François) is a souk-styled courtyard.

troupe, the *Théâtre de Soleil,* performs in the Cartoucherie — an abandoned munitions factory just outside of Paris. Even more than Brook, Mnouchkine is celebrated for mixing Eastern themes and performing traditions with Western works. And she has gone much further than Brook in dispensing with traditional theatrical hierarchy in favor of creative collaboration: in the Soleil, all productions emerge from an extended process of improvisation, discussion, and group study, with all twenty-five members of her company — who live and work together as a community — sharing the various responsibilities of research, scriptwriting, staging, interpretation, design, construction, and even house management. Indeed, all company members are allocated the same

salary — including Mnouchkine, who, perhaps alone among the world's artistic directors, has steadily worked to diminish the formal status of the director in the theatre. (Even today, at the height of her fame, Mnouchkine might be tearing the tickets at the door or clearing away paper plates at the theatre's buffet bar.) The audience, too, is treated as a participant at Soleil performances; before each show, the actors put on their costumes and makeup in open dressing areas located beneath the audience gallery, where they chat quietly with each other and with entering spectators.

Under Mnouchkine, the Soleil earned national esteem from the early 1970s for a trilogy of plays, titled *1789, 1793,* and *The Golden Age,* that traced major events of the French revolution. And the Soleil's reputation broadened immeasurably in the early 1980s with a trilogy of Asian-inspired Shakespearean productions — particularly a kabuki-inspired *Richard II* and a kathakali-inspired *Twelfth Night* that were also performed to great acclaim at the 1984 Los Angeles Olympics. In the 1990s, Mnouchkine extended her play groupings to a tetralogy of ancient Greek plays — Euripides' *Iphigeneia at Aulis* followed by the three plays of Aeschylus' *Oresteia*, collectively titled *The House of Atreus (Les Atrides)*. "You will be fortunate if you ever see a more exhilarating production of the first great tragedies in European drama," said the *New York Times* of this production.

Mnouchkine's work seeks a new language of theatre, based in equal parts on Artaudian freedom, Brechtian political commitment, collective improvisation, a commitment to multiplay series, and a passionate commitment to interculturalism whereby Eastern performance traditions are blended with Western texts. A 1995 production of Molière's *Tartuffe*, employing an international and interracial cast, is a thrilling revisitation of religious hypocrisy as seen in the light of North African Islamic fundamentalism.

Four subsequent Asian-themed plays by Hélène Cixous — *Norodom Sihanouk* about Cambodia, *L'Indiade* about India, *Suddenly, Nights of Awakening* about Tibet, and *Drums on the Dyke* about China — each dealing with political, gender, and ethnic issues, combine ancient themes with contemporary struggles on Mnouchkine's stylized stage. *Drums on the Dyke*, for example, a play for masked actors who are "operated" like marionettes, with continuous music and sound played on Asian instruments, is based on a 4,000-year-old work by legendary Chinese poet Hsi-Xhou, exploring the relations between humans and nature as the ancient Chinese try to contain the rampaging Yellow and Blue Rivers. In fact, however, the play was inspired by the current Beijing government's deliberate flooding of

Ariane Mnouchkine's 1998 production of *Suddenly, Nights of Awakening (Et soudain, des nuits d'éveil)* at the Théâtre de Soleil in Paris takes the form of a touring Tibetan acting troupe seeking — in midperformance — political asylum from its audience. The play was created through company improvisations (which were then shaped into a text by author-critic Hélène Cixous) and employs a unique mix of Tibetan dance, Buddhist ritual, commedia dell'arte *lazzi* (clowning), current political discourse, and actors wandering freely among the audience, speaking and passing out faxes. The scenery was designed by Guy-Claude François.

Frank Castorf's radical reconstruction of Tennessee Williams's *A Streetcar Named Desire*, retitled *Endstation Amerika* at the Berlin Volksbühne in 2001, alters dialogue, characters, situation, and language but retains, and in some cases expands and intensifies, fundamental aspects of the characters' relationships. From left, Stanley (now a rock guitarist) is played by Henry Hübchen, and Stella (his abused and deeply distracted wife) by Kathrin Angerer, while Mitch and Steve (Bernhard Schütz and Fabian Hinrichs) complete Stanley's musical combo. The video monitor shows what is happening in the bathroom behind the door.

large areas of farmland without warning its local citizens. As this book goes to press, *Drums on the Dyke* is touring on three continents. Like its name, the Soleil (meaning "the sun") brings both light and heat to the pressing issues of our time.

FRANK CASTORF: BERLIN VOLKSBÜHNE   After studying dramaturgy at Humboldt University in East Berlin, Frank Castorf earned a strong public following with startling productions of classical dramas (Sophocles' *Ajax,* Ibsen's *A Doll's House* and *Enemy of the People,* Shakespeare's *Othello* and *Hamlet,* Goethe's *Tasso*) and adaptations of novels (Anthony Bur-

gess's *A Clockwork Orange*) at major theatres throughout Germany in the 1980s, leading to his current appointment, as artistic director of the Berlin Volksbühne, or People's Theatre, in 1992. There, and increasingly in guest productions throughout Europe, Castorf's reputation has soared, as has the controversy his works induce. "A master of ruination" is one of the critical brickbats he has faced.

Castorf's first directorial act is to dismember the script. Improvising with the actors, he fragments and reconstructs the text as virtually a new work, often unrecognizable from its former self. Characters are deleted, combined, and added; speeches are rewritten, translated into different languages, or turned into songs; words are changed, chanted, and often repeated (all but endlessly); gestures and stage business are freely invented; music and songs are freely interpolated; and whole storylines are eliminated while wholly new ones emerge. Castorf's production of *Endstation Amerika* (2001) is a classic example of this process: An adaptation of Tennessee Williams's *A Streetcar Named Desire* (the Williams estate required the title be changed for this presentation), the cast has been drastically pared to six characters — Stanley and Stella, Blanche and Mitch, Steve and Eunice — each of whom are given approximately the same weight in the play's action, which now centers on three dysfunctional couples. Themes of sexual longings and abuse remain, but are largely switched around: Stanley (played by the young and sultry Marlon Brando in the famous 1948 New York premiere) is here presented as a violent, middle-aged, beer-bellied thug, a Polish veteran of the anticommunist Solidarity movement, while a hyperanimated Stella, not a predatory Blanche, is now his principal victim. Music adds a constant (and wholly new) theme: Steve lugs his base viol around the house, joining with Stanley on his guitar, in a rendition (in English) of Lou Reed's "Just A Perfect Day." Eunice spouts cultural commentary in French, while Mitch, as if imagining himself a character in Alfred Hitchcock's *Psycho,* carts what he believes is his mother's corpse around the stage in a wheelchair. Responding to Blanche's accusation that he's an animal, Stanley saunters into their home in a head-to-toe gorilla suit. *Endstation*'s design is deconstructed as well. The garish and trashy set consists of a narrow one-room flat, divided from right to left into kitchen, bathroom door, and double bed, but we're invited to see right into the bathroom — where Stella changes her clothes and Mitch takes a (real) shower — on a large-screen video monitor facing the audience. When, in the final scene, the reality of the characters' lives turns topsy-turvy, the entire set suddenly tilts a full 45 degrees backward, with the actors sliding awkwardly against its back wall. At the play's end, the actors are scrambling up the "floor" — which is now a virtual fourth wall of their apartment — to show their heads while they speak to one another and to nod at the audience during the riotous curtain call. And amazingly, all of this works, in its fashion, showing a world in which there is tenderness and carnality, romance and commercialism, interethnic violence and attraction that Williams himself probably would have admired (even if his estate attorneys did not).

Since taking over the Volksbühne, Castorf has vastly expanded the theatre's namesake mission. Intermixed with the company's stage productions, an ambitious series of public discussions, symposia, lectures, films, rock bands, and electronic music concerts are also presented there on a regular basis, and new films are beginning to emerge from an on-premises film studio initiated in 2000. The Volksbühne, located in the heart of old — and newly fashionable — "Mitte" (central) Berlin, is clearly not merely a place for deconstructing classic dramas, but also for reconstructing — or at least reinvigorating — urban German culture at large.

CHRISTOPH MARTHALER: ZURICH SCHAUSPIELHAUS Swiss-born Christoph Marthaler was trained as a classical musician specializing in early wind instruments, beginning his career as a concert composer in the 1970s and 80s. Starting in 1988, however, Marthaler began to create — first as theatre composer and then as director at Theater Basel in Switzerland — new and wholly original blends of action and music that have since become his unique theatre. Deconstructed texts — à la Castorf — are interspersed with songs and trancelike choreography; the stylistic tone alternates between the poetic and the farcical, and the play is structured more through varied rhythms than forward-moving dramaturgy.

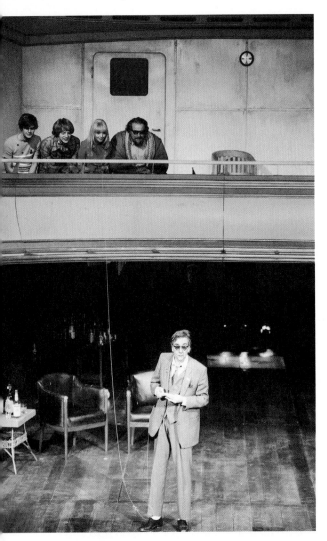

Christoph Marthaler's modern-dress production of Shakespeare's *Twelfth Night* at the Zurich Schauspielhaus was set on a sort of ship of fools, with the "ship" being a mirror image of the schauspielhaus in which the play was performed. Here, Feste, Sir Andrew, Maria, and Toby (played by Lars Rudolph, Oliver Mallison, Olivia Grigolli, and Josef Ostendorf) on the "upper deck" snare Malvolio (Ueli Jaeggi) with a trick letter in a barroom below deck. The consistently imaginative and innovative production toured to the Berlin *Theatertreffen* ("theatre meeting") – a collection of the twelve best productions in the German-speaking theater – in 2001.

Marthaler's theatre projects a dreamlike sur-reality: a stage picture (invariably co-created by his longtime collaborator, set and costume designer Anna Viebrock) rarely explainable but, at its best, profoundly engaging. Brought by Castorf to the Berlin Volksbühne in 1993, Marthaler quickly became a multiple-prize-winning European theatre celebrity, touring his productions widely and twice being voted "Director of the Year" by *Theater Heute,* the distinguished German theatre magazine. In 2000, Marthaler returned to his native country to take up the artistic directorship of the Zurich Schauspielhaus in Switzerland's largest city.

In his first — and so far only — Shakespearean production, *Twelfth Night* (2001), Marthaler has retained the play's basic situations (mostly revolving around feigned and mistaken sexual identities, contrasting social order versus alcoholic chaos), but only fragments of its specific dialogue, actions, and sequences. Characters in this production come and go, seemingly at will, on the set's two distinct levels, which appear to be the upper and lower decks of a seagoing ferryboat (and are also a near-replica of the Zurich Schauspielhaus auditorium and balcony), while key scenes are only minimally isolated amidst an overall panorama of the play's fourteen characters sitting, standing, and lying around, sometimes sleeping, sometimes reading, sometimes making love, and almost always drinking. Extended passages of group chanting — with which, in fact, the production begins — are occasionally punctuated by the entire cast violently and inexplicably hurling themselves on the floor, as if the "boat" in which they sailed had suddenly run upon a reef. And the play's famous climaxes — long-lost twins discovering each other in the final scene, Orsino finding out that Caesario is really Viola and hence female — are completely omitted in lieu of a communal singing of an 1888 American hymn (in English), beginning, "Throw out the lifeline, Throw out the lifeline, Someone is drifting away . . ." Neither words nor photographs can begin to convey the theatrical impact of Marthaler's adventurous stagings, but admirers, who are numerous, find them breathtaking.

Theatre of Today: Where Can You Find It?

The current theatre happens all over the world: in villages, campuses, prisons, resorts, and parks; at local and international festivals; on ocean liners and at suburban dinner theatres; on temporary stages in rural churchyards or within historic ruins; and, increasingly, at so-called site-specific venues, as a Manhattan apartment, a worker's meeting hall, or, in the case of one recent Russian production, inside an interurban railway car.

But mostly current theatre is found in cities — particularly in the traditionally great theatrical capitals such as New York City, Moscow, London, Paris, Vienna, Toronto, Tokyo, Budapest, and Berlin, as well as in cities of more modest theatrical repute, such as Kyoto, Zurich, Munich, Edinburgh, Milan, Buenos Aires, Johannesburg, Helsinki, Mexico City, Chicago, San Francisco, Seattle, Minneapolis, New Haven, Louisville, Los Angeles, Hartford, Boston, and Washington, D.C.

In the United States, New York City is without question the primary locus of the nation's theatrical activity. Every year Manhattan is the site of more performances, more openings, more revivals, more tours, and more dramatic criticism than any half-dozen other American cities put together; theatrically, it is the showcase of the nation. In the minds of many Americans, the Big Apple is simply *the* place to experience theatre; thus the town's hundred-plus playhouses are a prime tourist attraction and a major factor in the local economy. And in the minds of most theatre artists — actors, directors, playwrights, and designers — New York is the town where the standards are the highest, the challenge the greatest, and the

rewards the most magnificent. "Will it play in Peoria?" may be the big question in the minds of film and television producers, but "Will it make it in New York?" remains a cardinal concern in the rarefied world of American professional theatre. Therefore the reality of New York is surrounded by a fantasy of New York, and in a "business" as laced with fantasy as is the theatre, New York commands a strategic importance of incomprehensible value.

Broadway

Broadway is the longest street in Manhattan, slicing diagonally down the entire length of the island borough. The outside world largely knows it, however, for its cluster of thirty-plus theatres congregated in the dozen blocks north of Times Square. Broadway has been the "Great White Way" (referring to its bright illumination) of the American theatre since the first years of the century: the place where Eugene O'Neill, Arthur Miller, Tennessee Williams, William Inge, and Edward Albee all saw their masterpieces first produced; where memories of George M. Cohan, Ethel Merman, Mary Martin, and Barbra Streisand — Broadway Babies all — sang and danced through the twentieth century; and where John Barrymore, Marlon Brando, Helen Hayes, Henry Fonda, Alfred Lunt, Lynn Fontanne, and thousands of others acted their way into America's hearts and, subsequently, into Hollywood's films.

Much of the Broadway theatre district fell into urban decay after World War II, however, becoming a haven for sex shops, crack houses, porno movie theatres, and videogame parlors for the best part of a generation. Massive redevelopment immediately before and after 2000, however, including the reclaiming of drug-riddled 42nd Street by the construction or reconstruction of the New Amsterdam, New Victory, Ford Center, and American Airlines (once Roundabout) Theatres, has made the Broadway district once again a glamorous, vibrant center for mainstream legitimate theatre and, arguably, the single most important focal point of America's cultural life.

Broadway's lure is its dazzling visual and social excitement, its heady mix of bright lights and famed celebrities, and its trend-setting fashions, big-buck entertainments, and high-toned Tony Awards. The stakes are higher on Broadway than anywhere else in theatre; if you can make it there, as the song says, you'll make it anywhere, and the energy that this lyric connotes — and attracts — makes the Broadway district unforgettably fascinating.

Broadway is no longer the place where new plays ordinarily originate, however, as it was in 1947 when Tennessee Williams's *A Streetcar Named Desire* and Arthur Miller's *All My Sons* debuted there. Rather, it has become, primarily, the staging ground for extravagantly produced musicals, both new ones (recently *The Producers, Rent, Ragtime, The Full Monty, The Lion King*) and revivals (*The Music Man, Chicago, Cabaret, Oklahoma!*). Secondarily, it is the showcase for the best (or at least most commercially promising) new plays from America's off-Broadway and regional theatres, such as David Auburn's *Proof* from the Manhattan Theatre Club, David Henry Hwang's *Golden Child* from the South Coast Repertory in California, Wendy Wasserstein's *An American Daughter* from the Seattle Repertory, David Mamet's *The Old Neighborhood* from the American Repertory Theatre in Cambridge, Alfred Uhry's *Last Night of Ballyhoo* from Atlanta's Alliance Theatre, as well as new plays from abroad, such as Tom Stoppard's *The Invention of Love,* Michael Frayn's *Copenhagen,* Martin McDonagh's *The Beauty Queen of Leenane,* Marie Jones's *Stones in His Pockets,* and Yasmina Reza's *Art.* Finally, it is the site of major revivals of classic dramas from the American and international repertory (Arthur Miller's *A View from the Bridge, The Crucible,* and *The Iceman Cometh,* plus Neil Simon's *The Sunshine Boys,* Frances Goodrich and Albert Hackett's *The Diary of Anne Frank,* Dale Wasserman's *One Flew Over the Cuckoo's Nest,* and Eugène Ionesco's *The Chairs*). Occasionally, too, you will find a star-heavy revival of a world classic on Broadway, such as George C. Wolfe's 1998 rendition of *Macbeth,* starring Alec Baldwin and Angela Bassett.

As mentioned, rarely does a new play by a young playwright premiere on Broadway; the costs are ordinarily far too high to risk on an unknown author. And despite high ticket prices, which in 2002 ascended to as much as $85 for straight plays and $100 for musicals (and a near-astronomical $480 for selected seats at *The Producers*), most new productions on Broadway are, in fact, financial failures. Increasingly, therefore, Broadway producers await the new plays whose worth has first been "proven" in the subsidized European (chiefly English) theatre or on the not-for-profit American regional stage. Only the star-studded revival or Tony Award–winning new musical is otherwise likely to be "bankable" and offer sufficient opportunity for commercial success. And Broadway, once at the cutting edge of the American theatre, is its glamorous but somewhat expectable museum.

Off-Broadway and Off-Off-Broadway

Not all of New York theatre is performed within the geographic and commercial confines of the Broadway district, however. There are literally hundreds of theatres far from the Great White Way. The symbolic centrality of Broadway, however, is so strong that these theatres are named not for what they are but for what they are not: they are "off-Broadway" theatres. *Off-Broadway,* a term that came into theatrical parlance during the 1950s, refers to professional theatres operating on significantly reduced budgets. They are found primarily in Greenwich Village, with some in the area south of Houston Street (SoHo) and others on the upper East and West sides of Manhattan. A few houses in the Broadway geographic area itself actually fall into this category (American Place, Manhattan Theatre Club, New 42nd Street), but only because they operate under off-Broadway financing structures. Yet another category of theatre is known as

Above: The very popular TKTS booth in New York's Duffy Square (Broadway at 47th Street – the heart of the New York theatre district) sells unsold tickets at a 25 percent or 50 percent discount for most Broadway and off-Broadway shows on the afternoon of the performance only.

Right: The annual Antoinette Perry – or "Tony" – Awards honor the plays, performers, and designers who, in the views of their peers, have made the most outstanding contributions to the preceding Broadway season, and capturing such a prestigious honor – in front of a national television audience – can be one of the most exciting events in a theatre artist's life at any age. Cady Huffman here unashamedly exults as she claims the 2001 "Best Featured Actress in a Musical" Tony Award for her performance as Ulla in the gigantic Broadway success, *The Producers,* which won an all-time record twelve Tony Awards that season.

off-off-Broadway, a term dating from the 1960s that denotes semiprofessional or even amateur theatres located in the metropolitan area, often in church basements, YMCAs, coffeehouses, and converted studios or garages.

Off- and off-off-Broadway theatres generate a great deal of fertile and vigorous activity; leaner and less costly than the Broadway stage, they attract specialized cadres of devotees, some of whom would never allow themselves to be seen in a Broadway house. Much of the original creative work in the American theatre since World War II has been done in these theatres, and their generally low ticket prices, and in many cases subscription seasons, have lured successive generations of theatre audiences their way to see original works before they are showcased to the Broadway masses, works still raw with creative energy and radiating the excitement of their ongoing development. There are many New Yorkers who attend off- and off-off-Broadway theatre all the time — and would never dream of going to a Broadway show.

In composite, the New York theatre provides almost every conceivable opportunity for theatrical exploration and achievement, offering close to a thousand new productions each year. And thanks to coverage in the national media — weekly news magazines, monthly journals, television talk shows and specials, and the annual televising of the Tony Awards ceremonies — the New York theatrical season does not long remain a strictly local phenomenon; it becomes a focal point of American cultural activity, and, before long, the world is privy to its innovations, its successes, its radical ideas, its catastrophes, and its gossip.

The Nonprofit Professional Theatre

But the nonprofit (or, technically, "not-for-profit") professional theatre is where, for the last forty years or so, America's theatre has

been truly happening. The nonprofit theatre, often called the "regional" or "resident" theatre (because the theatres generally are in regions outside of New York, with resident staffs and at least some resident company members), is a phenomenon of the last third of the twentieth century, an outpouring of theatrical activity that at first diversified the American theatre and has since remade it.

Nonprofit means "non-commercial," not "non-professional." Nonprofit theatres are fully professional, but have funding sources other than the box office, including some mix of state or local grants, national foundation or corporate support, and private donations. But in return for having no owners and making no profits, the nonprofit theatre is exempt from most taxes, and its donors receive tax deductions for their support. In all other aspects, the theatres are professional in every sense, employing professional artists, sometimes year-round, at every level. There were no such theatres at the end of World War II, and only four — one each in Washington, Houston, San Francisco, and Minneapolis — by the mid-1960s. But there are well over four *hundred* today — many with multiple stages — and they exist in every major city in America, including New York. They produce over two thousand productions each year (which translates into tens of thousands of performances), providing Americans in every part of the country an opportunity to see professional theatre, often at its best.

Nonprofit theatres vary enormously in character: some concentrate on classics, some on the contemporary international repertoire, some on American classics, others on new plays. Some operate on tiny stages with tiny budgets, and although engaging professional artists, reduce their costs by negotiating salary waivers with the professional unions. Other theatres operate several stages simultaneously and are enormous operations: the New York Shakespeare Festival has an annual budget of more than $10 million and often has its pro-

Carrie Luft's *Goodbye Stranger* is "the episodic and slightly surreal story of Glad, a young person who tries to be good even though life in the city can feel so bad." This production, directed by Polly Noonan at the Steppenwolf Theatre in 1998, was aimed at reaching audiences from every stratum of Chicago society.

ductions running in many parts of the city. Among America's best-known regional theatres — and web connections at the back of this chapter can connect you to many more of them — are these in the following nine cities.

BOSTON   The American Repertory Theatre, actually in Cambridge, was founded by Robert Brustein in 1980. The ART has been one of America's most experimental companies since its founding and has been known particularly for giving free rein to many of the most creative directors working in the United States, including Andrei Serban, Peter Sellars, Adrian Hall, Jonathan Miller, Anne Bogart, Susan Sontag, Des McAnuff, JoAnne Akalaitis, and Robert Wilson.

CHICAGO   With as many as two hundred theatre companies, a thriving "loop" theatre district (six major theatres within five blocks in the heart of downtown), seven half-price ticket booths, 1,400 professional actors, and at least a score of nationally distinguished directors and playwrights, Chicago rightfully stands as America's "second city" for theatrical culture. Chicago has been the breeding ground for literally hundreds of bright and creative American actors and directors, including Alan Arkin, Gilda Radner, Dan Aykroyd, Alan Alda, Mike Nichols, and Elaine May (all former members of the famed "Second City" improvisational troupe) and the more recent Dennis Franz, Joe Mantegna, David Schwimmer, John Mahoney, John Malkovich, Gary

Athol Fugard is South Africa's most internationally prominent playwright, having both chronicled and participated in his country's agonizing struggle against apartheid since the very early 1960s. In his more recent, postapartheid, plays, Fugard (who is white) has wrestled with the profoundly complex issues of racial assimilation. Here, in his beautiful and sad *Valley Song*, Fugard plays two roles: "the author," namely himself (shown here), and a mixed-race tenant farmer named Buks; LisaGay Hamilton (also shown here) plays Buks's granddaughter, who plans to move from the family's Karoo desert farm to start a singing career in Johannesburg. What will happen to her? and to Buks? and to author Fugard? and to South Africa? Fugard makes us focus on the smallest detail and the largest implication. This photograph comes from the 1997 production directed by Fugard himself at the Mark Taper Forum in Los Angeles.

Sinese, and Joan Allen. Chicago is also the home (and setting) for plays by David Mamet and dramatizations by Mary Zimmerman (see earlier discussion) and Frank Galati. The Goodman Theatre, now in sparkling new quarters, is Chicago's oldest and largest nonprofit company and is known for its production of new plays, particularly Mamet's, while the Steppenwolf is known for intense naturalistic acting and for pioneering what is frequently called a "Chicago style" of fervently emotional performances. With many smaller distinguished theatres as well (one of which, Victory Gardens, won the 2001 Tony Award for outstanding regional theatre), Chicago has now become a "destination town" for theatregoers from all over the Midwest and beyond.

LOS ANGELES   The Mark Taper Forum was founded in 1967 by Gordon Davidson, who continues to serve as its artistic director. The Taper is distinguished primarily for its production of new American plays, many of which have subsequently received national recognition: George C. Wolfe's *Jelly's Last Jam*, Tony Kushner's *Angels in America*, Robert Schenkkan's *The Kentucky Cycle*, Mark Medoff's *Children of a Lesser God*, Luis Valdez's *Zoot Suit*, Marsha Norman's *Getting Out*, Michael Christopher's *The Shadow Box*, and Daniel Berrigan's *The Trial of the Catonsville Nine* had either their premieres or major developmental productions at the Taper. These works constitute a remarkable diversity of authorial interests and backgrounds. Forty-five miles south of Los Angeles,

South Coast Repertory vies for attention with its only slightly older rival. Founded by David Emmes and Martin Benson, who remain as the company's artistic codirectors, SCR's success has been built on excellent productions and a superb knack at finding (and commissioning) outstanding new plays, including Craig Lucas's *Prelude to a Kiss,* David Henry Hwang's *Golden Child,* Richard Greenberg's *Three Days of Rain,* Margaret Edson's *Wit,* and Amy Freed's *Freedomland* and, in 2001, *The Beard of Avon.*

LOUISVILLE   The Actors Theatre of Louisville, under the guidance of longtime artistic director Jon Jory (who, however, retired from ATL in 2000), has achieved a fine reputation both for a "Classics in Context" series and, even more significantly, for its annual Humana New Play Festival, in which five to ten new plays are produced simultaneously, attracting a large audience of theatre critics from around the country. Many of these plays, including *The Gin Game, Getting Out, Crimes of the Heart, Agnes of God, Extremities, Talking With, Marisol,* and *Execution of Justice,* have enjoyed long subsequent lifetimes in the national American repertory.

MINNEAPOLIS   The Guthrie Theatre was founded by the celebrated English director Tyrone Guthrie in 1963 and, with a continuing series of distinguished artistic directors, has maintained the highest artistic and creative standards in staging world theatre classics from all periods in the heart of America's Midwest.

African American playwright Suzan-Lori Parks won a slot at the 1992 Humana New Play Festival at the Actors Theatre of Louisville, where her *Devotees in the Garden of Love* was well received. Shown here are the actors Esther Scott (*left*) and Margarette Robinson.

NEW HAVEN   The Long Wharf Theatre has become widely known for its fine, sensitive productions — sometimes with stellar actors such as Al Pacino — of mid-twentieth-century American and English classics, several of which moved to nearby New York. Playwright Arthur Miller chose the Long Wharf for the premiere of his 1994 play *Broken Glass*. And the nearby Yale Repertory Theatre has also proven nationally influential, particularly when Lloyd Richards held the artistic leadership and the YRT became the first American presenter of several plays by South African Athol Fugard (*A Lesson from Aloes, Master Harold . . . And the Boys, The Road to Mecca*), Nigerian Wole Soyinka (*A Play of Giants*), and American August Wilson (*Ma Rainey's Black Bottom, Fences, The Piano Lesson, Joe Turner's Come and Gone,* and *Two Trains Running*).

NEW YORK CITY   The New York Shakespeare Festival was founded by Joseph Papp in 1954 with the goal of presenting free Shakespeare productions on trestles in Central Park. By the time Papp died in 1991, the company had a permanent theatre (the Delacorte) in the park plus six performance spaces in its downtown New York Public Theatre. The NYSF has also mounted full-scale Broadway productions, including *A Chorus Line, The Pirates of Penzance, Macbeth, Bring in 'Da Noise, Bring in 'Da Funk,* and, most recently, *On the Town*.

There are more than fifty other not-for-profit theatres in New York City. The Manhattan Theatre Club, which has been under the artistic directorship of Lynne Meadow since 1972, is one of the foremost. Under Meadow, MTC has regularly presented major new works by Terrence McNally (*Love! Valour! Compassion!, A Perfect Ganesh*), Beth Henley (*Crimes of the Heart, Miss Firecracker Contest*), Athol Fugard (*The Blood Knot*), Donald Margulies (*Sight Unseen, Collected Stories*), Arthur Miller (*The Last Yankee*), and Richard Greenberg (*Eastern Standard*), while more recently David Auburn's *Proof* won the 2001 Pulitzer Prize; indeed, MTC productions have among them won, as

of 2002, ten Tony Awards and three Pulitzer Prizes. The Lincoln Center Theatre Company is also a not-for-profit operation; it has premiered major plays by John Guare, Wendy Wasserstein, John Robin Baitz, and Richard Nelson, as well as lavish musical theatre revivals and an annual international summer theatre festival. The Wooster Group and the La Mama Theatre, on the other hand, are among many veteran New York theatres that specialize in highly experimental new plays, both American and foreign, and reinvestigations of older classics.

SEATTLE   With seven professional companies, Seattle is arguably the most exciting theatre city on the West Coast. Its major stages include the Seattle Repertory Theatre, which premiered the Broadway-bound productions of Wendy Wasserstein's *The Heidi Chronicles* and *The Sisters Rosensweig* as well as Herb Gardner's *Conversations with My Father*; the Intiman, which initially premiered Schenkkan's *The Kentucky Cycle*; and the more avant-garde Empty Space and ACT Theatre (formerly A Contemporary Theatre). Scoring an international coup, Seattle's four major theatres collaborated to present — in a sports arena — the first American showing of Peter Brook's *Hamlet* (see earlier discussion) in 2001.

WASHINGTON, D.C.   The Arena Stage, founded in 1950 and one of America's oldest and most distinguished, owes its name to the shape of the original stage, in which the audience surrounds the actors. Now several times removed from its original location, and augmented by more conventional staging configurations, Washington's Arena is increasingly dedicated to echoing the racial and ethnic mix of its city, emphasizing its "long-standing commitment to encourage participation by people of color in every aspect of the theatre's life."

But there are hundreds of theatre towns in the United States. The American nonprofit professional theatre, which was a "movement" during the 1960s and 70s, has become, quite simply, America's national theatre: it is the theatre where the vast majority of America's plays are first shaped and first exposed. More and more, the American national press is attuned to major theatre happenings in the nonprofit sector; more and more the Broadway audience, while admiring the latest "hit," is aware that they are seeing that hit's second, third, or fourth production. National theatre prizes like the Pulitzer, once awarded only for New York productions, are now seized by theatres around the country; world-renowned actors, once seen live only on the Broadway stages and on tour, are appearing in the country's more than four hundred nonprofit theatres in the fifty states. Most important: for the first time in America's history, the vast majority of Americans can see first-class professional theatre created in or near their hometowns, and professional theatre artists can live in any major city in the country — not only in New York.

Shakespeare Festivals

In Broadway's midcentury heyday there was also *summer stock,* a network of theatres, mainly located in resort areas throughout the mountains of the Northeast, that provided summer entertainment for tourists and assorted local folks. This "straw-hat circuit," as it was called, produced recent and not-so-recent Broadway shows, mainly comedies, with a mix of professional theatre artists from New York and young theatrical hopefuls from around the country; it was both America's vacation theatre and professional training ground.

Summer stock is mostly gone today, but in its place has arisen another phenomenon that, like summer stock, is unique to the United States. This is the vast array of Shakespeare festivals, begun during the Great Depression and now flourishing in almost every state in the nation. The Oregon Shakespeare Festival, in rural Ashland, is the much-heralded (and Tony Award–winning) grandparent of this

movement. Founded by local drama teacher Angus Bowmer, whose three-night amateur production of *The Merchant of Venice* in 1935 was preceded by an afternoon boxing match "to draw the crowds," the OSF, which immediately discovered that Shakespeare outdrew the pugilists, now produces (under Libby Appel, who became artistic director in 1996) 750 fully professional performances of 11 plays (and a free, outdoor "green show") each year, attracting 350,000 spectators during a 10-month season — all in a town of less than 20,000 people! There are over a hundred other North American Shakespeare festivals, many of which are largely or partially professional; particularly notable are the Stratford Festival in Canada, the Utah Shakespearean Festival (also Tony Award–winning), and the Alabama, New Jersey, California, Colorado, Illinois, Santa Cruz (California), and New York Shakespeare festivals. Characteristic of all of these operations is a core of two to four Shakespearean productions, normally performed outdoors, together with more contemporary plays, often performed on adjacent indoor stages: a setup resembling that of Shakespeare's original company, the King's Men, which, by the end of his career, was performing plays of many authors at both the outdoor Globe and the indoor Blackfriars.

In addition to providing exciting classical (and sometimes contemporary) theatre to audiences around the nation, often in rural areas and always at reasonable prices, Shakespeare festivals provide a wonderful bridge, for aspiring performers and designers, from college or community training to actual professional employment. And more than the old summer stock, the festivals offer opportunities to work in an ambitious theatre repertory as well.

Summer and Dinner Theatres

There remain some notable professional summer theatres without the word *Shakespeare* in their names. The Williamstown Theatre Festival in Massachusetts is probably the best of these, employing many of New York's better-known actors, designers, and directors, eager to leave the stifling city in July and August to spend a month or two in this beautiful Berkshire village, where they may play Chekhov (for which the theatre is justly famous), Brecht, O'Neill, and Williams in elegantly mounted productions. The Berkshire Theatre Festival in Stockbridge, Massachusetts, is also a highly accomplished professional summer theatre, located in a culturally rich area just two hours north of New York, where, in the afternoons, visitors can also drop in at Tanglewood to see the Boston Symphony Orchestra rehearsing in their shirtsleeves.

Dinner theatres were introduced to suburban America in the 1970s, offering a "night-on-the-town" package of dinner and a play in the same facility. Their novelty has worn thin, however, and only a few remain, generally offering light comedies, mystery melodramas, and pared-down productions of golden-age Broadway musicals. Never high in its artistic aspirations (the format virtually excludes adventurous dramaturgy, challenging themes, or even elaborate staging), dinner theatre nevertheless has played a role in bringing theatre to those otherwise unacquainted with it and in providing employment (and certainly performance experience) to hundreds of theatre artists each year.

Amateur Theatre: Academic and Community

Finally, there is an active amateur theatre in America, some of which operates in conjunction with educational programs. More than one thousand U.S. colleges and universities have drama (or theatre) departments offering degrees in theatre arts, and another thousand collegiate institutions put on plays, or give classes in drama, without having a full curriculum of studies. And several thousand high schools, summer camps, and private schools teach drama and mount plays as well. Much of this dramatic activity is directed toward general education, as the staging of plays has been pursued at least since the Renaissance as an excellent way to explore dramatic literature, human behavior, and cultural history, as well as to teach skills such as public speaking, self-presentation, and foreign languages. Practical instruction in drama has the virtue of making the world's greatest literature physical and emotional; it gets drama not only into the mind, but into the muscles — and into the heart and loins as well. Some of the world's great theatre has, in fact, emerged from just such academic activity. Four or five "University Wits" dominated Elizabethan playwriting before Shakespeare arrived on the scene, and Shakespeare's company competed with publicly presented school plays that had become popular in London (such plays "are now the fashion," says a character in *Hamlet*) during his career. Several plays that changed theatre history — such as Alfred Jarry's *Ubu Roi*, Tom Stoppard's *Rosencrantz and Guildenstern Are Dead*, and Arthur Kopit's *Oh Dad, Poor Dad* . . . — were first conceived as extracurricular college projects.

The founding of the Yale Drama Department (now the Yale School of Drama) in 1923 signaled an expanded commitment on the part of American higher education: to assume not merely the role of theatre educator and producer, but also that of theatre trainer. Today, the vast majority of American professional theatre artists receive their training in American college and university departments devoted, in whole or in part, to that purpose. As a result, academic and professional theatres have grown closer together, with many artists working interchangeably in both kinds of institutions. For this reason, the performances at many university theatres may reach sophisticated levels of excellence and, on occasion, equal or surpass professional productions of the same dramatic material.

Community theatres are amateur groups that put on plays for their own enjoyment and

Above: This University of California at Irvine production of Shakespeare's *As You Like It* featured giant (and bleating!) yellow balls that represent sheep in the pastures of Arden. The set designer was Douglas-Scott Goheen.

Right: Universities often produce new dramas as well as classics and revivals. Here the University of California at Irvine stages *The Prince,* a new play about Niccolò Machiavelli, with Joe Osheroff (*seated*) as Machiavelli and Jeff Takacs as Cesare Borgia.

for the entertainment or edification of their community. There are occasions when these theatres, too, reach levels of excellence; some community theatres are gifted with substantial funding, handsome facilities, and large subscription audiences; some (Theatre Virginia in Richmond and the Laguna Playhouse in California are examples) become professional. One should always remember that many of the greatest companies in the theatre's history, including Konstantin Stanislavsky's Moscow Art Theatre and André Antoine's Parisian Théâtre Libre, began, essentially, as amateur community theatres. One should also remember that the word *amateur* means "lover" and that the artist who creates theatre out of love rather than commercial expedience may in fact be headed for the highest, not lowest, levels of art. Community theatre has, then, a noble calling: it is the theatre a community makes out of itself and for itself, and it can therefore tell us a lot about who we are and what we want.

International Theatre

One of the greatest movements in current theatre is its growing internationalism; few spectator experiences are as challenging and fascinating as seeing plays from a culture — and a country — other than your own.

International theatre festivals are common abroad: there are now major such festivals in Avignon, France; Edinburgh, Scotland; Spoleto, Italy; Tampere, Finland; Amsterdam, Holland; Ibeza, Spain; Berlin, Germany; Toga, Japan; Adelaide, Australia; Curitiba, Brazil; and the city-state of Singapore. North America has been relatively slow to respond, but there is now a major international festival at Lincoln Center in New York every summer, and there have been successful international festivals in Baltimore, Denver, Chicago, Montreal, and Los Angeles over the years as well, often with audio translations (by earphones) or supertitles above the stage. A distinguished organi-

zation — the International Theatre Institute (www.iti-worldwide.org) — has been the coordinating overseer of much of this activity and can provide current information. It is possible that nothing could prove more valuable for the world today than global theatre exchanges, for drama's capacity to serve as a vehicle for international communication — a communication that goes beyond mere rhetoric — is one of its greatest potential gifts to humanity. Drama, in performance, can transcend ideologies, making antagonists into partners and strangers into friends. As theatre once served to unite the thirteen tribes of ancient Greece, so it may serve in the coming decades to unite a world too often fractured by prejudice and divided by ignorance. The theatre's greatest virtue is to explore the fullest potential of humankind and to lay before us all the universality of the worldwide human experience: human hopes, fears, feelings, and compassion for the living. Nothing could be more vital in the establishment of true world peace than a shared, cross-cultural awareness of what it means to be human on this planet.

A trip to an international drama festival, either in the United States or abroad, is the best way to sample the theatres of several other countries, but in truth nothing can match a theatre tour abroad, whereby the adventurous theatregoer can see not only the dramatic productivity of a given culture but also the "theatre scene" in its own local setting. Each year millions of Americans find a way to go to London for this purpose; indeed, Americans often comprise up to a third of the theatre audiences at mainstream London productions, which, in addition to classics and musicals, may in any given year feature new works by such celebrated current English dramatists as Tom Stoppard, Edward Bond, Harold Pinter, Mark Ravenhill, Patrick Marber, Simon Gray, Alan Ayckbourn, Pam Gems, David Hare, Caryl Churchill, or Peter Shaffer. Highlighting England's theatre scene is the Royal National Theatre, operating three stages in a large complex

London's Leicester (pronounced "Lester") Square has two half-price ticket booths – an "official" one in the square itself and this commercial one on a side street, which does twice the business. Ticket prices are in British pounds.

on the south side of the Thames; the nearby Globe — a replica of Shakespeare's original playhouse — which offers Shakespearean-era drama during the summers; and the more commercial "West End" theatre district, on and around Shaftesbury Avenue, comparable to New York's Broadway in its mix of musicals, dramas, and the occasional classical revival. There is also a London "fringe" of smaller theatres, roughly comparable to off-Broadway, which is often where the most exciting action is, particularly at the always-adventurous Almeida Theatre, Donmar Warehouse, and Royal Court. Also often in London, though no longer on a regular basis, is the legendary and ambitious Royal Shakespeare Company, which you are more likely to catch at its home base in Shakespeare's birthplace, Stratford-

upon-Avon, only a little more than an hour's train ride away. Tickets in London are somewhat cheaper than in New York, and an official half-price, day-of-performance ticket office, comparable to New York's TKTS booth, can be found in the small park centering Leicester (pronounced "Lester") Square, with several commercial discount booths (though with higher prices) right nearby.

The international theatregoer can also travel to other English-speaking dramatic centers. Ireland has provided a vast repertoire to the stage since the seventeenth century; indeed, most of the great "English" dramatists of the eighteenth and nineteenth centuries — George Farquhar, Oliver Goldsmith, Richard Sheridan, Oscar Wilde, and George Bernard

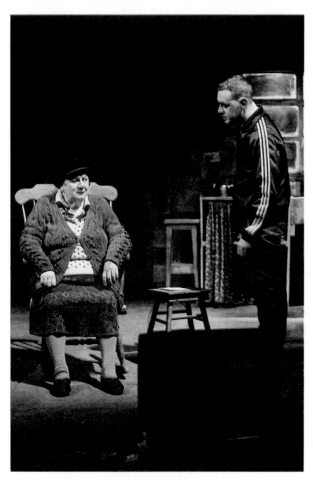

English/Irish Martin McDonagh electrified New York with two hit plays in 1998, one of which, *The Beauty Queen of Leenane,* won the best-play Tony Award. *The Beauty Queen* tells the gruesome and tragic story of an aging mother (played here by also-Tony-winning Anna Manahan) who cruelly dominates not only her daughter but any man who comes into her life. The production was created by the Druid Theatre Company of Ireland and directed by Garry Hynes. Francis O'Connor designed the set and costumes.

Shaw — were in fact Irish. In the twentieth century, a truly Irish drama became immensely popular under the hands of William Butler Yeats, Sean O'Casey, and Brendan Behan. But possibly no period of Irish drama is as rich as the current one, which includes major established playwrights such as Brian Friel (*Phila-*

delphia, Here I Come; Translations; Dancing at Lughnasa) and newer ones such as Sebastian Barry (*The Steward of Christendom, Our Lady of Sligo*) and English/Irish Martin McDonagh (*The Beauty Queen of Leenane, The Cripple of Inishmaan*). The production of these works, issuing from theatres as abundantly active as the Gate Theatre of Dublin and the Druid Theatre of Galway, foretells a brilliant future for Irish theatre.

Plays have been staged in Canada since the beginning of the seventeenth century. Today, theatre flourishes in every Canadian province. Toronto alone claims 200 professional theatre companies and is now, after London and New York, the largest theatre metropolis in the English-speaking world. With its celebrated dramatists David French (writing in English) and Michael Trombley (in French), its internationally prominent Stratford Festival Theatre in Ontario, Shaw Festival at Niagara-on-the-Lake, and Théâtre du Nouveau Monde in Montreal, plus a strong network of repertory companies and avant-garde groups throughout the provinces, Canada today enjoys a virtual flood of new Canadian playwrights, directors, and theatre critics who are developing global reputations.

Half a world away, another former British colony, Australia, has a fine theatrical tradition and a lively contemporary scene. Established playwrights David Williamson and Louis Nowra, now supplemented by a host of younger writers, flourish in both standard repertory and offbeat, alternative theatres in Melbourne, Sydney, and Brisbane, as well as Australia's great biennial Adelaide Arts Festival.

Nor is English playwriting limited to Europe and North America. The Market Theatre of Johannesburg, South Africa, has won its reputation not only for the outstanding quality of its productions but also for its courageous and effective confrontation of that country's now-concluded policy of apartheid; its most notable productions include Athol Fugard's *Sizwe Banzi Is Dead, The Island, Master Harold . . . And the*

Boys, A Lesson from Aloes, Valley Song, My Children! My Africa!, and *Playland.* Since the demise of apartheid, Fugard has written two plays dealing with his continuing struggles to reconcile contemporary Africa with its roots: *Valley Song* (1996) and *The Captain's Tiger* (1998). Fugard's plays, along with those of Mbongeni Ngema (*Woza Albert* and *Asinamali!*), toured internationally during the 1980s and 90s and were crucial in shaping world opinion on these vital South African (but universal) issues.

And, though you won't be likely to see his works in his native country, Nobel laureate Wole Soyinka, of tormented Nigeria, has played an equally important role in the politics and theatre art of his country and the international scene. Jailed for his radical political activity, Soyinka has helped shape his country's destiny since the mid-1960s with plays that both reexamine his country's colonial past (*Death and the King's Horseman*) and savagely parody postindependence African tyranny and corruption (*Opera Wonyosi* and *A Play of Giants,*

in which African dictators are portrayed as dim-witted clowns). Soyinka's 1995 play, *The Beatification of Area Boy,* portrays the homeless squatters and corrupt government officials of present-day Lagos. Such protest does not come without enormous risk, however, and Soyinka has been forced into political exile in the United States.

And for those able to manage a foreign language, theatres in France and Germany — the countries that spawned the theatre of the absurd and the theatre of alienation, respectively — are immensely rewarding theatre destinations, each country providing an outstanding mix of traditional and original theatre, though rarely in English. French and German theatre, along with that of most European countries, also enjoys strong government support, which keeps ticket prices at a fraction of what they are in the United States and England. France has five fully supported national theatres, four of them — including the historic Comédie Française, founded in

Like her other plays, *Art* and *Life × Three,* Yasmina Reza's 1995 *The Unexpected Man* (*L'Homme du hasard*) explores interpersonal anguish in a social context; here, in a railroad car, a young woman finds herself awkwardly seated across from a celebrated novelist whom she admires. The play mostly consists of the characters' internal monologues. This photograph shows the original Parisian production, starring Françoise Fabian and Michel Aumont.

1680 out of the remains of Molière's company shortly after his death, and the Odeon, which is now a "theatre of nations" presenting plays from all over the world — in Paris, plus more than a dozen regional ones. Germany, where major dramatic activity is spread more broadly throughout the country (there is no recognized German cultural "capital" comparable to London or Paris), supports more than 150 theatres, and about 60 theatre

Left: New Latin American theatre is usually experimental and often intensely political. Here, in the 1998 Teatro Ubu (San José, Costa Rica) premiere of Argentinian-Quebecer Luis Thenon's *Los Conquistadores*, Maria Bonilla (director-actor at Costa Rica's National Theatre) kneels in anguish at the plight of her son, whom she discovers listed among citizens who mysteriously "disappeared" but were generally known to have been tortured and killed by official goon squads.

Below: Theatregoers study the billboards for upcoming performances at Tokyo's Kabuki-za theatre.

festivals, in just about every large city on the map.

We end this mini-travelogue with the reminder that only cultural insularity causes us to imagine ourselves as the center of the universe, as the true and legitimate heirs of those who invented theatre. The truth, however, is that theatre is happening throughout the world and in forms so diverse as to defy accounting or assimilation. Every component of theatre — from architecture to acting, from dramaturgy to directing — is in the process of change: theatre is always learning, rebelling from convention, building anew. The theatre's diversity is its very life, and change is the foremost of its vital signs. We must not think to pin it down but rather to seek it out, to produce it ourselves, and to participate in its growth.

Conclusions on the Current Theatre?

Can there be any conclusions concerning the current theatre? No, there cannot — simply because what is current is never concluded.

Above right: Although traditional dramatic forms dominate in most Asian countries, Western-style realism gained a foothold in the late nineteenth century and has grown steadily in popularity. This 1997 production of Raymond To's *Love in a Teahouse*, produced by the Hong Kong Repertory Theatre, was directed by Daniel S. P. Yang and starred the celebrated Hong Kong actress Lisa Wang Ming-chuan.

Below right: The Gesher ("Bridge") Theatre consists entirely of Russian theatre artists who have emigrated to Israel; the company performs internationally in both Hebrew and Russian, creating a unique intercultural political aesthetic. In this production of Joshua Sobol's *K'far*, or *Village*, set on the slopes of Mount Carmen (Palestine) during World War II, Israel Demidov plays Yossi, "the eternal child," encountering his schoolteacher (played by Vladimir Vorobyev) as he cycles to synagogue and the Jewish underground prepares to make their last stand against the approaching Germans. From the 1998 Lincoln Center (NYC) Festival performance.

The current theatre is in process; it is like a book we are just beginning to read. The plays and playwrights discussed in this chapter may not, in the end, be accorded significant positions in our era of theatre; even the movements they now seem to represent may prove minor and transitory. We are not in a position even to hazard guesses at this point. We can only take note of certain directions and look for clues as to where the future will lead us.

Meanwhile, the evidence plays nightly on the stages of the theatre worldwide. It is there to apprehend, to enjoy, to appreciate, and, finally, to be refined by opinion and encapsulated into critical theory and aesthetic categorization — if that is our wish. More than being a play, or a series of plays, or a spectrum of performances, the current theatre is a worldwide event, a communication between people and peoples that raises the level of human discourse and artistic appreciation wherever it takes place. The current theatre responds to the impulses of creativity and expression and to the demands of human contact and understanding. It synthesizes the impulses of authors and artists, actors and audiences, to foster a medium of focused interaction that incorporates the human experience and embodies each culture's aspirations and values. No final chapter can be written on this medium, no last analysis or concluding categorization. All that is certain is that the art, and the feeling, of theatrical life will endure.

11

The Critic

I t is eleven o'clock; the lights fade a final time, the curtain falls, the audience applauds, and the play is over. The actors go back to their dressing rooms, take off their makeup, and depart. The audience disperses into the night.

But the theatrical experience is not over; in important ways, it is just beginning. A play does not begin and end its life on a stage. A play begins in the mind of its creator, and its final repository is in the minds and memories of its audiences. The stage is simply a focal point where the transmission takes place — in the form of communication we know as theatrical performance.

After the performance is over, the play's impact remains. It is something to think about, talk about, fantasize about, and live with for hours, days, and years to come. Some plays we remember all our lives: plays whose characters are as indelible in our memories as the people in our personal lives, plays whose settings are more deeply experienced than were many of our childhood locales, and plays whose themes abide as major object lessons behind our decision making. Should we take up arms against a sea of troubles? Can we depend on the kindness of strangers? What's in a name? Shall we be as defiant as Prometheus? as determined as Oedipus? as passionate as Romeo? as accepting as Winnie? as noble as Hecuba? What is Hecuba to us, or we to Hecuba? We talk about these matters with our friends.

And we also talk about the production — about the acting, the costumes, the scenery, the sound effects. Were we convinced? impressed? moved? transported? changed? Did the production hold our attention throughout? Did our involvement with the action increase during the play, or did we feel a letdown after the intermission? Did we accept the actors as the characters they were playing, or were we uncomfortably aware that they were simply "acting" their parts rather than embodying their roles?

The formalization of postplay thinking and conversation is known as *dramatic criticism*. When it is formalized into writing it can take many forms: production reviews in newspapers or periodicals, essays about plays or play productions written as academic assignments, commentaries in theatre programs or theatre journals, magazine feature articles on theatre artists, and scholarly articles or books on dramatic literature, history, or theory. All of these and more fall under the category of dramatic criticism, which is nothing other than an informed, articulate, and communicative response to what the critic has seen in the theatre or read in the theatre's vast literature.

Critical Perspectives

What makes a play particularly successful? What gives a theatrical production significance and impact, and what makes it unforgettable? What should we be looking for when we read a play or see a dramatic production? We have, of course, complete freedom in making up our minds, for response, by definition, can never be dictated: the price of theatrical admission carries with it the privilege of thinking what we wish and responding as we will. But five perspectives can be particularly useful in helping us focus our response to any individual theatrical event. These perspectives relate to a play's social significance, its human or personal significance, its artistic quality, its theatrical expression, and its capacity to entertain.

A Play's Relation to Society

Theatre, as we have seen throughout this book, is always tied to its culture. Many theatres have

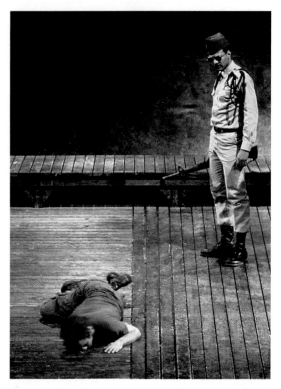

Realism, by "making real" the personal consequences of public policy, often develops a genuine political impact. American policy was certainly influenced during the Vietnam War by a series of realistic dramas portraying the human dimensions of the conflict, including this powerful 1972 production of Thomas Rabe's *The Basic Training of Pavlo Hummel* at the New York Public Theatre.

been directly created or sustained by governments and ruling elites: the Greek theatre of the fifth century B.C. was a creation of the state; the medieval theatre was generated by the church, the township, and the municipal craft guilds; and the Royal theatre was a direct extension of a monarchical reign. Even in modern times, government often serves as sponsor or cosponsor or silent benefactor of the theatre. But the intellectual ties between a theatre and its culture extend well beyond merely political concerns: thematically, the theatre has at one time or another served as an arena for the discussion of every social issue imaginable. In modern times, the theatre

THE INDOMITABLE THEATRE

There are places in the world where theatre has, at times, been made illegal, either for political or religious reasons. But the theatre's spirit has never been totally extinguished. The Puritan government of Oliver Cromwell outlawed all theatre in England in 1642 and burned down London's playhouses, but theatre was quickly restored after the Puritans fell from power in 1660. China abolished its ancient *xiqu* – apart from eight new plays strictly spouting the party line – during the Cultural Revolution in the 1960s and 70s, only to see this glorious traditional drama quickly return with the emergence of new leaders. And the Taliban government of Afghanistan outlawed theater when it assumed rule over that long-tortured country in 1995, punishing actors with beatings and imprisonment. By the time the Taliban was routed in 2001, Kabul's National Theatre was in ruins – its roof bombed into oblivion, its walls bullet-scarred or fallen, and its stage literally blasted away – yet the Afghan theatre quickly re-emerged with the advent of a new government in 2002.

At the National Theatre's reopening, a new play celebrated the country's renewal. "My compatriots, God is great. We're still alive, and peace will definitely come. God, please have mercy on us," cried actress Roya Naqibullah on the ruins of the Kabul stage. Several hundred Afghan men, women, and children – many of the women having shed their hated burqas in public for the first time in years – responded with wild applause, as reported by MSNBC's Yuka Tachibana. Theatre is a voice of freedom everywhere, but it is never so precious as in cultures where such freedoms have been suppressed.

In a performance at Kabul's National Theatre shortly following the country's 2001 liberation from Taliban rule, an actor portrays a Taliban soldier burning down that same theatre, which remains in a ruined state. Nineteen-year-old actress Roya Naqibullah, in white,

symbolizes Peace in this first post-Taliban performance to be presented in Kabul's National Theatre. "Watching this performance is like watching a flower bloom from beneath the ashes," said a former schoolteacher in the audience, as reported on MSNBC.

has approached from different perspectives such issues as alcoholism, homosexuality, venereal disease, prostitution, public education, racial prejudice, capital punishment, thought control, prison reform, character assassination, civil equality, political corruption, and military excess. The best of these productions have presented the issues in all of their complexity and have proffered solutions not as dogma but as food for thought — for great theatre has never sought to purvey pure propaganda.

The playwright is not necessarily brighter than the audience nor even better informed: he and his collaborators, however, may be able to focus public debate, stimulate dialogue, and turn public attention and compassion towards social injustices, inconsistencies, and irregularities. The theatre artist traditionally is something of a nonconformist; her point of view is generally to the left or right of the social mainstream, and her perspective is of necessity somewhat unusual. Therefore, the theatre is in a strong position to force and focus public confrontation with social issues, and at its best it succeeds in bringing the audience into touch with its own thoughts and feelings about those issues.

A Play's Relation to the Individual

The theatre is a highly personal art, in part because it stems from the unique (and often oblique) perspectives of the playwrights who initiate it and the theatre artists who execute it and in part because its audiences all through history have decreed that it be so.

The greatest plays transcend the social and political to confront the hopes, concerns, and conflicts faced by all humankind: personal identity, courage, compassion, fantasy versus practicality, kindness versus self-serving, love versus exploitation, and the inescapable problems of growing up and growing old, of wasting and dying. These are some of the basic themes of the finest of plays and of our own stray thoughts as well: the best plays simply link up with our deepest musings and help us to put our random ideas into some sort of order or philosophy. The theatre is a medium in which we invariably see reflections of ourselves, and in the theatre's best achievements those reflections lead to certain discoveries and evaluations concerning our own individual personalities and perplexities.

THE PEOPLE OF THE THEATRE MUST WIN

Theatre is not just another genre, one among many. It is the only genre in which, today and every day, now and always, living human beings address and speak to other human beings. Because of that, theatre is more than just the performance of stories or tales. It is a place for human encounter, a space for authentic human existence, above all the kind of existence that transcends itself in order to give an account of the world and of itself. It is a place of living, specific, inimitable conversation about society and its tragedies; about man, his love and anger and hatred. Theatre is a point at which the intellectual and spiritual life of the human community crystallizes.

… There is another war going on in Sarajevo besides the one we see on television. It is an unarmed conflict between those who hate and kill others only because they are different; and people of the theatre who bring the uniqueness of human beings alive and make dialogue possible. In this war, the people of the theatre must win. They are the ones who point towards the future as a peaceful conversation between all human beings and societies — about the mysteries of the world and of Being itself.

— Václav Havel
*playwright and president of the
Czech Republic, 1994*

A Play's Relation to Art

The theatre is an art of such distinctive form that even with the briefest exposure we can begin to develop certain aesthetic notions as to what that form should be. We quickly come to know — or think we know — honesty onstage, for without being experts we feel we can recognize false notes in acting, in playwriting, and even in design.

Beyond that, we can ask a number of questions of ourselves. Does the play excite our emotions? Does it stimulate the intellect? Does it surprise us? Does it thrill us? Does it seem complete and all of a piece? Are the characters credible? Are the actors convincing? en-

The Liberation of Skopje, by the Zagreb Theatre Company of Croatia, previewed the war and devastation that has since overwhelmed much of the Balkan Peninsula. Shown here is the 1995 World Theatre Festival production in Denver.

chanting? electrifying? Does the play seem alive or dead? Does it seem in any way original? Is it logically sound? Is the action purposeful, or is it gratuitous? Are we transported, or are we simply waiting for the final curtain? In the last analysis, does the play fit our idea of what a play should be — or, even better, does it force us, by its sheer luster and power, to rewrite our standards of theatre?

Aesthetic judgments of this sort are necessarily comparative, and they are subjective as well. What seems original to one member of the audience may be old hat to another; what seems an obvious gimmick to a veteran theatregoer can seem brilliantly innovative to a

less-jaded patron. None of this should intimidate us. An audience does not bring absolute standards into the theatre — and certainly such standards as it brings are not shared absolutely. The theatrical response is a composite of many individual reactions. But each of us has an aesthetic sensibility and an aesthetic response. We appreciate colors, sights, sounds, words, actions, behaviors, and people that please us. We appreciate constructions that seem to us balanced, harmonic, expressive, and assured. We appreciate designs, ideas, and performances that exceed our expectations, that reveal patterns and viewpoints we didn't know existed. We take great pleasure in sensing underlying structure: a symphony of ideas, a sturdy architecture of integrated style and action.

A Play's Relation to Theatre

As we've already discussed, plays are not simply things that happen *in* the theatre; they *are* theatre — which is to say that each play or play production redefines the theatre itself and makes us reconsider, at least to a certain extent, the value and possibilities of the theatre itself. In some cases the playwright makes this reconsideration mandatory, by dealing with theatrical matters in the play itself. Some plays are set in theatres where plays are going on (Luigi Pirandello's *Six Characters in Search of an Author,* Michael Frayn's *Noises Off,* Richard Nelson's *Two Shakespearean Actors*); other plays are about actors (Jean-Paul Sartre's *Kean*) or about dramatic characters (Tom Stoppard's *Rosencrantz and Guildenstern Are Dead*); still other plays contain plays within themselves (Anton Chekhov's *The Seagull,* William Shakespeare's *Hamlet*) or the rehearsals of such plays (Shakespeare's *A Midsummer Night's Dream,* Molière's *The Versailles Rehearsal,* Jean Anouilh's *The Rehearsal*).

We use the term *metatheatre,* or *metadrama,* to describe those plays that specifically refer back to themselves in this manner, but in fact all plays and play productions can be analyzed and evaluated on the way they use the theatrical format to best advantage and the way they make us rethink the nature of theatrical production. For all plays stand within the spectrum of a history of theatre and a history of theatrical convention (see Chapter 2). All plays and productions can be studied, often with illuminating results, from the perspective of how they adopt or reject prevailing theatrical conventions, how they fit into or deviate from prevailing dramatic genres, and how they echo various elements of past plays or productions — and what theatrical effects, good and bad, such historical resonances may have.

A Play as Entertainment

Finally, we look upon all theatre as entertainment. Great theatre is never less than pleasing. Even tragedy delights. People go to see *Hamlet* not for the purpose of self-flagellation or to wallow in despair but, rather, to revel in the tragic form and to experience the liberating catharsis of the play's murderous finale. Hamlet himself knows the thrill of staged tragedy:

HAMLET: What players are they?

ROSENCRANTZ: Even those you were wont to take such delight in, the tragedians . . .

What is this entertainment value that all plays possess? Most obviously the word *entertainment* suggests "amusement," and so we think immediately of the hilarity of comedy and farce; indeed, most of the literature regarding theatrical entertainment concentrates on the pratfalls and gags that have been part of the comic theatre throughout its history. But entertainment goes far beyond humor. Another definition for *entertainment* is "that which holds the attention." This definition casts more light on our question. It means that entertainment includes the enchantment of romance, which stimulates our curiosity about our own emotions and longings. It takes in the dazzle of brilliant debate, witty epigram, and biting repartee; the exotic appeal of the foreign and the grotesque; the beauty and grandeur of spectacle; the nuance and crescendo of a musical or rhythmic line. It accommodates suspense and adventure, the magic of sex appeal, and the splendor of sheer talent. Finally, of course, it includes any form of drama that profoundly stirs our feelings and heightens our awareness of the human condition. It is no wonder that Hamlet delights in the performance of tragedians — and that we delight in *Hamlet* — for the concatenation of ideas, language, poetry, feelings, and actions that constitute great tragedy confers one of life's sublime entertainment experiences.

Indeed, the theatre is a storehouse of pleasures, not only for the emotional, intellectual, spiritual, and aesthetic stimulation it provides but also for its intrinsic social excitement. It is a favored public meeting place for people who care about each other. "Two on the aisle" implies more than a choice seating location; it implies companionship in the best theatrical experience. For the theatre is a place to commune in an especially satisfying way with strangers. When in the course of a dramatic performance we are gripped by a staging of romantic passion or stunned by a brilliantly articulated argument or moved by a touching denouement, the thrill is enhanced a hundredfold by the certainty that we are not alone in these feelings, that possibly every member of the audience has been stirred to the same response. Theatre, in its essence, serves to rescue humankind from an intellectual and emotional aloneness; and therein lies its most profound "entertainment" value.

Critical Focus

These five perspectives on the theatre experience — on its social, personal, artistic, theatrical, and entertainment values — are all implicit in the responses of any audience, regardless of its training or theatrical sophistication. These are the five angles from which we view and judge plays — and judge them we do, for our involvement with a play naturally generates a series of comparisons: the play vis-à-vis other plays, the play vis-à-vis our personal experiences, the play vis-à-vis other things we might have done that evening. Judging plays and performances, which has been done formally since ancient Greek times and continues today through the well-publicized Tony and Obie Awards, Pulitzer Prizes, and Critics Circle citations, is one of the fundamental aspects of theatrical participation — and yet it is a participation open to amateur and professional alike.

A CRITIC'S TASTES

Somebody recently wrote one of my editors to the effect that I had no sense whatever of the tastes of my readers or the public at large. He was, unintentionally, paying me a great tribute which I can only hope I deserve. For it is extremely hard not to be influenced by the tastes of one's milieu; yet resisting them is precisely the critic's duty. It is only in being uncompromisingly himself that a critic performs a true service, and as a man of taste (not infallible taste, for there can be no such thing), goes down in history, or as a man of no taste, goes down the drain.

— John Simon

Professional Criticism

Professional criticism takes the basic form of production reviews and scholarly books and articles written, for the most part, by persons who specialize in this activity, often for an entire career.

Newspaper reviews of play productions are common throughout the theatre world; indeed, the box-office success of most theatres depends on receiving favorable press coverage. In the commercial Broadway theatre, favorable reviews — particularly from the influential *New York Times* — are all but absolutely necessary in order to guarantee a successful run. Where theatre audiences are generated by subscriptions and where institutional financing secures the production funds, newspaper reviews play a less-crucial, short-term role, but they still bear weightily in a theatre's ultimate success or failure.

In New York, newspaper reviews have traditionally been written immediately following the opening-night performance and are published the following morning; actors and producers gather after opening night at Sardi's restaurant, in the Broadway theatre district, awaiting the first edition of the next morning's *Times* to see how their show fared with the current critic. This is "instant criticism,"

Contrasting Reviews

Play reviewers have their individual styles; they also write for different audiences. Compare, for example, these two reviews — each by a celebrated veteran reviewer — of the 1992 New York premiere of Wendy Wasserstein's *The Sisters Rosensweig*. Mel Gussow, in the high-brow *New York Times*, provides a sensitive and balanced analysis of the text and production. Doug Watt, writing for the *Daily News*, a popular tabloid, gives a more succinct description that focuses on the play's entertainment values. Neither represents *the* way to write a review; each is responsive to the writer's interest and the expectations of his readers.

Wasserstein: Comedy, Character, Reflection

By Mel Gussow

"The Sisters Rosensweig" is Wendy Wasserstein's captivating look at three uncommon women and their quest for love, self-definition and fulfillment. Unified by their sisterhood, they are as different as only sisters (or brothers) can be, as each tries to live up to an image imposed by her family. At the same time, each performs her own act of rebellion — or is it penitence? Because of their disparities, they are heroines to one another.

Ms. Wasserstein's generous group portrait (at the Mitzi E. Newhouse Theater) is not only a comedy but also a play of character and shared reflection as the author confronts the question of why the sisters behave as they do. The immediate answer is that they are Rosensweigs and are only doing what is expected of them. The play offers sharp truths about what can divide relatives and what can draw them together.

The oldest sister is Sara (Jane Alexander), an overachiever, the only woman ever to head an international Hong Kong bank. She is an expatriate in England who is, we are told, "assimilated beyond her wildest dreams." Second is Gorgeous (Madeline Kahn), a triple threat as "housewife, mother and radio personality" in Newton, Mass. The youngest is Pfeni, née Penny (Frances McDormand), a globe-trotting journalist who lives her life as if she were on "an extended junior year abroad."

The three come together in London for Sara's 54th birthday. One of the show's surprises is that in a play essentially about women, the sisters are subtly upstaged by two of the men in their lives, characters enhanced in performance by Robert Klein and John Vickery.

The play is steeped in Jewish culture and humor, but the emotional subtext is broader. None of the sisters can find happiness; they have all been nurtured in a family in which heartbreak has been confused with heartburn. With effort, the women arrive at a new understanding. Bonding as siblings, they can anticipate a more promising future.

With Sara, additional hope comes from a most unlikely source: a wealthy New York furrier (Mr. Klein) who in politically correct parlance manufactures "synthetic animal protective covering." In dealing with social and cultural paradoxes, Ms. Wasserstein is, as always, the most astute of commentators. Along the way, she shatters the myth that Jewish men don't drink ("a myth made up by our mothers to persuade innocent women that Jewish men make superior husbands") as well as national patterns of speech (when an Englishman praises a stew as "brilliant," Mr. Klein adds, "the chicken was very bright, too"). But underlying the comedy is an empathetic concern for the characters and for the prospects of women today.

At the same time, the play has its imperfections. There are gratuitous remarks and irrelevancies. Both Ms. Wasserstein and her director, Daniel Sullivan, should have been more judicious in their editing, especially in dealing with the author's penchant for labeling characters and offering information in the guise of conversation. There is no need, for example, to keep saying that Sara is so intelligent; the character and the actress should speak for themselves. In addition, two stock characters represent the polarities of English society: an upper-class snob and a young radical with incredible gaps in his knowledge (and too many easy jokes made at his expense).

These flaws do not substantially detract from a play with wit as well as acumen. "The Sisters Rosensweig" grows naturally out of the author's previous work. With its Jewish themes and reference to a mother's strong influence on her adult daughters, it looks back to "Isn't It Romantic?" In contrast to the title character in "The Heidi Chronicles," each sister is focused on her life to an obsessive degree. But as with Heidi, each has difficulty with men. Those they meet seldom seem worthy of the Rosensweigs. It is in this area that the play is at its funniest and most observant, with Mr. Klein's faux furrier and Mr. Vickery as a flamboyant theater director. Both roles could lead actors into excess, but the pitfalls are assiduously avoided.

Acting as armchair counselor, the furrier sees through Sara's protective screen. As written, and as played by Mr. Klein, he is an unpretentious wise man who forces Sara to see herself as he sees her. Shrewdly, the actor plays the role straight, eradicating all thought of his background as a stand-up comic. Mr. Vickery's character is Pfeni's man of many moments, who is unable to commit himself either in love or in art. Evidently a serious man of the theater, he has made his reputation by staging an Andrew Lloyd Webber-like musical of "The Scarlet Pimpernel," from which we hear exuberant excerpts. Mr. Vickery is both dashing and self-mocking, winning laughs with looks and pauses as well as with Ms. Wasserstein's lines.

The women also rise above stereotype. As the expatriate, Ms. Alexander assumes an artful Englishness. Despite her admission of being humorless, she wryly observes her post-marital situation: because her second husband has been married so many times, his wives, past and present, could form a club with "branches in Chicago, New York, London and Tokyo." In the course of the play, Ms. Alexander reveals a vulnerability beneath the ladylike veneer.

For Ms. Kahn, Dr. Gorgeous (who advises everyone including her sisters) is the choicest of the roles. Restlessly changing her costumes and interrupting conversations, she is a delirious combination of extravagant plumage and native intuition.

Of the three, Pfeni is the most problematic, and the problem is in the character as well as the performance. Given Pfeni's eccentric life style, one would have imagined a more vivid, Auntie Mame-ish personality instead of someone overshadowed by her sisters and by her suitor.

Although Rex Robbins is miscast as the English snob, Patrick Fitzgerald manages to invest the young radical with a certain zeal; and Julie Dretzin, in her professional stage debut (as Ms. Alexander's daughter), easily holds her own with her more experienced colleagues. On John Lee Beatty's tasteful townhouse set, Mr. Sullivan leads the actors to play scenes for their reality rather than for their comic effect. As he did with his production of Herb Gardner's "Conversations With My Father," the director reveals his expertise in dealing with a Jewish milieu.

Overlooking the play is the symbolic figure of Anton Chekhov, smiling. Although the characters do not directly parallel those in "The Three Sisters," the comparison is intentional. The Rosensweigs have their own dreams of reclamation by romance, of escaping to a metaphorical Moscow. Ms. Wasserstein does not overstate the connection but uses it like background music while diverting her attention to other cultural matters, as in Mr. Vickery's statement that he would like to make a film entitled, "Three Days That Shook the Rosensweigs." For the two acts, the Rosensweigs (and friends) are entertaining company.

As the characters in Ms. Wasserstein's plays have become older, moving on from college to New York careers to the international setting of the current work, the author has remained keenly aware of the changes in her society and of the new roles that women play. In her writing, she continues to be reflexively in touch with her times. Drawing upon his strength as a nurturer of plays and playwrights, André Bishop has made an auspicious debut as artistic director of Lincoln Center Theater.

— The New York Times,
October 23, 1992

Wasserstein Pens a Pointed Drawing-Room Comedy

By Doug Watt

Here's a play that sparkles like the autumn air. "The Sisters Rosensweig," ideally in Lincoln Center's cozy Newhouse, finds author Wendy Wasserstein at the top of her game, or very near it.

A smart drawing-room comedy, it calls to mind Philip Barry, as filtered through S. N. Behrman.

The play, about upper middle-class Jewish manners, is set in the John Lee Beatty-designed London townhouse of the twice-married and divorced Sara Goode (Jane Alexander). It is her 54th birthday.

There to celebrate are her two sisters Pfeni (Frances McDormand), a travel writer in her 40s eager to wed and have children by the campy, bisexual Geoffrey (John Vickery), the British director of a splashy "Scarlet Pimpernel"; and Gorgeous, a Newton, Mass., wife and radio talk-show personality, the only halfway devout Jew of the three. It is a role in which Madeline Kahn is at her hilarious best.

The sexually repressed Sara, international rep of a Hong Kong bank, has a one-night affair (a somewhat quick quickie) with a drop-by American, Mervyn Kant (Robert Klein), a successful "furrier" dealing in synthetic animal outerwear. And in the end, the gabby, fluttery Gorgeous has a sad confession to make, after which the three sisters, Chekhovian only in their emotional losses, lovingly embrace to the strains of "Shine On, Harvest Moon."

The time is late August 1991, when the Soviet Union is breaking up.

Several supporting players, who include Sara's near-radicalized daughter, Tess (Julie Dretzin), drift through this warm, humorous, witty play — the author's most sustained piece of writing.

It is superbly directed by Daniel Sullivan.

— Daily News, October 30, 1992

CRITICAL PERVERSITY

The critical voice in its ever-changing moods sometimes effects reversals that seem exceptionally perverse. In an article titled "The Curious Case of *Time* and Tennessee Williams," *Esquire* magazine demonstrated the way in which *Time* continued to accord the celebrated playwright negative notices right up to the moment it chose to call him America's greatest living dramatic author.

> The play [*A Streetcar Named Desire*] could stand more discipline; along with an absence of formulas there is sometimes an absence of form. And it could stand more variety: only the clash between Blanche and Stanley . . . gets real emotion and drama into the play. — December 15, 1947

> *Summer and Smoke* . . . is all too plainly — but not too happily — by the author of *The Glass Menagerie* and *A Streetcar Named Desire*. What stamps, and sometimes rubber-stamps, it as his is the nature of the story and the style of the storytelling; far too often missing is the talent of the storyteller. — October 18, 1948

> [In] *The Rose Tattoo* . . . Williams has never seemed so blatantly himself. . . . Often the play . . . is lush, garish, operatic, decadently primitive, a salt breeze in a swamp, a Banana Truck Named Desire. — February 12, 1951

> *Camino Real* is perhaps excessively pessimistic in reaction against Williams' previous *Rose Tattoo*, with its factitious "affirmation." But very excessive it is — and not only excessively black, but excessively purple. *Camino Real* lacks philosophic or dramatic progression (on that score, it might claim the deadendedness of a wasteland), but it also lacks all discipline and measure, so that the wasteland becomes a swamp. What makes the play ultimately unacceptable is not that it is often dull and even more often arty, but that it exposes decadence with decadent means. — March 30, 1953

> [T]he play [*Cat on a Hot Tin Roof*], closing on a lame, stagy note, lacks stature. Perhaps there is a little too much of everything: Williams is not only lavish of suffering, but voluble in articulating it. There might well be less emotionalism and should certainly be fewer words, particularly profane ones: the profanity often seems to relieve Williams' own feelings rather than his characters'. But more important, *Cat* never quite defines itself as chiefly a play about a marriage, about a family, or about a man. . . . It needs sharper form, greater unity, a sense of something far more deeply interfused. — April 4, 1955

> Unhappily, Williams' story [*Garden District*] dies with his telling it, for though he weaves a spell he cannot validate a vision. It matters less that noisomely misanthropic symbols keep recurring in his work than that they nowhere seem purgative. — January 20, 1958

and the journalist who tackles these assignments has to be very fluid at articulating his or her immediate impressions. Outside of New York, newspaper critics frequently take two or three days to review a production, allowing themselves the luxury of considered opinions and more polished essays. Some New York newspaper critics have recently begun to emulate this practice; although their reviews are still published the day after opening night, they have actually attended a preview performance two or three days earlier and have had the opportunity to write their review at some leisure.

Still, the journalist's review must be limited to a brief, immediate reaction rather than to a detailed or exhaustive study. It provides a firsthand, audience-oriented response to the production, often vigorously and wittily expressed, and may serve as a useful consumer guide for the local theatregoing public. Writing skill rather than dramatic expertise is often the newspaper critic's principal job qualification, and at many smaller papers, staff reporters with little dramatic background are assigned to the theatre desk. But many fine newspaper critics throughout the years — New York's Walter Kerr and Boston's Elliot

In *Period of Adjustment,* which opened last week at Miami's Coconut Grove Playhouse, Playwright Tennessee Williams repaired no cracking masonry in his familiar dramatic neighborhood, but at least he slapped on a coat of whitewash. Billed as a "Serious Comedy," *Period* sounds more like a mad Gothic anecdote.   — January 12, 1959

Sweet Bird of Youth ... is very close to parody, but the wonder is that Williams should be so inept at imitating himself. The sex violence, the perfumed decay, the hacking domestic quarrels, the dirge of fear and self-pity, the characters who dangle in neurotic limbo — all are present — but only like so many dramatic dead cats on a cold tin roof.   — March 23, 1959

Many serious, liberal-minded intellectuals worry profoundly about the unattractive impression the U.S. often makes abroad, blaming everyone from unimaginative ambassadors to loud tourists with star-spangled sport shirts. But few would ever admit that some of their own heroes — for example, Playwright Tennessee Williams — can be the worst ambassadors of all. Last week two Williams plays, presented by a free-lance theatrical troupe called the New York Repertory Company (which claimed association with Manhattan's Actors Studio) had left a fairly indelible stain in Rio de Janeiro.   — September 1, 1961

Summer and Smoke. ... Playwright Tennessee Williams often writes like an arrested adolescent who disarmingly imagines that he will attain stature if (as short boys are advised in Dixie) he loads enough manure in his shoes. In his most famous plays, he has hallucinated a vast but specious pageant of depravity in which fantasies of incest, cannibalism, murder, rape, sodomy and drug addiction constitute the canon of reality.... Nevertheless, the film conspicuously possesses Playwright Williams' characteristic virtue: a pathetic-romantic atmosphere that lingers from scene to scene like an ineffable sachet of self-pity.   — December 1, 1961

The fact is that Tennessee Williams ... is a consummate master of theatre. His plays beat with the heart's blood of the drama: passion. He is the greatest U.S. playwright since Eugene O'Neill, and, barring the aged Sean O'Casey, the greatest living playwright anywhere.... Williams has peopled the U.S. stage with characters whose vibrantly durable presences stalk the corridors of a playgoer's memory: ... Williams' dialogue sings with a lilting eloquence far from the drab, disjunctive patterns of everyday talk. And for monologues, the theatre has not seen his like since the god of playwrights, William Shakespeare.   — March 9, 1962

Norton, for example — have proven extremely subtle and skillful at transcending the limitations of their particular profession and have written highly intelligent dramatic criticism that remains pertinent long after its consumer-oriented function has run its course.

More scholarly critics, writing without the deadlines or strict space restrictions of journalists, are able to analyze plays and productions within detailed, comprehensive, and rigorously researched critical contexts. They are therefore able to understand and evaluate, in a more complex way, the achievements of playwrights and theatre artists within any or all of the five perspectives we have discussed. Scholarly critics (and by *scholarly* we mean only "one who studies") seek to uncover hidden aspects of a play's structure, to analyze its deep relationships to social or philosophical issues, to probe its various meanings and dramatic possibilities, to define its place in cultural history, to amplify its resonance of earlier works of art, to shape its future theatrical presentations, and to theorize about larger issues of dramaturgy, art, and human understanding. Such criticism is itself a literary art, and the great examples of dramatic criticism have included brilliantly styled essays that have outlasted the theatrical works that were their presumed subjects: Aristotle, Goethe, Shaw, and Nietzsche are among the drama critics who, simply through their analyses of drama, have helped shape our vision of life itself.

The scholarly critic, ordinarily distinguished by her or his broad intellectual background and exhaustive research, writes with a comprehensive knowledge of the specific subject — a knowledge that includes the work of all important previous scholars who have studied the same materials. The professional scholar is not content to repeat the opinions or discoveries of others but seeks to make fresh insights from the body of literature (playtexts and productions, production records, previous scholarship) that constitutes the field of study.

Scholarly critics tend to work within accepted methodologies, which develop and change rapidly in contemporary academic life. Traditional methodologies include historical and biographical approaches ("the man and his work"), thematic and rhetorical analyses, studies of character and plot, examinations of staging and theatrical styles, and detailed exegeses of meaning, or *explication de texte*. More contemporary methodologies include systems and theories developed since the 1970s, particularly structuralist, semiotic, and deconstructive approaches; these bypass traditional questions of history, biography, character, theme, and meaning and focus instead on the internal relationships of various dramatic ingredients and their particular combination in a self-referential dramaturgic system. Contemporary methodologies, which draw heavily from the fields of philosophy, linguistics, anthropology, and critical theory, are intellectually demanding and difficult to master; they provide, however, stunning insights to those properly initiated.

Student Criticism

One does not expect of beginning theatre students a thoroughly comprehensive back-

---

> ## IS IT ART . . . OR TRASH?
>
> The theatre critic spends most of his time with trash. But the trash is as much a part of his subject as the non-trash. . . . Part of his function is to make sure that false messiahs and peddlers and charlatans are shown as such. Hope — non-delusionary, non-inflationary, non-self-aggrandizing hope — is the core of the critic's being: hope that good work will recurrently arrive, hope that (partly by identifying trash) he may help it to arrive, hope that he may have the excitement and privilege of helping to connect that good work with its audience.
>
> — Stanley Kauffman

ground in the subject; indeed, students writing class papers are likely to be looking seriously at the subject for the very first time. Naturally, different standards apply.

Such beginning students will characteristically analyze plays from any of the five perspectives cited earlier but without the need for a very sophisticated or advanced methodology. Some simple but effective methodologies, for writing both class essays and production reviews for local or school newspapers, are provided in the appendix to this book.

We Are the Critics

Whether we are professional writers, students, or just plain theatregoers, we are all the critics of the theatre. We the audience are a party to the theatrical experience, not a mere passive receptacle for its contrived effects. The theatre is a forum of communication, and communication demands mutual and active participation.

To be an *observant* critic, one need only go to the theatre with an open mind and sharply tuned senses. Unfettered thinking should be a part of every theatrical experience, and provocative discussion should be its aftermath.

To be an *informed* critic, one needs sufficient background to provide a context for opinion and evaluation. A play may be moving, but is it as moving as *The Three Sisters?* as passionate as *The Trojan Women?* as romantic as *Romeo and Juliet?* as funny as *The Bourgeois Gentleman?* as intriguing as *Happy Days?* An actor's voice may be thrillingly resonant, but how does it compare with the voice of Ian McKellen? If our opinions are to have weight and distinction, they may do so only against a background of knowledge and experience. If we are going to place a performance on a scale of one to ten, our friends (or readers) must know just what is our "one" and what is our "ten."

To be a *sensitive* critic, one must be receptive to life and to artistic experience. The most sensitive criticism comes from a compassionate approach to life, to humankind, and to artistic expression; this approach elicits and provokes a personalized response to dramatic works. Sensitive criticism admits the critic's needs: it begins from the view that life is difficult and problematical and that relationships are demanding. Sensitive critics are questing, not smug; humane, not self-absorbed; eternally eager for personal discovery and the opportunity to share it. They recognize that we are all groping in the dark, hoping to encounter helping hands along the way in the adventure of life — that this indeed is the hope of theatre artists too.

To be a *demanding* critic is to hold the theatre to the highest standards of which it is capable. For, paradoxically, in the theatre's capacity to entertain, to supply immediate gratification, lies the seed of its own destruction. As we have seen so often in the preceding pages, the theatre wants to be liked. It has tried from its very beginning to assimilate what is likable in the other arts. Almost scavenger-like, it has appropriated for itself in every era the most popular music and dance forms, the most trendy arguments, vocabularies, philosophies, and fashions in dress. In the process, alas, it often panders to tastelessness and propagates the meanest and most shallow values of its time. And here the drama critic in each

of us can play a crucial role. The very need of the theatre to please its patrons tends to beget a crass insecurity: a tendency to resort to simple sensationalism in exchange for immediate approval. Cogent, fair-minded, penetrating criticism keeps the theatre mindful of its own artistic ideals and its essential responsibility to communicate. It prevents the theatre from either selling out completely to the current whim or bolting the other way into a hopelessly abstract and arcane self-absorption.

To be an *articulate* critic is to express one's thoughts with precision, clarity, and grace. "I loved it" or "I hated it" is not criticism but rather a crude expression of opinion and a wholly general opinion at that. Articulation means the careful building of ideas through a presentation of evidence, logical argument, the use of helpful analogy and example, and a style of expression neither pedantically turgid nor idiosyncratically anarchic. Good criticism should be a pleasure to write, a pleasure to read; it should make us want to go deeper into the mysteries of the theatre and not suffocate us with the prejudices or egotistical displays of the critic.

In sum, the presence of a critical focus in the audience — observant, informed, sensitive, demanding, and articulate — keeps the theatre honest. It inspires the theatre to reach its highest goals. It ascribes importance to the theatrical act. It telegraphs the expectations of the audience to producer, playwright, director, and actor alike, saying, "We are out here, we are watching, we are listening, we are hoping, we care: we want your best — and then we want you to be better yet." The theatre needs such demands from its audience. The theatre and its audience need to be worthy coparticipants in a collective experience that enlarges life as well as art.

If we are to be critics of the theatre, then, we must be knowledgeable, fair, and open-minded; receptive to stimulation and excitement; open to wisdom and love. We must also admit that we have human needs.

In exchange, the theatre must enable us to see ourselves in the characters of the drama and in the performers of the theatre. We must see our situations in the situations of plays and our hopes and possibilities in the behavior staged before us. We must be drawn to understand the theatre from the *inside* and to participate in thought and emotion in a play's performance.

Thus do we become critics, audience, and participants in one. The theatre is then no longer simply a remote subject encountered in a book, or in a class, or in the entertainment columns of the world press; the theatre is part of us.

It is *our* theatre.

Appendix: Writing on Theatre

If you study theatre in an academic setting, sooner or later you may be required to write a critical paper on a play (or plays) that you read or see. The word *critical* is used here not in the everyday sense of "finding fault" but in the scholarly sense of "examining closely."

Writing such a paper is, of course, a test of your perception, but it is also much more than that: it is an opportunity to organize and focus your thoughts, to investigate drama with a specific purpose, and to communicate your considered opinion to someone else. The act of writing is an act of clarification, for the author as well as for the reader. You usually will learn much more by writing a paper than by reading one.

You will also remember the subject of your paper long after the course is over. The acts of researching a topic and organizing, clarifying, and writing up your ideas will make the subject an important part of your own life. And although you will ultimately "give" the paper to the instructor, the ideas in it will remain yours: they will represent your contribution to the literature of drama.

Your instructor will give you a specific assignment for your paper, often detailing its proper length and an acceptable range of topics. The instructor will also usually guide you on appropriate procedures, some of which may differ markedly from the suggestions that follow. Barring instructions to the contrary, however, the advice given here may serve as a general guide to writing an undergraduate paper.

Your Purpose

Your purpose in writing a paper is to *demonstrate* something to someone: to present a *clear* point of view about your topic that leads to some *conclusions*. "Demonstration" involves more than merely citing facts or opinions; it requires the arrangement of these facts and opinions in a careful and persuasive way. "Conclusions" are what the paper is finally all about. Your paper should end by persuading its readers that your point of view is, if not the definitive truth, at least worthy of further consideration. A coherent set of conclusions is usually called your paper's "thesis." "Clarity" is simply the quality of good writing, plus good rewriting. A clear paper requires a good structure and an uncluttered use of language. A good paper is clear; a fine paper is both clear and convincing; an excellent paper is clear, convincing, and original.

Your Audience

The actual readership of your paper is usually limited to your instructor (and perhaps a reader or teaching assistant). But you should remember that the assigned paper is an exercise, and, as with an acting exercise, you should write the paper as if the readership were a more general one, including the theatre students in your class, theatre students and teachers at other institutions, and theatre artists and theatre enthusiasts in and out of the academic world.

Your assumption of a general audience will prevent your paper from becoming merely a letter to the instructor. At the same time, the assumption that your audience already possesses a basic theatre background means that you can use theatrical terms and cite major dramatists without detailed preamble. Your readers already know what a proscenium is and who Anton Chekhov is; you don't have to define the former or identify the latter unless it serves your purpose to do so. You can also assume that your readership is interested in the basic subject: you do not have to "sell" the notion that drama is a worthwhile artistic form.

Your Working Method

Generally, the writing of a paper consists of seven steps: choosing a topic, limiting the topic, conducting research, developing a thesis, organizing the argument, writing the draft, and revising the draft. In practice, these steps do not always proceed neatly or in this order: the topic is often chosen during the research phase, and the thesis is developed (and refined) continually throughout the process.

Choosing Your Topic

Often, this is the single most difficult part of writing a paper; certainly it is the one most subject to procrastination and deferral. You have read or seen a play, but what then? What is there to say about it?

What you might not realize is that your reading or viewing of a play, even when shared with a class or an audience, is a unique experience. What you receive from a play is a combination of two things — the play and you. The uniqueness of either your reading or your viewing comes from your contribution to the experience: your social background, your personal preoccupations, your particular hopes and fears, your unique perspective on human behavior. Your individuality gives you a view of the play that no one else has. If you can

develop that view in an intelligent manner, you already have begun the search for a topic without knowing it.

In hunting for a topic, you might discuss a play that interests you with fellow students. How do they see the play differently than you? What do you see (or focus on) that they don't? What important aspect of the play have they missed? What has the instructor missed? What has the director of the play or the editor of the play anthology missed?

There are six general topic approaches that you should consider as well; most good papers fall into one of these:

1. *The contextual analysis.* This sort of paper analyzes one or more plays according to their historical, social, and/or philosophical context: for example, *Hamlet* as a Renaissance tragedy or *Happy Days* as a masterpiece of the twentieth-century avant-garde. Such essays are often seen as the introductory matter in play anthologies or as a director's or dramaturge's notes in production programs. Beware, however: this is ordinarily the *least* interesting sort of paper you can write, for unless the assignment is purely to create a "research paper" or unless you are particularly passionate about the specified context, you might try something a little more adventurous.

The contextual paper must be marked with thorough research, which includes at least one source of recent scholarship; be certain that you are at least aware of current thinking on your topic, even if you disagree with it. Also, try to focus the contextual approach toward some sort of conclusion and evaluation so that something is finally demonstrated: it is not very interesting to say that *Hamlet* is a Renaissance tragedy, which we already know; you might explore instead why that does (or doesn't) make *Hamlet* a fine play or why it does (or doesn't) make Hamlet revenge his father in act 5 rather than in act 3.

2. *The comparative analysis.* Comparisons are the most basic building blocks of learning: if you can understand similarities and differ-

ences at the deepest levels, you can discover untold fields of wisdom. It was Newton's comparison of the fall of an apple and the motions of the planets that led to the theory of gravity and its consequent application to rocket travel; it was Pasteur's comparison of the incidence of disease and the incidence of hygienic procedures that led to the discovery of bacterial infection and the development of rubber gloves. In the same way, the study of literature is basically the study of similarities (which define genres and styles) and differences (which define creative departures and imaginative leaps).

Comparative papers might demonstrate the similarities and differences between two or more plays or authors — or between one or more plays and a nondramatic idea. For example, you could compare plays by Tennessee Williams and Arthur Miller, or you could compare Aristophanes' attitudes toward war to the antiwar movement of ancient Athens.

The comparative paper is not, however, merely a mechanical listing of observed similarities and differences. Your comparison should point up possible influences, conscious or unconscious. It might also demonstrate how two compared plays were subject to the same influences. Mere coincidental similarities are of no importance — although if you probe deeply enough, you might find the coincidences are, in fact, not coincidences at all.

A comparison is worth investigating when you discover an interesting similarity. This can be as simple as recognizing that Williams and Miller are both midcentury American playwrights, that they both write a form of poetic realism, that they both have dealt with problems of modern urban life, that they both have written autobiographical plays dealing with themselves as young writers working in impersonal surroundings, and that they both had successful Broadway hits in the same decade. Or, more originally, perhaps you read Hamlet's

And you, my sinews, be not instant old,
But bear me stiffly up,

and it made you think of the line from *Henry V:*

Stiffen the sinews, summon up the blood.

What do stiff sinews have in common, and why did Shakespeare use the same expression in these two plays? Are there any other similarities between Prince Hamlet and King Henry? Entire books have been based on curious musings such as this.

3. *A problem investigation.* Often you will read or see a play and, while liking it, find yourself bothered by something. Perhaps the story seems faulty, the characters are unlikable, or you don't understand what the playwright was driving at. You ask one or two classmates, and they have the same problems with the play, although they, perhaps, are not as preoccupied with them as you. You may have found fertile ground for an investigation.

Why, for example, does Othello suspect Desdemona of unfaithfulness when there has not been time for her to be alone with Cassio? Some eighteenth-century critics dismissed *Othello* out of hand because of this and similar problems; it might bother you too. You could work on this problem itself, for although you would not be the first to do so, there is no definitive answer. But there are an infinite number of such problems in the world's dramatic literature to investigate; and although the answers are not, so to speak, in the back of the book (final answers don't exist for most literary problems), your work on the subject may prove illuminating for both you and what will be your readership.

Problem investigations provide good opportunities for research into specialized critical literature. A reference librarian can help you find articles on your topic and on related topics that will help guide you deeper into the subject.

4. *An observed peculiarity in a play.* "Tragedy in *Hamlet*" is not an intriguing title, but "Comedy in *Hamlet*" is. Everyone knows that *Hamlet* is a tragedy, but there is also a peculiarly heavy dose of comedy in the play, right up to the last act — unlike in *Macbeth, King Lear,* and

even *Romeo and Juliet,* where the comedy is limited to the first half of the play or so. Why is this? What does it do to the tragic conclusion of the play? Why might Shakespeare have written *Hamlet* this way? Was it a mistake? Why or why not?

5. *A confrontation with higher authority.* Ordinarily you will turn to critical literature for facts and for expert opinion on subjects that interest you, but there may also be times when you feel that experts, no matter how well recognized, are wrong in their opinions or evaluations. If you can back up an interesting though contrary point of view, you might have a chance at rewriting critical opinion. Of course this is a dangerous field; you will be matching wits with scholars of wide literary background and proven critical judgment. Still, in the final analysis, the best opinion will out, and it might very well be yours. All opinions are ultimately reversed, refined, or revoked anyway; there is no reason not to try to "set the matter straight."

A confrontational paper, if you have the heart for it, can elicit your most dedicated research, persuasive writing, and passionate attention to detail; it can also give you a confidence in your ideas unattainable simply by quoting learned authority. It is certainly worth a try — when in fact you find yourself in considered disagreement with a published expert.

6. *A discovered pattern.* Perhaps through a series of comparisons, contextual analyses, and investigations into observed problems you will discover some fundamental pattern in an author's writing (or in a director's direction or a designer's design). This is not usually the sort of thing one finds in an undergraduate paper — rather, it is more often the subject of a book-length doctoral dissertation — but it is the deepest goal of writing on the theatre or on any other scholarly subject. Discovering aesthetic or dramaturgical patterns in individual dramatic works not only makes clear the nature of the works considered but also throws light on the art of theatre itself. Such discoveries require, of course, a broad background

in theatre studies, plus a sustained intellectual investigation. Still, several such papers, on limited topics, are written by undergraduate students every year.

Limiting Your Topic

After making the initial choice of a topic, be careful to limit it to what you can realistically cover in the time allotted and what you can, in all good conscience, write about in the paper. To deal with more than one or two plays in a six-to-eight-page paper is probably a mistake; such a paper should have only one principal topic and no more than two or three subordinate ones.

Conducting Your Research

Having initially selected your topic (and remember, you will continually refine the topic as you work), reread everything that pertained to your having selected the topic in the first place, noting everything in your rereading that might be relevant to the topic you have chosen. If the material that generated the topic is a play you have seen, get a copy of the play. (If it is an unpublished play, go to the theatre office, explain your purpose, and see if you can borrow a script copy.)

Make notes any way you choose, but be sure they are easily retrievable. There are computer programs for collecting and arranging material like this; ordinary three-by-five-inch cards may also be used.

Understand your basic material in as much detail as possible. Look up words and references that you don't know, using historical dictionaries (such as the *Oxford English Dictionary*) and well-annotated editions (such as the Arden Shakespeare) when necessary to study the meanings of older words and obsolete allusions.

Then expand your reading to include material that might be related: some other play(s) by the same playwright(s), essays on the play(s) by the playwright(s), and essays on the play(s) and related subjects by scholars, critics, and editors. Get help from a reference librarian to ferret out pertinent books and essays that will help you probe deeper into your analysis, investigation, and/or comparison. Write down important facts and interesting and well-expressed opinions of others, being careful to record such opinions in their exact words, putting quotation marks around them. Such "citations" should be identified in your notes by their source (including the author, title of the book or article, facts of publication, and page reference) so that you don't have to hunt up that information all over again when writing your footnotes.

Research need not take place only in your school library, of course. There are specialized libraries containing theatre works, including one-of-a-kind production books and manuscripts. Using a search engine on the Internet (such as www.google.com) or accessing the Online Learning Center for *Theatre* at www.mhhe.com/cohen will lead you to an enormous amount of information on almost every subject imaginable — although because the Internet is unhosted and unedited, you will have to be very careful in determining the accuracy and relevance of what you find there. You may also wish to correspond with living authors, directors, designers, or actors if such communications could prove useful to your subject. Seeing one or more of the plays under consideration and talking about it afterward with the director or dramaturge could certainly prove an invaluable aid to your developing investigation.

Developing Your Thesis

Somewhere in this process — probably starting at the point when you selected the topic — you will be arriving at a conclusion about your research, in terms of both what it seems to indicate about the subject and why your conclusion might be important. Where does your research lead? What observations are you drawing from your study? Are the experts right? Have they missed something? Are they ignoring the most important part?

A thesis need not be earth-shattering (for example, "Shakespeare's plays were really written by Queen Elizabeth"), but it should have at least some element of surprise, some conclusion the average reader or viewer would not arrive at on his or her own. This will follow easily and naturally if you have responded to the play yourself, with your own unique set of attributes, and have not simply tried to "find" your thesis in existing essays.

Organizing Your Argument

All papers are organized in the form of an "argument" — a logical series of suppositions, elaborations, demonstrations, proofs, and conclusions that argue your position coherently, perhaps even convincingly. Some form of outline is usually helpful in creating this organization. Following is a sample outline, which includes some headings that are usually omitted from student papers (and are so identified) but which are fundamental to advanced critical writing:

I. Initial statement of the topic (problem, peculiarity, subjects of comparison)
   A. Major questions posed by topic
   B. Indications of why these questions have attracted your attention
II. General review of earlier scholarly attempts to deal with the topic (ordinarily omitted in an undergraduate paper)
III. General review of the limitation of these earlier scholarly attempts (ordinarily omitted in an undergraduate paper)
IV. Presentation of specific material to be critically considered
   A. Citations of primary materials (the texts considered)
   B. Citations of secondary analyses (historical sources, critical interpretations, reference materials)
V. Presentation of proofs and conclusions
VI. Final statement of thesis

This outline, bare-bones as it is, provides a starting point for arranging your paper and presenting your ideas as a structured argument rather than a random collection of unrelated notions that, however brilliant, can never lead to new discoveries. When the outline is done, you can rearrange your notes according to the outline's structure — which will be your paper's structure as well.

Writing Your First Draft

The first draft involves more than fleshing out the outline; it tests your ability to articulate, on paper, what is by now buzzing about in your head and organized in your outline.

Writing is a skill that you learn from the time you begin to speak. There are hundreds of ways of saying the same thing, each with its own slight variation:

These are the times that try men's souls.

These times are trying to men.

Men have a trying time of it these days.

Men's souls are sorely tried by modern times.

These are trying times to the soul of man.

And so forth. All of these sentences have probably been uttered at one time or another, but only Tom Paine's, the first one, has entered the history books.

No essay is going to teach you to be a good writer, but the more strongly you want to demonstrate something, the more cogently and persuasively you will write. Good writing is not an end in itself; good writing serves your argument, your thesis, your point of view. If you want to develop your writing, write essays (or letters) that explain to somebody else something that is important to you.

A well-written paper is always divided into paragraphs, each having its own central point — usually broached in the opening sentence, or "topic sentence." Look at the first sentence of the preceding paragraph. The remainder of the paragraph develops and explains the topic idea. When the author thinks the idea is satisfactorily expressed and communicated, the paragraph is brought to a close, often with a slight shift in tone that signals closure and gives the reader a little breathing space (such as "entered the history books," two paragraphs above).

Cite all quoted material inside quotation marks, *always,* and identify all quoted material by author and published source. This is important for two reasons: (1) you don't want to be accused of stealing another author's direct ideas, which is a serious academic crime (plagiarism), and (2) you want to direct the reader to the original author, who probably has more to say on the subject. Your instructor might have specific instructions on footnoting; if not, you can follow any of several standard formats, such as those used in any scholarly journal or textbook. Footnotes should always include page references — except for well-known classic plays from which lines can usually be cited, directly in the text of your paper, by act, scene, and line reference (an initial footnote should identify the edition used).

When should you cite an outside authority? There are basically four situations when this is useful: (1) when you want to establish a standard critical opinion that provides a background to your argument, (2) when you want to state facts you haven't directly uncovered yourself, (3) when you want to disagree with an outside authority, and (4) when you want to support your first steps toward your conclusion. It is in this last situation that you must be careful, because you cannot use an outside authority to state your conclusion or even to support your final finding. The final finding must be yours alone. Indeed, if your conclusion is the same as a leading critic's, then why should I read *your* essay?

Revising the Paper

Revising does *not* mean turning all the simple words into fancy ones or turning to the thesaurus. In fact, effective revising is not fancying up but paring down. Read each sentence — aloud if that helps — and ask yourself, Am I saying that as clearly as possible? Am I being persuasive, or am I just filling in blanks?

You should know that authors rewrite everything, and rewrite many times. Leo Tolstoy wrote out the 1,800 pages of *War and Peace* seven times — in longhand. (Actually, his wife did most of the writing out.) And he was a professional writer with great experience at the time. I've written this section five times — at least. So you mustn't be embarrassed to rewrite nor be so cocky as to think you've said things perfectly the first time around. "These times are sure trying for men's souls" — sounds okay, but don't you think you could make it better?

Some Final Thoughts

Writing a paper is a creative task, not a duty. (Answering essay questions on exams, by contrast, is pretty much a duty.) You choose the topic; you choose the method of investigation; and you dig into the material and into the relevant research field as deeply as time and inclination permit. Perspicacity, organizational skill, writing ability, and stick-to-it-iveness are all required, but so is imagination and originality. Fine papers explore new ground, and you can always be sure that if you really dig into yourself, as well as into the material at hand, you will be very much on that new ground. Nobody else could ever go precisely where you go — that is a fundamental principle. Consequently, the potential results for someone interested in pursuing scholarship are substantial. You really can uncover things yet unearthed by your instructors and the world of outside experts. Undergraduate essays, particularly those that thoroughly and creatively address specific comparisons, problems, patterns, or peculiarities, are published in scholarly literature each year; this author's writing career began with just such an undergraduate paper. And, apart from publication, the excitement of treading where no scholar or critic has ever trod before may prove to be one of the highlights of your many years of higher education.

Glossary

Terms within the definitions that are themselves defined in this glossary are in *italic*.

absurd The notion that the world is meaningless, derived from an essay, "The Myth of Sisyphus," by Albert Camus, which suggests that man has an unquenchable desire to understand but that the world is eternally unknowable. The resulting conflict puts man in an "absurd" position, like Sisyphus, who, according to Greek myth, was condemned for eternity to push a rock up a mountain, only to have it always fall back down before it reached the top. The philosophical term gave the name to a principal postwar dramatic genre: theatre of the absurd.

act (verb) To perform in a play. (noun) A division of a play. Acts in modern plays are bounded by an *intermission* or by the beginning or end of the play on each side. Full-length modern plays are customarily divided into two acts, sometimes three. Roman, Elizabethan, and neoclassic plays were usually printed in five acts, but the actual productions were not necessarily divided by intermissions, only stage clearings.

ad lib A line improvised by an actor during a performance, usually because the actor has forgotten his or her line or because something unscripted has occurred onstage. Sometimes an author directs the actors to ad lib, as in crowd scenes during which individual words cannot be distinguished by the audience.

aesthetic distance The theoretical separation between the created artifice of a play and the "real life" the play appears to represent.

agon "Action," in Greek; the root word for "agony." Agon refers to the major struggles and interactions of Greek tragedies.

alienation effect A technique, developed by German playwright Bertolt Brecht (1898–1956), by which the actor deliberately presents rather than represents his or her character and "illustrates" the character without trying to embody the role fully, as *naturalistic* acting technique demands. This technique may be accomplished by "stepping out of character" — as to sing a song or to address the audience directly — and by developing a highly objective and *didactic* mode of expression. The actor is alienated from the role (*estranged* and *distanced* are perhaps better terms — all translations of the German word *Verfremdung*) in order to make the audience more directly aware of current political issues. This technique is highly influential today, particularly in Europe.

amphitheatre In Rome, a large elliptical outdoor theatre, originally used for gladiatorial contests. Today the term is often used to designate a large outdoor theatre of any type.

anagnorisis "Recognition," in Greek. Aristotle claimed that every fine *tragedy* has a recognition scene, in which the *protagonist* discovers either some fact unknown to her or him or some moral flaw in her or his character. Scholars disagree as to which of these precise meanings Aristotle had in mind. See also *hamartia*.

antagonist In certain Greek tragedies, the opponent of the *protagonist*.

Apollonian That which is beautiful, wise, and serene, in the theories of Friedrich Nietzsche, who believed *drama* sprang from the junction of Apollonian and *Dionysian* forces in Greek culture.

apron The part of the stage located in front of the *proscenium;* the forwardmost portion of the stage. The apron was used extensively in the English *Restoration* period, from whence the term comes. Today, it is usually called the *forestage*.

aragoto The flamboyant and exaggerated masculine style of acting employed in certain *kabuki* roles.

arena stage A stage surrounded by the audience; also known as "theatre-in-the-round." *Arena* is a latin term meaning "sand," and it originally referred to the dirt circle in the midst of an *amphitheatre.*

aside A short line in a play delivered directly to the audience; by dramatic convention, the other characters onstage are presumed not to hear it. Popular in the works of William Shakespeare (1564–1616) and of the *Restoration* period, the aside has made a comeback in recent years and is used to good effect, in conjunction with the longer *direct address,* by contemporary American playwrights such as Lanford Wilson (born 1937) and Neil Simon (born 1927).

audition The process whereby an actor seeks a role by presenting to a director or casting director a prepared reading or by "reading cold" from the text of the play being presented.

avant-garde In military terms, the "advance-battalion" of an army that goes beyond the front lines to break new ground; in theatre terms, those theatre artists who abandon conventional models and create works that are in the forefront of new theatrical movements and styles.

backstage The offstage area hidden from the audience that is used for *scenery* storage, for actors preparing to make entrances, and for stage technicians running the show. "Backstage plays," such as *The Torchbearers* and *Noises Off,* "turn the set around" and exploit the furious backstage activity that takes place during a play production.

biomechanics An experimental acting system, characterized by expressive physicalization and bold gesticulation, developed by Russian play director Vsevolod Meyerhold (1874–1940) in the 1920s.

black musical See *black theatre.*

black theatre In America, theatre that is generally by, with, and about African Americans.

black-box theatre A rectangular room with no fixed seating or stage area; this theatre design allows for a variety of configurations in staging plays.

blocking The specific staging of a play's movements, ordinarily by the director. "Blocking" refers to the precise indications of where actors are to move, moment by moment, during the performance. Often this is worked out ("blocked out") on graph paper by the director beforehand.

book In a *musical,* the *dialogue* text, apart from the music and song lyrics.

border A piece of flat *scenery,* often black velour but sometimes a *flat,* which is placed horizontally above the set, usually to *mask* the lighting instruments. Borders are often used with side *wings,* in a scenery system known as "wing and border."

box set A stage set consisting of hard scenic pieces representing the walls and ceiling of a room, with one wall left out for the audience to peer into. This set design was developed in the nineteenth century and remains in use today in realistic plays.

Broadway The major commercial theatre district in New York, bordered by Broadway, 8th Avenue, 42nd Street, and 52nd Street.

bunraku A Japanese puppet theatre, founded in the seventeenth century and still performed today.

burlesque Literally, a parody or mockery, from an Italian amusement form. Today the term implies broad, coarse humor in *farce,* particularly in *parodies* and *vaudeville*-type presentations.

business The minute physical behavior of the actor, such as fiddling with a tie, sipping a drink, drumming the fingers, lighting a cigarette, and so forth. Sometimes this is controlled to a high degree by the actor and/or the director for precise dramatic effect; at other times the business is improvised to convey a *naturalistic* verisimilitude.

callback After the initial *audition,* the director or casting director will "call back" for additional — sometimes many — readings those actors who seem most promising. Rules of the actors' unions require that actors be paid for callbacks exceeding a certain minimum number.

caricature A character portrayed very broadly and in a stereotypical fashion, ordinarily objectionable in *realistic* dramas. See also *character.*

catharsis In Aristotle's *Poetics,* the "purging" or "cleansing" of terror and pity, which the audience develops during the *climax* of a *tragedy.*

character A "person" in a play, as performed by an actor. Hamlet, Oedipus, Juliet, and Willy Loman are characters. Characters may or may not be based on real people.

chiton The full-length gown worn by Greek tragic actors.

chorus (1) In classic Greek plays, an ensemble of characters representing the general public of the play, such as the women of Argos or the elders of Thebes. Originally, the chorus numbered fifty; Aeschylus is said to have reduced it to twelve and Sophocles to have increased it to fifteen. More recent playwrights, including Shakespeare and Jean Anouilh (1910–1987), have occasionally employed a single actor (or small group of actors) as "Chorus," to provide narration between the scenes. (2) In *musicals,* an ensemble of characters who sing and/or dance together (in contrast to soloists, who sing and/or dance independently).

chou In *xiqu,* clown characters and the actors who play them.

classical drama Technically, plays from classical Greece or Rome. Now used frequently (if incorrectly) to refer to masterpieces of the early and late Renaissance (Elizabethan, Jacobean, French *neoclassical,* and so on).

climax The point of highest tension in a play, when the conflicts of the play are at their fullest expression.

comedy Popularly, a funny play; classically, a play that ends happily; metaphorically, a play with some humor that celebrates the eternal ironies of human existence ("divine comedy").

comic relief In a *tragedy,* a short comic scene that releases some of the built-up tension of the play — giving the audience a momentary "relief" before the tension mounts higher. The "porter scene" in Shakespeare's *Macbeth* is an often-cited example; following the murder of Duncan, a porter jocularly addresses the audience as to the effect of drinking on sexual behavior. In the best tragedies, comic relief also provides an ironic counterpoint to the tragic action.

commedia dell'arte A form of largely improvised, masked street theatre that began in northern Italy in the late sixteenth century and still can be seen today. The principal characters — Arlecchino, Pantalone, Columbine, Dottore, and Scapino among them — appear over and over in thousands of commedia stories.

company A group of theatre artists gathered together to create a play production or a series of such productions.

convention A theatrical custom that the audience accepts without thinking, such as "when the curtain comes down, the play is over." Each period and culture develops its own dramatic conventions, which playwrights may either accept or violate.

cue The last word of one speech that then becomes the "cue" for the following speech. Actors are frequently admonished to speak "on cue" or to "pick up their cues," both of which mean to begin speaking precisely at the moment the other actor finishes.

cycle plays In medieval England, a series of *mystery plays* that, performed in sequence, relate the story of religion, from the Creation of the universe to Adam and Eve to the Crucifixion to Doomsday. The York Cycle includes forty-eight such plays.

cyclorama In a *proscenium theatre,* a large piece of curved *scenery* that wraps around the rear of the stage and is illuminated to resemble the sky or to serve as an abstract neutral background. It is usually made of fabric stretched between curved pipes but is sometimes a permanent structure made of concrete and plaster.

Dada A provocative and playful European art movement following World War I — characterized by seemingly random, unstructured, and "anti-aesthetic" creativity — that was briefly but deeply influential in poetry, painting, and theatre.

dan In *xiqu,* the female roles and the actors who play them.

denouement The final *scene* or scenes in a play devoted to tying up the loose ends after the *climax* (although the word originally meant "the untying").

deus ex machina In Greek *tragedies,* the resolution of the *plot* by the device of a god ("deus") arriving onstage by means of a crane ("machina") and solving all the characters' problems.

Today, this term encompasses any such contrived play ending, such as the discovery of a will. This theatrical element was considered clumsy by Aristotle and virtually all succeeding critics; it is occasionally used ironically in the modern theatre, as by Bertolt Brecht in *The Threepenny Opera.*

dialogue The speeches — delivered to each other — of the *characters* in a play. Contrast with *monologue.*

diction One of the six important features of a *drama,* according to Aristotle, who meant by the term the intelligence and appropriateness of the play's speeches. Today, this term refers primarily to the actor's need for articulate speech and clear pronunciation.

didactic drama Drama dedicated to teaching lessons or provoking intellectual debate beyond the confines of the play; the dramatic form espoused by Bertolt Brecht. See also *alienation effect.*

dim out To fade the lights gradually to blackness.

dimmer In lighting, the electrical device (technically known as a potentiometer) that regulates the current passing through the bulb filaments and, thereby, the amount of light emitted from the lighting instruments.

Dionysia Or "Great Dionysia" or "City Dionysia"; the week-long Athenian springtime festival in honor of *Dionysus,* which was, after 534 B.C., the major play-producing festival of the Greek year.

Dionysian Passionate revelry, uninhibited pleasure-seeking; the opposite of *Apollonian,* according to Friedrich Nietzsche, who considered *drama* a merger of these two primary impulses in the Greek character.

Dionysus The Greek god of drama as well as the god of drinking and fertility. Dionysus was known as Bacchus in Rome.

direct address A character's speech delivered directly to the audience, common in Greek Old Comedy (see *parabasis*), in Shakespeare's work (see *soliloquy*), in *epic theatre,* and in some otherwise *realistic* modern plays (such as Neil Simon's *Broadway Bound*).

discovery A *character* who appears onstage without making an entrance, as when a curtain opens.

Ferdinand and Miranda are "discovered" playing chess in Shakespeare's *The Tempest* when Prospero pulls away a curtain that had been hiding them from view.

dithyramb A Greek religious rite in which a *chorus* of fifty men, dressed in goatskins, chanted and danced; the precursor, according to Aristotle, of Greek *tragedy.*

documentary drama Drama that presents historical facts in a nonfictionalized, or only slightly fictionalized, manner.

domestic tragedy A *tragedy* about ordinary people at home.

double (1) An actor who plays more than one role is said to "double" in the second and following roles. Ordinarily the actor will seek, through a costume change, to disguise the fact of the doubling; occasionally, however, a production with a *theatricalist* staging may make it clear that the actor doubles in many roles. (2) To Antonin Artaud, the life that drama reflects, as discussed in his book *The Theatre and Its Double.* See also *theatre of cruelty.*

downstage That part of the stage closest to the audience. The term dates back to the eighteenth century, when the stage was *raked* so that the front part was literally below the back (or *upstage*) portion.

drama The art of the theatre; plays, playmaking, and the whole body of literature of and for the stage.

dramatic Plays, scenes, and events that are high in conflict and believability and that would command attention if staged in the theatre.

dramatic irony The situation when the audience knows something the characters don't, as in Shakespeare's *Macbeth,* when King Duncan remarks on his inability to judge character — while warmly greeting the man (Macbeth) we already know plans to assassinate him.

dramaturge A specialist in *dramatic* construction and the body of dramatic literature; a scientist of the art of *drama.* Dramaturges are frequently engaged by professional and academic theatres to assist in choosing and analyzing plays, develop production concepts, research topics pertinent to historic period or play production *style,* and write program essays. The dramaturge has been a mainstay of the German theatre since the eighteenth century and is becoming increasingly popular in the English-speaking world. Sometimes identified by the German spelling "Dramaturg."

dramaturgy   The science of *drama;* the art of play construction; sometimes used to refer to play structure itself.

dress rehearsal   A *rehearsal,* perhaps one of several, in full costume; usually also with full *scenery, properties,* lighting, sound, and technical effects. This is ordinarily the last rehearsal(s) prior to the first actual performance before an audience.

drop   A flat piece of *scenery* hung from the *fly gallery,* which can "drop" into place by a *flying system.*

empathy   Audience members' identification with dramatic characters and their consequent shared feelings with the plights and fortunes of those characters. Empathy is one of the principal effects of good drama.

ensemble   Literally, the group of actors (and sometimes directors and designers) who put a play together; metaphorically, the rapport and shared sense of purpose that bind such a group into a unified artistic entity.

environmental theatre   Plays produced not on a conventional stage but in an area where the actors and the audience are intermixed in the same "environment" and where there is no precise line distinguishing stage space from audience space.

epic theatre   As popularized by Bertolt Brecht, a *style* of theatre in which the play presents a series of semi-isolated episodes, intermixed with songs and other forms of *direct address,* all leading to a general moral conclusion or set of integrated moral questions. Brecht's *Mother Courage* is a celebrated example. See also *alienation effect.*

epilogue   In Greek *tragedy,* a short concluding *scene* of certain plays, generally involving a substantial shift of tone or a *deus ex machina.* Today, the epilogue is a concluding scene set substantially beyond the time frame of the rest of the play, in which characters, now somewhat older, reflect on the preceding events.

existential drama   A play based on the philosophical notions of existentialism, particularly as developed by Jean-Paul Sartre (1905–1980). Existentialism, basically, preaches that "you are your acts, and nothing else" and that people must be held fully accountable for their own behavior. *No Exit* contains Sartre's most concise expression of this idea.

exodos   In Greek *tragedy,* the departure ode of the *chorus* at the end of the play.

exposition   In play construction, the conveyance, through *dialogue,* of story events that have occurred before the play begins.

expressionism   An artistic *style* that greatly exaggerates perceived reality in order to express inner truths directly. Popular mainly in Germany between the world wars, expressionism in the theatre is notable for its gutsy dialogue, piercing sounds, bright lighting and coloring, bold scenery, and shocking, vivid imagery.

farce   Highly comic, lighthearted, gleefully contrived drama, usually involving *stock situations* (such as mistaken identity or discovered lovers' trysts), punctuated with broad physical stunts and pratfalls.

flat   A wooden frame covered in fabric or a hard surface and then painted, often to resemble a wall or portion of a wall. The flat is a traditional staple of stage *scenery,* particularly in the realistic theatre, since it is exceptionally lightweight, can be combined with other flats in various ways, and can be repainted and reused many times over several years.

fly   (verb) To raise a piece of *scenery* (or an actor) out of sight by a system of ropes and/or wires. This theatre practice dates back at least to ancient Greek times (see also *deus ex machina*).

fly gallery   The operating area for flying scenery, where fly ropes are tied off (on a pinrail) or where ropes in a counterweight system are clamped in a fixed position.

follow-spot   A swivel-mounted lighting instrument that can be pointed in any direction by an operator.

footlights   In a *proscenium theatre,* a row of lights across the front of the stage, used to light the actors' faces from below and to add light and color to the setting. Footlights were used universally in previous centuries but are employed only on special occasions today.

forestage A modern term for *apron,* the small portion of the stage located in front of the *proscenium.*

found object In scene or costume design (and art in general), an item that is found rather than created and subsequently incorporated into the finished design.

full house Audience seating filled to capacity. See also *house.*

genre French for "kind"; a term used in dramatic theory to signify a distinctive class or category of play, such as *tragedy, comedy, farce,* and so on.

geza The *stage right,* semi-enclosed musicians' box in *kabuki* theatre. This term also refers to the music that is played in this box.

gidayu The traditional style of chanting in *kabuki* and *bunraku* theatre. This term also refers to the singer-chanter himself.

greenroom A room near the stage where actors may sit comfortably before and after the show or during scenes in which they do not appear. This room is traditionally painted green; the custom arose in England, where the color was thought to be soothing.

ground plan A schematic drawing of the stage setting, as seen from above, indicating the location of stage-scenery pieces and furniture on (and sometimes above) the floor. A vital working document for directors in *rehearsal,* as well as for technicians in the installation of *scenery.*

hamartia In Aristotle's *Poetics,* the "tragic flaw" of the *protagonist.* Scholars differ as to whether Aristotle was referring primarily to a character's ignorance of certain facts or to a character's moral defect.

hanamichi In the *kabuki* theatre, a long narrow runway leading from the stage to a door at the back of the auditorium that is used for highly theatrical entrances and exits right through the audience.

Hellenistic theatre Ancient Greek theatre during the fourth and third centuries B.C. The surviving stone theatres of Athens and Epidaurus date from the Hellenistic period, which began well after the great fifth-century tragedies and comedies were written. The Hellenistic period did produce an important form of comedy (*New Comedy*), however, and Alexandrian scholars during this period collected, edited, and preserved the masterpieces of the golden age.

high comedy A comedy of verbal wit and visual elegance, usually peopled with upper-class characters. The *Restoration* comedies of William Congreve (1670–1729) and the Victorian comedies of Oscar Wilde (1854–1900) are often cited as examples.

hikimaku The traditional striped curtain of the *kabuki* theatre.

himation The gownlike basic costume of the Greek tragic actor.

house The audience portion of the theatre building.

hubris In Greek, an excess of pride; the most common *character* defect (one interpretation of the Greek *hamartia*) of the *protagonist* in Greek *tragedy.* "Pride goeth before a fall" is an Elizabethan expression of this foundation of tragedy.

improvisation *Dialogue* and/or stage *business* invented by the actor, often during the performance itself. Some plays are wholly improvised, even to the extent that the audience may suggest situations that the actors must then create. More often, improvisation is used to "fill in the gaps" between more traditionally memorized and rehearsed scenes.

inciting action In play construction, the single action that initiates the major conflict of the play.

ingenue The young, pretty, and innocent girl role in certain plays; also used to denote an actress capable of playing such roles.

interlude A *scene* or staged event in a play not specifically tied to the *plot;* in medieval England, a short moral play, usually comic, that could be presented at a court banquet amid other activities.

intermission In England, "interval"; a pause in the action, marked by a fall of the curtain or a fade-out of the stage lights, during which the audience may leave their seats for a short time, usually ten or fifteen minutes. Intermissions divide the play into separate *acts.*

jing In *xiqu,* the "painted-face" roles, often of gods, nobles, or villains.

jingju "Capital theatre" in Chinese; the Beijing (or Peking) Opera, the most famous form of *xiqu*.

kabuki One of the national theatres of Japan. Dating from the seventeenth century, the kabuki features magnificent flowing costumes; highly stylized scenery, acting, and makeup; and elaborately styled choreography.

kakegoe Traditional shouts that *kabuki* enthusiasts in the audience cry out to their favorite actors during the play.

kathakali A traditional dance-drama of India.

kōken Black-garbed and veiled actors' assistants who perform various functions onstage in *kabuki* theatre.

lazzo A physical joke, refined into traditional *business* and inserted into a play, in the *commedia dell'arte*. "Eating the fly" is a famous lazzo.

Lenaea The winter dramatic festival in ancient Athens. Because there were fewer foreigners in town in the winter, comedies that might embarrass the Athenians were often performed at this festival rather than at the springtime *Dionysia*.

liturgical drama *Dramatic* material that was written into the official Catholic Church liturgy and staged as part of regular church services in the medieval period, mainly in the tenth through twelfth centuries.

low comedy Comic actions based on broad physical humor, scatology, crude punning, and the argumentative behavior of ignorant and lower-class *characters*. Despite the pejorative connotation of its name, low comedy can be inspired, as in the "mechanicals" scenes of Shakespeare's *A Midsummer Night's Dream*. Good plays, such as this one, can mix low comedy with *high comedy* in a highly sophisticated pattern.

mask (noun) A covering of the face, used conventionally by actors in many periods, including Greek, Roman, and *commedia dell'arte*. The mask was also used in other sorts of plays for certain occasions, such as the masked balls in Shakespeare's *Romeo and Juliet* and *Much Ado about Nothing*. The mask is a symbol of the theatre, particularly the two classic masks of Comedy and Tragedy. (verb) To hide backstage storage or activity by placing in front of it neutrally colored *flats* or drapery (which then become "masking pieces").

masque A minor dramatic form combining dance, music, a short allegorical *text,* and elegant *scenery* and costuming; often presented at court, as in the royal masques written by Ben Jonson (1572–1637), with scenery designed by Inigo Jones (1573–1652), during the Stuart era (early seventeenth century).

melodrama Originally a term for musical theatre, by the nineteenth century this became the designation of a suspenseful, plot-oriented drama featuring all-good heroes, all-bad villains, simplistic *dialogue,* soaring moral conclusions, and bravura acting.

metaphor A literary term designating a figure of speech that implies a comparison or identity of one thing with something else. It permits concise communication of a complex idea by use of associative imagery, as with Shakespeare's "morn in russet mantle clad."

metatheatre Literally, "beyond theatre"; plays or theatrical acts that are self-consciously theatrical, that refer back to the art of the theatre and call attention to their own theatricality. Developed by many authors, including Shakespeare (in plays-within-plays in *Hamlet* and *A Midsummer Night's Dream*) and particularly the twentieth-century Italian playwright Luigi Pirandello (*Six Characters in Search of an Author, Tonight We Improvise*), thus leading to the term "Pirandellian" (meaning "metatheatrical"). See also *play-within-the-play*.

mie A "moment" in *kabuki* theatre in which the actor (usually an *aragoto* character) suddenly freezes in a tense and symbolic pose.

mime A stylized art of acting without words. Probably derived from the *commedia dell'arte*, mime was revived in France during the mid-twentieth century and is now popular again in the theatre and in street performances in Europe and the United States. Mime performers traditionally employ whiteface makeup to stylize and exaggerate their features and expressions.

modern classic A term used to designate a play of the past hundred years that has nonetheless passed the test of time and seems as if it will last into the century or centuries beyond, such as the major works of Anton Chekhov, George Bernard Shaw, and Samuel Beckett. Contrast with *classical drama*.

monologue A long unbroken speech in a play, often delivered directly to the audience (when it is more technically called a *soliloquy*).

morality play An allegorical medieval play form, in which the characters represent abstractions (Good Deeds, Death, and so on) and the overall impact of the play is moral instruction. The most famous of these plays in English is the anonymous *Everyman* (fifteenth century).

motivation That which can be construed to have determined a person's (or *character's*) behavior. Since Konstantin Stanislavsky (1863–1938), actors have been encouraged to study the possible motivations of their characters' actions. See also *objective*.

musical A generic name for a play with a large number of songs, particularly when there is also dancing and/or a chorus.

musical comedy A popular form of twentieth-century theatre, with singing and dancing, designed primarily for entertainment.

mystery play The most common term referring to medieval plays developed from liturgical drama that treated biblical stories and themes. (They were also known as pageant plays in England, as passion plays when dealing with the Crucifixion of Jesus, and as Corpus Christi plays when performed in conjunction with that particular festival.) Unlike *liturgical dramas,* which were in Latin, mystery plays were written in the vernacular (English, French, German, Italian, Spanish, and Russian versions exist) and were staged outside the church.

naturalism An extreme form of *realism,* which advanced the notion that the natural and social environment, more than individual will power, controlled human behavior. Its proponents, active in the late nineteenth and early twentieth centuries, sought to dispense with all theatrical convention in the search for complete verisimilitude: a *slice of life,* as the naturalists would say.

neoclassicism Literally, "new classicism," or a renewed interest in the literary and artistic theories of ancient Greece and Rome and an attempt to reformulate them for the current day. A dominant force in seventeenth-century France, neoclassicism promoted restrained passion, balance, artistic consistency, and formalism in all art forms; it reached its dramatic pinnacle in the tragedies of Jean Racine (1639–1699).

New Comedy Greek comic dramas — almost all of which are now lost — of the late fourth to the second centuries B.C. Considerably more realistic than the Old Comedy of Aristophanes, New Comedy employed *stock characters* and domestic scenes; it strongly influenced Roman author Plautus and, through him, Renaissance comedy.

nō The classical dance-drama of Japan. Performed on a bare wooden stage of fixed construction and dimension and accompanied by traditional music, nō is the aristocratic forebear of the more popular *kabuki* and remains generally unchanged since its fourteenth-century beginnings.

objective The basic "goal" of a *character.* Also called "intention" or "victory." Since Konstantin Stanislavsky, the actor has been urged to discover his or her character's objectives and, by way of "living the life of that character," to pursue that character's objective during the course of the play.

off-Broadway The New York professional theatre located outside the *Broadway* district; principally in Greenwich Village and around the upper East and West Sides. Developed in the 1950s, when it was considered highly experimental, the off-Broadway theatre is now more of a scaled-down version of the Broadway theatre, featuring *musicals* and commercial revivals as much as (or more than) original works.

off-off-Broadway A term designating certain theatre activity in New York City, usually nonprofessional (although with professional artists involved) and usually experimental and *avant-garde* in nature. Off-off-Broadway developed in the 1970s as a supplement to the commercialism of both Broadway and, increasingly, off-Broadway.

onnagata "Women-type" roles in *kabuki,* which, like all the roles, are played by men.

open the house A direction to admit the audience. See also *house.*

orchestra (1) In the ancient Greek or Roman theatre, the circular (in Rome, semicircular) ground-level acting area in front of the stagehouse, or *skene*. It was used primarily by the *chorus*. (2) In modern theatre buildings, the main ground-level section of the audience, which usually slopes upward at the rear. Distinct from the mezzanine and balconies and ordinarily containing the more expensive seats.

parabasis A "coming-forward" of a *character* in Greek Old Comedy who then gives a *direct address* to the audience in the middle of the play. In Aristophanes' plays, the parabasis is often given in the author's name and may have been spoken by Aristophanes himself. The parabasis was often unrelated to the *plot* and dealt with the author's immediate political or social concerns.

parados The ode sung by the chorus entering the orchestra in a Greek tragedy; the space between the stagehouse (*skene*) and audience seating area (*theatron*) through which the chorus entered the orchestra.

parody Dramatic material that makes fun of a dramatic genre or mode or of specific literary works; a form of theatre that is often highly entertaining but rarely has lasting value.

pathos "Passion," in Greek; also "suffering." The word refers to the depths of feeling evoked by *tragedy;* it is at the root of our words "sympathy" and "empathy," which also describe the effect of drama on audience emotions.

peripeteia In the Anglicized form, "peripety"; the reversal of the *protagonist's* fortunes that, according to Aristotle, is part of the *climax* of a *tragedy*.

pièce bien faite See *well-made play*.

play-within-the-play A play that is "presented" by characters who are already in a play; like "The Murder of Gonzago," which is presented by "players" in *Hamlet*. Many plays are in part about actors and plays and contain such plays-within-plays; these include Anton Chekhov's *The Seagull*, Jean Anouilh's *The Rehearsal*, and Shakespeare's *A Midsummer Night's Dream* and *The Taming of the Shrew*.

plot The events of the play, expressed as a series of linked dramatic actions; more generally, and in common terms, the story of the play. The plot is the most important aspect of play construction, according to Aristotle.

postmodern A wide-ranging term describing certain post–World War II artistic works, characterized by nonlinearity, self-referentiality if not self-parody, and multiple/simultaneous sensory impressions.

practical In stage terminology, a *property* that works onstage the way it does in life. For example, a "practical" stove, in a stage setting, is one on which the characters can actually cook. A "nonpractical" stove, by contrast, is something that only looks like a stove (and may in fact be a stove without insides).

problem play A realistic play that deals, often narrowly, with a specific social problem. George Bernard Shaw's *Mrs. Warren's Profession,* for example, is virtually a dramatic tract on prostitution. The term was most popular around the beginning of the twentieth century; today it is mostly descriptive of certain movies for television.

producer (1) In America, the person responsible for assembling the ingredients of a play production: financing, staff, theatre, publicity, and management. Not ordinarily involved in the day-to-day artistic direction of the production, the American producer nonetheless controls the artistic process through her or his authority over personnel selection and budgeting. (2) Until recently, in the English theatre, the theatre artist Americans refer to as the director.

prologue In Greek *tragedy,* a speech or brief scene preceding the entrance of the *chorus* and the main action of the play, usually spoken by a god or gods. Subsequently, the term has referred to a speech or brief *scene* that introduces the play, as by an actor in certain Elizabethan plays (often called the chorus) and in the *Restoration*. The prologue is rarely used in the modern theatre.

properties Or "props"; the furniture and handheld objects (hand props) used in play productions. These are often real items (chairs, telephones, books, etc.) that can be purchased, rented, borrowed, or brought up from theatre storage; they may also, particularly in period or stylized plays, be designed and built in a property shop.

proscenium arch The arch separating the audience area from the main stage area. The term derives from the Roman playhouse, in which the proscenium (literally, *pro skene,* or "in front of the stage") was the facing wall of the stage. Modern *thrust* and *arena stages* have no proscenium.

proscenium theatre A rectangular-roomed theatre with the audience on one end and the stage on the other, with both areas separated by a *proscenium arch.* The proscenium theatre was first popular in the late seventeenth century and reached its apogee in the late nineteenth and early twentieth centuries. Still the basic theatre architecture of America's Broadway and of major European theatre companies.

protagonist In Greek *tragedy,* and subsequently in any drama, the principal *character,* often opposed by an *antagonist.*

raked stage A sloped stage, angled so that the rear (*upstage*) area is higher than the forward (*downstage*) area. A raked stage was standard theatre architecture in the seventeenth century and is often used today in scene design but rarely in a theatre's permanent architecture.

realism The general principle that the stage should portray, in a reasonable facsimile, ordinary people in ordinary circumstances and that actors should behave, as much as possible, as real people do in life. Although realism's roots go back to Euripides, it developed as a deliberate contrast to the florid *romanticism* that swept the European theatre in the mid-nineteenth century. See also *naturalism,* which is an extreme version of realism.

recognition See *anagnorisis.*

rehearsal The gathering of actors and director to put a play into production; the period in which the director stages the play and the actors develop and repeat their *dialogue* and actions; etymologically, a "reharrowing," or repeated digging into. In French, the comparable term is *répétition.*

repertory The plays a theatre company produces. A company's current repertory consists of those plays available for production at any time.

Restoration In England, the period following the restoration of the monarchy in 1660. In the theatre, the period is particularly noted for witty and salacious comedies, through to William Congreve's brilliant *The Way of the World* in 1700.

revival The remounting of a play production after its initial closing, usually by the same theatre *company* and/or employing many or most of the same artists. The term is not normally used to describe fresh restagings, by other artists, of older plays.

rising action In dramatic structure, the escalating conflict; events and actions that follow the *inciting action.*

ritual A traditional cultural practice, usually religious, involving precise movements, music, spoken text, and/or gestures, that serves to communicate with deities. Ritual is often incorporated into plays, either as *conventions* of the theatre or as specific dramatized actions.

romanticism A nineteenth-century European movement away from *neoclassic* formalism and toward outsized passions, exotic and grotesque stories, florid writing, and all-encompassing worldviews. Supplanted in the late century by *realism,* romanticism survives today primarily in grand opera and nineteenth-century-based *musicals.*

rotating repertory The scheduling of a series of plays in nightly rotation. This is customary in most European theatres and in many American Shakespeare festivals; it is otherwise rare in America. See also *repertory.*

samisen The three-stringed banjolike instrument used in *kabuki* and *bunraku.*

satire A play or other literary work that ridicules social follies, beliefs, religions, or human vices, almost always in a lighthearted vein. Satire is not usually a lasting theatre form, as summed up by dramatist George S. Kaufman's classic definition: "Satire is what closes on Saturday night."

satyr A mythological Greek creature, half man and half goat, who attended *Dionysus* and represented male sexuality and drunken revelry; goatskin-clad followers of Dionysus who served as the *chorus* of the *satyr play.*

satyr play The fourth play in a Greek *tetralogy.* Satyr plays were short bawdy *farces* that parodied the events of the trilogies that preceded them.

scansion The study of verse for patterns of accented and unaccented syllables; also known as "metrics."

scene (1) The period of stage time representing a single space over a continuous period of time, now usually marked either by the rise or fall of a curtain or by the raising or lowering of lights but in the past often marked simply by a stage clearing; often the subdivision of an *act*. (2) The locale where the events of the play are presumed to take place, as represented by *scenery* (as in "the scene is the Parson's living room"). (3) Of scenery, as "scene design."

scenery The physical constructions that provide the specific acting environment for a play and that often indicate, by representation, the locale where a scene is set; the physical *setting* for a scene or play.

scenography *Scene* design, particularly as it fits into the moving pattern of a play or series of plays. Scene design is four-dimensional, comprising three physical dimensions plus time.

scrim A theatrical fabric woven so finely that when lit from the front it appears opaque and when lit from behind it becomes transparent. A scrim is often used for surprise effects or to create a mysterious mood.

script A play's *text* as used in and prior to play production, usually in manuscript or typescript rather than in a published version.

semiotics The study of signs, as they may be perceived in literary works, including plays. Semiotics is a contemporary tool of dramaturgical analysis that offers the possibility of identifying all the ingredients of *drama* (staging as well as language) and determining the precise conjunctions between them.

setting Or "set," the fixed (stable) stage scenery.

sheng In *xiqu,* the male roles and the actors who play them.

shite The principal *character* (the "doer") in *nō*.

skene The Greek stagehouse (and root word of our *scene*). The skene evolved from a small changing room behind the *orchestra* to a larger structure with a raised stage and a back wall during the Greek period.

slapstick Literally, a prop bat made up of two hinged sticks that slap sharply together when the bat is used to hit someone; a staple gag of the *commedia dell'arte*. More generally, slapstick is any sort of very broad physical stage humor.

slice-of-life Pure *naturalism:* stage action that merely represents an ordinary and arbitrary "slice" of the daily activity of the people portrayed.

soliloquy A *monologue* delivered by a single actor with no one else onstage, sometimes played as the *character* "thinking aloud" and sometimes as a seeming *dialogue* with the (silent) audience.

stage business See *business*.

stage directions Scene descriptions, *blocking* instructions, and general directorial comments written, usually by the playwright, in the script.

stage left Left, from the actor's point of view.

stage right Right, from the actor's point of view.

stock character A character recognizable mainly for his or her conformity to a standard ("stock") dramatic stereotype: the wily servant, the braggart soldier, the innocent virgin, and so on. Most date from at least Roman times.

stock situation One of a number of basic *plot* situations, such as the lover hiding in the closet, twins mistaken for each other, and so on, which, like *stock characters,* have been used in the theatre since Plautus and before.

style The specific manner in which a play is shaped, as determined by its genre, its historical period, the sort of impact the director wishes to convey to the audience, and the skill of the artists involved. The term generally refers to these aspects inasmuch as they differ from *naturalism,* although it could be said that naturalism is a style.

stylize To deliberately shape a play (or a setting, a costume, or so on) in a specifically non-naturalistic manner.

subplot A secondary *plot* in a play, usually related to the main plot by play's end. The Gloucester plot in *King Lear* and the Laertes plot in *Hamlet* are examples.

subtext According to Konstantin Stanislavsky, the deeper and usually unexpressed "real" meanings of a *character's* spoken lines. Of particular importance in the acting of realistic plays, such as those of Anton Chekhov, where the action is often as much between the lines as in them.

surrealism An art movement of the early twentieth century, in which the artist sought to go beyond *realism* into *superrealism* (of which surrealism is a contraction).

symbolism The first major antirealistic movement in the arts and in the theatre. Symbolism, which emphasizes the symbolic nature of theatrical presentation and the abstract possibilities of drama, flourished as a significant movement from the late nineteenth century to the early twentieth century, when it broke into various submovements: *expressionism, surrealism, theatricalism,* and so on.

tableau A "frozen moment" onstage, with the actors immobile, usually employed at the end of a *scene,* as the curtain falls or the lights dim.

tetralogy Four plays performed together in sequence. In ancient Greek theatre, this was the basic pattern for the tragic playwrights, who presented a *trilogy* of tragedies, followed by a *satyr play.*

text A playscript; sometimes used to indicate the spoken words of the play only, as apart from the stage directions and other material in the script.

theatre of alienation See *alienation effect, epic theatre.*

theatre of cruelty A notion of theatre developed by the French theorist Antonin Artaud (1896–1948). Artaud's goal was to employ language more for its sound than for its meaning and to create a shocking stream of sensations rather than a coherent *plot* and cast of *characters.* Although Artaud's practical achievement was slight, his theories have proven extraordinarily influential.

theatre of the absurd See *absurd.*

theatre-in-the-round See *arena stage.*

theatricalist A style of contemporary theatre that boldly exploits the theatre itself and calls attention to the theatrical contexts of the play being performed. This term is often used to describe plays about the theatre that employ a *play-within-the-play.*

theatron From the Greek for "seeing place"; the original Greek theatre.

thespian Actor; after Thespis, the first Greek actor.

thrust stage A stage that projects into the seating area and is surrounded by the audience on three sides.

tragedy From the Greek for "goat song"; originally meant a serious play. The tragedy was refined by Greek playwrights (Thespis, sixth century B.C., being the first) and subsequently the philosopher Aristotle (384–322 B.C.) into the most celebrated of dramatic genres: a play that treats, at the most uncompromising level, human suffering. The reason for the name is unclear; a goat may have been the prize, and/or the *chorus* may have worn goatskins.

tragic flaw See *hamartia.*

tragicomedy A play that begins as a *tragedy* but includes comic elements and ends happily. Tragicomedy was a popular genre in the eighteenth century but is rarely employed, at least under that name, in the modern theatre.

traveler A curtain that, instead of flying out (see *fly*), moves horizontally and is usually opened by dividing from the center outward.

trilogy Three plays performed in sequence; the basic pattern of ancient Greek tragedies, of which one — Aeschylus' *The Oresteia* (*Agamemnon, The Libation Bearers,* and *The Eumenides*) — is still extant.

trope A written text, usually in dialogue form, incorporated into the Christian church service. In the tenth century A.D. these became the first *liturgical dramas.*

troupe A group of actors who perform together, often on tour. See also *company.*

unit set A set that, by the moving on or off of a few simple pieces and perhaps with a change of lights, can represent all the scenes from a play. The unit set is a fluid and economical staging device, particularly useful for Shakespeare productions.

unities The unity of place, unity of time, unity of action, and unity of tone were the four "unities" that *neoclassic* critics of the seventeenth century claimed to derive from Aristotle; plays said to "observe the unities" were required to take place in one locale, to have a duration of no more than one day (in an extreme interpretation, in no more time than the duration of the play itself), and to concern themselves with no more than one single action. Aristotle made no such demands on playwrights, however, and very few authors have ever succeeded in satisfying these restrictive conventions.

upstage (noun) In a *proscenium theatre,* that part of the stage farthest from the audience; the rear of the stage, so called because it was in fact raised ("up") in the days of the *raked stage.* (verb) To stand upstage of another actor. Upstaging is often considered rude, inasmuch as it forces the *downstage* actor to face upstage (and away from the audience) in order to look at the actor to whom she or he is supposed to be speaking. Figuratively, the term may be used to describe any sort of acting behavior that calls unwarranted attention to the "upstaging" actor and away from the "upstaged" one.

vaudeville A stage variety show, with singing, dancing, comedy skits, and animal acts; highly popular in America from the late 1880s to the 1930s, when it lost out to movies, radio, and subsequently television.

verisimilitude The appearance of actual reality (as in a stage setting).

wagoto In *kabuki,* "gentle-style" acting performed by certain male romantic characters.

waki The secondary *character* in *nō.*

well-made play *Pièce bien faite* in French; in the nineteenth century, a superbly plotted play, particularly by such gifted French playwrights as Eugène Scribe (1791–1861) and Victorien Sardou (1831–1908); today, generally used pejoratively, as to describe a play that has a workable *plot* but shallow characterization and trivial ideas.

West End The commercial theatre district of London, England.

wings In a *proscenium theatre,* the vertical pieces of *scenery* to the left and right of the stage, usually parallel with the footlights.

xiqu Chinese for "tuneful theatre"; the general term for all varieties of traditional Chinese theatre, often called "Chinese Opera."

zadacha Russian for "task"; (though commonly translated as "objective"); according to Konstantin Stanislavsky, the character's (fictional) tasks (or goals) that the actor must pursue during the play.

Selected Bibliography

Historical Surveys of Theatre and Drama

Banham, Martin, ed. *The Cambridge Guide to Theatre.* Cambridge: Cambridge University Press, 1995.

Brockett, Oscar G. *History of the Theatre.* 7th ed. Boston: Allyn & Bacon, 1995.

Duerr, Edwin. *The Length and Depth of Acting.* New York: Holt, Rinehart & Winston, 1962.

Dukore, Bernard F., ed. *Dramatic Theory and Criticism: Greeks to Grotowski.* New York: Holt, Rinehart & Winston, 1974.

Hartnoll, Phyllis, ed. *The Oxford Companion to the Theatre.* 4th ed. New York: Oxford University Press, 1983.

Hill, Errol. *The Theatre of Black Americans.* New York: Applause Books, 1987.

Kanellos, Nicolás, ed. *Hispanic Theatre in the United States.* Houston: Arte Público Press, 1984.

——. *Mexican American Theater: Legacy and Reality.* Pittsburgh: Latin American Literary Review Press, 1987.

Leacroft, Richard, and Helen Leacroft. *Theatre and Playhouse.* London: Methuen, 1984

Nagler, Alois M. *Sources of Theatrical History.* New York: Dover, 1952.

Nicoll, Allardyce. *World Drama from Aeschylus to Anouilh.* Rev. ed. London: Harrap, 1976.

Pottlitzer, Joanne. *Hispanic Theater in the United States and Puerto Rico.* New York: Ford Foundation, 1988.

Sanders, Leslie C. *The Development of Black Theater in America.* Baton Rouge: Louisiana State University Press, 1988.

General Studies of Theatre and Drama

Beckerman, Bernard. *Dynamics of Drama: Theory and Method of Analysis.* New York: Knopf, 1970.

——. *Theatrical Presentation: Performer, Audience, and Act.* Edited by Gloria Brim Beckerman and William Coco. New York: Routledge, 1990.

Bentley, Eric. *The Life of the Drama.* New York: Atheneum, 1964.

Chinoy, Helen, and Linda Jenkins, eds. *Women in American Theatre.* New York: Crown, 1981.

Esslin, Martin. *An Anatomy of Drama.* New York: Hill & Wang, 1976.

Granville-Barker, Harley. *On Dramatic Method.* New York: Hill & Wang, 1956.

Hayman, Ronald. *How to Read a Play.* New York: Grove Press, 1977.

Laughlin, Karen, and Catherine Schuler, eds. *Theatre and Feminist Aesthetics.* Madison, WI: Fairleigh Dickinson University Press, 1995.

Rokem, Freddie. *Performing History: Theatrical Representations of the Past in Contemporary Theatre.* Iowa City: University of Iowa Press, 2000.

Schechner, Richard. *Environmental Theatre.* 2d ed. New York: Applause Books, 1994.

Schechner, Richard, and Willa Appel, eds. *By Means of Performance: Intercultural Studies of Theatre and Ritual.* Cambridge: Cambridge University Press, 1990.

Styan, J. L. *Drama, Stage, and Audience.* New York: Cambridge University Press, 1975.

——. *The Elements of Drama.* New York: Cambridge University Press, 1960.

Specialized Studies

GREEK AND ROMAN THEATRE

Arnott, Peter D. *Public and Performance in the Greek Theatre.* New York: Routledge, 1989.

Burkert, Walter. *Greek Religion.* Oxford: Basil Blackwell, 1985.

Butler, James H. *The Theatre and Drama of Greece and Rome.* San Francisco: Chandler, 1972.

Pickard-Cambridge, A. W. *Dithyramb, Tragedy, and Comedy.* 2d ed., revised by T. B. L. Webster. Oxford: Clarendon Press, 1962.

——. *The Dramatic Festivals of Athens.* 2d ed., revised by John Gould and D. M. Lewis. Oxford: Clarendon Press, 1968.

Taplin, Oliver. *Greek Tragedy in Action.* Berkeley: University of California Press, 1978.

——. *The Stagecraft of Aeschylus.* New York: Oxford University Press, 1977.

Toepfer, Karl. *Theatre, Aristocracy, and Pornocracy: The Orgy Calculus.* New York: PAJ Publications, 1991.

Zimmerman, Bernhard. *Greek Tragedy: An Introduction.* Translated by Thomas Marier. Baltimore: Johns Hopkins Press, 1991.

MEDIEVAL THEATRE

Chambers, E. K. *The Medieval Stage.* 2 vols. Oxford: Clarendon Press, 1903.

Collier, Richard J. *Poetry and Drama in the York Corpus Christi Play.* New York: Archon, 1978.

Harisson, O. B. *Christian Rite and Christian Drama in the Middle Ages: Essays in the Origin and Early History of Modern Drama.* Baltimore: Johns Hopkins Press, 1965.

Johnston, Alexandra F., and Margaret Rogerson. *Records of Early English Drama: York.* Toronto: University of Toronto Press, 1979.

Kolve, V. A. *The Play Called Corpus Christi.* Stanford, CA: Stanford University Press, 1966.

Muir, Lynette R. *The Biblical Drama of Medieval Europe.* Cambridge: Cambridge University Press, 1995.

Nagler, A. M. *The Medieval Religious Stage: Shapes and Phantoms.* New Haven, CT: Yale University Press, 1976.

Nelson, Alan H. *The Medieval English Stage: Corpus Christi Pageants and Plays.* Chicago: University of Chicago Press, 1974.

Southern, Richard. *The Medieval Theatre in the Round.* London: Faber & Faber, 1957.

Tydeman, W. *The Theatre in the Middle Ages.* New York: Cambridge University Press, 1979.

Wickham, Glynne. *The Medieval Theatre.* London: St. Martin's Press, 1974.

Woolf, Rosemary. *The English Mystery Play.* Berkeley: University of California Press, 1972.

SHAKESPEAREAN THEATRE

Beckerman, Bernard. *Shakespeare at the Globe, 1599–1609.* New York: Macmillan, 1962.

Bentley, Gerald E. *The Profession of Dramatist in Shakespeare's Time, 1590–1642.* Princeton, NJ: Princeton University Press, 1971.

Boom, Harold. *Shakespeare: The Invention of the Human.* New York: Riverhead Books, 1998.

Chambers, E. K. *The Elizabethan Stage.* 4 vols. London: Oxford University Press, 1923.

Dash, Irene G. *Wooing, Wedding and Power: Women in Shakespeare's Plays.* New York: Columbia University Press, 1981.

David, Richard. *Shakespeare in the Theatre.* New York: Cambridge University Press, 1978.

Hildy, Franklin J., ed. *New Issues in the Reconstruction of Shakespeare's Theatre.* New York: Peter Lang, 1990.

Hodges, C. Walter. *The Globe Restored.* 2d ed. New York: Oxford University Press, 1968.

——. *Shakespeare's Second Globe.* New York: Oxford University Press, 1973.

Hotson, Leslie. *Shakespeare's Wooden O.* New York: Macmillan, 1960.

Kahn, Coppélia. *Man's Estate: Masculine Identity in Shakespeare.* Berkeley: University of California Press, 1981.

Kiernan, Pauline. *Staging Shakespeare in the New Globe.* New York: St. Martins Press, 1999.

Mann, David. *The Elizabethan Player.* New York: Routledge, 1991.

Nagler, A. M. *Shakespeare's Stage.* New Haven, CT: Yale University Press, 1958.

Neely, Carol T. *Broken Nuptials in Shakespeare's Plays.* New Haven, CT: Yale University Press, 1985.

Southern, Richard. *The Staging of Plays before Shakespeare.* New York: Theatre Arts Books, 1973.

Speaight, Robert. *Shakespeare on the Stage.* New York: William Collins Sons, 1972.

Weimann, Robert. *Author's Pen and Actor's Voice: Playing and Writing in Shakespeare's Theatre.* Cambridge: Cambridge University Press, 2000.

ASIAN THEATRE

Akihiko, Senda. *The Voyage of Contemporary Japanese Theatre.* Honolulu: University of Hawai'i Press, 1997.

Benegal, Som. *A Panorama of Theatre in India.* Bombay: Popular Prakashan, 1968.

Brandon, James R., ed. *No and Kyogen in the Contemporary World.* Honolulu: University of Hawai'i Press, 1997.

Chen, Jingson. "To Make People Happy, Drama Imitates Joy," *Asian Theatre Journal* (Spring 1997).

Dunn, Charles J., and Bunzoh Torigoe. *The Actors' Analects.* New York: Columbia University Press, 1969.

Emmert, Richard. "Expanding Nō's Horizons." In *Nō and Kyogen in the Contemporary World,* ed. James R. Brandon. Honolulu: University of Hawai'i Press, 1997.

Ernst, Earle. *The Kabuki Theatre.* New York: Grove Press, 1956.

Gunji, Masakatsu. *Kabuki.* Tokyo: Kodansha International, 1988.

Immoos, Thomas. *Japanese Theatre.* Translated by Hugh Young, photographs by Fred Mayer. London: Studio Vista, 1977.

Keene, Donald. *No and Bunraku.* New York: Columbia University Press, 1970.

Kenny, Don. *On Stage in Japan*. Tokyo: Shufunotomo Co., 1974.

Kominiz, Laurence R. *The Stars Who Created Kabuki*. Tokyo: Kodansha International, 1997.

Leiter, Samuel L. *New Kabuki Encyclopedia*. Westport, CT: Greenwood Press, 1997.

Loc, Nguyen. *Vietnam's Hat Boi Theatre Art*. Hanoi, Vietnam: Culture Publishers, 1994.

Mackerras, Colin. *The Performing Arts in Contemporary China*. London: Routledge, 1981.

Mackerras, Colin, Pradeep Taneja, and Graham Young. *China since 1978*. New York: St. Martin's Press (Longman Cheshire), 1994.

Maruoka, Daiji, and Tatsuo Yoshikoshi. *No*. Translated by Don Kenny. Osaka: Hoikusha Publishing, 1992.

Miettinen, Jukka O. *Classical Dance and Theatre in South-East Asia*. Oxford: Oxford University Press, 1992.

Nakamura, Matazo. *Kabuki, Backstage, Onstage: An Actor's Life*. Translated by Mark Oshima. Tokyo: Kodansha International, 1990.

Ortolani, Benito. *The Japanese Theatre: From Shamanistic Ritual to Contemporary Pluralism*. Leiden: E. J. Brill, 1990.

Peterson, William. *Theatre and the Politics of Culture in Contemporary Singapore*. Middletown, CT: Wesleyan University Press, 2001.

Pronko, Leonard. *Theatre East and West: Perspectives Toward a Total Theatre*. Berkeley: University of California Press, 1967.

Quiang, Ma. *The Pictorial Album of Costumes in Chinese Traditional Opera*. Shanxi Education Press, 1992.

Richmond, Farley P., Darius L. Swann, and Phillip B. Zarilli, eds. *Indian Theatre: Traditions of Performance*. Honolulu: University of Hawai'i Press, 1990.

Scott, A. C. *The Classical Theatre of China*. London: Simson Shand, 1957.

——. *The Theatre in Asia*. London: Weidenfeld and Nicholson, 1972.

Shindo, Shigero. *Kunisada (The Kabuki actor portraits)*. Tokyo: Graphic-sha Publishing, 1993.

Toita, Yasuji, and Chiaki Yoshida. *Kabuki*. Translated by Don Kenny. Osaka: Hoikusha Publishing, 1992.

Van Erven, Eugène. *The Playful Revolution: Theatre and Liberation in Asia*. Bloomington: Indiana University Press, 1992.

Varadpande, M. L. *Ancient Indian and Indo-Greek Theatre*. New Delhi: Shakti Malik Abhinav Publications, 1981.

Wang-ngai, Siu, with Peter Lovrick. *Chinese Opera*. Vancouver: University of British Columbia Press, 1997.

Wichmann, Elizabeth. *Listening to Theatre: The Aural Dimension of Beijing Opera*. Honolulu: University of Hawai'i Press, 1991.

Zugang, Wu, Huang Zuolin, and Mei Shaowu. *Peking Opera and Mei Lanfang*. Beijing: New World Press, 1981.

ROYAL THEATRE

Holland, Peter. *The Ornament of Action: Text and Performance in Restoration Comedy*. New York: Cambridge University Press, 1979.

Lancaster, H. C. *A History of French Dramatic Literature in the Seventeenth Century*. 5 vols. Baltimore: Johns Hopkins Press, 1929–42.

Lawrenson, T. E. *The French Stage in the XVIIth Century*. Manchester, England: Manchester University Press, 1957.

McBride, Robert. *Aspects of 17th Century French Drama and Thought*. Totowa, NJ: Rowman & Littlefield, 1980.

Nicoll, Allardyce. *History of English Drama, 1660–1900*. 6 vols. London: Cambridge University Press, 1955–59.

Wiley, W. L. *The Early Public Theatre in France*. Cambridge, MA: Harvard University Press, 1960.

MODERN AND POSTMODERN THEATRE

Artaud, Antonin. *The Theatre and Its Double*. Translated by Mary C. Richards. New York: Grove Press, 1958.

Bentley, Eric. *The Playwright as Thinker*. New York: Reynal, 1946.

Bigsby, C. W. E. *A Critical Introduction to Twentieth-Century American Drama*. 3 vols. Cambridge: Cambridge University Press, 1985.

Birringer, Johannes H. *Theatre, Theory, Postmodernism*. Bloomington: Indiana University Press, 1991.

Bordman, Gerald. *American Musical Theatre*. New York: Oxford University Press, 1978.

Bradby, David. *Modern French Drama 1940–1980*. Cambridge: Cambridge University Press, 1984.

Brecht, Bertolt. *Brecht on Theatre*. Translated by John Willett. New York: Hill & Wang, 1965.

Brook, Peter. *The Empty Space*. New York: Atheneum, 1968.

——. *Threads of Time*. Washington, DC: Counterpoint, 1998.

Brown-Guillory, Elizabeth. *Their Place on the Stage: Black Women Playwrights in America*. New York: Greenwood Press, 1988.

Brustein, Robert. *The Theatre of Revolt: An Approach to Modern Drama*. Boston: Little, Brown, 1964.

Craig, Edward Gordon. *On the Art of the Theatre*. 2d ed. Boston: Small, Maynard, 1924.

Croyden, Margaret. *Lunatics, Lovers and Poets: The Contemporary Experimental Theatre*. New York: McGraw-Hill, 1974.

de Jongh, Nicholas. *Not in Front of the Audience: Homosexuality on Stage*. London: Routledge, 1992.

Esslin, Martin. *Brecht: The Man and His Work*. New York: Doubleday, 1960.

——. *The Theatre of the Absurd*. Rev. ed. New York: Doubleday, 1969.

Gaggi, Silvio. *Modern/Postmodern*. Philadelphia: University of Pennsylvania Press, 1989.

Gordon, Mel. *Dada Performance*. New York: PAJ Publications, 1987.

Grotowski, Jerzy. *Towards a Poor Theatre*. New York: Simon & Schuster, 1968.

Harris, Andre B. *Broadway Theatre*. London: Routledge, 1994.

Houghton, Norris. *Moscow Rehearsals*. New York: Harcourt Brace, 1936.

Innes, Christopher. *Modern German Drama: A Study in Form*. New York: Cambridge University Press, 1979.

Kerensky, Oleg. *The New British Drama: Fourteen Playwrights since Osborne and Pinter*. New York: Taplinger, 1979.

Kirby, Michael, ed. *The New Theatre: Performance Documentation*. New York: New York University Press, 1974.

Marranca, Bonnie, and Gautam Dasgupta, eds. *Interculturalism and Performance*. New York: PAJ Publications, 1991.

Natalle, Elizabeth J. *Feminist Theatre: A Study in Persuasion*. Metuchen, NJ: Scarecrow Press, 1985.

Roose-Evans, James. *Experimental Theatre: From Stanislavski to Peter Brook*. New York: Universe Books, 1984.

Shaw, George Bernard. *The Quintessence of Ibsenism*. London: Constable, 1913.

Trachtenberg, Stanley, ed. *The Postmodern Moment*. Westport, CT: Greenwood Press, 1985.

Vanden Heuvel, Michael. *Performing Drama/Dramatizing Performance*. Ann Arbor: University of Michigan Press, 1991.

Willett, John. *The Theatre of Bertolt Brecht*. New York: New Directions, 1959.

Williams, Mance. *Black Theatre in the 1960s and 1970s*. Westport, CT: Greenwood Press, 1985.

MUSICAL THEATRE

Bloom, Ken. *American Song*. 2d ed. New York: Schirmer, 1996.

Bordman, Gerald. *American Musical Theatre*. 2d ed. New York: Oxford, 1992.

Bradley, Ian, ed. *The Complete Annotated Gilbert and Sullivan*. New York: Oxford University Press, 1996.

Ewen, David. *New Complete Book of the American Musical Theatre*. New York: 1970.

Ganzl, Kurt. *The Encyclopedia of Musical Theatre*. Oxford, England: Blackwell, 1994.

Hammerstein, Oscar. *Lyrics*. New York: Simon and Schuster, 1949.

Hollis, Alpert. *125 Years of Musical Theatre*. New York: Arcade Publications, 1991.

Peterson, Bernard L. *A Century of Musicals in Black and White*. Westport, CT: Greenwood Press, 1993.

Woll, Allen L. *Black Musical Theatre*. Baton Rouge, Louisiana State University Press, 1989.

ACTING AND DIRECTING

Acker, Barbara, and Marion Hampton, eds. *The Vocal Vision*. New York: Applause, 1997.

Barish, Jonas. *The Anti-Theatrical Prejudice*. Berkeley: University of California Press, 1981.

Barrault, Jean-Louis. *Reflections on the Theatre*. London: Salisbury Square, 1951.

Benedetti, Jean. *Stanislavsky*. London: Methuen, 1988.

Berry, Cecily. *Voice and the Actor*. London: Harrap, 1973.

Boleslavski, Richard. *Acting: The First Six Lessons*. New York: Theatre Arts Books, 1933.

Brook, Peter. *Between Two Silences*. Dallas: Southern Methodist University Press, 1999.

Carnicke, Sharon Marie. *Stanislavsky in Focus*. Amsterdam: Harwood Press, 1998.

Chaikin, Joseph. *The Presence of the Actor*. New York: Atheneum, 1972.

Cohen, Robert. *Acting Power*. Palo Alto, CA: Mayfield, 1978.

——. *Acting Professionally*. 5th ed. Mountain View, CA: Mayfield, 1997.

Cohen, Robert, and John Harrop. *Creative Play Direction*. 2d ed. Englewood Cliffs, NJ: Prentice-Hall, 1984.

Cole, Toby, and Helen K. Chinoy, eds. *Actors on Acting*. Rev. ed. New York: Crown, 1970.

——. *Directors on Directing*. Rev. ed. Indianapolis: Bobbs-Merrill, 1963.

Diderot, Denis. "The Paradox of Acting." In William Archer, *Masks or Faces?* New York: Hill & Wang, 1957.

Goldman, Michael. *The Actor's Freedom*. New York: Viking, 1975.

Hagen, Uta. *Respect for Acting*. New York: Macmillan, 1973.

Hethmon, Robert. *Strasberg at the Actors Studio*. New York: Viking, 1965.

Jory, Jon. *Tips: Ideas for Acting*. Lyme, NH: Smith & Krause, 2000.

Lewis, Robert. *Advice to the Players*. New York: Harper & Row, 1980.

——. *Method or Madness*. London: Heinemann, 1960.

Linklatter, Kristin. *Freeing the Natural Voice*. New York: DBS Publications, 1976.

Marowitz, Charles. *The Act of Being: Toward A New Theory of Acting*. New York: Taplinger, 1978.

McGaw, Charles J. *Acting Is Believing*. 4th ed. New York: Holt, Rinehart & Winston, 1980.

Roach, Joseph R. *The Player's Passion: Studies in the Science of Acting*. Newark: University of Delaware Press, 1985.

Spolin, Viola. *Improvisation for the Theatre*. Evanston, IL: Northwestern University Press, 1963.

Stanislavsky, Konstantin. *An Actor Prepares*. Translated by Elizabeth Reynolds Hapgood. New York: Theatre Arts Books, 1936.

DESIGN

Aronson, Arnold. *American Set Design*. New York: Theatre Communications Group, 1985.

Bablet, Denis. *Revolutions of Stage Design in the Twentieth Century*. New York: L. Amiel, 1976.

Barton, Lucy. *Historic Costume for the Stage*. Boston: Baker's Plays, 1935.

Bay, Howard. *Stage Design*. New York: DBS Publications, 1974.

Bellman, Willard F. *Scenography and Stage Technology: An Introduction*. New York: Harper & Row, 1977.

Bergman, Gosta M. *Lighting in the Theatre*. Totowa, NJ: Rowman & Littlefield, 1977.

Burdick, Elizabeth B., et al., eds. *Contemporary Stage Design*. Middletown, CT: Wesleyan University Press, 1975.

Corson, Richard. *Stage Make-up*. 8th ed. Englewood Cliffs, NJ: Prentice Hall, 1989.

Goodwin, John, ed. *British Theatre Design: The Modern Age*. London: Weidenfeld & Nicholson, 1989.

Izenour, George C. *Roofed Theaters of Classical Antiquity*. New Haven, CT: Yale University Press, 1996.

——. *Theatre Design*. 2d ed. New Haven, CT: Yale University Press, 1996.

Jones, Robert Edmund. *The Dramatic Imagination*. New York: Meredith, 1941.

Mielziner, Jo. *Designing for the Theatre*. New York: Atheneum, 1965.

Motley. *Designing and Making Stage Costumes*. London: Studio Vista, 1964.

——. *Theatre Props*. New York: DBS Publications, 1976.

Oenslager, Donald. *Stage Design: Four Centuries of Scenic Invention*. New York: Viking, 1975.

Payne, Darwin Reid. *Computer Scenographics*. Carbondale: Southern Illinois University Press, 1994.

——. *Scenographic Imagination*. Carbondale: Southern Illinois University Press, 1993.

Pecktal, Lynn. *Costume Design*. New York: Back Stage Books, 1993.

Pilbrow, Richard. *Stage Lighting*. New York: DBS Publications, 1979.

Reid, Francis. *Designing for the Theatre*. New York: Routledge, 1996.

——. *The Stage Lighting Handbook*. 5th ed. New York: Routledge, 1996.

Smith, Ronn. *American Set Design 2*. New York: Theatre Communications Group, 1991.

Svoboda, Joseph. *The Secret of Theatrical Space*. New York: Applause Theatre Books, 1993.

Walne, Graham, ed. *Effects for the Theatre*. New York: Drama Book Publishers, 1995.

Text Credits

Chapter 4   Page 87, from Harold Pinter, *Silence*. Copyright © 1969 by Harold Pinter Limited. Used by permission of Grove/Atlantic, Inc.; From Tom Stoppard, *Dirty Linen*. Copyright © 1976 by Tom Stoppard. Used by permission of Grove/Atlantic, Inc.; p. 87 from *Glengarry Glen Ross* by David Mamet. Copyright © 1982, 1983. Used with permission of Grove Press; p. 90, from *Major Barbara*. Copyright © 1907, 1913, 1930, 1941 by George Bernard Shaw. Copyright © 1957, The Public Trustee as Executor of the Estate of George Bernard Shaw; p. 92, from *Wit* by Margaret Edson. Copyright © 1993, 1999 by Margaret Edson. Reprinted by permission of Faber and Faber, Inc., an affiliate of Farrar, Straus, and Giroux, LLC; p. 93, from *Cat on a Hot Tin Roof* by Tennessee Williams. Copyright © 1954, 1955, 1971, 1975 by Tennessee Williams. Reprinted by permission of New Directions Publishing Corporation; p. 94, from *Joe Turner's Come and Gone* by August Wilson. Copyright © 1988 by August Wilson. Used by permission of New American Library, a division of Penguin Books USA Inc.; p. 114, from *Imperceptible Mutabilities in the Third Kingdom* by Suzan-Lori Parks. Copyright © 1995, 1989, 1986 by Suzan-Lori Parks.

Chapter 8   Page 254, from Alfred Jarry, *Ubu Roi*, translated by Michael Benedikt and George E. Wellwarth. From *Modern French Theatre: The Avant-Garde, Dada and Surrealism* by Michael Benedikt and George E. Wellwarth. Play translation copyright © 1964 by Michael Benedikt and George E. Wellwarth. Reprinted by permission of Georges Borchardt, Inc. for the translators; page 258, from Luigi Pirandello, *Six Characters in Search of an Author*, translated by Edward Storer. Copyright © 1922 by E. P. Dutton. Renewed 1950 in the names of Stefano, Fausto, and Lietta Pirandello. From *Naked Masks: Five Plays* by Luigi Pirandello, edited by Eric Bentley. Translation copyright © 1922 by E. P. Dutton. Renewed 1950 in the names of Stefano, Fausto, and Lietta Pirandello. Used by permission of Dutton, a division of Penguin Putnam Inc.; page 259, from Antonin Artaud, *Jet of Blood*, translated by George E. Wellwarth. From *Modern French Theatre: The Avant-Garde, Dada and Surrealism*, by Michael Benedikt and George E. Wellwarth. Play translation copyright © 1966 by George E. Wellwarth. Reprinted by permission of Georges Borchardt, Inc. for the translator; page 268, from *Bedroom Farce* in *Absurd Person Singular* by Alan Ayckbourn. Copyright © 1975 by Alan Ayckbourn. Reprinted by permission of Grove Press, Inc. and Chatto and Windus; page 269, from *Buried Child* in *Seven Plays* by Sam Shepard. Copyright © 1979 by Sam Shepard. Used by permission of Bantam Books, a division of Random House, Inc.; page 272, *Catastrophe* from *Wings* by Arthur Kopit. Copyright © 1978 by Arthur Kopit. Reprinted by permission of Hill and Wang, a division of Farrar, Straus & Giroux, Inc.; page 275, from *Serious Money* by Caryl Churchill, Methuen Publishing Ltd., 1987. Reprinted by permission of the publisher.

Chapter 9   Page 281, from "Ol' Man River" written by Jerome Kern and Oscar Hammerstein II. Copyright © 1927 PolyGram International Publishing, Inc. Copyright renewed. Used by permission. All rights reserved; page 284, from "'S Wonderful" written by George and Ira Gershwin. Copyright © 1927 Warner/Chappell Music. Copyright renewed. Reprinted by permission; From "Bewitched, Bothered and Bewildered" by Richard Rodgers and Lorenz Hart. Copyright © 1940 Williamson Music/Warner Chappell. Copyright renewed. Reprinted by permission; page 285, from "Oh, What A Beautiful Mornin'" by Richard Rodgers and Oscar Hammerstein II. Copyright © 1943 by Williamson Music. Copyright renewed. International copyright secured. Reprinted by permission. All rights reserved; From "The Little Things You Do Together" by Stephen Sondheim. Copyright © 1970 Range Road Music Inc., Quartet Music Inc., and Rilting Music Inc. All rights administered by Herald Square Music Inc. Used by permission. All rights reserved; From "Contact," words and music by Jonathan Larson. Copyright © 1996 Finster & Lucy Music Ltd. Co. All rights controlled and administered by EMI April Music Inc. All rights reserved. International copyright secured. Used by permission.

Chapter 10   Page 301, from Samuel Beckett, *Rockabye* in *Rockabye and Other Short Pieces*, Grove/Atlantic, 1981. Copyright © 1981 by Samuel Beckett. Reprinted by permission

Chapter 11   Page 372, from Mel Gussow, *Wasserstein: Comedy, Character, Reflection, The New York Times*, October 23, 1992. Copyright © 1992 by The New York Times Co. Reprinted by permission; From Doug Watt, *Wasserstein Pens a Pointed Drawing Room Comedy, New York Daily News*, October 30, 1992. Copyright © 1992 New York Daily News L. P. Reprinted by permission.

Photo Credits

Index